THE NEW
AMERICAN
COMMENTARY

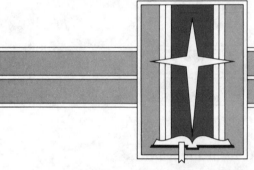

An Exegetical and Theological
Exposition of Holy Scripture

THE NEW
AMERICAN
COMMENTARY

Volume
9

1, 2 CHRONICLES

J. A. Thompson

BROADMAN
& HOLMAN
PUBLISHERS

© Copyright 1994 • Broadman & Holman Publishers
All rights reserved
4201-9
ISBN 0-8054-0109-1
Dewey Decimal Classification: 222.6
Subject Heading: BIBLE. O.T. CHRONICLES
Library of Congress Catalog Card Number: 94-36020
Printed in the United States of America

Library of Congress Cataloging-in-Publication Data

Thompson, J. A. (John Arthur), 1913–
    1, 2 Chronicles / J. A. Thompson.
      p.   cm. — (The new American commentary ; v. 9)
    Includes bibliographical references and indexes.
    1. Bible. O.T. Chronicles—Commentaries. I. Bible. O.T. Chronicles. English. New International. 1994. II. Title.
III. Title: 1, 2 Chronicles. IV. Series.
BS1345.3.T48   1994
222'.6077—dc20

To my beloved wife, constant companion, loyal and loving
friend over our long life together

Editors' Preface

God's Word does not change. God's world, however, changes in every generation. These changes, in addition to new findings by scholars and a new variety of challenges to the gospel message, call for the church in each generation to interpret and apply God's Word for God's people. Thus, THE NEW AMERICAN COMMENTARY is introduced to bridge the twentieth and twenty-first centuries. This new series has been designed primarily to enable pastors, teachers, and students to read the Bible with clarity and proclaim it with power.

In one sense THE NEW AMERICAN COMMENTARY is not new, for it represents the continuation of a heritage rich in biblical and theological exposition. The title of this forty-volume set points to the continuity of this series with an important commentary project published at the end of the nineteenth century called AN AMERICAN COMMENTARY, edited by Alvah Hovey. The older series included, among other significant contributions, the outstanding volume on Matthew by John A. Broadus, from whom the publisher of the new series, Broadman Press, partly derives its name. The former series was authored and edited by scholars committed to the infallibility of Scripture, making it a solid foundation for the present project. In line with this heritage, all NAC authors affirm the divine inspiration, inerrancy, complete truthfulness, and full authority of the Bible. The perspective of the NAC is unapologetically confessional and rooted in the evangelical tradition.

Since a commentary is a fundamental tool for the expositor or teacher who seeks to interpret and apply Scripture in the church or classroom, the NAC focuses on communicating the theological structure and content of each biblical book. The writers seek to illuminate both the historical meaning and contemporary significance of Holy Scripture.

In its attempt to make a unique contribution to the Christian community, the NAC focuses on two concerns. First, the commentary emphasizes how each section of a book fits together so that the reader becomes aware of the theological unity of each book and of Scripture as a whole. The writers, however, remain aware of the Bible's inherently rich variety. Second, the NAC is produced with the conviction that the Bible primarily belongs to the church. We believe that scholarship and the academy provide an indispensable foundation for biblical understanding and the service of Christ, but the editors and authors of this series have attempted to communicate the findings of their research in a manner that will build up the whole body of Christ. Thus, the commentary concentrates on theological exegesis while providing practical, applicable exposition.

THE NEW AMERICAN COMMENTARY's theological focus enables the reader to see the parts as well as the whole of Scripture. The biblical books vary in content, context, literary type, and style. In addition to this rich variety, the editors and authors recognize that the doctrinal emphasis and use of the biblical books differs in various places, contexts, and cultures among God's people. These factors, as well as other concerns, have led the editors to give freedom to the writers to wrestle with the issues raised by the scholarly community surrounding each book and to determine the appropriate shape and length of the introductory materials. Moreover, each writer has developed the structure of the commentary in a way best suited for expounding the basic structure and the meaning of the biblical books for our day. Generally, discussions relating to contemporary scholarship and technical points of grammar and syntax appear in the footnotes and not in the text of the commentary. This format allows pastors and interested laypersons, scholars and teachers, and serious college and seminary students to profit from the commentary at various levels. This approach has been employed because we believe that all Christians have the privilege and responsibility to read and seek to understand the Bible for themselves.

Consistent with the desire to produce a readable, up-to-date commentary, the editors selected the *New International Version* as the standard translation for the commentary series. The selection was made primarily because of the NIV's faithfulness to the original languages and its beautiful and readable style. The authors, however, have been given the liberty to differ at places from the NIV as they develop their own translations from the Greek and Hebrew texts.

The NAC reflects the vision and leadership of those who provide oversight for Broadman Press, who in 1987 called for a new commentary series that would evidence a commitment to the inerrancy of Scripture and a faithfulness to the classic Christian tradition. While the commentary adopts an "American" name, it should be noted some writers represent countries outside the United States, giving the commentary an international perspective. The diverse group of writers includes scholars, teachers, and administrators from almost twenty different colleges and seminaries, as well as pastors, missionaries, and a layperson.

The editors and writers hope that THE NEW AMERICAN COMMEN-

TARY will be helpful and instructive for pastors and teachers, scholars and students, for men and women in the churches who study and teach God's Word in various settings. We trust that for editors, authors, and readers alike, the commentary will be used to build up the church, encourage obedience, and bring renewal to God's people. Above all, we pray that the NAC will bring glory and honor to our Lord who has graciously redeemed us and faithfully revealed himself to us in his Holy Word.

SOLI DEO GLORIA
The Editors

Author's Preface

When I received an invitation in June 1988 to participate in *The New American Commentary* by writing a commentary on 1, 2 Chronicles, I responded to the invitation very happily. It seemed to be a good opportunity for an Australian to become involved in an American Enterprise. I was happy also to be invited to participate in an Old Testament commentary since this has been my area of research and teaching in theological colleges and in a secular university over many years, where I have taught Old Testament, Hebrew, and Aramaic for much of my teaching life. Another attraction to become involved in such a project was that I would be participating in a joint enterprise with fellow Baptists from other parts of the world, I myself being from Melbourne in the Southern Hemisphere. Further, I have identified myself very happily and with deep conviction with a conservative and evangelical theological stance. For me, the Bible is the Word of God bringing to humankind the mind of God on all sorts of issues and constituting a challenge to human thought and life, calling its readers to an understanding of how God would have them live in the contemporary world.

The Books of Chronicles present the commentator with their own particular problems. For instance, the question of the historicity of these sections of Chronicles that are not dependent on Samuel-Kings is often raised, and questions are asked about the historical value of other sources the Chronicler may have used. The questions of the original author's intention in producing the work and of his main theological perspectives present their own challenges. Also, what was the author's own preferred vocabulary in developing his main themes? In addition, a number of important technical questions need to be explored; the reason for the chronological tables, the literary forms, the unity of the work, its authorship, and date. These and other issues will need to be investigated.

Sometimes the commentary will take up important philological, syntactical, and exegetical concerns. Most of these will be taken up in footnotes. Frequently, comparison will be made with other works that deal with similar material. The Books of Samuel and Kings are important in this respect. In making such comparisons, the distinctive emphasis of the writer of 1, 2 Chronicles will become much clearer. Because of the nature of this particular commentary series, references to important bibliography, whether books or articles, are kept to a minimum, although a certain number seemed to be essential. Most of these are in English. But these will have their own footnotes that will enable the readers of this commentary on Chronicles to expand their horizons. However, no important issue will be avoided altogether. Since the target readership is the pastor and student rather than the technical scholar, there will be gaps in the treatment from the viewpoint of some readers.

I am grateful to those who have helped in the production of this commentary. First of all, I thank the producers of *The New American Commentary,* especially Kenneth Mathews, David Dockery, and Tom Clark, with whom I first had contact, and the rest of the staff at Broadman & Holman who provided help and encouragement.

My typist, Mrs. Bronwyn Donald, has been a great help in deciphering my difficult manuscript and in helping me to draw together the various strands that go to making a unified whole out of a number of parts.

My wife, Marion, has been the "good woman" who stands behind my literary work. This she has done with preliminary typing and has given constant encouragement as the work proceeded. I am grateful to God that despite periods of illness, including a stroke and a prostate operation, this commentary has been brought to completion.

My hope is that this commentary will convey to the modern readers of the text of 1, 2 Chronicles the thought of its original writer as he sought to make clear to us the mind of God in the areas of his concern. For its modern exponent, the present writer, the task of these years has been a glad offering to the Lord himself for his mercy towards me, his servant. My prayer is that the work will help others as much as it has helped me.

J. A. Thompson
Melbourne, Australia

Abbreviations

Bible Books

Gen	Isa	Luke
Exod	Jer	John
Lev	Lam	Acts
Num	Ezek	Rom
Deut	Dan	1,2 Cor
Josh	Hos	Gal
Judg	Joel	Eph
Ruth	Amos	Phil
1,2 Sam	Obad	Col
1,2 Kgs	Jonah	1,2 Thess
1,2 Chr	Mic	1,2 Tim
Ezra	Nah	Titus
Neh	Hab	Phlm
Esth	Zeph	Heb
Job	Hag	Jas
Ps (pl. Pss)	Zech	1,2, Pet
Prov	Mal	1,2,3 John
Eccl	Matt	Jude
Song	Mark	Rev

Apocrypha

Add Esth	*The Additions to the Book of Esther*
Bar	*Baruch*
Bel	*Bel and the Dragon*
1,2 Esdr	*1,2 Esdras*
4 Ezra	*4 Ezra*
Jdt	*Judith*
Ep Jer	*Epistle of Jeremiah*
1,2,3,4 Mac	*1,2,3,4 Maccabees*
Pr Azar	*Prayer of Azariah and the Song of the Three Jews*
Pr Man	*Prayer of Manasseh*
Sir	*Sirach, Ecclesiasticus*
Sus	*Susanna*
Tob	*Tobit*
Wis	*The Wisdom of Solomon*

Commonly Used Sources

AASOR	Annual of the American Schools of Oriental Research
AB	Anchor Bible
ABD	*Anchor Bible Dictionary*
ABW	*Archaeology and the Biblical World*
AC	An American Commentary, ed. A. Hovey
AcOr	*Acta orientalia*
AEL	M. Lichtheim, *Ancient Egyptian Literature*
AJSL	*American Journal of Semitic Languages and Literature*
Akk.	Akkadian
AnBib	Analecta Biblica
ANET	J. B. Pritchard, ed., *Ancient Near Eastern Texts*
AOAT	Alter Orient und Altes Testament
AOTS	*Archaeology and Old Testament Study,* ed. D. W. Thomas
ArOr	Archiv orientální
ATD	Das Alte Testament Deutsch
ATR	*Anglican Theological Review*
AusBR	*Australian Biblical Review*
BA	*Biblical Archaeologist*
BAGD	W. Bauer, W. F. Arndt, F. W. Gingrich, and F. W. Danker, *Greek-English Lexicon of the New Testament*
BARev	*Biblical Archaeology Review*
BASOR	*Bulletin of the American Schools of Oriental Research*
BDB	F. Brown, S. R. Driver, and C. A. Briggs, *Hebrew and English Lexicon of the Old Testament*
BETL	Bibliotheca ephemeridum theologicarum lovaniensium
BFT	Biblical Foundations in Theology
BHS	*Biblia hebraica stuttgartensia*
Bib	*Biblica*
BKAT	Biblischer Kommentar: Altes Testament
BO	*Bibliotheca orientalis*
BSac	*Bibliotheca Sacra*
BSC	Bible Study Commentary
BT	*Bible Translator*
BurH	*Buried History*
BZ	*Biblische Zeitschrift*
BZAW	Beihefte zur ZAW
CAD	*The Assyrian Dictionary of the Oriental Institute of the University of Chicago*
CAH	*Cambridge Ancient History*

CBSC	Cambridge Bible for Schools and Colleges
CBC	Cambridge Bible Commentary
CBQ	*Catholic Biblical Quarterly*
CC	The Communicator's Commentary
CCK	*Chronicles of Chaldean Kings,* D. J. Wiseman
CHAL	*Concise Hebrew and Aramaic Lexicon,* ed. W. L. Holladay
COT	Commentary on the Old Testament, C. F. Keil and F. Delitzsch
CTR	*Criswell Theological Review*
DOTT	*Documents from Old Testament Times,* ed. D. W. Thomas
EAEHL	*Encyclopedia of Archaeological Excavations in the Holy Land,* ed. M. Avi-Yonah
DSS	Dead Sea Scrolls
EBC	Expositor's Bible Commentary
Ebib	Etudes bibliques
ETL	*Ephermerides theologicae lovanienses*
FB	Forschung zur Bibel
FOTL	Forms of Old Testament Literature
GKC	Gesenius' Hebrew Grammar, ed. E. Kautzsch, tr. A. E. Cowley
GTJ	*Grace Theological Journal*
HAR	*Hebrew Annual Review*
HAT	Handbuch zum Alten Testament
HBT	*Horizons in Biblical Theology*
HDR	Harvard Dissertations in Religion
Her	Hermeneia
HKAT	Handkommentar zum Alten Testament
HSM	Harvard Semitic Monographs
HT	Helps for Translators
HTR	*Harvard Theological Review*
HUCA	*Hebrew Union College Annual*
IB	*Interpreter's Bible*
ICC	International Critical Commentary
IDB	*Interpreter's Dictionary of the Bible,* ed. G. A. Buttrick, et al.
IDBSup	Supplementary volume to *IDB*
IBHS	B. K. Waltke and M. O'Connor, *Introduction to Biblical Hebrew Syntax*
IEJ	*Israel Exploration Journal*
IES	Israel Exploration Society

Int	*Interpretation*
INT	Interpretation: A Bible Commentary for Teaching and Preaching
ITC	International Theological Commentary
IOS	*Israel Oriental Society*
ISBE	*International Standard Bible Encyclopedia*, rev. ed. G. W. Bromiley
IJT	*Indian Journal of Theology*
ITC	International Theological Commentary
JANES	*Journal of Ancient Near Eastern Society*
JAOS	*Journal of the American Oriental Society*
JBL	*Journal of Biblical Literature*
JBR	*Journal of Bible and Religion*
JCS	*Journal of Cuneiform Studies*
JEA	*Journal of Egyptian Archaeology*
JETS	*Journal of the Evangelical Theological Society*
JJS	*Journal of Jewish Studies*
JNES	*Journal of Near Eastern Studies*
JNSL	*Journal of Northwest Semitic Languages*
JPOS	*Journal of Palestine Oriental Society*
JSJ	*Journal for the Study of Judaism in the Persian, Hellenistic, and Roman Period*
JSOR	*Journal of the Society for Oriental Research*
JSOT	*Journal for the Study of the Old Testament*
JSOTSup	JSOT—Supplement Series
JSS	*Journal of Semitic Studies*
JTS	*Journal of Theological Studies*
JTSNS	*Journal of Theological Studies, New Series*
KAT	Kommentar zum Alten Testament
KB	Koehler and W. Baumgartner, *Lexicon in Veteris Testamenti libros*
LCC	Library of Christian Classics
LLAVT	E. Vogt, *Lexicon Linguae Aramaicae Veteris Testamenti*
LTQ	*Lexington Theological Quarterly*
MT	Masoretic Text
NAC	New American Commentary
NB	*Nebuchadrezzar and Babylon*, D. J. Wiseman
NBD	*New Bible Dictionary*
NCBC	New Century Bible Commentary
NICOT	New International Commentary on the Old Testament
NJPS	New Jewish Publication Society Version
NKZ	*Neue kirchliche Zeitschrift*

NovT	*Novum Testamentum*
NTS	*New Testament Studies*
Or	*Orientalia*
OTL	Old Testament Library
OTS	*Oudtestamentische Studiën*
OTWSA	*Ou-Testamentiese Werkgemeenskap in Suid-Afrika*
PCB	*Peake's Commentary on the Bible,* ed. M. Black and H. H. Rowley
PEQ	*Palestine Exploration Quarterly*
POTT	*Peoples of Old Testament Times,* ed. D. J. Wiseman
PTR	*Princeton Theological Review*
Pss. Sol.	*Psalms of Solomon*
RA	Revue d'assyriologie et d'archéologie orientale
RB	*Revue biblique*
ResQ	*Restoration Quarterly*
RevExp	*Review and Expositor*
RSR	Recherches de science religieuse
SANE	Sources from the Ancient Near East
SBLDS	Society of Biblical Literature Dissertation Series
SOTI	*A Survey of Old Testament Introduction,* G. L. Archer
SBT	Studies in Biblical Theology
SJT	*Scottish Journal of Theology*
SP	Samaritan Pentateuch
SR	Studies in Religion/Sciences religieuses
ST	*Studia theologica*
STJD	Studies on the Texts of the Desert of Judah
Syr	Syriac
TDOT	*Theological Dictionary of the Old Testament,* ed. G. J. Botterweck and H. Ringgren
Tg	Targum
TJNS	Trinity Journal—New Series
TrinJ	*Trinity Journal*
TLZ	*Theologische Literaturzeitung*
TOTC	Tyndale Old Testament Commentaries
TS	*Theological Studies*
TWAT	*Theologisches Wörterbuch zum Alten Testament,* ed. G. J. Botterweck and H. Ringgren
TWOT	*Theological Wordbook of the Old Testament*
TynBul	*Tyndale Bulletin*
UF	*Ugarit-Forschungen*
Vg	Vulgate
VT	*Vetus Testamentum*
VTSup	Vetus Testamentum, Supplements

Contents

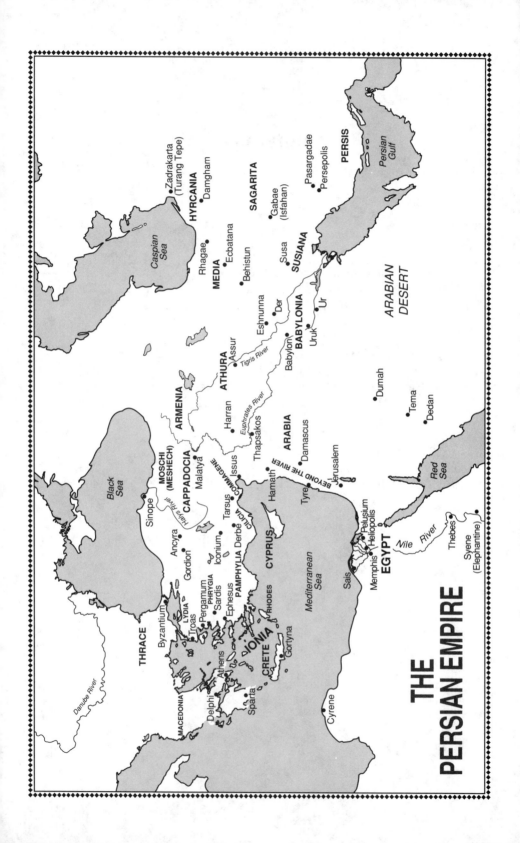

THE
PERSIAN EMPIRE

1, 2 Chronicles

1. Name and Place in the Canon

In the Christian canon of Scripture, Chronicles has been divided into two books. In the Hebrew Bible it is called "words [or events] of the days," although in the Hebrew canon the two books were counted as one. The division into two books was made when the Hebrew text was translated into Greek in pre-Christian times. One reason for this may have been that in Hebrew only the consonants are written (the vowels are implied) whereas in Greek both consonants and vowels are written. Hence in Greek there are approximately double the number of characters to be recorded. As a result the Greek Chronicles came to be spread over two scrolls.

In the Hebrew Bible these two books normally stand at the end of the third division of the Bible known as the Writings. Jesus' words in Matt 23:35 referring to the death of the priest Zechariah suggest that by New Testament times these books were considered as Scripture and stood at, or near, the end of the collection (cf. 2 Chr 24:20–22).[1] But the English Bible followed the Greek LXX (which named these books "the things left over") and attached them to the historical books after Samuel and Kings. This is unfortunate because the church has tended to see 1 and 2 Chronicles as a sort of appendix to Samuel-Kings, a supplement containing a collection of priestly observations, and has ignored the unique contents and message of 1 and 2 Chronicles.

If Chronicles is treated as a whole, there is a major break after the genealogies at 1 Chronicles 9. Another major break comes after 2 Chronicles 9, which records the death of Solomon. The stories of David and Solomon should not be split. Solomon's work was complementary to that of David.

2. The Text of Chronicles

The original Hebrew text is always important in the study of an Old Testament book. For Chronicles we have the usual resources: parallel passages elsewhere in the Hebrew Bible notably in Samuel and Kings; the Greek translation, the LXX; other versions like the Latin and Syriac texts; and, recently, fragments of Chronicles in the Qumran scrolls. Most studies in the past have concentrated on those portions of Chronicles that are paralleled by sections in the Pentateuch or in Samuel-Kings, the so-called synoptic portions. Where Chronicles differs from its original source (*Vorlage*) in Samuel or Kings scholars assumed that the Chronicler, because of his theological viewpoint, modified the text.

---

[1] Cf. R. K. Harrison, *Introduction to the Old Testament* (Grand Rapids: Eerdmans, 1969), 268.

But recent studies have shown that the Chronicler did not modify his sources at will. Rather, some of his sources arose from a different Hebrew tradition from that of the MT.[2] In addition to the Masoretic tradition preserved in the MT, there also existed a "Palestinian" tradition of the texts of the Pentateuch and Samuel-Kings. It is now clear from comparison of Chronicles with the Samaritan Pentateuch and the Greek translations of the Pentateuch that the text Chronicles used was more like these texts than the MT. Similarly, comparison of Chronicles with parallel passages in Samuel-Kings from 4QSam[a], 4QSam[b], and 4QSam[c], and the LXX show that the Chronicles text is more like these than the MT version of Samuel-Kings. The Palestinian text tradition can be identified in the Lucianic LXX, Chronicles, the Dead Sea Scrolls fragments, and the Jewish writer Josephus. In short, the Chronicler faithfully used the sources he had.[3]

3. The Chronicler's Sources

It seems clear, and it is generally agreed, that the Chronicler's primary source was the books of Samuel-Kings in the Palestinian tradition. It may appear that we are given a clear pointer to at least some other sources in various citations from official annals like "The Book of the Kings of Judah and Israel" (2 Chr 16:11) or references to prophetic records like those of "Iddo the Seer" (2 Chr 12:15). But the Chronicler almost always refers to his "sources" at the precise points where the author of Kings cites his sources. For example, compare 2 Chr 12:15 with 1 Kgs 14:29; 2 Chr 16:11 with 1 Kgs 15:23; 2 Chr 20:34 with 1 Kgs 22:45; and 2 Chr 25:26 with 2 Kgs 14:18.[4]

Thus we need to use the citation formula with some care. In particular, reference to prophetic records may in fact be to Samuel-Kings and not to some other, independent sources. Evidently other sources were utilized by the Chronicler although we are somewhat uncertain about these. A significant source evidently was that in which the genealogical lists were preserved.[5] Military and census type lists such as we find incorporated in 1 Chronicles 11–12 also existed. Soggin comments that "in Chronicles we

---

[2] Cf. S. Japhet, *I & II Chronicles*, OTL (Louisville: Westminster/John Knox, 1994), 29.

[3] For further discussion see G. F. Hasel, "Chronicles, Book of," *ISBE* 1.667; F. M. Cross, "The History of the Biblical Text in the Light of Discoveries in the Judaean Desert," *HTR* 57 (1964) 281–99; R. W. Klein, *Textual Criticism of the Old Testament* (Philadelphia: Fortress, 1974) 42–50; and E. Tov, *Textual Criticism of the Hebrew Bible* (Minneapolis: Fortress, 1992).

[4] See H. G. M. Williamson, *1 and 2 Chronicles,* NCBC (Grand Rapids: Eerdmans, 1982), 18, and D. M. Howard, Jr., *An Introduction to the Old Testament Historical Books* (Chicago: Moody, 1993), 238–42.

[5] A discussion of the nature of genealogies follows (see "Genealogies," p. 23).

have a series of notes from a reliable source, perhaps even at first hand, which complement what we know only partially from the books of Samuel and Kings."[6]

The fact that the Chronicler used Samuel-Kings as a source for his work does not mean that he slavishly followed it. Chronicles is not an exposition of Samuel-Kings, nor does it have the same structure. It is a separate work with an independent purpose.[7]

Basing himself broadly on a variety of Old Testament traditions, the Chronicler, with considerable literary skill, drafted his history, building upon Samuel-Kings and interpreting, supplementing, and deleting as he felt compelled by his own theological perspectives. His intention was not to rewrite the history of Judah nor to gather what had not been covered by his predecessors, but it was to provide lessons for the people of his time drawn from the history of his people. The speeches of David in 1 Chronicles 22; 28–29, the speech of Abijah in 2 Chronicles 13, and the account of Uzziah's prosperity and punishment in 2 Chronicles 26 reflect a common point of view that we may identify as that of the Chronicler.

He made use of a variety of exegetical techniques such as harmonization, typology, and explanation of difficult passages by appeal to other passages. He was not attempting, however, simply to expound his source material in its own right. He did not use all the source material available but made a selective use of Samuel and Kings. He was intent on presenting some theological perspectives from the written sources that were available. More of these were at hand than some modern writers allow in their tendency to propose later additions. The Chronicler saw patterns that were repeated at various points in Israel's history, for example, the pattern of the "exile" and "restoration" motif exemplified in 1 Chronicles 10, with the death of Saul leaving Israel totally defeated and in a state of "exile" from which only the faithfulness of a David could rescue them. Another discernible motif was that of "all Israel" (to be discussed later). In presenting these patterns, the Chronicler used without distinction biblical sources, other materials, and his own personal composition in the interests of a wider purpose.

The Chronicler was highly skilled in composition, being able to shape material within a shorter narrative unit to make it serve a wider purpose. Examples of this are the growing support shown for David before and at his coronation at Hebron (1 Chr 11–12) and patterning the transition of rule from David to Solomon after the transition from Moses to Joshua (1 Chr 22; 28–29).[8] He was able to use his sources creatively and utilize them to teach

---

[6] J. A. Soggin, *Introduction to the Old Testament* (Philadelphia: Westminster, 1974), 416.

[7] See T. Sugimoto, "Chronicles as Independent Literature," *JSOT* 55 (1992): 61–74.

the developing community of Israel important principles that had guided his nation in the past and were still relevant for Israel in the future.

4. The Literary Forms in Chronicles

Chronicles contains a wide variety of literary forms, but four deserve special mention: (1) genealogies, such as chaps. 1–8; (2) lists, such as 1 Chr 9:3–23; 11:10–17; 12; (3) speeches, sermons, and prayers, such as 1 Chronicles 22; 28–29; (4) a miscellaneous group of literary forms comprising extracts from Samuel-Kings. These forms were often related verbatim but sometimes with alterations, additions, and deletions that reflected the mind of the Chronicler himself as he sought in yet other ways to use his sources to give expression to his special theological concerns.

(1) Genealogies

The fact that the author of 1 and 2 Chronicles devoted nine chapters out of sixty-five to genealogies (1 Chr 1–9) makes clear that these were of great importance to him and bear significantly on his purpose in writing his work. This purpose needs to be understood by any commentator who would elucidate the nature of these volumes.

We may define a genealogy as "a written or oral expression of the descent of a person or persons from an ancestor or ancestors."[9] They may display breadth ("These were the sons of Israel: Reuben, Simeon, Levi, Judah," 1 Chr 2:1) and depth (the sons of Solomon: "Rehoboam, Abijah his son, Asa his son," 1 Chr 3:10). This latter genealogy and others of its type that display depth alone are termed "linear." Biblical genealogies, like the extrabiblical ones, are normally quite limited in depth, rarely extending beyond ten or twelve generations but often from four to six. In 1 Chronicles 2–9 we have an exception. Perhaps the writer sometimes joined separate genealogies.

If a genealogy displays breadth as well as depth, it is termed "segmented," or "mixed." In Chronicles multiple descendants of an ancestor are frequently named, but not all the lives are pursued to later generations. Genealogies may proceed from parent to child (descending, as in 1 Chr 9:39–44) or from child to parent (ascending, as in 1 Chr 9:14–16).[10]

The two types of genealogy, linear and segmented, serve different pur-

---

[8] H. G. M. Williamson, "The Accession of Solomon in the Books of Chronicles," *VT* 26 (1976): 351–61.

[9] R. R. Wilson, *Genealogy and History in the Biblical World* (New Haven: Yale University Press, 1977), 9.

[10] This discussion is based on R. Braun, *1 Chronicles*, WBC (Waco: Word, 1986), 1–5, which in turn summarizes Wilson, *Genealogy and History*, 9f.

poses. The linear genealogy seeks to legitimize an individual by relating him to an ancestor whose status is established. The segmented genealogy is designed to express relationships between the various branches of a family. These relationships may be of a domestic, political, or religious kind, areas that are multiple or interpenetrating. These kinship relationships are variously expressed. (1) The most common is, "The descendants of X, Y his son, Z his son," and so on (1 Chr 3:10–14). (2) A second way of expressing relationship is "X begat [caused to bring forth] Y." Of the same general type is "X gave birth to Y," where the emphasis is on the mother. In the same group we should include "the father of" (1 Chr 2:49). (3) "X the son of Y" is ascending order. (4) "X, his son Y" is descending order (1 Chr 3:10–14; 7:25–27).

These genealogies performed several functions. They were used to demonstrate existing relations between Israel and neighboring tribes with whom there was some degree of kinship. They also demonstrated relationships between Israel and isolated traditional elements by creating a coherent and inclusive genealogical system. At times they provided a continuity over periods of time not covered by material in the traditions. The genealogies also allowed for chronological speculation concerning world cycles. Some genealogies were military in content and purpose. They demonstrated the legitimacy of individuals in their office and provided individuals of rank with connections to a worthy family or individual in the past. Taken as a whole, they provided support for the "all Israel" concept so important to the Chronicler. Finally, they exhibited a sense of movement in Israel's history toward a divine goal. The course of history was shown to be governed by the providence of God.

The genealogies of 1 Chronicles 1–9 are designed to demonstrate the relationships that existed between the various components of the people of Israel in the past and the people who claimed to be part of Israel at the time of the writer of Chronicles. Concepts such as "your father's household" (Gen 12:1), representing the extended family; the "clan," roughly equivalent to our "relatives"; and the "tribe," of which, originally, Israel contained twelve, were all important in Israel and feature in the genealogies. At times these family structures are well marked, as in the family of Achan in Josh 7:16–18.

Important in interpreting the genealogies is recognizing that they reflect not only blood relationships but geographical, social, economic, religious, and political realities as well. Not all these are expressed at one time. The relationship changes from time to time. That is, there is a fluidity in their mode of expression. Thus theoretically Israel consisted of twelve tribes in the canonical tradition. But there were variations. The tribe of Joseph became divided into Ephraim and Manasseh. Levi is at times not counted. Simeon was absorbed by Judah. Dan and Zebulun, although listed in 1 Chr

2:1–2, are virtually neglected in the rest of chaps. 1–9. At times additional names could be added and others deleted. A name may lose its functional importance or reflect changes in the structure of the lineage. Names may be integrated into a genealogy not formerly included. Examples of all these and others can be found in Chronicles and from time to time will be referred to in this commentary.

The source of this genealogical information is not always clear to us. It is too simplistic a solution to propose that the Chronicler, or someone else, concocted a genealogy. Even in the twentieth century tribal peoples trace their family for many generations through oral memories. Also there were written records that could be consulted, although the Chronicler's sources have not always survived.

(2) Lists

Chronicles contains sufficient lists to group them together as a recognizable literary form. Among these was the list of the people of Judah, Benjamin, Ephraim, and Manasseh; leaders of fathers' houses; priests, Levites and gatekeepers; the list of those who resettled on their own lands after exile (1 Chr 9:3–23); the chiefs of David's mighty men (1 Chr 11:10–47); the warriors who joined David at Ziklag, at his stronghold in the desert; men of Manasseh who defected to David, and men who came to David at Hebron (1 Chr 12); and others. The sources from which these lists derived are quite unknown to us. Possibly they were preserved in temple lists, but they evidently were accessible to the Chronicler and served an important function in the Chronicler's overall purpose.

(3) Speeches, Sermons, and Prayers

At several points in Chronicles the speeches of kings and others are recorded, for example, speeches of David and Solomon and various utterances from the later kings of Judah. Some of these might easily be regarded as sermons. In other areas prayers are recorded, for example, Solomon's prayer of dedication before the altar of the temple in front of the whole assembly of Israel (2 Chr 6:14–42) and Jehoshaphat's prayer on the occasion of the attack by the troops of Ammon, Moab, and Mount Seir (2 Chr 20:6–12).

(4) Prophetic Utterances of "Minor Prophets"

A succession of prophets in Israel delivered God's word to the people at different times. We do not have a literary record of their utterances like the classical prophets in the Bible, but the Chronicler had access to their words. Among these were Nathan (1 Chr 17:1–14), Gad (1 Chr 21:9–19; and see esp. 29:29), Shemaiah (2 Chr 11:2–4), Azariah (2 Chr 15:2–7), and Hanani (2 Chr 16:7–9).

(5) The Levitical Sermons

Some scholars have isolated a particular literary form that has been called "The Levitical Sermon," so named by G. von Rad. This is a prose form in which a confessional statement is made with a quotation from the canonical prophets in support[11] (2 Chr 15:2–7; 16:7–9; 19:6–7; 20:15–17,20; 29:5–11). This literary form is widely accepted by scholars as a genuine form, but some have thought it to be a rather artificial idea.[12] A modern commentator like H. G. M. Williamson refers to it frequently.[13]

(6) Psalms and Poetry

While in general, poetry is not a literary feature of Chronicles, it is not entirely lacking. David's psalm of thanks in 1 Chr 16:7–36 is a notable example. The list of names in 1 Chr 25:4–5 has been identified as poetic in form (see commentary). Snatches of psalm verses also are here and there in these books.

5. The Authorship and Unity of Chronicles

In the study of the Books of Chronicles commentators frequently have postulated that behind this work lie the efforts and ingenuity of an individual we can call the Chronicler. While this is a reasonable position, a number of questions have arisen. What was the extent of the Chronicler's work? Was he responsible also for the whole or part of the books of Ezra and Nehemiah as well as Chronicles? In particular regard to the books of Chronicles themselves, to what extent are they a unity, or is there evidence of secondary material within the books of Chronicles? The decisions arrived at in regard to these issues will profoundly affect the interpretation of the material that lies before the commentator on the books of Chronicles.

---

[11] G. von Rad, *The Problem of the Hexateuch and Other Essays* (London: SCM, 1984), 267–80.

[12] R. Braun, *1 Chronicles,* xxiv–xxv.

[13] Williamson, *1 and 2 Chronicles,* 11,15,31, 179, 266–68, 274–75, 299, 306, 346, 355, 366, 379, 382, 409, 415. On the other hand, some have argued these "levitical sermons" are neither "levitical" nor "sermonic." See D. Mathias "'Levitische Predigt' und Deuteronomistmus," *ZAW* 96 (1984): 23–49; R. Mason, "Some Echoes of the Preaching in the Second Temple," *ZAW* 96 (1984): 221–35; and Japhet, *I & II Chronicles,* 36–37.

(1) The Relation of Chronicles to Ezra-Nehemiah

The view that the books of Chronicles are directly continued in the books of Ezra and Nehemiah and that the same author was responsible for them has been regarded as scholarly orthodoxy for well over a century. Indeed the view of the Talmud and church fathers was that Ezra was the author. S. R. Driver prepared a list of characteristic vocabulary that is prominent in Chronicles, Ezra, and Nehemiah, suggesting that they were authored by one person.[14]

In recent years that view has been challenged by scholars such as S. Japhet[15] and H. G. M. Williamson.[16] Japhet noted four phenomena that were used to argue for common authorship: (1) the presence of the opening verses of Ezra at the end of Chronicles; (2) the fact that 1 Esdras begins with 2 Chronicles 35–36 and continues through Ezra; (3) common vocabulary, style, and syntax; and (4) uniform theological ideas expressed in the material and its selection. While it may be admitted that a number of themes and a good deal of common vocabulary, style, and syntax are common to Chronicles and Ezra-Nehemiah, important differences exist in theological themes, such as the doctrine of retribution and the assessment of Solomon. In the matter of vocabulary, style, and syntax much of this was simply characteristic of postexilic Hebrew as a whole. But a close study of the vocabulary lists of Chronicles and Ezra-Nehemiah reveals significant differences of usage between the two bodies of writing.[17] The Ezra-Nehemiah work has problems of its own, but at no point are these dependent on the books of Chronicles, which, for its part, can be well understood as a work in its own right.[18]

(2) The Unity of Chronicles

A further question needs to be raised, namely, the question of internal unity. Various approaches to this question have been made. Some scholars have argued that Chronicles has been subjected to a measure of secondary

---

[14] S. R. Driver, *An Introduction to the Literature of the Old Testament* (Gloucester, Mass.: Peter Smith, 1972), 535–39.

[15] S. Japhet, "The Supposed Common Authorship of Chronicles and Ezra-Nehemiah Investigated Anew," *VT* 18 (1968): 332–72.

[16] Williamson, *1 and 2 Chronicles*, 5–11.

[17] For a careful rebuttal of Japhet and Williamson and an attempt to show that the unity of Chronicles and Ezra-Nehemiah can be maintained on linguistic grounds, see D. Talshir, "A Reinvestigation of the Linguistic Relationship between Chronicles and Ezra-Nehemiah," *VT* 38 (1988): 165–93.

[18] For further discussion of this issue, see P. R. Ackroyd, "Chronicles-Ezra-Nehemiah: The Concept of Unity," *BZAW* 100 (1988): 189–201.

editing. For example, 1 Chronicles 1–9 is held by some writers as entirely secondary to the original work. Others see in Chronicles essentially the work of a single author that has been subjected to a wide variety of later additions.[19] Others have proposed three separate editions of the Chronicler's work that they have named Chronicles 1, Chronicles 2, Chronicles 3.[20] The commentary of Williamson to which we have referred presents a moderate view. He regards Chronicles as a substantial unity including 1 Chronicles 1–9. He rejects many of the secondary additions proposed by other writers. He does allow, however, some cases of secondary expansion of the Chronicler's work by a priestly reviewer as in 1 Chronicles 15–16 and 23–27 and a few other less extensive passages.[21]

While some relatively slight redaction of the Chronicler's work may be allowed, a wholesale editing of the Chronicler's text is not warranted. Where it is allowed, it needs to be based on internal literary-critical considerations and not on speculative theories.

We might add that the Chronicler structures his work very carefully. L. C. Allen has isolated three types of literary design. First, the Chronicler often used an inclusio pattern to define the limits of a text, as in 2 Chr 29:2 and 31:20. Second, he often used recurring motifs; and third, he often used contrasting motifs. All of these are evident in the Hebrew text.[22]

6. The Historical Situation of the Chronicler

By the time the Chronicler wrote, much had happened in Israel's history. From the tribal days of the Judges, through the period of the establishment of the United Kingdom under David and Solomon (ca. 1000–931 B.C.), through the schism after Solomon's death and the period of the Divided Kingdom (931–722 B.C.), and on through the period of the kingdom of Judah (722–587 B.C.), the people of Israel had experienced many vicissitudes including two major political tragedies. The destruction of the Northern Kingdom as a separate political entity and the exile of many of its people[23] at the hands of the Assyrian ruler Sargon II (721–705 B.C.) or perhaps Shal-

---

[19] For a list of proposed glosses, see S. J. De Vries, *1 and 2 Chronicles*, FOTL (Grand Rapids: Eerdmans, 1989), 13.

[20] For a succinct summary of the various approaches to unity, see Williamson, *1 and 2 Chronicles,* 12–15.

[21] See Williamson, *1 and 2 Chronicles,* 14–15.

[22] L. C. Allen, "Kerygmatic Units in 1 & 2 Chronicles," *JSOT* 41 (1988): 21–36. Also S. D. Waters believes that the bulk of Chronicles is included in an inclusio formed by the use of the Hebrew word גלה in 1 Chr 9:1 and again in 2 Chr 36:14,21 ("Saul of Gibeon," *JSOT* 52 [1991]: 61–76).

[23] The records of Sargon II (721–705 B.C.) give the number as 27,290 (*ANET,* 285).

maneser V (726–722 B.C.) took place in the late summer or autumn of the year 722/721 B.C. After that, the Southern Kingdom, Judah, survived as the sole representative of the people of Israel until it too, after surviving 134 years, came to an end in July 587 and more of the people of old Israel went into exile.[24]

Politically the old Israel had ceased to exist. But in God's mind there was more to its story yet to unfold. The great empires of Assyria and Babylonia passed from the stage of history. During their period of ascendancy, numbers of God's people languished in a foreign land. Some, of course, never left their homeland. But in 539 B.C. Cyrus, ruler of Persia, overthrew Babylon. In the first year of his reign in Babylon, in 538 B.C., he issued a decree ordering the restoration of the Jewish community and its cult in Palestine (Ezra 1:2–4; 6:3–5). The exiles were free to return, and many did, although some stayed in Babylonia.

When they returned, there were years of hardship and frustration ahead of them. The community was at first very small, perhaps only twenty thousand. It was to be a "day of small things" (Zech 4:10).[25] Jerusalem was still thinly populated seventy-five years later (Neh 7:4). The land at the disposal of the Jews was tiny (about twenty-five miles from north to south); there was no temple. The newcomers faced years of privation and insecurity. They experienced poor seasons, partial crop failures (Hag 1:9–11; 2:15–17). Nor is it likely that Jews who were still resident in the land in every case welcomed the influx of immigrants with enthusiasm. They had regarded the land as theirs (Ezek 33:24). Their neighbors, especially the aristocracy of Samaria, resented the limitation of their prerogatives there and were openly hostile. To aggravate matters the returning exiles considered themselves as the true Israel and tended to separate themselves both from the Samaritans and their less orthodox brethren as from men unclean (Hag 2:10–14).

In addition to these physical problems, a real spiritual emergency existed in the community. The morale of the community was dangerously low as revealed in Haggai and Zechariah. The second temple was built by March 515 and dedicated with great rejoicing (Ezra 6:13–18). David's throne, however, was not reestablished. Among the returning exiles questions arose about the legitimacy of the membership of individuals in the community of Israel. Men of spiritual insight like the Chronicler had even deeper concerns—the spiri-

---

[24] For details of the history of these times consult one of the histories of Israel such as J. Bright, *A History of Israel*, 3d ed. (Philadelphia: Westminster, 1981), or E. H. Merrill, *Kingdom of Priests: A History of Old Testament Israel* (Grand Rapids: Baker, 1987).

[25] W. F. Albright, *The Biblical Period from Abraham to Ezra* (New York: Harper & Row, 1963), 87, 110–11.

tual health of the community and the proper recognition of Jerusalem as the authentic place of worship. The returnees were the legitimate successors of the people of Judah. But the issue was wider in the Chronicler's view with his concept of "all Israel." He needed to demonstrate by resort to genealogical records the total composition of Israel—not merely Judah and the returning exiles but legitimate descendants of the authentic Israel both north and south. He also needed to establish the legitimacy of the priests and Levites from the extant genealogies of which, it seems, there were many.

7. The Date of Chronicles

As did many other biblical authors, the Chronicler left few clues to help us date his work with any certainty. We can set some upper and lower limits and propose that the date of Chronicles lies within these limits. Thus the reference in 2 Chr 36:20 to the "the kingdom of Persia" coming to power sets 539 B.C. as the earliest possible date. The latest possible date is 180 B.C. Eupolemos, a Greek writer, quoted from the LXX of Chronicles about the middle of the second century B.C. Ben Sira, a scholar and teacher living in Jerusalem, published his book (Sirach) about 180 B.C. It was taken by his grandson to Egypt and translated into Greek. The description of King David in Sirach (47:8–10) seems to be based on Chronicles. This would exclude a Maccabean date for Chronicles. This provides at best a date somewhere within a 350 year period.

Yet commentators have proposed a wide variety of dates within these limits. Those who regard Chronicles as having been written by the author of Ezra-Nehemiah date the book to the Persian period on the basis of the Aramaic of Ezra as compared to that of the Elephantine material.[26] While there is no consensus about the exact date, a number of scholars incline towards the fourth century B.C.[27]

8. Important Theological Themes

Some writers frankly consider Chronicles to be an inferior piece of work. Pfeiffer claimed that it was an inferior supplement to the priestly code and commented that "the Chronicler made no important contributions to theological thought."[28] D. Howard, on the other hand, begins his treatment of Chronicles by saying, "The books of Chronicles are Wonderful," and that

---

[26] J. M. Myers, *I Chronicles*, AB (New York: Doubleday, 1974), LXXXVII–LXXXIX.

[27] For fuller discussion consult Williamson (*1 and 2 Chronicles*, 15–17), who accepts the middle of the fourth century B.C., about 350 B.C.; Braun suggests 350–300 B.C. (*I Chronicles*, XXV–XXIX); Myers suggests a date around 400 B.C. (*I Chronicles*, IXXXVI–IXXIX).

the theological message of Chronicles is very relevant to our time.[29] In fact, the intention of the Chronicler was neither to rewrite the history of Judah, nor to supplement the so-called P document, nor to gather together what had been omitted by his predecessors. He had to deal with the pressing theological issues of his day. One of the problems of the restored community was to delineate the precise extent of those who could rightly be counted as legitimate members of God's people. For that reason care was taken to legitimize an individual in terms of his family tree. In this a genealogy was of enormous importance. The same search for legitimacy was a concern of priests and Levites who also sought legitimacy in a genealogy. It was important for the Chronicler to develop his concept of "all Israel," which we will discuss in due course.

But there was something more important than physical descent and biological relationship. The Chronicler attempted to interpret to the restored community in Jerusalem the history of Israel as the working out of the eternal covenant between God and the people that demanded an obedient response to the divine law. Using David as a model he could show that Israel prospered when it was obedient but came under divine judgment when it abandoned God's law (2 Chr 36:15–19). After the judgment God once again restored his people, who continued to stand under the divine imperatives.

The Chronicler's theology was not basically at variance with that of other biblical writers though there were variations on some themes and certainly different emphases. Writing in the latter part of the Old Testament period the Chronicler was heir to most of the traditions which form Old Testament thought. He did not set out to write a systematic presentation of all that had gone before but assumed a knowledge of much of Israel's history and thought. His own thought emerges in the course of his work. Indeed, there is a certain artificiality in attempting even the degree of systematization which we shall now undertake.

(1) "All Israel"

The Chronicler viewed the whole nation, both north and south together, as the people of God and referred on numerous occasions to "all Israel." At the time of his writing, a major issue was the composition of the restored exiles in relation to the people of Israel. There was even some disagreement about how "open" or how "exclusive" the official stand should be. But for

---

[28] R. H. Pfeiffer, *Introduction to the Old Testament* (New York: Harper & Brothers, 1941), 785–86, 789.

[29] Howard, *Introduction to the Old Testament Historical Books,* 231.

the Chronicler there was no problem. His presumption was that Israel, the people of God, was made up of those who formed part of "all Israel," which included both north and south.

He opens his book with a genealogical portrayal of Israel in its ideal extent of twelve tribes. The first nine chapters are not to be viewed as a later addition to the work but as an essential part of a whole argument. The line of God's election of his people is traced directly from Adam to the "sons of Israel" (Jacob) in 1:1–2:1. Jacob, the father of the tribal ancestors, is always called "Israel" in Chronicles and is given a prominence that is virtually unique in the Old Testament. In chaps. 2–8 the descendants of Jacob are presented in their various tribal groups by means of genealogical tables. They are organized around the primary groups of the community (Judah, Benjamin, and Levi), which act as a framework for the other tribes. The final chapter (1 Chr 9) focuses on the postexilic Jerusalem community. The genealogy of Saul is presented at the end of chap. 9 as an introduction to Israel's line of kings. The total introduction in chaps. 1–9 is an essential part of the whole picture of Israel, the people of God.

As the story unfolds, the Chronicler is at great pains to show that "all Israel" accepted the kingship of both David and Solomon. "All Israel" came together to David at Hebron (1 Chr 11:1). It was David and "all Israel" who proceeded to Jerusalem to take the city (1 Chr 11:4). The "all-Israel" theme seems to lie behind the various lists of chaps. 11–12, for representatives of the various tribes were involved. "All Israel" was involved in the transfer of the ark to Jerusalem (1 Chr 13:1–6; 15:3; 16:3). All of Israel's officials were present when David made his speech to Solomon (1 Chr 28:1). When Solomon became king, "all Israel" gave their unanimous support (29:21–26). "All Israel" was present at the dedication of the temple (2 Chr 7:8).

In the period after Solomon we catch glimpses of the same motif. Rehoboam appeared before "all Israel" at Shechem to be made king (2 Chr 10:1). In the period after Solomon's death there is some variety in the use of the terms "Israel" and "all Israel." Both are used for the northern tribes (2 Chr 13:4-5,15,18), and in 2 Chr 24:5–6 the term "all Israel" refers to portions of the south. It is not possible to follow this question through within the scope of this commentary.[30] But throughout 1 Chronicles 10 to 2 Chronicles 36 various southern kings are pictured as active in the north both in warfare and in religious activities (2 Chr 13:18; 15:8; 17:2; 31:1; 34:6). On the other hand, there was religious contact between north and south at times when people from the north came to worship at Jerusalem (2 Chr 11:16; 15:9–10;

---

[30] A full discussion is given in H. G. M. Williamson, *Israel in the Books of Chronicles*, (Cambridge: Cambridge University Press, 1977).

30:11,18,21,25).

Some of the Chronicler's readers might have thought that when the schism came after Solomon's death the unity of Israel was lost forever. The Chronicler, however, was at pains to show that the division did not mean that either north or south was irretrievably divided from the other, certainly not from a religious point of view. The northern tribes did not forfeit their position as children of Israel even if they were people who had "forsaken" Yahweh. They could be restored and could return by way of repentance (2 Chr 13:4–12). Actually, the southern tribes also fell away at times and were restored after repentance.

But evidence that the division was not irretrievable came from the fact that in the days of Hezekiah the whole population was reunited in worship at Jerusalem when a Davidic king was on the throne. Hezekiah was something like a second Solomon. Even in preexilic times there had been a reunification of the people of Israel, a foretaste of that of which the prophets spoke (Ezek 37:15–23). The repeated thrust of the Chronicler's work was that north and south, "all Israel," ought to be and finally would be one in a unity based on their common worship of Yahweh centered in the Jerusalem temple.

(2) The Temple and Worship

Obviously one of the Chronicler's central concerns was the temple of Jerusalem and the worship conducted there. It was incumbent on all who were members of the family of Israel that they loyally adhered to the temple cult. The sin of Jeroboam I was that he neglected his adherence to the temple in Jerusalem and replaced it by another loyalty. King Abijah of Judah gave full expression to the fact that the worship of the temple made exclusive demands on all who claimed to be a member of Israel (2 Chr 13:10–12).

Another aspect of the temple and its worship was the importance of a Davidic king for the successful maintenance of the temple cult. David and Solomon were of focal significance in the building of the temple and in the establishment of its rituals. Generally speaking, as the reigns of Hezekiah and Josiah demonstrate and as the careful preparations to restore Joash to the Davidic kingship show, the Chronicler believed that a Davidic king was necessary for the successful maintenance of the temple cult. On great occasions such as the dedication of the temple, the Passover of Hezekiah, and the Passover of Josiah, the contribution of the king was considerable, and the Chronicler pointed out this fact.

The last four kings of Israel brought the king and the temple together in an interesting way. When the Lord's judgment fell finally on Judah, the Chronicler focused his interest on the punishment of the king personally and on the plundering of the temple (2 Chr 36).

Some writers have wanted to portray the place of the high priest in post-exilic times in an exalted position. But it is striking how little attention the Chronicler gives to the role of high priest. The most distinguished of all the high priests was Jehoiada, but he is singled out because he worked for the restoration of the Davidic monarchy at a time when it was under great threat (2 Chr 23–24). For the Chronicler the Davidic king was necessary for the successful maintenance of the temple cult and could not be replaced by the high priest.

Another important observation is that the Chronicler did not at any stage seek to supercede the Mosaic rituals that were ordered in conformity with the prescriptions of the Pentateuch. Sacrifices and festivals were conducted according to the law. Yet the Chronicler had an appreciation of historical development. He saw the need of redefining the tasks of the Levites once the significance of the ark and tabernacle had been taken over by the temple.

Finally, the Chronicler was not a strict and unyielding ritualist. He stressed the note of great joy at the conclusion of nearly all major religious celebrations. Joyless ritualism was not characteristic of him (1 Chr 29:22; 2 Chr 7:8–10; 30:21–26). Further, in a number of passages he put considerable emphasis on faith in God as the way to blessing but rarely on ritual perfection.

(3) The Concept of Kingship

We have just observed that the king was important in the leadership of and provision for the temple cult although there were strict limits on the part the king could play in the ritual. But in the Chronicler's concept of kingship in Israel were some more general aspects.

Kingship in Israel could be equated with the kingdom of God. King David addressing the officials in Israel about the future, declared that God had chosen Solomon to sit upon the throne of the kingdom of the Lord over Israel (1 Chr 28:5). In due course Solomon sat on the throne of the Lord as king after his father (1 Chr 29:23). Abijah rebuked Jeroboam I for planning to resist "the kingdom of the Lord which is in the hands of David's descendants" (2 Chr 13:8). There is a view of kingship in Israel being expressed in such passages that is extremely high. It is expressed in different terms in other passages. In 1 Chr 17:14 God speaks of "my house" and "my kingdom" through the prophet Nathan, who conveyed the divine word to David. In 2 Chr 9:8 the queen of Sheba tells Solomon that God has "placed you on his throne as king to rule for the LORD your God." The import of these passages is that God's kingship was exercised in Israel through human representatives chosen by God himself. As a consequence Israel's kingdom was secure and everlasting because it was in God's hands. In the Chronicler's thinking there was a continuity of kingship in Israel since it was grounded in God himself. If there were a change in the earthly kingship, God had the matter in hand. He could "turn the kingdom over to David" in order to rescue Israel after Saul's death (1 Chr 10:14).

In fact, kingship was entrusted to David and his dynasty. Nathan made the promise to David at God's bidding that his throne would be established forever (1 Chr 17:13; cf. 2 Chr 13:5; 21:7; 23:3). This is more than a nostalgia for the good old days;[31] it is a theological assertion that the house of David is for all time the only legitimate ruling house over Israel.

Inevitably, once the Davidic dynasty was firmly established there could have been a minimizing of the earlier exodus and Sinai traditions. But the Chronicler did not allow the idea of a Davidic covenant to push aside the fundamental importance of the Mosaic covenant that was basic for Israel's self-understanding (1 Chr 17:20–22). If need be, both of the two covenants had to be held in tension. The covenantal basis for Israel's existence, harking back to the Sinai covenant, needed to be held alongside the new Davidic covenant. Israel's roots ran back to Sinai. Their continuing existence was to be under the kingship of God exercised through the human representative of his choice. The Chronicler wrote at a time when Israel had a temple but no king. His lessons from history were to demonstrate that God had not abandoned his people—he was present among them and the future was open before them. Because of the biblical covenants they could have a legitimate hope in God's work on their behalf. A glorious future lay ahead, although the Chronicler was content to point only to its foundations.

(4) Retribution and Repentance

One of the striking features of the Chronicler's theology is his attempt to correlate blessing with faithfulness and judgment with disobedience. He returned to the theme time and again, and almost every interpreter at some point reckons with this theological axiom in Chronicles.[32]

It was specially applicable to the kings of Judah. Where a king demonstrates faithfulness to Yahweh and his covenant, he is rewarded in standard ways—success in building and military operations, the blessing of a large family, wealth, respect from his own subjects, and the respect of foreign

---

[31] Contrary to G. Fohrer, *Introduction to the Old Testament* (Nashville: Abingdon, 1968), 248.

[32] E.g., W. H. Schmidt, *Introduction to the Old Testament* (London: SCM Press, 1984), 168.

nations. By contrast a king who "forsakes" God suffers military defeat, sickness, conspiracy, lack of loyalty from his own subjects, and lack of respect from foreigners. The Chronicler goes even further than the writers of Samuel and Kings. A good illustration of his method is seen in the case of King Saul, who "died because he was unfaithful to the LORD; he did not keep the word of the LORD and even consulted a medium for guidance, and did not inquire of the LORD. So the LORD put him to death and turned the kingdom over to David son of Jesse" (1 Chr 10:13–14). This is the negative expression of the doctrine. On the positive side Solomon was urged to "acknowledge the God of your father, and serve him with wholehearted devotion and with a willing mind. . . . If you seek him, he will be found by you; but if you forsake him, he will reject you forever" (1 Chr 28:9).

The doctrine has sometimes been called the doctrine of "immediate retribution," which is to state it too exactly. Sometimes the retribution is delayed for a period. The possibility of repentance (2 Chr 7:14), which averted or at least moderated the threatened judgment, always was present. In this passage God's people are exhorted to humble themselves, to pray, to seek God's face, and to turn from their wicked ways. In such cases God would hear from heaven, forgive their sin, and heal their land. To the Chronicler's mind God was more willing to bless than to bring judgment on his people. In addition, the Chronicler's doctrine was not a facile theology of the sort associated with Job's three friends. He knew that there were exceptions, and he told of some of these.

One other facet of his doctrine of retribution is important. God gives a warning through a prophet before judgment falls. Often such a warning led to repentance as in the case of the prophet Shemaiah, who warned Rehoboam and the leaders of Judah of the approach of Pharaoh Shishak. As a result, they humbled themselves and said, "The LORD is just," so the sentence was lessened (2 Chr 12:5–12). Other examples will be given in the course of the commentary. In cases where the prophetic warning went unheeded, judgment fell as in the case of King Asa's rejection of the word of the prophet Hanani (2 Chr 16:7–10; cf. 24:19–22; 25:15–16; 26:16–21). Any doctrine of retribution in the Chronicler must therefore be removed from a purely mechanical sphere. God was compassionate (36:15–16). There was truth in a doctrine of divine judgment on evildoers, but there was truth also in a doctrine of repentance. Each individual had to answer to God for his own misdeeds. The present generation need not be heir to the judgments on their predecessors. The Chronicler's doctrine of retribution and repentance leaves the way open to future hope and blessing. For Israel there was always hope for a restoration of one people united under one king around one temple. A responsive faith arising out of repentance will call down the mercy of God (2 Chr 20:20).

(5) The Response of the People

The Chronicler's belief in the importance of repentance naturally led him to assert the importance of the spiritual attitudes of the heart. While the Chronicler stressed the importance of the temple rituals, the offering of sacrifices, the observance of the festivals like the Passover, the bringing of contributions to the temple, and the keeping of the law, it was not sufficient for God's people merely to observe the letter of the law. A deeper spiritual response was just as important, if not more so, than purely legal requirements. Three important attitudes were expected in Israel—not merely obedience but obedience with a perfect heart[33] (1 Chr 28:9; 29:9,17); not merely contributions to the temple for its repair and upkeep and the support of its personnel but willing contributions (1 Chr 29:1–9,14,17); and not merely temple rituals but ritual participation with joy (1 Chr 29:9,17,22).

These emphases are made somewhat sparsely in 1 Chronicles because the subject matter does not lend itself so readily to them (although 1 Chr 29 stresses these themes). They are, however, prominent throughout 2 Chronicles. In later areas of 2 Chronicles the phrases "with a perfect heart" and "with all the heart" are used twenty-one times of kings whose conduct won the Chronicler's approval, for example, Asa (2 Chr 15:17), Hezekiah (2 Chr 31:21), and Josiah (2 Chr 34:31). It is surprising that the Chronicler did not state explicitly that David and Solomon were perfect in Yahweh's service, although this is implied.

The characteristic of joy is evident in the disposition of the people as they rendered their service, noted in 1 Chr 12:38–40, first of all, where it marks the mood of the people making their contributions to the temple and at the feast accompanying Solomon's coronation. The theme does occur elsewhere, but Chronicles employs the root śmḥ ("be glad, rejoice") some fifteen times. It reflects the mood both of the Levites and singers in the temple services (1 Chr 15:16; 2 Chr 23:18; 29:30) and particularly of the people in various kinds of cultic activity (2 Chr 7:10; 15:15; 24:10; 29:36; 30:21,23,25). The Chronicler showed his own joy in such ceremonies.[34]

A closely related emphasis is the generosity of the people and its leaders in their support of the monarchy and the cult. This generosity is shown on the occasion of the recognition of David as king over all Israel at Hebron (1 Chr 12:38–40). It is described in 1 Chr 29:1–9 when the people gave freely and wholeheartedly to the Lord as they brought their gifts for the

---

[33] On the significance of "heart" for Chronicles, see Howard, Jr., *Introduction to the Old Testament Historical Books,* 264–66.

[34] See Japhet, *I & II Chronicles,* 38–40, for a discussion of ceremonies in Chronicles.

building of the temple. Again, on the occasion of Hezekiah's reform (2 Chr 31:2–13) the people brought "heaps" of gifts. Further evidence of the generosity of kings and princes is furnished on the occasion of major feasts and reform movements (2 Chr 29:20–24,31–35; 30:24–25; 31:4–10; 35:7–9).

We sense the enthusiastic support, the great joy, and the willing generosity shown by everyone—king, leaders, temple personnel, and people—on such occasions. This is a far cry from a barren legalism. It is an evidence of the disposition of the hearts of people who are involved at a deep level in the worship of Yahweh.

(6) The Chronicler and Messianism

In view of the discussion on "Retribution and Repentance," we have argued that the Chronicler had an eye for the future. By his understanding of the united monarchy of David and Solomon, the Chronicler intended his readers to understand that the dynasty had been eternally established.

The content of God's promise to David was not exhausted with Solomon's building of the temple (2 Chr 7). In fact, the completion of the temple was only a factor in the establishment of the promise. The variation of the Chronicler's account of Solomon's dedicatory prayer in 2 Chr 6:41–42 from that recorded in 1 Kings 8 reemphasizes the imperialist interpretation of the promise to David. The passage refers to the Davidic dynasty rather than to the people as a whole. Again, in 2 Chr 13:5–8 the speech of Abijah in vv. 5–12 reflects the Chronicler's viewpoint. "The kingdom of the LORD is in the hands of David's descendants" (v. 8). It was useless for the rebellious northerners to withstand Davidic rule. Another passage, 2 Chr 21:7, stresses the permanence of the house of David. Likewise, according to 2 Chr 23:3 when Jehoiada presented the king's son Joash to the people, he declared, "The king's son shall reign, as the LORD promised concerning the descendants of David."

In these instances it is clear that the house of David survived three critical situations. The promise to David, confirmed by the obedience of his son Solomon, was of eternal validity. The Chronicler had evidence from the nation's past and was therefore able to pass on a continuing tradition of hope, centered on the Davidic family. How far into the future this hope continued is not spelled out. It was not "messianic" in the strict sense of the word or in the manner conceived of in other parts of the Old Testament (notably by some of the prophets, e.g., Isa 9:6–7; 11:1–10; and elsewhere). He did not look into the distant future for the fulfillment of a vision in which Jerusalem would be seen as the center of the world governed by Israel to which the nations were welcomed (Isa 2:1–4). But he did have a "royalist" hope[35] and presented a "realized or inaugurated eschatology," that is, as far as the story had unfolded in his day. The future still lay open, as Jehoshaphat had declared in the Desert of Tekoa on the day he was attacked by the Moabites, the Edomites, and the Meunites (2 Chr 20:1). "Listen to me, Judah and people of Jerusalem! Have faith in the LORD your God and you will be upheld; have faith in his prophets and you will be successful."

The fully developed doctrine of Messiah had to await the future, when Christian interpreters made much of the fulfillment of the Davidic hope in the person of Jesus Christ, the Messiah.

(7) The Repetition of Historical Patterns

In developing his story the Chronicler used models around which to shape his account of individual kings. Working on the basis of material that lay before him in the earlier records in Samuel and Kings but wishing to point up theological issues he wanted to make clear, he used the earlier records as models to lend support to his theological concerns. His methodology is pervasive, and one can identify his intentions in many areas. It is not possible within the scope of this book to develop the question in detail. It must suffice to illustrate by reference to Solomon, Jehoshaphat, and Hezekiah.

1. Solomon is seen as a second David.[36] The succession from David to Solomon is patterned on the succession of Moses to Joshua. In the Chronicler's distinctive treatment of Solomon, he omits a good deal of the unfavorable material found in Kings that might tarnish the image of both David and Solomon and portrays the glorious, obedient, all-conquering figures who enjoy both divine blessing and the total support of the people.

Solomon, like David, was king by divine choice. He enjoyed the complete and immediate support of all the people. Solomon, like David, had a profound concern for the cult, the temple, and its personnel. Solomon's succession of David parallels with the example of Moses and Joshua. Numerous phrases in Deuteronomy and Joshua are paralleled in Chronicles.[37]

The Chronicler also fashioned his account of Solomon as temple builder, with his helper Huram-Abi (2 Chr 4:16), on that of Bezalel, the tabernacle supervisor of building, and his helper Oholiab (Exod 36:1–2). Solomon is

---

[35] The term is used by H. G. M. Williamson, "Eschatology in Chronicles," *TB* 28 (1977): 154.

[36] R. B. Dillard gives an excellent statement of "The Chronicler's Solomon" (*2 Chronicles,* WBC [Waco: Word, 1987], 1–7).

[37] This is worked out in the article of H. G. M. Williamson, "The Accession of Solomon in the Books of Chronicles," 351–61.

seen as the new Bezalel and Huram-Abi as the new Oholiab.[38]

2. A second example of the Chronicler's use of a model around which to shape his version of a particular reign is the use of Asa's story as a paradigm for Jehoshaphat's story. The Chronicler considerably expanded his account of the reign of Asa, and comparison of his accounts of Asa and Jehoshaphat will indicate that there are several strong parallels between the two reigns. Both were pious kings whose reigns followed similar patterns. Both kings enjoyed the rewards of their piety in building programs, peace, and large armies. God was with them both, and the fear of Yahweh was on the nations in their day. Also both were rebuked by prophets for foreign alliances.[39]

3. For Hezekiah also the Chronicler used the model of David and Solomon. Under Hezekiah Israel was united under a Davidic king. Hezekiah showed a great concern for the temple and for its rituals (e.g., the Passover) and its personnel, the priests and Levites. He had enormous wealth. He received gifts from the nations. He did what was right in the eyes of Yahweh. His intercessory prayer at the Passover observance (2 Chr 30:18–20) recalls the prayer of Solomon at the temple dedication (2 Chr 6). For his fidelity Hezekiah enjoyed the blessing of God in the loyalty and support of his people, in the reunification of the nation, in his building projects, in the support of his people, in his military victories, and in his recognition among the nations. He is presented as almost as blameless as Solomon, although he had a proud spirit. Yet he repented and was therefore saved from the divine wrath (32:24–26).[40]

The description of the models the Chronicler chose to portray Solomon, Jehoshaphat, and Hezekiah do not exhaust this theme. It was an important part of the Chronicler's repertoire as he developed his theological emphasis.

(8) The Chronicler as an Exegete of Scripture and the Past

B. Childs has pointed out that the Chronicler's work may be described as an exegesis of authoritative Scripture. He harmonized, supplemented, and looked for types and lessons. In his writings we see a kind of early example of how lessons may be drawn from Scripture and history for the modern reader. In so doing, he "bears witness to the unity of God's will for his people," and he points to the importance of Scripture in guiding the lives of the modern believer.[41]

---

[38] The detailed comparisons are provided in Dillard, *2 Chronicles.*

[39] See Dillard, ibid., 129–30, for other parallels.

[40] Ibid., 227–29.

[41] See B. Childs, *Introduction to the Old Testament as Scripture* (Philadelphia: Fortress, 1979), 647–55.

9. The Chronicler's Theological Vocabulary

With his own specific interests in view, it was inevitable that the Chronicler should use a vocabulary that best served his purpose. An important feature of his treatment of the story of Israel was to demonstrate that not only the kings but often the people also had turned aside from their allegiance to Yahweh their God and had worshiped and served other gods. A particular group of words was regularly used to describe this apostasy. Another group of words was used to describe the response of those who were obedient to Yahweh or who returned to him after turning aside. A particular vocabulary also is used to describe the response of God to those who repented.

(1) Vocabulary of Apostasy

The verb *māʿal* ("to be unfaithful") and its noun *maʿal* ("unfaithfulness") occur frequently in Chronicles to describe how individual kings as well as the people and the priests had turned aside from their allegiance to Yahweh (verb: 1 Chr 5:25; 10:13; 2 Chr 12:2; 26:16,18; 28:19,22; 29:6; 30:7; 36:14; noun: 2 Chr 28:19; 29:19; 33:19; 36:14). In addition, commonly used phrases that form part of his vocabulary are "to do evil in the eyes of the LORD" and "to walk in the ways of the kings of Israel" (2 Chr 21:6; 28:2; 33:2,22; 36:5,9,12).

(2) Vocabulary of Obedience

These experiences have a particular distinctiveness, often in sharp contrast to that used to describe those who were unfaithful. Typical phrases are "to do what was good and right in the eyes of the LORD his God," "to walk in the ways of his father David" (2 Chr 17:3; 20:32; 24:2; 26:4; 27:2; 29:2; 34:2), "to humble oneself" (2 Chr 7:14; 12:6–7,12; 30:11; 33:12; 34:27).

A significant passage that uses several of the Chronicler's common phrases is the Lord's reply to Solomon after the dedication of the temple in 2 Chr 7:14: "If my people, who are called by my name, will humble themselves and pray and seek my face and turn from their wicked ways, then will I hear from heaven and will forgive their sin and will heal their land." This verse is of vital significance for the Chronicler's theology. Four avenues of repentance are mentioned that will lead God to forgive and restore. Each of these is taken up at appropriate places in the later narrative of Chronicles, often in connection with one of the remarkable interventions of God. The verb "to humble oneself" occurs earlier in Chronicles in a theologically neutral sense (1 Chr 17:10; 18:1; 20:4), but later it is a key element on several occasions. It occurs four times in the account of Shishak's invasion during the reign of Rehoboam (2 Chr 12:6–7,12; 30:11; 33:12,19,23; 34:27; 36:12).

The verb *pālal* ("pray") appears in several passages (2 Chr 32:20,24; 33:13; cf. 1 Chr 17:25; 2 Chr 7:1). The verb is used more generally of "pray" in other contexts (1 Chr 17:25; 2 Chr 6:19–21,24,26,32,34,38; 30:18; 32:20,24; 33:13). The phrase "to seek God's face," "to seek God" also is used often by the Chronicler (2 Chr 11:16; 15:4,15; 20:4). The same verb *bqsˊ*("to seek") also is used in a more general sense (1 Chr 4:39; 14:8; 16:10–11). The verb *šûb* ("to turn") frequently is used but with the theological significance "to turn from wicked ways." It occurs in 2 Chr 15:4; 30:6,9; 36:13. The combination of the verbs "pray" and "turn" occurs a number of times in Solomon's prayer in 1 Chronicles 6, and this verse in 1 Chr 7:14 is God's answer to Solomon's prayer.

(3) Vocabulary of Divine Response

The divine promise for those who make the four responses of repentance in 7:14a is that God will "hear," "forgive their sin," and "heal their land," a divine response of full restoration. The request that God would "forgive" occurs several times in Solomon's prayer, and this verse in 2 Chr 7:14b gives the answer to that plea (2 Chr 6:21,25,27,30,39).

Another term that the Chronicler used some fifteen times, three times in the plural, is the Hebrew word *ḥesed,* variously translated as "love," "kindness." It occurs in the liturgical formula "for his love endures for ever" (1 Chr 16:34,41; 2 Chr 5:13; 7:3,6; 20:21), which the Chronicler frequently used. But the word is often used in contexts where a covenant is involved and denotes "loyalty." Thus David sought to demonstrate "loyalty" to his covenant with Hanun, the Ammonite, who had shown "loyalty" to him (1 Chr 19:2). God showed covenant loyalty to David (2 Chr 1:8). Solomon's prayer refers to the "covenant love" God showed to his servants (2 Chr 6:14). The term was evidently close to the Chronicler's thinking about God. One fascinating use of this noun in the plural is that the Chronicler found it useful in three contexts. In his prayer in 2 Chronicles 6, Solomon concludes with the words: "Remember the great love [kindnesses] promised to David your servant" (2 Chr 6:42).[42] Other aspects of the Chronicler's vocabulary concern his description of the activities and personnel of the cult, but these are hardly distinctive of the Chronicler because they appear in other writers who referred to the religious life of Israel.

---

[42] See Japhet, *I & II Chronicles,* 44–49, for other themes closely related to those mentioned here.

The purpose of Chronicles is intimately connected with the very reason we need to read and study it. In the words of S. Japhet: "The past is explained so that its institutions and religious principles become relevant to the present, and the ways of the present are legitimized anew by being connected to the prime source of authority—the formative period in the people's past."[43]

———————— *OUTLINE OF THE BOOK* ————————

---

[43] S. Japhet, *The Ideology of the Book of Chronicles and Its Place in Biblical Thought* (New York: Peter Lang, 1989), 515–16.

1 Chronicles

--------- **I. GOD'S PEOPLE IN GOD'S WORLD (1:1–9:34)** ---------

1. The Genealogical Prologue from Adam to Israel (Jacob) (1:1–2:2)

This section may be regarded as a preamble to the main genealogy in 2:3–9:1. In 1:1–2:2 the name "Israel" does not appear. The nation yet to come into being was hidden within the general body of humankind. Meanwhile the genealogies of chaps. 1–9 pursue their way, giving a panorama of the human background out of which the people of Israel emerged. The nation yet to be born emerged in due course from the Semites, one of the three great families of humankind: the Japhethites, the Hamites, and the Semites.

The Chronicler established Israel's place in the world through the lengthy genealogies of chaps. 1–9 so that his audience might understand anew their role among the nations. Their mission was universal in nature, enabling all peoples to know the Lord through God's appointed means, the Jerusalem temple. It was temple more so than kingship that indicated the presence of God's rule on earth. As long as there was the temple, Israel had its peculiar role among the nations.

The genealogies provided for the reconstituted Israel a sense of God's universal and ongoing work in the world. This continuity of design fueled Israel's ambition to be the holy vessel that God had envisioned for it (Exod 19). This same sense of continuity with God's work through the ages motivated the apostles to found the church in the shadow of Israel's religious tradition. But more importantly, it was the universal setting that explained the drive to bring the gospel to the Gentiles (Acts 13). God's people whether in past generations or in the present have this same commission to reach beyond themselves with the gospel to all the peoples of God's created world (Rom 1:16-17).

The main source of information for the Chronicler was the Book of Genesis.[1] Following his usual pattern, he dealt first with what to him were secondary lines within the family of humankind: first the Japhethites (vv. 5–7), then the Hamites (vv. 8–16), and finally what to him was the major family—the Semites (vv. 17–27), narrowing down this family to Abraham and his sons (v. 28). From his sons Isaac and Ishmael came three lines of descendants. The family of Ishmael came first (vv. 29–31), then the family of Keturah, Abraham's concubine (vv. 32–33), and finally the family of Sarah and her two descendants, Esau and Israel, the sons of Isaac (v. 34), the second of these being the most significant for the Chronicler. The descendants of Esau are then presented (vv. 35–37) and linked with the people of Seir (vv. 38–42) and the people of Edom (vv. 43–54). Only after these listings are completed does the Chronicler take up again the sons of Israel. But he had established links in a very broad sense with other branches of the human race.

We may ask why this book burdens the reader with seemingly endless genealogies. Perhaps the best answer is provided by M. Wilcock, who observes that the generations after the exile needed a sense of history and legitimacy. In other words, they needed roots. Using the analogy of a tree, Wilcock observes that the genealogies reach from the very deepest root—Adam—to the very topmost branches of the tree—people who were living in the Chronicler's lifetime. With these roots God's people knew who they were and how they were to live. They may have felt like the most insignificant of peoples (a small, backwater country in the great Persian Empire), but the genealogies served to remind them that they were not only a people with a rich history but that their history was God's history.[2]

(1) Adam to Noah's Sons (1:1–4)

[1]Adam, Seth, Enosh, [2]Kenan, Mahalalel, Jared, [3]Enoch, Methuselah, Lamech, Noah.

[4]The sons of Noah:
Shem, Ham and Japheth.

The Chronicler proceeded directly from Adam to Noah by way of a bare list of names taken from Genesis 5 and in the same order.

---

[1] See the discussion in S. Japhet, *I & II Chronicles,* OTL (Louisville: W/JKP, 1994), 15–16.

[2] M. Wilcock, *The Message of Chronicles,* BST (Downers Grove: InterVarsity, 1987), 19–31.

(2) The Descendants of Japheth (1:5–7)

⁵The sons of Japheth:
Gomer, Magog, Madai, Javan, Tubal, Meshech and Tiras.
⁶The sons of Gomer:
Ashkenaz, Riphath and Togarmah.
⁷The sons of Javan:
Elishah, Tarshish, the Kittim and the Rodanim.

The list follows Gen 10:2–4 with minor differences.

1:5–6 Following a number of Hebrew manuscripts, the LXX, the Vg, and Gen 10:13, the NIV reads "Riphath" (v. 6) for the MT *dîpat*. In Hebrew the *r* and the *d* are very similar.

1:7 The Rodanim were the inhabitants of Rhodes.[3] Only Gomer and Javan are carried further due no doubt to the source. As L. C. Allen notes, the reference to Tarshish is one of seventeen names in chap. 1 that "recur in the Chronicler's narratives of David and Solomon as subject to their control or influence"[4] (cf. 2 Chr 9:21; also "Sheba" in vv. 9,22,32 and in 2 Chr 9:9). These may be hints of the significance the Chronicler placed on the united monarchy. As the theme of God's kingdom as represented in the Davidic-Solomonic empire would resound with promise for the future (cf. 1 Chr 17:14; 28:5; Pss 2:8; 72:10), so it found quiet introduction in this first chapter.

(3) The Descendants of Ham (1:8–16)

⁸The sons of Ham:
Cush, Mizraim, Put and Canaan.
⁹The sons of Cush:
Seba, Havilah, Sabta, Raamah and Sabteca.
The sons of Raamah:
Sheba and Dedan.
¹⁰Cush was the father of Nimrod, who grew to be a mighty warrior on earth.
¹¹Mizraim was the father of the Ludites, Anamites, Lehabites, Naphtuhites,
¹²Pathrusites, Casluhites (from whom the Philistines came) and Caphtorites.
¹³Canaan was the father of Sidon his firstborn, and of the Hittites,
¹⁴Jebusites, Amorites, Girgashites, ¹⁵Hivites, Arkites, Sinites,
¹⁶Arvadites, Zemarites and Hamathites.

The individuals named are those of Gen 10:6–20.

1:10 Most of the additional material from Genesis has been omitted,

---

[3] H. G. M. Williamson, *1 and 2 Chronicles*, NCBC (Grand Rapids: Eerdmans, 1982), 42.
[4] L. C. Allen, *1, 2 Chronicles*, CC (Waco: Word, 1987), 34–36.

although space is devoted to Nimrod, who is described as a mighty warrior on earth. This is equivalent to the Greek "tyrant" or "hero." The reference to the mighty hunter of Gen 10:9 is omitted, although in the ancient Near East hunting was a sport of kings, and a powerful ruler also was a man of might and power because he subdued wild animals.

It would be interesting to know why the Chronicler, not usually including details about individuals, made an exception in the case of Nimrod. Perhaps in a world where powerful rulers were common, he wanted to show that the practice was ancient. It should be noted that it was Nimrod who founded the Mesopotamian cities which became the arch enemies of Israel. In his own day the Persians were powerful rulers. But the spiritual ancestors of David should remember God's promise to him, "I will make your name like the names of the greatest men of the earth" (1 Chr 17:8). Greatness is in God's hands to bestow, to deny, or to take away.

1:11–12 The Philistines were Israel's archrivals over the centuries. Egypt, another nation in the background of Israel's story, rates a mention here.

1:13 Among the descendants of Ham was Canaan, the father of several groups including the Hittites. These were not the Hittites of Asia Minor but a local West Asiatic group. It was from one of the sons of Heth that Abraham bought a burial place for Sarah (Gen 10:15; 23:3).

(4) The Descendants of Shem (1:17–27)

¹⁷The sons of Shem:
Elam, Asshur, Arphaxad, Lud and Aram.
The sons of Aram:
Uz, Hul, Gether and Meshech.
¹⁸Arphaxad was the father of Shelah, and Shelah the father of Eber.
¹⁹Two sons were born to Eber:
One was named Peleg, because in his time the earth was divided; his brother was named Joktan.
²⁰Joktan was the father of Almodad, Sheleph, Hazarmaveth, Jerah, ²¹Hadoram, Uzal, Diklah, ²²Obal, Abimael, Sheba, ²³Ophir, Havilah and Jobab. All these were sons of Joktan.

²⁴Shem, Arphaxad, Shelah,
²⁵Eber, Peleg, Reu,
²⁶Serug, Nahor, Terah
²⁷and Abram (that is, Abraham).

1:17 The source of this material was Gen 10:21–29 but with some omissions, notably the phrase "the father of all the children of Eber, the elder brother of Japheth" (Gen 10:21, NRSV). We might have expected the

Chronicler to emphasize the seniority of Shem among Noah's sons in order to stress that the people of Israel had come from the Semitic branch of the human family.[5] The Chronicler had his own reasons for this omission that are not clear to us.

1:18–27 The line of Shem is traced through Arphaxad, Shelah, Eber, and Peleg to Abram, that is, Abraham (v. 27), although Abraham was not nearly as significant to the Chronicler later in the story as Jacob (Israel).

The name "Abram" is preserved from Gen 11:26 as son of Terah along with Nahor and Haran. The shorter name Abram (ʾabram) is of uncertain meaning, though probably it means "the father is exalted." The name rarely was used in the Old Testament. The name Abraham (ʾabrāhām) probably means "father of a multitude," and from the late perspective of the Chronicler in this genealogical context it testified to the verity of God's promises and to his faithfulness.

(5) The Descendants of Abraham (1:28–37)

²⁸The sons of Abraham:
   Isaac and Ishmael.
²⁹These were their descendants:
   Nebaioth the firstborn of Ishmael, Kedar, Adbeel, Mibsam, ³⁰Mishma, Dumah, Massa, Hadad, Tema, ³¹Jetur, Naphish and Kedemah. These were the sons of Ishmael.

³²The sons born to Keturah, Abraham's concubine:
   Zimran, Jokshan, Medan, Midian, Ishbak and Shuah.
   The sons of Jokshan:
   Sheba and Dedan.
³³The sons of Midian:
   Ephah, Epher, Hanoch, Abida and Eldaah.
   All these were descendants of Keturah.

³⁴Abraham was the father of Isaac.
   The sons of Isaac:
   Esau and Israel.
³⁵The sons of Esau:
   Eliphaz, Reuel, Jeush, Jalam and Korah.
³⁶The sons of Eliphaz:
   Teman, Omar, Zepho, Gatam and Kenaz;
   by Timna: Amalek.
³⁷The sons of Reuel:
   Nahath, Zerah, Shammah and Mizzah.

---

[5] R. Braun, *1 Chronicles,* WBC (Waco: Word, 1986), 17.

ABRAHAM'S SONS (1:28).   **1:28**   Verses 24–27 trace the line of Shem to Abraham, but at v. 28 the Chronicler reaches the point he was aiming for with the person of Abraham. In a mere twenty-seven verses he is poised to take up the story of Abraham's family, having traced the development of the human race from Adam to Noah to Abraham.

ABRAHAM'S DESCENDANTS THROUGH ISHMAEL (1:29–31).   **1:29–31**   After introducing Abraham's two sons, Isaac and Ishmael, the Chronicler deals first with what to him were the secondary lines of descent from Abraham, namely, the descendants[6] through Hagar (vv. 29–31) and through Keturah (vv. 32–33). The most important descendants of Abraham were, of course, those who formed the line of promise through Isaac.

The list of Hagar's descendants here is taken from Gen 25:13–16a, although as is usual with the Chronicler some details are omitted, for example, "the descendants of Dedan" (Gen 25:3b).

ABRAHAM'S DESCENDANTS THROUGH KETURAH (1:32–33).   **1:32–33**   Keturah was Abraham's concubine, a term used loosely for "wife" (Gen 25:1). The sons of "Keturah" (meaning "frankincense") are appropriately named. They came from an area to the east and southeast of Israel that produced frankincense. They are here recognized as kindred to Israel but less closely connected than the Ishmaelites. Only the descendants of Jokshan (v. 32) and Midian (v. 33) are listed, those of Dedan being ignored (cf. Gen 25:3–4). The descendants of Dedan were South Arabians. Perhaps the Chronicler thought they were only peripheral to his main theme.

ABRAHAM'S DESCENDANTS THROUGH SARAH (1:34–37).   The genealogical list picks up from v. 28b.

1:34   From Sarah came Isaac, whose sons were Esau and Israel (Jacob). The shortest description of Abraham comes in v. 34, "Abraham was the father of Isaac."

1:35–37   Esau's descendants are listed first. Some of these touch the story of Israel elsewhere in Genesis in a peripheral way. The Chronicler used the name "Israel" twelve times and "Jacob" only occasionally (1 Chr 16:13,17). The name "Israel" represented the whole nation to which he referred many times as "all Israel." The list of Esau's family comes from Gen 36:4–5,10–14 and is taken up first, the less significant before the more significant.

1:36   In Gen 36:11–12 Timna is presented slightly differently as Eliphaz's "concubine" (cf. the NIV text note).

---

[6] The term "descendant" translates תֹּלְדֹת, "generations" in the AV. This term occurs frequently in Genesis and is the key word in that book. It occurs here in 1 Chronicles for the first time.

(6) The Edomites: The Line of Esau and Seir (1:38–54)

³⁸The sons of Seir:
　Lotan, Shobal, Zibeon, Anah, Dishon, Ezer and Dishan.
³⁹The sons of Lotan:
　Hori and Homam. Timna was Lotan's sister.
⁴⁰The sons of Shobal:
　Alvan, Manahath, Ebal, Shepho and Onam.
　The sons of Zibeon:
　Aiah and Anah.
⁴¹The son of Anah:
　Dishon.
　The sons of Dishon:
　Hemdan, Eshban, Ithran and Keran.
⁴²The sons of Ezer:
　Bilhan, Zaavan and Akan.
　The sons of Dishan:
　Uz and Aran.

⁴³These were the kings who reigned in Edom before any Israelite king
　reigned:
　Bela son of Beor, whose city was named Dinhabah.
⁴⁴When Bela died, Jobab son of Zerah from Bozrah succeeded him as king.
⁴⁵When Jobab died, Husham from the land of the Temanites succeeded him
　as king.
⁴⁶When Husham died, Hadad son of Bedad, who defeated Midian in the
　country of Moab, succeeded him as king. His city was named Avith.
⁴⁷When Hadad died, Samlah from Masrekah succeeded him as king.
⁴⁸When Samlah died, Shaul from Rehoboth on the river succeeded him as
　king.
⁴⁹When Shaul died, Baal-Hanan son of Acbor succeeded him as king.
⁵⁰When Baal-Hanan died, Hadad succeeded him as king. His city was
　named Pau, and his wife's name was Mehetabel daughter of Matred,
　the daughter of Me-Zahab. ⁵¹Hadad also died.
　The chiefs of Edom were:
　Timna, Alvah, Jetheth, ⁵²Oholibamah, Elah, Pinon, ⁵³Kenaz, Teman,
　Mibzar, ⁵⁴Magdiel and Iram. These were the chiefs of Edom.

THE PEOPLE OF SEIR (1:38–42).　**1:38–42**　Seir is not listed as a
descendant of Esau in any of the genealogies available to us. However, both
Seir and Esau dwelt in Edom (cf. 2 Chr 25:11,14). Perhaps the Chronicler's
interest here was geographical. The material in Gen 36:20–28 was omitted.
He seems to have assumed his readers had a knowledge of Genesis, so he
could omit much of its detail. But the passage suggests there was a broad but
perhaps tenuous link between Israel and these tribal groups to the southeast.

THE EDOMITE KINGS (1:43–51a) AND CHIEFS (1:51b–54). The list follows Gen 36:31–39 almost verbatim. It is not clear why the Chronicler should have included this list unless it was that having mentioned the people of Seir he decided to add some remarks about their neighbors, the Edomites, in order to complete his picture of these peoples to the southwest of Israel. The Edomites played a major role in the history of Israel and were closely related to them. The Chronicler did not feel he could pass them by without comment. He did, however, omit "the chiefs among Esau's descendants" (Gen 36:15–19).[7]

1:43 The historical note about the "kings who reigned in Edom before any Israelite king reigned" suggests a time reference to conditions that obtained in Israel in the days of the judges. Later, when David was king, Edom fell under Israel's control (1 Chr 18:13), although later Israel lost its control.

1:44–54 The list of the kings who reigned in Edom does not suggest any kind of dynastic line. The residences of the kings were at different places. Evidently these rulers were something like the "judges" in the Bible. The establishment of a strong dynasty was a later development. The term used for "chief" (*ʾallûp*) is different from the word for "king" (*melek*).

(7) Israel's Sons (2:1–2)

¹These were the sons of Israel: Reuben, Simeon, Levi, Judah, Issachar, Zebulun, ²Dan, Joseph, Benjamin, Naphtali, Gad and Asher.

2:1–2 The elaborate genealogical scheme of chap. 1 reaches its climax with the words, "These were the sons of Israel." The genealogical story of Israel proper could now begin.

2. The Line of Judah (2:3–4:23)

With 2:3 the Chronicler takes up his genealogical résumé of the sons of Israel, which will occupy him until 9:1, that is, for approximately eight chapters. The material deals with the sons of Israel: Judah (2:3–4:23), Simeon (4:24–43), Reuben (5:1–10), Gad (5:11–17), the Transjordan tribes including the half-tribe of Manasseh (5:18–26), Levi (6:1–81), Issachar (7:1–5), Benjamin (7:6–12), Naphtali (7:13), Manasseh (7:14–19), Ephraim (7:20–29), Asher (7:30–40), and Benjamin (8:1–40). At 9:1 the Chronicler sums up with the words, "All Israel was listed in the genealogies recorded in the book of the kings of Israel." Thereafter he takes up the postexilic community in chap. 9.

---

[7] Williamson, *1 and 2 Chronicles*, 44.

The questions of the Chronicler's sources and of the order in which the tribes are presented are of some interest. As to the sources of his material, we must give high priority to Old Testament lists such as Genesis 46 and Numbers 26. Information about geographical material, pastures, intertribal skirmishes, and so forth (4:39–43; 5:9–10,19–21; 7:21) could have been culled from a variety of sources preserved in ancient tribal traditions. Evidently the writer also had access to military census material, for he included data about army units and personnel.

A variety of explanations has been offered about the arrangement of the tribes. Did the writer follow the order of Numbers 26 or was it according to some geographical order? No solution is entirely satisfactory. The proposal of H. G. M. Williamson is helpful. He proposes that since Judah was the strongest of his brothers and a ruler came from him (5:2), he was given pride of place. Then came Simeon, who always was associated with Judah (4:24–43). At this point the Chronicler drew in the Transjordan tribes, Reuben (5:1–10), Gad (5:11–17), and half the tribe of Manasseh (5:23–26), probably to ensure that these tribes were not overlooked.[8]

Placing Judah first among the tribes prepares the reader for the prominence of the house of David in Chronicles as the text moves quickly to the Davidic line (2:11–15). In this we see in part the messianic program of Chronicles.

Next comes the genealogy of Levi (6:1–81), the second major postexilic group to occupy the Chronicler's attention. This genealogy occupies the central place in the scheme. The priestly tribe of Levi was of very great importance in the postexilic period because of the temple and the rituals. The placing of Levi in the central position no doubt reflects the enormous significance of this tribe both for the Chronicler himself and for the postexilic community.

The emphasis on Judah and Levi in the genealogies marks the center of the Chronicler's hope and faith. Two things marked the true Israel: the king and the priest. These two men, or perhaps better institutions, reflected God's choice for the leadership of the people and the establishment of the kingdom of God. Although the king had passed from the scene already in the Chronicler's day, the author obviously wanted to hold up this as the ideal and goal.[9] The ultimate fulfillment, in fact, would be the uniting of both king and priest in the one man, Christ Jesus.

The third major tribe was Benjamin (chap. 8), but between Levi (chap. 6) and Benjamin is material on Issachar (7:1–5), some military material on

---

[8] H. G. M. Williamson, *1 and 2 Chronicles,* NCB (Grand Rapids: Eerdmans, 1982), 46–47.
[9] See Wilcock, *Message of Chronicles,* 48–50.

Benjamin (7:6–12; cf. chap. 8), Naphtali (7:13), Western Manasseh (7:14–19), Ephraim (7:20–29), and Asher (7:30–40). The genealogies of Zebulun and Dan are lacking, and that of Naphtali is brief (7:13). The reason for this is not clear, but perhaps the Chronicler did not include all the material he had at his disposal but made use of just enough to allow the general sweep of the tribal genealogies to cover the whole. His main purpose was achieved by giving full attention to the main postexilic tribes of Judah (2:3–4:23), Levi (6:1–81), and Benjamin (8:1–40), which covered between them the royal descent, the priestly group, and the Benjamites from which Saul, the first king of Israel, came (1 Sam 9:1). He gathered round those three tribes representative material from the other tribes so as to preserve the concept of "all Israel." The postexilic community known to the Chronicler consisted largely of members of Judah, Levi, and Benjamin, but the whole included representatives of all the tribes. In fact, at no time did all of the people go into exile; and since there would always have been some intertribal migration, it was extremely likely that the true picture was one of an "all-Israel" distribution in postexilic times—even if the tribal picture in the central area was predominantly a Judah-Levi-Benjamin composition.

The analysis and discussion of the tribes of Israel begins at 2:3 with the tribe of Judah, to which the Chronicler devoted by far his longest coverage. It was this line that gave rise to Israel's kings. David, a key figure for the Chronicler, came from the tribe of Judah. The emphasis on the line of David here signals the major emphasis of the Chronicler. He was looking to the Davidic monarchy as the model for the future hope of his people. In contrast, he ignored the exodus almost entirely.

(1) The Sons of Judah up to Hezron and His Sons (2:3–9)

³The sons of Judah:

Er, Onan and Shelah. These three were born to him by a Canaanite woman, the daughter of Shua. Er, Judah's firstborn, was wicked in the Lord's sight; so the Lord put him to death. ⁴Tamar, Judah's daughter-in-law, bore him Perez and Zerah. Judah had five sons in all.

⁵The sons of Perez:

Hezron and Hamul.

⁶The sons of Zerah:

Zimri, Ethan, Heman, Calcol and Darda—five in all.

⁷The son of Carmi:

Achar, who brought trouble on Israel by violating the ban on taking devoted things.

⁸The son of Ethan:

Azariah.

> **⁹The sons born to Hezron were:**
> **Jerahmeel, Ram and Caleb.**

From a genealogical perspective, the royal clan of Judah did not show much promise. His eldest son Er died because of wickedness. As a familiarity with the account would show (Gen 38), it did not get much better since Judah's second and third sons did not bear sons either. It was rather through the sordid incident of Judah and his daughter-in-law Tamar, disguised as a prostitute, that the promised heritage was perpetuated through their twin sons, Perez and Zerah. Ironically, the Chronicler could in one and the same breath show the consequences of sin (death of Er) and also the grace of God abounding in the midst of it as two sons were born by means of Judah's wicked deed. Out of this union came the ancestral father of Israel's greatest king (Ruth 4:18-22).

2:3 The Chronicler disposed of the sons of Judah in a brief space (2:3–9) before embarking on his peculiar chronological scheme at 2:9 with the sons of Hezron. The source of this information is Genesis 38, where the Canaanite mother of Er, Onan, and Shelah appears as Shua. Nothing more is said about Onan, but Er, Judah's firstborn, is described as "wicked in the LORD'S sight; so the LORD put him to death." Shelah is referred to in 4:21–23. Another Canaanite woman, Tamar, appears in the genealogy of David's family, demonstrating the more generous attitude to foreigners than is shown in some postexilic writers. The Chronicler evidently had no inhibitions about this fact and displayed thereby some of the perspectives of the New Testament. That Judah had two sons by his Canaanite daughter-in-law Tamar was contrary to the law of Lev 18:15; 20:12. But divine grace can overrule such restrictions, and divine election will move forward despite human failure (cf. Matt 1:3). Evidently the Chronicler did not regard marriage to a Canaanite woman as a hindrance to the development of the Davidic line.

A contrast appears here with the slaying of Er for his wickedness in the eyes of the Lord. Perhaps Er showed a persistent attitude toward evil. God is the God of both judgment and mercy. The Chronicler may have had a deliberate theological intention in stating that Er was wicked in the Lord's sight. Here is the first reference to the divine name "Yahweh" ("LORD") in 1 Chronicles.

2:4 The Chronicler noted that Judah had five sons in all. All five were born in unusual circumstances, three to a foreign mother and two as a result of sexual irregularity. Divine grace was able to deal with each case—an important emphasis. No circumstance is beyond the reach of God's grace.

2:5 As the genealogy develops, concentration falls briefly on the fourth son, Perez, and his sons, Hezron and Hamul (cf. Gen 46:12; Num 26:21). No more is said of Hamul, and the emphasis falls on Hezron and his family because David came from this line (2:9–17; note vv. 13–15). J. G. McConville notes here the theme of the *fresh start*. The Chronicler "makes no attempt to disguise the fact that it [the promise to the patriarchs] had its beginning in Judah's illicit relationship with his daughter-in-law Tamar."[10] Despite such an event, God begins anew, i.e., provides a fresh start, in fulfilling his promise to his people.

2:6–8 The five sons of Zerah evidently were of some importance to the Chronicler because of their connection with musical guilds. Zimri[11] seems to link with a group of individuals with musical connections. Ethan (lit., "a native") is listed with Heman, Calcol, and Darda, "sons of Mahol" in 4:31, the traditional "wise men" of Solomon's court. They are associated with musical guilds, as in the headings to Pss 88 and 89.[12] In no other biblical tradition are Ethan, Heman, Calcol, and Darda attached to Zerah of the tribe of Judah. Some writers have conjectured that this group of five (v. 6) may have been members of a guild of musicians who were "adopted" into the tribe of Judah because of their musical skills. As v. 3 shows, a Canaanite woman was the mother of three of Judah's sons. Similarly, Rahab of Jericho was a Canaanitess, and Ruth the Moabitess became part of the family of Israel. Evidently in earlier times in Israel there was a degree of flexibility in regard to the composition of families.

The name "Carmi" is known from Josh 7:1,18 as the father of Achan (or Achar). The Chronicler added the note "who brought trouble on Israel by violating the ban on taking devoted things."[13]

Azariah is not known from elsewhere, but the Chronicler may have used a version of the Hebrew text different from the MT, a feature of Chronicles (see Introduction).

2:9 The sons of Hezron were Jerahmeel, Ram, and Kelubai (Caleb). At this point in the genealogy an interesting pattern emerges. The Chronicler made use of the literary device known as chiasmus in which there is a reversal of a sequence. The genealogy of the sons of Hezron is broken up in this way as follows:

---

[10] J. McConville, *I & II Chronicles*, DSB (Philadelphia: Westminster, 1984) 10.

[11] The name derives from the root זמר, "to make music."

[12] W. F. Albright, *Archaeology and the Religion of Israel* (Baltimore: Johns Hopkins University Press, 1946), 126–28.

[13] This is paranomasia: עָכַר עוֹכֵר, "*Achar,* who brought *trouble*" (cf. Josh 7:24–26; the Achan of Joshua has become Achar ["trouble"]).

> A   Descendants of Ram (as far as David) 2:10–17;
>   B   Descendants of Caleb 2:18–24;
>   C   Descendants of Jerahmeel 2:25–33;
>   C'   Supplementary material on Jerehmeel 2:34–41;
>   B'   Supplementary material on Caleb 2:42–55;
> A'   Supplementary material on Ram (David's descendants) chap. 3.

A comprehension of this pattern helps the reader to follow some of the complexities of these genealogies which are something of a puzzle from 2:10 to 3:24. The figure of David who lies squarely in the tribe of Judah embraces this whole genealogical arrangement in a large inclusio.[14]

(2) The Sons of Judah from Ram, Son of Hezron, as Far as David (2:10–17)

[10]Ram was the father of Amminadab, and Amminadab the father of Nahshon, the leader of the people of Judah. [11]Nahshon was the father of Salmon, Salmon the father of Boaz, [12]Boaz the father of Obed and Obed the father of Jesse.
[13]Jesse was the father of Eliab his firstborn; the second son was Abinadab, the third Shimea, [14]the fourth Nethanel, the fifth Raddai, [15]the sixth Ozem and the seventh David. [16]Their sisters were Zeruiah and Abigail. Zeruiah's three sons were Abishai, Joab and Asahel. [17]Abigail was the mother of Amasa, whose father was Jether the Ishmaelite.

The family of Hezron brought the Chronicler to one of his key concerns, the family of David (v. 15). Hezron's genealogy has no parallel in Old Testament sources. Hezron, son of Perez, is mentioned in Gen 46:12 and Num 26:21, but no genealogy is developed. The name is given to a town between Kadesh Barnea and Addar (Josh 15:3) and in the composite name Kerioth-Hezron in Josh 15:25. It is also associated with Reuben in Gen 46:9 and 1 Chr 5:3. The name evidently was well known and had links with southern Canaan. But the precise genealogy in 1 Chr 2:10–1725–33,42–50 is lacking elsewhere. Possibly the Chronicler composed his genealogy from independent sources such as vv. 10–17,25–33,42–50 in order to present his argument in a chiastic framework.[15] Hezron's sons were Jerahmeel, Ram, and Chelubai (Caleb; v. 9). Ram, the middle son, is taken up first (vv. 10–17). His genealogy is developed through Jesse (v. 13) and David (v. 14). The order in which these three sons are presented is Ram, Caleb, and Jerahmeel.

---

[14] An inclusio is a bracketing device to hold together a variety of related material. It is used elsewhere by the Chronicler.
[15] Williamson, *1 and 2 Chronicles*, 51.

The main line of descent is presented first, although Ram was the second son. This was in accord with the Chronicler's literary plan. There is no reason to postulate a later literary expansion.

2:10–17   The genealogy of Ram here is to be compared with Ruth 4:19–22; Num 2:3; and 1 Sam 16:6–8, though the connection between the Chronicler and these passages is not clear. Each of these texts may go back to an original temple source.

The Samuel material refers to eight sons of Jesse (1 Sam 16:10–11; 17:12) while the Chronicler mentions only seven (v. 15). One rabbinical interpretation is that perhaps one died childless and so was not mentioned by the Chronicler. The Syriac version adds Elihu as a brother of David (1 Chr 27:18) though this may be a variant of Eliab or even an otherwise unnamed eighth son of Jesse. The presence of David in a list reaching back through Jesse to Hezron and Judah provides the vital genealogical link for the Chronicler. Zeruiah and Abigail are listed as sisters of David (v. 16; cf. 1 Sam 26:6; 2 Sam 17:25). These evidently were listed here because they occur in the story of Abigail later on.

Nahshon, son of Amminadab, is described as a "leader" (tribal prince) of Judah. He was a contemporary of Moses and Aaron (Exod 6:23; Num 2:3). These verses fill in important details of David's life although they are far from complete. Evidently this did not matter to the Chronicler provided the general shape of the line was established.

(3) *The Descendants of Caleb, Son of Hezron (2:18–24)*

18Caleb son of Hezron had children by his wife Azubah (and by Jerioth). These were her sons: Jesher, Shobab and Ardon. 19When Azubah died, Caleb married Ephrath, who bore him Hur. 20Hur was the father of Uri, and Uri the father of Bezalel.

21Later, Hezron lay with the daughter of Makir the father of Gilead (he had married her when he was sixty years old), and she bore him Segub. 22Segub was the father of Jair, who controlled twenty-three towns in Gilead. 23(But Geshur and Aram captured Havvoth Jair, as well as Kenath with its surrounding settlements—sixty towns.) All these were descendants of Makir the father of Gilead.

24After Hezron died in Caleb Ephrathah, Abijah the wife of Hezron bore him Ashhur the father of Tekoa.

The descendants of Caleb (Chelubai), the third son of Hezron, are now listed, the most important of these being Bezalel because of his association with the tabernacle and its furnishings. The logical arrangement of vv. 18–24 is not entirely clear to us now. Probably fragments have been taken from their original and fuller context. Thus vv. 18–19 have their continuation in

vv. 50b–52, and v. 20 is related to Exod 31:2 and 35:30 while v. 23b is a formula without a context.

2:18 The Caleb referred to is not the Caleb of Num 13:6, who was a contemporary of Bezalel, the great-grandson of the Caleb listed here (v. 20). Caleb the spy is mentioned in a different context (4:15). Further, some textual problems are found here. By a small emendation Jerioth is shown to be the daughter of Caleb and Azubah.[16]

2:19–20 Caleb married Ephrath after the death of Azubah, and she bore him Hur, the grandfather of Bezalel, the builder of the tabernacle (Exod 31:1–11; 2 Chr 1:5). The Chronicler here placed side by side the genealogies of Ram and Caleb from whom came the royal line and the temple, thus stressing the close connection between these key ideas.

2:21-24 Hezron later married the daughter of Makir, a son of Manasseh (Num 32:39–41), when he was sixty years old. She bore him Segub, father of Jair, who controlled twenty-three towns in Gilead. Jair is known from Judg 10:3–4 as a Gileadite. This link between Judah and Manasseh shows how the tribes became mixed, probably quite early. There were evidently encroachments into this area from Geshur and Aram (v. 23a) long before the western expansion of Aram-Damascus. The Chronicler evidently regarded these early associations between Judah's family and Transjordan as significant. Unfortunately we do not have enough data to analyze vv. 21–24 in detail.

A further question arises in regard to the geographical interpretation of these verses. There is information here about intertribal and interclan relationships. The genealogical form in which these verses are cast cannot always be studied properly apart from the domestic, political, and religious relationships of the area. The genealogies in Chronicles are highly complex.[17]

What may appear to be a heavy emphasis on geographical material in vv. 21–24 could be understood as an accurate expression of the perception of the Chronicler. "The comparative data now available suggests that at many points the Bible's genealogical views are quite similar to those of living societies where genealogies are still created, preserved, and used. A recognition of these similarities can add new dimensions to the biblical genealogies and can allow the modern reader to enter more fully into the world of the ancient Israelites."[18]

---

[16] Read אֲשֶׁת־חֹתִוֹ for אֶת־אֵשֶׁת. See Williamson, *1 and 2 Chronicles,* 53. The NEB has "Caleb . . . had Jerioth by Azubah his wife."

[17] See Introduction on Chronologies.

[18] R. R. Wilson, "Between 'Azel' and 'Azel': Interpreting Biblical Genealogies," *BA* 42 (1979): 21.

(4) The Sons of Jerahmeel, Firstborn Son of Hezron (2:25–33)

   ²⁵The sons of Jerahmeel the firstborn of Hezron: Ram his firstborn, Bunah,
      Oren, Ozem and Ahijah. ²⁶Jerahmeel had another wife, whose name
      was Atarah; she was the mother of Onam.
   ²⁷The sons of Ram the firstborn of Jerahmeel:
      Maaz, Jamin and Eker.
   ²⁸The sons of Onam:
      Shammai and Jada.
    The sons of Shammai:
      Nadab and Abishur.
   ²⁹Abishur's wife was named Abihail, who bore him Ahban and Molid.
   ³⁰The sons of Nadab:
      Seled and Appaim. Seled died without children.
   ³¹The son of Appaim:
      Ishi, who was the father of Sheshan. Sheshan was the father of Ahlai.
   ³²The sons of Jada, Shammai's brother: Jether and Jonathan. Jether died
      without children.
   ³³The sons of Jonathan:
      Peleth and Zaza.
    These were the descendants of Jerahmeel.

The ominous repetition of "died without children" (2:30,32) and the
absence of male offspring for Sheshan (2:34) spoke volumes to readers anxious about their future. The linkage from Adam to Abraham to Jacob-Israel
to David and so forth was never automatic. The harsh realities of life were
that some families did not enjoy perpetuation. These startling exceptions to
the rule showed how the genealogical survival of the appointed, such as the
royal and high priestly houses, were a tribute to the sustaining grace of
God's hand across the ages. This was the case for the house of Jesse and his
"seventh son" David (2:13) whose male offspring were also numerous (3:1–
9). There must have been a growing sense of confidence in the Lord's sovereignty as each clan and family's names resounded in the mind of the ancient
reader. No person was incidental to Israel's life, past or present. The Church
has always experienced the same triumphant note in a future for God's people because of the testimony of the past.

2:25–33   The genealogy is presented in a straightforward manner. It evidently goes back to a well-preserved source, but it lacks Old Testament parallels. The Jerahmeelites came from an area to the south of Judah (1 Sam
27:10; 30:29), and to judge from names like Ahijah (v. 25) and Jonathan
(v. 33) they shared the faith of Israel, whose God was Yahweh. They originally may have been non-Israelites who became absorbed into Judah. In any
case this strong association with Judah could provide a sufficient link with

Judah to enable them to claim a place in the postexilic community.

Between vv. 25–33 and vv. 42–50a is a parallel in literary expression. The opening and closing formulae are similar, but the arrangement of the names differs. In vv. 25–33 the descendants of Jerahmeel by his two wives are presented in segments arranged in horizontal form, while in vv. 34–41 the arrangement is vertical and linear in form, without opening and closing formulae. Little is known about the clan of Jerahmeel, but there is no reason to doubt the general reliability of this record.

(5) Supplementary Material on Jerahmeel (2:34–41)

> [34]Sheshan had no sons—only daughters.
>> He had an Egyptian servant named Jarha. [35]Sheshan gave his daughter in marriage to his servant Jarha, and she bore him Attai.
> [36]Attai was the father of Nathan,
>> Nathan the father of Zabad,
> [37]Zabad the father of Ephlal,
>> Ephlal the father of Obed,
> [38]Obed the father of Jehu,
>> Jehu the father of Azariah,
> [39]Azariah the father of Helez,
>> Helez the father of Eleasah,
> [40]Eleasah the father of Sismai,
>> Sismai the father of Shallum,
> [41]Shallum the father of Jekamiah,
>> and Jekamiah the father of Elishama.

2:34–41 These verses consist of a vertically arranged genealogy. It leads from Sheshan (v. 34) to Elishama (v. 41), giving the pedigree of Elishama, who had no sons but only daughters (v. 34). One of the daughters was given in marriage to an Egyptian slave, Jarha. From this union one branch of the family led to Elishama (v. 41), fourteen generations later, perhaps about the time of David although there is no certainty about this.

(6) Supplementary Material on Caleb, Brother of Jerahmeel (2:42–55)

> [42]The sons of Caleb the brother of Jerahmeel:
>> Mesha his firstborn, who was the father of Ziph, and his son Mareshah, who was the father of Hebron.
> [43]The sons of Hebron:
>> Korah, Tappuah, Rekem and Shema. [44]Shema was the father of Raham, and Raham the father of Jorkeam. Rekem was the father of Shammai. [45]The son of Shammai was Maon, and Maon was the father of Beth Zur.

⁴⁶Caleb's concubine Ephah was the mother of Haran, Moza and Gazez. Haran was the father of Gazez.
⁴⁷The sons of Jahdai:
Regem, Jotham, Geshan, Pelet, Ephah and Shaaph.
⁴⁸Caleb's concubine Maacah was the mother of Sheber and Tirhanah. ⁴⁹She also gave birth to Shaaph the father of Madmannah and to Sheva the father of Macbenah and Gibea. Caleb's daughter was Acsah. ⁵⁰These were the descendants of Caleb.

The sons of Hur the firstborn of Ephrathah:
Shobal the father of Kiriath Jearim, ⁵¹Salma the father of Bethlehem, and Hareph the father of Beth Gader.
⁵²The descendants of Shobal the father of Kiriath Jearim were:
Haroeh, half the Manahathites, ⁵³and the clans of Kiriath Jearim: the Ithrites, Puthites, Shumathites and Mishraites. From these descended the Zorathites and Eshtaolites.
⁵⁴The descendants of Salma:
Bethlehem, the Netophathites, Atroth Beth Joab, half the Manahathites, the Zorites, ⁵⁵and the clans of scribes who lived at Jabez: the Tirathites, Shimeathites and Sucathites. These are the Kenites who came from Hammath, the father of the house of Recab.

Verses 42–50a begin with an introduction, "The sons of Caleb," and conclude with "these were the descendants of Caleb" (v. 50). Verses 50b–55 begin with "the sons of Hur" (cf. 1 Sam 30:14,29). A particular formula is used in these verses, namely, "*X* the father of *Y*," where *Y* represents a place name, for example, "Mareshah, who was the father of Hebron" (v. 42). This is a different way of expressing a genealogy in which a person is considered "the father" of a city rather than of an individual. Several of these cities are known in lists of cities allotted to Judah (Josh 15). Thus Ziph (Josh 15:55) has sometimes been identified with Tell Ziph about five miles southeast of Hebron (or Khirbet-ez-Zaifeh, southwest of Kurnub).[19]

2:42–49 The name "Hebron" is important here. His relationship to Caleb is known elsewhere in the Old Testament (Josh 14:13; 15:13; Judg 1:20). The area of Calebite settlement lay near Hebron with several of the settlements lying beyond the postexilic province of Judah in the days of the Chronicler. The material in these verses may reflect an earlier situation. There are further references in these verses to concubines being the mothers of some of the individuals listed (vv. 46,48). Such a state of affairs did not destroy the validity of descent.[20]

---

[19] For other identifications see the index in Y. Aharoni, *The Land of the Bible* (Philadelphia: Westminster, 1966), 300.
[20] There is a textual problem in v. 42. The NIV "his son Mareshah" is "the sons of Mareshah" in the MT. Several options are offered in Japhet, *I & II Chronicles*, 86. Although the MT is difficult to interpret it is best to go with "the sons of Mareshah."

2:50–51 Verses 50b–55 should be linked with 2:18–19,24 and 4:4b. Hur was the firstborn of Ephrathah, the second wife of Caleb (2:19). Each of the three sons of Hur (vv. 50–51) is called "the father of" a well-known city, namely, Kiriath Jearim, Bethlehem, and Beth Gader.

2:52–54 "Shobal" is an Edomite name (cf. Gen 36:20,23,29; 1 Chr 1:38,40). His descendants were Haroeh (the seer or perhaps Reaiah; cf. 4:2), half the Manahathites, and the clans of Kiriath Jearim. These names suggest associations between Judah and its neighbors to the south.[21] The genealogy in vv. 50b–55 may well reflect the ongoing amalgamation of previously unrelated tribal elements into the mainstream of Judah.

The genealogies up to this point in chap. 2 have brought together under Hezron's sons Jerahmeel and Caleb (vv. 5,18) a wide variety of genealogical, geographical, and general cultural information, some of which is derived from the biblical sources and some from other sources.

The line of David was derived from Ram, the son of Hezron (vv. 10–17). Other details about this tribe are gathered under the other two sons of Hezron, Caleb (vv. 18–24) and Jerahmeel (vv. 25–41). The aim of the Chronicler was to attach all of these diverse elements to the tribe of Judah through Hezron and his descendants. There evidently was some prestige as well as political, economic, and social advantage belonging to the only tribe restored to its own territory by official decree. Many of those who had become attached to the tribe of Judah shared in the status by adoption, and the present genealogy served to recognize that adoption.

2:55 The reference to the clans of scribes (v. 55) is puzzling. Some commentators understand them to be the residents of a town like Kiriath-sefer (book city). The associated names are not known otherwise. They are called "the Kenites," who came from Hammath. Perhaps they were connected by marriage with the ancestors of "the house of Rechab," the Rechabites, people who espoused a nonsedentary life (Jer 25); but certainty is not possible. In fact, there may be no connection between the Kenites and the Rechabites.[22]

(7) Supplementary Material on Ram, David's Descendants (3:1–24)

¹These were the sons of David born to him in Hebron:
The firstborn was Amnon the son of Ahinoam of Jezreel;
the second, Daniel the son of Abigail of Carmel;

---

[21] See Braun, *1 Chronicles*, 42–43.
[22] See C. H. Knights, "Kenites = Rechabites?: 1 Chronicles ii 55 Reconsidered," *VT* 43 (1993): 10–18. He argues that the Hebrew בֵּית־רֵכָב is a place name, not a tribal name, and that the verse does not identify the Kenites and Rechabites as one tribe.

²the third, Absalom the son of Maacah daughter of Talmai king of Geshur; the fourth, Adonijah the son of Haggith;
³the fifth, Shephatiah the son of Abital;
and the sixth, Ithream, by his wife Eglah.
⁴These six were born to David in Hebron, where he reigned seven years and six months.
David reigned in Jerusalem thirty-three years, ⁵and these were the children born to him there:

Shammua, Shobab, Nathan and Solomon. These four were by Bathsheba daughter of Ammiel. ⁶There were also Ibhar, Elishua, Eliphelet, ⁷Nogah, Nepheg, Japhia, ⁸Elishama, Eliada and Eliphelet—nine in all. ⁹All these were the sons of David, besides his sons by his concubines. And Tamar was their sister.

¹⁰Solomon's son was Rehoboam,
Abijah his son,
Asa his son,
Jehoshaphat his son,
¹¹Jehoram his son,
Ahaziah his son,
Joash his son,
¹²Amaziah his son,
Azariah his son,
Jotham his son,
¹³Ahaz his son,
Hezekiah his son,
Manasseh his son,
¹⁴Amon his son,
Josiah his son.
¹⁵The sons of Josiah:
Johanan the firstborn,
Jehoiakim the second son,
Zedekiah the third,
Shallum the fourth.
¹⁶The successors of Jehoiakim:
Jehoiachin his son,
and Zedekiah.

¹⁷The descendants of Jehoiachin the captive:
Shealtiel his son, ¹⁸Malkiram, Pedaiah, Shenazzar, Jekamiah, Hoshama and Nedabiah.
¹⁹The sons of Pedaiah:
Zerubbabel and Shimei.
The sons of Zerubbabel:
Meshullam and Hananiah. Shelomith was their sister.

20There were also five others:
　Hashubah, Ohel, Berekiah, Hasadiah and Jushab-Hesed.
21The descendants of Hananiah:
　Pelatiah and Jeshaiah, and the sons of Rephaiah, of Arnan, of Obadiah
　and of Shecaniah.
22The descendants of Shecaniah:
　Shemaiah and his sons:
　Hattush, Igal, Bariah, Neariah and Shaphat—six in all.
23The sons of Neariah:
　Elioenai, Hizkiah and Azrikam—three in all.
24The sons of Elioenai:
　Hodaviah, Eliashib, Pelaiah, Akkub, Johanan, Delaiah and Anani—
　seven in all.

This chapter deals with the descendants of David. Following the literary device of chiasmus, the last element in the pattern outlined above (see at 2:9) is supplementary material on Ram (cf. 2:10–17, where the descendants of Ram as far as David are given), sons born to David in Hebron (3:1–4a), and those born in Jerusalem (3:4b–8). The effect of beginning and ending the chiasmus with Ram is to draw attention to this line, which was David's. The sources for this material were 2 Sam 3:2–5 and 5:14–16. David reigned in Hebron seven years and six months, and he reigned thirty-three years "over all Israel and Judah" (2 Sam 5:5). This listing of the two groups of David's sons does not occur elsewhere in Chronicles. The Chronicler does not seem to have been anxious to refer to David's rule over only part of the land. His perspective is from the viewpoint of "all Israel."

This account contains a number of textual variants and some simplifying of details about David's wives in comparison with the Samuel account, but the two lists are essentially the same.

3:1–9　The list of David's sons born in Jerusalem also differs from 2 Sam 5:14–16 and 1 Chr 14:3–7. The verses in 1 Chronicles 3 refer to Shammua, Shobab, Nathan, and Solomon born to Bethshua (Bathsheba).[23]

Among the variations, this list also refers to nine sons (v. 8) born in Jerusalem. A daughter Tamar is also mentioned (v. 9). The name "Daniel" (3:1), David's second son, here is unusual. In 2 Sam 3:3 it is Chileab. Various Greek texts offer other renderings.

Eliphelet and Nogah do not appear in 2 Samuel. Eliphelet appears also in v. 8. Both names appear in 1 Chronicles 14. The name Eliada (v. 8) appears in 1 Chr 14:7 as Beeliada. The change from the element Beel-(Baal) to El

---

23 Most Hebrew MSS have "Bethshua," but one Hebrew MS, the LXX, the Vg, and 2 Sam 11:3 have "Bathsheba."

reflects a tendency known elsewhere in the Old Testament to avoid the offensive name of Baal, a tendency with which the Chronicler would agree.

3:10–16 The Davidic dynastic line up to the exile is well known from the books of Kings. The name of Athaliah is omitted (cf. 2 Kgs 11:1–16) because she was a usurper and a Canaanite princess. The true Davidic succession was through Joash, who was kept in hiding during Athaliah's interregnum. The normal opening and closing notes for a ruler are omitted for Athaliah in Kings as though to emphasize her illegality.

Some other features of this list are worthy of mention. Uzziah's throne name, Azariah, is used in v. 12 (cf. 2 Chr 26). Similarly Shallum (v. 15) is given his throne name, Jehoahaz (cf. Jer 22:11). Josiah's firstborn Johanan is not known elsewhere. He may have died young and is not listed because he was never in contention for the throne. The other three sons of Josiah, Jehoiakim, Zedekiah (whose name originally was Mattaniah; cf. 2 Kgs 24:17), and Shallum are listed here in the order of their age and not in the order of their accession to the throne, which was Jehoahaz (2 Kgs 23:30), Jehoiakim (Eliakim, 2 Kgs 23:34), and Zedekiah. Jehoiachin (whose name in the Heb. text here is Jeconiah; cf. Esth 2:9; Jer 24:1; 27:20; 28:4; 29:2), the son of Jehoiakim, however, was king for a brief period (2 Kgs 24:17) but was succeeded by his uncle Zedekiah. Jehoiakim was friendly with Egypt and would have been the successor to Josiah had not "the people of the land" chosen Shallum (Jehoahaz).

There are some difficulties in this section about ages, the solution to which is not now clear. Jehoiakim reigned until the attack of Nebuchadnezzar on Jerusalem. About that time Jehoiakim met his death (2 Kgs 24:1–6), and Jehoiachin became king (2 Kgs 24:8–10). It is difficult to interpret the texts at this point. Both 2 Kgs 24:17 and the LXX of 2 Chr 36:10 regard Zedekiah as the son of Josiah and therefore Jehoiachin's uncle (Jer 37:1). However, whereas 2 Chr 36:10 appears to regard Zedekiah as Jehoiachin's brother, 1 Chr 3:16 is ambiguous. The most likely solution is that Zedekiah was Josiah's son and the uncle of Jehoiachin, but that perhaps Jehoiakim had a son Zedekiah, which led to confusion.

Good external documentation exists for Jehoiachin's exile and imprisonment. The Babylonian Chronicle[24] refers to Jehoiachin, king of Judah, and his five sons (seven sons in 1 Chr 3:17–18) to whom rations were allotted by the authorities in Babylon.

3:17 These verses trace the line of Davidic descent from the exile in the days of Jehoiachin into postexilic times down to the time of the Chronicler. This period was of great importance to postexilic Israel. Parts of this list are

---

[24] *ANET*, 308.

not found elsewhere, and most of the names are unknown to us so that detailed analysis is not possible.

3:18   Some commentators have linked the name Sheshbazzar in Ezra 1:8,11; 5:14,16 with Shenazzar, but there probably is no connection.

3:19   Zerubbabel is named in Ezra-Nehemiah (Ezra 3:2,8; 5:2; Neh 12:1), Haggai (1:1,12,14; 2:2), and the New Testament (Matt 1:12; Luke 3:27) as the son of Shealtiel, Jehoiachin's oldest son (1 Chr 3:17). Here he is called the son of the younger Pedaiah, one apparently less significant in status. The explanation may be that Shealtiel died childless and Zerubbabel was born to Pedaiah by a levirate marriage with Shealtiel's widow.

3:20   The children of Zerubbabel are divided into two groups, three in v. 19 and five in v. 20. The names of Zerubbabel's children may have been symbolic, giving expression to the hopes of Israel in postexilic times. Hasadiah (v. 20) means "the Lord is kind," Jushab-Hesed, "may kindness be returned." The name "Shelomith" occurs on a postexilic seal found near Jerusalem, "Shelomith, maidservant/wife of Elnathan the governor." The occurrence of such a seal may indicate she was a woman of special status, perhaps as daughter of Zerubbabel. Additional evidence for the connection comes from her mention in this predominantly male genealogy, perhaps because she married the governor.[25]

3:21   This verse contains textual difficulties. We follow the MT.[26] In the second half of the verse "the sons of Rephaiah" begins a list of contemporaries who were not connected to the line of Zerubbabel and his grandsons in 3:21a. The important point is that we do not have a list here of four or six generations but only two and that this verse cannot be used to date the book of Chronicles.[27]

3:22–24   Other textual questions arise and uncertainty exists about the identity of the persons, although some names are known in extrabiblical sources of the same period. Dating is difficult although J. M. Myers attempts to provide approximate dates for the people listed in vv. 17–24. It would seem that Anami, the last name in the list, may provide a clue to the date of the Chronicler since names like these were common in the sixth and fifth centuries B.C. A date at the end of the fifth century may be proposed with some confidence.[28]

With v. 24 the list of David's descendants comes to an end. It stretches for

---

[25] E. Meyers, "The Shelomith Seal and the Judean Restoration: Some Additional Considerations." *EI* 18 (1985) 33-38.

[26] See Williamson, *1 and 2 Chronicles,* 58.

[27] R. K. Harrison, *Introduction to the Old Testament* (Grand Rapids: Eerdmans, 1969), 1155.

[28] J. M. Myers, *I Chronicles,* AB (Garden City: Doubleday, 1965), 21.

eight generations beyond the exile. The Davidic line played an important role in the early days of the restoration from the exile. Haggai 2 indicates the importance of this emphasis on David: his was the line of the Messiah. Although the present text has no explicit messianic intent, the emphasis on David is significant. The Chronicler has traced David's line from its roots down to the descendants of the royal line who lived after the exile. The kingdom may have been gone, but David's line was still the royal line. The hope of Israel still lived. As Wilcock has remarked, the kingdom still existed in mystery form.[29]

(8) Other Clans of Judah (4:1–23)

¹The descendants of Judah: Perez, Hezron, Carmi, Hur and Shobal.
²Reaiah son of Shobal was the father of Jahath, and Jahath the father of Ahumai and Lahad. These were the clans of the Zorathites.
³These were the sons of Etam:
Jezreel, Ishma and Idbash. Their sister was named Hazzelelponi.
⁴Penuel was the father of Gedor, and Ezer the father of Hushah.
These were the descendants of Hur, the firstborn of Ephrathah and father of Bethlehem.
⁵Ashhur the father of Tekoa had two wives, Helah and Naarah.
⁶Naarah bore him Ahuzzam, Hepher, Temeni and Haahashtari. These were the descendants of Naarah.
⁷The sons of Helah:
Zereth, Zohar, Ethnan, ⁸and Koz, who was the father of Anub and Hazzobebah and of the clans of Aharhel son of Harum.

⁹Jabez was more honorable than his brothers. His mother had named him Jabez, saying, "I gave birth to him in pain." ¹⁰Jabez cried out to the God of Israel, "Oh, that you would bless me and enlarge my territory! Let your hand be with me, and keep me from harm so that I will be free from pain." And God granted his request.

¹¹Kelub, Shuhah's brother, was the father of Mehir, who was the father of Eshton. ¹²Eshton was the father of Beth Rapha, Paseah and Tehinnah the father of Ir Nahash. These were the men of Recah.

¹³The sons of Kenaz:
Othniel and Seraiah.
The sons of Othniel:
Hathath and Meonothai. ¹⁴Meonothai was the father of Ophrah.
Seraiah was the father of Joab,
the father of Ge Harashim. It was called this because its people were

---

[29] Wilcock, *Chronicles*, 43.

craftsmen.
¹⁵The sons of Caleb son of Jephunneh:
    Iru, Elah and Naam.
  The son of Elah:
    Kenaz.
¹⁶The sons of Jehallelel:
    Ziph, Ziphah, Tiria and Asarel.
¹⁷The sons of Ezrah:
    Jether, Mered, Epher and Jalon. One of Mered's wives gave birth to
    Miriam, Shammai and Ishbah the father of Eshtemoa. ¹⁸(His Judean
    wife gave birth to Jered the father of Gedor, Heber the father of Soco,
    and Jekuthiel the father of Zanoah.) These were the children of Pha-
    raoh's daughter Bithiah, whom Mered had married.
¹⁹The sons of Hodiah's wife, the sister of Naham:
    the father of Keilah the Garmite, and Eshtemoa the Maacathite.
²⁰The sons of Shimon:
    Amnon, Rinnah, Ben-Hanan and Tilon.
  The descendants of Ishi:
    Zoheth and Ben-Zoheth.
²¹The sons of Shelah son of Judah:
    Er the father of Lecah, Laadah the father of Mareshah and the clans of
    the linen workers at Beth Ashbea, ²²Jokim, the men of Cozeba, and
    Joash and Saraph, who ruled in Moab and Jashubi Lehem. (These
    records are from ancient times.) ²³They were the potters who lived at
    Netaim and Gederah; they stayed there and worked for the king.

Chapter 4 consists of a number of apparently unrelated fragments, but
evidently it was felt necessary to mention the particular people and places in
the interests of giving a complete picture.

4:1   The chapter begins with additional material on Judah from preexilic
times in which both Hur and Shobal are traced to Judah. Shobal was the son
of Hur by Ephrathah (2:5). This list of Judah's descendants through Hur is
mentioned in 2:50,52 but is here expanded somewhat, no doubt to explain
the background to the Zorathites (2:53). Demonstrating the origins of the
Zorathites seems to have been important to the writer or to his source. Zorah
is known as one of the cities built by Rehoboam (2 Chr 11:10) and as a vil-
lage inhabited by postexilic Judeans (Neh 11:29).

4:2   Among Reaiah's descendants, Jahath was a common Levitical
name in Chronicles (6:20,43; 23:10–11; 24:22; 2 Chr 34:12), but Ahumai
and Lahad are unique. They were Zorathites.

4:3–4   These verses present another list of the sons of Hur, but there are
some textual questions. The MT reads, "These were the *father* of Etam."
The LXX and Vulgate are probably correct to read, "These were *the sons* of

Etam."[30] Some commentators propose that we have here a listing of the family of Hur's third son Hareph (cf. 2:51). The Etam mentioned here is the son of Hareph, who is listed with Tekoa (cf. 2:24; 4:5) and Zorah (cf. 2:54; 4:2) in cities fortified by Rehoboam (2 Chr 11:5–10). The Greek text of Josh 15:59a gives Etam as one of eleven cities in the district around Bethlehem.

4:5–8 Ashhur had two wives, Helah and Naarah, and was the younger brother of Hur.

4:6 The name "Haahashtari" carries an article, suggesting a clan, "the Ahashtarites." It seems to be a foreign word, perhaps Persian.

4:7 Possibly the words "and Koz" have fallen out at the end of v. 7 by haplography. Some Targum texts retain it because it supplies a link with what follows in v. 8, where the phrase "and Koz" is repeated.

4:9–10 The name Jabez recurs as a place name in 2:55, but it is not unusual in the Chronicler and elsewhere in the Old Testament for a name to represent both a person and a place. In the present context vv. 9–10 are not connected with preceding verses nor with vv. 11–12. It seems to be an independent pericope that is theological in character. The name "Jabez" (Heb. $ya^cb\bar{e}\d{s}$) was given to the child because his mother bore him "in pain" (Heb. $b\breve{e}^c\bar{o}\d{s}eb$). Jabez is described as "more honorable than his brothers." But following an ancient belief that the name represents the character, there was a fear that evil consequences might follow for the boy (cf. Gen 35:18). Jabez called on the God of Israel to turn any possible disaster into blessing. God granted his request and responded to an earnest prayer. The power of God can overcome the liabilities of the past and the present. The Chronicler believed in the efficacy of prayer and spoke of this often in later chapters.

4:11–12 These verses often have been taken to refer to the Calebites under the formulae "X the father of Y," but without success. The identity of Kelub is not known. The Greek text reads "Caleb," but none of the information listed here would support an identification with Caleb the companion of Joshua. The name "Ir Nahash" means "city of Nahash" or "city of the craftsman."

4:13–15 These were the Kenizzites, evidently another southern tribe that became attached to Judah. Othniel and Caleb "son of Jephunneh" are named as brothers (perhaps half-brothers or simply relatives) in Josh 15:17 and Judg 1:13. Caleb is referred to in Num 32:12 and Josh 14:6,14 as a Kenizzite.

4:13 The name "Menothai" occurs in the LXX and the Vulgate but was lost in the MT by haplography.

4:14 Seraiah, son of Kenaz, was the grandfather of Ge Harashim (lit.,

---

[30] Cf. the discussion in Japhet, *I & II Chronicles*, 107, who provides a succinct statement on the problem.

"valley of craftsmen"). Perhaps Ge Harashim represents a place or region "because its people were craftsmen" (cf. Neh 11:35). Evidently a guild of craftsmen lived in the area. The place is associated with Lod, Ono, and other Benjamite cities after the return from exile. These places lay some thirty miles northwest of Jerusalem. This reference to craftsmen in v. 14 may point to a link with the Kenites, who had moved north.

4:15　Caleb is here identified with the son of Jephunneh. The word "Elah" could be translated as "these," thus a transposition of the three words at the end of this verse to read "these are the sons of Kenaz" provides a better translation.

4:17–18　The whole passage in vv. 16–20 seems to have suffered somewhat in transmission, and various devices have been proposed to meet the difficulties. But any suggestion is at best tentative. A further example of descendants from a non-Israelite mother, Pharaoh's daughter, comes in v. 18.

4:21–23　The sons of Shelah conclude the genealogy of Judah. Shelah was the oldest surviving son of Judah (cf. 2:3). The reference to "clans of linen workers" seems to throw light on early guilds of craftsmen. The claim that records were preserved from ancient times points to preexilic records.

4:22　The meaning of the text may be that the linen workers married Moabites (cf. Ruth 1).[31] There is some possibility that the men who were in Moab returned to Bethlehem.[32]

4:23　Another guild is that of the "potters," who lived at Netaim and Gederah and worked for the king. They were royal potters.

3. The Tribe of Simeon (4:24–43)

24The descendants of Simeon:
　　Nemuel, Jamin, Jarib, Zerah and Shaul;
　25Shallum was Shaul's son, Mibsam his son and Mishma his son.
　26The descendants of Mishma:
　　Hammuel his son, Zaccur his son and Shimei his son.
　27Shimei had sixteen sons and six daughters, but his brothers did not have many children; so their entire clan did not become as numerous as the people of Judah. 28They lived in Beersheba, Moladah, Hazar Shual, 29Bilhah, Ezem, Tolad, 30Bethuel, Hormah, Ziklag, 31Beth Marcaboth, Hazar Susim, Beth Biri and Shaaraim. These were their towns until the reign of David. 32Their surrounding villages were Etam, Ain, Rimmon, Token and Ashan—five towns—33and all the villages around these towns as far as Baalath. These were their set-

---

[31] Taking the verb בעל to mean "marry."

[32] This would require a small emendation. Williamson, *1 and 2 Chronicles*, 61; Braun, *1 Chronicles*, 57.

tlements. And they kept a genealogical record.

[34]Meshobab, Jamlech, Joshah son of Amaziah, [35]Joel, Jehu son of Joshibiah, the son of Seraiah, the son of Asiel, [36]also Elioenai, Jaakobah, Jeshohaiah, Asaiah, Adiel, Jesimiel, Benaiah, [37]and Ziza son of Shiphi, the son of Allon, the son of Jedaiah, the son of Shimri, the son of Shemaiah.

[38]The men listed above by name were leaders of their clans. Their families increased greatly, [39]and they went to the outskirts of Gedor to the east of the valley in search of pasture for their flocks. [40]They found rich, good pasture, and the land was spacious, peaceful and quiet. Some Hamites had lived there formerly.

[41]The men whose names were listed came in the days of Hezekiah king of Judah. They attacked the Hamites in their dwellings and also the Meunites who were there and completely destroyed them, as is evident to this day. Then they settled in their place, because there was pasture for their flocks. [42]And five hundred of these Simeonites, led by Pelatiah, Neariah, Rephaiah and Uzziel, the sons of Ishi, invaded the hill country of Seir. [43]They killed the remaining Amalekites who had escaped, and they have lived there to this day.

The second major tribal grouping was that of Levi (6:1–80). But according to the Chronicler's plan, he gathered up between Judah and Levi some details about Simeon, Reuben, Gad, and the half-tribe of Manasseh. In a sense the material in chap. 5 comprises the Transjordan tribes.

4:24–33 The sons of Simeon appear in other Old Testament lists, in Gen 46:10; Exod 6:15; and Num 26:12–14. The unit in 1 Chr 4:24–43 is presented in three segments: (1) the genealogy proper (4:24–27), (2) geographical material combining towns and cities (4:28–33), and (3) a fragment of tribal history (4:34–43) that includes a list of "princes" (Heb. $nāś^ʾî$). The names in these lists contain few variants.[33] The reference in v. 27 to the fact that some of Simeon's descendants did not have large families may point to the fact that Simeon lost its identity early as it became absorbed into Judah (Josh 19:1,9). The name "Simeon" is absent from the blessing of Moses in Deuteronomy 33 and from the list of places to which David sent booty in 1 Sam 30:27–31. But even so, Simeon was a son of Israel and was correctly represented in the genealogy of Israel.

The list of Simeonite settlements (vv. 28–33) is dependent largely on Josh 19:2–8. Another list in Josh 15:26–32 forms part of a description of Judah's

---

[33] The Genesis and Exodus names correspond; Numbers and Chronicles omit Ohad. Chronicles has "Jarib" (v. 24) for "Jachin." Chronicles and Numbers have "Zerah" for "Zohar." According to Gen 46:10 and Exod 6:15, Shaul was the son of a Canaanite woman. In Gen 25:13 Ishmael was the father of Mibsam and Mishma, which seems to reflect the absorption of some Ishmaelites into the people of Israel. Evidently the Chronicler had access to a source otherwise unknown that preserved more details, although even this was abbreviated (v. 27).

southern territory. These places lay in the general area of Beersheba, with Ain-Rimmon, Moladah, Ashan, and Hormah not far distant. Ziklag is to be identified with Tel esh-Shariah, twelve miles northwest of Beersheba. It was given to David by King Achish of Gath (1 Sam 27:6). Shaaraim may represent Shariah, known in Egyptian records from the time of the Hyksos rulers, which was twenty miles west of Beersheba. Not all of these towns are identifiable today, although tentative identification is suggested for several of them.

The historical note that "these were their towns until the reign of David" (v. 31) points back to a period earlier than David. In fact Josh 19:2–7 refers to a time when Simeon was independent of Judah. The Chronicler evidently wished to stress that Simeon once had a tribal identity before it was absorbed into Judah. The RSV expression "they kept a genealogical record" (lit., "and *their* genealogical registration was *theirs*") grammatically includes the pronoun of ownership twice as though the writer wanted to stress that Simeon once had its own official registration and was part of the total Israel.

We may ask in passing whether or not David, in the days when he was an outlaw, exercised authority over a considerable area of the Negeb. Certainly some of these areas were included among cities occupied by the returning exiles in Neh 11:26–29.

4:34–43 The last part of the Simeon list deals with the problem that beset Simeon in the matter of overpopulation and the need for pasture for the flocks. Under pressure of increasing population the people of Simeon expanded to the east to seek pasture and space "to the outskirts of Gedor." The place appears as Gerar in the LXX, which seems likely (the *r* and *d* are similar in Hebrew). Gerar lay near Gaza and was more appropriately situated with regard to Ham, which could represent Egyptians, Ethiopians, or even Canaanites (Gen 10:6; 1 Chr 1:8). In that case the Simeonites expanded into Philistine areas. Both Philistines and Canaanites would have inhabited these areas, and both were regarded as descendants of Ham (Gen 10:6,14).

There was also expansion to the southeast in the direction of Edom (Mount Seir), where they encountered "the remaining Amalekites" (v. 43), those who survived the campaigns of Saul and David and perhaps others (1 Sam 14:48; 15:3; 2 Sam 8:12).

The Chronicler, wishing to give the complete picture, noted that in Hezekiah's day there was a campaign into Philistine territory (2 Kgs 18:8) further to the west of Gerar. It was into this area that Simeon expanded.

There is one particular textual problem in v. 41. The LXX, like the NIV, understands the proper name "Meunites." The Vulgate and Targum translate "dwellings."[34]

---

[34] In view of the proximity of "their tents," this minor emendation of הַמְּעוּנִים to מְעוֹנֵיהֶם "their dwellings" is plausible.

The section on Simeon serves to underline several features of the Chronicler's thinking. In the beginning of his discussion about the sons of Israel (2:1–2) he refers to the twelve tribes. The concept of twelve tribes was an ideal. Simeon, in fact, disappeared as a geographical and political entity long before the Chronicler wrote. Simeon's earlier history is also obscure, but its association with southern Judah was remembered. He is given a place among the lots set out in Josh 19:1–9, where the point is made that "Judah's portion was more than they needed. So the Simeonites received their inheritance within the territory of Judah."

It seems odd to us that the Chronicler should detail the genealogical history of a tribe that, by his day, had all but vanished. But he is presenting the ideal of Simeon as one of the tribes of Israel in tension with the historical reality of Simeon as a nonentity. He selectively portrays the vitality of Simeon in order to show that historical circumstances have not brought an end to the ideal plan of God.[35] By extension, the whole nation of Israel was a mere shadow of its Davidic glory by the time the Chronicler wrote, and yet he is asserting that ideal of Israel has not perished in God's eyes.

Beersheba was a focal point for Simeon, though his area was absorbed into Judah in David's time. Expansion of Simeon into Philistine areas (vv. 39–41) and into Edomite areas (vv. 42–43) brought them once again into regions occupied by Judah. It was evidently well known that Simeon was incorporated into Judah. Whether Simeon continued to maintain its tribal identity is impossible to say. Some of the towns referred to in 1 Chr 4:24 are mentioned in Nehemiah 11 as being resettled by the returning exiles in areas to the south of Judah. They may have found people in these areas whom they recognized as their kinsmen. But enough has been recorded to secure the place of Simeon within the family of Israel and to stress the significance of the idea of "all Israel."

4. The Transjordan Tribes (5:1–26)

(1) The Tribe of Reuben (5:1–10)

¹The sons of Reuben the firstborn of Israel (he was the firstborn, but when he defiled his father's marriage bed, his rights as firstborn were given to the sons of Joseph son of Israel; so he could not be listed in the genealogical record in accordance with his birthright, ²and though Judah was the strongest of his brothers and a ruler came from him, the rights of the firstborn belonged to Joseph)— ³the sons of Reuben the firstborn of Israel:

---

[35] See Wilcock, *Chronicles,* 34–35.

Hanoch, Pallu, Hezron and Carmi.
⁴**The descendants of Joel:**

Shemaiah his son, Gog his son, Shimei his son, ⁵**Micah his son, Reaiah his son, Baal his son, ⁶and Beerah his son, whom Tiglath-Pileser king of Assyria took into exile. Beerah was a leader of the Reubenites.**

⁷**Their relatives by clans, listed according to their genealogical records:**

Jeiel the chief, Zechariah, ⁸**and Bela son of Azaz, the son of Shema, the son of Joel. They settled in the area from Aroer to Nebo and Baal Meon. ⁹To the east they occupied the land up to the edge of the desert that extends to the Euphrates River, because their livestock had increased in Gilead.**

¹⁰**During Saul's reign they waged war against the Hagrites, who were defeated at their hands; they occupied the dwellings of the Hagrites throughout the entire region east of Gilead.**

By the time of the Chronicler the tribes which originally lay in Transjordan were remote from Judah and had probably lost a lot of their tribal identity. Yet descendants of the "sons of Israel" lived in Transjordan as part of "all Israel." An interesting comment on the Moabite Stone refers to "the men of Gad."[36] So Mesha, King of Moab in about 830 B.C. was aware of one of the Israel tribes in Transjordan in the middle of the ninth century B.C.

Up to this point the Chronicler has dealt with Judah and Simeon. But following his scheme of giving the total tribal picture built around the three central tribes of Judah, Levi, and Benjamin who remained faithful to the Davidic kingship and the temple, he needed to give attention also to the other tribes. The first of these in his order was the tribe of Reuben (5:1–10). We may postulate that the Chronicler had a source which preserved some personal details about Reuben and his descendants and brief notes of a very localized nature concerning pastures for their flocks.

5:1–2 Normally the firstborn son would have taken precedence. But Reuben, Jacob's eldest son, born to Leah (Gen 29:32; 35:23; 49:3; Exod 6:14; Num 1:20; 26:5) defiled his father's bed (Gen 35:22; 49:4b) and was displaced from the first place in favor of Judah. Further, Reuben was associated with Gad and the half-tribe of Manasseh. As a result, Reuben was not listed in the genealogical record in accordance with his birthright. Perhaps another factor that influenced the Chronicler in dropping Reuben from his place in the tribal list in favor of Joseph was that Joseph was the firstborn son of Rachel, Jacob's favorite wife. Fathers could determine who was the "eldest" son, especially when the normal heir had committed an offense.

The birthright was given to Joseph's sons. The Northern Kingdom was

---

thus preserved within the whole family of Israel. Yet Judah became strong among his brothers, and a ruler (*nāgîd*) came from him, namely David (cf. 11:2; 17:7; 2 Sam 5:2; 6:21; 7:8).

5:3   The list of the sons of Reuben follows Num 26:5–6.

5:4–5   This is a brief fragment which cannot be tied into the main genealogy of Reuben. The name Baal points to a northern link where the name Baal was well known, especially in names which had more than one element.

5:6   The list extends down to the days of the Assyrian conqueror Tiglath-Pileser III (745–727 B.C.).[37] A number of communities in Transjordan were carried captive at the same time (2 Kgs 15:29).

5:7–8   The relatives are given in a list that refers back to Beerah. In the region of Reuben, lists were evidently preserved. The area where these settled was from Aroer, which stood perched on the edge of the Wadi Arnon (Deut 2:36), and northwards to Nebo and Baal Meon (Num 32:38; Josh 13:15-18). According to the Moabite Stone these areas fell into the hands of the Moabite ruler, Mesha.[38]

5:9   Reuben expanded eastward up to the edge of the desert under the pressure of pastoral expansion.

5:10   It was during Saul's reign that Reuben became involved in a war with the Hagrites (cf. vv. 19-22; Ps 83:6). This campaign is not recorded elsewhere. According to Ps 83:7 they, with Moab, Edom, the Ishmaelites, and others were enemies of Israel. Other details are not known. Verses 9–10 reflect the unsettled conditions that prevailed in these areas occupied by Reuben. Reuben was eventually absorbed by Gad.

(2) The Tribe of Gad (5:11–17)

[11]**The Gadites lived next to them in Bashan, as far as Salecah:**
  [12]**Joel was the chief, Shapham the second, then Janai and Shaphat, in Bashan.**
[13]**Their relatives, by families, were:**
  Michael, Meshullam, Sheba, Jorai, Jacan, Zia and Eber—seven in all.
  [14]**These were the sons of Abihail son of Huri, the son of Jaroah, the son of Gilead, the son of Michael, the son of Jeshishai, the son of Jahdo, the son of Buz.**
[15]**Ahi son of Abdiel, the son of Guni, was head of their family.**
[16]**The Gadites lived in Gilead, in Bashan and its outlying villages, and on all the pasturelands of Sharon as far as they extended.**

---

[37] The MT in Chronicles reads "Pilneser" (1 Chr 5:26; 2 Chr 28:20) whereas Kings reads "Pileser" (2 Kgs 15:29; 16:7,10), probably for euphonic reasons.
[38] *ANET,* 320.

[17]All these were entered in the genealogical records during the reigns of Jotham king of Judah and Jeroboam king of Israel.

The discussion on Gad is short, a mere seven verses. It does not contain material from the lists of Gen 46:6; Num 26:15–18 or from the list of those in David's army in 1 Chr 12:9–13. The Chronicler must have had access to an independent source. The list contains some important geographical information and an account of the Hagrite war.

5:11 The genealogy opens with a geographical note, the only one to do so. Their area was Bashan and Gilead. They lived "over against" Reuben.

5:12 Their leaders were Joel, the chief; Shapham, the second; and Janai, who was a judge.[39]

5:13–15 The kinsmen are listed by families, seven in all.

5:16 The Gadites lived in Gilead, a rather elastic term. A word used in several places in the Old Testament appears here to describe "outlying villages," literally, "daughters." The reference to Sharon must be to a place mentioned on the Moabite Stone (line 13) and not to the coastal plain.

5:17 We are informed that these names were entered into the genealogical records in the days of King Jotham (742–745 B.C.) of Judah and King Jeroboam II (786–746 B.C.) of Israel. This provides information about some of the sources of the Chronicler's material and also about the fact that Judah and Israel preserved records, guaranteeing the historical integrity of the Chronicler's records. Jotham, of course, ruled as co-regent after his father Uzziah contracted leprosy (2 Kgs 15:5), although Gad was part of the Northern Kingdom. How these records about Gad came to be found in records in both Judah and Israel is a matter of debate.[40]

(3) The Transjordan Wars with Arab People (5:18–22)

[18]The Reubenites, the Gadites and the half-tribe of Manasseh had 44,760 men ready for military service—able-bodied men who could handle shield and sword, who could use a bow, and who were trained for battle. [19]They waged war against the Hagrites, Jetur, Naphish and Nodab. [20]They were helped in fighting them, and God handed the Hagrites and all their allies over to them, because they cried out to him during the battle. He answered their prayers, because they trusted in him. [21]They seized the livestock of the Hagrites—fifty thousand camels, two hundred fifty thousand sheep and two thousand donkeys.

---

[39] Although the NIV reads the MT שָׁפָט as a personal name "Shaphat," the Targum and LXX reads שֹׁפֵט, thus making Janai a judge.

[40] J. Myers suggests that between 750 and 745 B.C. there was one official list, and Jotham was mentioned with Jeroboam in a plan for making the Davidic dynasty the chronologico-religious backbone of the Chronicler's work (*I Chronicles*, 37).

They also took one hundred thousand people captive, ²²and many others fell slain, because the battle was God's. And they occupied the land until the exile.

In v. 10 reference is made to a war waged against the Hagrites. The Chronicler gives more details in these verses and wedges these details in between his account of Gad (vv. 11–17) and his account of the half-tribe of Manasseh (vv. 23–26). This was appropriate because Reuben and Gad were associated with the people of Manasseh in this campaign.

The report of the battle follows the pattern of other battle reports (cf. 2 Chr 13:13–19; 14:9–15; 18:31; 20:1–27; 26:7; 32:7–8,20–22). Though not all elements are present in every report, they characteristically include an ambush (the battle being before and behind Israel), the trumpets and the battle shout, the course of the battle (5:20–22), the booty and captives, and the attribution of success to God (v. 21).

5:18 The numbers 44,760 represent the combined forces of the three groups. This seems to us to be a very large force. Questions arise about the meaning of the terms "thousand" and "hundred," which often stand for military groupings rather than for numerical values (cf. 1 Chr 12).[41] By comparison with Numbers 1 and 26, however, the numbers here are considerably less. It would seem that the Chronicler had access to military census figures of some kind. We are given a glimpse of the composition of these military forces in three descriptions: "men who could handle shield and sword," "who could use a bow," and "who were trained for battle."

5:19 For the Hagrites see v. 10. The other groups were evidently Arab tribes (Gen 25:15 lists Jetur and Naphish as sons of Ishmael).

5:20 What is transparent from this report is that the impressive military credentials of the Transjordan tribes were not the deciding factor in their victory. God's response to their prayer prompted his intervention and their final victory (cf. 2 Chr 6:34–39). Here is another piece of evidence collected by the Chronicler to demonstrate his ardent belief that kingship was not necessary for Israel to regain its lands and restore its good fortunes. What was required was a people devoted to God. A feature of the Chronicler's theology was that when God's people called on God in the day of battle, he helped them and handed their foes over to them. They cried out to God, they trusted him, and he answered their prayers.

5:21 The numbers of animals captured seem to be very great. We may have here another example of the use of the terms "thousand," "hundred," and "fifty," which represent groups rather than arithmetic realities.

5:22 The same applies to the figure of 100,000 captives. Many were

---

[41] R. B. Allen, "Numbers," EBC (Grand Rapids: Zondervan, 1990), 2:681–83.

killed also. "The battle was God's." The phrase implies that the armies of Israel were victorious because God's favor was with them. When the people are in sin, God does not go out with them, and defeat follows. The tribes of Israel occupied these areas until the exile. The exile in question probably is the deportation of Transjordanian tribes in 734 B.C. (2 Kgs 15:29) in the days of Tiglath-Pileser III (745–727 B.C.). No date for this campaign can be given, and independent records are lacking. Perhaps it is a general picture of prolonged skirmishings in the region between rival settlers. Postexilic readers surely would have received here encouragement to trust God alone and to look to him for deliverance from Gentile domination. As the following verses indicate, exile resulted from failure to trust God.

(4) The Half-tribe of Manasseh (5:23–26)

²³**The people of the half-tribe of Manasseh were numerous; they settled in the land from Bashan to Baal Hermon, that is, to Senir (Mount Hermon).**

²⁴**These were the heads of their families: Epher, Ishi, Eliel, Azriel, Jeremiah, Hodaviah and Jahdiel. They were brave warriors, famous men, and heads of their families. ²⁵But they were unfaithful to the God of their fathers and prostituted themselves to the gods of the peoples of the land, whom God had destroyed before them. ²⁶So the God of Israel stirred up the spirit of Pul king of Assyria (that is, Tiglath-Pileser king of Assyria), who took the Reubenites, the Gadites and the half-tribe of Manasseh into exile. He took them to Halah, Habor, Hara and the river of Gozan, where they are to this day.**

Manasseh is dealt with again in 7:14–19. How the two parts of the Manasseh record came to be separated is not now known.

5:23 The people of the half-tribe of Manasseh were, in any case, numerous and were settled in northern Transjordan from Bashan to Senir, which is Mount Hermon (Deut 3:9).

5:24 The seven tribal leaders mentioned here are not otherwise known. The descriptions of these men as "brave warriors, famous men, and heads of their families" are well known, but the first two names regularly have military associations. It is possible that the material came from an old military list.

5:25 Because they were "unfaithful to the God of their fathers and prostituted themselves to [local gods]," they went into exile at the hands of the Assyrians. The Chronicler here sets up a contrast to 5:20, which records a victory by the tribes across the Jordan during the reign of Saul (5:10). Why were they victorious over the Hagrites and yet taken captive by Assyria? The obvious answer might be that the Assyrians were a greater power than the Hagrites, but this would not be the correct answer. The real reason for the demise of the Transjordan tribes is that instead of calling on the Lord as they had done some three hundred years earlier (5:20), they committed apostasy against him. These two incidents form a microcosm of the Chronicler's philosophy of history.

5:26 King Pul of Assyria is here identified as Tiglath-Pileser III (745–727 B.C.; cf. 2 Kgs 15:19,29). The Chronicler notes that representatives of the three Transjordan tribal groups were led into exile. Other lists of the areas to which they were exiled come in 2 Kgs 17:6 and 18:11 although Hara is absent from these lists, and many commentators delete Hara as a corruption of "the river of" or "the mountains of Maday [Media]." But Halah, Habor, and the river of Gozan are well known in Upper Mesopotamia. These exiles were still there in the days of the Chronicler. Unfaithfulness (v. 25) has an inevitable consequence, the judgment of God.

5. The Tribe of Levi (6:1–81)

The tribe of Levi was one of the three tribes that occupied the central place in the thinking of the Chronicler. It was one of the tribes that in his view remained faithful to the Davidic kingship and to temple worship in the preexilic period. Far more attention is given to their genealogy than to the other tribes (Naphtali has one verse, 7:13). Levi was scattered throughout "all Israel" and was in every era their clergy. In the words of Wilcock, "Levi thus provides a religious leadership which acts as a binding force through the length of Israel's history and the breadth of its territory."[42]

Also the tribe of Levi represented Israel's central concern, the worship of God. The temple and its rituals stood at the heart of Israel's life. It was the tribe of Levi that cared for the temple and administered its rituals. No doubt the Chronicler owed something to the Book of Numbers when he placed Levi in the center of the genealogies of Israel, for, according to Numbers, the tribes of Israel as they were encamped in the wilderness were arranged in a square with the clans of Levi in the center around the tabernacle (Num 1:44–2:34). Moses, Aaron, and his sons "were responsible for the care of the sanctuary on behalf of the Israelites" (Num 3:38).

First Chronicles 6 is comprised of several different lists dealing with priests and Levites and their positions and functions. The material is prefaced by an account of the high-priestly line from Levi (v. 1) to the exile (v. 15).

(1) The Line of the High Priests (6:1–15)

¹The sons of Levi:
    Gershon, Kohath and Merari.
²The sons of Kohath:

---

[42] Wilcock, *Chronicles,* 38.

Amram, Izhar, Hebron and Uzziel.
³The children of Amram:
Aaron, Moses and Miriam.
The sons of Aaron:
Nadab, Abihu, Eleazar and Ithamar.
⁴Eleazar was the father of Phinehas,
Phinehas the father of Abishua,
⁵Abishua the father of Bukki,
Bukki the father of Uzzi,
⁶Uzzi the father of Zerahiah,
Zerahiah the father of Meraioth,
⁷Meraioth the father of Amariah,
Amariah the father of Ahitub,
⁸Ahitub the father of Zadok,
Zadok the father of Ahimaaz,
⁹Ahimaaz the father of Azariah,
Azariah the father of Johanan,
¹⁰Johanan the father of Azariah (it was he who served as priest in the
temple Solomon built in Jerusalem),
¹¹Azariah the father of Amariah,
Amariah the father of Ahitub,
¹²Ahitub the father of Zadok,
Zadok the father of Shallum,
¹³Shallum the father of Hilkiah,
Hilkiah the father of Azariah,
¹⁴Azariah the father of Seraiah,
and Seraiah the father of Jehozadak.
¹⁵Jehozadak was deported when the LORD sent Judah and Jerusalem into
exile by the hand of Nebuchadnezzar.

In vv. 1–15 we have listed the sons of Levi who were the high priests in the preexilic period. The list here is based on Exod 6:16–25. The Chronicler adds little detail. He has a vertical chronology and moves through this to Jehozadak, who was deported by Nebuchadnezzar (v. 15). His list is the most extensive found in the Old Testament as well as the latest. Even so, several high priests are omitted here, including Jehoiada (2 Chr 22:11–24:17), Azariah (2 Chr 26:20), and Uriah (2 Kgs 16:11ff.). Azariah (v. 9) according to 1 Kgs 4:2 is the son of Zadok, not the grandson. This difference is due, no doubt, because complete lists were not always made. It was sufficient to preserve the line.[43]

In the arrangement of the names of the Levites in this chapter, the first

---

[43] The high priests of Israel are listed in five places: Neh 11:10–11; 1 Chr 9:11; Ezra 7:1–5; 1 Chr 6:1–15; 1 Chr 6:50–53. For a valuable comparative table see Braun, *1 Chronicles,* 84.

place is given to the priests (vv. 1–15). Then vv. 16–30 dealing with the three Levitical families are closely related to the temple musicians in vv. 31–48.[44] This arrangement is artificially constructed since not all the material that was available to the Chronicler was used. But he was making a point. The perfectly arranged, artistic pattern of priests and Levites gave a special significance to the priestly family and stressed the importance of the temple and its rituals in the life of God's people.

6:1 [5:27] "Gershon" sometimes is written as "Gershom" (cf. Gen 6:16–17). The Chronicler, however, used "Gershom" on occasion (1 Chr 23:15–16; 26:4) but "Gershon" on others (cf. 1 Chr 6:1,16–17,20,43,62; 15:7; 23:6; 2 Chr 26:21; 29:12).

6:2–9 [5:28–35] The line of Kohath that followed via Amram and Aaron to ensure that the very important figure of Zadok was preserved.

6:10–15 [5:36–41] With this reference we have twelve generations between Aaron and the building of the temple. This would give twelve times forty, or four hundred and eighty years to agree with 1 Kgs 6:1. This is a feasible reconstruction. The expression "the father," which appears several times in these verses, is best understood as denoting succession in office.

(2) The Sons of Levi (6:16–30) [6:1-15]

16The sons of Levi:
   Gershon, Kohath and Merari.
17These are the names of the sons of Gershon:
   Libni and Shimei.
18The sons of Kohath:
   Amram, Izhar, Hebron and Uzziel.
19The sons of Merari:
   Mahli and Mushi.
   These are the clans of the Levites listed according to their fathers:
20Of Gershon:
   Libni his son, Jehath his son, Zimmah his son, **21**Joah his son, Iddo his son, Zerah his son and Jeatherai his son.
22The descendants of Kohath:
   Amminadab his son, Korah his son, Assir his son, **23**Elkanah his son, Ebiasaph his son, Assir his son,
   24Tahath his son, Uriel his son, Uzziah his son and Shaul his son.
25The descendants of Elkanah:
   Amasai, Ahimoth,
   26Elkanah his son, Zophai his son, Nahath his son, **27**Eliab his son, Jeroham his son, Elkanah his son and Samuel his son.

---

[44] See Williamson, *1 and 2 Chronicles,* 69, for a tabular presentation of the data.

²⁸**The sons of Samuel:**
   Joel the firstborn and Abijah the second son.
²⁹**The descendants of Merari:**
   Mahli, Libni his son, Shimei his son, Uzzah his son,
   ³⁰**Shimea his son, Haggiah his son and Asaiah his son.**

6:16–24 [6:7–9]   Whereas the line of high priests is preserved in a vertical chronology, ignoring other lines of descent, in this section the three lines of Levi are followed up, namely, those of Gershon, Kohath, and Merari. Of these Gershon (v. 20) and Merari (v. 29) are followed for seven generations through the line of the elder sons Libni (v. 17) and Mahli (v. 19). The Kohath tradition develops through Amminadab for ten generations.

Amminadab is otherwise unknown. He is not listed among the sons of Kohath in v. 18 or elsewhere. Because Exod 6:21 has Korah as the son of Izhar, it may be that Izhar originally stood in the place of Amminadab in this verse (cf. vv. 18,38). There may be further problems as well, accounting for the ten generations of Kohath compared to the pattern of seven for Gershon and Merari.[45]

6:25 [6:10]   Ahimoth is possibly to be read "and his brother Mehath." A slight emendation is necessary (cf. v. 35).

6:26 [6:11]   It is noteworthy that Samuel is placed among the Levites, since 1 Sam 1:1 says his ancestor Zuph (here Zophai) was an Ephraimite. Either Samuel was a Levite whose family was from the territory of Ephraim (cf. Josh 21:20–22),[46] or he was an Ephraimite who was reckoned with or "adopted" into the Levites because of his services in the tabernacle and the performance of certain priestly duties (1 Sam 2:11,26; 3:15; 7:9–10). In the latter case, vv. 26–28 is considered a parenthesis in the surrounding genealogy.[47]

6:28 [6:13]   "Joel" is absent in the MT but is present in the LXX and in MT of 1 Sam 8:2. Although "firstborn" without a name is still appropriate, the NIV supplies the information to aid the reader.

(3) The Temple Musicians (6:31–47)

³¹**These are the men David put in charge of the music in the house of the LORD after the ark came to rest there. ³²They ministered with music before the tabernacle, the Tent of Meeting, until Solomon built the temple of the LORD in**

---

[45] Williamson, *1 and 2 Chronicles*, 71–72.

[46] Payne, *1, 2 Chronicles*, 4:351; R. F. Youngblood, *1, 2 Samuel* (Grand Rapids: Zondervan, 1992) 3:570.

[47] Japhet, *I & II Chronicles*, 153–56; Braun, *1 Chronicles*, 88. Cf. Williamson, *1 and 2 Chronicles*, 72.

Jerusalem. They performed their duties according to the regulations laid down for them.

³³Here are the men who served, together with their sons:
From the Kohathites:
  Heman, the musician,
  the son of Joel, the son of Samuel,
  ³⁴the son of Elkanah, the son of Jeroham,
  the son of Eliel, the son of Toah,
  ³⁵the son of Zuph, the son of Elkanah,
  the son of Mahath, the son of Amasai,
  ³⁶the son of Elkanah, the son of Joel,
  the son of Azariah, the son of Zephaniah,
  ³⁷the son of Tahath, the son of Assir,
  the son of Ebiasaph, the son of Korah,
  ³⁸the son of Izhar, the son of Kohath,
  the son of Levi, the son of Israel;
³⁹and Heman's associate Asaph, who served at his right hand:
  Asaph son of Berekiah, the son of Shimea,
  ⁴⁰the son of Michael, the son of Baaseiah,
  the son of Malkijah, ⁴¹the son of Ethni,
  the son of Zerah, the son of Adaiah,
  ⁴²the son of Ethan, the son of Zimmah,
  the son of Shimei, ⁴³the son of Jahath,
  the son of Gershon, the son of Levi;
⁴⁴and from their associates, the Merarites, at his left hand:
  Ethan son of Kishi, the son of Abdi,
  the son of Malluch, ⁴⁵the son of Hashabiah,
  the son of Amaziah, the son of Hilkiah,
  ⁴⁶the son of Amzi, the son of Bani,
  the son of Shemer, ⁴⁷the son of Mahli,
  the son of Mushi, the son of Merari,
  the son of Levi.

6:31–32 [6:16–17]   These introductory verses refer to David, who set up and organized the Levitical musical guilds for worship in the tabernacle, later transferred to the temple. These men were charged with ministering with music before the tabernacle until Solomon built the temple. They performed their duties according to the regulations laid down for them. There are the strongest traditions in the Bible that David was associated with music. Some of these are quite early (e.g., 2 Sam 6:5; 23:1). Several early stories tell of David playing the harp to Saul in 1 Samuel. By analogy with other systems of worship in other lands, Israel would have had its own equivalent of cultic music in which David the great reformer naturally played his part. The Chronicler mentions David more than once in connection with temple music (1 Chr 15:16,27; 25:1ff.; 2 Chr 29:26ff.) The tradition of David's influence on tabernacle and temple is strongly represented in the headings to many of the psalms.[48]

6:33–38 [6:18–23]   The Kohath group of singers is traced from Heman through Joel, Samuel, and others back to Levi, son of Israel (v. 38). The family of Samuel is clearly a part of this list of twenty-two generations. The list is longer than the next two lists, those of Asaph (v. 39) and the Merarites (v. 44). This list in vv. 33–38 is virtually the same as that in vv. 22–27, although there are some variations.

6:39–43 [6:24–28]   The name "Asaph" appears on a seal found at Megiddo belonging to the time of Jeroboam II (ca. 786–746 B.C.). The source of this list is not known although there are some parallels with vv. 20–21.

6:44–47 [6:29–32]   At the top of the list is Ethan, traced through Merari's younger son Mushi (v. 46) back to Levi.

(4) The Chief Duties of the Levites and the Priests (6:48–49)

[48]**Their fellow Levites were assigned to all the other duties of the tabernacle, the house of God. [49]But Aaron and his descendants were the ones who presented offerings on the altar of burnt offering and on the altar of incense in connection with all that was done in the Most Holy Place, making atonement for Israel, in accordance with all that Moses the servant of God had commanded.**

6:48–49 [6:33–34]   Aaron and his descendants made atonement for sin. The verb "to make atonement" was of special theological significance. Basically the verb root *kpr* means "to cover," i.e., "to cover over sin," by the offering of a sacrifice whether for individuals (Lev 4:29,31; 8:24; 10:17) or for the entire people on the day of atonement (Lev 16, esp. v. 14). Sin must be covered over in order that it not be an affront to God. But the atonement can only be done in the manner prescribed by God as he gave directions to his servant, Moses. Human efforts to deal with sin are of no avail.

(5) The List of the High Priests (6:50–53)

[50]**These were the descendants of Aaron:**
    Eleazar his son, Phinehas his son, Abishua his son, [51]Bukki his son, Uzzi his son, Zerahiah his son,

---

[48] Whatever the exact intention in the psalm headings "of David," whether the meaning is "by David," "belonging to David," "dedicated to David," or "belonging to the collection of psalms ascribed to David," there can be no doubt that there was a very strong tradition in Israel that David was closely associated with temple music.

[52]Meraioth his son, Amariah his son, Ahitub his son, [53]Zadok his son and
Ahimaaz his son.

6:50–53 [6:35–38]   The high priests are listed from Aaron down to
David, repeating the list from 6:3-8. Certainly this is tied to vv. 31–32. The
priests David put in charge of worship were descendants of Aaron.

(6) The List of Levitical Cities (6:54–81)

[54]These were the locations of their settlements allotted as their territory
(they were assigned to the descendants of Aaron who were from the Kohathite
clan, because the first lot was for them):
  [55]They were given Hebron in Judah with its surrounding pasturelands.
  [56]But the fields and villages around the city were given to Caleb son of
  Jephunneh.
  [57]So the descendants of Aaron were given Hebron (a city of refuge), and
Libnah, Jattir, Eshtemoa, [58]Hilen, Debir, [59]Ashan, Juttah and Beth Shemesh,
together with their pasturelands. [60]And from the tribe of Benjamin they were
given Gibeon, Geba, Alemeth and Anathoth, together with their pasturelands.
  These towns, which were distributed among the Kohathite clans, were thirteen in all.
  [61]The rest of Kohath's descendants were allotted ten towns from the clans
of half the tribe of Manasseh.
  [62]The descendants of Gershon, clan by clan, were allotted thirteen towns
from the tribes of Issachar, Asher and Naphtali, and from the part of the tribe
of Manasseh that is in Bashan.
  [63]The descendants of Merari, clan by clan, were allotted twelve towns from
the tribes of Reuben, Gad and Zebulun.
  [64]So the Israelites gave the Levites these towns and their pasturelands.
[65]From the tribes of Judah, Simeon and Benjamin they allotted the previously
named towns.
  [66]Some of the Kohathite clans were given as their territory towns from the
tribe of Ephraim.
  [67]In the hill country of Ephraim they were given Shechem (a city of refuge), and Gezer, [68]Jokmeam, Beth Horon, [69]Aijalon and Gath Rimmon,
together with their pasturelands.
  [70]And from half the tribe of Manasseh the Israelites gave Aner and
Bileam, together with their pasturelands, to the rest of the Kohathite clans.
  [71]The Gershonites received the following:
  From the clan of the half-tribe of Manasseh they received Golan in Bas-
     han and also Ashtaroth, together with their
     pasturelands;
  [72]from the tribe of Issachar they received Kedesh, Daberath, [73]Ramoth and
     Anem, together with their pasturelands;

74from the tribe of Asher they received Mashal, Abdon, 75Hukok and Rehob, together with their pasturelands;

76and from the tribe of Naphtali they received Kedesh in Galilee, Hammon and Kiriathaim, together with their pasturelands.

77The Merarites (the rest of the Levites) received the following:
From the tribe of Zebulun they received Jokneam, Kartah, Rimmono and Tabor, together with their pasturelands;

78from the tribe of Reuben across the Jordan east of Jericho they received Bezer in the desert, Jahzah, 79Kedemoth and Mephaath, together with their pasturelands;

80and from the tribe of Gad they received Ramoth in Gilead, Mahanaim, 81Heshbon and Jazer, together with their pasturelands.

This list is parallel to Josh 21:5–39. Both lists combine the cities of refuge with the Levitical cities and follow the familiar pattern of allotment to the Kohathites, the Gershonites, and the Merarites in that order. The Aaronite line is represented by Kohath, followed by Gershon, the oldest of Levi's sons, and Merari, the youngest son. The Levites, as we will see, were scattered through the tribal territory of Israel. They were important to the life and well being of the whole nation ("all Israel").

6:54–59 [6:39–44] The list of allotments to the descendants of Aaron is now given. These are their dwelling places throughout their settlements in their territory given by lot to the sons of Aaron from the Kohathite clan, to whom, according to Josh 21:10, the first lot fell.

The Aaronites were given Hebron in Judah and the surrounding pasture lands. The fields of the city and the villages were given to Caleb. The nine cities of vv. 55–59 seem to be the combined contribution of Simeon and Judah (v. 65; Josh 21:4,9). However, Simeon is not mentioned, although Ashan (v. 59) is attributed to Simeon in Josh 19:7. This may point to the early absorption of Simeon by Judah. The writer considers it significant that Hebron was a city of refuge.

6:60 [6:45] The contribution of Benjamin is listed here, three towns each with its common lands. The text names thirteen though the Chronicler lists only eleven. Juttah and Gibeon can be restored to vv. 59 and 60 on the basis of Josh 21:16–17.

6:61 [6:46] This completes the list, giving the rest of the Kohathite allotment—ten cities from the half-tribe of Manasseh. Some commentators suggest the restoration of Ephraim and Dan with Josh 21:5.

6:62 [6:47] Issachar, Asher, Naphtali, and the half-tribe of Manasseh that was in Bashan provided thirteen towns for the descendants of Gershon.

6:63 [6:48] Twelve towns from Reuben, Gad, and Zebulun were for Merari.

6:64–65 [6:49–50]   The children of Israel gave cities and common lands to the Levites. It was God's special provision for those who had been set apart for the service of the temple.

6:66–70 [6:51–55]   The Kohathites, comprising the descendants of Aaron and the "remaining Kohathites," had their allotted cities in the center of the land, that of the Aaronites in Judah and Benjamin and the "remaining Kohathites" in Ephraim, Dan, and West Manasseh.

6:71–77 [6:56–62]   The cities of the Gershonites were allotted, two in east Manasseh, four each from Issachar and Asher, and three in Naphtali.

6:78–81 [6:63–66]   The cities of Merari were in Zebulun, Reuben, and Gad.

6. The Tribes of Issachar, Benjamin, Naphtali, Manasseh, Ephraim, and Asher (7:1–40)

These may be classified broadly as the northern tribes. The preceding chapters have dealt with Judah, Simeon, Reuben, Gad, the half-tribe of Manasseh, and Levi with its priestly and Levitical families and their possessions and dwelling areas. But in giving the total picture of Israel to the postexilic community, mention had to be made of the northern tribes of Issachar, Benjamin, Naphtali, Manasseh, Ephraim, and Asher. The Chronicler still needed to give more detail about Benjamin. He devoted some space in 7:6–12 but reserved a much fuller treatment for chap. 8.

Chapter 7 consists of smaller genealogies within the framework of the Chronicler's major interests of Judah, Levi, and Benjamin. The source of this material was largely Numbers 26, but something was culled from a military census list. The order of presentation escapes us now. It may have been the order he found in his sources, which were in any case inadequate. They had to be "supplemented" from available archives, largely contemporary Judean. There is nothing about Dan or Zebulun despite a brief notice in 2:1–2 (but see comments at 7:12). Yet during the periods of exile, that of the northern tribes in the Assyrian exile of 721 B.C. and of the tribes of Judah, Benjamin, and Levi in the Babylonian exile in the Nebuchadnezzar period, by no means all the people of Israel were taken from the land even if only "the poorest people of the land" remained (2 Kgs 24:14). At least some memories must have remained even if detailed records were lost. The conviction of the Chronicler was that "all Israel" mattered (1 Chr 9:1; 11:1; 12:38; 13:5–8; 14:8; 15:3; 17:6; 18:14; 21:4; 28:4; 29:25–26; 2 Chr 1:2; 7:6; 9:30; 12:1,13).

An interesting possibility is that the Chronicler had his own way of maintaining the ideal of twelve tribes. If Dan is restored by emending 7:12, then only Zebulun is missing. If Levi and the two Joseph tribes are all included in the list, then the total number for the tribes is twelve. If Dan is considered to be absent but the two half-tribes of Manasseh are each counted separately, the number of tribes again is twelve.[49] Elsewhere in the Bible there are different ways of maintaining the number twelve for the tribes of Israel. Revelation 7:5–8, for example, omits Dan but counts Manasseh and Joseph (Ephraim).

Another feature about the Chronicler's teaching regarding the whole area Israel once covered is that this people was the God-appointed occupant of certain areas of Western Asia. God promised the land to the patriarchs (Gen 28:13–15; 35:12; Deut 6:10–11; 8:7–10).[50] The two categories, "the people" and "the land," were inseparable. The extent of the land was "from the river of Egypt to the great river, the Euphrates" (Gen 15:18–20). That was the promise. It was not always realized, but it stood as an ideal. It was by no means confined to the narrow limits defined by postexilic Judah. For the postexilic "Israel" the land that was promised comprised the whole tribal area, and the people comprised the whole tribal spectrum. The Chronicler therefore included six northern tribes.

(1) The Tribe of Issachar (7:1–5)

¹The sons of Issachar:
   Tola, Puah, Jashub and Shimron—four in all.
²The sons of Tola:
   Uzzi, Rephaiah, Jeriel, Jahmai, Ibsam and Samuel—heads of their families. During the reign of David, the descendants of Tola listed as fighting men in their genealogy numbered 22,600.
³The son of Uzzi:
   Izrahiah.
 The sons of Izrahiah:
   Michael, Obadiah, Joel and Isshiah. All five of them were chiefs. ⁴According to their family genealogy, they had 36,000 men ready for battle, for they had many wives and children.
⁵The relatives who were fighting men belonging to all the clans of Issachar, as listed in their genealogy, were 87,000 in all.

7:1–5 This list is to be compared with Num 26:23–25 and Gen 46:13. The Chronicler's text and these texts contain some variants. "Puah" occurs as "Puwwah" in Numbers and Jashub as Job in Genesis. It is common to find various spellings of names in the Old Testament. Four sons of Issachar are listed, and the fighting strength of one of them, Tola, is given for the time of

---

[49] Wilcock, *Chronicles*, 40.
[50] See the extended discussion in W. Brueggemann, *The Land* (Philadelphia: Fortress, 1977).

David (v. 2). Numbers of fighting men are also given for some of the other descendants of Tola, and reference is made to their many wives and children. Probably a military census is behind this material.[51]

(2) The Tribe of Benjamin (7:6–12)

⁶Three sons of Benjamin:
  Bela, Beker and Jediael.
⁷The sons of Bela:
  Ezbon, Uzzi, Uzziel, Jerimoth and Iri, heads of families—five in all. Their genealogical record listed 22,034 fighting men.
⁸The sons of Beker:
  Zemirah, Joash, Eliezer, Elioenai, Omri, Jeremoth, Abijah, Anathoth and Alemeth. All these were the sons of Beker. ⁹Their genealogical record listed the heads of families and 20,200 fighting men.
¹⁰The son of Jediael:
  Bilhan.
The sons of Bilhan:
  Jeush, Benjamin, Ehud, Kenaanah, Zethan, Tarshish and Ahishahar. ¹¹All these sons of Jediael were heads of families. There were 17,200 fighting men ready to go out to war.
¹²The Shuppites and Huppites were the descendants of Ir, and the Hushites the descendants of Aher.

7:6–11 Benjamin is given a brief introduction here. A fuller treatment is reserved for chap. 8. The MT is peculiar here. It starts with the word "Benjamin," breaking the pattern "the sons of Benjamin." These introductory words evidently have dropped out through haplography. Otherwise vv. 6–11 are presented normally with the genealogies of the three sons Bela, Beka, and Jediael following one another. Attention is paid again to fighting men (vv. 7,9,11). The numbers are not round numbers but exact numbers, suggesting a dependence on a census list no longer available to us.

7:12 The Shuppites and Huppites probably are to be identified with the sons of Benjamin mentioned in Gen 46:21 and the Shephupham and Hupham in Num 26:39. We noted earlier that Dan seems to be missing. One commentator has proposed an emendation at the end of v. 12 to give a reading "the sons of Dan: Hushim, his son, one."[52] This is rejected by other commentators.

---

[51] J. B. Payne suggests that because of the exceptionally high numbers here and in eight other places in Chronicles (12:24–37; 25:1–15; 2 Chr 13:3,17; 14:8–9; 17:14–18; 25:5–6; 26:12–13; 28:6,8) the word אֶלֶף usually translated "thousand" perhaps should be understood as "captain of a thousand," similar to אַלּוּף "chief." See Payne, *1, 2 Chronicles,* 4:357–58, 562; id., "The Validity of the Numbers in Chronicles," *BSac* 136 (1979): 217.

[52] See Williamson, *1 and 2 Chronicles,* 78.

(3) The Tribe of Naphtali (7:13)

¹³The sons of Naphtali:
Jahziel, Guni, Jezer and Shillem—the descendants of Bilhah.

7:13   The sons of Naphtali are exactly the same as those in Gen 46:24–25 and Num 26:48-49. The Chronicler notes that these were the sons of Bilhah, one of Jacob's concubines. It is a very truncated genealogy. Perhaps this did not matter to the Chronicler. He was satisfied to mention the tribe of Naphtali, filling in a gap in the tribal list of "all Israel." Such lacunae (i.e., gaps) are known elsewhere, as for example in the cases of Zebulun and Dan (but see comment on 7:12).

(4) The Tribe of Manasseh (7:14–19)

¹⁴The descendants of Manasseh:
Asriel was his descendant through his Aramean concubine. She gave birth to Makir the father of Gilead. ¹⁵Makir took a wife from among the Huppites and Shuppites. His sister's name was Maacah.
Another descendant was named Zelophe had, who had only daughters.
¹⁶Makir's wife Maacah gave birth to a son and named him. His brother was named Sheresh, and his sons were Ulam and Rakem.
¹⁷The son of Ulam:
Bedan.
These were the sons of Gilead son of Makir, the son of Manasseh. ¹⁸His sister Hammoleketh gave birth to Ishhod, Abiezer and Mahlah.
¹⁹The sons of Shemida were: Ahian, Shechem, Likhi and Aniam.

7:14–19   The tribe of Manasseh was split into two sections, one in Transjordan (5:23–26) and one in Cisjordan, which is described in the present passage. The list is drawn from various sources. The Chronicler evidently knew the census list of Num 26:29–33 and the allotment list of Josh 17:1–13, but there are some difficulties here.[53]

Maacah is named as the sister of Makir in v. 15 but as his wife in v. 16. Makir took a wife from among the Huppites and Shuppites (v. 15). How are these related to the people of v. 12 who were the descendants of Ir? Again the MT in v. 15 refers to "the second" who was named Zelophehad. Who was the "first"? Also the Gilead of v. 16 is not referred to in the list of vv. 16–17a. Some textual abbreviation or faulty transmission has been suggested by many commentators.[54]

---

[53] For an attempt to reckon with the inconsistencies and postulate a source for the Chronicler, see D. Edelman, "The Manassite Genealogy in 1 Chronicles 7:14–19," *CBQ* 53 (1991): 179–201.

[54] See Williamson, *1 and 2 Chronicles,* 79, and he translation of Braun, *1 Chronicles,* 110.

Some points of special interest to us may be noted. According to Joshua 17, Makir was given territory in Gilead and Bashan and the remaining "sons of Manasseh" were settled west of Jordan, as is clear from names such as Shechem and Tirzah. Some of the names here, Shemida, Abiezer, and Helek, occur in the Samaria ostraca.[55] A tradition of descendants of Manasseh in Transjordan has been met in 5:23–26. We find here, also, a further indication of Israelite links with Arameans. After the rise of Aram-Damascus there was, of course, open conflict.

(5) The Tribe of Ephraim (7:20–29)

[20] The descendants of Ephraim:

Shuthelah, Bered his son, Tahath his son, Eleadah his son, Tahath his son, [21]Zabad his son and Shuthelah his son.

Ezer and Elead were killed by the native-born men of Gath, when they went down to seize their livestock. [22]Their father Ephraim mourned for them many days, and his relatives came to comfort him. [23]Then he lay with his wife again, and she became pregnant and gave birth to a son. He named him Beriah, because there had been misfortune in his family. [24]His daughter was Sheerah, who built Lower and Upper Beth Horon as well as Uzzen Sheerah.

[25]Rephah was his son, Resheph his son,

Telah his son, Tahan his son,

[26]Ladan his son, Ammihud his son, Elishama his son, [27]Nun his son and Joshua his son.

[28]Their lands and settlements included Bethel and its surrounding villages, Naaran to the east, Gezer and its villages to the west, and Shechem and its villages all the way to Ayyah and its villages. [29]Along the borders of Manasseh were Beth Shan, Taanach, Megiddo and Dor, together with their villages. The descendants of Joseph son of Israel lived in these towns.

This pericope is composed of three major parts: (1) the genealogy from Ephraim to Joshua (vv. 20–21a,25–27); (2) a historical notice concerning the birth of Beriah which interrupts the genealogy of Joshua (vv. 21b–24); and (3) a list of villages occupied by the sons of Joseph (vv. 28–29).

7:20–21 The genealogy reaching from Ephraim to Joshua is presented as a vertical genealogy of the form "*X, his son Y, his son Z,*" in itself a unity though interrupted by the mention of Ezer and Elead in v. 21b, who were killed by the native-born men of Gath when they went down to seize their livestock. The Gath mentioned here probably is the Gittaim of 2 Sam 4:3 rather than Gath, one of the Philistine cities. The "native-born" men were lit-

---

[55] J. Myers, *I Chronicles,* 54–55.

erally "those who were born in the land," natives and not migrants.

7:22   Ephraim had only one brother, so the translation "relatives" (lit., "brothers") in the NIV is correct.

7:23–24   Ephraim's wife subsequently became pregnant with a son, whom they named Beriah "because misfortune had come upon his house" (NASB). The Heb. for Beriah, *bĕrî'â*, is a wordplay on "misfortune," *bĕrā'â*. The daughter of Beriah, Sheerah, is credited with the building of Lower and Upper Beth-Horon as well as the unidentified Uzzen Sheerah. These towns represent the limit of Ephraim's westward expansion. They evidently lay close together.

7:25–27   The vertical chronology of Ephraim's descendants continues to Joshua.

7:28–29   The material on Manasseh and Ephraim is here drawn together into a section that gives the dwelling places of the descendants of Joseph (cp. Josh 16–18). The Chronicler himself was not greatly concerned with problems of historical geography. His point was made when he had provided a picture of God's people in their land. Only modern scholars have concerned themselves with such details. Nevertheless, v. 28 is in general agreement with Josh 16:5–10, which gives the cities of Ephraim, and v. 29 follows Josh 17:11 for the cities of Manasseh. The list represents the southern and northern boundaries of the territory of Ephraim-Manasseh. Bethel was conquered by Joseph's tribes (Judg 1:22) and was regarded as a boundary city (Josh 16:1–2; 18:13) and as belonging to Benjamin (Josh 18:22). Shechem was within the limits of Manasseh (Josh 17:7ff.) but assigned to Ephraim (Josh 20:7). It was a city of refuge for the central tribes and was shared between Ephraim, Manasseh, and Benjamin. The line from Naaran (Naarath) to Gezer runs near Bethel. The line on the north from Beth-shean via Taanach and Megiddo to Dor is clear.[56]

(6) The Tribe of Asher (7:30–40)

³⁰The sons of Asher:
   Imnah, Ishvah, Ishvi and Beriah. Their sister was Serah.
³¹The sons of Beriah:
   Heber and Malkiel, who was the father of Birzaith.
³²Heber was the father of Japhlet, Shomer and Hotham and of their sister Shua.
³³The sons of Japhlet:
   Pasach, Bimhal and Ashvath. These were Japhlet's sons.
³⁴The sons of Shomer:

---

[56] See Myers, *I Chronicles*, 56; and Braun, *1 Chronicles*, 116.

Ahi, Rohgah, Hubbah and Aram.
³⁵The sons of his brother Helem:
    Zophah, Imna, Shelesh and Amal.
³⁶The sons of Zophah:
    Suah, Harnepher, Shual, Beri, Imrah, ³⁷Bezer, Hod, Shamma, Shilshah,
    Ithran and Beera.
³⁸The sons of Jether:
    Jephunneh, Pispah and Ara.
³⁹The sons of Ulla:
    Arah, Hanniel and Rizia.

⁴⁰All these were descendants of Asher—heads of families, choice men, brave warriors and outstanding leaders. The number of men ready for battle, as listed in their genealogy, was 26,000.

7:30–40 Asher was a peripheral tribe, descended from Zilpah, the handmaid of Leah (Gen 46:17). Evidently they furnished a useful body of fighters for Israel's army, 26,000, a reduced number from the 41,500 of Num 1:40–41; 2:27–28, and 53,400 of Num 26:47, perhaps reflecting accurately the situation at a later date.[57]

7. The Tribe of Benjamin (8:1–9:1a)

¹Benjamin was the father of Bela his firstborn,
    Ashbel the second son, Aharah the third,
   ²Nohah the fourth and Rapha the fifth.
³The sons of Bela were:
    Addar, Gera, Abihud, ⁴Abishua, Naaman, Ahoah, ⁵Gera, Shephuphan
    and Huram.
⁶These were the descendants of Ehud, who were heads of families of those
    living in Geba and were deported to Manahath:
   ⁷Naaman, Ahijah, and Gera, who deported them and who was the father
    of Uzza and Ahihud.
⁸Sons were born to Shaharaim in Moab after he had divorced his wives
    Hushim and Baara. ⁹By his wife Hodesh he had Jobab, Zibia, Mesha,
    Malcam, ¹⁰Jeuz, Sakia and Mirma. These were his sons, heads of fami-
    lies. ¹¹By Hushim he had Abitub and Elpaal.
¹²The sons of Elpaal: Eber, Misham, Shemed (who built Ono and Lod with
    its surrounding villages), ¹³and Beriah and Shema, who were heads of

---

[57] An unnecessarily pessimistic assessment of the historical value of these genealogies is N. Na'aman, "Sources and Redaction in the Chronicler's Genealogies of Asher and Ephraim," *JSOT* 49 (1991): 99–111. Na'aman does believe that it is possible to isolate units that are older and of historical worth, but he believes that the rest of the material constitutes the Chronicler's additions and elaborations on the genealogies and that they are of little historical value.

families of those living in Aijalon and who drove out the inhabitants of Gath.

[14]Ahio, Shashak, Jeremoth, [15]Zebadiah, Arad, Eder, [16]Michael, Ishpah and Joha were the sons of Beriah.

[17]Zebadiah, Meshullam, Hizki, Heber, [18]Ishmerai, Izliah and Jobab were the sons of Elpaal.

[19]Jakim, Zicri, Zabdi, [20]Elienai, Zillethai, Eliel, [21]Adaiah, Beraiah and Shimrath were the sons of Shimei.

[22]Ishpan, Eber, Eliel, [23]Abdon, Zicri, Hanan, [24]Hananiah, Elam, Anthothijah, [25]Iphdeiah and Penuel were the sons of Shashak.

[26]Shamsherai, Shehariah, Athaliah, [27]Jaareshiah, Elijah and Zicri were the sons of Jeroham.

[28]All these were heads of families, chiefs as listed in their genealogy, and they lived in Jerusalem.

[29]Jeiel the father of Gibeon lived in Gibeon.
His wife's name was Maacah, [30]and his firstborn son was Abdon, followed by Zur, Kish, Baal, Ner, Nadab, [31]Gedor, Ahio, Zeker [32]and Mikloth, who was the father of Shimeah. They too lived near their relatives in Jerusalem.

[33]Ner was the father of Kish, Kish the father of Saul, and Saul the father of Jonathan, Malki-Shua, Abinadab and Esh-Baal.

[34]The son of Jonathan:
Merib-Baal, who was the father of Micah.

[35]The sons of Micah:
Pithon, Melech, Tarea and Ahaz.

[36]Ahaz was the father of Jehoaddah, Jehoaddah was the father of Alemeth, Azmaveth and Zimri, and Zimri was the father of Moza. [37]Moza was the father of Binea; Raphah was his son, Eleasah his son and Azel his son.

[38]Azel had six sons, and these were their names:
Azrikam, Bokeru, Ishmael, Sheariah, Obadiah and Hanan. All these were the sons of Azel.

[39]The sons of his brother Eshek: Ulam his firstborn, Jeush the second son and Eliphelet the third. [40]The sons of Ulam were brave warriors who could handle the bow. They had many sons and grandsons—150 in all.
All these were the descendants of Benjamin.

[1]All Israel was listed in the genealogies recorded in the book of the kings of Israel.

The tribe of Benjamin is mentioned briefly in 7:6–12, where the Chronicler probably continued the source he was using for Issachar in 7:1–5. But he felt he needed to give a more extended treatment of the tribe of Benjamin to conclude his Judah–Levi–Benjamin concept for the framework that enclosed the whole of Israel. Indeed, the Chronicler gave a great deal of attention to Benjamin. In his mind the Southern Kingdom, composed of Judah and Benjamin, was the legitimate "Israel" because of the Davidic monarchy. Similarly, the tribe of Levi was the legitimate clergy (in contrast to the nonlevitical priesthood of Jeroboam).

Even a cursory reading of this chapter reveals significant differences between this genealogy of Benjamin and that in 7:6–12. The formula used is "*A* fathered *B*," as distinct from "the sons of *A* were . . ." This list is similar to Num 26:38–41 whereas the list in 7:6–12 is closer to Gen 46:21, but no two lists of Benjamin's sons are the same. Here and in Numbers, Benjamin is credited with five sons. In 7:6 there were only three. Only the name "Bela" appears in all four lists.

The material here is composite. Thus after vv. 7,12,28 there are breaks in the genealogy, and the subsections include geographical material. Do we have here parallel lists of Benjamite families at particular periods of time?[58] Another proposal is that the genealogy of Saul (vv. 29–40) may reflect the social and ethnic background of Gibeon at the end of the monarchy.[59] There are different types of material in the chapter: (a) the sons of Benjamin (vv. 1–5) and the sons of Ehud at Geba (vv. 6–7); (b) the sons of Shaharaim in Moab, Ono, and Lod (vv. 8–12); (c) the Benjamites in Aijalon, Gath, and Jerusalem (vv. 13–28); (d) the Benjamites in Gibeon and Jerusalem (vv. 29–32); (e) the genealogy of Saul (vv. 33–40).

Elsewhere in the Old Testament the Benjamites are linked with other tribal groups like Ephraim and Manasseh (Num 2:18–24), although the border between Benjamin and Ephraim fluctuated. The border with Judah also fluctuated (2 Chr 11:1,3,10,12,23; 14:8; 15:2,8–9; 25:5).

8:1–2 Several of the names in this passage occur in the Genesis and Numbers genealogies. Benjamites are associated with Ehud of Geba (v. 6). The present-day Jiba lies about six miles north of Jerusalem. The deportation of the sons of Ehud to Manahath cannot now be placed historically. Was Ehud the Benjamite judge of Judg 3:15?

8:3–5 The reference to two sons of Bela each named Gera may point to a scribal slip. A feasible emendation is to read, "Gera, even the father of Ehud." Then v. 6a follows smoothly, "These were the descendants of Ehud."[60]

8:6 While no independent reference to this deportation is known and by

---

[58] A suggestion of W. Rudolph. See Williamson, *1 and 2 Chronicles,* 82.

[59] A. Damsky, "The Genealogy of Gibeon (1 Chronicles 9:35–44): Biblical and Epigraphic Considerations," *BASOR* 202 (1971): 16–23.

[60] Payne suggests that the first Gera may be a son who died prematurely ("1, 2 Chronicles," EBC 4:360).

whom the deportation was carried out, it is possible that the Benjamites expelled the native inhabitants to Manahath in Judah (cf. 2:52,54). A similar expulsion of the inhabitants of Gath is mentioned in 2:13. There must have been numerous such expulsions in ancient times.

8:7 There may be some confusion in the Hebrew text here. Some commentators omit Naaman and Ahijah as a duplication of Naaman and Ahoah (almost identical to Ahijah in Heb. in v. 4). But the text is difficult to follow. So also is v. 7b. The NIV gives a widely accepted translation.

8:8–12 Moab broke free from Israel eventually. This reference may be concerned with earlier times when some people of Israel lived in Moab, as in the days of Ruth (Ruth 1) and David (1 Sam 22:3–4). We cannot be specific in the absence of other details. There is no information elsewhere that Benjamin had any connection with Moab. The name "Mesha" is used of a king of Moab on the Mesha stele (cf. 2 Kgs 3:4).

The Shaharaim of v. 9 had marital problems and divorced two women, one of whom, Hushim, was the mother of Elpaal, who gave rise to a genealogy (vv. 12–13). The use of the verb "built" raises a question. The towns Ono and Lod are known in Egyptian records from the days of Thutmose III (1490–1436 B.C.) before Israelite times.[61] "Built" here must mean "rebuilt," or "fortified." Certainly Ono and Lod were resettled in the postexilic period (Ezra 2:33; Neh 7:37; 11:35) by families who had lived there formerly. These towns are in the west of the land, and the question arises about how they could be counted in Benjamin. In earlier times they were in Dan and later in Ephraim. In Josh 19:40–46 Dan is "opposite Joppa" (NRSV). It is possible that the area of Dan was absorbed by Judah and Ephraim and, since Judah coalesced with Benjamin about the time of the division of the kingdom, it is feasible that Ono and Lod could be seen as part of Benjamin since the returning exiles were said to have gone back to their former places (Ezra 2:1). Benjamites lived at Ono and Lod (Neh 11:35).

8:13–28 These verses refer to Benjamites living in Aijalon who "drove out the inhabitants of Gath" (v. 13), possibly Gittaim. At least two of these, Beriah and Shema, were heads of families. Aijalon was assigned to Dan (Josh 19:42) but lay on Ephraim's border. It was fortified by Rehoboam (2 Chr 11:10) but was taken by the Philistines in the reign of Ahaz (2 Chr 28:18). The fact that Benjamites lived in Jerusalem (v. 28) shows how closely Judah and Benjamin were linked after the division of the kingdom.

For "Ahio" (*wʾhyw*; v. 14) the LXX reads "and their brothers" (translating *wʾhyhm*). The text then reads "their brothers were Shashak, Jeremoth, Arad, Zebadiah . . . the sons of Beriah." The sons of Elipaal follow in vv.

---

[61] *ANET*, 243, where "Lod" appears as "Lydda."

17–18. "Shimei" (v. 21) is the same as the Shema of v. 13. "Jeroham" (v. 27) probably is the same as Jeremoth of v. 14.

The summarizing note in v. 28 compares with 9:34; in both the claim is made that certain individuals lived in Jerusalem. Benjamites and Judahites during the period of the divided monarchy tended to mix in the same location. Jerusalem lay on the border between Judah and Benjamin. It may seem that v. 28 refers only to the sons listed in vv. 15–26 and not to v. 13 or vv. 6–12, yet the all-inclusive nature of v. 28 is clear. The Hebrew text reads literally "the heads of the fathers according to their generations, heads." To clinch the point that their dwelling place was Jerusalem, this phrase is now the normal one covering all Benjamite settlements (cf. 9:3 and the symbolic statements of 8:32 and 9:38).

8:29–40 The rest of chap. 8 deals with the Benjamites centered in Gibeon, the well-known el-Jib, six miles northwest of Jerusalem, assigned to Benjamin in Josh 18:25. These people helped rebuild the walls of Jerusalem after the exile (Neh 3:7). It was resettled in Nehemiah's time (Neh 7:25). The list combines both vertical and horizontal elements. Failure to appreciate this has led some scholars to deny unity to the section.[62] S. Waters argues that the line of Saul is given a geographical rather than a genealogical connection to the tribe of Benjamin here. This serves to imply that Saul was unfit to rule Israel.[63]

The word "father" (v. 29) may mean "civic leader" or "military leader." The individual "Jeiel" is lacking in the Hebrew text. It is restored on the basis of the LXX (cf. 9:35). The name of his wife, "Maacah," suggests a link with an Aramean (non-Israelite) group. It was from this union that Kish, the father of Saul, came (v. 30).

The name "Baal" (v. 30) points to an early origin of this section since in later days it was anathema (cf. 5:5). "Ner" is restored by the NIV in front of Nadab following some LXX manuscripts and 1 Chr 9:36. He was the father of Kish, the father of Saul (v. 33). In v. 30 Ner is named as brother of Kish. That is not an impossible scenario since Ner may well have given his son the name of his own brother. But in any case the very name Kish provided a good reason to introduce the family of Saul (vv. 33–40).

---

[62] Damsky ("Genealogy of Gibeon," 16–23) and A. Malamat ("King Lists of the Old Babylonian Period and Biblical Genealogies," *JAOS* 88 [1968]: 163–73) compare biblical and Babylonian royal genealogies that support the unity of the list.

[63] S. D. Waters, "Saul of Gibeon," *JSOT* 52 (1991): 61–76. J. Sailhamer also understands the message here that Saul was from the Benjamite family that came from Gibeon rather than from the city of David, God's chosen city, Jerusalem (*First and Second Chronicles* [Chicago: Moody, 1983], 27). There is then a subtle contrast here between Saul, Gibeon, and human plans on the one hand and David, Jerusalem, and divine plans on the other.

From v. 32 it seems that some of the people of Gibeon moved to Jerusalem, but how many is not specified.

Saul's family continues to v. 40. It is taken up again in 9:35–10:14. The name Esh-Baal ("man of Baal") is known as Ishvi in 1 Sam 14:49 and Ishbosheth ("man of shame") in 2 Sam 2:8 and elsewhere. This latter name is used to cover up religious scruples because pious Israelites objected to the name Baal and made a theological correction to the name (the LXX has "*Ishyo*, man of the Lord"). This genealogy is the most extensive one for Saul in the Hebrew Bible. It shows fifteen generations.[64]

The name "Merib-Baal" (v. 34; "Baal contends") provides another example of the abhorred name "Baal."[65] "Baal" was probably left on these names to cast a shadow over the Saulide family. In other words, the Chronicler subtly offers a condemnation of the reign of Saul.

Merib-Baal's son Mica (2 Sam 9:12) evidently was of some significance. Four sons are mentioned, the fourth of whom was Azel, whose six sons are mentioned in v. 38. The list from v. 35 on is paralleled in 9:35–44, taken from an unknown source. This brings the genealogy down to somewhere near the exile. The names in vv. 29–40 do not occur at the end of chap. 9. They are unattached to the preceding verses and may have come from a military list. The sons of Eshek lead into a list of brave warriors who could handle the bow.

The extensive listing of the Benjamites in chap. 8 reflects the widespread interest in that tribe in the postexilic period. The widespread locations where Benjamites were to be found—Geba, Moab, Ono, Lod, Gibeon, and Jerusalem itself—indicates that over the centuries members of this tribe were scattered through other tribal areas.

9:1a   The conclusion to Israel's genealogical lists is brief. It refers only to the official register of Israel's families and their situations. The northern tribes had been deported to foreign parts (5:25–26), but finally the state of

---

[64] J. Van Seters claims that Ishbosheth is not mentioned in the list of Saul's three sons in 1 Sam 14:49 (Jonathan, Ishvi, and Malki-Shua) or the list in 1 Sam 31:2 (Jonathan, Abinadab, and Malki-Shua) of Saul's sons who died with him at Gilboa. He considers the section on Ishbosheth in 2 Sam 2:8–4:12 to be part of the "Court History of David," which "made use of, and supplemented, the Dtr history" and whose account of events "may all be imaginary" (*In Search of History* [New Haven: Yale University Press, 1983], 281–87). The Chronicler's naming four sons "simply points to this author's 'correction' of the record subsequent to the addition of the Court History" (p. 281). He thus treats Ishvi and Abinadab as the same person, which, as R. P. Gordon notes, "is not the only or even the obvious way of dealing with the data" ("In Search of David," in *Faith, Tradition, and History*, ed. A. R. Millard et al. [Winona Lake, Ind.: Eisenbrauns, 1994], 293). Also see comments at 1 Chr 10:6.

[65] The name appears elsewhere as Mephibosheth (e.g., 2 Sam 4:4; 9:6,10,12–13; cf. Judg 6:31–32).

Judah, despite the presence of the temple in its midst as a witness to God and to his claim on their lives, suffered the unthinkable. Judah too was carried away to Babylon because of their unfaithfulness (cf. 6:15). They too knew the mental anguish of displaced people, torn from their roots, far from home and from God. But their God could reach out and restore them and their city and their land. That is the story that follows in subsequent chapters in Chronicles.

8. The Postexilic Community (9:1b–34)

The people of Judah were taken captive to Babylon because of their unfaith-fulness. [2]Now the first to resettle on their own property in their own towns were some Israelites, priests, Levites and temple servants.

[3]Those from Judah, from Benjamin, and from Ephraim and Manasseh who lived in Jerusalem were:

[4]Uthai son of Ammihud, the son of Omri, the son of Imri, the son of Bani, a descendant of Perez son of Judah.

[5]Of the Shilonites:

Asaiah the firstborn and his sons.

[6]Of the Zerahites:

Jeuel.

The people from Judah numbered 690.

[7]Of the Benjamites:

Sallu son of Meshullam, the son of Hodaviah, the son of Hassenuah;

[8]Ibneiah son of Jeroham; Elah son of Uzzi, the son of Micri; and Meshullam son of Shephatiah, the son of Reuel, the son of Ibnijah.

[9]The people from Benjamin, as listed in their genealogy, numbered 956. All these men were heads of their families.

[10]Of the priests:

Jedaiah; Jehoiarib; Jakin;

[11]Azariah son of Hilkiah, the son of Meshullam, the son of Zadok, the son of Meraioth, the son of Ahitub, the official in charge of the house of God;

[12]Adaiah son of Jeroham, the son of Pashhur, the son of Malkijah; and Maasai son of Adiel, the son of Jahzerah, the son of Meshullam, the son of Meshillemith, the son of Immer.

[13]The priests, who were heads of families, numbered 1,760. They were able men, responsible for ministering in the house of God.

[14]Of the Levites:

Shemaiah son of Hasshub, the son of Azrikam, the son of Hashabiah, a Merarite; [15]Bakbakkar, Heresh, Galal and Mattaniah son of Mica, the son of Zicri, the son of Asaph; [16]Obadiah son of Shemaiah, the son of Galal, the son of Jeduthun; and Berekiah son of Asa, the son of Elkanah, who lived in the villages of the Netophathites.

¹⁷The gatekeepers:

Shallum, Akkub, Talmon, Ahiman and their brothers, Shallum their chief ¹⁸being stationed at the King's Gate on the east, up to the present time. These were the gatekeepers belonging to the camp of the Levites. ¹⁹Shallum son of Kore, the son of Ebiasaph, the son of Korah, and his fellow gatekeepers from his family (the Korahites) were responsible for guarding the thresholds of the Tent just as their fathers had been responsible for guarding the entrance to the dwelling of the LORD. ²⁰In earlier times Phinehas son of Eleazar was in charge of the gatekeepers, and the LORD was with him. ²¹Zechariah son of Meshelemiah was the gatekeeper at the entrance to the Tent of Meeting.

²²Altogether, those chosen to be gatekeepers at the thresholds numbered 212. They were registered by genealogy in their villages. The gatekeepers had been assigned to their positions of trust by David and Samuel the seer. ²³They and their descendants were in charge of guarding the gates of the house of the LORD—the house called the Tent. ²⁴The gatekeepers were on the four sides: east, west, north and south. ²⁵Their brothers in their villages had to come from time to time and share their duties for seven-day periods. ²⁶But the four principal gatekeepers, who were Levites, were entrusted with the responsibility for the rooms and treasuries in the house of God. ²⁷They would spend the night stationed around the house of God, because they had to guard it; and they had charge of the key for opening it each morning.

²⁸Some of them were in charge of the articles used in the temple service; they counted them when they were brought in and when they were taken out. ²⁹Others were assigned to take care of the furnishings and all the other articles of the sanctuary, as well as the flour and wine, and the oil, incense and spices. ³⁰But some of the priests took care of mixing the spices. ³¹A Levite named Mattithiah, the firstborn son of Shallum the Korahite, was entrusted with the responsibility for baking the offering bread. ³²Some of their Kohathite brothers were in charge of preparing for every Sabbath the bread set out on the table.

³³Those who were musicians, heads of Levite families, stayed in the rooms of the temple and were exempt from other duties because they were responsible for the work day and night.

³⁴All these were heads of Levite families, chiefs as listed in their genealogy, and they lived in Jerusalem.

9:1b It would seem that 9:1a refers to the preexilic period and that the reference to "the kings of Israel" is an all-inclusive reference to kings, whether from political Judah or political Israel, who ruled over God's people. However, with 9:1b we are clearly concerned with Judah. Just as in 1 Chronicles 1 there is a line of election that narrows down to Israel and his sons (2:1), so here the postexilic community represents a narrowing of "all Israel" to the people of Judah who were taken to Babylon. Because of their "unfaithfulness" judgment fell, a concept used several times by the Chronicler. The basic structure of chap. 9 is paralleled by Nehemiah 11, although there are numerous differences in detail. In fact, the differences are extensive enough to conclude that whatever the original source, they probably came to the writers by different channels or by independent choice of the materials offered.[66]

9:2–3 The Hebrew text allows for more than one translation—"the first living on their property," "the first citizens who returned to their property" (understanding the verb as *haššābîm,* "return," rather than the MT *hayyôšĕbîm,* "live"), "the first to resettle" (NIV). Regardless, the verse is a reference to the returning exiles. The term "Israelite" here seems to mean laypeople because the text proceeds to distinguish priests, Levites, and temple servants. The last group, described as "temple servants" or *nĕtînîm,* is often referred to in Ezra and Nehemiah (Ezra 2:43; 7:7,24; 8:20). These are known as a social class in texts from ancient Ugarit, where they were temple slaves. Perhaps they originally were foreigners captured in war and may have been gatekeepers or other types of functionaries (cf. vv. 17–21). The Chronicler himself did not refer to them elsewhere by name. The mention of Ephraim and Manasseh living in Jerusalem with those from Judah and Benjamin may be intended to show that the postexilic community was representative of "all-Israel," not simply of Judah and Benjamin.

9:4–6 The returnees from Judah are listed under the names of the patriarchs mentioned in 2:3–4, Perez, Shelah, and Zerah. The idea of a continuity from ancient times is presented. The Shilonites were descendants of Shelah. Numbers 26:20 refers to them as Shelanites. The number 690 contrasts with 468 in Neh 11:6, which, however, does not refer to Zerah. The LXX names vary somewhat.[67]

9:7–9 Chronicles names four family heads with a total of 956 people. This list differs considerably from Neh 11:7–9, which mentions only one line of descent. As F. C. Fensham has written regarding the differences between 1 Chronicles 9 and Nehemiah 11: "We might presume that various genealogical lists were present in the archives. Each author made use of it in his own way, omitting material which he did not regard as relevant and adding new material to bring the list up to date. It is also clear that with the transmission of genealogical lists many scribal errors had crept in."[68] E. H.

---

[66] Braun (*1 Chronicles,* 132) proposes a list to show the two are in some way dependent on one another, probably 1 Chronicles 9 on Nehemiah 11. Payne thinks the list in Nehemiah is later, which based the order of categories on 1 Chronicles 9. He also thinks this chapter still concerns preexilic Benjamin, preferring the NASB translation of the beginning of v. 2, "Now the first who lived in," i.e., "the former, preexilic Jerusalemites" ("1, 2 Chronicles," EBC 4:365–66).

[67] A useful comparative table of the MT and the LXX occurs in Myers, *I Chronicles,* 68.

[68] F. C. Fensham, *The Books of Ezra and Nehemiah* (Grand Rapids: Eerdmans, 1982), 244.

Merrill also notes that since we do not know the basis for the Chronicler's 956 or Nehemiah's 928 (Neh 11:8), "we cannot account for the differences."[69]

9:10–13 The passage is comparatively close to Neh 11:10–14 although it is abbreviated and shows spelling differences.[70]

9:14–16 The list of Levites is now given, a little longer than the list in Nehemiah 11. The reason may be that it is an updating.[71] The families of Shemaiah, Mattaniah, and Obadiah are singled out for special mention. These were descended from the chief Levitical families of Merari, Asaph, and Jeduthun. Netophath was somewhere near Jerusalem. The villages of the Netophathites were the home of Levitical singers (Neh 12:28). The town is closely identified with Bethlehem (2:54; Ezra 2:21–22; Neh 7:26) and is sometimes identified with a site some three and a half miles southeast of Bethlehem.[72]

9:17–19 Four gatekeepers[73] are listed by name: Shallum, Akkub, Talmon, and Ahiman, though there were others. Shallum was chief and occupied an especially honored position as the gatekeeper of the east gate through which the king usually entered (cf. Ezek 46:2). This gate faced the entrance to the sanctuary. These gatekeepers were reckoned with the Levites (v. 26; 1 Chr 23:4). They formed a separate class in the list of priests, Levites, gatekeepers, and temple slaves in several places. They were Korahites. These verses stress the Levitical descent of the gatekeepers (vv. 18b,26). Their task was "guarding the thresholds of the tent [ʾōhel] just as their fathers had" (v. 19).

9:20 In earlier times Phinehas [the high priest] son of Eleazar was in charge of the gatekeepers, and the LORD was with him." This is an allusion to the heroic faith of Phinehas in Num 25:7–13. Because of his courageous opposition to the fertility cult of Baal, God gave him a "covenant of peace."

9:21 Zechariah, son of Meshelemiah (cf. 26:2,14), had duties at the north gate and the east gate respectively. Perhaps Zechariah succeeded his father. These chief gatekeepers had charge of the gates on the four sides and apparently lived in Jerusalem. Their brothers (assistants) lived in their villages (v. 23). According to 26:12–18, there was a total of twenty-four guard

---

[69] E. H. Merrill, "1 Chronicles," in *The Bible Knowledge Commentary: Old Testament*, ed. J. F. Walvoord and R. B. Zuck (Wheaton: Victor, 1985), 602.

[70] Ibid., 70.

[71] Ibid., 71.

[72] W. H. Morton, "Netophah," *IDB* 3.54.

[73] A valuable recent appraisal of their place in the temple is given in J. W. Wright, "Guarding the Gates: I Chronicles 26:1–19 and the Roles of Gate-keepers in Chronicles," *JSOT* 48 (1990): 69–81.

posts to be manned all the time in relays of a week each.

9:22–26a   In all there were 212 gatekeepers. This assignment had been undertaken by David and Samuel the seer. Samuel, of course, died before David (1 Sam 25:1; 28:3), so the statement has to be understood in a general sense. Samuel's influence was far reaching because he strove to guard the purity of Israel's worship in his day.

9:26b–34   There is a break in the prescriptions at v. 26b. The emphasis changes from the specific duties of the gatekeepers to a more general discussion of the duties of the Levites. This can be made clearer by translating vv. 25–26a: "Their brothers in their villages had to come from time to time and share their duties for seven-day periods because they were faithful. The four chief gatekeepers were Levites." The general outline of Levitical duties follows, beyond that of being gatekeepers. In addition to the opening of the temple each morning, they also were responsible for the implements used in the temple service, the care of the furnishings and all other articles of the sanctuary, and the handling of the flour, wine, oil, incense, and spices.

An actual list of Levitical singers is not provided. They were, in any case, exempt from other duties because they were responsible for the work day and night. In this respect they were not outdone by the gatekeepers who also ministered day and night (Ps 134; Isa 30:29). Verse 34 is a transitional verse between the Levitical musicians and the genealogy of Saul. It is preparatory to the accounts of the death of Saul related in chap. 10.

Chapter 9 begins with a sad testimony to sin and judgment (v. 1). Not only had the northern tribes been deported to foreign lands (5:25–26), but now Judah, despite the presence of the temple in its midst as a witness to God and to his claim on the people, was carried away captive to Babylon because of their unfaithfulness. But with God, there is hope of a return. The passage from vv. 2–24 is the story of a restored people in a restored city and land. The Chronicler, with his overall concern for the Davidic monarchy from David to Zedekiah, takes a moment to concern himself with the postexilic period. The whole history of God's people is the story of fresh starts by God's grace. God always picks up the broken pieces and puts them together again. There is ever a way back to God, and so it proved again in the sixth century B.C. Chapter 9 gives evidence of a continuation of God's purposes for Israel.

II. SAUL (9:35–10:14)
  1. The Ancestry of Saul (9:35–44)
  2. Saul Takes His Own Life (10:1–14)

II. SAUL (9:35–10:14)

The reigns of Saul, David, and Solomon over a united Israel were of great concern to the Chronicler. About half of his total space is taken up with the story of these three kings. The material is concerned with the abortive period of Saul, which is dealt with in brief compass, followed by a major consideration of David (1 Chr 11–29, nineteen chapters), and a substantial consideration of Solomon (2 Chr 1–9, nine chapters).

The Chronicler hardly could ignore Saul—he was too closely connected to David and too well known as the first king—but clearly Saul was not at the center of his interest. The history in Samuel, by contrast, devotes enormous attention to Saul (1 Sam 9–2; Sam 1). For the Chronicler, the disobedient Saul (v. 13) was if anything a foil meant to show the faithfulness of David.[1]

1. The Ancestry of Saul (9:35–44)

[35]Jeiel the father of Gibeon lived in Gibeon.
  His wife's name was Maacah, [36]and his firstborn son was Abdon, followed by Zur, Kish, Baal, Ner, Nadab, [37]Gedor, Ahio, Zechariah, and Mikloth. [38]Mikloth was the father of Shimeam. They too lived near their relatives in Jerusalem.
[39]Ner was the father of Kish, Kish the father of Saul, and Saul the father of Jonathan, Malki-Shua, Abinadab, and Esh-Baal.
[40]The son of Jonathan:
  Merib-Baal, who was the father of Micah.
[41]The sons of Micah:
  Pithon, Melech, Tahrea, and Ahaz.
  [42]Ahaz was the father of Jadah, Jadah was the father of Alemeth, Azmaveth and Zimri, and Zimri was the father of Moza. [43]Moza was the father of Binea; Rephaiah was his son, Eleasah his son and Azel his son.

---

[1] M. Wilcock, *The Message of Chronicles,* BST (Downers Grove: InterVarsity, 1987), 54.

[44]Azel had six sons, and these were their names:

Azrikam, Bokeru, Ishmael, Sheariah, Obadiah and Hanan. These were the sons of Azel.

9:35–44   Before dealing with the story of Saul, the Chronicler repeats his genealogy from 8:29–38, although there are differences. This text has Ner between Baal and Nadab in v. 36; it includes the name "Mikloth" in v. 37, has "Shimeam" for Shimeah in v. 38, and adds Ahaz to the sons of Micah (v. 41). Some spellings also are different. It may seem unusual to us to repeat the genealogy of Saul, but in a sense it is quite appropriate as an introduction to 1 Chronicles 10.

2. Saul Takes His Own Life (10:1–14)

[1]Now the Philistines fought against Israel; the Israelites fled before them, and many fell slain on Mount Gilboa. [2]The Philistines pressed hard after Saul and his sons, and they killed his sons Jonathan, Abinadab and Malki-Shua. [3]The fighting grew fierce around Saul, and when the archers overtook him, they wounded him.

[4]Saul said to his armor-bearer, "Draw your sword and run me through, or these uncircumcised fellows will come and abuse me."

But his armor-bearer was terrified and would not do it; so Saul took his own sword and fell on it. [5]When the armor-bearer saw that Saul was dead, he too fell on his sword and died. [6]So Saul and his three sons died, and all his house died together.

[7]When all the Israelites in the valley saw that the army had fled and that Saul and his sons had died, they abandoned their towns and fled. And the Philistines came and occupied them.

[8]The next day, when the Philistines came to strip the dead, they found Saul and his sons fallen on Mount Gilboa. [9]They stripped him and took his head and his armor, and sent messengers throughout the land of the Philistines to proclaim the news among their idols and their people. [10]They put his armor in the temple of their gods and hung up his head in the temple of Dagon.

[11]When all the inhabitants of Jabesh Gilead heard of everything the Philistines had done to Saul, [12]all their valiant men went and took the bodies of Saul and his sons and brought them to Jabesh. Then they buried their bones under the great tree in Jabesh, and they fasted seven days.

[13]Saul died because he was unfaithful to the LORD; he did not keep the word of the LORD and even consulted a medium for guidance, [14]and did not inquire of the LORD. So the LORD put him to death and turned the kingdom over to David son of Jesse.

The narrative is based on 1 Samuel 31. The Chronicler does not devote space to Saul's reign in its own right, although an assessment of his reign is provided in vv. 13–14. The Saul experiment ended in disaster, and Israel was left without a king, a state of affairs to be repeated in later days. Indeed, in the Chronicler's day Israel had no king and no national independence but was under the rule of strangers. At this juncture at the death of Saul, David appeared on the scene. The people of the postexilic community, by analogy, could look for another deliverer from the line of David. Chapter 10 need not be seen as a later insertion. It is not merely a prelude to David's reign but is a pattern of the way God acted for Israel.

10:1–2 While the story is based on 1 Samuel 31, it contains a few slight differences in wording, mostly stylistic.

10:3 Some translators render the text here in v. 3b in the passive, "He was wounded by the archers."

10:4 There clearly was great apprehension in Saul's mind about what his fate would be if he fell into the hands of the uncircumcised Philistines. Humiliation, torture, and mutilation surely would be likely to follow Saul's capture. Death at his own hands or at the hands of his armor bearer would be preferable. Suicide practically was unknown in Israel although 1 Sam 31:3–6 has preserved the story of Saul's own suicide. Second Samuel 1:10 has preserved the account of an Amalekite who claims to have killed Saul out of mercy. The Amalekite was apparently lying, and, as a result, David had the Amalekite put to death.

10:5–8 The point is made several times in these verses that Saul was dead. It is also stressed that his three sons died. So the dynasty of Saul had finally concluded. The army fled, the Israelites who lived in the valley of Jezreel abandoned their towns, and the Philistines took over.

As R. P. Gordon has pointed out (against Van Seters), the author of 1 Sam 31:2 understood that Saul was survived by his son Ishbosheth, and the Chronicler knew that as well (see note on 1 Chr 8:33). Whereas 1 Sam 31:6 says that Saul and three of his sons died "that same day," the Chronicler, whose attention was on the end of the kingdom of Saul, added "and all his house." But his omission of "that same day" shows that he was summarizing the consequent events to make the point that "the house of Saul as good as perished at Gilboa: Ishbosheth and his remnant Saulide kingdom counted for nothing from the perspective of later history."[2]

10:9–10 The Samuel account mentions the decapitation of Saul but does not include the detail that the head was put in the temple of Dagon along with his armor. The story in Chronicles, on the other hand, does not mention hanging Saul's body on the wall of Bethshan (1 Sam 31:10). Excavations at Bethshan have brought to light several foreign temples from the

---

[2] R. P. Gordon, "In Search of David: The David in Recent Study," in *Faith, Tradition, and History*, ed. A. R. Millard et al. (Winona Lake, Ind.: Eisenbrauns, 1994), 293–94.

Iron Age, the time of Saul's death. One of these temples may have been the temple referred to here and in 1 Samuel.

10:11–12 The men of Jabesh Gilead displayed their loyalty to the house of Saul by removing the corpses of Saul and his sons and taking them to Jabesh. There they buried their bones under the great tree in Jabesh and held a fast for seven days.

10:13–14 The assessment of Saul's reign is here given. Saul died because he was unfaithful to Yahweh.[3] He did not keep Yahweh's word and even consulted a medium for guidance (cf. 1 Sam 13:1–23; 15:1–35; 28:8–25). The charge of unfaithfulness is frequently employed by the Chronicler in reference to religious matters referring to the Jerusalem temple or the impurity of rituals (cf. 2 Chr 26:16,18; 28:19,22; 29:5–6,19; 30:7; 33:19; 36:14).[4] Such unfaithfulness would lead to military defeat and exile, which included the final exile of both the Northern and Southern Kingdoms (1 Chr 5:25–26; 9:1; 2 Chr 36:20). The consulting of a medium was as grievous an act of unfaithfulness as any ritual offense. The practice of consulting mediums was expressly forbidden in Israel (Deut 18:9–14; cf. 1 Sam 15:23). It was a phenomenon recognized by twittering communications from within a man (Lev 20:27; Isa 29:4).[5]

Saul should have taken his problems to the Lord, but he did not "inquire" (*šāʾal*) of the Lord.[6] It meant for him not merely seeking information but a deep dependence on God born out of a trustful attitude of personal faith and loyalty. Failure to inquire of the Lord on this occasion was a further indication of Saul's whole attitude. Godly leadership is characterized by complete obedience to the Lord and by seeking guidance from him in faith. Saul failed on both counts.

---

[3] See S. Zalewski, "The Purpose of the Story of the Death of Saul in 1 Chronicles X," *VT* 39 (1989): 449–67, for further discussion. Zalewski sees this text as in effect asserting that Saul was executed by Yahweh and that David was fully exonerated of any wrongdoing in assuming the throne.

[4] Williamson, *1 and 2 Chronicles*, 94.

[5] See J. A. Thompson, *Deuteronomy*, TOTC (Downers Grove: InterVarsity, 1974), 211.

[6] See the discussion of seeking the Lord at 2 Chr 14:4.

III. DAVID (11:1–29:30)
1. David's Early Years (11:1–12:40)
   (1) David Becomes King over "All Israel" (11:1–3)
   (2) The Capture of Jerusalem (11:4–9)
   (3) David's Mighty Men (11:10–47)
   (4) David's Early Supporters (12:1–22)
   (5) David's Coronation at Hebron (12:23–40)
2. The Ark Brought to Jerusalem (13:1–16:43)
   (1) The Transfer of the Ark to Jerusalem: First Attempt (13:1–14)
   (2) David's House and Family (14:1–17)
   (3) The Successful Transfer of the Ark to Jerusalem (15:1–16:6)
   (4) David's Psalm of Thanksgiving (16:7–36)
   (5) Ministry before the Ark (16:37–43)
3. God's Promise to David: The Dynastic Oracle (17:1–27)
   (1) David's Plan to Build the Temple and Yahweh's Disapproval (17:1–15)
   (2) David's Prayer in Response to the Oracle (17:16–27)
4. David's Wars (18:1–20:8)
   (1) David's Victories (18:1–13)
   (2) David's Officials (18:14–17)
   (3) David's Campaigns against the Ammonites (19:1–20:3)
   (4) Wars against the Philistines (20:4–8)
5. David's Census and the Choice of Jerusalem for the Temple Site (21:1–22:1)
6. David's First Speech: Solomon Chosen to Build the Temple (22:2–19)
   (1) Materials Needed for the Building of the Temple (22:2–5)
   (2) David's Charge to Solomon (22:6–16)
   (3) David's Charge to the Leaders of Israel (22:17–19)
7. David's Organization of the Priests and Levites (23:1–27:34)
   (1) Divisions of the Levites (23:1–32)
   (2) Divisions of the Priests and the Rest of the Levites (24:1–31)
   (3) The Temple Musicians (25:1–31)
   (4) The Gatekeepers (26:1–19)
   (5) Treasurers and Other Officials (26:20–32)

III. DAVID (11:1–29:30)

With chap. 11 the Chronicler comes to the heart of his story: the rise of David and the establishment of the Davidic kingdom. The source of his material was 2 Sam 5:1–10. Some aspects of the full story are ignored. The long struggle of David with Saul (1 Sam 16–26) and the remnants of his kingdom (2 Sam 2–4) are left aside not because they were unimportant but because the Chronicler was concerned to develop the story of the legitimate line of Israel's kings as represented by David and his successors. After Solomon these were represented by the kings of Judah.

The Chronicler's religious purpose and the theological thrust of his work was to stress for the people of his own day the significance of David and the Davidic kingdom. What made the difference between Saul's failure on the one hand and David's and Solomon's success on the other was seeking the Lord (cf. 1 Chr 13:3; 14:10,16; 2 Chr 14:4). Furthermore, David had the task of reuniting the tribes into "all Israel," but it was "all Israel" that raised David to the throne (11:1–9). After the defeat and death of Saul and the collapse of his house, David was recognized as the Lord's anointed (11:1–3,10; 12:23,31,38). If his military successes brought him honor, these were for Israel's sake and in the will of God and according to his word (11:10; 12:23). A further point is stressed that at Hebron "all Israel" was involved. As "all Israel" had been united under David, they could be again, in a glorious future.

The account of David's reign is generally much more favorable here than in 2 Samuel. This is not because the Chronicler was trying to hide something; he knew that his readers were familiar with the sordid stories of David's sins. Rather, he wanted to forcefully present the equally true side of David, that he loved the Lord God with all his heart and provided an ideal for future kings to follow (cf. 2 Chr 29:2). M. Wilcock rightly remarks that David's passing left a "David-shaped blank" that the Chronicler longed to see filled.[1] His Davidic ideal is also a messianic ideal. "It is in that sense that much of the perspective of the books of Chronicles is messianic. They look *forward* with anticipation to the coming King who will bring in God's final salvation and blessing."[2]

Stylistically, the device of chiasmus is used in presenting the story in 11:1 to 12:40.

A   All Israel gathers   11:1–10
  B   According to God's Word   11:10
  B'   According to God's Word   12:23
A'   All Israel gathers   12:23

Another chiasmus structure is found in 12:1–22. The Chronicler made use of this literary device more than once in the course of his work.

1. David's Early Years (11:1–12:40)

(1) David Becomes King over "All Israel" (11:1–3)

[1]All Israel came together to David at Hebron and said, "We are your own flesh and blood. [2]In the past, even while Saul was king, you were the one who led Israel on their military campaigns. And the LORD your God said to you, 'You will shepherd my people Israel, and you will become their ruler.'"

[3]When all the elders of Israel had come to King David at Hebron, he made a compact with them at Hebron before the LORD, and they anointed David king over Israel, as the LORD had promised through Samuel.

The anointing of David is based on 2 Sam 5:1–3. The Chronicler omits any reference to the failure of Ishbosheth's kingdom (2 Sam 2–4) because this was seen from the perspective of the final outcome as incidental.[3]

11:1–3 David's kingship was confirmed by national recognition, mili-

---

[1] M. Wilcock, *The Message of Chronicles,* BST (Downers Grove: InterVarsity, 1987), 52.

[2] J. Sailhamer, *First and Second Chronicles* (Chicago: Moody, 1983), 32.

[3] For a good summary of the events see C. F. Keil, *The Books of Chronicles* (Grand Rapids: Eerdmans, n.d.), 173–74; H. G. M. Williamson, *1 and 2 Chronicles,* NCBC (Grand Rapids: Eerdmans, 1982), 97.

tary success, and prophetic announcement.[4] The "all Israel" theme is presented at once. The people recognized that they were David's own flesh and blood. They were a unity under David, their legitimate head. This took place at Hebron. The Chronicler, however, did not see Hebron as David's capital over a separate kingdom. David's first children were born at Hebron merely because he lived there (3:1–9; 29:26–27). His short reign of seven years and six months at Hebron was nevertheless part of his forty-year reign over "all Israel." God had appointed him to "shepherd" his people and to become their "ruler." This term was used in preference to the term "king" in many passages because "king" often had unfortunate political overtones. In the covenant ceremony that followed, the people "anointed" David king over Israel according to the Lord's promise through Samuel (2 Sam 7). God's choice had been fulfilled. Wilcock sees four motifs in the people's speech: (1) they recognized their oneness with David, (2) they acknowledged that by his achievements he had proved himself able to lead Israel, (3) they accepted him as king by anointing him, and (4) they confessed that all had been by the will and word of God.[5]

(2) The Capture of Jerusalem (11:4–9)

[4]**David and all the Israelites marched to Jerusalem (that is, Jebus). The Jebusites who lived there [5]said to David, "You will not get in here." Nevertheless, David captured the fortress of Zion, the City of David.**

[6]**David had said, "Whoever leads the attack on the Jebusites will become commander-in-chief." Joab son of Zeruiah went up first, and so he received the command.**

[7]**David then took up residence in the fortress, and so it was called the City of David. [8]He built up the city around it, from the supporting terraces to the surrounding wall, while Joab restored the rest of the city. [9]And David became more and more powerful, because the LORD Almighty was with him.**

No question of the chronology of events is involved in the placing of the capture of Jerusalem at this point in the story. The focus is rather political than chronological. A united Israel would need a center of government. This was to be Jerusalem. The religious significance of Jerusalem as the site of the temple came later.

11:4–5 David and all Israel went to Jerusalem, the Canaanite "Jebus," a rocky site surrounded by valleys, which gave its occupants a great sense of security. With an irony born of confidence in God, the Chronicler could

---

[4] Sailhamer, *First and Second Chronicles,* 34.
[5] Wilcock, *Chronicles,* 54.

comment "nevertheless, David captured the fortress of Zion, the City of David." That the stronghold would be taken was in the purpose of God. The mention of Jebusites is reminiscent of the early divine promises of possessing the land (e.g., Deut 7:1). The Chronicler considers it significant that David was the one to drive out these obstinate enemies (cf. Judg 1:21) and complete the task begun by Joshua.[6] The reference to the blind and the lame found in 2 Sam 5:6 is lacking here. This was nevertheless an overconfident assertion by David's opponents. The fortress was taken and became the city of David by right of conquest.

11:6 The place of Joab in this story raises some questions. David looked for someone to lead the attack on the Jebusite stronghold. That man would become commander-in-chief. The man was Joab, son of Zeruiah. The expression "went up first" has been variously understood. It may have been a general military expression common in Old Testament usage for the leader of an enterprise. Some commentators have seen in the words "he went up" an indication that he climbed up a Jebusite water shaft that led to the underground water supply for the city. Several such shafts that enabled inhabitants of walled Canaanite towns on hills above springs to reach the town water supply have been found.[7]

One other possibility is that Joab gained entrance to the stronghold by frontal attack on the walls of the city without making use of the water shaft. A breach of the walls would call for a later repair (v. 7). Also a problem is the word translated "water shaft" in 2 Sam 5:8.[8] Two main suggestions are offered, a water tunnel or a grappling hook. Either Joab scrambled up the water tunnel or attacked the surrounding wall of the stronghold with some siege tool. In the present state of our knowledge it is not possible to be dogmatic. Certainly Joab played a leading part in the capture of Jebus and held a significant place in David's chain of command shortly after (2 Sam 8:16; 11:1). But he was to incur David's displeasure when he murdered Abner, the previous commander (2 Sam 3:29; 1 Kgs 2:5–6).

11:7–8 David took up his residence in the fortress in due course. There are some exegetical difficulties in v. 8. In what sense did David "build up the city"? It was hardly a case of a total building but rather a repair. The archaeologist K. M. Kenyon has shown that on its eastern slope Jerusalem was sup-

---

[6] J. G. McConville, *I & II Chronicles,* DSB (Philadelphia: Westminster, 1984), 21.

[7] J. A. Thompson, *Handbook of Life in Bible Times* (Leicester, England: InterVarsity, 1987), 118–124, nn. 120–21.

[8] The Hebrew word in 2 Sam 5:8 is בַּצִּנּוֹר, which can mean "water shaft." A related Aramaic cognate is צִנּוֹרְדָה, which means "hook." The NEB translates "grappling iron." Some commentators regard it as some kind of tool. The LXX translated the phrase as "with a dagger." Another cognate of the root is צֹר, "(flint) knife."

ported by an elaborate system of terraces that required continuous repair. These "supporting terraces" are aptly noted in the NIV.

Another problem is the translation of the Hebrew text rendered in the NIV as "he built up the city around it, from the supporting terraces to the surrounding wall." Only here in the Hebrew Bible does the noun *sābîb* have the article. Normally this noun is in the plural and means "the surroundings." The NIV translates it "the surrounding wall." The NEB renders the phrase "starting at the Millo [supporting terraces] and including its neighbourhood." Emendations to the text suggest "as far as the palace." A degree of uncertainty remains about the exact meaning. Clearly the city of David needed both repair and extension. Joab also was involved in the repair work and is said to have literally "restored to life" the rest of the city.

11:9   David was becoming stronger all the time because the "LORD Almighty" was with him.

(3) David's Mighty Men (11:10–47)

[10]These were the chiefs of David's mighty men—they, together with all Israel, gave his kingship strong support to extend it over the whole land, as the LORD had promised— [11]this is the list of David's mighty men:

Jashobeam, a Hacmonite, was chief of the officers; he raised his spear against three hundred men, whom he killed in one encounter.

[12]Next to him was Eleazar son of Dodai the Ahohite, one of the three mighty men. [13]He was with David at Pas Dammim when the Philistines gathered there for battle. At a place where there was a field full of barley, the troops fled from the Philistines. [14]But they took their stand in the middle of the field. They defended it and struck the Philistines down, and the LORD brought about a great victory.

[15]Three of the thirty chiefs came down to David to the rock at the cave of Adullam, while a band of Philistines was encamped in the Valley of Rephaim. [16]At that time David was in the stronghold, and the Philistine garrison was at Bethlehem. [17]David longed for water and said, "Oh, that someone would get me a drink of water from the well near the gate of Bethlehem!" [18]So the Three broke through the Philistine lines, drew water from the well near the gate of Bethlehem and carried it back to David. But he refused to drink it; instead, he poured it out before the LORD. [19]"God forbid that I should do this!" he said. "Should I drink the blood of these men who went at the risk of their lives?" Because they risked their lives to bring it back, David would not drink it.

Such were the exploits of the three mighty men.

[20]Abishai the brother of Joab was chief of the Three. He raised his spear against three hundred men, whom he killed, and so he became as famous as the Three. [21]He was doubly honored above the Three and became their commander, even though he was not included among them.

²²Benaiah son of Jehoiada was a valiant fighter from Kabzeel, who performed great exploits. He struck down two of Moab's best men. He also went down into a pit on a snowy day and killed a lion. ²³And he struck down an Egyptian who was seven and a half feet tall. Although the Egyptian had a spear like a weaver's rod in his hand, Benaiah went against him with a club. He snatched the spear from the Egyptian's hand and killed him with his own spear. ²⁴Such were the exploits of Benaiah son of Jehoiada; he too was as famous as the three mighty men. ²⁵He was held in greater honor than any of the Thirty, but he was not included among the Three. And David put him in charge of his bodyguard.

²⁶The mighty men were:

Asahel the brother of Joab, Elhanan son of Dodo from Bethlehem,
²⁷Shammoth the Harorite,
Helez the Pelonite,
²⁸Ira son of Ikkesh from Tekoa,
Abiezer from Anathoth,
²⁹Sibbecai the Hushathite,
Ilai the Ahohite,
³⁰Maharai the Netophathite,
Heled son of Baanah the Netophathite,
³¹Ithai son of Ribai from Gibeah in Benjamin,
Benaiah the Pirathonite,
³²Hurai from the ravines of Gaash,
Abiel the Arbathite,
³³Azmaveth the Baharumite,
Eliahba the Shaalbonite,
³⁴the sons of Hashem the Gizonite,
Jonathan son of Shagee the Hararite,
³⁵Ahiam son of Sacar the Hararite,
Eliphal son of Ur,
³⁶Hepher the Mekerathite,
Ahijah the Pelonite,
³⁷Hezro the Carmelite,
Naarai son of Ezbai,
³⁸Joel the brother of Nathan,
Mibhar son of Hagri,
³⁹Zelek the Ammonite,
Naharai the Berothite, the armor-bearer of Joab son of Zeruiah,
⁴⁰Ira the Ithrite,
Gareb the Ithrite,
⁴¹Uriah the Hittite,
Zabad son of Ahlai,
⁴²Adina son of Shiza the Reubenite,
who was chief of the Reubenites, and the thirty with him,

⁴³Hanan son of Maacah,
  Joshaphat the Mithnite,
⁴⁴Uzzia the Ashterathite,
  Shama and Jeiel the sons of Hotham the Aroerite,
⁴⁵Jediael son of Shimri,
  his brother Joha the Tizite,
⁴⁶Eliel the Mahavite,
  Jeribai and Joshaviah the sons of Elnaam,
  Ithmah the Moabite,
⁴⁷Eliel, Obed and Jaasiel the Mezobaite.

11:10   The "all Israel" theme is taken up again. Already at Hebron the warriors joined with all Israel to support David (cf. 11:1,3; 12:23). They were the "chiefs of David's mighty men" and gave David strength (*ḥzq*). This list of David's mighty men is based on 2 Sam 23:8–39 although details contain some differences. More important for us is that David had significant support.[9]

11:11   The first verse covering this list raises a number of questions. The name "Jashobeam" is a variant of "Josheb-Basshebeth," in 2 Sam 23:8, and both may be corruptions of an original "Ishbaal" (found in the LXX), sometimes changed to "Ishbosheth."[10] He is described as "chief of the thirty" in the MT and some versions. The NIV translates "officers" (*haššālîšîm*) because the Hebrew word is so translated in other contexts and is like a similar word that denotes a military official in some Old Testament texts. Jashobeam is said to have brandished his spear against three hundred men whom he killed in one encounter. The numeral "hundred" may denote a military group rather than a number.[11]

11:12–14   Eleazar, son of Dodai the Ahohite, was another of the three mighty men who stood with David at Pas Dammim at a barley field. The troops of Israel fled before the Philistines, but David and Eleazar took their stand in the midst of the field and achieved a great victory.

A third mighty man, Shammah, son of Agee the Hararite, is mentioned in 2 Sam 23:11–12 but omitted in Chronicles. The story of Eleazar is like the story of Shammah.

11:15–19   This moving little pericope portrays the bravery of three of the thirty chiefs who came to David at the cave of Adullam when the Philis-

---

[9] Some scholars have undertaken detailed studies of this list of the mighty men of David. E.g., B. Mazar, "The Military Elite of King David," *VT* 13 (1963): 310–20.

[10] E. Tov, *Textual Criticism of the Hebrew Bible* (Minneapolis: Fortress, 1992), 268.

[11] Second Samuel 23:8 has "eight hundred." Payne suggests that an original "eight" may have been misread and inadvertently changed to "three" ("1, 2 Chronicles," EBC [Grand Rapids: Zondervan, 1988], 4:275).

tines were spread out in the valley of Rephaim. It is tempting to identify these three with the three warriors of vv. 13–14 though this is not specifically stated. The story shows the love of David's men for their leader and their willingness to take risks to satisfy his desire. But David himself is shown to have such gratitude to these warriors that he refused to drink the water they brought to him from Bethlehem at such a risk to their lives. He poured it out as a libation to Yahweh, who alone was worthy of such a sacrifice.

11:20–21 Two additional heroes are given here, Abishai and Benaiah (cf. 2 Sam 23:18–23). Abishai, the brother of Joab, is described here as "chief of the Three" (the Syriac text has thirty). But there is considerable uncertainty about the correct text. Most commentators make Abishai and Benaiah leaders among the thirty but perhaps not among the three (v. 21). Abishai was "doubly honored above the Three and became their commander, even though he was not included among them."

Abishai might have belonged to and been the leader of another "three." Some have suggested that the three heroes of vv. 15–19 may be intended. L. C. Allen proposes: "Of the three he was more honored than the other two. Therefore he became their captain."[12]

11:22 Benaiah also performed great exploits, striking down two of Moab's best warriors and killing a lion on a snowy day.

11:23 Two of the details about the Egyptian, "seven and a half feet tall" and "like a weaver's rod," are lacking in 2 Sam 17:4–7. The Egyptian had a huge spear like a weaver's rod in his hand, but Benaiah disarmed him and killed him, huge man that he was.

11:24–25 Although Benaiah was "as famous as the three mighty men" and greater in honor than any of the thirty, he was not included among the three. David appointed him over his bodyguard.

11:26–41a A list of mighty men begins with v. 26 and names thirty-one individuals.[13] Naturally some names and spellings have variations. The Chronicles list contains thirty-one names; and the Samuel list, thirty. Most of the thirty came from the Judah-Simeon and Old Dan areas, two came from Mount Ephraim, one came from the Jordan Valley, and three were from Transjordan. The bulk of these evidently were strong leaders from David's own area, and others were carefully selected from other areas.

11:41b–47 This seems to be a supplementary list because the names do not appear in the list in 2 Samuel. Of some interest is that several of these

---

[12] L. C. Allen, *1, 2 Chronicles,* CC (Dallas: Word, 1987), 84.

[13] Helpful lists in which 1 Chr 11 is set beside 2 Sam 23 occur in J. M. Myers, *I Chronicles,* AB (New York: Doubleday, 1974), 90; and R. Braun, *1 Chronicles,* WBC (Waco: Word, 1986), 161–62. Tov compares 1 Chr 11:24–28 and 2 Sam 23:22–27 (*Textual Criticism,* 225).

sixteen extra heroes came from Transjordan, for example, a Reubenite (v. 42) and a Moabite (v. 46). An addition like this would serve to magnify the standing of David. The source of this material is not known.

(4) David's Early Supporters (12:1–22)

[1]These were the men who came to David at Ziklag, while he was banished from the presence of Saul son of Kish (they were among the warriors who helped him in battle; [2]they were armed with bows and were able to shoot arrows or to sling stones right-handed or left-handed; they were kinsmen of Saul from the tribe of Benjamin):

[3]Ahiezer their chief and Joash the sons of Shemaah the Gibeathite; Jeziel and Pelet the sons of Azmaveth; Beracah, Jehu the Anathothite, [4]and Ishmaiah the Gibeonite, a mighty man among the Thirty, who was a leader of the Thirty; Jeremiah, Jahaziel, Johanan, Jozabad the Gederathite, [5]Eluzai, Jerimoth, Bealiah, Shemariah and Shephatiah the Haruphite; [6]Elkanah, Isshiah, Azarel, Joezer and Jashobeam the Korahites; [7]and Joelah and Zebadiah the sons of Jeroham from Gedor.

[8]Some Gadites defected to David at his stronghold in the desert. They were brave warriors, ready for battle and able to handle the shield and spear. Their faces were the faces of lions, and they were as swift as gazelles in the mountains.

[9]Ezer was the chief, Obadiah the second in command, Eliab the third,
[10]Mishmannah the fourth, Jeremiah the fifth,
[11]Attai the sixth, Eliel the seventh,
[12]Johanan the eighth, Elzabad the ninth,
[13]Jeremiah the tenth and Macbannai the eleventh.

[14]These Gadites were army commanders; the least was a match for a hundred, and the greatest for a thousand. [15]It was they who crossed the Jordan in the first month when it was overflowing all its banks, and they put to flight everyone living in the valleys, to the east and to the west.

[16]Other Benjamites and some men from Judah also came to David in his stronghold. [17]David went out to meet them and said to them, "If you have come to me in peace, to help me, I am ready to have you unite with me. But if you have come to betray me to my enemies when my hands are free from violence, may the God of our fathers see it and judge you."

[18]Then the Spirit came upon Amasai, chief of the Thirty, and he said:

"We are yours, O David!
We are with you, O son of Jesse!
Success, success to you,
and success to those who help you, for your God will help you."

So David received them and made them leaders of his raiding bands.

[19]Some of the men of Manasseh defected to David when he went with the Philistines to fight against Saul. (He and his men did not help the Philistines

because, after consultation, their rulers sent him away. They said, "It will cost us our heads if he deserts to his master Saul.") [20]When David went to Ziklag, these were the men of Manasseh who defected to him: Adnah, Jozabad, Jediael, Michael, Jozabad, Elihu and Zillethai, leaders of units of a thousand in Manasseh. [21]They helped David against raiding bands, for all of them were brave warriors, and they were commanders in his army. [22]Day after day men came to help David, until he had a great army, like the army of God.

Chapter 12 falls into two parts: 12:1–22 and 12:23–41. The chapter shows in four brief sections how support grew for David until he had "a great and mighty army" (v. 22; cf. vv. 1,8,16,19,22). A poem spoken by Amasai, chief of the Thirty, stresses the fact and adds a prayer for success. The Chronicler's well-known chiastic structure is again pressed into use, linking back to 11:10. It is built around three geographical points—Hebron, Ziklag, and the stronghold.

A   Hebron   11:10
 B   Ziklag   12:1
    C   The Stronghold   12:8
    C'   The Stronghold   12:16
 B'   Ziklag   12:20
A'   Hebron   12:23[14]

Some of David's support was displayed when men "came to him." Other support resulted from desertions. These men came from many places, indeed from "all Israel." This gives further confirmation of the legitimacy of David's kingship and Samuel's prophetic word (11:1–3).

We probably should not be looking for any chronological presentation here but rather the development of a theme, namely, that the men of Israel came as part of a concerted movement to stand with David to ensure that Saul's kingdom was handed over to him according to the plan and purpose of God (v. 23).

12:1–2 Ziklag was given to David by Achish, king of Gath, when David was fleeing from Saul (1 Sam 27:6). From this center David made raids against various groups. David's allies were armed with bows and arrows and sling stones, an interesting comment on some of the arms carried by Israel's warriors in the tenth century B.C. David's warriors were ambidextrous, a useful skill in small armies. Remarkably, they were from Saul's tribe of Benjamin, and their leaders were from Gibeah, Saul's hometown (v. 3, "Gibeathite"). Whether they were politically discerning (sensing that Saul's power was in decline), spiritually discerning (recognizing the godliness of

---

[14] Williamson, *1 and 2 Chronicles*, 105.

David over against Saul), or both, their defection to David was proof that loyalty to the rightful ruler of Israel can overcome tribal jealousies. David was truly a king for all Israel.

12:3–7 Some of the place names mentioned here are readily identifiable—Gibeah, Azmaveth, Anathoth (Ras el-Karrubeh), about three miles northeast of Jerusalem, home of Jeremiah in later days, Gibeon (el-Jib), Gederah (probably Jedireh, near Gibeon). All these fell in the area of Benjamin.

12:8–13 Here is a second group that joined David, this time defectors from Gad. Before fleeing to the Philistines with Ziklag as his center, David hid from Saul in his stronghold in the wilderness. Here brave warriors, ready for battle and able to handle a shield and spear (additional weapons to those in v. 2), joined him. The comparison of these brave warriors with animals, lions and gazelles, makes use of a well-known metaphor in the Hebrew Bible. Seven Gadites, army commanders, are listed in the manner of 2:13–15; 3:1–3.

12:14 The Hebrew text here is staccato and cryptic and has been variously translated. It probably is best translated "the least of them a match for a hundred, the greatest a match for a thousand" (NEB; cf. Lev 26:8; Deut 32:30; Isa 30:17).

12:15 The first month of the year was springtime, when the melting snows from Mount Hermon brought floods to the Jordan (cf. Josh 3:13).

The latter part of this verse poses some translation problems. The translation of J. M. Myers captures the sense: "The Jordan overflowed all its banks and made impassable all the lowlands to the east and to the west."[15]

12:16–17 Others from Benjamin and Judah, evidently a group demanding special mention, joined David at the stronghold. The identity of the stronghold (fortress) is not known. The term "stronghold" is used in vv. 8,16. Some commentators have proposed Engedi as the location (cf. 1 Sam 24:1). David was at first cautious about accepting this group and asked whether they had come in peace to help him or whether they had come to betray him to his enemies. He was eager to make an alliance with them but had been betrayed on three previous occasions—by Doeg the Edomite (1 Sam 21–22), by the people of Keilah (1 Sam 23), and by the Ziphites (1 Sam 26). So David responded with an oath, "May the God of our fathers see it and judge you" (1 Chr 12:17).

12:18 Amasai's reply was inspired by the Spirit, as indicated by the expression found several times in the Old Testament, literally, "The Spirit clothed himself with Amasai" (cf. Judg 6:34; 2 Chr 24:20). Amasai may have been the same as Absalom's general Amasa. David was satisfied when

---

[15] Myers, *I Chronicles,* 92.

he heard this powerful affirmation of loyalty to himself and a clear statement of their acknowledgment that David was God's man as much as Abraham had been (cf. Gen 12:3). Again and again Israel reaffirmed the legitimacy of David's assumption of the crown. The best warriors came to David, Saul's own fellow Benjamites acknowledged him (1 Chr 12:1–7), and now a soldier-prophet declared he was God's anointed over the nation.[16] The word translated "success" is *šālôm,* often rendered "peace" but more broadly denoting the well-being, wholeness, and fullness of life coming to those who know God. It also included a prayer and assurance that David would experience rest from his enemies (Deut 12:10; 2 Sam 7:1; 1 Chr 17:1).[17]

12:19–22 Seven defectors from Manasseh are listed. These men must have joined David just before the battle of Mount Gilboa, where Saul was killed. David was sent away by the Philistines because they mistrusted him, though Achish did not (cf. 1 Sam 29). Apparently David accompanied the Philistines part of the way, at least as far as Aphek (1 Sam 29:1), which lay near Manasseh. The term "thousand" (1 Chr 12:20; cf. note at 5:18) probably denotes a tribal subdivision. These men assisted David in his raids against the Amalekites who attacked Ziklag during David's absence (1 Sam 30).

(5) David's Coronation at Hebron (12:23–40)

[23]These are the numbers of the men armed for battle who came to David at Hebron to turn Saul's kingdom over to him, as the LORD had said:
[24]men of Judah, carrying shield and spear—6,800 armed for battle;
[25]men of Simeon, warriors ready for battle—7,100;
[26]men of Levi—4,600, [27]including Jehoiada, leader of the family of Aaron, with 3,700 men, [28]and Zadok, a brave young warrior, with 22 officers from his family;
[29]men of Benjamin, Saul's kinsmen—3,000, most of whom had remained loyal to Saul's house until then;
[30]men of Ephraim, brave warriors, famous in their own clans—20,800;
[31]men of half the tribe of Manasseh, designated by name to come and make David king—18,000;
[32]men of Issachar, who understood the times and knew what Israel should do—200 chiefs, with all their relatives under their command;
[33]men of Zebulun, experienced soldiers prepared for battle with every type of weapon, to help David with undivided loyalty—50,000;
[34]men of Naphtali—1,000 officers, together with 37,000 men carrying shields and spears;
[35]men of Dan, ready for battle—28,600;

---

[16] See Wilcock, *Message of Chronicles,* 58–63.
[17] McConville, *I & II Chronicles,* 30.

³⁶**men of Asher, experienced soldiers prepared for battle—40,000;**
³⁷**and from east of the Jordan, men of Reuben, Gad and the half-tribe of Manasseh, armed with every type of weapon—120,000.**
³⁸**All these were fighting men who volunteered to serve in the ranks. They came to Hebron fully determined to make David king over all Israel. All the rest of the Israelites were also of one mind to make David king.** ³⁹**The men spent three days there with David, eating and drinking, for their families had supplied provisions for them.** ⁴⁰**Also, their neighbors from as far away as Issachar, Zebulun and Naphtali came bringing food on donkeys, camels, mules and oxen. There were plentiful supplies of flour, fig cakes, raisin cakes, wine, oil, cattle and sheep, for there was joy in Israel.**

12:23–25 A further list of units supporting David's kingship is provided here. Men came, armed for battle, to hand over Saul's kingdom to David in the plan and purpose of God.

A general comment about the large numbers seems to be called for. The word translated as meaning *thousand* may, in some circumstances, have indicated a military unit of some kind (see 12:19–22). Thus v. 24 could be translated, "The men of Judah, carrying shield and spear numbered six units with eight hundred armed men."[18]

Alternatively, each tribal clan may have been intended to provide a contingent of a thousand men.[19] The word indicating *thousand* can be retained in translation but interpreted loosely. Another proposal is to vocalize *ʾelep,* "thousand," to read *ʾallûp,* "chief" or "military officer" (see note on 7:1–5). In that case Judah would have provided eight hundred armed troops under six leaders.[20] In the absence of clear definition our view must remain uncertain.

Appraisal of the list will show that warriors came to David from "all Israel." They were battle ready, "armed with every type of weapon, fighting men who volunteered to serve in the ranks."

12:26–30 A contingent of Levites was included. This made up thirteen tribes. Normally Levites were not included in the armies of Israel. Only here in vv. 27–28 are individuals named.

The Zadok of v. 28 sometimes has been identified with the one who became priest under Solomon when Abiathar was banished. He was a young man of standing, a brave young warrior who was accompanied by twenty-two commanders. Not all commentators accept this identification, although his association with Jehoiada, of Aaron's family, may lend support to this view.

---

[18] Myers, *I Chronicles,* 98.

[19] R. de Vaux, *Ancient Israel: Its Life and Institutions* (New York: Macmillan, 1965), 216.

[20] J. Wenham, "Large Numbers in the Old Testament," *TB* 18 (1967): 44–53. Payne reads it as "six (commanders of) thousands, eight (commanders of) hundreds," as we might speak of the group coming to make David king would be 398 officers ("1, 2 Chronicles," 4:378).

12:32   The intention of this verse seems to be that the men of Issachar had some skill in discerning the meaning of current political events, not an astrological skill (as in Esth 1:13) but resulting from shrewd observation.

12:33–40   When the time was up, the volunteers came to Hebron to make David king over "all Israel." But "the rest of Israel" was of one mind with the warriors to make David king. They held a large celebratory banquet with large contributions of food from the northern tribes of Issachar, Zebulun, and Naphtali. It is easy to see in these days of "eating and drinking" a covenant meal. On such occasions joy was a regular accompaniment of the celebrations. The Chronicler noticed this on other occasions (1 Chr 29:22; 2 Chr 7:8–10; 30:21–26).

Now that David was established as king over all Israel, the Chronicler could take up his second great concern, the restoration of the ark from its exile in readiness for its housing in the temple, which at this stage still remained to be built.

2. The Ark Brought to Jerusalem (13:1–16:43)

(1) The Transfer of the Ark to Jerusalem: First Attempt (13:1–14)

¹David conferred with each of his officers, the commanders of thousands and commanders of hundreds. ²He then said to the whole assembly of Israel, "If it seems good to you and if it is the will of the LORD our God, let us send word far and wide to the rest of our brothers throughout the territories of Israel, and also to the priests and Levites who are with them in their towns and pasturelands, to come and join us. ³Let us bring the ark of our God back to us, for we did not inquire of it during the reign of Saul." ⁴The whole assembly agreed to do this, because it seemed right to all the people.

⁵So David assembled all the Israelites, from the Shihor River in Egypt to Lebo Hamath, to bring the ark of God from Kiriath Jearim. ⁶David and all the Israelites with him went to Baalah of Judah (Kiriath Jearim) to bring up from there the ark of God the LORD, who is enthroned between the cherubim—the ark that is called by the Name.

⁷They moved the ark of God from Abinadab's house on a new cart, with Uzzah and Ahio guiding it. ⁸David and all the Israelites were celebrating with all their might before God, with songs and with harps, lyres, tambourines, cymbals and trumpets.

⁹When they came to the threshing floor of Kidon, Uzzah reached out his hand to steady the ark, because the oxen stumbled. ¹⁰The LORD'S anger burned against Uzzah, and he struck him down because he had put his hand on the ark. So he died there before God.

¹¹Then David was angry because the LORD'S wrath had broken out against Uzzah, and to this day that place is called Perez Uzzah.

¹²**David was afraid of God that day and asked, "How can I ever bring the ark of God to me?"** ¹³**He did not take the ark to be with him in the City of David. Instead, he took it aside to the house of Obed-Edom the Gittite.** ¹⁴**The ark of God remained with the family of Obed-Edom in his house for three months, and the LORD blessed his household and everything he had.**

The ark was brought to Jerusalem in two stages. It had been taken by the Philistines in the encounter at Ebenezer (1 Sam 5) and removed to their territory. But it caused so much embarrassment there that they decided to send it back to the land of Judah with a guilt offering (1 Sam 6:1–9). It was brought to Beth-Shemesh, where prying eyes "looked into the ark" and the offenders were stricken down (1 Sam 6:10–20). Messengers were sent to Kiriath Jearim requesting its removal (1 Sam 6:21–7:1). It was taken to the house of Abinadab and there remained until David removed it.

The main part of the story comes from 2 Sam 6:2–11. Only here in 1 Chr 13:1–5, however, do we find details of David's call to the people of Israel to bring back the ark. It was to prove a difficult task.

13:1   The Chronicler was at pains to point out that the enterprise was a joint effort of all Israel. David consulted with each of his leaders, the commanders of the thousands and the commanders of the hundreds.

13:2–3   The comprehensive nature of the call to the "whole assembly" of Israel is here spelled out. Word was to be sent far and wide to the rest of the people throughout the territories of Israel, to the priests, the Levites, in the towns and in the pasturelands to join together in a great enterprise to bring back the ark. Neglect of the ark in the days of Saul was at least in part the reason for the defeat of Israel in Saul's day. The people had failed to "inquire" of the Lord as they should have. The verb "inquire" has strong overtones of that sincere worship of and commitment to Yahweh that was expected of Israel.

13:4   The "whole assembly" agreed to the proposal. It seemed right to "all the people."

13:5   "All the Israelites" (mentioned three times in vv. 5–8) throughout the land from the Shihor River in Egypt to Lebo-Hamath (the entrance of Hamath), that is, in the full extent of the land of Israel from Beersheba to Dan (cf. 1 Chr 21:2), assembled to bring the ark of God from Kiriath Jearim, the present-day Tell el-Azhar, about eight miles west of Jerusalem. It was one of four Gibeonite towns located on the Judah-Benjamin border (Josh 18:15). In Josh 18:14 it is called Kiriath-baal (city of Baal), in Josh 15:9 it is called Baalah, and here in 1 Chr 13:6 it is called Baalah of Judah (cf. 2 Sam 6:2, Baal-Judah). It was later the home of Uriah, the prophet of Jeremiah's day (Jer 26:20) and figured in postexilic history (Neh 7:29).

13:6   The ark is here described as "the ark of God, the LORD, who is enthroned between the Cherubim."[21] The ark was a central feature of Israel's temple worship because it represented the presence of God among his people (cf. Exod 25:22). It was both the throne of God and a receptacle for the law. In 1 Chr 28:2 it is referred to as "the footstool of God."[22]

13:7–8   Uzzah and Ahio moved the ark from Abinadab's house on a new cart while David and "all" celebrated before God with songs and music. "All the Israelites" stresses again the involvement of all God's people in this rescue. The term "Israel" is more theological than political. While the expression "before the LORD [Yahweh]" is frequently found elsewhere, the terms "LORD [Yahweh]" and "God [Elohim]" are synonymous.

13:9–10   At the threshing floor of Kidon the oxen drawing the cart on which the ark rested stumbled and evidently rocked the ark. Uzzah reached out his hand to steady it. This was a serious ritual offense since only authorized persons, the Levites, were to carry the tabernacle and all its furnishings. The wrath of the Lord flared forth against Uzzah, and he died.

13:11   David's response to this action of the Lord was anger because the Lord's wrath had broken out against Uzzah (the verb translated "had broken out" also is found in 14:11; 15:13). The place was called Perez Uzzah (the rending asunder of Uzzah, or outbreak against Uzzah).

13:12   David was afraid of God and despaired of restoring the ark to the City of David. He needed to learn that there was a proper way to carry out God's will. When David and the people went to get the ark, the excitement of the moment and the sense that they were doing God's will gave the event a festive atmosphere.[23] This very excitement gave them a sense of familiarity with the things of God that became unhealthy, and they neglected to give the ark the respect God demanded. David, in his fear, came back to sobriety about this issue. The whole incident reminds us that even our enthusiasm for God can cause us to forget the holiness of God and the need to fear him. Doing what we believe to be God's will in a way that violates God's Word is wrong and displeases God.

13:13–14   The ark was lodged in the home of Obed-Edom, the Gittite (man of Gath), for three months. Blessing came to Obed-Edom's house as a result. While a question may be raised about the propriety of lodging the ark with such a man, it is to be noted that in 15:18,21 there is mention of an Obed-Edom, who was a Levite and a gatekeeper.

---

[21] Myers, *I Chronicles*, 100.

[22] See de Vaux, *Ancient Israel*, 298–300.

[23] S. J. De Vries, *1 and 2 Chronicles*, FOTL (Grand Rapids: Eerdmans, 1989), 104.

(2) David's House and Family (14:1–17)

[1]Now Hiram king of Tyre sent messengers to David, along with cedar logs, stonemasons and carpenters to build a palace for him. [2]And David knew that the LORD had established him as king over Israel and that his kingdom had been highly exalted for the sake of his people Israel.

[3]In Jerusalem David took more wives and became the father of more sons and daughters. [4]These are the names of the children born to him there: Shammua, Shobab, Nathan, Solomon, [5]Ibhar, Elishua, Elpelet, [6]Nogah, Nepheg, Japhia, [7]Elishama, Beeliada and Eliphelet.

[8]When the Philistines heard that David had been anointed king over all Israel, they went up in full force to search for him, but David heard about it and went out to meet them. [9]Now the Philistines had come and raided the Valley of Rephaim; [10]so David inquired of God: "Shall I go and attack the Philistines? Will you hand them over to me?"

The LORD answered him, "Go, I will hand them over to you."

[11]So David and his men went up to Baal Perazim, and there he defeated them. He said, "As waters break out, God has broken out against my enemies by my hand." So that place was called Baal Perazim. [12]The Philistines had abandoned their gods there, and David gave orders to burn them in the fire.

[13]Once more the Philistines raided the valley; [14]so David inquired of God again, and God answered him, "Do not go straight up, but circle around them and attack them in front of the balsam trees. [15]As soon as you hear the sound of marching in the tops of the balsam trees, move out to battle, because that will mean God has gone out in front of you to strike the Philistine army." [16]So David did as God commanded him, and they struck down the Philistine army, all the way from Gibeon to Gezer.

[17]So David's fame spread throughout every land, and the LORD made all the nations fear him.

At first sight it might seem that after David's failure to bring back the ark to Jerusalem he should have been rebuked. Rather, he received blessing in his dealings with Hiram, ruler of Tyre, his defeat of the Philistines, his spreading fame, and his growing family, all sure signs of blessing. These events are not necessarily in chronological order, but the Chronicler used them to make some observations about David that are basically theological. He was a savior figure for Israel in the Chronicler's view. He would yet restore the ark to the City of David, and, despite the abortive attempt to bring back the ark, he still had God's approval as the various incidents gathered together here show. The material is drawn from 2 Sam 5:11–25 but was used for the Chronicler's own purpose.[24] The theme of divine blessing is to be seen throughout but especially at the beginning and end of the chapter in vv. 2,17.

---

[24]WIlliamson, *1 and 2 Chronicles*, 116.

The Chronicler presents a theological contrast between David and Saul. David, unlike Saul, was concerned for the ark (13:3). By incorporating indications of David's prosperity and success against the Philistines, the Chronicler demonstrated God's blessing on his servant for his faithfulness. By contrast, Saul's defeat because of his unfaithfulness (chap. 10) stresses the point. It is a theme that runs throughout Chronicles. The reigns of faithful kings are marked by divine blessing.

14:1 Hiram's delegation brought assistance to David. He gave David recognition, respect, and gifts—each a sign of God's blessing. The embassy of Hiram was accompanied by cedar logs, stone masons, and carpenters to assist in the building of a palace for David. The word used for "palace" (*bayit*, the normal word for "house") is also used for "temple," but here it must refer to palace. The time to build the temple had not yet arrived. There is a subtle play on words here because the term can mean "palace," "dynasty," and "temple." The theme will be expounded again in chap. 17 with the prophecy of Nathan.

14:2 The Chronicler makes a slight change in the text of 2 Sam 5:12 in order to give more prominence to the exaltation of David's kingdom "for the sake of his people Israel."[25] David was aware that Yahweh had established him as king over Israel and that he had been "highly exalted for the sake of his people Israel." The Chronicler seems here to be saying that not only David but the whole of the people were enjoying God's favor.

14:3–7 Further evidence of God's blessing on David was his large family born in Jerusalem, both sons and daughters. Among his sons was Solomon, through whom David's dynasty would be established. He was born during or shortly after the Ammonite campaign (2 Sam 12:24). The list of thirteen sons follows 3:5–8 but deviates from 2 Sam 5:14–16, primarily in the addition of two sons, Elpelet and Nogah.[26]

14:8–11 David had two encounters with the Philistines and was successful in both (vv. 8–12 and vv. 13–16). The first attack came after the Philistines learned that David had been anointed king over "all Israel," a favorite expression of the Chronicler as we have noted several times. The place they struck was in the valley of Rephaim, southwest of Jerusalem on the old boundary between Judah and Benjamin (Josh 15:8). David went to meet them, but he first "inquired" (*šāʾal*) of God and gained the assurance

---

[25] See S. Japhet, "Interchanges of Verbal Roots in Parallel Texts in Chronicles," *HS* 28 (1987): 22–23.

[26] A useful comparison of the three lists of David's children (2 Sam 5:14–16; 1 Chr 3:5–8; 1 Chr 14:4–7) is given in Myers, *I Chronicles*, 107. E. H. Merrill suggests that their omission in 2 Samuel may have been because of their early deaths ("1 Chronicles," The Bible Knowledge Commentary, ed. J. F. Walvoord and R. B. Zuck [Wheaton, Ill.: Victor, 1985], 1:594).

that God would hand them over to him (v. 10). A further contrast with Saul appears here. Saul "inquired" (*šāʾal*) of a medium at Endor. The encounter took place at Baal-Perazim, where God "broke out" against David's enemies (v. 11). The incident gave its name to the place.

14:12 The gods (idols) of the Philistines were taken into battle but failed them in the encounter, and the Philistines abandoned them. They were not taken as booty but were burned on David's orders (cf. Deut 7:5; 12:3).

14:13–16 There was a second Philistine encounter in which David again was victorious. The Philistines raided the valley, defined in 2 Sam 5:22 as "the Valley of Rephaim." David acted appropriately again and "inquired" (same verb as in v. 10) of God, who assured him of success although the plan of attack was different. God assured David of victory. He was to circle round and listen for the sound of marching in the tops of the balsam trees. That would indicate that God had gone out in front of David to strike the Philistine army. Other examples of divine intervention on behalf of his people occur in later narratives in Chronicles. It was a sign that the holy war was being discharged. David obeyed and struck down the Philistines all the way from Gibeon to Gezer. David's fame spread abroad, and the fear he engendered reached into every land. Under God's blessing and in keeping with David's faithfulness, David became famous.

(3) The Successful Transfer of the Ark to Jerusalem (15:1–16:6)

¹After David had constructed buildings for himself in the City of David, he prepared a place for the ark of God and pitched a tent for it. ²Then David said, "No one but the Levites may carry the ark of God, because the LORD chose them to carry the ark of the LORD and to minister before him forever."

³David assembled all Israel in Jerusalem to bring up the ark of the LORD to the place he had prepared for it. ⁴He called together the descendants of Aaron and the Levites:

⁵From the descendants of Kohath,
    Uriel the leader and 120 relatives;
⁶from the descendants of Merari,
    Asaiah the leader and 220 relatives;
⁷from the descendants of Gershon,
    Joel the leader and 130 relatives;
⁸from the descendants of Elizaphan,
    Shemaiah the leader and 200 relatives;
⁹from the descendants of Hebron,
    Eliel the leader and 80 relatives;
¹⁰from the descendants of Uzziel,
    Amminadab the leader and 112 relatives.
¹¹Then David summoned Zadok and Abiathar the priests, and Uriel, Asaiah,

Joel, Shemaiah, Eliel and Amminadab the Levites. ¹²He said to them, "You are the heads of the Levitical families; you and your fellow Levites are to consecrate yourselves and bring up the ark of the LORD, the God of Israel, to the place I have prepared for it. ¹³It was because you, the Levites, did not bring it up the first time that the LORD our God broke out in anger against us. We did not inquire of him about how to do it in the prescribed way." ¹⁴So the priests and Levites consecrated themselves in order to bring up the ark of the LORD, the God of Israel. ¹⁵And the Levites carried the ark of God with the poles on their shoulders, as Moses had commanded in accordance with the word of the LORD.

¹⁶David told the leaders of the Levites to appoint their brothers as singers to sing joyful songs, accompanied by musical instruments: lyres, harps and cymbals.

¹⁷So the Levites appointed Heman son of Joel; from his brothers, Asaph son of Berekiah; and from their brothers the Merarites, Ethan son of Kushaiah; ¹⁸and with them their brothers next in rank: Zechariah, Jaaziel, Shemiramoth, Jehiel, Unni, Eliab, Benaiah, Maaseiah, Mattithiah, Eliphelehu, Mikneiah, Obed-Edom and Jeiel, the gatekeepers.

¹⁹The musicians Heman, Asaph and Ethan were to sound the bronze cymbals; ²⁰Zechariah, Aziel, Shemiramoth, Jehiel, Unni, Eliab, Maaseiah and Benaiah were to play the lyres according to *alamoth,* ²¹and Mattithiah, Eliphelehu, Mikneiah, Obed-Edom, Jeiel and Azaziah were to play the harps, directing according to *sheminith.* ²²Kenaniah the head Levite was in charge of the singing; that was his responsibility because he was skillful at it.

²³Berekiah and Elkanah were to be doorkeepers for the ark. ²⁴Shebaniah, Joshaphat, Nethanel, Amasai, Zechariah, Benaiah and Eliezer the priests were to blow trumpets before the ark of God. Obed-Edom and Jehiah were also to be doorkeepers for the ark.

²⁵So David and the elders of Israel and the commanders of units of a thousand went to bring up the ark of the covenant of the LORD from the house of Obed-Edom, with rejoicing. ²⁶Because God had helped the Levites who were carrying the ark of the covenant of the LORD, seven bulls and seven rams were sacrificed. ²⁷Now David was clothed in a robe of fine linen, as were all the Levites who were carrying the ark, and as were the singers, and Kenaniah, who was in charge of the singing of the choirs. David also wore a linen ephod. ²⁸So all Israel brought up the ark of the covenant of the LORD with shouts, with the sounding of rams' horns and trumpets, and of cymbals, and the playing of lyres and harps.

²⁹As the ark of the covenant of the LORD was entering the City of David, Michal daughter of Saul watched from a window. And when she saw King David dancing and celebrating, she despised him in her heart.

¹They brought the ark of God and set it inside the tent that David had pitched for it, and they presented burnt offerings and fellowship offerings

before God. ²After David had finished sacrificing the burnt offerings and fellowship offerings, he blessed the people in the name of the LORD. ³Then he gave a loaf of bread, a cake of dates and a cake of raisins to each Israelite man and woman.

⁴He appointed some of the Levites to minister before the ark of the LORD, to make petition, to give thanks, and to praise the LORD, the God of Israel: ⁵Asaph was the chief, Zechariah second, then Jeiel, Shemiramoth, Jehiel, Mattithiah, Eliab, Benaiah, Obed-Edom and Jeiel. They were to play the lyres and harps, Asaph was to sound the cymbals, ⁶and Benaiah and Jahaziel the priests were to blow the trumpets regularly before the ark of the covenant of God.

The setback at Perez-uzzah delayed the return of the ark to Jerusalem. The account is based on 2 Sam 6:12–20. The Chronicler, however, gives the story a different perspective in several respects. David's intention always was to bring the ark back to Jerusalem despite delays. He needed to prepare a home for the ark (15:1) and also to order and prepare the Levites for their task. This could not be hurried. It was not simply that David sought blessings similar to those enjoyed by Obed-Edom, in whose home the ark had rested. David had a deeper purpose. The ark was to be brought to Jerusalem irrespective of any hope for his own personal blessing.

Further, the Chronicler stresses the work of the Levites. They were to have special duties after the ark had found a resting place, namely, to take responsibility for the music of Israel's worship (6:31–32). The Chronicler shows that David had initiated the plans that Solomon brought to fruition. The bearers of the ark became the temple singers in a later day (16:4–40). But already in David's day the plans had been laid (15:11–22). The Chronicler stressed certain elements in which David was involved: the preparation of a place for the ark to rest, the appointment of singers and musical instruments, and the preparation of the vestments to be worn by the Levites.

The most arresting feature of this narrative is not obvious to the modern reader. The Chronicler was devoting great time and attention to describing incidents surrounding the ark and the need to treat it as a holy object even though by the time of the Chronicler *it had already ceased to exist*. In other words, the original readers of this book had no more opportunity to worship God before the ark than we do. Why would the Chronicler stress the joy and holiness associated with it if his readers would never have opportunity to emulate David's obedience?

The answer must be that for the Chronicler it was not the object itself but what the object represented that mattered. The ark represented two great truths. First, God was with them and would go with them wherever they went. The ark traveled with the exodus generation, was with Joshua's generation as they entered Canaan, and had been in various locations now in their land. Second, the ark represented the holiness of God. It contained the tablets of the Ten Commandments—the essence of the law—and they had seen for themselves that God's ark was not to be trifled with (13:10). These two truths, that God is with us and that God is holy, are what really mattered to the Chronicler. We need to keep this in mind lest we think of the Chronicler simply as one full of nostalgia for the good old days. Finally, the chapter teaches God's compassionate forgiveness in allowing Israel a second chance. Israel's initial failure was not final and God's judgment was not just positive but instructive.

We can discern the steps taken to restore the ark to Jerusalem. The narrative becomes the occasion for spelling out the organization and installation of the Levitical families and in particular the temple musicians (15:1–24). The arrival of the ark in Jerusalem (15:25–16:3) was celebrated by the gathering of "all Israel" and the singing of a lengthy hymn by the Asaphites (16:4–36), after which the priests and Levites were assigned their various duties (16:37–42). Once this was complete, the scene was set for a new stage in the story of the ark and the history of King David and Israel.

15:1–3 These verses are unique to the Chronicler. Important aspects of the preparations for bringing the ark to Jerusalem were: (1) the ark and its tent, (2) the role of the Levites, and (3) the reassembling of "all Israel."[27]

The buildings David erected for himself were a palace and other yet-unnamed structures. Details of these were not regarded as particularly important. The focus is on the place he had prepared for the ark of God and the tent he had pitched for it although details about the nature of this tent are not given (cf. 2 Sam 6:17). This must have been a new construction. The old Mosaic tabernacle was still at Gibeon (16:39; 2 Chr 1:3; cf. 1 Kgs 8:4). The term "place" often carries overtones of a holy place.

Great care had to be taken that the proper personnel, namely, the Levites, should carry the ark. Their failure to do this at the first attempt at its removal to Jerusalem was the reason for the failure of that attempt. The law of Deut 10:8 was clear in this respect (Num 4:1–18). Transport by ox-cart was fraught with danger. The Chronicler, however, here stressed the significance of the Levites in temple worship (cf. 16:4–7; 2 Chr 5–6).

"All Israel" (v. 3) was assembled in Jerusalem to bring up the ark of the Lord to the place prepared for it. It was a national occasion.

15:4–10 The three Levitical groups—Kohath, Merari, and Gershon, and the numbers of their families—are mentioned along with descendants of three other families—Elizaphan, Hebron, and Uzziel, who must have attained sufficient numbers or prestige to gain independent status. They all

---

[27] Braun, *1 Chronicles,* 188.

derive from Kohath (Exod 6:18,22). This sixfold division of Levites is otherwise unknown and may represent an updated statement nearer to the time of the Chronicler.[28] The name of Joel (v. 7) is lacking in the list of Gershonites in 6:16–30 but is present at 23:8 and 26:22. However, Hebron and Uzziel (vv. 9–10) are not listed elsewhere as heads of Levitical families though they may have been descendants of Kohath (6:18; Exod 6:22).

The work of the Levites is in focus in this list although priests and Levites are associated in vv. 11,14. Not until 16:39–40 is the distinctive work of the priests taken up as they presented burnt offerings to the Lord on the altar of burnt offerings.

15:11–15 The religious leaders were then summoned—the priests, Zadok and Abiathar, and six Levites. The Levites, who carried the ark, were charged to consecrate themselves before they brought up the ark to the place prepared for it (v. 12). The Chronicler offers an explanation for the failure to bring up the ark earlier, which caused the Lord to break forth in anger against Israel. Ritual propriety and action according to the regulations laid down were always important but particularly to the Chronicler. These things helped to guarantee an appreciation for the sanctity and sovereignty of God.

The priests and Levites alike consecrated themselves for the significant task of bringing up the ark of Yahweh, the God of Israel. The Levites carried the ark with the poles on their shoulders according to the word the Lord delivered through Moses (Exod 25:13–15; Num 7:9). Even in matters of ritual it is important to follow God's directions.

15:16–24 Having brought up the ark to its place, it was time for the people to break out into joyous celebration with the help of singers and musical instruments. It had been a joyous occasion when David was accepted as king over all Israel (12:39–40). Now with the ark restored, the note of joy is sounded again (15:16,25). So vv. 16–24 lay stress on the singing of joyful songs accompanied by music. Arrangements were necessarily interim in character until the temple was built. Continuing worship was being enjoyed at the sanctuary in Gibeon (2 Chr 1:3). Priestly personnel were appointed for the sacrificial system to be operated according to the Torah (16:40), and two of the Levitical guilds, those of Heman and Jeduthun, were commissioned to carry out a musical ministry (16:42). Asaph came to be a composer of Psalms (cf. 16:4–5; Pss 73–83).

Three lists of Levitical personnel are in chaps. 15–16: (1) 15:17–18; (2) 15:19–24; (3) 16:5–6, the longest being 15:19–24.[29] It is difficult now to account for the differences. Lists (1) and (2) give some indication of the

---

[28] Williamson, *1 and 2 Chronicles*, 123.
[29] For an analysis of these lists see Braun, *1 Chronicles*, 190–91.

instruments some individuals used. We cannot now be sure why the Chronicler included parts of three different lists, although no doubt each in its way was authentic. The list of Levites may be divided into three groups according to the instruments they played.

15:16 We can probably see here the practice of family tradition. Certain families were specialists in particular instruments, much as they were in wider life. The leaders of the Levites were to appoint their "brothers" as singers and musicians. That David was an originator of musical guilds and services is well known.[30]

15:17–18 Most of these names are known in other Levitical lists although the question of identity is uncertain. Some occurrences have slight changes; for example, "Kushaiah" (v. 17) appears as "Kishi" in 6:44; and Obed-Edom (v. 18), who appears as a Levitical musician in v. 21 and 16:5, later has a change of status to gatekeeper (26:1–11). This was not necessarily a demotion.

15:19–24 The Levites who provided music are here listed as players of bronze cymbals, lyres, and harps. A number of technical terms used here have been variously understood.[31] The doorkeepers for the ark seem to have been a special group not included in the list in v. 16.[32] Seven priests were to blow trumpets before the ark of God (cf. Num 10:8; 31:6; Neh 12:35,41).

15:25 David, the elders of Israel, and the commanders of units of a thousand went to bring up the ark of the covenant of the Lord from the house of Obed-Edom. David was not operating alone but in cooperation with other leaders of Israel. The "all Israel" motif is clear, as is the motif of joy.

15:26–27 Samuel had referred to "the bearers of the ark" (2 Sam 6:13, NASB) and to "shouts and the sound of trumpets" (v. 15). Chronicles makes clear that it was the Levites who carried the ark and also refers to the singers, their leader (v. 27), and the wide range of instruments usually associated with the Levites and priests (v. 28). God responded to Israel's ritual faithfulness by helping the Levites in their duty of carrying the ark. The sacrifices were then an expression of thanks for God's help.

The question about who offered the sacrifices may be asked. This was normally a priestly act. The fact that David was clothed in "a robe of fine linen" (v. 27), which is also described as a "linen ephod," as did the Levites who carried the ark, has raised the question of whether David had assumed

---

[30] See W. F. Albright, *Archaeology and the Religion of Israel* (Baltimore: The Johns Hopkins University Press, 1946), 125f.

[31] See A. A. Anderson, *Psalms,* NCB (Grand Rapids: Eerdmans, 1972), 48–50.

[32] J. W. Wright, "Guarding the Gates: 1 Chronicles 26:1–18 and the Roles of Gatekeepers in Chronicles," *JSOT* 48 (1990): 69–81.

priestly garments. The wearing of the ephod was restricted to the high priest in the Chronicler's day (Exod 28:4ff.; Lev 8:7). In the parallel text in 2 Sam 6:14,20 the reference may be to a loin cloth, which would explain Michal's rebuke.[33] The occasion was special, and the full temple rituals were yet in the future when the rituals and offices could be regulated.

Probably we should see some priestly function for David here, but not as a pretext for Israelite kings to assume Levitical prerogatives. This was, in the history of Israel, an exceptional but significant event. David functioned as the type for the Messiah as a king who is also a priest.

15:28 "All Israel" thus transported the ark of the covenant of Yahweh with music and shouts of joy.

15:29 The Chronicler's perspective on Michal is slightly different than that of the longer account in 2 Sam 6:16,20,23. There it might appear that Michal's reaction to David's behavior was motivated by jealousy and by a misinterpretation of David's motive. But here it is clear that like her father, Saul, Michal had no appreciation for the things of God.

16:1–3 Following the parallel record in 2 Sam 6:17–19, the Chronicler describes the successful conclusion of the task of restoring the ark. Here again David was involved in the presentation of burnt offerings and fellowship offerings before God. Then he blessed the people in the name of the Lord and presented them with gifts: a loaf of bread, a cake of dates, and a cake of raisins to each. Some translators take the Hebrew of "cake of dates" to mean a "portion" (of meat).[34]

The Levitical ministrations are next set out (16:4–42). Until the temple had been dedicated, the sacrificial aspects of Israel's worship were confined to the altar at Gibeon (vv. 39–40). In the passage before us the Levites, whom David appointed to minister before the ark of the covenant, performed restricted duties.

16:4 The Levites' main responsibilities were the musical aspects of worship: to make petitions through psalms of lament, to give thanks in thanksgiving psalms, and to praise the Lord, the God of Israel, in song. Elements of each of these three are to be found in the composite psalm of Asaph and his associates in vv. 8–36.[35]

16:5–6 Only some of those listed in 15:16–22 are listed in these verses. The others evidently were engaged at Gibeon (v. 41).

In a passage concerned with Levites the reference to priests may seem out of place. But since the general context is concerned with music and not with

---

[33] See de Vaux, *Ancient Israel,* 349–50.
[34] Myers, *I Chronicles,* 114, n. b.
[35] Williamson, *1 and 2 Chronicles,* 127.

the sacrificial aspects of priestly duties, the priestly task of blowing the trumpets before the ark of the covenant is all that is required. The priest Benaiah was mentioned in 15:24, although his companion, Jaheziel, is not mentioned there.

(4) David's Psalm of Thanksgiving (16:7–36)

[7]That day David first committed to Asaph and his associates this psalm of thanks to the LORD:

[8]Give thanks to the LORD, call on his name;
    make known among the nations what he has done.
[9]Sing to him, sing praise to him;
    tell of all his wonderful acts.
[10]Glory in his holy name;
    let the hearts of those who seek the LORD rejoice.
[11]Look to the LORD and his strength;
    seek his face always.
[12]Remember the wonders he has done,
    his miracles, and the judgments he pronounced,
[13]O descendants of Israel his servant,
    O sons of Jacob, his chosen ones.
[14]He is the LORD our God;
    his judgments are in all the earth.
[15]He remembers his covenant forever,
    the word he commanded, for a thousand generations,
[16]the covenant he made with Abraham,
    the oath he swore to Isaac.
[17]He confirmed it to Jacob as a decree,
    to Israel as an everlasting covenant:
[18]"To you I will give the land of Canaan
    as the portion you will inherit."
[19]When they were but few in number,
    few indeed, and strangers in it,
[20]they wandered from nation to nation,
    from one kingdom to another.
[21]He allowed no man to oppress them;
    for their sake he rebuked kings:
[22]"Do not touch my anointed ones;
    do my prophets no harm."
[23]Sing to the LORD, all the earth;
    proclaim his salvation day after day.
[24]Declare his glory among the nations,
    his marvelous deeds among all peoples.
[25]For great is the LORD and most worthy of praise;

he is to be feared above all gods.
²⁶For all the gods of the nations are idols,
　　but the LORD made the heavens.
²⁷Splendor and majesty are before him;
　　strength and joy in his dwelling place.
²⁸Ascribe to the LORD, O families of nations,
　　ascribe to the LORD glory and strength,
²⁹　ascribe to the LORD the glory due his name.
　Bring an offering and come before him;
　　worship the LORD in the splendor of his holiness.
³⁰Tremble before him, all the earth!
　　The world is firmly established; it cannot be moved.
³¹Let the heavens rejoice, let the earth be glad;
　　let them say among the nations, "The LORD reigns!"
³²Let the sea resound, and all that is in it;
　　let the fields be jubilant, and everything in them!
³³Then the trees of the forest will sing,
　　they will sing for joy before the LORD,
　　for he comes to judge the earth.
³⁴Give thanks to the LORD, for he is good;
　　his love endures forever.
³⁵Cry out, "Save us, O God our Savior;
　　gather us and deliver us from the nations,
　that we may give thanks to your holy name,
　　that we may glory in your praise."
³⁶Praise be to the LORD, the God of Israel,
　from everlasting to everlasting.
Then all the people said "Amen" and "Praise the LORD."

16:7　This verse serves to stress the role of Asaph and his kinsmen and to establish that their appointment went back to David. The NASB translation is closer to the Hebrew: "Then on that day David first assigned Asaph and his relatives to give thanks to the LORD" (cf. NRSV). The NIV translates *lĕhōdôt* (lit. "to give thanks") as "this psalm of thanks." The NIV suggests that the psalm which follows was given by David to Asaph, but the Hebrew does not say that a psalm was given, only that the act of "giving thanks" was placed into the hand (*bĕyad*) of Asaph.

The psalm which follows is a psalm of thanksgiving. The psalm given here contains material found in three well-known psalms: Pss 105:1–15 (vv. 8–22); 96:1–13 (vv. 23–33); 106:1 (v. 34); and 106:47–48 (vv. 35–36).

16:8–13　These verses provide a hymnlike introduction to Asaph's hymn of thanksgiving. Israel is exhorted to give thanks to the Lord, to call upon his name, and to make known (publicize) among the peoples his deeds (v. 8); to sing to him, sing praise to him, and talk of all his wonderful works

(v. 9); to glory in his holy name, to let those who seek rejoice (v. 10); to look to the Lord and his strength, and seek his face continually (v. 11); to remember the marvelous works he has done, his miracles, and the judgments of his mouth (v. 12). The psalm then addresses the people: "O descendants of Israel his servant, O sons of Jacob, his chosen ones" (v. 13).[36]

16:14–22 This material is also dependent on Psalm 105. It takes up from Ps 105:14 and continues through to Ps 105:22. Particular emphasis is placed on Yahweh's covenant with Israel (1 Chr 16:15–17) and on the patriarchs. Israel is commanded to remember the covenant.[37]

Verse 19 reads (in Hebrew) "when you were but few," rather than Ps 105:12 "when they were but few." The second person "you" would encourage a sense of unity with the patriarchs and their experience with God. When Israel was few and strangers, wandering from nation to nation and from one kingdom to another, the Lord allowed no one to oppress them and rebuked any who tried to do them harm. This would have been an encouragement to the relatively small community of Jews in the Chronicler's age who found themselves not only few but under foreign domination.

16:23–29 The theme changes. The kingship of Yahweh comes to the fore. If the Chronicler's readers could identify themselves with their forebears, the patriarchs, who were a politically insignificant group that grew to a significant people as their story unfolded, the people of Israel of the Chronicler's day might well take hope and look to a brighter future. Their God was a great God whose salvation was to be proclaimed from day to day. He was great and most worthy of praise, to be revered above all gods. The gods of the nations were but idols, but Israel's God made the heavens. Before him was splendor and majesty; strength and joy were in his dwelling place.

The latter words of v. 29 have been variously understood.[38] The probable meaning of the phrase is that the Lord's actions always display his holy splendor, for which he deserves holy worship (cf. 2 Chr 20:21; Pss 29:2; 96:9).

16:30–33 "Tremble before him, all the earth! . . . let them say among the nations, "The LORD reigns!" These words are a powerful statement asserting that Israel's God, Yahweh, is the supreme ruler over all. All nature

---

[36] The reading of Ps 105:6 has "Abraham" here, but the reading "Israel" stresses the point that all Israel comprises the people of God.

[37] A slight textual variant occurs in v. 15. Some LXX manuscripts have "he remembers" his covenant (so also Ps 105:8 in Hebrew). The MT uses the imperative plural "remember," which better fits the context.

[38] The KJV renders the Heb בְּהַדְרַת־קֹדֶשׁ "in the beauty of holiness"; NASB has "in holy array" (also RSV); NEB has "in the splendor of holiness"; NCV has "because he is holy." The identical phrase is found in 2 Chr 20:21, but with the preposition לְ "for" rather than בְ "in."

responds with joy (vv. 31–33). The Lord will come to judge the earth.

16:34   This verse appears in many settings in the Old Testament (see the refrain in Ps 136). It found its way into various liturgical settings, where it probably had its origin.

16:35–36   These thoughts are similar to Ps 106:47. As Williamson notes, here is a prayer that could have been particularly appropriate to the Chronicler's own day though not at all inappropriate for David's day.[39]

(5) Ministry before the Ark (16:37–43)

[37]David left Asaph and his associates before the ark of the covenant of the LORD to minister there regularly, according to each day's requirements. [38]He also left Obed-Edom and his sixty-eight associates to minister with them. Obed-Edom son of Jeduthun, and also Hosah, were gatekeepers.

[39]David left Zadok the priest and his fellow priests before the tabernacle of the LORD at the high place in Gibeon [40]to present burnt offerings to the LORD on the altar of burnt offering regularly, morning and evening, in accordance with everything written in the Law of the LORD, which he had given Israel. [41]With them were Heman and Jeduthun and the rest of those chosen and designated by name to give thanks to the LORD, "for his love endures forever." [42]Heman and Jeduthun were responsible for the sounding of the trumpets and cymbals and for the playing of the other instruments for sacred song. The sons of Jeduthun were stationed at the gate.

[43]Then all the people left, each for his own home, and David returned home to bless his family.

16:37–40   These verses provide a concluding observation or summarizing remark on the way David ordered the Levites. Asaph and his associates were left before the ark to minister there regularly as each day required. Obed-Edom and his sixty-eight associates ministered with them although Obed-Edom and Hosah were gatekeepers. Zadok and his fellow priests were at the tabernacle at Gibeon to attend to the morning and evening burnt offerings in accordance with the law of the Lord.

Some dismiss the tradition of a tent sanctuary at Gibeon as the Chronicler's fabrication designed to justify Solomon's early visit to Gibeon (1 Kgs 3:4; 2 Chr 1:3) and bring it into line with the priestly law in Lev 17:8–9.[40] This is unnecessary. The Chronicler may well have had access to older traditions.

16:41   This verse seems to refer to the list in 15:17–22 not specifically mentioned in 16:5, as Levites who ministered before the ark in Jerusalem.

---

[39] Williamson, *1 and 2 Chronicles,* 130.
[40] Ibid., 130–31.

The well-known liturgical phrase "for his love endures forever" appears again here. The word "love" (*ḥesed*) gathers up the ideas of "loyalty," "faithfulness," "steadfast love," an appropriate description of the Lord's character.

16:42 The sons of Jeduthun were not involved in the playing of music but were gatekeepers. Jeduthun himself was head of one of the guilds of singers. The reason for the change is not given.

16:43 The section on the restoration of the ark is concluded at this point. The Chronicler could now return to his story by describing the important dynastic oracle of Nathan the prophet (cf. 2 Sam 7). The note on the people returning home and David returning to his home to bless his family comes from 2 Sam 6:19b–20a. However, the Chronicler omitted the story of David's dispute with Michal (2 Sam 6:20b–23). David's encounter with Michal is mentioned briefly in 15:29, where Michal is said to have despised David. The explanation of 2 Sam 6:20–23 is not given. It is clear, however, from 1 Chr 15:29 that a representative of Saul's family, Michal, disapproved of David's care of the ark, a theme that has appeared already in chaps. 13–14.

3. God's Promise to David: The Dynastic Oracle (17:1–27)

The Chronicler was ready to embark on his primary theme—the building of the temple—but certain steps had yet to be taken. The individual who would actually build the temple had to be identified (chap. 17), the political conditions had to be propitious (chaps. 18–20), the precise site had to be chosen (chap. 21), the materials and plans had to be in hand (chaps. 22; 28–29), and the personnel to undertake the proper functioning of the temple had to be selected and authorized (chaps. 23–27). All of these important items are taken up in the last part of 1 Chronicles, which closes with David's prayer, the recognition of Solomon as king, and the death of David (chap. 29). The present chapter describes David's desire to build the temple, a desire that failed to receive God's blessing (17:1–15).

(1) David's Plan to Build the Temple and Yahweh's Disapproval (17:1–15)

¹**After David was settled in his palace, he said to Nathan the prophet, "Here I am, living in a palace of cedar, while the ark of the covenant of the LORD is under a tent."**

²**Nathan replied to David, "Whatever you have in mind, do it, for God is with you."**

³**That night the word of God came to Nathan, saying:**

⁴**"Go and tell my servant David, 'This is what the LORD says: You are**

not the one to build me a house to dwell in. [5]I have not dwelt in a house from the day I brought Israel up out of Egypt to this day. I have moved from one tent site to another, from one dwelling place to another. [6]Wherever I have moved with all the Israelites, did I ever say to any of their leaders whom I commanded to shepherd my people, "Why have you not built me a house of cedar?'"

[7]"Now then, tell my servant David, 'This is what the LORD Almighty says: I took you from the pasture and from following the flock, to be ruler over my people Israel. [8]I have been with you wherever you have gone, and I have cut off all your enemies from before you. Now I will make your name like the names of the greatest men of the earth. [9]And I will provide a place for my people Israel and will plant them so that they can have a home of their own and no longer be disturbed. Wicked people will not oppress them anymore, as they did at the beginning [10]and have done ever since the time I appointed leaders over my people Israel. I will also subdue all your enemies.

"'I declare to you that the LORD will build a house for you: [11]When your days are over and you go to be with your fathers, I will raise up your offspring to succeed you, one of your own sons, and I will establish his kingdom. [12]He is the one who will build a house for me, and I will establish his throne forever. [13]I will be his father, and he will be my son. I will never take my love away from him, as I took it away from your predecessor. [14]I will set him over my house and my kingdom forever; his throne will be established forever.'"

[15]Nathan reported to David all the words of this entire revelation.

Some interesting political and religious background material from the ancient Near East helps us understand the nature of events in chaps. 17–19. In Near Eastern thought there was a widely recognized relationship between the earthly kingship and the temple of the protecting deity of the city-state. The state was seen as a reflection of the cosmic reality of the divine government, which stood behind the state. The state, with its various hierarchies, culminated in the earthly kingship at its apex. This was thought to be parallel to a cosmic state of affairs with its own gradations in which the major deity headed a pantheon of lesser deities. The ultimate kingship of the protecting deity was thought to be expressed through, and paralleled by, the empirical kingship exercised by the ruler of the city-state on earth. This concept was given concrete expression in the relationship that existed between the temple of the city-state and the palace of the king of the city-state. The temple was the earthly residence of the deity, and the palace was the residence of the earthly representative of the deity, that is, the king.

A remarkable fact about this chapter is that while it sets in motion the events that would culminate in the building of the temple, it actually shows that the temple was not what really was important. David wanted to build a house for God, but God himself would do something far greater in building a house for David. This house, the Davidic dynasty with its eternal and messianic implications, was of far greater importance than any building. This chapter reminds the reader that the house God builds surpasses any human house however grand it may be and however honorable the motivations were behind its building. This should once again remind us that it is superficial to think of the Chronicler as someone who could not see beyond legal and ceremonial religion.

The place where the temple stood was of paramount importance, for it was the point of contact between two worlds—the city-state and the cosmic state. The city-state was the property of, and under the control of, the deity. The choice of a temple site was therefore significant and was preceded by the divine disclosure to the state of the intention of the deity to reside at a particular place. The erection of the temple was an assertion of the divine control over the political and religious life of the state (v. 22).

In 2 Samuel 6 Yahweh, Israel's King, indicated that he would take up residence in the new Davidic capital. The return of the ark confirmed this. The presence of the ark represented the rule of Yahweh over Israel from Jerusalem. The ark was the footstool of the divine throne (Ps 132:7b; 1 Chr 28:2). The presence of the covenant document here (the tables of stone carrying the Ten Commandments), has a parallel with the depositing of the covenant document at the feet of the gods in the ancient Near East.

The parallels between Near Eastern ideas about the kings of city-states and the titular deity of the state are, to say the least, interesting but may provide important clues about the significance of the return of the ark to Jerusalem and the oracle of Nathan in 2 Sam 7:4–14. We return to the text of 1 Chronicles 17.

17:1 After David had settled in his own palace, he turned his attention to the important matter of the temple. This chapter is based largely on 2 Samuel 7 although there are differences. The Samuel story notes that it was after the Lord had given David rest from all his enemies round about that Nathan delivered his oracle. That remark, which is lacking in Chronicles, implies a lapse of time between the bringing back of the ark to Jerusalem and the expression of David's desire to build a temple. Nathan the prophet was the intermediary between David and Yahweh. He and his contemporary Gad were typical of God's spokesmen in the early tenth century B.C. God had his spokesmen in every age, but there were notable prophets in the centuries before the so-called classical prophets of the eighth and following centuries B.C.

David's concern arose from the fact that while he himself lived in a "palace of cedar," the ark was in a tent. In keeping with Near Eastern practice, palaces and other grand buildings made lavish use of cedar that often came from Lebanon. Indeed, Hiram, ruler of Tyre, cooperated in supplying this valuable timber all over the east (1 Kgs 5:8,10; 6:9–10,15–16,18; 1 Chr 14:1; 22:4; 2 Chr 2:3,8). It was incongruous that the ark of the covenant of the Lord should be housed in a tent while the king lived in a fine palace.

17:2-4 Nathan, the prophet, gave approval to David's place (cf. 2 Sam 7:3). It was, however, an approval Yahweh rejected. In the Samuel account David's proposal is rejected with a question (2 Sam 7:4–5), but in Chronicles the reply is in the form of a strong command (v. 4). The building of "the house" (note the article) was not forbidden, but David was not the one to undertake the building. The term "house" is used in two senses here. In one sense it refers to a physical structure like a temple or a palace. In the other sense the reference is to a dynasty. God would secure the house of David, that is, the dynasty of David, first of all. The physical house (temple) would come later.

17:5–6 The reference in the first instance is to the wilderness wanderings (Num 33) but could also apply to the pretemple localizations of the shrine at Gibeon, Shiloh, and Nob or even to the wanderings of the ark after the fall of Shiloh. The text in v. 5b requires a second use of "dwelling place," a different word from "house"—from one tent site to another, from one dwelling place to another.

The "leaders" of v. 6 are literally "judges" (*šōpĕṭîm*). The traditional "judges" in the Book of Judges were leaders, some of whom were real shepherds of God's people. Yahweh did not require any of these leaders to build a house of cedar for him.

17:7–10 David was originally a shepherd taken from the pastures and from following the flock to become "ruler" over Israel. This term was deliberately chosen in preference to the word "king," which had overtones of autocratic rule familiar among the surrounding nations. One of the outstanding marks of David was that he was regarded by many in Israel as a leader, but not as an autocratic king. The divine word through Nathan reminded David that the Lord had been with him wherever he had gone and had cut off his enemies from before him. The Lord's plan was to grant him a great name and provide his people a place and a secure home free from oppression by wicked people who once harassed them. These words would have conjured up a great sense of longing and encouragement on the part of the Chronicler's postexilic readers.

17:11–15 The Lord's intention was to build a house, that is, a "dynasty," for David and his offspring (lit., Heb. *zera*ᶜ, "seed") to succeed him when his days were over. This would be one of his own sons whose kingdom the Lord would establish. The Lord would be his father, and he would be Yahweh's son (Ps 2:7). Nor would the love of the Lord ever be taken away from him as it was removed from Saul, David's predecessor. David's heir would have a double significance. He would demonstrate the continuity of David's throne, and he would be the verification of the Lord's continuing presence, fulfilling the promise that David's son would build a "house" (temple) for Yahweh. L. C. Allen notes that v. 12, in its dual focus on temple and dynasty, forms the "focal point" not only of Nathan's oracle but also of the Chronicler's message, if taken together with the call to seek God in 2 Chr 7:14. Allen summarizes that these "two verses are Chronicles in a nutshell."[41]

The Samuel text has an additional comment in 2 Sam 7:14b. "When he does wrong, I will punish him with the rod of men, with floggings inflicted by men. But my love [Heb. *ḥesed,* "faithfulness"] will never be taken away from him, as I took it away from Saul." The reason for this omission by the Chronicler is probably that Solomon is pictured in a special way because it was he who would build the temple. To be sure, Solomon perpetrated some misdemeanors, but the dynasty continued. This was the important thing to the Chronicler.

Another difference from the parallel text in 2 Samuel is that here reference is made to "my house and my kingdom" while 2 Sam 7:16 refers to "your house and your kingdom," that is, David's house and David's kingdom. The Chronicles reference is far wider. God is the real King of Israel, and the kingdom is his. It is his right to establish the throne of Israel's kings, and successful kings of the future could appeal to this idea. It was futile for the Northern Kingdom to resist the descendants of David and Solomon (2 Chr 13:8). Israel's hope in times of despair was that God would intervene to reestablish his kingdom in the hands of the sons of David.

In the oracle of Nathan there is a messianic significance that can hardly be overestimated. Both 1 Chronicles 17 and 2 Samuel 7 stress that the divine decree indicated that Solomon, David's son, would build the temple and that his throne would be established forever. But was this oracle relevant to Solomon alone or was there some greater, even some "messianic" significance? A variety of opinions have been offered, but these gather round two perspectives: (1) that the focus is on Solomon alone and (2) that the focus is on "David's greater son." The Chronicler gives prominence to the "eternal" reference of the oracle. The phrase "forever" occurs several times. From the days of Nathan a regular feature of messianic thinking has been to refer to David's descendants (cf. Isa 11:1–5; Jer 17:24–27; Ezek 34:20–24; Amos

---

[41] Allen, *1, 2 Chronicles,* 124.

9:11–12; Mic 5:2–4). In light of Old Testament insights, the New Testament pictures Jesus as the son of David (cf. Matt 1:1; Luke 1:30-31). The church in every century has celebrated the reign of Jesus Christ, whose kingdom will have no end (vv. 17–23).

(2) David's Prayer in Response to the Oracle (17:16–27)

[16]Then King David went in and sat before the LORD, and he said:

"Who am I, O LORD God, and what is my family, that you have brought me this far? [17]And as if this were not enough in your sight, O God, you have spoken about the future of the house of your servant. You have looked on me as though I were the most exalted of men, O LORD God.

[18]"What more can David say to you for honoring your servant? For you know your servant, [19]O LORD. For the sake of your servant and according to your will, you have done this great thing and made known all these great promises.

[20]"There is no one like you, O LORD, and there is no God but you, as we have heard with our own ears. [21]And who is like your people Israel— the one nation on earth whose God went out to redeem a people for himself, and to make a name for yourself, and to perform great and awesome wonders by driving out nations from before your people, whom you redeemed from Egypt? [22]You made your people Israel your very own forever, and you, O LORD, have become their God.

[23]"And now, LORD, let the promise you have made concerning your servant and his house be established forever. Do as you promised, [24]so that it will be established and that your name will be great forever. Then men will say, 'The LORD Almighty, the God over Israel, is Israel's God!' And the house of your servant David will be established before you.

[25]"You, my God, have revealed to your servant that you will build a house for him. So your servant has found courage to pray to you. [26]O LORD, you are God! You have promised these good things to your servant. [27]Now you have been pleased to bless the house of your servant, that it may continue forever in your sight; for you, O LORD, have blessed it, and it will be blessed forever."

The text of David's prayer here is substantially the same as in 2 Sam 7:18–29 although there are some alterations and omissions. The prayer is offered in the newly established tent shrine in Jerusalem to which the ark has been brought. It acknowledges the greatness and uniqueness of God and refers to the election and deliverance of Israel, revealed especially in the exodus. The continuity of David's throne also is acknowledged (vv. 23–24). The reference to the exodus in vv. 21–22 is important. The saving events of the exodus were basic in Israel's theology although they were not always made explicit by the Chronicler. Even Solomon's prayer of dedication (2 Chr 6) of the temple pays scant attention to the exodus, which is mentioned only in passing (2 Chr 6:5). Those earlier events seem to be lost sight of in the new emphasis on the Davidic covenant.

17:16 David referred to the insignificance of his own family in contrast to the high position he now held. More than that, there was an exciting future hope.

17:17-24 Verse 17b has textual problems, and translators give different renderings. The general drift of the passage seems to be that God has marked out a significant future for David, but there is uncertainty about the exact translation. In the parallel in 2 Sam 7:19, David proclaims that God's decree is "instruction for the people" (NRSV), a phrase that may have profound messianic implications.[42] The text here, however, is unclear.

In any case David expressed thanks that God had honored him (v. 19). David's prayer is that the Lord's promise should be established forever. The frequent use of "forever" and similar phrases points forward to a future beyond David's time. So David prayed that God's "name" (fame) should be sure and great forever so that "the LORD Almighty, the God over Israel, is Israel's God." Thus will the house of David be established forever before God.

17:25-27 The prayer closes with the invocation: "O LORD, you are God! You have promised these good things to your servant." Assurance of the Lord's continuing blessing comes in the final words, "Now you have been pleased to bless the house of your servant, that it may continue forever in your sight; for you, O LORD, have blessed it, and it will be blessed forever."

4. David's Wars (18:1–20:8)

The chief reason David was not permitted to build the temple was that he was a man of war (22:8; 28:3). Yet these wars were important to David and to Israel, for they gave security to David and to the nation. It was necessary to establish "rest" before the temple could be built. David himself needed to be "settled in his palace" (17:1), and peace would need to be secured by subduing Israel's enemies (17:10). All that was not in place till the days of Solomon. But first, David, the man of war and of blood, needed to prepare the way.

Another requirement for the building of the temple was adequate

---

[42] See W. C. Kaiser, *Toward an Old Testament Theology* (Grand Rapids: Zondervan, 1978), 152–5.

resources. These were a corollary of David's military exploits (18:8–11). The booty David took in his military campaigns was available to Solomon to build the temple.

(1) David's Victories (18:1–13)

¹In the course of time, David defeated the Philistines and subdued them, and he took Gath and its surrounding villages from the control of the Philistines.

²David also defeated the Moabites, and they became subject to him and brought tribute.

³Moreover, David fought Hadadezer king of Zobah, as far as Hamath, when he went to establish his control along the Euphrates River. ⁴David captured a thousand of his chariots, seven thousand charioteers and twenty thousand foot soldiers. He hamstrung all but a hundred of the chariot horses.

⁵When the Arameans of Damascus came to help Hadadezer king of Zobah, David struck down twenty-two thousand of them. ⁶He put garrisons in the Aramean kingdom of Damascus, and the Arameans became subject to him and brought tribute. The LORD gave David victory everywhere he went.

⁷David took the gold shields carried by the officers of Hadadezer and brought them to Jerusalem. ⁸From Tebah and Cun, towns that belonged to Hadadezer, David took a great quantity of bronze, which Solomon used to make the bronze Sea, the pillars and various bronze articles.

⁹When Tou king of Hamath heard that David had defeated the entire army of Hadadezer king of Zobah, ¹⁰he sent his son Hadoram to King David to greet him and congratulate him on his victory in battle over Hadadezer, who had been at war with Tou. Hadoram brought all kinds of articles of gold and silver and bronze.

¹¹King David dedicated these articles to the LORD, as he had done with the silver and gold he had taken from all these nations: Edom and Moab, the Ammonites and the Philistines, and Amalek.

¹²Abishai son of Zeruiah struck down eighteen thousand Edomites in the Valley of Salt. ¹³He put garrisons in Edom, and all the Edomites became subject to David. The LORD gave David victory everywhere he went.

A survey of David's victories is provided in vv. 1–13. It is drawn from 2 Sam 8:1–14. Here again we must remind ourselves of how these chapters must have looked to the Chronicler's original readers. Wilcock has drawn attention to the glorious character of the Davidic monarchy in chaps. 14; 18–20—his fame, prestige among the nations, and many victories—and to the fact that the postexilic community in Jerusalem had none of these things. We can sympathize here. Just as the Jews have seen their nation diminished to insignificance on the world stage, so also we can see the waning influence of the church in Western society. The point in Chronicles is surely not that the Jews of the Chronicler's day should aspire to military greatness again; they were genuinely puny in comparison to Persia. Rather, the message here is that God continues to be God of all nations. Just as he could raise up a David, so also he could control events in the heart of the Persian Empire (as illustrated by the Book of Esther). Rather, for the Chronicler's original readers and for us, the message is that we should see that the real prestige of the people of God is in the person of David's greater son, the Messiah.[43]

18:1 Israel had encountered the Philistines on a number of occasions in defensive wars (chaps. 10–11; 14). But defensive wars were not enough. David needed to take the offensive (2 Sam 8:1). Details are lacking though Gath and its surrounding villages were snatched from the control of the Philistines. This secured David's west flank.

18:2 Moab was defeated and brought into subjection and compelled to bring tribute.

18:3–4 To the northeast of David's domain lay the Aramean states. One of these was the kingdom of Hadadezer of Zobah, whose kingdom reached to Hamath. David encountered Hadadezer when he went to establish his control along the Euphrates River. He captured chariots, charioteers, and foot soldiers. The parallel list in 2 Sam 8:4 of what David captured is slightly different due to apparent copyist errors. Where Chronicles reads (literally) "a thousand chariots and seven thousand charioteers," 2 Sam 8:4 has "a thousand [missing word?] and seven hundred charioteers." That seven thousand charioteers is also given in 1 Chr 19:18 and that the LXX of 2 Sam 8:4 and a Qumran text (4QSam[a]) agrees with 1 Chr 18:4 leads us to suspect that it is the Samuel text which has suffered in transmission.[44]

18:5–6 The help sent by the Arameans of Damascus to assist the king of Zobah was neutralized when David struck down twenty-two thousand of them (the word for "thousand" may refer to a military grouping—see on 5:18; 7:1-5) and placed garrisons in the Aramean kingdom of Damascus, which became subject to him and brought him tribute. The Lord gave victory to David everywhere he went, a further sign of God's blessing.

18:7–8 Reference is made to the booty David obtained, gold shields from Hadadezer and bronze from Tibhath and Cun. The bronze was used in the preparation of items for Solomon's temple.

18:9–10 Others had suffered under Hadadezer. The gifts brought by Tou, king of Hamath, expressed thanks not only to David but to David's God.

18:11 These gifts and the booty taken from Edom, Moab, Ammon, the

---

[43] See Wilcock, *Message of Chronicles*, 80–86.

[44] Japhet, *I & II Chronicles*, 346. She explains that after "chariots" was lost, the number of charioteers was adjusted.

Philistines, and Amalek were dedicated to the Lord. They would find their way into the collection of metals required for the temple. Edom appears in 2 Sam 8:12 as Aram. The confusion between these two results from the fact that the Hebrew consonants *r* (ר) and *d* (ד) are very much alike. Both Aram and Edom had been subjected to raids from David, and either name would be acceptable. In the list of nations here, neither the Ammonites nor the Amalekites has been previously mentioned.

18:12–13 There is a mention of the activities of Abishai, son of Zeruiah, in Edom, where he struck down eighteen thousand Edomites in the Valley of Salt. Again the word for "thousand" may refer to some military grouping and not a numerical usage. David put garrisons in Edom, and the Edomites became his vassals. The heading to Psalm 60 refers to an event when Joab returned from war in Aram and killed twelve thousand in the Valley of Salt. Joab was also a son of Zeruiah and was in command of David's army (1 Chr 18:15). According to 2 Sam 8:13, David was responsible for the Edomites' defeat, but both Joab and Abishai may have acted in concert under David's direction. Alternately, there may have been a textual corruption of 2 Sam 8:13 and Psalm 60. The point is made again that "The LORD gave David victory everywhere he went," further stressing how God blessed David for his faithfulness.

(2) David's Officials (18:14–17)

14David reigned over all Israel, doing what was just and right for all his people. **15**Joab son of Zeruiah was over the army; Jehoshaphat son of Ahilud was recorder; **16**Zadok son of Ahitub and Ahimelech son of Abiathar were priests; Shavsha was secretary; **17**Benaiah son of Jehoiada was over the Kerethites and Pelethites; and David's sons were chief officials at the king's side.

18:14 The growth of David's domains necessitated some organization to care for their administration. The Chronicler notes that it was over "all Israel" that David reigned. The character of his rule was that he ruled with justice and rectitude. This statement enhanced still further David's reputation. He was an ideal ruler. Justice and right doing marked his whole administration.

18:15–17 David's leading administrators were Joab, son of Zeruiah, as commander-in-chief of the army; Jehoshaphat, son of Ahilud, his recorder (spokesman or chief of protocol); Zadok, son of Ahitub, and Ahimelech were priests; Shavsha was the secretary or royal scribe; Benaiah, son of Jehoiada, was in charge of the professional military corps. He was over the mercenaries, the Kerethites, and Pelethites; David's sons were lieutenants or personal adjutants. Second Sam 8:18 names David's sons as priests, but the Chronicler evidently did not regard this as legitimate because they were laymen even though both David and Solomon exercised what were strictly priestly duties on some official occasions. It is possible, however, that the term for priest (*kōhēn*) was confused with the term for "administrator" (*sōkēn*). The evidence of the versions and the context would support this. By the Chronicler's day this latter term was rare and had largely fallen out of use.

This was a carefully planned administration, a sort of cabinet. Certain parallels with Egyptian models have been noted. The "recorder" was parallel to the royal herald in the Egyptian court whose duties included regulation of the palace ceremonies, admission to royal audiences, reporting to the king matters concerning the people and the country, reporting the orders of the king to the people as the official interpreter, accompanying the king on his travels as his personal secretary, arranging for the stages of his itinerary, and serving as chief of police for the pharaoh.[45]

(3) David's Campaigns against the Ammonites (19:1–20:3)

[1]In the course of time, Nahash king of the Ammonites died, and his son succeeded him as king. [2]David thought, "I will show kindness to Hanun son of Nahash, because his father showed kindness to me." So David sent a delegation to express his sympathy to Hanun concerning his father.

When David's men came to Hanun in the land of the Ammonites to express sympathy to him, [3]the Ammonite nobles said to Hanun, "Do you think David is honoring your father by sending men to you to express sympathy? Haven't his men come to you to explore and spy out the country and overthrow it?" [4]So Hanun seized David's men, shaved them, cut off their garments in the middle at the buttocks, and sent them away.

[5]When someone came and told David about the men, he sent messengers to meet them, for they were greatly humiliated. The king said, "Stay at Jericho till your beards have grown, and then come back."

[6]When the Ammonites realized that they had become a stench in David's nostrils, Hanun and the Ammonites sent a thousand talents of silver to hire chariots and charioteers from Aram Naharaim, Aram Maacah and Zobah. [7]They hired thirty-two thousand chariots and charioteers, as well as the king of Maacah with his troops, who came and camped near Medeba, while the Ammonites were mustered from their towns and moved out for battle.

[8]On hearing this, David sent Joab out with the entire army of fighting men. [9]The Ammonites came out and drew up in battle formation at the entrance to their city, while the kings who had come were by themselves in the open country.

[10]Joab saw that there were battle lines in front of him and behind him; so he selected some of the best troops in Israel and deployed them against the Arameans. [11]He put the rest of the men under the command of Abishai his

---

[45] Myers, *I Chronicles*, 138f.

brother, and they were deployed against the Ammonites. [12]Joab said, "If the Arameans are too strong for me, then you are to rescue me; but if the Ammonites are too strong for you, then I will rescue you. [13]Be strong and let us fight bravely for our people and the cities of our God. The LORD will do what is good in his sight."

[14]Then Joab and the troops with him advanced to fight the Arameans, and they fled before him. [15]When the Ammonites saw that the Arameans were fleeing, they too fled before his brother Abishai and went inside the city. So Joab went back to Jerusalem.

[16]After the Arameans saw that they had been routed by Israel, they sent messengers and had Arameans brought from beyond the River, with Shophach the commander of Hadadezer's army leading them.

[17]When David was told of this, he gathered all Israel and crossed the Jordan; he advanced against them and formed his battle lines opposite them. David formed his lines to meet the Arameans in battle, and they fought against him. [18]But they fled before Israel, and David killed seven thousand of their charioteers and forty thousand of their foot soldiers. He also killed Shophach the commander of their army.

[19]When the vassals of Hadadezer saw that they had been defeated by Israel, they made peace with David and became subject to him.

So the Arameans were not willing to help the Ammonites anymore.

[1]In the spring, at the time when kings go off to war, Joab led out the armed forces. He laid waste the land of the Ammonites and went to Rabbah and besieged it, but David remained in Jerusalem. Joab attacked Rabbah and left it in ruins. [2]David took the crown from the head of their king—its weight was found to be a talent of gold, and it was set with precious stones—and it was placed on David's head. He took a great quantity of plunder from the city [3]and brought out the people who were there, consigning them to labor with saws and with iron picks and axes. David did this to all the Ammonite towns. Then David and his entire army returned to Jerusalem.

This section contains the account of David's wars against potential invaders of his territory. It further illustrates the fact that David was a man of war and thus disqualified from building the temple. Nevertheless, just as he was successful in campaigns against the Philistines, Moab, Aram, and Edom, so also in his war against Ammon he was granted victory and success, enjoying Yahweh's further blessing on his enterprises. The Chronicler devoted considerable space to the Ammonite campaigns. The account is based on 2 Sam 10:1–11:1; 12:26,30–31 although it omits the disgraceful affair of David's seduction of Bathsheba. We are not able to place the Ammonite campaign into a chronological perspective although it would seem that David had taken care of Moab and Edom before this so as to obviate any attacks on his southern flank. Perhaps also a secure southern flank would give him confidence to undertake his Aramean campaigns. Perhaps Ammon was also well in control before he embarked on his Aramean adventure.

19:1–2 The conflict with Ammon was provoked by a foolish act on the part of the new king, Hanun. On the death of Hanun's father, Nahash, David sought to secure good relations with Hanun in return for the kindness shown to David earlier, in the days of Saul. So David sent a delegation to Hanun to express his sympathy.

19:3 Hanun was suspicious, no doubt because he had witnessed that acts of kindness sometimes were a cover for treachery. His nobles interpreted the visit as a not-too-subtle attempt to explore and to spy out the country with a view to attacking Ammonite territory.

19:4 For the ancient Israelites, it was a matter of great shame to have one's beard shaved off and buttocks exposed.[46]

19:5 David was not a man to trifle with, and Hanun soon set about organizing help. At the same time, David showed sensitivity about the humiliation of his own men and gave them a leave of absence until their beards grew back.

19:6–7 Realizing that David would be greatly offended, Hanun and the Ammonites set about hiring chariots and charioteers from Mesopotamia (Aram Naharaim) and from two other Aramean states, Maacah and Zobah. The huge number of chariots and charioteers, thirty-two thousand, may be expressed in terms of some military unit of uncertain magnitude (see on 5:18; 7:1-5). The assembly of Arameans at Medeba in Moab, south of Ammon, seems to be too far south. Other places have been conjectured such as "the water of Rabbah" (2 Sam 12:27), but such suggestions are speculative. It seems that a considerable force comprising Aramean troops as well as Ammonites prepared for battle.

19:8–9 David's enemies intended to trap him with a two-flank attack and pin his army between the Ammonites on one side and their allies on the other.

19:10–15 Joab prepared to fight a battle on two fronts. He decided to fight on the front against the Arameans, and he needed someone he could trust to command the troops at the other front, against Ammon. His brother Abishai was the man. He realized that a smaller force could fight a two-front battle to its own advantage if both commanders kept their heads and supplied reinforcements to the other front as needed. He also committed the outcome to God. The enemy was outdone by superior leadership in the Israelite army and the purpose of God.

19:16–19 This was not the final defeat of the Arameans; for hearing of the rout of those helping the Arameans, they brought others from beyond the

---

[46] See D. A. Garrett, *Proverbs, Ecclesiastes, Song of Songs,* NAC (Nashville: Broadman, 1993), 212.

Euphrates River commanded by Shophach, the commander of Hadadezer's army, to help them in a new offensive. On this occasion David himself apparently led the army. It was time for the Arameans to make peace with David and become his vassals. They ceased to help the Ammonites (another example of the Lord helping David wherever he went; 18:6,13; cf. 17:8).

20:1 The Ammonite war dragged on. In the spring the war was taken up again when Joab led Israel's forces on a campaign in which the land of the Ammonites was laid waste and Rabbah their capital was attacked and left in ruins, although the citadel seems to have remained. King David did not participate in these events. He remained in Jerusalem and became involved in the Bathsheba affair (2 Sam 11–12), which the Chronicler omits because his focus was on David's divinely empowered achievements. Nevertheless, no one familiar with the story of David's fall, as the Chronicler's readers surely were, would miss the ominous allusion to it in this verse, which repeats from 2 Sam 11:1, "In the spring, at the time when kings go off to war. . . . But David remained in Jerusalem." Where the Samuel account spotlights David's troubles resulting from his sin, the Chronicler shows God's grace at work at the same time. Though David's personal life was in turmoil, God continued to use his faltering servant to bless the nation.[47]

20:2 David made a sudden and unexpected appearance on the scene. According to 2 Sam 12:27, Joab sent messengers to David to invite him to participate in the final assault on Rabbah so as to have the honor of this victory. The order of events in this final defeat of Ammon is not easy to follow. The Samuel material states that Joab raided the land of Ammon, besieged the capital, and took "the city of waters" (2 Sam 12:27, NASB), probably a portion of the city. Then he advised David to come and direct the final assault against the acropolis and so enjoy the honor resulting from this. David heeded Joab's advice and was present at the fall of Rabbah. He took the crown from their king (or their god; see NIV text note) and took a great deal of booty. The god of the Ammonites is given as *Milkom* ("Molech," NIV) in 1 Kgs 11:5; 2 Kgs 23:13, having the same consonants as the word *malkam*, here translated "their king." The term *malkam* at times must be translated "their king" (Ps 149:2; Jer 30:9; Hos 3:5), but in other places it appears to be an alternative designation for the Ammonite god (Jer 49:1,3; Zeph 1:5; and probably Amos 1:15). In this verse it could be either, but the weight of the crown would suggest that it refers to the god.[48]

---

[47] McConville, *I & II Chronicles*, 63–64.

[48] On Molech/Milcom see E. R. Clendenen, "Religious Background of the Old Testament," in *Foundations for Biblical Interpretation*, ed. D. Dockery et al. (Nashville: Broadman & Holman, 1994), 298–99.

20:3 The citizens of Rabbah were brought out and consigned to forced labor with saws, iron picks, and axes (cf. 2 Sam 12:31). One more kingdom was thus added to David's jurisdiction, and his prestige was further enhanced.

(4) Wars against the Philistines (20:4–8)

⁴In the course of time, war broke out with the Philistines, at Gezer. At that time Sibbecai the Hushathite killed Sippai, one of the descendants of the Rephaites, and the Philistines were subjugated.
⁵In another battle with the Philistines, Elhanan son of Jair killed Lahmi the brother of Goliath the Gittite, who had a spear with a shaft like a weaver's rod.
⁶In still another battle, which took place at Gath, there was a huge man with six fingers on each hand and six toes on each foot—twenty-four in all. He also was descended from Rapha. ⁷When he taunted Israel, Jonathan son of Shimea, David's brother, killed him.
⁸These were descendants of Rapha in Gath, and they fell at the hands of David and his men.

To conclude his survey of David's wars, the Chronicler returns to further victories over the Philistines. His material is based on 2 Sam 21:18–22. Three episodes are mentioned in these verses, but there doubtless were many skirmishes during the early part of David's reign. One by one David subdued centers of trouble. Each of the three incidents mentioned in these verses features the "giants" of the area.

20:4 The first encounter mentioned was at Gezer, one of the walled cities of the area. Also called Gob in 2 Sam 21:8, it is a place not otherwise known, but the Amarna letters mention a site called Gubba in the vicinity of the better-known Gezer. Evidently some fighting had taken place in the area when Sibbecai, the Hushathite, killed Sippai, one of the Rephaites (a giant). We are not told how David became involved, but the Philistines were subjugated, another victory for David.

20:5 In another encounter Elhanan, son of Jair, killed Lahmi, brother of Goliath the Gittite (i.e., a person from of Gath), who had a spear with a shaft like a weaver's rod. This verse presents some textual problems. According to 2 Sam 21:19, Elhanan slew Goliath. The text of 2 Sam 21:19 names the father of Elhanan as Jaareoregim. The word *oregim* is identical in the Hebrew text to the last word of the verse, "weavers," in the phrase "like a rod of weavers."[49] Furthermore, in 2 Sam 21:19 Elhanan's father is called a Bethlehemite, written *bêt hallaḥmî*, which easily could be confused with the name *laḥmî* ("Lahmi"). All this suggests the verse has suffered transcrip-

---

[49] See Williamson, *1 and 2 Chronicles,* 142.

tional difficulties. We do not know the exact reading of the original, but it likely is to have been closer to this text in Chronicles (note the NIV translation of 2 Sam 21:19).

20:6–8 A third encounter took place at Gath, where Jonathan, son of Shimea, David's brother, killed a giant, a huge man with six fingers on each hand and six toes on each foot. All these unusually large men were descendants of Rapha of Gath, but they fell at the hands of David and his men, who were able to flush out Philistine resistance.

The closing words of vv. 3,8 and the statement in v. 4 that the Philistines were subjugated completes the account of how God blessed David's work and provide a fitting climax to the Chronicler's story of all the work he had done prior to the building of the temple. One further insight into the methods of the Chronicler comes in the omission of the incident where Ishbibenob, another giant, sought to kill David (2 Sam 21:16–17). According to 2 Sam 21:17, David's men adjured him not to go out to battle again lest the lamp of Israel be quenched. The Chronicler bypassed several of David's personal faults and family history. Nothing was allowed to interrupt God's plan to have a home in Jerusalem where he could dwell among his people. God's plans were brought to fruition despite the frailties of those through whom he carried out his work.

5. David's Census and the Choice of Jerusalem for the Temple Site (21:1–22:1)

¹Satan rose up against Israel and incited David to take a census of Israel. ²So David said to Joab and the commanders of the troops, "Go and count the Israelites from Beersheba to Dan. Then report back to me so that I may know how many there are."

³But Joab replied, "May the LORD multiply his troops a hundred times over. My lord the king, are they not all my lord's subjects? Why does my lord want to do this? Why should he bring guilt on Israel?"

⁴The king's word, however, overruled Joab; so Joab left and went throughout Israel and then came back to Jerusalem. ⁵Joab reported the number of the fighting men to David: In all Israel there were one million one hundred thousand men who could handle a sword, including four hundred and seventy thousand in Judah.

⁶But Joab did not include Levi and Benjamin in the numbering, because the king's command was repulsive to him. ⁷This command was also evil in the sight of God; so he punished Israel.

⁸Then David said to God, "I have sinned greatly by doing this. Now, I beg you, take away the guilt of your servant. I have done a very foolish thing."

⁹The LORD said to Gad, David's seer, ¹⁰"Go and tell David, 'This is what the

LORD says: I am giving you three options. Choose one of them for me to carry out against you.'"

¹¹So Gad went to David and said to him, "This is what the LORD says: 'Take your choice: ¹²three years of famine, three months of being swept away before your enemies, with their swords overtaking you, or three days of the sword of the LORD—days of plague in the land, with the angel of the LORD ravaging every part of Israel.' Now then, decide how I should answer the one who sent me."

¹³David said to Gad, "I am in deep distress. Let me fall into the hands of the LORD, for his mercy is very great; but do not let me fall into the hands of men."

¹⁴So the LORD sent a plague on Israel, and seventy thousand men of Israel fell dead. ¹⁵And God sent an angel to destroy Jerusalem. But as the angel was doing so, the LORD saw it and was grieved because of the calamity and said to the angel who was destroying the people, "Enough! Withdraw your hand." The angel of the LORD was then standing at the threshing floor of Araunah the Jebusite.

¹⁶David looked up and saw the angel of the LORD standing between heaven and earth, with a drawn sword in his hand extended over Jerusalem. Then David and the elders, clothed in sackcloth, fell facedown.

¹⁷David said to God, "Was it not I who ordered the fighting men to be counted? I am the one who has sinned and done wrong. These are but sheep. What have they done? O LORD my God, let your hand fall upon me and my family, but do not let this plague remain on your people."

¹⁸Then the angel of the LORD ordered Gad to tell David to go up and build an altar to the LORD on the threshing floor of Araunah the Jebusite. ¹⁹So David went up in obedience to the word that Gad had spoken in the name of the LORD.

²⁰While Araunah was threshing wheat, he turned and saw the angel; his four sons who were with him hid themselves. ²¹Then David approached, and when Araunah looked and saw him, he left the threshing floor and bowed down before David with his face to the ground.

²²David said to him, "Let me have the site of your threshing floor so I can build an altar to the LORD, that the plague on the people may be stopped. Sell it to me at the full price."

²³Araunah said to David, "Take it! Let my lord the king do whatever pleases him. Look, I will give the oxen for the burnt offerings, the threshing sledges for the wood, and the wheat for the grain offering. I will give all this."

²⁴But King David replied to Araunah, "No, I insist on paying the full price. I will not take for the LORD what is yours, or sacrifice a burnt offering that costs me nothing."

²⁵So David paid Araunah six hundred shekels of gold for the site. ²⁶David built an altar to the LORD there and sacrificed burnt offerings and fellowship offerings. He called on the LORD, and the LORD answered him with fire from heaven on the altar of burnt offering.

[27]Then the LORD spoke to the angel, and he put his sword back into its sheath. [28]At that time, when David saw that the LORD had answered him on the threshing floor of Araunah the Jebusite, he offered sacrifices there. [29]The tabernacle of the LORD, which Moses had made in the desert, and the altar of burnt offering were at that time on the high place at Gibeon. [30]But David could not go before it to inquire of God, because he was afraid of the sword of the angel of the LORD.

[1]Then David said, "The house of the LORD God is to be here, and also the altar of burnt offering for Israel."

Having cut off David's enemies, God then provided for Israel a place (cf. 1 Chr 17:8–9). It may also be said that having empowered Israel to defeat their human foes, God provided a place of atonement and divine manifestation whereby they could defeat (or hold at bay) their nonhuman enemy, Satan.

The temple site was designated following an incident in which David called for a census. Because of inadequate ritual preparations for the calling of a census, David's action incurred the Lord's wrath. This led to the purchase of a farmer's threshing floor on which to offer an expiatory sacrifice and on which eventually to build the temple and the altar of burnt offering. The Chronicler made use of 2 Samuel 24 but did so with his own unique perspective.[50] It becomes clear that the basic reason for using this story was not so much that David had failed to observe certain ritual requirements but that David's offense led to the purchase of the threshing floor of Araunah, which became the site for the temple.

We need to understand some facts about the conduct of a census in Israel. The precise reason for this particular census is not given. The major reason for taking a census in Israel was to lay the basis for levying taxes (Exod 30:12; Num 3:40–51) or registering men for military service (Num 26:1–4). But a census for the purpose of conducting an unauthorized military campaign was hardly likely to be approved. In the present case it may have been a census to be used as a basis for corvée (forced or unpaid labor for some national enterprise) in view of the building of the temple. There always was a risk in the assembly of a large body of men that an epidemic might break out. Ritual precautions were needed, involving confession, penitence, and the offering of sacrifices and prayers. Such ritual preparations were not peculiar to Israel but were known in Mesopotamia.[51] In Israel people enrolled for military service were required to pay a ransom and to be ritually purified. Otherwise a plague would result. The half-shekel of Exod 30:12 was a precaution against a breach of purity laws. In David's case there

---

[50] Braun, *1 Chronicles*, 216–18 lists eight variations between 2 Sam 24 and 1 Chr 21.
[51] P. K. McCarter, *II Samuel*, AB (Garden City: Doubleday, 1984), 512ff.

apparently was not only a problem with motive[52] but also some breach in ritual preparation, although the reason for the plague is not spelled out.

21:1 The figure of Satan appears clearly only in three passages in the Old Testament (Job 1:12; 2:6; Zech 3:1–2). The word generally has the article and means "The Accuser." Here it is without the article (*śāṭān*), suggesting that it was used as a proper name. In Zech 3:1–2 he appears in the heavenly court to accuse Joshua, the high priest. In Job 1–2 he appears among "the sons of God" to accuse Job and then to afflict Job, but within limits imposed by God (Job 1:12; 2:6).[53] In 2 Sam 24:1 it was the Lord whose anger against Israel (the reason is not given) led him to "incite" David to count Israel. Satan is not mentioned there. At any rate, the Samuel passage suggests that the sinful designs of Satan and David were used by the Lord as agents of his wrath. The Chronicler's focus, however, is on the immediate rather than the ultimate cause. Joab and his commanders (military personnel) were given the task of counting Israel.

21:3 While the exact nature of the offense involved in taking a census is unclear to us, Joab had no doubt that it would bring guilt on the nation and expressed himself strongly. David's persistence left him without excuse since he had been forewarned.

21:4–7 The military nature of the census is suggested not only by General Joab's involvement but also from the report of its results. The number of fighting men in all Israel that David could muster was 1,100,000, including 470,000 from Judah.[54] The tribes of Levi and Benjamin were omitted. The exclusion of Levi is explained because they were excluded from military service (Num 1:49; 2:33). Benjamin's exclusion may have been because the tabernacle rested at Gibeon (1 Chr 21:29).

---

[52] See R. B. Dillard, "David's Census: Perspectives on 2 Samuel 24 and 1 Chronicles 21," in *Through Christ's Word,* ed. W. R. Godfrey and J. L. Boyd III (Phillipsburg: Presbyterian & Reformed, 1985), 104–5.

[53] An alternative interpretation is given in J. Sailhamer, "1 Chronicles 21:1—A Study in Inter-Biblical Interpretation," *TJ* 10 (1989): 33–48. He takes שָׂטָן as the common noun "adversary" (cf. 1 Sam 29:4; 2 Sam 19:23; 1 Kgs 5:4; 11:9–14,23,25) and understands that David was incited by imminent attack to number his troops. The ultimate cause for such an attack was the Lord's anger at Israel. Against this view see R. F. Youngblood, "1, 2 Samuel," EBC 3:1095–96.

[54] J. B. Payne ("1, 2 Chronicles," 407) explains that the discrepancy between these numbers and those in 2 Sam 24:9 may be the result of different groups being counted and of numbers being rounded. For example, the 1,100,000 of Chronicles may include (note "all Israel") a standing army of about 500,000 (cf. 1 Chr 27:1–15) not included in the 800,000 given in Samuel. Also the Chronicler's 470,000 may be rounded to 500,000 in Samuel. Furthermore, the possibility must be reckoned with here again that the word translated "thousand" may actually mean "tribal chief" or "military leader," yielding "a muster of 1,570 outstanding military figures" rather than an army of over a million men. See also Dillard, "David's Census," 97–98; Youngblood, "1, 2 Samuel," 3:1098–99.

21:8–14 The narrative telling of David's choice of punishment is based on 2 Sam 24:10b–15. How David recognized that he had done wrong in taking the census is not explained, but Gad may have rebuked him. Gad was one of those early prophets, like Nathan, who exercised a prophetic ministry but whose utterances were never recorded in a written record like the latter prophets. He brought Yahweh's word and offered David one of three options: (a) three years of famine, (b) three months of fleeing before his enemies, (c) three days of pestilence. David did not choose but cast himself on the mercy of God. This is a sign of true repentance—he left all in God's hands and did not seek to determine the way that might have seemed easiest for him.

It is important to recognize here also that regardless of what or who "incited" David to take the census, he is held accountable for the action, which is judged as sin (cf. also v. 17).

21:15–19 The verb translated in the NIV as "was grieved" (*nḥm*) appears many times in the Old Testament and frequently is translated as "repented" (Gen 6:6; see 1 Sam 15:11,29,35). But at least in human terms God does not repent or change his mind. It is better to think of a divine decree going forth that would be fulfilled unless a change of circumstance came about, such as repentance. In that case there was no need to carry out the threatened judgment. In the incident before us there was evidence of a deep repentance on David's part. In this he was joined by the elders, all clothed in sackcloth. But David's repentance cut deeply into his own conscience since the people were suffering for his sin.[55] At the time the angel of the Lord was standing at the threshing floor of Araunah (or alternatively, Ornan),[56] the prophet Gad was sent to tell David to build an altar to the Lord on the threshing floor of Araunah, the Jebusite. This, of course, had to be negotiated. An interesting difference between the accounts in Chronicles and Samuel is that in 2 Samuel 24 God himself gives the command to David whereas here it is the angel of the Lord who orders the prophet Gad to tell David to build an altar on the threshing floor of Araunah.

21:20–21 Some commentators have seen parallels between this story and the story of Gideon in Judges 6. The themes are similar—the encounter of an angel with a man threshing wheat and the consumption of an offering with a supernatural fire (cf. Judg 6:11–21). There are parallels, to be sure,

---

[55] The text of the Greek LXX for 2 Sam 24:17 and more recently the pieces of Samuel found in the Qumran caves reads, "I am the shepherd who did wrong," which provides an interesting counterpart to, "These are but sheep."

[56] The Hebrew text in vv. 15–16,20–25 and 2 Chr 3:1 uses אׇרְנׇן, "Ornan," which is a regular variant for אֲרַוְנׇה, "Araunah."

but what significance should be attached to these is by no means certain.

21:22–26 There was an urgent need to build an altar to the Lord so that the plague on the people might be stopped. David paid a fairly high price[57] for the land in spite of Araunah's offer and showed himself to be above the selfish conniving that seeks to avoid personal payment or loss (cf. Mal 1:8–14). We are reminded of Abraham's purchase of the cave of Machpelah for Sarah's burial in spite of Ephron's generous response (Gen 23). The text does not indicate whether David personally made the sacrifice or whether a priest was present to officiate, although on superficial reading it appears that David himself made the sacrifice. This seems surprising in light of the Chronicler's concern with ritual purity (contrast 1 Sam 13:1–15). In any case, the consumption of the sacrifice by fire from heaven served to confirm God's acceptance of David's sacrifice (see 1 Kgs 18:36–40) and pointed forward to the successful completion and dedication of the temple (cf. 2 Chr 7:1).

21:27–22:1 The plague was lifted, the angel returned his sword to its sheath, and the site for the temple had been determined. The Chronicler now gives an explanation of why the center of worship in Israel could be moved from Gibeon to Jerusalem. Through the centuries continuity had been preserved. The worship at the altar of the Mosaic tabernacle (cf. Lev 9:24) gave way to the worship at Gibeon and finally at the Jerusalem temple. Thus David could declare, "The house of the LORD God is to be here, and also the altar of burnt offering for Israel." Furthermore, in 2 Chr 3:1 we are told that this site was none other than Moriah, the place where Abraham offered his son Isaac as a sacrifice (Gen 22:2). Many years later Jesus would die in Jerusalem on Calvary, completing the work of atonement and defeating Satan "once for all" (Heb 7:26–28; Col 2:15). The events that led to the choice of this place were of God's doing. This was the place where divine wrath and divine mercy would meet.[58]

6. David's First Speech: Solomon Chosen to Build the Temple (22:2–19)

The Chronicler includes three speeches by David: (1) 22:2–19; (2) 28:1–21; (3) 29:1–9. Chapters 22–29 are unique to Chronicles, having no parallel in the Bible.

---

[57] The discrepancy between the "six hundred shekels of gold" in 1 Chr 21:25 and "fifty shekels of silver" often has been explained on the basis of the different objects in view. Chronicles gives this as the price of "the site," which included land for the whole temple complex, whereas the fifty shekels of silver covered only the threshing floor and the oxen.

[58] See Wilcock, *Message of Chronicles*, 94–96.

(1) Materials Needed for the Building of the Temple (22:2–5)

²So David gave orders to assemble the aliens living in Israel, and from among them he appointed stonecutters to prepare dressed stone for building the house of God. ³He provided a large amount of iron to make nails for the doors of the gateways and for the fittings, and more bronze than could be weighed. ⁴He also provided more cedar logs than could be counted, for the Sidonians and Tyrians had brought large numbers of them to David.

⁵David said, "My son Solomon is young and inexperienced, and the house to be built for the LORD should be of great magnificence and fame and splendor in the sight of all the nations. Therefore I will make preparations for it." So David made extensive preparations before his death.

22:2 The stone probably was limestone, which was readily available near Jerusalem. Indeed, numbers of ancient stone quarries can still be seen in the neighborhood of Jerusalem. David drew upon the resident aliens to prepare stone for the temple structure. The resident aliens appointed stonecutters to prepare dressed stone, large ashlar masonry, for building the house of God. Those resident aliens or sojourners formed an important group in ancient Israel. Israel had significant obligations toward them. They were allowed to join in the Passover, for example. But they were called upon for the permanent corvée, although the Israelites could be called upon for temporary conscription. David appointed Adoniram over the forced labor contingent (2 Sam 20:24), a task he continued under Solomon and Rehoboam (1 Kgs 12:18).[59]

22:3 Iron sounds cheap to us, but in the early Iron Age it was of great value (see Deut 3:11 and 2 Kgs 6:6). These large quantities of metal came from the booty David captured in his wars.

22:4 Over the centuries cedar from Lebanon found its way into many lands for construction of temples, palaces, and other large buildings. Inscriptions in the buildings of Assyria, Babylonia, and other lands bear testimony to this fact.

22:5 One can almost say that the temple was prefabricated by David. He knew that a young man or boy, however intelligent, is not ready for certain jobs. Solomon's age at this time cannot be determined.

(2) David's Charge to Solomon (22:6–16)

⁶Then he called for his son Solomon and charged him to build a house for the LORD, the God of Israel. ⁷David said to Solomon: "My son, I had it in my heart to build a house for the Name of the LORD my God. ⁸But this word of the

---

[59] de Vaux, *Ancient Israel, Its Life and Institutions,* 74–76.

LORD came to me: 'You have shed much blood and have fought many wars. You are not to build a house for my Name, because you have shed much blood on the earth in my sight. [9]But you will have a son who will be a man of peace and rest, and I will give him rest from all his enemies on every side. His name will be Solomon, and I will grant Israel peace and quiet during his reign. [10]He is the one who will build a house for my Name. He will be my son, and I will be his father. And I will establish the throne of his kingdom over Israel forever.'

[11]"Now, my son, the LORD be with you, and may you have success and build the house of the LORD your God, as he said you would. [12]May the LORD give you discretion and understanding when he puts you in command over Israel, so that you may keep the law of the LORD your God. [13]Then you will have success if you are careful to observe the decrees and laws that the LORD gave Moses for Israel. Be strong and courageous. Do not be afraid or discouraged.

[14]"I have taken great pains to provide for the temple of the LORD a hundred thousand talents of gold, a million talents of silver, quantities of bronze and iron too great to be weighed, and wood and stone. And you may add to them. [15]You have many workmen: stonecutters, masons and carpenters, as well as men skilled in every kind of work [16]in gold and silver, bronze and iron—craftsmen beyond number. Now begin the work, and the LORD be with you."

22:6–10 David is here to Solomon much like Moses was to Joshua. David could do all the preparations for the temple but could not build it, just as Moses could not lead Israel into Canaan. A life of violence, even in God's service, had disqualified him. The one who built God's house must be a man of peace. The name "Solomon" (Heb. *šĕlōmōh*) is a cognate of the word for "peace" (*šālôm*). Israel would have peace and quiet during his reign (v. 9). On the other hand, we should not forget that it was David's warfare and many victories that enabled Solomon and the nation to have the peace in which they could build the temple. David was not qualified to build the temple, but he was not thereby condemned in the text.[60]

22:11–13 This invocation includes encouragement, a definition of the task ahead, and the assurance of divine help. It is reminiscent of the charge to Joshua by Moses (Deut 31:23; Josh 1:6–9). In similar fashion Solomon himself prayed for the wisdom necessary for the job that lay ahead of him (1 Kgs 3:9). Without the wisdom that comes from above (Jas 1:5), no one can do God's work.

22:14–16 The list of materials available to Solomon to build the temple (v. 14) and of the wide variety of artisans ready at hand for the work indicated that there need be no further delay. The quantities specified here seem to be exceptionally large. One explanation is that it was a standard figure of speech for stressing the magnificence of the temple and drawing attention to

---

[60] See Wilcock, *Message of Chronicles*, 99–100.

David's vast preparations for the temple that was soon to be erected. This sort of hyperbole is often used in ancient literature and speeches, and the round numbers further imply that they are not to be taken literally. Our western propensity to be precise allows little room for a characteristic feature of the literary methods of the ancient Near East. A comparison may be made with the amount of gold that Solomon's fleet brought to Israel from Ophir (1 Kgs 10:14).[61]

(3) David's Charge to the Leaders of Israel (22:17–19)

[17]Then David ordered all the leaders of Israel to help his son Solomon. [18]He said to them, "Is not the LORD your God with you? And has he not granted you rest on every side? For he has handed the inhabitants of the land over to me, and the land is subject to the LORD and to his people. [19]Now devote your heart and soul to seeking the LORD your God. Begin to build the sanctuary of the LORD God, so that you may bring the ark of the covenant of the LORD and the sacred articles belonging to God into the temple that will be built for the Name of the LORD."

22:17–19 David's charge to Solomon was private, preceding the public assembly at which he addressed the leaders of Israel. He ordered the leaders to help his son Solomon, reminding them that God was with them. His primary charge to them, however, was that they should devote their hearts and souls to the Lord. He knew that if they were faithful to God they would be faithful to Solomon. If one places a human duty above duty to God, one will fail at both.

7. David's Organization of the Priests and Levites (23:1–26:32)

Chapters 23–27 sometimes are looked upon as an interruption, if not an interpolation, in this narrative. In fact, they are very important for showing that David fulfilled all his duties as a good king by seeing to it that the proper worship of the Lord would continue. From the Chronicler's perspective, the account of David's reign would be truncated if this material were not included.[62]

---

[61] L. C. Allen suggests the sense intended by these large numbers is that "no expense was spared in David's generous provision of raw materials (*1, 2 Chronicles,* 151).

[62] See J. W. Wright, "The Legacy of David in Chronicles: The Narrative Function of 1 Chronicles 23–27," *JBL* 110 (1991): 229–42. Wright has examples of similar cultic legacies from Egypt and cites the Nehemiah memoirs as parallel also. According to S.De Vries, the real purpose behind the writing of Chronicles was to establish David as an inspired founder of Israel's worship, alongside Moses, and thereby to increase the legitimacy and standing of the Levites over against the Aaronite priests (S. J. De Vries, "Moses and David as Cult Founders in Chronicles," *JBL* 107 [1988]: 619–39). But it is the subordinate role of the Levites that is stressed in vv. 28,32.

The total preparations for the temple included the allocation of personnel to undertake the various spiritual ministries of the temple. These were more crucial than the material structure alone—a perspective that David understood better than many of his modern Christian counterparts. Chapters 23–26 take up various branches of the Levites (chap. 23), priests (chap. 24), musicians (chap. 25), and the gatekeepers and treasury officials (chap. 26). These chapters form a unit in themselves. It seems likely that the Chronicler used for his composition some traditions that were reduced to writing earlier although in their present form they bear unmistakable signs of the Chronicler's hand.

(1) Divisions of the Levites (23:1–32)

[1]When David was old and full of years, he made his son Solomon king over Israel.

[2]He also gathered together all the leaders of Israel, as well as the priests and Levites. [3]The Levites thirty years old or more were counted, and the total number of men was thirty-eight thousand. [4]David said, "Of these, twenty-four thousand are to supervise the work of the temple of the LORD and six thousand are to be officials and judges. [5]Four thousand are to be gatekeepers and four thousand are to praise the LORD with the musical instruments I have provided for that purpose."

[6]David divided the Levites into groups corresponding to the sons of Levi: Gershon, Kohath and Merari.

[7]Belonging to the Gershonites:
   Ladan and Shimei.
   [8]The sons of Ladan:
   Jehiel the first, Zetham and Joel—three in all.
   [9]The sons of Shimei:
   Shelomoth, Haziel and Haran—three in all.
   These were the heads of the families of Ladan.
[10]And the sons of Shimei:
   Jahath, Ziza, Jeush and Beriah.
   These were the sons of Shimei—four in all.
   [11]Jahath was the first and Ziza the second, but Jeush and Beriah did not have many sons; so they were counted as one family with one assignment.
[12]The sons of Kohath:
   Amram, Izhar, Hebron and Uzziel—four in all.
[13]The sons of Amram:
   Aaron and Moses.
   Aaron was set apart, he and his descendants forever, to consecrate the most holy things, to offer sacrifices before the LORD, to minister

before him and to pronounce blessings in his name forever. ¹⁴The sons of Moses the man of God were counted as part of the tribe of Levi.

¹⁵The sons of Moses:
Gershom and Eliezer.

¹⁶The descendants of Gershom:
Shubael was the first.

¹⁷The descendants of Eliezer:
Rehabiah was the first.
Eliezer had no other sons, but the sons of Rehabiah were very numerous.

¹⁸The sons of Izhar:
Shelomith was the first.

¹⁹The sons of Hebron:
Jeriah the first, Amariah the second, Jahaziel the third and Jekameam the fourth.

²⁰The sons of Uzziel:
Micah the first and Isshiah the second.

²¹The sons of Merari:
Mahli and Mushi.
The sons of Mahli:
Eleazar and Kish.

²²Eleazar died without having sons: he had only daughters. Their cousins, the sons of Kish, married them.

²³The sons of Mushi: Mahli, Eder and Jerimoth—three in all.

²⁴These were the descendants of Levi by their families—the heads of families as they were registered under their names and counted individually, that is, the workers twenty years old or more who served in the temple of the LORD. ²⁵For David had said, "Since the LORD, the God of Israel, has granted rest to his people and has come to dwell in Jerusalem forever, ²⁶the Levites no longer need to carry the tabernacle or any of the articles used in its service." ²⁷According to the last instructions of David, the Levites were counted from those twenty years old or more.

²⁸The duty of the Levites was to help Aaron's descendants in the service of the temple of the LORD: to be in charge of the courtyards, the side rooms, the purification of all sacred things and the performance of other duties at the house of God. ²⁹They were in charge of the bread set out on the table, the flour for the grain offerings, the unleavened wafers, the baking and the mixing, and all measurements of quantity and size. ³⁰They were also to stand every morning to thank and praise the LORD. They were to do the same in the evening ³¹and whenever burnt offerings were presented to the LORD on Sabbaths and at New Moon festivals and at appointed feasts. They were to serve before the LORD regularly in the proper number and in the way prescribed for them.

³²And so the Levites carried out their responsibilities for the Tent of Meet-

ing, for the Holy Place and, under their brothers the descendants of Aaron, for the service of the temple of the LORD.

23:1 This verse seems to be a heading that introduces the final chapters of 1 Chronicles. After the organizational details of chaps. 23–27 this verse is resumed in 28:1. The expression "old and full of years" implies a status of great honor (cf. 29:28; Gen 25:8; 35:29; Job 42:17). It was not that Solomon became king at the very close of David's life. Indeed, there may have been a period of co-regency between David and Solomon based on Egyptian models.[63] The statement means simply that as David grew older and in order to protect the succession, he installed Solomon as king (cf. 1 Kgs 1-2). There is no indication of Solomon's age at this time.

23:2 David gathered the three leading segments of Israelite society— princes, priests, and Levites. These groups were a stereotyped division of the people current at the time (cf. 13:2; 2 Chr 30:25; 35:8; Ezra 2:70). They will be dealt with in the reverse order in the following chapters: Levites (chap. 23), priests (chap. 24), and others (chaps. 25–27).

23:3–6a The first group to be specified was the Levites. The Chronicler was always anxious to give the Levites an important place. Provision for the temple services begins with the Levites, here specified as men thirty years old and upwards. There is no consistency in the age when a man became a ministering Levite. The age of thirty agrees with the age given in Num 4:3 (but see Num 8:24), although later in 1 Chr 23:24,27; 2 Chr 31:17 and Ezra 3:8 it is only twenty. The reason for this is not given, but it seems that some variation in age was allowable for the needs at a particular time, especially where Levitical families were depleted. The two ages given in this chapter could be the result of the Chronicler drawing together material from different eras or we could assume that some tasks required a higher age.[64] Of the thirty-eight thousand listed, twenty-four thousand were set apart to supervise the work of the temple, six thousand were to be officials and judges, four thousand were to be gatekeepers, and four thousand were to be musicians to praise the Lord with musical instruments.

The thirty-eight thousand is larger than the number of Levites given elsewhere in Chronicles. It may, of course, be a way of saying that by David's time the population had grown and was greater also in wealth and power than in the days of Moses. However, there can be no certainty about such suggestions. The Chronicler possibly had access to much earlier material.[65] The "judges" and "officials" represent Levites involved in judicial work.

---

[63] E. Ball, "Co-Regency of David and Solomon (1 Kings 1)," *VT* XXVII (1977): 268–79.

[64] McConville, *I & II Chronicles*, 90, 92.

[65] Williamson, *1 and 2 Chronicles*, 159–60.

These two terms often are found together in the Old Testament. The "officials" perhaps were record keepers. The reference to supervising the work of the temple (v. 4) does not here refer to the construction of the temple but to activities concerned with the discharge of aspects of general administration of the temple and its services of worship.

The organization of the Levites was based on the three traditional families of Levi in the order followed by all lists (Exod 6:17–18; Num 3; 1 Chr 6).

23:6b–11   Gershon's first son was Libni (6:17; Exod 6:17; Num 3:18). His second son, as here, was Shimei. The origin of the name "Ladan" is not known although it appears also in 26:21. He may have been a descendant of Libni, who was prominent in later times. Ladan had three sons, Jehiel, Zetham, and Joel (v. 8). The brother of Ladan, Shimei, had four sons, two of whom had small families (v. 11) and were counted as one family, a strange observation but by its nature suggests authenticity.

23:12–24   The sons of Amram included Aaron and Moses. The line of Aaron was excluded from the Levites because it was the priestly family. Verse 13 contains a small explanatory expansion. On the other hand, Moses is regarded as a Levite. It is not clear whether v. 22 was intended to include Eleazar as a father's house because he had no sons, although Num 27:4 and 36:6 allowed legitimate descent through daughters.

23:25–27   There was a need to change the nature of Levitical service from one of transporting the ark and its implements to one of service in a permanent arrangement in Jerusalem. David had foreseen this. The duty of the Levites was to help Aaron's descendants in the service of the temple. The Levites were assigned cultic responsibilities, particularly in the area of providing music for the services.

23:28–32   The Levitical duties listed here were only on the periphery of the temple cult and reflect less responsibility than in 9:28–32. They appear to be subordinate to the priests, for they are to stand beside the sons of Aaron, that is, to assist them morning and evening when offerings were presented in the temple. Part of their duty was to provide thanksgiving and praise in the temple, that is, to carry out musical duties. If some of the details of this and subsequent chapters appear trivial and even irrelevant to us, they were evidently important to the Chronicler and his postexilic audience. The details of God's relationship with his people are significant in every age. Organization and planning is not necessarily contrary to sincerity in worship. As J. G. McConville has written, "Worship can be sublime and spiritual without becoming disorganized; and the converse is probably not true" (cf. 1 Cor 14:48).[66] These chapters also remind us of the many tasks and the

---

[66] McConville, *I & II Chronicles*, 93.

many people necessary for proper worship and service (cf. 1 Cor 12:14–31).

(2) Divisions of the Priests and the Rest of the Levites (24:1–31)

[1]These were the divisions of the sons of Aaron:

The sons of Aaron were Nadab, Abihu, Eleazar and Ithamar. [2]But Nadab and Abihu died before their father did, and they had no sons; so Eleazar and Ithamar served as the priests. [3]With the help of Zadok a descendant of Eleazar and Ahimelech a descendant of Ithamar, David separated them into divisions for their appointed order of ministering. [4]A larger number of leaders were found among Eleazar's descendants than among Ithamar's, and they were divided accordingly: sixteen heads of families from Eleazar's descendants and eight heads of families from Ithamar's descendants. [5]They divided them impartially by drawing lots, for there were officials of the sanctuary and officials of God among the descendants of both Eleazar and Ithamar.

[6]The scribe Shemaiah son of Nethanel, a Levite, recorded their names in the presence of the king and of the officials: Zadok the priest, Ahimelech son of Abiathar and the heads of families of the priests and of the Levites—one family being taken from Eleazar and then one from Ithamar.

[7]The first lot fell to Jehoiarib,
  the second to Jedaiah,
[8]the third to Harim,
  the fourth to Seorim,
[9]the fifth to Malkijah,
  the sixth to Mijamin,
[10]the seventh to Hakkoz,
  the eighth to Abijah,
[11]the ninth to Jeshua,
  the tenth to Shecaniah,
[12]the eleventh to Eliashib,
  the twelfth to Jakim,
[13]the thirteenth to Huppah,
  the fourteenth to Jeshebeab,
[14]the fifteenth to Bilgah,
  the sixteenth to Immer,
[15]the seventeenth to Hezir,
  the eighteenth to Happizzez,
[16]the nineteenth to Pethahiah,
  the twentieth to Jehezkel,
[17]the twenty-first to Jakin,
  the twenty-second to Gamul,
[18]the twenty-third to Delaiah,
  and the twenty-fourth to Maaziah.

¹⁹This was their appointed order of ministering when they entered the temple of the LORD, according to the regulations prescribed for them by their forefather Aaron, as the LORD, the God of Israel, had commanded him.

²⁰As for the rest of the descendants of Levi:
from the sons of Amram: Shubael;
    from the sons of Shubael: Jehdeiah.
    ²¹As for Rehabiah, from his sons:
    Isshiah was the first.
²²From the Izharites: Shelomoth;
from the sons of Shelomoth: Jahath.
²³The sons of Hebron: Jeriah the first, Amariah the second, Jahaziel the
third and Jekameam the fourth.
²⁴The son of Uzziel: Micah;
from the sons of Micah: Shamir.
²⁵The brother of Micah: Isshiah;
    from the sons of Isshiah: Zechariah.
²⁶The sons of Merari: Mahli and Mushi.
The son of Jaaziah: Beno.
²⁷The sons of Merari:
from Jaaziah: Beno, Shoham, Zaccur and Ibri.
²⁸From Mahli: Eleazar, who had no sons.
²⁹From Kish: the son of Kish:
Jerahmeel.
³⁰And the sons of Mushi: Mahli, Eder and Jerimoth.

These were the Levites, according to their families. ³¹They also cast lots, just as their brothers the descendants of Aaron did, in the presence of King David and of Zadok, Ahimelech, and the heads of families of the priests and of the Levites. The families of the oldest brother were treated the same as those of the youngest.

Chapter 24 moves on to give a description of the priestly courses. Hints from later documents suggest that the priestly order depicted here remained in use for many centuries during the second temple period. This chapter deals first with the priestly divisions of the sons of Aaron (24:1–19) and finally returns to some additional Levites (24:20–31). Twenty-four priestly courses are listed. It has been suggested by some commentators that vv. 1–19 in the midst of material on the Levites is out of place and represents an insertion by a reviser. But it is not wise in principle to assume that because we cannot discern an author's purpose for his literary structure that he did not have one. The section on priests is probably placed here because of the preceding emphasis on the Levites as their helpers "in the service of the temple of the LORD" (23:28).

24:1–2   These divisions of the sons of Aaron follow the biblical tradition found in 1 Chr 6:3; Exod 6:23; Num 3:2–4 with some omissions such as the death of Nadab and Abihu, who died before their father (and before the Lord, Num 3:4). This incident meant that only the families of Eleazar and Ithamar remained for priestly service. Here again the Chronicler has chosen not to include a sinful detail that the informed Jewish reader already would have known.[67] It is not correct to speak of the Chronicler as suppressing this information since there is no indication that he sought to change the historical record. Wilcock compares him to an artist painting a landscape but leaving out an ugly building; he is not trying to fool anyone; he simply does not want anything to distract from the image he is creating.[68]

24:3 Descendants of the two remaining sons of Aaron assisted David in the organization of the priests Zadok, a descendant of Eleazar, and Ahimelech, a descendant of Ithamar (cf. 18:16). Zadok was prominent under both David and Solomon and became firmly established in tradition. He was to become the head of the Zadokite priesthood.[69]

24:4–6 Although the Eleazar line had twice as many representatives as the Ithamar line, duties were divided impartially by drawing lots (cf. 24:31; 25:8; 26:13). The details of the lot drawing are not given, but the larger group was not given any advantage over the smaller since there were officials from both lines. The precise significance of their titles is not certain. The "and" may mean "even," as in, "There were officials of the sanctuary, even officials of God" (v. 5). Or this latter phrase may have a superlative sense as "outstanding leaders." The scribe Shemaiah (not otherwise known), a Levite, recorded the names in the presence of the king and the officials— Zadok the priest, Ahimelech, son of Abiathar, and the heads of the priestly and Levitical families, one family being taken from Eleazar and then one from Ithamar. The alternating draw would continue for the first sixteen names, and the remaining eight would have to come from Eleazar.

24:7–18 A list of twenty-four families is given in these verses. These names represent families and not individuals as such. Some of these names do not occur elsewhere: Seorim, Huppah, Jeshebeab, Happizzez, Gamul, and Delaiah, while Jakim and Pethahiah occur only here as names of priests. The list seems to reflect the final stage in the postexilic development of the priestly courses for which there is evidence. The name Abijah (v. 10) is known in Luke 1:5 as the division to which Zechariah the priest, father of John the Baptist, belonged. After his angelic vision in the temple Zechariah was not able to utter the blessing mentioned in 1 Chr 23:13.

---

[67] Williamson, *1 and 2 Chronicles,* 163.
[68] Wilcock, *Message of Chronicles,* 102.
[69] See R. Corney, "Zadok the Priest," *IDB* 4.428–29.

24:19 This statement is intended to establish the activities of priests prescribed not merely by David but by Aaron their forefather. Ultimately the choice of these priests goes back to Yahweh himself. It is of some interest that in other ancient Near Eastern lands the practice of assigning priests to specific periods (watches) was well known. In some cases such service was hereditary.[70]

24:20–31 The list of Levites here presupposes and updates the list in 23:6–23 by recapitulating parts of it in the same order and extending them by one generation. Thus to the family of Kohath the line of Shubael is extended to Jehdeiah (v. 20); the line Rehabiah, to Isshiah (v. 21); that of Izhar, to Jahath (v. 22). The Hebron line is not changed (v. 23; 23:19); Uzziel extended to Shamir (v. 24), and so on.[71] A new line is added to Merari, that of Jaaziah, who had three sons. Ten more names were added, apparently reflecting the situation at the time of the author. The addition of only one name in most cases suggests a generation later than the list in chap. 23.

(3) The Temple Musicians (25:1–31)

¹David, together with the commanders of the army, set apart some of the sons of Asaph, Heman and Jeduthun for the ministry of prophesying, accompanied by harps, lyres and cymbals. Here is the list of the men who performed this service:

²From the sons of Asaph:
 Zaccur, Joseph, Nethaniah and Asarelah. The sons of Asaph were under the supervision of Asaph, who prophesied under the king's supervision.
³As for Jeduthun, from his sons:
 Gedaliah, Zeri, Jeshaiah, Shimei, Hashabiah and Mattithiah, six in all, under the supervision of their father Jeduthun, who prophesied, using the harp in thanking and praising the LORD.
⁴As for Heman, from his sons:
 Bukkiah, Mattaniah, Uzziel, Shubael and Jerimoth; Hananiah, Hanani, Eliathah, Giddalti and Romamti-Ezer; Joshbekashah, Mallothi, Hothir and Mahazioth. ⁵All these were sons of Heman the king's seer. They were given him through the promises of God to exalt him. God gave Heman fourteen sons and three daughters.
 ⁶All these men were under the supervision of their fathers for the music of the temple of the LORD, with cymbals, lyres and harps, for the ministry at the house of God. Asaph, Jeduthun and Heman were under the supervision of the king. ⁷Along with their relatives—all of them trained and skilled in music for

---

[70] See Myers, *I Chronicles,* 167–68.
[71] These are listed in more detail in Myers, *I Chronicles,* 166.

the LORD—they numbered 288. [8]Young and old alike, teacher as well as student, cast lots for their duties.

[9]The first lot, which was for Asaph, fell to Joseph,

his sons and relatives,	12
the second to Gedaliah,	
he and his relatives and sons,	12
[10]the third to Zaccur,	
his sons and relatives,	12
[11]the fourth to Izri,	
his sons and relatives,	12
[12]the fifth to Nethaniah,	
his sons and relatives,	12
[13]the sixth to Bukkiah,	
his sons and relatives,	12
[14]the seventh to Jesarelah,	
his sons and relatives,	12
[15]the eighth to Jeshaiah,	
his sons and relatives,	12
[16]the ninth to Mattaniah,	
his sons and relatives,	12
[17]the tenth to Shimei,	
his sons and relatives,	12
[18]the eleventh to Azarel,	
his sons and relatives,	12
[19]the twelfth to Hashabiah,	
his sons and relatives,	12
[20]the thirteenth to Shubael,	
his sons and relatives,	12
[21]The fourteenth to Mattithiah,	
his sons and relatives,	12
[22]the fifteenth to Jerimoth,	
his sons and relatives,	12
[23]the sixteenth to Hananiah,	
his sons and relatives,	12
[24]the seventeenth to Joshbekashah,	
his sons and relatives,	12
[25]the eighteenth to Hanani,	
his sons and relatives,	12
[26]the nineteenth to Mallothi,	
his sons and relatives,	12
[27]the twentieth to Eliathah,	
his sons and relatives,	12
[28]the twenty-first to Hothir,	
his sons and relatives,	12

²⁹**the twenty-second to Giddalti,**
    his sons and relatives,   12
³⁰**the twenty-third to Mahazioth,**
    his sons and relatives,   12
³¹**the twenty-fourth to Romamti-Ezer,**
    his sons and relatives,   12

Chapter 25 is devoted to the temple musicians. They are arranged into twenty-four courses (vv. 9–31) like the priests in chap. 24. The chapter falls into two parts, (1) vv. 1–7 and (2) vv. 8–31. The first part arranges the personnel associated with the music of the temple into three groups—the sons of Asaph, the sons of Jeduthun, and the sons of Heman. The Chronicler placed this list close to the Levites (24:20–31) because of their close association in the cult. The genealogies were designed to show how the contemporary occupants of these posts were linked to their origins in the time of David.[72]

The establishment of a temple choir is in one sense surprising. Elsewhere the Chronicler is profoundly concerned that the worship be carried on in strict accord with the law, which makes no provision for a choir. How then does he justify a levitical choir in David's reign? J. W. Kleinig observes that the Chronicler uses several strategies to support the validity of this institution. Above all, it was authorized by a prophetic word from Nathan and Gad (2 Chr 29:25). Three other sources of justification for the choir, however, are possible. First, in Num 10:10 the priests are to proclaim the Lord's grace by blowing trumpets at the altar, and this serves to vindicate the use of music in praise. Second, Deut 10:8 and 18:5 say that the Levites "pronounce blessings" in God's name (cf. Deut 18:5); hence the use of a levitical choir is reasonable. Third, the general admonitions in Scripture to rejoice in God's presence allow for worship in song.[73]

25:1   The translation of v. 1 presents some difficulties. David's helpers were "commanders of the army" or perhaps "cult officials" (AB), "chiefs of the service" (RSV), or "chief officers" (NEB). No doubt these were some of the leaders of the Levites. The Hebrew word for "army" is flexible in meaning. Members of the three families of Asaph, Jeduthun, and Heman—were set apart for service of various kinds, prophesying accompanied by harps, lyres, and cymbals (vv. 2–3,5; see also 2 Chr 20:14; 29:25–30; 35:15). The nature of their prophesying is not spelled out. But the Levites, or at least their leaders, are referred to with prophetic terminology such as the verb

---

[72] R. Braun, 1 Chronicles, WBC (Waco: Word, 1986), 243. See E. L. Curtis and A. A. Madden, *The Books of Chronicles,* ICC (London: T & T Clark, 1910), 275–76.

[73] J. W. Kleinig, "The Divine Institution of the Lord's Song in Chronicles," *JSOT* 55 (1992): 75–83.

"prophesy" (vv. 1–3) and the noun "seer" (v. 5). At least we are to understand that through the ministry and music of the Levites, God revealed his
will to the people, and the people gave thanks and praise to him (v. 3; cf.
Num 11:25–30). Some commentators postulate a class of cultic prophets in
preexilic Israel with whom the Levitical singers stood in direct continuity.[74]
It is noteworthy that the prophesying was done "under the supervision" of
temple personnel. In other words, even the prophetic gift was not allowed to
disrupt the ceremony and worship in the temple. Similarly, Paul abhorred
chaotic worship done in the name of the Spirit (1 Cor 14).

The musical instruments listed here are variously translated: "harps, lyres
and cymbals" (NIV); "lyres, harps, and cymbals" (RSV); "zithers, harps and
cymbals" (Myers); "harps, lutes and cymbals" (NEB). In a number of areas
of translation there are similar problems—plants, precious stones, diseases,
clothing, and others. We lack specific samples in many cases.

25:2 Generally speaking the names recorded in chap. 25 are recorded
elsewhere as levitical singers. Asharelah may be a conflation of "Asharel"
and "these are" in Hebrew.

25:3 The NIV inserts "Shimei" in accordance with the LXX and a
Hebrew manuscript (see NIV text note and cf. v. 17).

25:4–5 The fact that Heman was the king's seer keeps the motif of
prophecy prominent among these singers (25:1–3,5). The gift of many children to Heman, fourteen sons and three daughters, emphasized God's blessing on him. The names in the second half of v. 4, namely, the last nine of
Heman's sons, differ from the first five and from the usual form of Hebrew
names. For example, Giddalti and Romamti look like verb forms, although
they were regarded as proper names by the author and were seen as necessary
to complete the fourteen sons of Heman.

Some regard vv. 4–5 as a poetic construction, perhaps part of a psalm
verse, used in the manner of 16:8–36. J. M. Myers' translation is:

> Be gracious to me, Yahweh, be gracious to me;
> My God art thou;
> I have magnified, and I will exalt [my] helper;
> Sitting [in] adversity I said,
> Clear signs give plentifully.[75]

Myers suggests that we have here a catalog of five "incipits," that is, the
first lines of five separate psalms, which served as their titles. Williamson
suggests that members of five separate families or sections of guilds were

---

[74] A. R. Johnson, *The Cultic Prophet in Ancient Israel* (Cardiff: University of Wales, 1944).
See 2 Chr 20:14–17. See also Japhet, *1 & 2 Chronicles,* 440–41.

[75] Myers, *I Chronicles,* 173; cf. Braun, *1 Chronicles,* 244–45.

named after the openings of psalms they were accustomed to singing regularly.[76]

25:6   This verse is a conclusion to vv. 4–5 and is parallel to vv. 2b and 3b. The names of the three leaders are lacking in the LXX and are often omitted by commentators. Such repetitions may simply indicate a stylistic feature of the Chronicler's writing.

25:7–8   The number 288 represents twenty-four courses of twelve each. There evidently was some kind of program of instruction for these singer-musicians although no details are given.

25:9–31   As S. Japhet has noted, the singers are the only group in these chapters to be identified by both descent (vv. 2–5) and division (vv. 9–31).[77] The order of the divisions is closely related to the first list in that the sons of Asaph formed divisions one, three, five, and seven; the sons of Jeduthun formed divisions two, four, eight, ten, twelve, and fourteen; and the sons of Heman formed divisions six, nine, eleven, thirteen, and fifteen through twenty-four (accounting for spelling variation; see NIV text notes).[78] Such an arrangement shows how the lots were cast, alternating between two groups beginning with Asaph and Jeduthun.[79]

(4) The Gatekeepers (26:1–19)

¹**The divisions of the gatekeepers:**
   From the Korahites: Meshelemiah son of Kore,
   one of the sons of Asaph.
²**Meshelemiah had sons:**
   Zechariah the firstborn,
   Jediael the second,
   Zebadiah the third,
   Jathniel the fourth,
³**Elam the fifth,**
   Jehohanan the sixth and Eliehoenai the seventh.
⁴**Obed-Edom also had sons:**
   Shemaiah the firstborn,
   Jehozabad the second,
   Joah the third,
    Sacar the fourth,
   Nethanel the fifth,

---

[76] Williamson, *1 and 2 Chronicles*, 167.
[77] S. Japhet, *I & II Chronicles*, OTL (Louisville: Westminster/John Knox, 1994), 457.
[78] See chart in Williamson, *1 and 2 Chronicles*, 168.
[79] Japhet, *I & II Chronicles*, 447.

⁵Ammiel the sixth,
Issachar the seventh
and Peullethai the eighth.
(For God had blessed Obed-Edom.)

⁶His son Shemaiah also had sons,
who were leaders in their father's family because they were very capable
men. ⁷The sons of Shemaiah: Othni, Rephael, Obed and Elzabad; his relatives Elihu and Semakiah were also able men. ⁸All these were descendants of Obed-Edom; they and their sons and their relatives were
capable men with the strength to do the work—descendants of Obed-
Edom, 62 in all.
⁹Meshelemiah had sons and relatives, who were able men—18 in all.

¹⁰Hosah the Merarite had sons: Shimri the first (although he was not the
firstborn, his father had appointed him the first), ¹¹Hilkiah the second,
Tabaliah the third and Zechariah the fourth. The sons and relatives of
Hosah were 13 in all.
¹²These divisions of the gatekeepers, through their chief men, had duties for
ministering in the temple of the LORD, just as their relatives had. ¹³Lots were
cast for each gate, according to their families, young and old alike.
¹⁴The lot for the East Gate fell to Shelemiah. Then lots were cast for his son
Zechariah, a wise counselor, and the lot for the North Gate fell to him. ¹⁵The
lot for the South Gate fell to Obed-Edom, and the lot for the storehouse fell to
his sons. ¹⁶The lots for the West Gate and the Shalleketh Gate on the upper
road fell to Shuppim and Hosah.
Guard was alongside of guard: ¹⁷There were six Levites a day on the east,
four a day on the north, four a day on the south and two at a time at the storehouse. ¹⁸As for the court to the west, there were four at the road and two at the
court itself.
¹⁹These were the divisions of the gatekeepers who were descendants of
Korah and Merari.

The list of gatekeepers follows the list of singers. In its present form chap.
26 can be divided into two sections: (1) a genealogically based list of gatekeepers (vv. 1–11) and their duties (vv. 12–19) and (2) a further listing of
Levites and their duties (vv. 20–32). The gatekeepers were composed of the
sons of Korah (vv. 1–3,9), that is, Kohathites through the line of Izhar (6:22–
25); the Obed-Edomites (vv. 4–8), for whom no genealogical connection
with the Levites is made; and the sons of Merari (vv. 10–11). The appointment of these by lot is given in vv. 12–19. Other appointments of treasurers
and judges follow in vv. 20–32.
Various questions have been raised about the literary arrangement of
these individuals. Verses 4–8 appear to represent a strange intrusion into the
family of Meshelemiah, which is resumed at v. 9. The reason for this is not

clear. Also there is an unexpected imbalance in the number of names. Obed-Edom has sixty-two (v. 8) whereas Meshelemiah has only eighteen (v. 9) and Hosah thirteen (v. 11). The gatekeepers are distributed among three families, but only two are linked with the Levitical genealogies, namely, Meshelemiah through Korah (v. 1) and Hosah through Merari (v. 10). Obed-Edom (v. 4) is not linked to the normal Levitical families.

What precisely did the gatekeepers do? They have generally been regarded by commentators as "cultic officials of a more or less peripheral nature,"[80] and yet they were regarded as important and were classified as Levites, even if of a somewhat lower order. Recent study, however, suggests that the gatekeepers were a paramilitary security force. They possessed three significant roles in the Jerusalem temple-state: (1) the governance of the state, (2) the administration of temple revenue, and (3) the maintenance of the temple and its paraphernalia. There is evidence for this in 1 Chr 26:1–19, and further confirmation is found in the activities of these individuals throughout Chronicles.[81] This information may be gained both in the list of names (vv. 1–11) and in their placement (vv. 12–18). They were stationed at entry ways to buildings and intersections within the city. They functioned as guards for the temple and its precincts from theft or from illegal entry into sacred areas. The vocabulary used by the Chronicler in relation to the gate-keepers ties them firmly to the Judean military establishment. Some of the soldiers who fought in David's army in 1 Chronicles 12 were Levites (1 Chr 12:27), and priests (1 Chr 12:28), including Zadok, were described in military terms. The priests and Levites were thus related to David's military organization in 1 Chronicles 12, which explains why chap. 27 fits into these chapters.

26:1–3 Gatekeepers are mentioned in 9:17–27, one of whom was Ebiasaph (9:19), son of Korah. In this verse Meshelemiah is listed as a descendant of Asaph and also as a Korahite. The Korahites belonged to the Levitical family of Kohath (cf. 6:22,37–38), but Asaph belonged to the family of Gershom (cf. 6:39–43). For "Asaph" here we should read "Ebiasaph," as in 9:19 and the LXX.

26:4–9 The list of Obed-Edom and his eight sons comes next. Obed-Edom appears as a musician in 15:18,24, and 16:38 groups him with Hosah among the gatekeepers. His large family provokes the comment that God had blessed him. This also may point back to 13:14, which states that the ark was taken to Obed-Edom's house after the Philistines returned it to Israel. He is known there as Obed-Edom the Gittite, a person from Gath. On two

---

[80] Myers, *I Chronicles,* 176.
[81] Wright, "Guarding the Gates," 69–81.

grounds, therefore, he was mentioned because he provided shelter for the ark and enjoyed God's blessing in the gift of a large family. We have drawn attention to the apparently intrusive reference of Obed-Edom and his sons into the family of Meshelemiah between vv. 3 and 8 and to the fact that he is not linked to any Levitical family. The description of Obed-Edom's descendants as "able men" (v. 7) and of Meshelemiah's descendants also as "able" men (v. 9) is further evidence of the military character of these people.

The figure sixty-two (v. 8) differs slightly from 16:38, which has sixty-eight. We have no way of knowing which figure is correct.[82] Verse 9 picks up after v. 3. The reason for the insertion of vv. 4–8 is not clear to us now.

26:10 Hosah, of the family of Merari, is known from 16:38, where he also is named as a gatekeeper in association with Obed-Edom. His father named him as "firstborn" though he was not firstborn. This practice is known elsewhere in the Old Testament (cf. Gen 48:14).

26:12–13 The gatekeepers were assigned to various gates by lot. The mention of "the temple of the LORD" shows that the material has a post-David influence. Lots were cast for each gate according to their families (cf. 1 Chr 7:11; 11:10) to judge from the vocabulary.

26:14–15 The duties were distributed by gate. We are told little about the gates of the first temple (Solomon's temple), although conjectures have been made on the basis of later temples like Ezekiel's visionary temple and Herod's temple (cf. Ezek 43). The gate of Shalleketh is not mentioned elsewhere. Second Chronicles 25:24 reveals the content of Obed-Edom's storehouse, where it is said that Jehoash of Israel took all the gold and silver and all the articles found in the temple of God that had been in the care of Obed-Edom. In 9:21 Zechariah is described as the gatekeeper to the Tent of Meeting.

26:16 Shuppim seems to be a dittograph of the preceding word and is deleted by many commentators.[83] To preserve the pattern of names in these verses, only one name is needed here. Some argue that there may have been no south gate in the period of Solomon's temple because the palace adjoined it on that side and no guard was needed. However, there is a reference to a south gate in Ezek 40:24,28 as part of a vision of things to come. In any case it would be important to have a guard at an entrance to the palace.

26:17–18 The meaning of the Hebrew word for "court," *parbar,* is unknown. The KJV gives this verse the memorable translation, "At Parbar westward, four at the causeway and two at the Parbar." The Temple Scroll from Qumran suggests this was an area of freestanding pillars to the west of

---

[82] As Williamson notes, both 62 and 68 are "orthographically similar" in Hebrew, hence the difference (*1 and 2 Chronicles,* 170).

[83] Ibid., 171.

the sanctuary used in connection with various types of offering.[84] The use of obscure terminology, by the way, indicates that the Chronicler had knowledge of the temple beyond what we now possess and lends credibility to his account.[85]

26:19   Only two families are mentioned here, the Korahites (i.e., the Kohathites) and the Merarites. These verses are best seen as a conclusion to vv. 1–3 and 9–11. The sons of Obed-Edom were attached to this list of Kohathites through Korah. There are topographical difficulties in reference to the gates. The original writer had an intimate knowledge of the temple precincts, and he took such knowledge for granted in the reader.

(1) Treasurers and Other Officials (26:20–32)

²⁰**Their fellow Levites were in charge of the treasuries of the house of God and the treasuries for the dedicated things.**

²¹**The descendants of Ladan, who were Gershonites through Ladan and who were heads of families belonging to Ladan the Gershonite, were Jehieli,** ²²**the sons of Jehieli, Zetham and his brother Joel. They were in charge of the treasuries of the temple of the LORD.**

²³**From the Amramites, the Izharites, the Hebronites and the Uzzielites:**

²⁴**Shubael, a descendant of Gershom son of Moses, was the officer in charge of the treasuries.** ²⁵**His relatives through Eliezer: Rehabiah his son, Jeshaiah his son, Joram his son, Zicri his son and Shelomith his son.** ²⁶**Shelomith and his relatives were in charge of all the treasuries for the things dedicated by King David, by the heads of families who were the commanders of thousands and commanders of hundreds, and by the other army commanders.** ²⁷**Some of the plunder taken in battle they dedicated for the repair of the temple of the LORD.** ²⁸**And everything dedicated by Samuel the seer and by Saul son of Kish, Abner son of Ner and Joab son of Zeruiah, and all the other dedicated things were in the care of Shelomith and his relatives.**

²⁹**From the Izharites: Kenaniah and his sons were assigned duties away from the temple, as officials and judges over Israel.**

³⁰**From the Hebronites: Hashabiah and his relatives—seventeen hundred able men—were responsible in Israel west of the Jordan for all the work of the LORD and for the king's service.** ³¹**As for the Hebronites, Jeriah was their chief according to the genealogical records of their families. In the fortieth year of David's reign a search was made in the records, and capable men among the Hebronites were**

---

[84] Williamson, *1 and 2 Chronicles,* 171; Braun, *1 Chronicles,* 249, v. 18a.

[85] Wilcock, *Message of Chronicles,* 106–7.

found at Jazer in Gilead. [32]Jeriah had twenty-seven hundred relatives, who were able men and heads of families, and King David put
them in charge of the Reubenites, the Gadites and the half-tribe of
Manasseh for every matter pertaining to God and for the affairs of
the king.

26:20–28 A group of treasurers and other officials concludes chap. 26.
It is a single unit comprising a list of fellow Levites. Two treasuries are distinguished, those of "the house of God" (vv. 21–22) and those of "the dedicated things" (vv. 25–28). Shubael, a Kohathite from the family of Amram
(cf. 23:12–18), is specially noted as the officer in charge of the treasuries,
which probably means both types of treasury (v. 39).

Shelomith and his relatives were in charge of the spoils of war (v. 27).
Treasures accumulated by great figures of the past—Samuel, the seer; Saul,
son of Kish; Abner; and Joab—were included. The reference to Saul does
not indicate any approval of Saul as a person but merely as one who
acquired spoils taken in battle.

26:29–32 The descendants of Izhar and Hebron were assigned "duties
away from the temple, as officials and judges over Israel." These outside
duties evidently were different from "the king's service" (v. 30) and "the
affairs of the king" (v. 32), both of which were taken over by the Hebronites.
The descendants of Izhar thus performed a judicial role. The "officials" were
the "helpers" of the judges, a kind of subordinate executive. The Hebronites
(vv. 30–32) may have been responsible for religious and secular taxes.[86]
Clearly the Levites had a much broader role than that of subordinate temple
servants.

A search of the records in the last year of David's reign, his fortieth (cf.
1 Kgs 2:11; 1 Chr 29:27), revealed that there were Hebronites living at Jazer,
one of the Levitical cities (6:81). Its precise location is uncertain though it
may be Khirbet Gazzir near the city of Salt. The town once belonged to
Sihon, king of the Amorites (Num 21:32).

8. David's Organization: Civil and Military Arrangements (27:1–34)

This chapter is composed of four separate, perhaps originally unrelated
lists: (1) commanders of the monthly courses (vv. 1–15), (2) officers of the
tribes (vv. 16–24), (3) stewards of David's property (vv. 25–31), and (4)
David's advisors (vv. 32–34).

Chapter 26 concludes by naming those Levites who were assigned to
semisecular duties. Chapter 27 moves naturally to other non-Levitical mili-

---

[86]Williamson, *1 and 2 Chronicles,* 173.

tary and administrative personnel. But while the contents of chaps. 23–26 deal mainly with preparations for the construction of the temple, chap. 27 has little if anything to do with the temple or the Levites. However, as observed at chap. 26 regarding the gatekeepers, there was a close connection between religious and military orders. Furthermore, J. Sailhamer has suggested that chaps. 23–27 are outlined in reverse by the statement in 23:2 that David "gathered together [organized] all the *leaders* of Israel, as well as the *priests* and *Levites*."[87] Some regard the chapter, however, as a series of appendixes included at the end of the account of David's reign to round out the record and to take note of some important features of his reign not mentioned in earlier chapters.

(1) The Commanders of the Monthly Relays (27:1–15)

[1]**This is the list of the Israelites—heads of families, commanders of thousands and commanders of hundreds, and their officers, who served the king in all that concerned the army divisions that were on duty month by month throughout the year. Each division consisted of 24,000 men.**

[2]**In charge of the first division, for the first month, was Jashobeam son of Zabdiel. There were 24,000 men in his division.** [3]**He was a descendant of Perez and chief of all the army officers for the first month.**
[4]**In charge of the division for the second month was Dodai the Ahohite; Mikloth was the leader of his division. There were 24,000 men in his division.**
[5]**The third army commander, for the third month, was Benaiah son of Jehoiada the priest. He was chief and there were 24,000 men in his division.** [6]**This was the Benaiah who was a mighty man among the Thirty and was over the Thirty. His son Ammizabad was in charge of his division.**
[7]**The fourth, for the fourth month, was Asahel the brother of Joab; his son Zebadiah was his successor. There were 24,000 men in his division.**
[8]**The fifth, for the fifth month, was the commander Shamhuth the Izrahite. There were 24,000 men in his division.**
[9]**The sixth, for the sixth month, was Ira the son of Ikkesh the Tekoite. There were 24,000 men in his division.**
[10]**The seventh, for the seventh month, was Helez the Pelonite, an Ephraimite. There were 24,000 men in his division.**
[11]**The eighth, for the eighth month, was Sibbecai the Hushathite, a Zerahite. There were 24,000 men in his division.**
[12]**The ninth, for the ninth month, was Abiezer the Anathothite, a Ben-**

---

[87] J. Sailhamer, *First & Second Chronicles*, 56.

jamite. There were 24,000 men in his division.

[13]The tenth, for the tenth month, was Maharai the Netophathite, a Zerahite. There were 24,000 men in his division.

[14]The eleventh, for the eleventh month, was Benaiah the Pirathonite, an Ephraimite. There were 24,000 men in his division.

[15]The twelfth, for the twelfth month, was Heldai the Netophathite, from the family of Othniel. There were 24,000 men in his division.

27:1 The names of the commanders are parallel to those in the list of David's heroes in 11:11–47 and 2 Sam 23:8–39.[88] This verse should be seen as a heading to vv. 2–15 rather than to the whole chapter. The groups mentioned—"heads of families," "commanders of hundreds, and their officers"—are well known in military contexts elsewhere and so form an appropriate heading to the military material of vv. 2–15. Many commentators think that there is a certain artificiality about this list. But surely David set up arrangements to call fighting men together (1 Chr 21) into a citizen's army. The compiler of this record presents a carefully ordered statement about David's army—twelve divisions each consisting of twenty-four thousand men, each obligated to serve the king's army for a month a year, each commanded by an officer bearing the name of one of David's heroes. The army was arranged in perfect order in a strictly systematic scheme.

27:2–3 Jashobeam, described here as the son of Zabdiel, a descendant of Perez, is referred to as "a Hacmonite" in 11:11. He is introduced as the chief of all the army officers for the first month. This formula is repeated with slight variations in the remaining verses in this section.

27:4–6 Benaiah, son of Jehoiada, is listed as a valiant fighter from Kabzeel who performed great exploits in 11:22.[89]

27:7–15 Asahel, the brother of Joab, met his death before David became king (2 Sam 2:18–23). In fact, his son and successor Zebadiah commanded the division. Shamhuth, the Izrahite, appears in v. 11 as Zerahite. The origins of several of the commanders show how they were drawn from various parts of the land: Tekoa (v. 9), Ephraim (v. 10), Anathoth (v. 12), and so forth.

(2) The Officers of the Tribes (27:16–24)

[16]The officers over the tribes of Israel:
over the Reubenites: Eliezer son of Zicri;

---

[88] A convenient comparison of 1 Chr 11:10–31 and the present chapter is provided in Braun, *1 Chronicles,* 259.

[89] The Hebrew text adds the phrase "and his division and Mikloth the leader" after "Dodai the Ahohite," but it is lacking in the LXX text, and some translators omit it. The NIV endeavors to accommodate the variations.

over the Simeonites: Shephatiah son of Maacah;
¹⁷over Levi: Hashabiah son of Kemuel;
   over Aaron: Zadok;
¹⁸over Judah: Elihu, a brother of David;
   over Issachar: Omri son of Michael;
¹⁹over Zebulun: Ishmaiah son of Obadiah;
   over Naphtali: Jerimoth son of Azriel;
²⁰over the Ephraimites: Hoshea son of Azaziah;
   over half the tribe of Manasseh: Joel son of Pedaiah;
²¹over the half-tribe of Manasseh in Gilead: Iddo son of Zechariah;
   over Benjamin: Jaasiel son of Abner;
²²over Dan: Azarel son of Jeroham.
   These were the officers over the tribes of Israel.

²³David did not take the number of the men twenty years old or less, because the LORD had promised to make Israel as numerous as the stars in the sky. ²⁴Joab son of Zeruiah began to count the men but did not finish. Wrath came on Israel on account of this numbering, and the number was not entered in the book of the annals of King David.

27:16 The order of the tribes in these verses does not correspond exactly to any other listing in the Old Testament, although the verses contain some parallels with 1 Chr 2:1–2 and Numbers 1, especially vv. 20–22.[90] The present list differs from the list in 1 Chronicles 2 in several ways. It places Napthali in Dan's position and sets Dan at the end of the list; Joseph in 1 Chronicles 2 becomes Ephraim, Half-Manasseh (east), and Half-Manasseh (west); and Gad and Asher in 1 Chronicles 2 are lacking in 1 Chronicles 27, probably to maintain the number of tribes at twelve. Differences between these lists make it clear that although there is general correspondence between them there was no slavish borrowing, although 1 Chronicles 27 is closer to 1 Chronicles 2 than to Numbers 1.

The similarity of style to Num 1:1–19 is perhaps another indication that the Chronicler considered David to be a second Moses (see the discussion of 22:11–13).

27:17 The tribe of Levi is counted as one of the tribes although it was set apart from the "secular" tribes because of its involvement with religious duties. It is something of a surprise, however, to discover that Aaron is listed as a tribe of which the leader was Zadok. No other evidence indicates that Aaron was ever reckoned as a tribe separate from Levi. Another fact is that the father of Zadok is not mentioned. Why these individuals were presented in this way is not clear, but perhaps the Chronicler intended to enhance the

---

[90] A useful comparative table is given in Braun, *1 Chronicles,* 260.

status of the Aaronic family.

27:18–22   There is no "Elihu" mentioned among David's brothers in the genealogy of 1 Chr 2:13–15. Either Eliab is meant (as in the LXX) or Elihu is the eighth brother not listed in the genealogy (1 Sam 16:10–11; 17:12). Perhaps also "brother" was used in the sense of "relative."

27:23–24   If one were to read these verses in isolation, they would imply that Joab was to blame for the census and that David was innocent. But this is an allusion to the account in chap. 21 where Joab acted under David's orders (21:2). Perhaps this points out the need for exercising caution in reading the Bible: the impression we get from one passage may not be the whole story. The census was intended for men twenty years old or more (cf. Num 1:3). The present text states that Joab did not finish; from 21:5–6 we learn that he did not count Levi and Benjamin.

(3) The Stewards of Crown Property (27:25–31)

²⁵Azmaveth son of Adiel was in charge of the royal storehouses.

Jonathan son of Uzziah was in charge of the storehouses in the outlying districts, in the towns, the villages and the watchtowers.

²⁶Ezri son of Kelub was in charge of the field workers who farmed the land.

²⁷Shimei the Ramathite was in charge of the vineyards.

Zabdi the Shiphmite was in charge of the produce of the vineyards for the wine vats.

²⁸Baal-Hanan the Gederite was in charge of the olive and sycamore-fig trees in the western foothills.

Joash was in charge of the supplies of olive oil.

²⁹Shitrai the Sharonite was in charge of the herds grazing in Sharon.
   Shaphat son of Adlai was in charge of the herds in the valleys.

³⁰Obil the Ishmaelite was in charge of the camels.
Jehdeiah the Meronothite was in charge of the donkeys.

³¹Jaziz the Hagrite was in charge of the flocks.
All these were the officials in charge of King David's property.

There is no indication of formal taxation in the modern sense. Crown expenditure was met by income from crown property. Kings in the ancient Near East acquired large areas of land, often as a result of military conquest,[91] and drew on these resources for state expenses. These verses provide an interesting insight into the range of income-producing activities that provided the economic strength of the kingdom. Exactly twelve names are

[91] de Vaux, *Ancient Israel*, 124–26.

listed, conforming to the pattern of twelves elsewhere in Chronicles.

27:25   Storehouses for spoils of war were set up in many areas. We may have a glimpse into the nature of these in excavated storehouses at Megiddo, Beersheba, and elsewhere.

27:26–31   The management of crown property also was important—the text mentions the farmers (v. 26), the vineyards and the wineries (v. 27), the olive and sycamore-fig trees and the production of olive oil (v. 28), the cattle herds (v. 29), the camels and she-asses (v. 30), and the flocks (v. 31). The far-reaching agricultural and pastoral activities of the king are striking, but the king needed considerable support for the maintenance of his court and his administration. All this wealth enhanced the prestige of the king and bore testimony to the way God had blessed his loyal and faithful servant. Some of these activities have been illustrated by modern archaeological excavations. Numerous ancient olive vats have come to light. Ancient quarries bear testimony to building activities. Excavations at Gibeon have uncovered a winery with wine jars, wine presses, and fermenters.[92]

(4) David's Personal Counselors (27:32–34)

[32]Jonathan, David's uncle, was a counselor, a man of insight and a scribe. Jehiel son of Hacmoni took care of the king's sons.

[33]Ahithophel was the king's counselor.

Hushai the Arkite was the king's friend. [34]Ahithophel was succeeded by Jehoiada son of Benaiah and by Abiathar.

Joab was the commander of the royal army.

Along with public counselors and administrative officials (18:14–17; cf. 2 Sam 8:15–18; 20:23–26), David had private advisers.

27:32   "Jonathan, David's uncle," is not otherwise known. We cannot be certain all that was involved in being a scribe during David's time. He was not necessarily in the same profession as the later scribes but perhaps was a secretary in the more general sense. Jehiel the Hacmonite is not otherwise known.

27:33   Ahithophel was the well-known counselor of David who committed suicide when his counsel was rejected (2 Sam 16:23; 17:23). He defected to Absalom during Absalom's rebellion. Hushai, the Arkite, remained loyal to David (2 Sam 15:32ff.). The description of him as "the king's friend" may have referred to a specific office, as in Egypt.

---

[92] W. L. Reed, "Gideon," *Archaeology and Old Testament Study,* ed. D. W. Thomas (Oxford: Clarendon, 1967), 234–35, 241.

27:34 Jehoiada, son of Benaiah (not otherwise known), and Abiathar, a long-standing associate of David (1 Sam 22:20–23), succeeded Ahithophel. Abiathar is not here called a priest; perhaps the writer believed that legitimate priesthood was assumed only through the line of Zadok, Abiathar's rival. Joab was not a close friend of David, but perhaps his skills were such that David could not afford to dismiss him. He incurred David's wrath for the murder of Abner, the previous commander (2 Sam 3:29,39; 1 Kgs 2:5–6,32).

With this list of the king's inner circle of advisors and counselors the description of David's administration comes to a close. The whole picture that emerges gives expression to the belief that Israel's total religious and governmental structure was inaugurated by David and provided a pattern for the future. The subsequent centuries showed that the pattern was not as static as may appear at first sight but was open to the possibility of change and development.

9. David's Final Instructions: His Second Speech (28:1–21)

Already in 22:6–16 David delivered a private charge to Solomon. In chap. 28 he resumes the thought of chap. 22, which was interrupted by chaps. 23–27. Now David summoned the people and addressed them as well as his son Solomon. There was a public commissioning of Solomon (28:1–10) and the handing over of the plans for the temple (28:11–21).

The chapter, after a brief introduction (vv. 1–2a), falls into three parts: (1) David's presentation of Solomon as the temple builder (vv. 2–10); (2) the temple plans are transferred to Solomon (vv. 11–19); and (3) the concluding exhortation is given (vv. 20–21). In both content and structure David's speech here is closely related to chap. 22 although there are differences.[93] It is not surprising to find these parallels since the subject matter is similar.

(1) Address to the People and to Solomon (28:1–10)

¹David summoned all the officials of Israel to assemble at Jerusalem: the officers over the tribes, the commanders of the divisions in the service of the king, the commanders of thousands and commanders of hundreds, and the officials in charge of all the property and livestock belonging to the king and his sons, together with the palace officials, the mighty men and all the brave warriors.

²King David rose to his feet and said: "Listen to me, my brothers and my people. I had it in my heart to build a house as a place of rest for the ark of the covenant of the LORD, for the footstool of our God, and I made plans to build

---

[93] A useful comparison of chap. 22 and chap. 28 is given in Braun, *1 Chronicles,* 267.

it. ³But God said to me, 'You are not to build a house for my Name, because you are a warrior and have shed blood.'

⁴"Yet the LORD, the God of Israel, chose me from my whole family to be king over Israel forever. He chose Judah as leader, and from the house of Judah he chose my family, and from my father's sons he was pleased to make me king over all Israel. ⁵Of all my sons—and the LORD has given me many— he has chosen my son Solomon to sit on the throne of the kingdom of the LORD over Israel. ⁶He said to me: 'Solomon your son is the one who will build my house and my courts, for I have chosen him to be my son, and I will be his father. ⁷I will establish his kingdom forever if he is unswerving in carrying out my commands and laws, as is being done at this time.'

⁸"So now I charge you in the sight of all Israel and of the assembly of the LORD, and in the hearing of our God: Be careful to follow all the commands of the LORD your God, that you may possess this good land and pass it on as an inheritance to your descendants forever.

⁹"And you, my son Solomon, acknowledge the God of your father, and serve him with wholehearted devotion and with a willing mind, for the LORD searches every heart and understands every motive behind the thoughts. If you seek him, he will be found by you; but if you forsake him, he will reject you forever. ¹⁰Consider now, for the LORD has chosen you to build a temple as a sanctuary. Be strong and do the work."

28:1 This verse repeats the material of 23:2. It is a literary device designed to resume the narrative from chap. 23 after the inclusion of the important data of chaps. 23–27.

28:2 "Listen to me" (šĕmāʿûnî) is plural imperative. Plural verb forms are used throughout v. 8 when David addressed the whole nation. Here David saw the assembly as "my brothers and my people." In a brief historical résumé David declares that it had been in his heart to build a house as a place of rest for the ark of the covenant of Yahweh so that God might be among his people. The ark is here called God's footstool as in cf. Ps 132:7.

28:3 These ideas are a reiteration of words in 22:8–9.

28:4–7 David legitimized his dynasty both retrospectively and prospectively by looking backward to the selection of Judah as the ruling tribe and forward to the selection of Solomon as his successor. The selection of Judah is recounted in Gen 49:8–12.[94] The dynastic oracle of Nathan (2 Sam 7) also lies in the background of this speech. David also sought to preclude the possibility that rivals would try to take the throne upon his death. Reverting to God's words to Nathan (17:12–13; 22:10), David asserted that Solomonic succession fulfilled the precise intention of God. At the same time, he reminded them all that the continued success of the dynasty depended upon faithfulness to God.

---

[94] See D. A. Garrett, *Rethinking Genesis* (Grand Rapids: Baker, 1991), 173–76.

28:8 The use of plural verb forms in the Hebrew behind "be careful to follow all the commands of the Lord your God, that you may possess this good land and pass it on as an inheritance to your descendants forever" indicates that this exhortation is still part of the address to the leaders of Israel. Within David's speech to the men before him—and to the readers of Chronicles—there lies a profound message. David, the great king and leader of Israel, must pass from the scene. What future or hope can the people have? Their hope must not be in David, whom they see but whose strength and wisdom are limited, but in God, whom they do not see but whose presence, power, goodness, and wisdom are forever. It was God who chose the house of David, God who determined who would build the temple, God who gave the commandments in which are life and peace, and God who would remain when David was gone. Israel must not despair the loss of their great king but realize that their only hope is in God.[95]

28:9–10 At this point the address is directed to Solomon with the assembled company as witnesses. He was to acknowledge (*daᶜ*)[96] the God of David and serve him with wholehearted devotion and with a willing mind. He also reminded Solomon of a specific area in which he needed to be faithful to God: he must finish the temple. The temple was the abode of Yahweh and the symbol of his presence in the land among his people.

(2) The Presentation of the Temple Plans to Solomon (28:11–19)

11Then David gave his son Solomon the plans for the portico of the temple, its buildings, its storerooms, its upper parts, its inner rooms and the place of atonement. **12**He gave him the plans of all that the Spirit had put in his mind for the courts of the temple of the LORD and all the surrounding rooms, for the treasuries of the temple of God and for the treasuries for the dedicated things. **13**He gave him instructions for the divisions of the priests and Levites, and for all the work of serving in the temple of the LORD, as well as for all the articles to be used in its service. **14**He designated the weight of gold for all the gold articles to be used in various kinds of service, and the weight of silver for all the silver articles to be used in various kinds of service: **15**the weight of gold for the gold lampstands and their lamps, with the weight for each lampstand and its lamps; and the weight of silver for each silver lampstand and its lamps, according to the use of each lampstand; **16**the weight of gold for each table for consecrated bread; the weight of silver for the silver tables; **17**the weight of pure gold for the forks, sprinkling bowls and pitchers; the weight of gold for each gold dish; the weight of silver for each silver dish; **18**and the weight of the

---

[95] See Wilcock, *Message of Chronicles,* 109.

[96] The verb יָדַע ("know") is used in a technical sense for legal recognition of an overlord in a political treaty where it means acknowledge, recognize (authority, claims). See H. B. Huffmon, "The Treaty Background of Hebrew *Yadaᶜ*," *BASOR* 181 (1966): 31–37.

refined gold for the altar of incense. He also gave him the plan for the chariot, that is, the cherubim of gold that spread their wings and shelter the ark of the covenant of the LORD.

[19]"All this," David said, "I have in writing from the hand of the LORD upon me, and he gave me understanding in all the details of the plan."

28:11 The Chronicler places David in the same position in reference to the temple as that which Moses occupied in reference to the tabernacle. (See comments at 22:11–13 and 27:16–24.) For the Chronicler the temple was a continuation of the tabernacle. The reference to the "plan" (*tabnît*) recalls the narrative in Exod 25:9,40, where the same Hebrew word is used. Three times he mentions the transference of the plans of the temple from David to Solomon (vv. 11–12a,19). More than that, the physical shape of the two was similar even though the tabernacle was made of timber and skins; and the temple, of stone.

We have no way of knowing what David gave to Solomon. It may very well have been some outline sketch, a descriptive plan produced under inspiration (v. 19), perhaps the main components of the temple. The "details of the plan" would be filled in by the architects.

28:12 A question of translation arises here. The word *rûaḥ* can mean "mind" or "spirit." Some translate this "the plan of all that was with him by the Spirit" and take this to mean "under inspiration." Others use the word "mind" and translate "the pattern of all that he had in mind."[97] The plans were for the courts of the temple and all the surrounding rooms, the treasuries of the temple of God, and the treasuries of the dedicated things. The treasuries have been discussed in 26:22–28.

28:13–19 In mentioning the Levitical duties, the articles of the temple, and the cherubim for the temple, the Chronicler is asserting that this was more David's temple than Solomon's. David was responsible for the entire project. The golden vessels are referred to in 2 Chr 4:7–8,19–22. By clearly stating that these plans were committed to writing (v. 19), the Chronicler further implies that David's instructions to Solomon were specific and were carried out in detail. They were not mere impressions or ideas.

Verse 18 contains a wordplay—*hammerkābâ hakĕrûbîm*, "the chariot, the cherubim." The ark between the cherubim frequently was referred to as God's throne (Exod 25:22; Num 7:89; 1 Sam 4:4; 2 Sam 6:2; 2 Kgs 19:15; Isa 37:16). Ezekiel 1:10 is the only other place where the idea occurs, although the word "chariot" does not occur there.[98]

---

[97] But does the expression עִמּוֹ בָרוּחַ ("by/in the spirit/mind with him") mean the same thing as בְרוּחוֹ ("by/in his spirit/mind")?

[98] See L. E. Cooper, Sr., *Ezekiel*, NAC (Nashville: Broadman & Holman, 1994), 68–69, 130.

The NIV translation of v. 19 seems to have missed the mark. The Hebrew syntax is better reflected by the NRSV rendering, "All this, in writing at the LORD'S direction, he made clear to me—the plan of all the works." The Lord guided David in recording the plans for the temple he had revealed, so that the temple was from God just as the tabernacle had been.

That the Chronicler never implies that the second temple, the temple that stood in his day, should be built according to the same plan is significant.[99] Again we are misreading Chronicles if we conclude that it teaches that the Davidic-Solomonic period was the once-for-all ideal for the kingdom of God and that any future manifestation of God's kingdom must follow this pattern exactly. The temple of Solomon, as Chronicles presents it, upholds the ideal of pure worship in the kingdom of God, but it does not assert that any future fulfillment of the ideal will be in all points the same.

(3) Concluding Exhortation (28:20–21)

[20]David also said to Solomon his son, "Be strong and courageous, and do the work. Do not be afraid or discouraged, for the LORD God, my God, is with you. He will not fail you or forsake you until all the work for the service of the temple of the LORD is finished. [21]The divisions of the priests and Levites are ready for all the work on the temple of God, and every willing man skilled in any craft will help you in all the work. The officials and all the people will obey your every command."

28:20–21 Once again Solomon is given a charge by David to be strong and courageous and to do the work (cf. 22:11–13; 28:10). Helpers lay ready to assist in the building who would obey Solomon's every command. The extent of this support is spelled out in 29:1–9. Solomon also was given the assurance by David that "the LORD God, my God, is with you."[100] David stressed that God is Yahweh, the God of Israel, but that he also is specifically the God of David and his dynasty. In this Solomon could take the throne with full confidence of success. The next major division of Chronicles, in 2 Chr 1–9, shows how Solomon undertook his task.

10. The Climax of David's Reign (29:1–30)

Only some concluding aspects of David's story remain to be recorded: (1) contributions of the people for the temple building (29:1–9), (2) David's

---

[99] Wilcock, *Message of Chronicles,* 111.

[100] The assurance of God's presence and the success that results is a common biblical theme. For example, see Gen 21:22; 24:40; 26:3,24; Exod 3:12; 33:14; Num 14:43; Deut 2:7; 20:1,4; 31:6,8,23; Josh 1:5,9,17; 3:7; 7:12; 2 Sam 7:9; 1 Kgs 11:38; 1 Chr 22:11.

prayer of thanksgiving (29:10–19), (3) Solomon's accession to the throne (29:20–25), and (4) the close of David's reign (29:26–30). David left the affairs of the kingdom in perfect readiness for his son Solomon to take up his own work.

(1) The Contributions of the People for the Temple Building (29:1–9)

¹Then King David said to the whole assembly: "My son Solomon, the one whom God has chosen, is young and inexperienced. The task is great, because this palatial structure is not for man but for the LORD God. ²With all my resources I have provided for the temple of my God—gold for the gold work, silver for the silver, bronze for the bronze, iron for the iron and wood for the wood, as well as onyx for the settings, turquoise, stones of various colors, and all kinds of fine stone and marble—all of these in large quantities. ³Besides, in my devotion to the temple of my God I now give my personal treasures of gold and silver for the temple of my God, over and above everything I have provided for this holy temple: ⁴three thousand talents of gold (gold of Ophir) and seven thousand talents of refined silver, for the overlaying of the walls of the buildings, ⁵for the gold work and the silver work, and for all the work to be done by the craftsmen. Now, who is willing to consecrate himself today to the LORD?"

⁶Then the leaders of families, the officers of the tribes of Israel, the commanders of thousands and commanders of hundreds, and the officials in charge of the king's work gave willingly. ⁷They gave toward the work on the temple of God five thousand talents and ten thousand darics of gold, ten thousand talents of silver, eighteen thousand talents of bronze and a hundred thousand talents of iron. ⁸Any who had precious stones gave them to the treasury of the temple of the LORD in the custody of Jehiel the Gershonite. ⁹The people rejoiced at the willing response of their leaders, for they had given freely and wholeheartedly to the LORD. David the king also rejoiced greatly.

29:1–6 There is a parallel between the account of the building of the tabernacle in Moses' day when the people responded with generous gifts and the gifts that the leaders and people give for the temple here (cf. Exod 25:1–7; 35:4–9,20–29).[101] It is a theme that has been touched on in 22:2–5. The divine choice of Solomon is stressed again (cf. 28:4–5), but David reminded the assembly of Solomon's youth and inexperience (especially in political matters) and went on to urge them to give him support (v. 5). Solomon's primary task would be to build the temple. It is called here a "palatial structure"[102] to remind the people and Solomon that the true King of Israel was

---

[101] Williamson, *1 and 2 Chronicles*, 183.

[102] The word here is בִּירָה, used only here and in v. 19 for the temple. It occurs fourteen times elsewhere (in Nehemiah, Esther, and Daniel) for a royal fortress or palace.

to be the Lord God. The degree to which Solomon and his royal successors were to succeed as kings and Israel was to flourish would depend upon the extent to which they remembered that fact. This is what made the task of temple building so great.

David's generosity was lavish and served as a catalyst for the generosity of the people. Leaders will never see openhanded giving from their people if they are not willing to take the lead in this as well. In addition to David's gifts from the spoils of war, which were considerable, David had a personal treasure of gold from Ophir.[103] The Hebrew word for "personal treasure" (*sĕgullâ*) occurs only seven times in the Hebrew Bible, elsewhere of Israel as the Lord's precious, private possession (Exod 19:5; Deut 7:6; 14:2; 26:18; Ps 135:4; Mal 3:17).

Following his own sacrificial giving, David challenged Israel to do the same (v. 5). The verb translated "be willing" (*nādab*) is used elsewhere in reference to making freewill offerings for building the tabernacle (Exod 25:2; 35:21,29) and the second temple (Ezra 1:6; cf. 7:16) and for volunteering for military service (Judg 5:2,9; 2 Chr 17:16). The related noun (*nidbâ*) is the word for "freewill offering" (Lev 7:16). It is used of gifts that were not required but prompted by one's heart (Exod 25:2) or spirit (Exod 35:21). The expression translated "consecrate" means literally to "fill the hand" and is used many times of ordination to the priesthood (cf. Exod 28:41; 29:9; 2 Chr 13:9) and once of the dedication of the altar (Ezek 43:26). Thus David viewed these gifts for the temple as symbols of Israel's giving themselves wholly to the Lord, pledging themselves afresh as "a kingdom of priests and a holy nation" (Exod 19:6; cf. 2 Chr 29:31).

29:7–9 This vast array of contributions on the part of the king stimulated the officials to offer their gifts, which, in quantity, exceeded those of the king. A daric was a Persian coin and was in current use in the days of the Chronicler. In terms of the way money was counted in Solomon's day, the use of the term was an anachronism; but it was no doubt an attempt to express money value in terms of a later equivalent, a practice that is common enough in our day when Bible translators express ancient measures in terms of a modern equivalent. Precious stones were given into the custody of Jahiel, the Gershonite (cf. 26:21f.), whose family had connections with the treasury of the house of the Lord. Such a generous response from the leaders caused the people to rejoice, a reaction that was quite characteristic of other major occasions in Israel as, for example, when the temple was dedicated (2 Chr 7:8–10; but cf. 1 Chr 15:25; 2 Chr 20:27–26). That the bringing of

---

[103] Ophir is now attested on an eighth-century ostracon from Tel Qasile; see B. Maisler, "Ancient Israelite Historiography," *IEJ* 1 (1951): 209f.

gifts to the Lord caused rejoicing is interesting. It implies that the people gave freely and wholeheartedly (cf. 2 Cor 9:7). J. G. McConville has written, "People are closest to God-likeness in self-giving, and the nearer they approach God-likeness the more genuinely and rightly they become capable of rejoicing."[104] As David had learned vividly and painfully, "The search for true happiness cannot be along the path of self-gratification."[105]

(2) David's Prayer (29:10–19)

[10]David praised the LORD in the presence of the whole assembly, saying,

"Praise be to you, O LORD,
   God of our father Israel,
   from everlasting to everlasting.
[11]Yours, O LORD, is the greatness and the power
   and the glory and the majesty and the splendor,
   for everything in heaven and earth is yours.
Yours, O LORD, is the kingdom;
   you are exalted as head over all.
[12]Wealth and honor come from you;
   you are the ruler of all things.
In your hands are strength and power
   to exalt and give strength to all.
[13]Now, our God, we give you thanks,
   and praise your glorious name.
[14]"But who am I, and who are my people, that we should be able to give as generously as this? Everything comes from you, and we have given you only what comes from your hand. [15]We are aliens and strangers in your sight, as were all our forefathers. Our days on earth are like a shadow, without hope. [16]O LORD our God, as for all this abundance that we have provided for building you a temple for your Holy Name, it comes from your hand, and all of it belongs to you. [17]I know, my God, that you test the heart and are pleased with integrity. All these things have I given willingly and with honest intent. And now I have seen with joy how willingly your people who are here have given to you. [18]O LORD, God of our fathers Abraham, Isaac and Israel, keep this desire in the hearts of your people forever, and keep their hearts loyal to you. [19]And give my son Solomon the wholehearted devotion to keep your commands, requirements and decrees and to do everything to build the palatial structure for which I have provided."

The presentation of such a wealth of gifts to the Lord called forth David's praise and thanksgiving to the Lord, who is the giver of every good and per-

---

[104] McConville, I & II Chronicles, 103.
[105] Ibid.

fect gift in the first place.

29:10 The words translated "praise" and "praised" are from the verb *bārak,* "bless." Usually it is God who blesses us, but the word is used of praise to God elsewhere in Neh 8:6; Ps 145:21.

29:11–13 The first part of this prayer has found its way into Christian liturgy as the doxology appended to the Lord's Prayer: "Yours, O LORD, is the greatness and the power and the glory," although this ascription of praise here adds "and the majesty and the splendor."[106] As Allen has noted, David's prayer "ransacks the theological dictionary" for terms expressing God's sovereign and boundless power and regal grandeur.[107] It ascribes to Yahweh the possession of everything in heaven and earth. His is the kingdom, and he is exalted as head over all (cf. 2 Chr 20:6). Wealth and honor come from him. He is ruler over all things, and in his hands are the strength and power to exalt and give strength to all.

29:14 David and the people had brought their gifts and had given generously. But they had only given back what had come from God's hand. David is recorded as asking, "Who am I?" twice elsewhere—once of Saul (1 Sam 18:18) and once more of the Lord (2 Sam 7:18; 1 Chr 17:16).

29:15–16 The terms translated "aliens" and "strangers" frequently were used of the patriarchs (Gen 17:8; 21:23; 23:4; 1 Chr 16:19; cf. Heb 11:13–14). They spoke of persons without property and therefore without security of their own who lived in an area only by the good graces of its citizens. Like widows and orphans, they were in need of protection (Lev 19:10,33–34; Deut 10:18–19). Even after possessing the land, Israel was to have this attitude about themselves, remembering that the land really belonged to the Lord (Lev 25:23). In his very nature man is only a resident alien and a sojourner on earth. His days are like a shadow and without hope. Not even the wealth and security that had been granted to David would alter man's lot (cf. Job 7:6; 8:9; Ps 144:4). D. J. Estes sees in this verse an advance toward a concept of a spiritual pilgrimage. The life of the foreigner serves as the analogy to the life of the pious man in a world estranged from God[108] (1 Pet 2:11).

29:17 Knowing that God examines the heart (Jer 11:20; 17:10; 20:12) and is pleased with uprightness (1 Kgs 9:4), David had given all his offerings willingly and with honest intent and had joyfully watched God's people contribute willingly to him.

29:18 Reference already has been made to the patriarchs in vv. 10,15.

---

[106] The Lord's Prayer in Matt 6:13 in Greek does not have these words in early manuscripts. The longer ending was based on 1 Chr 29:11.

[107] Allen, *1, 2 Chronicles,* 191.

[108] D. J. Estes, "Metaphorical Sojourning in 1 Chronicles 29:15," *CBQ* 53 (1991): 45–49.

The Chronicler had dwelt on this theme in Asaph's psalm of thanks to the Lord (16:8–36). Several of the themes taken up there reappear here.[109] Israel had received a promise long ago. They were the benefactors of God's favor toward them and had thus been able to bring gifts. David's prayer was that this desire to give willingly to the Lord in return for all his past favors should remain in their hearts forever and that God might keep their hearts loyal to him.

29:19 David's special supplication was that the Lord himself would establish a perfect heart in both Israel and Solomon so that God's commandments might be kept and the temple built. It is noteworthy that the keeping of the law is set alongside the building of the temple. These two were indissolubly bound together. A temple without wholehearted devotion to the law was an empty gesture.

David's prayer remains a model of piety for worshipers in every age. A comparison of this prayer with the Psalms will reveal many similarities (see esp. Ps 39).[110]

(3) Solomon's Accession to the Throne (29:20–25)

[20]Then David said to the whole assembly, "Praise the LORD your God." So they all praised the LORD, the God of their fathers; they bowed low and fell prostrate before the LORD and the king.

[21]The next day they made sacrifices to the LORD and presented burnt offerings to him: a thousand bulls, a thousand rams and a thousand male lambs, together with their drink offerings, and other sacrifices in abundance for all Israel. [22]They ate and drank with great joy in the presence of the LORD that day.

Then they acknowledged Solomon son of David as king a second time, anointing him before the LORD to be ruler and Zadok to be priest. [23]So Solomon sat on the throne of the LORD as king in place of his father David. He prospered and all Israel obeyed him. [24]All the officers and mighty men, as well as all of King David's sons, pledged their submission to King Solomon.

[25]The LORD highly exalted Solomon in the sight of all Israel and bestowed on him royal splendor such as no king over Israel ever had before.

The Chronicler presents not one but two great kings as the ideal for Israel. The one was David, the warrior-king, who subdued the enemies of the people of God and established a secure domain. He was now passing, and the other, Solomon, was taking his place. Solomon was a man of peace who would build up the prosperity of the nation. These two things together—vic-

---

[109] See Williamson, *1 and 2 Chronicles*, 128–30, 185.

[110] Braun draws out a table of vocabulary comparisons with the Psalms (*1 Chronicles*, 284).

tory over enemies and a reign of peace—are both essential. For Christian readers these two ideals are fulfilled in the one man, Jesus Christ. He conquers all his foes but at the same time establishes a reign of peace for his own people. In this the tandem of David and Solomon are a type of Christ.[111]

29:21–22a   The term "sacrifices" (*zābaḥ*) is a general word. The nature of these sacrifices is spelled out immediately as "burnt offerings." But there may have been "peace offerings" also in which the worshipers shared. There were, as well, drink offerings. The people ate and drank with great joy in the presence of the Lord that day. We are reminded of the occasion when fighting men came to Hebron to make David king and spent three days eating and drinking (12:38–40). Vast numbers of animals were presented on the occasion of Solomon's anointing: a thousand bulls, a thousand rams, and a thousand male lambs. The mention of sacrifices for "all Israel" recalls the common motif formed so often in Chronicles (see also 29:23,25–26). This enormous number of sacrifices (at least three thousand animals) points to the significance of the event (cf. 2 Chr 7:4–5; 30:23–27; 35:7–9).

29:22b–23   The suggestion that this acknowledgment of Solomon took place a second time raises a question. The phrase "a second time" is lacking in the LXX and is omitted by some commentators as a gloss. But it is a true statement of the facts. In a time of uncertainty, when the rebel Adonijah was trying to usurp David's throne by a great display of religious fervor and the offering of sacrifices (1 Kgs 1:9), Nathan the prophet, Zadok the priest, and Benaiah the army commander with David's permission anointed Solomon king (1 Kgs 1:32–40). But that anointing was a hurried and semiprivate arrangement lacking the pomp and ceremony of a great national occasion. Hence Solomon had to be anointed a second time with proper solemnity and appropriate religious decorum. Assuming that the phrase is original, it shows that the Chronicler, while focusing on the successful transference of the throne to God's chosen "man of peace," was not unaware of the conflict surrounding Solomon's accession. At the same time, Zadok was acknowledged as high priest.[112]

29:23–25   David's final act was witnessing the anointing of Solomon. At what point David died we are not told. But the Lord prospered him, and Israel obeyed him. Solomon was exalted in the sight of all Israel over his

---

[111] Wilcock, *Message of Chronicles*, 140–42.

[112] Zadok already was prominent according to 1 Chr 16:39 when he officiated before the tabernacle of the Lord at the high place in Gibeon, and of course he was involved in the "first" anointing of Solomon (1 Kgs 1:34,39).

rivals and enjoyed royal splendor such as no king over Israel ever had before him, even David. Yet Jesus was to say of himself in Luke 11:31, "One greater than Solomon is here."

(4) The Death of David and the Close of His Reign (29:26–30)

²⁶David son of Jesse was king over all Israel. ²⁷He ruled over Israel forty years—seven in Hebron and thirty-three in Jerusalem. ²⁸He died at a good old age, having enjoyed long life, wealth and honor. His son Solomon succeeded him as king.

²⁹As for the events of King David's reign, from beginning to end, they are written in the records of Samuel the seer, the records of Nathan the prophet and the records of Gad the seer, ³⁰together with the details of his reign and power, and the circumstances that surrounded him and Israel and the kingdoms of all the other lands.

29:26–27 The "all Israel" motif continues. David's rule had been over "all Israel" forty years, seven in Hebron and thirty-three in Jerusalem.

29:28 This verse echoes 23:1. David's enjoyment of long life, wealth, and honor and the accession of Solomon in his place were all marks of divine approval of and divine blessing for his faithful servant. The summation of David's long and healthy life is comparable to that given for Moses (Deut 34:7).

29:29–30 The use of written records preserved by Samuel, Nathan the prophet, and Gad the seer may be a reference to material now found in the canonical books of Samuel and Kings. Whether or not that is the case, the point here is that the facts to which Chronicles bears witness are well attested and that in fact David did much more than is written here.[113] The phrase "the kingdoms of all the other lands" is peculiar to the Chronicler. It refers to other countries close to Israel, especially those over which David held dominion—Philistia, Moab, the Aramean States, Edom, Ammon, and Tyre. David's task was completed. His dynasty was established with the enthronement of Solomon. Plans for the building of the temple were in hand. Completion of that task was part and parcel of the eternal establishment of the Davidic dynasty.

---

[113] De Vries, *1 and 2 Chronicles,* 232.

2 Chronicles

IV. SOLOMON (1:1–9:31)

1. The Greatness of Solomon (1:1–17)

Nine chapters are devoted to Solomon (ca. 961–922 B.C.), but of these the major portion is given to the building of the temple (2:1–8:16). In a sense these chapters may be viewed as a direct continuation and fulfillment of David's preparatory work (1 Chr 17–29). While the material in 2 Chronicles is based on 1 Kings 1–11, the Chronicler told the story, under divine supervision, in his own way. The story of the building of the temple (chaps. 2–8) is enclosed between chaps. 1 and 9, both of which deal with Solomon's greatness (1:1–17; 8:17–9:31).[1] The point is made again that the eternal establishment of the Davidic dynasty was conditional on the completion of the temple, the tangible evidence that the Lord dwelt in the midst of his people, and that the occupant of the Davidic throne should be obedient to God's commandments. Throughout the Chronicler's work the assessment of the Davidic kings was based on their having God's presence in the temple and his will in the law.

In his build-up to Solomon's reign, covered only in chaps. 8–9, the Chronicler devotes considerable space to the plans David made for building the temple (chap. 28), the lavish gifts provided by the people (chap. 29), the preparations for the building of the temple (2 Chr 2), the actual building of the temple and the preparation of its furnishings (chaps. 3–4), the bringing of the ark to the temple (chap. 5), and the dedication of the temple (chaps. 6–7).

Chapter 1 serves primarily as an introduction to Solomon's reign. He is shown as carrying on the work of David as it pertained to the religious aspects of the kingdom. Here note is taken of his accession and his wealth (a subject to be amplified in chap. 9) probably to emphasize the way God blessed him for his concern for and attention to the cult. Special attention is given to Solomon's request for wisdom (1:7–13), but three aspects of Solomon's reign are introduced: his worship (vv. 2–6), his wisdom (vv. 7–13), and his wealth (vv. 14–17).

Above all else, this chapter reminds us that Solomon began his reign by seeking God (v. 5). Here, as elsewhere, it is not the specific facts of Solomon's reign but the principles behind it that the Chronicler stresses. The postexilic Jews, like Israel after the death of David, faced an uncertain future. The right place to begin was with God. His favor and direction alone could give health and peace to the nation. Once again, therefore, the king is portrayed in a favorable light not in order to obscure his sins but in order to make the point that the good things he did are what we should imitate.

(1) Solomon's Worship (1:1–6)

[1]Solomon son of David established himself firmly over his kingdom, for the LORD his God was with him and made him exceedingly great.

[2]Then Solomon spoke to all Israel—to the commanders of thousands and commanders of hundreds, to the judges and to all the leaders in Israel, the heads of families— [3]and Solomon and the whole assembly went to the high place at Gibeon, for God's Tent of Meeting was there, which Moses the LORD'S servant had made in the desert. [4]Now David had brought up the ark of God from Kiriath Jearim to the place he had prepared for it, because he had pitched

---

[1] R. B. Dillard proposes a chiastic scheme (2 Chronicles, WBC [Waco: Word, 1987], 5–6).

a tent for it in Jerusalem. **⁵But the bronze altar that Bezalel son of Uri, the son of Hur, had made was in Gibeon in front of the tabernacle of the LORD; so Solomon and the assembly inquired of him there. ⁶Solomon went up to the bronze altar before the LORD in the Tent of Meeting and offered a thousand burnt offerings on it.**

1:1 At the close of 1 Chronicles (9:23–30) Solomon is presented as sitting on the Lord's throne as king in place of David, his father, while the officials, the warriors, and King David's sons pledged submission to him. The expression translated "established himself firmly" (*hitpael* of *ḥāzaq*) frequently is found where the new king assumed power after a time of difficulty (12:13; 13:21; 17:1; 21:4).[2] Despite problems at the time of his accession, Solomon experienced help from the Lord (cf. 1 Chr 22:11,16; 28:20), who made him great (cf. 1 Chr 29:25; Josh 3:7; 4:14).

1:2 Whereas 1 Kgs 3:4 provides only a brief account of Solomon's worship and proceeds quickly to the account of the dream, the Chronicler devotes several verses to Solomon's worship at the high place of Gibeon. In the process he includes information regarding the military and tribal organization under Solomon in early monarchic Israel. The military units comprised the "hundreds" and "thousands" raised by levy along ancient tribal and clan lines led by the "heads of families."[3] King Solomon spoke to "all Israel." That description is a recurrent feature of the Chronicler. When David brought back the ark, he conferred with each of his officers, the commanders of the thousands and the commanders of the hundreds, and spoke to the whole assembly of Israel (1 Chr 13:1–5; cf. 1 Chr 28:1). The first assembly in Solomon's reign is thus patterned on the assemblies of David's reign.

1:3–4 Solomon and the whole assembly proceeded to Gibeon, where God's tent of meeting stood (v. 3). The information in v. 4 has already been given in 1 Chronicles 13; 15–16. The ark was lodged at that time in the tent David had prepared in Jerusalem at a time when the temple had not yet been built. The bronze altar that Bezalel had made (Exod 38:1–8) stood at Gibeon in front of the tabernacle of Yahweh. Bezalel is mentioned only in Chronicles and Exodus. He had been granted the gifts of wisdom and skill in his day (Exod 35:30–33). The mention of Bezalel in the present context enabled the Chronicler to associate Solomon's gift of wisdom for building the temple with the earlier model of the man who was associated with the construction of the tabernacle.

---

[2] H. G. M. Williamson, *1 and 2 Chronicles*, NCBC (Grand Rapids: Eerdmans, 1982), 193.

[3] Dillard notes that "the number of men at arms in each unit would be a function of the size of the clan and need not correspond in a literal way to the number one hundred or one thousand (*2 Chronicles*, 71).

1:5-6 In front of the tabernacle of the Lord, Solomon and the assembly "inquired of the LORD" (v. 5). The altar provided a symbolic picture of the one in whose honor the altar was erected. The offering of a thousand burnt offerings was considerable, appropriate to the occasion. It was the first event of Solomon's reign, which thus began with a national act of worship.

A king in Israel was to be distinguished by piety, wisdom, and wealth, as well as military leadership. These verses tell again the story of 1 Kgs 3:5-15 although it is abbreviated. For example, Solomon's display of wisdom in handling the case of the two women and their babies (1 Kgs 3:16-28) is omitted by the Chronicler. Evidently the incident was not regarded as of paramount importance in the ruling of Solomon's kingdom. His greatest wisdom would be displayed in his building, furnishing, and dedicating the temple (chaps. 2-7).

(2) Solomon's Wisdom (1:7-13)

[7]That night God appeared to Solomon and said to him, "Ask for whatever you want me to give you."

[8]Solomon answered God, "You have shown great kindness to David my father and have made me king in his place. [9]Now, LORD God, let your promise to my father David be confirmed, for you have made me king over a people who are as numerous as the dust of the earth. [10]Give me wisdom and knowledge, that I may lead this people, for who is able to govern this great people of yours?"

[11]God said to Solomon, "Since this is your heart's desire and you have not asked for wealth, riches or honor, nor for the death of your enemies, and since you have not asked for a long life but for wisdom and knowledge to govern my people over whom I have made you king, [12]therefore wisdom and knowledge will be given you. And I will also give you wealth, riches and honor, such as no king who was before you ever had and none after you will have."

[13]Then Solomon went to Jerusalem from the high place at Gibeon, from before the Tent of Meeting. And he reigned over Israel.

1:7 This verse is based on 1 Kgs 3:6-7 though it is abbreviated. The account there provides the information that God appeared to Solomon in a dream. God's offer to Solomon may sound something like a genie's offer to grant any wish, and we may tend to think of it as a one-time favor that was given to Solomon alone. This, however, would be incorrect. While few have ever received such a direct offer from God, M. Wilcock is correct to observe that the Lord has promised all his people, "Ask, and it will be given you" (Matt 7:7).[4] Every believer is entitled to make requests of God, and every

---

[4] M. Wilcock, *The Message of Chronicles,* BST (Downers Grove: InterVarsity, 1987), 124.

believer receives a favorable hearing. Solomon's prayer is important not because he had an opportunity that was spectacularly better than what God offers the rest of us but because his response is a model for all of us. He did not ask for external things that would make his job easier (e.g., victory in every battle) but for wisdom that would make him a person better equipped to do a hard job. We too have freedom to ask whatever we wish, but often we surrender to the temptation to ask for things or for an easy life rather than seeking for the gifts of wisdom, perseverance, faith, and virtue, whereby we might overcome the trials of life. Finally, Solomon's prayer shows great humility (v. 10), a quality that God never despises.

1:8 The important word translated in the NIV "kindness" is the Hebrew noun *hesed,* which carries many significant overtones—loyalty, loving-kindness, and faithfulness. It denotes a sense of the deep commitment God had to his covenant with David. As part of that commitment, God had placed David's son Solomon as king in David's place.

1:9 Solomon's repeated reference to his father, David, shows that he was in a sense praying in David's name. That is, he was relying on his relationship as David's son for favor with God. Israel had become a people "as numerous as the dust of the earth," an expression used elsewhere in the Old Testament (Gen 13:16; 28:14).

1:10 Solomon's request for "wisdom and knowledge" to lead and govern "this great people of yours" is an acknowledgment of his own weakness in the tasks of government and of the fact that Israel was God's people, not Solomon's.

1:11–12 Because Solomon had requested wisdom and knowledge rather than what one might have expected—wealth, honor, the death of his enemies, and long life for himself—God promised him the wisdom and knowledge he had asked for and these other gifts as well.

1:13 The Chronicler omits any reference to Solomon sacrificing before the ark on his return to Jerusalem (1 Kgs 3:15). Perhaps he wanted to avoid any confusion in the picture of legitimate worship that he had taken such trouble to develop.

(3) Solomon's Wealth (1:14–17)

¹⁴**Solomon accumulated chariots and horses; he had fourteen hundred chariots and twelve thousand horses, which he kept in the chariot cities and also with him in Jerusalem. ¹⁵The king made silver and gold as common in Jerusalem as stones, and cedar as plentiful as sycamore-fig trees in the foothills. ¹⁶Solomon's horses were imported from Egypt and from Kue—the royal merchants purchased them from Kue. ¹⁷They imported a chariot from Egypt for six hundred shekels of silver, and a horse for a hundred and fifty. They also**

exported them to all the kings of the Hittites and of the Arameans.

God's promise in v. 12 was fulfilled. Wealth of considerable dimensions was needed to build the temple, and this was granted to Solomon.

1:14 Under Solomon the chariot became a standard part of Israel's military equipment. According to 2 Chr 9:25 and the LXX of 1 Kgs 4:26, Solomon had 4,000 stalls. If two horses were available for each of the 1,400 chariots, he would need 2,800 horses. The 4,000 stalls would then allow for 1,200 additional horses. The word *pārāšîm* ("horses") also can mean "horsemen" (e.g., Gen 50:9).

Discussion has arisen about the nature of certain structures with pillars uncovered at Megiddo and identified by the original excavators as stables and associated with Solomon's chariot cities (1 Kgs 9:17; 10:26–29; 2 Chr 8:6). Subsequent excavation led to a reassessment of the dating, and the structures were assigned to King Ahab's time. Later research still has questioned whether these structures were stables at all and has described them as storehouses by comparison with similar buildings at Beersheba, where a large number of pottery vessels were discovered in similar buildings. Similar structures have been excavated at sites both within Israel and outside Palestine. More recently the subject has been opened up again, and the claim has been made that these structures were indeed stables.[5] Whether they were stables or storehouses, the fact is that Solomon built both "store-cities" and "cities for his chariots" (1 Kgs 9:19).

1:15 The reference to silver and gold being as common in Jerusalem as stones is a hyperbole and a reminder of the rocky terrain of Israel. Cedar trees, highly prized in building, grew in the foothills (Shephelah). The timber was, of course, also imported from Lebanon (1 Kgs 5:8–9). The comparison with the common and widely distributed sycamore-fig was an apt one and helped to enhance the picture of Solomon's wealth.

1:16–17 Solomon's kingdom lay across the only land bridge between Asia and Africa so that he was able to control the trade routes over a wide area, particularly between Syria and Egypt. The NIV follows a number of modern translators by referring to the land of Kue (Heb. *qĕwēʾ*, probably Cilicia, to judge from ancient documents). But it retains "Egypt" (Heb. *miṣrāyim*), where some modern commentators translate "from Musri." Both Kue and Musri are mentioned together in Assyrian texts, suggesting Cilicia and Cappadocia as the location of these regions.

The picture then suggests some sort of trade with horses and chariots as the commodities—a chariot from Egypt at 600 silver shekels and a horse

---

[5] A succinct discussion of the issue with bibliography is given in Dillard, *2 Chronicles*, 13.

from Cilicia or Cappadocia at 250 shekels. The picture is enhanced by including the Hittites and the Arameans in these trading arrangements. There is, however, some uncertainty about the exact translation and meaning of these verses, and at present dogmatism should be avoided.[6]

Several theological issues are raised in this chapter. In contrast with the account in Kings, where Solomon's visit to the high place at Gibeon was an act of private devotion, the Chronicler sees it as a national cultic assembly that involved "all Israel." This emphasis is maintained throughout the Chronicler's account of Solomon's reign. The writer does not display any concern about Solomon's visit to Gibeon but legitimizes it by reference to the tabernacle and Bezalel's altar at that site. As part of his idealization of David and Solomon, he emphasizes the patriarchal promises (Gen 15:5; 22:17; 26:4 used in 1 Chr 27:23; and Gen 13:16; 28:14 used in 2 Chr 1:9).

2. The Building of the Temple (2:1–7:22)

With 2 Chronicles 2 the writer reaches the point to which he has been aiming, the building of the temple. The events recorded in 2 Chr 2:1–7:22 were central for the Chronicler's work as a whole. In fact, since the introduction of David in 1 Chronicles 11 the story leads to its focal point in the erection of the temple, its physical building, its dedication with prayer and sacrifice, and God's acceptance of it when he appeared to Solomon and declared some important theological values for which the temple was intended to stand. Having established the pedigree of the true Israel in 1 Chronicles 1–9 and having dealt with Israel's experimental king, Saul, son of Kish, the crucial story begins in 1 Chronicles 11. Thereafter the narrative is bent toward the planning and building of the temple, the physical symbol of God's presence among his people Israel and the place where he might be worshiped according to his divine prescriptions.

(1) The Preparations (2:1–18)

[1]Solomon gave orders to build a temple for the Name of the LORD and a royal palace for himself. [2]He conscripted seventy thousand men as carriers and eighty thousand as stonecutters in the hills and thirty-six hundred as foremen over them.

[3]Solomon sent this message to Hiram king of Tyre:

"Send me cedar logs as you did for my father David when you sent him cedar to build a palace to live in. [4]Now I am about to build a temple for

---

[6] Dillard gives a splendid summary of the debate (*2 Chronicles*, 13–14).

the Name of the LORD my God and to dedicate it to him for burning fragrant incense before him, for setting out the consecrated bread regularly, and for making burnt offerings every morning and evening and on Sabbaths and New Moons and at the appointed feasts of the LORD our God. This is a lasting ordinance for Israel.

[5]"The temple I am going to build will be great, because our God is greater than all other gods. [6]But who is able to build a temple for him, since the heavens, even the highest heavens, cannot contain him? Who then am I to build a temple for him, except as a place to burn sacrifices before him?

[7]"Send me, therefore, a man skilled to work in gold and silver, bronze and iron, and in purple, crimson and blue yarn, and experienced in the art of engraving, to work in Judah and Jerusalem with my skilled craftsmen, whom my father David provided.

[8]"Send me also cedar, pine and algum logs from Lebanon, for I know that your men are skilled in cutting timber there. My men will work with yours [9]to provide me with plenty of lumber, because the temple I build must be large and magnificent. [10]I will give your servants, the woodsmen who cut the timber, twenty thousand cors of ground wheat, twenty thousand cors of barley, twenty thousand baths of wine and twenty thousand baths of olive oil."

[11]Hiram king of Tyre replied by letter to Solomon:

"Because the LORD loves his people, he has made you their king."

[12]And Hiram added:

"Praise be to the LORD, the God of Israel, who made heaven and earth! He has given King David a wise son, endowed with intelligence and discernment, who will build a temple for the LORD and a palace for himself.

[13]"I am sending you Huram-Abi, a man of great skill, [14]whose mother was from Dan and whose father was from Tyre. He is trained to work in gold and silver, bronze and iron, stone and wood, and with purple and blue and crimson yarn and fine linen. He is experienced in all kinds of engraving and can execute any design given to him. He will work with your craftsmen and with those of my lord, David your father.

[15]"Now let my lord send his servants the wheat and barley and the olive oil and wine he promised, [16]and we will cut all the logs from Lebanon that you need and will float them in rafts by sea down to Joppa. You can then take them up to Jerusalem."

[17]Solomon took a census of all the aliens who were in Israel, after the census his father David had taken; and they were found to be 153,600. [18]He assigned 70,000 of them to be carriers and 80,000 to be stonecutters in the hills, with 3,600 foremen over them to keep the people working.

INTRODUCTION (2:1–2).   **2:1 [1:18]**[7]   Solomon's instructions were to build a temple for the name of Yahweh, that is, for the honor of the LORD (cf. Deut 12:5), and a royal palace for himself.

2:2 [2:1]   According to 1 Kgs 5:13, there was a levy of forced labor from all Israel. A question arises about whether Solomon imposed corvée labor on Israelites or whether the compulsory labor was imposed only on aliens. The text in v. 17 (Heb. v. 16) refers to "aliens." It would appear from 2 Chr 2:17–18; 8:7–10; 1 Kgs 9:15,20–22 that this labor was extracted from the resident aliens alone. Israel imposed such labor on subservient people just as it had been imposed on them (Gen 49:15; Exod 1:11; Deut 20:11; Josh 9:21–25; 16:10; Judg 6:28,34). It has been argued that the purpose of the census under both David and Solomon was to register those liable for compulsory labor among the Canaanites.[8] The people conscripted in the present case were carriers, stonecutters, and foremen.

In this chapter is the Chronicler's further use of a chiastic structure, one of his favorite literary devices.

Conscription of laborers   2:2
   Solomon's letter   2:3–10
   Hiram's letter   2:11–16
Conscription of laborers   2:17–18

The use of this device so many times by the Chronicler suggests deliberate design rather than later redactional activity.

SOLOMON'S LETTER (2:3–10).   **2:3[2:2]**   This letter and Hiram's reply provide examples of international communication in the tenth century B.C. Solomon here takes the initiative (cf. 1 Kgs 5:1). At times the Hebrew refers to "Hiram" as "Huram." Solomon refers to previous dealings of Hiram with David (cf. 1 Chr 14:1). Solomon is thus presented as the dominant partner (cf. v. 14). Some commentators suggest that Hiram's dispatch of cedar logs to both David and Solomon may have been an obligation on the part of the king of Tyre, who was required to provide tribute to the king of Israel as his vassal.

2:4[2:3]   The Chronicler provides a list of cultic activities here instead of an account of the reason David was not allowed to build the temple as in 1 Kgs 5:3–5. That theme had, of course, been developed in 1 Chr 17:1–27; 22:7–10; 28:2–3. But it was the function of the temple in the worship of Israel's God that finally was important. This was a perpetual duty resting on Israel. The items specified provide a comprehensive summary of what was

---

[7] The Hebrew Bible verse numbers are one less than the English so that in the Hebrew Bible the English 2:1 is numbered as 1:18.

[8] A. Rainey, "Compulsory Labor Gangs in Ancient Israel," *IEJ* 20 (1970): 191–202.

undertaken by Israel in the worship of their transcendent God—the burning of fragrant incense; the setting out of consecrated bread regularly; and the presentation of burnt offerings every morning and evening and on Sabbaths, New Moons, and appointed feasts. The purpose of each of these is spelled out in the Pentateuch in such passages as Exod 25:6,30; 30:7–8; 40:23; Lev 24:5–9; Numbers 28–29.

2:5[2:4] God's transcendence is affirmed strongly. A great temple befits an almighty God.

2:6[2:5] "Who am I?" is a well-known protestation of humility in the Old Testament (Exod 3:11; 1 Sam 18:18; 2 Sam 7:18; 1 Chr 29:14). It was an appropriate comment for Solomon to make in view of the character the Chronicler portrayed for him. The temple was designated as a place to burn sacrifices before the Lord. It was indeed Israel's focus for the worship of the Lord. Yet the Lord was not confined to the temple. Even the highest heavens cannot contain him.

2:7[2:6] The introductory words in the Hebrew text, "And now" or "So now," were a normal part of literary debate. After laying down a number of preliminary statements, the exact issue or demand is introduced with this well-known phrase that marks the main point (Exod 19:4–5). In the passage before us Solomon explains that he purposes to build a temple for his God and adds "so now," which is a transition marker between his introductory remarks and his request.

The request is for a man skilled to work in metals and fabrics and in the art of engraving to work in Judah and Jerusalem with his own artisans. Solomon's father, David, had assembled a workforce of his own (1 Chr 22:14–16; 28:21; 29:5). This work was the internal decorative and artistic work of the temple. The various fabrics are reminiscent of the tabernacle fabrics (Exod 35:35). The word used here for purple is an Aramaic form of the Hebrew word, and the word used for crimson may be a Persian loan word. Both words would suit the Chronicler's contemporary vocabulary.

2:8–9[2:7–8] The timber for the framework of the temple—cedar, pine, algum—were imported from Lebanon. The algum wood is not easily identifiable but is known from a Ugaritic list of tribute and may be the Akkadian *alammakku,* a valuable wood known in Akkadian texts though not identifiable at present. It would seem that Hiram dealt in prized domestic woods like cedar and pine but also in exotic timbers. There is some evidence that the algum wood came from northern Syria.

The arrangement was that Solomon's men would work with Hiram's men to provide abundant timber for the large and magnificent temple Solomon planned to build. This was to honor God but also to add to his own prestige (1 Chr 22:5; 2 Chr 2:5).

2:10[2:9]   Solomon fixed the payment to Hiram's servants, the workmen who cut the timber, at twenty thousand cors of ground wheat, twenty
thousand cors of barley, twenty thousand baths of wine, and twenty thousand
baths of olive oil.[9] It would seem that these quantities represent a total figure, not an annual payment. The picture is somewhat different from that
given in 1 Kgs 5:6, where Hiram set the amount, but all the facts are not
given. The treaty of friendship between Solomon and Hiram (1 Kgs 5:13)
would have given precise details no doubt. The "ground" or "crushed"
wheat referred to in this verse is regarded by some translators simply as
"food" or "provisions" on the basis of the parallel in 1 Kgs 5:11 and several
versions.

Several aspects of worship emerge from Solomon's letter. First, true worship cannot abandon all tradition. On the one hand, of course, the temple
would be a new thing in Israel. On the other hand, it would include worship—the sacrifice, incense, and prayers—with which the people were
familiar and indeed which had been decreed by God himself (v. 4). Novelty
can be good, but not if neither Scripture nor the people of God recognize it
as true worship. Second, true worship is spiritual and recognizes that the
architecture and ceremony of human houses of worship cannot capture what
God himself is (v. 6). If we ever think that some place, ceremony, or object
has captured the essence of the God we worship, we are in idolatry. Third,
true worship pays attention to quality. Solomon demanded that Hiram send
only the best (vv. 7–10). We make a mockery of worship if we suppose that
God is indifferent to shabbiness and laziness in our preaching, singing, and
even our preparation of the place of worship.[10] Finally, true worship bears
witness to the outside world of the great God whom we worship (v. 5).

HIRAM'S REPLY (2:11–16).   **2:11[2:10]**   Hiram's letter commences
with an acknowledgment that Solomon had become king because Israel's
God loved his people. In a similar diplomatic context the Queen of Sheba
recognized Solomon's rule over Israel as a sign of the Lord's love for his
people (2 Chr 9:8).[11]

2:12[2:11]   Although this may be only diplomatic language (cf. Ezra
1:2–4), Hiram acknowledged that the God of Israel made heaven and earth.
It was he who had given David a wise son endowed with "intelligence and
discernment" (the identical phrase in Heb. is found in 1 Chr 22:12, where it

---

[9] The cor was a large dry measure of about 220 liters in volume; and the bath, a liquid measure of about 22 liters (see *IBD*, 1637–39).

[10] See Wilcock, *Message of Chronicles,* 128–30.

[11] Both Hiram and the Queen of Sheba use the Heb. word בָּרוּךְ ("blessed"), translated
"praise." The word is found elsewhere in Chronicles only on the lips of David (1 Chr 16:36;
29:10) and Solomon (2 Chr 6:4).

is translated "discretion and understanding"). Solomon is thus presented as the dominant partner in the treaty between him and Hiram.

2:13–14[2:12–13]   These words are based on 1 Kgs 7:13–14 but speak here of events at the beginning of the building operations. Huram-Abi's skills are given in more detail, and his family links are spelled out. His mother came from Dan and his father from Tyre. The comparison with Bezalel, who assisted in building the tabernacle and was helped by Oholiab, of the tribe of Dan (Exod 31:6; 35:34), is apt. The Chronicler wished to compare the gifted Bezalel with Huram-Abi, both of whom were involved in building a structure where God might be worshiped. The name "Huram-Abi" is related to "Hiram," the builder of 1 Kgs 7:13,40,45; the additional *abi* here (and in 4:16) could be part of his name or perhaps a title, to be translated as "my [or his] master [craftsman]." It has even been proposed that the use of this longer name with the ending *-ab* may be an additional effort to see a parallel between Huram-Abi and Oholiab by giving the names the same ending.[12]

The use of "my lord" in vv. 14–15 of both David and Solomon has been taken to indicate a vassal relationship between Hiram and the king of Israel. This may have been so, but it may also have been the language of a shrewd merchant to a client (cf. Gen 23:5–6).

2:15–16[2:14–15]   The terms of the treaty between Solomon and Hiram included the exchange of commodities—wheat, barley, olive oil, and wine—for timber logs. Was there also a diplomatic marriage (1 Kgs 11:1,5)? The Chronicler notes that the logs would be cut in Lebanon and floated down in rafts to Joppa by sea. Thereafter they would be transported by land up to Jerusalem (see 1 Kgs 5:9; Ezra 3:7), no doubt via Gezer, which had been given to Solomon at the time of his marriage to Pharaoh's daughter (1 Kgs 9:16–17). Some commentators have conjectured that the small river leading to the ancient site of Tell el Qasile on the northern outskirts of Tel Aviv, not far from Joppa, represents the point of entry to Solomon's domains. Bas-relief from Khorsabad, a city of King Sargon of Assyria, depicts Phoenician ships with their horse-head bows and horsetail sterns transporting logs by sea. The logs were carried on the decks and towed on rafts behind the ships.

SOLOMON'S CENSUS (2:17–18).   **2:17–18[2:16–17]**   Solomon took a census of all the resident aliens in Israel, in Hebrew called "the land of Israel." This phrase occurs ten times in the Old Testament, four of them in Chronicles in the reigns of David (1 Chr 22:2—also in connection with a census of aliens), Solomon (here at 2:17), Hezekiah (30:25), and Josiah (34:7). All

---

[12] See the useful discussions in Williamson, *1 and 2 Chronicles*, 200–201; and in Dillard, *2 Chronicles*, 20.

these were occasions when the geographical extent of Israel was great.

As noted at 2:2, Solomon's forced levy did not include any Israelites. Indeed an Israelite was forbidden to rule over another "with harshness" (Lev 25:43,46,53). And yet it seems possible that some people from Israel may have been used at times in a temporary capacity (1 Kgs 5:13–14) and different from the main levy of Gentile conscripts. The notice in 1 Kgs 5:13 that there was a levy "out of all Israel" points in the direction of a certain number of Israelites, some thirty thousand, a group not mentioned by the Chronicler. In support of this is the record that Jeroboam was in charge of the forced labor of the house of Joseph (1 Kgs 11:28; cf. 12:4). The stoning of Adoniram, the officer in charge of the corvée, points in the same direction (1 Kgs 12:3–4,18–19).[13]

The expression in v. 17, "after the census his father David had taken," may not have been a backward look to 1 Chronicles 21 but rather a description of how and why the census was taken, that is, "on the model of" or "similar to." Both in Chronicles and in 2 Samuel 24 that census referred to Israelites themselves whereas the census referred to in v. 17 was concerned with the resident aliens.[14]

(2) The Construction (3:1–7)

[1]Then Solomon began to build the temple of the LORD in Jerusalem on Mount Moriah, where the LORD had appeared to his father David. It was on the threshing floor of Araunah the Jebusite, the place provided by David. [2]He began building on the second day of the second month in the fourth year of his reign.

[3]The foundation Solomon laid for building the temple of God was sixty cubits long and twenty cubits wide (using the cubit of the old standard). [4]The portico at the front of the temple was twenty cubits long across the width of the building and twenty cubits high.

He overlaid the inside with pure gold. [5]He paneled the main hall with pine and covered it with fine gold and decorated it with palm tree and chain designs. [6]He adorned the temple with precious stones. And the gold he used was gold of Parvaim. [7]He overlaid the ceiling beams, doorframes, walls and doors of the temple with gold, and he carved cherubim on the walls.

---

[13] The title "over the corvée" has been found on a seal bearing the words, "Belonging to Pelayahu, son of Mattityahu who is over the corvée" (cf. 1 Kgs 4:6).

[14] The number varies from 1 Kgs 5:16, where the number of supervisors is 3,300 instead of 3,600. An additional group of 250 in 2 Chr 8:10 is counted in 1 Kgs 9:23 as 550. Variations in the Greek texts may be due to problems in transmission. Or there may be a group of 300 counted differently in the two books. See J. W. Wenham ("Large Numbers in the Old Testament," *TynBul* 18 [1967], 34).

This account of the building of the temple, which is safer than the parallel account in 1 Kgs 6:1–7:51 by almost half, is divided into two parts. The first concerns the building itself (3:1–7); and the second, the temple furnishings (3:8–5:1).

The details here are apt to be tedious and anything but edifying to the modern reader. Why would the Chronicler include so much minutia? The problem is not in the Chronicler but in us; we are unfamiliar with the details and terminology of ancient Jewish temple worship. We are in the position of amateurs listening to one professional musician describe a performance of a Beethoven symphony to another. We hear all kinds of technical terms we do not understand, we hear names of musical instruments that we only vaguely identify, and we are not familiar enough with the score to imagine how it must have sounded. To us, the outsiders, the marvel is that anyone could find this discussion interesting. To the insider, however, who appreciates the detail and can form a mental image of all that is said, the words are charged with meaning and are even exciting. Thus the ancient audience of this book, particularly the Levites, would have found here something to admire and wonder at. We cannot imitate their experience, but we can see here a picture of the worship of God carried out in a manner that is both grand and exact.

THE TEMPLE SITE AND THE BEGINNING OF THE CONSTRUCTION (3:1–2). **3:1** The first two verses in this chapter, concerned mainly with the temple's location, are the Chronicler's own and are not dependent on 1 Kgs 6:1, which is concerned only with the date when the work began relative to the exodus. He identifies the temple site with Mount Moriah, where Abraham was commanded to offer up Isaac (Gen 22:2). There is an important question for the commentator to address here, that is, the location of Mount Moriah. There is little help from Gen 22:2. Abraham was to go to the "region [or "land"] of Moriah" and offer up Isaac on "one of the mountains" (v. 2). "On the mountain of the LORD" a sacrifice was to be provided. This latter description may suggest that the site was associated with a well-known location. But for us the precise place is not specified. The Chronicler, however, identified Moriah with the temple site,[15] where the Lord appeared to David at the threshing floor of Araunah (or Ornan).

3:2 Solomon began building on the second day of the second month in the fourth year of his reign. Where only the Kings account gives the date relative to history, only the Chronicler gives the exact day. The important thing was that the temple was built finally in accordance with the divine promise.

MAIN STRUCTURE (3:3–7). The Chronicler draws a distinction between the main temple's structure (vv. 3–7) and its internal contents (3:8–5:1).

---

[15] A helpful discussion is provided by Williamson, *1 and 2 Chronicles,* 203–5.

3:3 It is evident that Israel used two standards for the cubit, a short cubit (17.4 inches) and a long cubit (20.4 inches), both based on an Egyptian dual standard of six and seven palms respectively (cf. Ezek 40:5; 45:13). It is not clear what the Chronicler meant by "the old standard,"[16] but excavations at the temple of Arad yielded evidence of these two standards. The temple of the tenth century had a north-south measurement of nine meters (twenty short cubits) for its main hall while the ninth-century temple had been lengthened to 10.5 meters (twenty long cubits).[17] The latter measurement is exactly the same as that of the Jerusalem temple, that is, twenty cubits.

3:4 The portico at the front of the temple is described in the NIV as "twenty cubits long across the width of the building and twenty cubits high." A glimpse at the variants given in the *BHS* will show that the Hebrew is uncertain. Various solutions have been offered.[18] The MT gives the length and height while 1 Kgs 6:3 provides the length and breadth. The MT of 3:4 reads literally, "And the portico which was on front of the length on front of the breadth of the house, which [was] twenty cubits," which is not clear in meaning. It also gives the height of a hundred and twenty cubits, which seems too great when the height of the rest of the temple was only thirty cubits (1 Kgs 6:2; see NIV text note). A feasible solution is offered in the ICC: "And (as to) the porch (portico) which was in front of the house (LXX): the length according to the breadth of the house was twenty cubits and the height twenty cubits."[19]

An important detail is that the inside of the portico was overlaid with pure gold to give the appearance of solid gold. Several grades of gold are mentioned in this and parallel passages (3:4,6,:8; 1 Kgs 6:20–21). It is arguable that the value of the gold increased as one approached the ark and the most holy place.

3:5 The main hall (the holy place) was paneled with pine ("cypress," RSV), covered with fine gold, and decorated with palm tree and chain designs. This type of decoration is also mentioned in 1 Kgs 6:18,29,32,35; 7:17. Probably the floor was made of cypress and the rest of the walls and roof of cedar.

3:6 No details are given of the precious stones used to adorn the temple, and no mention is made of these in 1 Kings, but 1 Chr 29:2 refers to various

---

[16] R. B. Y. Scott, *JBL* 77 (1958): 205–14.

[17] Dillard provides a helpful discussion (*2 Chronicles,* 28).

[18] See E. L. Curtis and A. A. Madden, *The Books of Chronicles,* ICC (London: T & T Clark, 1910), 326, for fuller discussion.

[19] Ibid. This translation follows the LXX and Syriac in reading אַמּוֹת ("cubits") for מֵאָה ("hundred"). These two words are *kethiv-qere* variants in Ezek 42:16.

precious stones given to use in the adornment of the temple. The gold came from Parvaim, a place that has not been identified.[20]

3:7 The various areas that were covered with gold are listed—ceiling beams, door frames, walls, and doors. Cherubim were carved on the walls (cf. 1 Kgs 6:29).

(3) The Temple Furnishings (3:8–5:1)

[8]He built the Most Holy Place, its length corresponding to the width of the temple—twenty cubits long and twenty cubits wide. He overlaid the inside with six hundred talents of fine gold. [9]The gold nails weighed fifty shekels. He also overlaid the upper parts with gold.

[10]In the Most Holy Place he made a pair of sculptured cherubim and over-laid them with gold. [11]The total wingspan of the cherubim was twenty cubits. One wing of the first cherub was five cubits long and touched the temple wall, while its other wing, also five cubits long, touched the wing of the other cherub. [12]Similarly one wing of the second cherub was five cubits long and touched the other temple wall, and its other wing, also five cubits long, touched the wing of the first cherub. [13]The wings of these cherubim extended twenty cubits. They stood on their feet, facing the main hall.

[14]He made the curtain of blue, purple and crimson yarn and fine linen, with cherubim worked into it.

[15]In the front of the temple he made two pillars, which [together] were thirty-five cubits long, each with a capital on top measuring five cubits. [16]He made interwoven chains and put them on top of the pillars. He also made a hundred pomegranates and attached them to the chains. [17]He erected the pil-lars in the front of the temple, one to the south and one to the north. The one to the south he named Jakin and the one to the north Boaz.

[1]He made a bronze altar twenty cubits long, twenty cubits wide and ten cubits high. [2]He made the Sea of cast metal, circular in shape, measuring ten cubits from rim to rim and five cubits high. It took a line of thirty cubits to mea-sure around it. [3]Below the rim, figures of bulls encircled it—ten to a cubit. The bulls were cast in two rows in one piece with the Sea.

[4]The Sea stood on twelve bulls, three facing north, three facing west, three facing south and three facing east. The Sea rested on top of them, and their hindquarters were toward the center. [5]It was a handbreadth in thickness, and its rim was like the rim of a cup, like a lily blossom. It held three thousand baths.

[6]He then made ten basins for washing and placed five on the south side and five on the north. In them the things to be used for the burnt offerings were

---

[20] See the lengthy discussion in Williamson, *1 and 2 Chronicles*, 207–8, and Dillard, *2 Chronicles*, 28–29.

rinsed, but the Sea was to be used by the priests for washing.

[7]He made ten gold lampstands according to the specifications for them and placed them in the temple, five on the south side and five on the north.

[8]He made ten tables and placed them in the temple, five on the south side and five on the north. He also made a hundred gold sprinkling bowls.

[9]He made the courtyard of the priests, and the large court and the doors for the court, and overlaid the doors with bronze. [10]He placed the Sea on the south side, at the southeast corner.

[11]He also made the pots and shovels and sprinkling bowls.

So Huram finished the work he had undertaken for King Solomon in the temple of God:

[12]the two pillars;

the two bowl-shaped capitals on top of the pillars;

the two sets of network decorating the two bowl-shaped capitals on top of the pillars;

[13]the four hundred pomegranates for the two sets of network (two rows of pomegranates for each network, decorating the bowl-shaped capitals on top of the pillars);

[14]the stands with their basins;

[15]the Sea and the twelve bulls under it;

[16]the pots, shovels, meat forks and all related articles.

All the objects that Huram-Abi made for King Solomon for the temple of the LORD were of polished bronze. [17]The king had them cast in clay molds in the plain of the Jordan between Succoth and Zarethan. [18]All these things that Solomon made amounted to so much that the weight of the bronze was not determined.

[19]Solomon also made all the furnishings that were in God's temple:

the golden altar;

the tables on which was the bread of the Presence;

[20]the lampstands of pure gold with their lamps, to burn in front of the inner sanctuary as prescribed;

[21]the gold floral work and lamps and tongs (they were solid gold);

[22]the pure gold wick trimmers, sprinkling bowls, dishes and censers; and the gold doors of the temple: the inner doors to the Most Holy Place and the

doors of the main hall.

[1]When all the work Solomon had done for the temple of the LORD was finished, he brought in the things his father David had dedicated—the silver and gold and all the furnishings—and he placed them in the treasuries of God's temple.

3:8–9 The most holy place (holy of holies) was included within the holy place and could thus be regarded as part of the temple furnishings. In a sense the whole structure of the temple was built to contain the "Most Holy Place." The details come from 1 Kgs 6:19–20, but neither there nor here is the height specified—only the floor dimensions at twenty cubits long and twenty cubits wide. This too was overlaid with gold, six hundred talents of fine gold. The amount is considerable, even enormous. The number may be symbolic, either a fifty-talent contribution from each of the twelve tribes or a year's revenue for Solomon (9:13). By way of comparison David paid six hundred talents of gold to Araunah for the temple site. Gold leaf, even if it is reasonably thick, must be fixed to a base by nails or tacks. These too were gold plated (cf. Exod 26:32,37).

3:10–13 A pair of sculptured cherubim overlaid with gold graced the most holy place (cf. 1 Kgs 6:23–28). They must have been a spectacular sight. Their wingspan was twenty cubits. One wing of each touched the temple wall; the other wing touched that of its partner. These cherubim stood upright and faced the main hall. According to the RSV, the cherubim were made of wood overlaid with gold.

3:14 The veil is not mentioned in the parallel text in 1 Kings 6. But the veil was present in the tabernacle and in Herod's temple (Matt 27:51) and was almost certainly present in Solomon's temple. In the parallel account in 1 Kings there is a lengthy passage (6:29–7:4), but this is omitted by the Chronicler. However, some of this material can be found elsewhere in Chronicles.

3:15–17 The two pillars, Jakin and Boaz, that stood in front of the temple have provoked some discussion. In Chronicles (v. 15) they were thirty-five cubits tall, whereas in 1 Kgs 7:15 they were eighteen cubits. Eighteen cubits also is given in 2 Kgs 25:17 and Jer 52:21 (except the LXX has thirty-five). Various proposals have been made to reconcile these two figures. The NIV adds the word "together" as an effort at harmonization. Another is that the Chronicler added to the eighteen cubits the circumference of the pillars (twelve cubits) and the height of the capital (five cubits) to make up thirty-five cubits. But nothing in the text suggests this. Another is that the letters representing the number *eighteen* were misread in the course of transmission.[21]

The decorated capital on top of the pillars was of "interwoven chains" (v. 16). The NRSV translates "encircling chains." The additional note that "he made a hundred pomegranates and attached them to the chains" gives an added perspective on the ornateness of these capitals.

These pillars were erected in front of the temple, one to the south and one to the north, that is, on either side of the entrance to the holy place rather

---

[21] J. B. Payne, "The Validity of the Numbers in Chronicles: Part One," *BSac* (1979): 121–22.

than outside the vestibule. A parallel has been found at Hazor and Arad.[22] The function of these pillars is debated. They apparently had a symbolic and decorative value rather than structural, that is, they were not part of the support structure. The names "Jakin" and "Boaz" may provide a clue, but here too there is wide disagreement.[23] A commonly held view is that the names are abbreviations for names of God, "He is the one who establishes" (Jakin), and "In him is strength" (Boaz).

The suggestion that these pillars were fire cressets (metal cups mounted on a pole and containing oil or pitch burnt to provide light) has been widely proposed.[24]

4:1 The parallel passage in the MT of Kings does not refer to the bronze altar in the temple court although it is referred to elsewhere (1 Kgs 8:64; 9:25; 2 Kgs 16:14). The large size of the altar, twenty cubits long, twenty cubits wide, and ten cubits high may represent its base from which steps led up to the altar (cf. Ezek 43:13–17).

4:2–5 The Sea of cast metal had an important place to play in the ritual cleansing of the priests. The Sea was the equivalent of the laver in the tabernacle (Exod 30:18–21). The parallel (in 1 Kgs 7:23–26) is followed closely. It was a roughly circular container ten cubits across, five cubits high, thirty cubits in circumference (a round number if the diameter was exactly ten cubits, or perhaps they are all approximations), and a handbreadth in thickness.[25] The volume was three thousand baths, about 17,500 gallons. Below the rim were "figures of bulls" (cf. NRSV "panels"), protuberances of some kind not fully understood. The RSV "gourds" is an emendation that has no textual support in the versions. The figure of three thousand baths does not agree with two thousand in 1 Kgs 7:26. The number three here may have been inadvertently transferred from v. 4, where it occurs four times.[26]

4:6 Reference is made here to the ten basins, five placed on the south side of the Sea and five on the north side. A distinction is made in the use to which these basins were put in contrast to that of the Sea. The basins were used for washing the utensils used for the burnt offerings, while the Sea was reserved for the priests. The parallel passage in Kings is longer and includes a section that deals with the portable stands for the basins (1 Kgs 7:27–37).

---

[22] See references in Williamson, *1 and 2 Chronicles,* 210; Dillard, *2 Chronicles,* 30.

[23] Dillard, *2 Chronicles,* 30–31.

[24] Dillard provides an extensive bibliography (p. 30).

[25] Dillard discusses the dimensions of the laver (p. 85).

[26] See Payne, "The Validity of Numbers in Chronicles," 122. Another view is that the conflict results from a difference in calculation, the figure in Kings assuming the Sea was hemispherical whereas the Chronicles figure assumes a cylindrical shape. See C. C. Wylie, *BA* 12 (1949): 86–90.

4:7 The use of the phrase "according to the specifications" suggests that the lampstands are singled out as of special importance (cf. v. 20). The lamps are not described in detail. Zechariah's vision (4:1–3) may reflect a memory of the lamps of the first temple. Each lampstand had at its top a bowl with seven lamps on its perimeter. The tabernacle had only one lampstand, which was seven-branched, whereas here there were ten. Details of their placement are here provided, five on the south side and five on the north. Over the centuries the practice changed. In the temple of the days of Antiochus Epiphanes IV (175–163 B.C.) there was only one lampstand (1 Macc 1:21; 4:49).

4:8 The ten tables and the hundred gold sprinkling bowls are mentioned only here. The context suggests that in the Chronicler's view the lampstands rested on the tables. However, the precise function of these tables is not given. Perhaps the tables held the Bread of the Presence (v. 19). But the tabernacle accounts (Exod 25:23–40; Lev 24:5–9) and Ezekiel's temple vision (Ezek 41:22) speak of only one table for this purpose. It would seem that the table that held the bread of the Presence was different from the rest. It is not mentioned here.

4:9 The courtyard hardly was part of the temple furniture as such, but the Chronicler included it at this point. Temple courts are mentioned in 1 Kgs 6:36; 7:12. A structural feature referred to in Kings is three courses of dressed stone and a course of cedar beams, which archaeologists have found in Megiddo and elsewhere. It is omitted in Chronicles. There was a courtyard for the priests and a large court for the nonpriests. The Hebrew word for "court" (ʿăzārâ) is unique to 2 Chr 4:9; 6:13; and Ezek 43:14,17,20; 45:19. It evidently was the terminology of the second-temple period. The doors are not referred to in Kings.

4:10–11 The disposition of the Sea was on the south side at the southeast corner. A few items are added here: pots (ash containers for the ashes from the altar offerings), shovels, and bowls. The bowls received the blood of the sacrifices (Exod 27:3; 38:3; Num 4:14). A succinct statement indicates that Huram finished the work he had undertaken for King Solomon in the house of God.

4:12–16 This summarizing statement gathers up Huram's achievements and gives some additional details. The verses follow 1 Kgs 7:41–50 with slight variations. The stands (v. 14) are not mentioned before this in Chronicles (cf. 1 Kgs 7:43). Huram-Abi has been mentioned in 2:13–14. The objects referred to in the summary were made of polished bronze.

4:17 Some details of the casting of these bronze items are here provided. The casting was done on the other side of Jordan between Succoth and Zarethan. This verse presents some textual difficulties. "Clay molds" sometimes is emended to "the ford at Adamah," a city in the Jordan plain

(Josh 3:9–17). Most commentators accept "clay beds" or "clay molds" (see 1 Kgs 7:46). Their location in the plain of Jordan between Succoth and Zarethan seems acceptable.

4:18 Considerable quantities of copper were required to prepare the bronze. There were, in ancient times, mines in the wadis of Timna and Amram in the valley north of Elath on the Gulf of Aqabah. The source of the copper for the large quantities of bronze required (4:16–18) is not really known, though there were accessible sources of copper ore in various places.

4:19–22 This is another summarizing passage. With minimal changes this list of temple equipment follows that of 1 Kings. Of special interest is the golden altar (v. 19) used for burning incense. It was modeled after that of the tabernacle in Exod 30:1–10. The reference in v. 19 to "the tables [plural] on which was the bread of the Presence" may be due to a scribal error since the parallel in 1 Kgs 7:48 is singular. The mistake could have been caused by the use of "tables" in v. 8. There was only one table for the bread of the Presence (cf. 13:11; 29:18). All of the utensils mentioned here were made of gold, as were the doors of the temple, the inner doors of the most holy place, and the doors to the main hall (v. 22). Everything was costly and grand.

5:1 This verse marks the transition between the story of the construction and that of the dedication of the temple. It follows 1 Kgs 7:51. The last action mentioned in this section is Solomon's moving to the treasuries of God's temple (1 Chr 18:8,10–11; 22:3–4,14,16; 26:26; 29:2–9) the things David, his father, had dedicated. The spoils taken from Egypt went into the building of the tabernacle. The spoils taken from Israel's enemies built the temple. The treasuries of God's temple are not described in the Chronicler's account of the temple construction (cf. 1 Kgs 6:5–10). The verb "was finished" (*watišalam*) may be a play on Solomon's name (*šělōmōh*), for it uses the same consonants. Solomon, the chosen temple builder, brings his task to fulfillment.

(4) The Removal and Installation of the Ark (5:2–14)

[2]Then Solomon summoned to Jerusalem the elders of Israel, all the heads of the tribes and the chiefs of the Israelite families, to bring up the ark of the LORD'S covenant from Zion, the City of David. [3]And all the men of Israel came together to the king at the time of the festival in the seventh month.

[4]When all the elders of Israel had arrived, the Levites took up the ark, [5]and they brought up the ark and the Tent of Meeting and all the sacred furnishings in it. The priests, who were Levites, carried them up; [6]and King Solomon and the entire assembly of Israel that had gathered about him were before the ark, sacrificing so many sheep and cattle that they could not be recorded or counted.

[7]The priests then brought the ark of the LORD'S covenant to its place in the

inner sanctuary of the temple, the Most Holy Place, and put it beneath the wings of the cherubim. [8]The cherubim spread their wings over the place of the ark and covered the ark and its carrying poles. [9]These poles were so long that their ends, extending from the ark, could be seen from in front of the inner sanctuary, but not from outside the Holy Place; and they are still there today. [10]There was nothing in the ark except the two tablets that Moses had placed in it at Horeb, where the LORD made a covenant with the Israelites after they came out of Egypt.

[11]The priests then withdrew from the Holy Place. All the priests who were there had consecrated themselves, regardless of their divisions. [12]All the Levites who were musicians—Asaph, Heman, Jeduthun and their sons and relatives—stood on the east side of the altar, dressed in fine linen and playing cymbals, harps and lyres. They were accompanied by 120 priests sounding trumpets. [13]The trumpeters and singers joined in unison, as with one voice, to give praise and thanks to the LORD. Accompanied by trumpets, cymbals and other instruments, they raised their voices in praise to the LORD and sang:

"He is good;

his love endures forever."

Then the temple of the LORD was filled with a cloud, [14]and the priests could not perform their service because of the cloud, for the glory of the LORD filled the temple of God.

With the completion of the temple it was time to bring the ark to the temple because once the ark was in place, the temple rituals could proceed. The bringing of the ark to the temple, Solomon's prayer of dedication, and the concluding ceremonies of dedication brought the climax toward which the Chronicler had been moving throughout his story.

5:2 The Chronicler's interest in the "all Israel" motif is supported in vv. 2–3, although the wording is the same in 1 Kgs 8:1–2. The ark was lodged at Zion, the City of David, and needed to be transported in the appropriate way from Zion to the temple.

5:3 The opportunity chosen to move the ark to its final resting place was the time of the festival of the seventh month, the Feast of Tabernacles. According to 1 Kgs 6:38, the temple actually was completed in the eighth month of Solomon's eleventh year. The dedication must have taken place during the month before the actual completion of the work. The seventh month is designated by its old Canaanite name in 1 Kgs 8:2, "Ethnaim," the later "Tishri."

5:4–5 Appropriately it was the Levites (v. 4) who took up the ark. The parallel text in 1 Kgs 8:3 gives the movers as "priests," which would be more precise, but the Chronicler is contrasting the first attempt to move the ark (cf. 1 Chr 13:9–10; 15:2). The involvement of the Levites in moving the tent of meeting is rooted in Kings with the expression "priests and Levites"

(1 Kgs 8:4). The Chronicler, in reverse, having removed the priests (who were, of course, also from the tribe of Levi) from v. 4, noted their importance in v. 5 by using the phrase "the priests, the Levites," which should be understood as referring to only one group, namely, the Levitical priests (cf. Deut 17:9; Josh 3:3). Hence the NIV translates "the priests, who were Levites." The Chronicler wished to accentuate the differences between priests and Levites (1 Chr 23:24–32) and to make much of the place of the Levites in Israel.

In the present incident the Levites were charged with the task of transferring the ark to the temple (5:4; 1 Chr 15:2,11–15; Num 4:24–28), but only the priests could enter the most holy place and handle the sacred vessels (5:7; Num 4:5–20). When the ark reached the sanctuary itself, the priests carried the ark, the tent of meeting, and all the sacred vessels since only the priests were allowed to enter the sanctuary (5:7; Num 4:5–20). No record has been found of the transfer of the tabernacle from Gibeon (1:3) to Jerusalem. The phrase "Tent of Meeting" is used exclusively to describe that structure and should not be confused with the temporary structure David erected for the ark (1 Chr 16:1; 2 Chr 1:4).

5:6–9 While the priests were bringing the ark of the covenant to its appropriate place, the king and the entire assembly of Israel were at the temple sacrificing great numbers of sheep and cattle. After the ark was in place, the cherubim could be seen from the holy place in front of the inner chamber though they could not be seen from outside.[27] Apparently the veil did not extend the full width of the sanctuary. The statement that they are "still there to this day" (v. 9) comes from the Chronicler's source (1 Kgs 8:8); it does not necessarily mean that the poles still existed in the Chronicler's day.

5:10 The ark was empty except for the two tablets that Moses placed there at Horeb. The New Testament had a tradition that referred to a jar of manna and Aaron's rod in the ark as well (Heb 9:4). The Old Testament speaks of the rod and the jar of manna being placed in front of the ark (Exod 16:32–34; Num 17:10–11).

5:11–14 Verses 11b ("All the priests . . .") through the song in v. 13 has been added to the Chronicler's source in the middle of 1 Kgs 8:10. The scene is one of great celebration and cooperation among all the priests and Levites. Priests from all the divisions were involved and were even helping with the music. One hundred and twenty priests sounded their trumpets while the Levites played cymbals, harps, and lyres (cf. 1 Chr 15:16; 25:1). Part of the ritual was to play these instruments when the ark moved. The singing and

---

[27] The verb וַיְכַסּוּ ("covered") is a variant of וַיָּסֹכּוּ ("overshadowed") in 1 Kgs 8:7. Whichever is original, the other arose through transposition of letters.

music were in unison (v. 13), and there was great joy as the people worshiped together and sang the well-known and often-sung words, "He is good; and his love endures forever."

A cloud symbolizing God's presence filled the house (cf. Exod 40:34-35; Ezek 43:4). This marked the acceptance by God of the temple as the place of sacrifice. The priests were not able to take their place to perform their service because the glory of the Lord filled the temple. The cloud as a symbol of the presence of Yahweh is mentioned several times in the Old Testament (Exod 13; Num 9; Ezek 10:3–4). The Chronicler's expanded account places the Lord's filling the temple in the context of a great celebration of praise and affirmation of faith as if to encourage future generations of Israel to continue praising and worshiping God until his glory returns.

(5) The Dedicatory Speeches (6:1–42)

¹Then Solomon said, "The LORD has said that he would dwell in a dark cloud; ²I have built a magnificent temple for you, a place for you to dwell forever."

³While the whole assembly of Israel was standing there, the king turned around and blessed them. ⁴Then he said:

"Praise be to the LORD, the God of Israel, who with his hands has fulfilled what he promised with his mouth to my father David. For he said, ⁵'Since the day I brought my people out of Egypt, I have not chosen a city in any tribe of Israel to have a temple built for my Name to be there, nor have I chosen anyone to be the leader over my people Israel. ⁶But now I have chosen Jerusalem for my Name to be there, and I have chosen David to rule my people Israel.'

⁷"My father David had it in his heart to build a temple for the Name of the LORD, the God of Israel. ⁸But the LORD said to my father David, 'Because it was in your heart to build a temple for my Name, you did well to have this in your heart. ⁹Nevertheless, you are not the one to build the temple, but your son, who is your own flesh and blood—he is the one who will build the temple for my Name.'

¹⁰"The LORD has kept the promise he made. I have succeeded David my father and now I sit on the throne of Israel, just as the LORD promised, and I have built the temple for the Name of the LORD, the God of Israel. ¹¹There I have placed the ark, in which is the covenant of the LORD that he made with the people of Israel."

¹²Then Solomon stood before the altar of the LORD in front of the whole assembly of Israel and spread out his hands. ¹³Now he had made a bronze platform, five cubits long, five cubits wide and three cubits high, and had placed it in the center of the outer court. He stood on the platform and then knelt down

before the whole assembly of Israel and spread out his hands toward heaven. [14]He said:

"O LORD, God of Israel, there is no God like you in heaven or on earth—you who keep your covenant of love with your servants who continue wholeheartedly in your way. [15]You have kept your promise to your servant David my father; with your mouth you have promised and with your hand you have fulfilled it—as it is today.

[16]"Now LORD, God of Israel, keep for your servant David my father the promises you made to him when you said, 'You shall never fail to have a man to sit before me on the throne of Israel, if only your sons are careful in all they do to walk before me according to my law, as you have done.' [17]And now, O LORD, God of Israel, let your word that you promised your servant David come true.

[18]"But will God really dwell on earth with men? The heavens, even the highest heavens, cannot contain you. How much less this temple I have built! [19]Yet give attention to your servant's prayer and his plea for mercy, O LORD my God. Hear the cry and the prayer that your servant is praying in your presence. [20]May your eyes be open toward this temple day and night, this place of which you said you would put your Name there. May you hear the prayer your servant prays toward this place. [21]Hear the supplications of your servant and of your people Israel when they pray toward this place. Hear from heaven, your dwelling place; and when you hear, forgive.

[22]"When a man wrongs his neighbor and is required to take an oath and he comes and swears the oath before your altar in this temple, [23]then hear from heaven and act. Judge between your servants, repaying the guilty by bringing down on his own head what he has done. Declare the innocent not guilty and so establish his innocence.

[24]"When your people Israel have been defeated by an enemy because they have sinned against you and when they turn back and confess your name, praying and making supplication before you in this temple, [25]then hear from heaven and forgive the sin of your people Israel and bring them back to the land you gave to them and their fathers.

[26]"When the heavens are shut up and there is no rain because your people have sinned against you, and when they pray toward this place and confess your name and turn from their sin because you have afflicted them, [27]then hear from heaven and forgive the sin of your servants, your people Israel. Teach them the right way to live, and send rain on the land you gave your people for an inheritance.

[28]"When famine or plague comes to the land, or blight or mildew, locusts or grasshoppers, or when enemies besiege them in any of their cities, whatever disaster or disease may come, [29]and when a prayer or plea is made by any of your people Israel—each one aware of his afflictions and pains, and spreading out his hands toward this temple— [30]then hear

from heaven, your dwelling place. Forgive, and deal with each man according to all he does, since you know his heart (for you alone know the hearts of men), 31so that they will fear you and walk in your ways all the time they live in the land you gave our fathers.

32"As for the foreigner who does not belong to your people Israel but has come from a distant land because of your great name and your mighty hand and your outstretched arm—when he comes and prays toward this temple, 33then hear from heaven, your dwelling place, and do whatever the foreigner asks of you, so that all the peoples of the earth may know your name and fear you, as do your own people Israel, and may know that this house I have built bears your Name.

34"When your people go to war against their enemies, wherever you send them, and when they pray to you toward this city you have chosen and the temple I have built for your Name, 35then hear from heaven their prayer and their plea, and uphold their cause.

36"When they sin against you—for there is no one who does not sin—and you become angry with them and give them over to the enemy, who takes them captive to a land far away or near; 37and if they have a change of heart in the land where they are held captive, and repent and plead with you in the land of their captivity and say, 'We have sinned, we have done wrong and acted wickedly'; 38and if they turn back to you with all their heart and soul in the land of their captivity where they were taken, and pray toward the land you gave their fathers, toward the city you have chosen and toward the temple I have built for your Name; 39then from heaven, your dwelling place, hear their prayer and their pleas, and uphold their cause. And forgive your people, who have sinned against you.

40"Now, my God, may your eyes be open and your ears attentive to the prayers offered in this place.

41"Now arise, O LORD God, and come to your resting place,
    you and the ark of your might.
May your priests, O LORD God, be clothed with salvation,
    may your saints rejoice in your goodness.
42O LORD God, do not reject your anointed one.
    Remember the great love promised to David your servant."

Once the ark had been deposited in the temple and the appearance of the glory cloud had indicated divine acceptance of the temple, Solomon could utter his prayer of dedication (6:14–42). Chapter 6 is presented in the form of three different addresses by Solomon: vv. 1–2, vv. 3–11, vv. 12–42, increasing in length from two verses, to nine verses, to thirty-one verses. The individual petitions of the dedicatory prayer form separate paragraphs. The whole chapter follows 1 Kgs 8:12–50 closely (omitting 1 Kgs 8:50b–53 and adding material in 2 Chr 6:5–6,13); 6:41–42 is included as is a fragment from Ps 132:8–10.

SOLOMON ADDRESSES GOD (6:1–2).   **6:1–2**   These two verses are Solomon's response to the appearance of the divine glory in the shape of a dark cloud. The cloud formerly had appeared at Sinai (Exod 20:21; Deut 4:11; 5:22). There God revealed his presence. The darkness of the most holy place was a dwelling suited to a thick darkness (Exod 20:21). The picture is thus linked with the cloud of 5:13–14 and also with the thick darkness of Sinai. Once again the Chronicler points out a continuity between past revelation and the temple. This small structure in Jerusalem, moreover, was the place where divine transcendence and divine immanence would meet. On the one hand, no building, not even the whole earth, could contain God. He dwells in thick darkness, and indeed he fills all. On the other hand, in some special way God would be here, in this temple, more than in any other place. Perhaps this helps us understand the mystery of the incarnation of God in Christ—while God fills the whole universe, he also is specially present in the person of Christ. This is why Jesus referred to his body as a "temple" (John 2:20–21).

SOLOMON ADDRESSES THE ASSEMBLY (6:3–11).   **6:3**   The motif of "all Israel," so significant for the Chronicler, is brought forward at this critical point as Solomon addressed "the whole assembly of Israel" in preparation for his prayer of dedication. Turning from facing the temple to face the assembly of Israel, Solomon blessed the people as David once had blessed a national cultic assembly, assuming what was usually a priestly function (1 Chr 16:2; cf. 16:43; 2 Chr 31:8; 1 Kgs 8:55).

6:4   Solomon's address to the people begins here. It concentrates on God's promise to David to provide a house (temple) as a permanent resting place for the ark, which was not achieved since the days of the exodus. The God of Israel (the whole nation) is praised because the fulfillment of God's promise has taken place (chap. 5).

6:5   While the Chronicler does not place as much stress on the exodus as did some of the earlier writers in Israel (cp. 1 Kgs 8:21,51,53 with 6:11), the deliverance of Israel from Egypt was important for him (cf. 1 Chr 17:21; 2 Chr 5:10; 6:5; 7:22; 20:10). However, in Solomon's address to the assembly he was stressing the fulfillment of God's promise to David more than the exodus. The building of the temple and the establishment of the Davidic dynasty as a consequence of the divine promise was the important focus for the Chronicler (cf. 1 Chr 17).[28]

---

[28] Two additional clauses are found at the end of 2 Chr 6:5 ("nor have I . . .") and the beginning of v. 6 that are missing in 1 Kgs 8:16. The Kings verse apparently is the result of scribal omission due to the repetition of the phrase translated "for my Name to be there." See E. Tov, *Textual Criticism of the Hebrew Bible* (Minneapolis: Fortress, 1992), 238-39.

6:6 The point is made that now, with the completion of the temple, it was clear that God had chosen Jerusalem as the place for his Name to be, and David (and his dynasty) was appointed to rule God's people Israel (that is, all Israel).

6:7–11 These verses are a reiteration of emphases made several times. Building the temple was in David's heart, but since he was a man of war, he was denied his desire (1 Chr 22:8–9; 28:3). The accession of Solomon and the completion of the temple were stages in the establishment of the Davidic covenant. Solomon, David's son, sat on the throne of Israel. He had built the temple and had placed there the ark in which lay the covenant of the Lord that God had made with the people of Israel. What mattered supremely to the Chronicler was that that covenant was effective at that time with the children of Israel. Solomon had in mind the whole of the people, all Israel, the descendants of the patriarch Jacob/Israel (1 Chr 2:1).

SOLOMON'S PRAYER OF DEDICATION (6:12–42). **6:12** Solomon's prayer of dedication is close to the version in 1 Kgs 8:22–53. It was delivered as Solomon stood before the altar of the Lord in front of the whole assembly of Israel with his hands spread out.

6:13 This verse is lacking in the parallel account in 1 Kgs 8:22. The bronze platform, five cubits long, five cubits wide, and three cubits high placed in the center of the outer court, has provoked some comments. Several representations from the ancient Near East portray dignitaries standing or kneeling on platforms while performing cultic duties.[29] The placing of the platform in the center of the outer court suggests that it was set up temporarily for this particular occasion though it probably was near the altar (v. 12). There is a question, however, about the court. The Chronicler distinguished between the court of the priests and the great court (4:9). In the present verse the word for court ($^c\bar{a}z\bar{a}r\hat{a}$) is the one used for the great court in 4:9. Therefore it probably was the great court where Solomon could be seen by the whole assembly. The spreading out of the hands as a gesture of prayer is known in other places in the Old Testament (Exod 9:29,33; 1 Kgs 8:54; Ezra 9:5; Job 11:13).

6:14–17 The prayer of Solomon is now given. God is addressed as "Lord, God of Israel," and his uniqueness is declared. The significant theological words "covenant" and "love" (*ḥesed*) feature prominently. These God keeps with those servants of his who walk before him (see comment at 7:17–18). The prayer then takes up God's promises to David, his father, and

---

[29] *ANET,* 490, fig. 576; C. James, *Old Testament Illustrations* (London: Cambridge University Press, 1971), fig. 173; W. F. Albright, *Archaeology and the Religion of Israel* (Baltimore: The Johns Hopkins University Press, 1946), 152–54; J. M. Myers, *II Chronicles,* AB (New York: Doubleday, 1965), 36.

to their fulfillment in the building of the temple. Those promises extended also to the establishment of the Davidic dynasty (vv. 16–17). Of course, a basic condition was that David's descendants should walk in God's law. That law, or Torah, was a permanent reference point for Israel.[30]

6:18–21 These verses raise the question of the relationship between the transcendence and immanence of God (cf. 2:45). God's transcendence is fully acknowledged, but the temple was the place of prayer where Israel could meet God. It was, in fact, both a place for the offering of sacrifices (2:5) and for the offering of prayer. The prayer asks God to hear from heaven, his dwelling place, and when he hears to forgive both his servant Solomon and his people Israel.

6:22–23 In vv. 22–39 the prayer gives expression to a number of petitions that cover the whole life of Israel. They were taken basically from 1 Kgs 8:31–50 but generally were applicable no less during Israel's history up to the time of the Chronicler than in the Chronicler's own day, although specific details about a particular period are not always known to us. But Solomon's prayer transfers to the temple procedures ordinarily administered at the tabernacle or other holy places. Thus when a man wrongs his neighbor and is required to take an oath, he is to go to the altar in the temple. Taking an oath was a solemn act ordinarily accompanied by a self-maledictory curse. Lifting the hand toward heaven was the common gesture while making the oath (Deut 32:40; Ps 142:8).

6:24–25 While the main themes in Solomon's prayer were the Davidic dynasty, the temple, and prayer itself, two other themes also occur—war (6:24–25; 34–37) and the land (6:25,27–28,31,38). Defeat in battle is the result of sinning against God. The people are required to turn back to God, confess his name, pray, and make supplication before him in the temple. Solomon made the plea that God would hear their confession, forgive their sin, and bring them back to the land he had given to them and their fathers. War, of course, often involved exile.

6:26–27 Drought and famine were common occurrences. Israel was largely an agrarian society dependent on regular seasonal rains, especially the early rains to soften the ground for plowing in autumn and the latter rains to swell the crop before harvest in the spring. Adequate rainfall was a sign of God's blessing, and poor rainfall was a sign of divine anger (Lev 26:3–4; Deut 11:13–14; 28:23–24; Prov 16:15; Jer 3:3; 5:24). God's response to the people's confession would be to send rain upon the land he had given Israel for an inheritance. He would heal their land (7:13–14).

---

[30] See B. S. Childs, *Introduction to the Old Testament as Scripture* (Philadelphia: Fortress, 1979), 648–49, on consciousness of an authoritative canon in Israel.

6:28–31   Famine or plague, blight or mildew, locusts or grasshoppers, and the ravages of war recurred from time to time. Famine in the ancient Near East derived from natural causes such as drought, disease, or insects (Gen 12:10; 26:1; 41:1–57; Ruth 1:1; 2 Sam 21:1; 24:13; 1 Chr 21:12; 1 Kgs 18:1–2); the ravages of warfare through the confiscation and burning of crops (Judg 6:3–6; 15:3–5); and through siege (Lev 26:25–26; 2 Kgs 6:24–25; 2 Kgs 25:1–3; 2 Chr 32:11; Isa 31:19; Jer 14:11–18; 16:4; 21:7–9). Plague or pestilence affected animals (Exod 9:3; Ps 78:48–50), men (Lev 26:25–26; Num 14:12; 1 Chr 21:12), and crops. Israel's special geographical location on the only land bridge between the continents of Europe, Asia, and Africa brought a lot of commercial traffic through the area and made the land subject to the easy spread of disease and epidemics from neighboring lands.

An important theological principle is set out in v. 30. God is requested to "deal with each man according to all he does, since you know his heart [for you alone know the hearts of men]." God is a God of justice and deals with people as individuals. The prayer of the nation (the people Israel) is in the final analysis the prayer of the needy individual.

6:32–33   There is a fine spirit of tolerance toward the foreigner who came from a distant land because of God's great name and his mighty hand and outstretched arm. Let God hear the foreigner and do whatever he asks so that the people of the earth may know his name and fear him as do God's own people Israel. The spirit of this prayer is different from that displayed so often in Ezra and Nehemiah. Later prophets envisaged Gentiles coming to Jerusalem to worship the Lord (Isa 56:6–8; Zech 8:20–23; 14:16–21).

6:34–35   These verses contain a plea for assistance in war against Israel's enemies. This was a frequent occurrence over the years; and the prayers of Israel against Egyptians, Arameans, Moabites, Ammonites, Edomites, and Assyrians all provided examples of victory and of God upholding their cause. The message that God responds to prayer in times of military tension was always relevant.

6:36–39   The prayer turns again to captivity after defeat in battle. In such a case if Israel turned back to God with all their heart in the land of their captivity, confessing their sin, let God hear and forgive.[31] Prayer was to be directed toward Jerusalem, toward the land God had given to their fathers (Dan 6:10; Jonah 2:4).

6:40–41   Verse 40 is reminiscent of 1 Kgs 8:52, although vv. 41–42 are based on Ps 132:8–10. In concluding his prayer, Solomon based his expectation of God's favorable response on the divine promises to David. In the

---

[31] For the word שֹׁבִים ("their captivity") in v. 37, the parallel text in 1 Kgs 8:47 has שֹׁבֵיהֶם ("their conquerors"). And for the same word in v. 38, 1 Kgs 8:48 has אֹיְבֵיהֶם ("their enemies").

Kings account of Solomon's prayer, the ground for God's answer is his unique relationship to Israel deriving from the exodus (1 Kgs 8:50–53). In place of a reference to the themes of election and redemption in the exodus, he finds an adequate basis of appeal to God in Ps 132:1,8–10. God is called upon to arise and come to his resting place.

This call follows the usual "and now," which is used to conclude an argument or an exposition. God is called, he and his mighty ark, to their resting place. The theme of rest is important for the Chronicler. Rest was needed before the temple could be built. Although David's wars contributed to the conditions for peace, he himself could not build a temple, a resting place for God, with blood on his hands. But Solomon was a man of peace and rest (1 Chr 22:9; 28:2). Later history, however, would show that the peace and rest acquired in Solomon's time did not last. If it were to be acquired, that state lay in the future, an eschatological rest in which the passing glory of Solomon's day would give way to a permanent dwelling of God among his people (cf. Ezek 48:35; Heb 4; Rev 21:3). Solomon's present prayer was that God's priests would be clothed with salvation and his saints (loyal ones) rejoice in what was good.[32]

6:42 This verse is based on Ps 132:10 but differs a little. The order of the lines is reversed, giving a particular emphasis to the last line. Then the wording of this line has been changed, reminding the reader of Isa 55:3–6 with its reference to God's steadfast love for his servant David. The line has been rephrased to make it refer to God's promise to David. Psalm 132:10 has a certain ambiguity. It could refer to David's faithfulness to God or to God's promise to David. The Chronicler has made clear his own belief that the reference is God's promise to David, which is the sense in Isa 55:3. This supports the request in vv. 4–11 that God would confirm his promise to David about a dynasty.

The phrase "kindnesses promised to David" makes use of the plural form of the important noun *hesed,* which stressed the faithfulness, loyalty, and loving-kindness of God. The task of temple building was completed, and the way was now clear for God to establish the eternal Davidic dynasty in accordance with his promise. While this is not a messianic promise in the full sense, it strongly suggests that there is an abiding validity for the Davidic line. The completion of the temple served to confirm such a hope. There was more to the promise to David than the mere building of a temple.

---

[32] The noun לְחַסְדֵי, translated by the NIV as "saints," is a derivative of the Heb. noun חֶסֶד, variously translated as "loyalty, faithfulness, loving-kindness." It occurs in the plural form in v. 42. The NIV translates these nouns as "anointed ones" and "kindnesses."

(6) The Dedication Ceremony (7:1–22)

¹When Solomon finished praying, fire came down from heaven and consumed the burnt offering and the sacrifices, and the glory of the LORD filled the temple. ²The priests could not enter the temple of the LORD because the glory of the LORD filled it. ³When all the Israelites saw the fire coming down and the glory of the LORD above the temple, they knelt on the pavement with their faces to the ground, and they worshiped and gave thanks to the LORD, saying,

"He is good;

his love endures forever."

⁴Then the king and all the people offered sacrifices before the LORD. ⁵And King Solomon offered a sacrifice of twenty-two thousand head of cattle and a hundred and twenty thousand sheep and goats. So the king and all the people dedicated the temple of God. ⁶The priests took their positions, as did the Levites with the LORD'S musical instruments, which King David had made for praising the LORD and which were used when he gave thanks, saying, "His love endures forever." Opposite the Levites, the priests blew their trumpets, and all the Israelites were standing.

⁷Solomon consecrated the middle part of the courtyard in front of the temple of the LORD, and there he offered burnt offerings and the fat of the fellowship offerings, because the bronze altar he had made could not hold the burnt offerings, the grain offerings and the fat portions.

⁸So Solomon observed the festival at that time for seven days, and all Israel with him—a vast assembly, people from Lebo Hamath to the Wadi of Egypt. ⁹On the eighth day they held an assembly, for they had celebrated the dedication of the altar for seven days and the festival for seven days more. ¹⁰On the twenty-third day of the seventh month he sent the people to their homes, joyful and glad in heart for the good things the LORD had done for David and Solomon and for his people Israel.

¹¹When Solomon had finished the temple of the LORD and the royal palace, and had succeeded in carrying out all he had in mind to do in the temple of the LORD and in his own palace, ¹²the LORD appeared to him at night and said:

"I have heard your prayer and have chosen this place for myself as a temple for sacrifices.

¹³"When I shut up the heavens so that there is no rain, or command locusts to devour the land or send a plague among my people, ¹⁴if my people, who are called by my name, will humble themselves and pray and seek my face and turn from their wicked ways, then will I hear from heaven and will forgive their sin and will heal their land. ¹⁵Now my eyes will be open and my ears attentive to the prayers offered in this place. ¹⁶I have chosen and consecrated this temple so that my Name may be there forever. My eyes and my heart will always be there.

¹⁷"As for you, if you walk before me as David your father did, and do all I command, and observe my decrees and laws, ¹⁸I will establish your

royal throne, as I covenanted with David your father when I said, 'You
shall never fail to have a man to rule over Israel.'

[19]"But if you turn away and forsake the decrees and commands I have
given you and go off to serve other gods and worship them, [20]then I will
uproot Israel from my land, which I have given them, and will reject this
temple I have consecrated for my Name. I will make it a byword and an
object of ridicule among all peoples. [21]And though this temple is now so
imposing, all who pass by will be appalled and say, 'Why has the LORD
done such a thing to this land and to this temple?' [22]People will answer,
'Because they have forsaken the LORD, the God of their fathers, who
brought them out of Egypt, and have embraced other gods, worshiping
and serving them—that is why he brought all this disaster on them.'"

The dedication of the temple was a grand occasion. Chapter 7 corresponds closely to the parallel text in 1 Kgs 8:54–9:9 although there are additions and omissions. The chapter is concerned with the actual dedication of
the house of the Lord in 7:1–10 and with the Lord's response in 7:11–22.

The Chronicler omits the account of Solomon's blessing of the people
given in 1 Kgs 8:54b–61. This was normally the prerogative of the priests
(but cf. 1 Chr 16:2; 2 Chr 6:3). Here Solomon was standing on a raised platform (6:13; cp. Neh 8:4), not before the altar. But as the dedication proceeded, God's positive response to the prayer of 6:41 showed his approval
on the proceedings.

DEDICATION (7:1–10). **7:1** At the conclusion of Solomon's prayer of
dedication "a gigantic holocaust ignited by fire from heaven"[33] (cp. 1 Kgs
18:38) was the Lord's response to Solomon's dedication, confirming his
acceptance of both the temple and the offerings. A similar though less spectacular response was made by the Lord to the sacrifice of burnt offerings and
fellowship offerings David offered up on the altar he built on Araunah's
threshing floor when the future temple site was purchased (1 Chr 21:26). At
last three important elements of the Israelite cult had been brought together.
The ark, the Mosaic tabernacle, and the bronze altar that had been at Gibeon
(1:5–6) were installed in the temple, which stood on the site designated by
God (1 Chr 21:26–22:1). God once had approved the earlier tabernacle in a
similar way (Lev 9:23–24).

7:2 A similar statement is in 5:14. L. C. Allen makes an interesting
comparison: "The double attestation of the temple, in 5:13,14 and 7:1–3a,
reminds one of the twofold divine endorsement of Jesus, with a voice from
heaven at his baptism and a voice from the cloud of glory at his transfigura-

---

[33] Myers uses this striking description of what happened on this occasion (*II Chronicles,*
40).

tion (Mark 1:11; 9:7).[34] There is a parallel also in Exod 40:35.

7:3 The people saw the fire coming down and the glory of the Lord above the temple. This assured the whole congregation that God had consecrated the temple as a place of sacrifice and prayer. The people responded with worship and giving of thanks, making use of the well-known liturgical phrase, "He is good; his love endures forever" (cf. 5:13). By comparison the parallel in Kings does not indicate that the glory was seen by the laity outside the sanctuary (cf. Lev 9:23–24). The reverse repetition in vv. 2–3 of the filling of the temple and the song of thanks that are found in 5:13–14 identifies this as a framing device enclosing Solomon's prayer.

7:4–7 The large number of sacrifices (cf. 1 Kgs 8:62–64) presumably provided food for the people during the fifteen days of celebration that followed (vv. 8–10). The fat was burned before the people could consume it (Lev 3). The considerable number of animals, 22,000 oxen and 120,000 sheep, would require twenty sacrifices a minute for ten hours a day for twelve days. A hyperbole probably is intended[35] (cf. the figures at the time of Hezekiah, 29:32–36, and Josiah, 35:7–9). It was not possible to present all the offerings on the bronze altar that Solomon had made (4:1), so he consecrated the middle part of the courtyard in front of the temple, and there he offered burnt offerings and the fat of the fellowship offerings (traditionally peace offerings). The details of this arrangement are not given. In v. 6 the Chronicler mentions the full range of people present at the ceremony of dedication—priests, Levites, and all Israel. The "LORD'S musical instruments, which King David had made" (cf. 1 Chr 25:1–6), were carried by the Levites.

7:8–10 The festival lasted for seven days, and on the eighth day they held an assembly. "All Israel" was involved in the festival, a vast assembly gathered from Lebo (the entrance to) Hamath to the Wadi of Egypt. This area enabled representatives from "all Israel" to be gathered.

The Chronicler understood this festival to be the Feast of Tabernacles, normally followed by a solemn assembly on the eighth day (Lev 23:34–36). The law in Deut 16:13–15 refers only to seven days. The precise sequence of events was seven days of dedication from the eighth to the fourteenth of the month, then the Feast of Tabernacles from the fifteenth to the twentieth day of the month. The eighth day (cf. Lev 23:39) would be the final assembly on the twenty-second, followed by dismissal on the twenty-third day of the month. Solomon avoided having the dedication of the temple during Tabernacles and so placed the dedication for seven days before the Feast of Tabernacles. Thus on the twenty-third day of the seventh month he sent the people

---

[34] Allen, *1, 2 Chronicles*, 236.
[35] J. W. Wenham, "Large Numbers in the Old Testament," *TB* 18 (1967): 49–53.

to their homes joyful and glad in heart for the good things God had done.

An important phrase occurs in v. 9, "the dedication of the altar." The temple was not merely a place of prayer (chap. 6) but a place for sacrifice (cf. 2:4–6).

GOD'S RESPONSE TO THE DEDICATION CEREMONY (7:11–22). God's reply came in a nocturnal visitation. The Lord's temple was now completed along with Solomon's own palace. God's reply came some time later. But in spite of the close proximity of Solomon's prayer to this second appearance of God in the text, both Kings and Chronicles separate the two events. In fact, it took some thirteen years to accomplish this double task (1 Kgs 7:1; 9:10). This section (7:11–22) is based on 1 Kgs 9:2–9.

7:11–12a Some commentators regard this verse as a summary conclusion to the dedication. Others take it to be an introduction to God's response to Solomon's dedicatory prayer and associated rituals. The parallel account in 1 Kgs 9:2 refers to this event as a second appearance of God to Solomon, the first being at Gibeon. It is possible that the use of the phrase "at night" is intended as a reminder of that earlier occasion (cf. 1:7). This time, however, God's purpose was different.

7:12b–15 These verses from the use of the verb "chosen" in v. 12 through its interpretation in v. 16 are not found in the parallel account in 1 Kgs 9:3. They echo many of Solomon's words in his prayer in 1 Chr 6:22–39, and the one quoted here is representative of them all. In a sense this statement is a summary of what will appear in 2 Chronicles 10–36, where the Chronicler gives his account of the divided kingdoms.[36] Both then and in years to come if this people, called by God's name, that is, carrying his mark of ownership, would repent and inquire of the Lord (see comments at 1 Chr 10:13–14; 13:2–3; 14:8–11), he would forgive them and heal this land. Such was God's response to the prayer of Solomon, who had repeated the phrase "if your people" often in his prayer in 6:24–35. God promises to keep his eyes open and his ears attentive to the prayers offered "in this place," that is, the temple. His concluding promise in v. 15 follows the regular phrase used to round off a discussion or an argument, "Now."

7:16 This verse provides further strengthening of God's affirmation that he had chosen and consecrated the temple where his Name would be forever.

7:17–18 The appeal is made to Solomon to walk before God[37] as David

---

[36] Allen understands v. 14 as "one of the two keys of Chronicles," along with 1 Chr 17:12. He sees the book from this point on as constructed around this second verse (*1, 2 Chronicles*, 238).

[37] Although 2 Chr 6:16 has לָלֶכֶת בְּתוֹרָתִי ("walk in my law"), 1 Kgs 8:25 has לָלֶכֶת לְפָנַי ("walk before me"). The expression "walk before me" in 1 Kgs 9:4 is also in this parallel verse in 2 Chr 7:17. As Japhet explains (*1 & 2 Chronicles*, 591), walking before the Lord is simply a more general and rare equivalent of walking in his law (cf. Jer 26:4; Dan 9:10; Neh 10:30).

had done and to be obedient to all of God's law. These things were essential for establishing and continuing the Davidic dynasty. Use of the verb "covenanted," for which 1 Kgs 9:5 has "promised," probably is significant. The Kings text reads "promised" (1 Kgs 9:5). Here there is a deliberate strengthening of the idea of God's covenant with David. The use of "covenanted" also creates a wordplay since the Hebrew word is *kāratî*, and the word for "fail" is *yikkārēt*.

The phrase "a man to rule over Israel" is parallel to "a man upon the throne of Israel" in 1 Kgs 9:5. Williamson[38] thinks there may be an echo here of Mic 5:2 (Heb. 5:1). This no doubt was intended to emphasize the promise to David of an eternal dynasty and could easily be seen as an incipient messianic hope.

7:19–22   In Hebrew, the pronoun "you" is plural. This moved the context from the second singular (see vv. 17–18), which referred to Solomon, to the second plural, which included both Solomon and the people. If they turned away and forsook God's laws to serve and worship other gods, there would be dire consequences. They would be separated from their land (exiled), the temple would be rejected, and they would become an object of ridicule among all peoples. The temple itself would become the object of taunting (Deut 28:37; Jer 24:9). This was to happen in the destruction brought about by Nebuchadnezzar. The Chronicler and the Israel of his day worshiped in a new temple. But though the temple had once been destroyed, God's choice of Jerusalem was still valid; and though no descendant of David sat on David's throne, the Davidic line had not failed (7:18).

3. Other Achievements of Solomon (8:1–16)

[1]**At the end of twenty years, during which Solomon built the temple of the LORD and his own palace, [2]Solomon rebuilt the villages that Hiram had given him, and settled Israelites in them. [3]Solomon then went to Hamath Zobah and captured it. [4]He also built up Tadmor in the desert and all the store cities he had built in Hamath. [5]He rebuilt Upper Beth Horon and Lower Beth Horon as fortified cities, with walls and with gates and bars, [6]as well as Baalath and all his store cities, and all the cities for his chariots and for his horses—whatever he desired to build in Jerusalem, in Lebanon and throughout all the territory he ruled.**

[7]**All the people left from the Hittites, Amorites, Perizzites, Hivites and Jebusites (these peoples were not Israelites), [8]that is, their descendants remaining in the land, whom the Israelites had not destroyed—these Solomon con-**

---

[38] Williamson gives a succinct statement of the way in which 8:1–16 may be linked into the story of the building of the temple (*1 and 2 Chronicles,* 227).

scripted for his slave labor force, as it is to this day. ⁹But Solomon did not make slaves of the Israelites for his work; they were his fighting men, commanders of his captains, and commanders of his chariots and charioteers. ¹⁰They were also King Solomon's chief officials—two hundred and fifty officials supervising the men.

¹¹Solomon brought Pharaoh's daughter up from the City of David to the palace he had built for her, for he said, "My wife must not live in the palace of David king of Israel, because the places the ark of the LORD has entered are holy."

¹²On the altar of the LORD that he had built in front of the portico, Solomon sacrificed burnt offerings to the LORD, ¹³according to the daily requirement for offerings commanded by Moses for Sabbaths, New Moons and the three annual feasts—the Feast of Unleavened Bread, the Feast of Weeks and the Feast of Tabernacles. ¹⁴In keeping with the ordinance of his father David, he appointed the divisions of the priests for their duties, and the Levites to lead the praise and to assist the priests according to each day's requirement. He also appointed the gatekeepers by divisions for the various gates, because this was what David the man of God had ordered. ¹⁵They did not deviate from the king's commands to the priests or to the Levites in any matter, including that of the treasuries.

¹⁶All Solomon's work was carried out, from the day the foundation of the temple of the LORD was laid until its completion. So the temple of the LORD was finished.

While this chapter may appear to be sort of a miscellany and to have little to do with the building of the temple, the words of v. 16 indicate that the Chronicler wished to round off a large program of Solomon's work until the temple was finished.

Chapter 8 is parallel to 1 Kgs 9:10–28, although the Chronicler made some changes. First Kings 9:11–16 is omitted, and 2 Chr 8:11b,13–16 is added material. The general sequence of the materials, however, is the same. It is convenient to take 8:1–16 as an appendix to the building of the temple and include 8:17–18 with 9:1–31, which gives more detail about Solomon's greatness.

Chapters 8–9 describe four glorious aspects of Solomon's reign: his power, his worship of God, his wealth, and his wisdom. Wilcock has pointed out that these aspects of Solomon's reign can only in a limited way serve as examples for us to follow; we cannot (and should not) aspire to his power and wealth, and even his wisdom and the worship he sponsored are in many respects different from what we might realistically imitate.[39] The true significance of this presentation of Solomon is that it is a model for the kingdom of God. When God's domain has been fully established, there will be no

---

[39] Wilcock, *Message of Chronicles,* 153–62.

want or ignorance. The powers of evil will be set in flight, but God will be truly worshiped. In this the greatness of Solomon's kingdom is a reminder that the kingdom of God must finally triumph. When that happens, all his people will live under a reign that is far greater than anything Israel experienced under Solomon. Still, Solomon serves as a pointer to what the kingdom of God will be.

8:1 Verses 1–16 parallel 2:17–5:1 in the overall chiastic structure of the Chronicler's account of Solomon.[40] Reference is here made to a state of affairs twenty years after Solomon's accession to the throne, during which the temple and the king's palace were built.

8:2 There is an apparent discrepancy between this statement and that in 1 Kgs 9:10–14, where Solomon tried to give twenty cities in Galilee to Hiram, king of Tyre, either to satisfy an outstanding debt (1 Kgs 9:11) or as payment for additional items needed to complete the work (1 Kgs 9:14). There may have been a contract entered into beyond that agreed to originally (2 Chr 2:10; 1 Kgs 5:10–11).

According to the Kings text, Hiram was not pleased with Solomon's gift. In that case Chronicles may provide the sequel to the story. Hiram may have returned the unsatisfactory cities to Solomon, who had given them originally as payment or collateral until he could pay Hiram in some other acceptable commodity.[41]

8:3–6 Solomon is recorded as having gone to Hamath Zobah and captured it. This is the only reference in Chronicles to any military activity by Solomon, who is known elsewhere as a man of peace (1 Chr 22:9). This military reference is lacking in 1 Kgs 9:17–19, although there are links between the two passages, suggesting that they are somehow related.[42]

It clearly was part of the Chronicler's record that the kingdom under David and Solomon had now reached its ideal borders (7:8; 1 Chr 13:5,18:3). If David had extended control as far as Hamath, it was natural that Solomon would consolidate his borders. We already have learned (7:8) that people came from Lebo Hamath to the dedication of the temple. This passage reports Solomon's extension of his borders to include Hamath. Solomon did not, however, maintain these borders so far north (1 Kgs

---

[40] See Dillard, *2 Chronicles,* 5–6.

[41] A valuable discussion of the issue is given in Williamson, *1 and 2 Chronicles,* 228–29.

[42] The two paragraphs have identical wording at their close (cp. 1 Kgs 9:19b; 2 Chr 8:6b). Certainly the towns listed in vv. 4–6—Tadmor, Hamath, Upper Beth Horon, and Lower Beth Horon as well as Baalath—are reminiscent of the list in Kings. But there are differences. The positions of Lower Beth Horon and Tadmor (Tamar) are reversed. Hamath (vv. 3–4) is absent from 1 Kgs 9:15–19. The introduction to the Kings account ("and this is the account of the forced labor") in 1 Kgs 9:15 does not appear in Chronicles.

11:23–25). Even so, it is evident also that Solomon controlled the major trade routes to Mesopotamia—the main overland route via Hamath and the shorter desert route via Tadmor (possibly Palmyra). Control of these trade routes was important for Solomon's commercial endeavors and therefore his wealth. The mention of store cities (v. 4) would fit this picture of trade.

Upper Beth Horon and Lower Beth Horon are situated on the ridge rising from the Valley of Aijalon to the plateau just north of Jerusalem. The road along this route linked Jerusalem to the coastal highway and was of great strategic importance. Invaders from the north attacked Jerusalem along this road. Both these cities were fortified with walls and gates and bars. The exact location of Baalath is not certain, but from the present context it seems to have lain on the Gezer-Beth Horon-Jerusalem road.

It seems clear that the Chronicler in vv. 2–6 is extending his picture of Solomon's building program. Store-cities and chariot-cities deal with trade and defense. The program covered wherever Solomon desired to build in Jerusalem, in Lebanon, and throughout all the territory that he ruled.

8:7–10 These verses deal with Solomon's levy and follow 1 Kgs 9:20–23 fairly closely (see comments on 2:17–18). Solomon's workmen were all non-Israelites. He did not make slaves of the Israelites but reserved them for fighting men, military officers, and chief officials who supervised the men.

8:11 The Chronicler assumed his readers knew of Solomon's diplomatic marriage with pharaoh's daughter (1 Kgs 9:16), who lived with him in Jerusalem. Solomon built a palace for her lest her close proximity to the temple while living in the king's palace might somehow defile the temple and the ark.

8:12–15 These verses are an expansion of 1 Kgs 9:25. They illustrate Solomon's cultic arrangements for the new temple with an emphasis on the detailed observance of Moses' commands in Lev 23:1–37 and Numbers 28–29 and on the prescriptions of David (1 Chr 23–26), with specific reference to the three annual festivals—the Feast of Unleavened Bread, the Feast of Weeks, and the Feast of Tabernacles (each mentioned in Kings). The Chronicler added the observance of the Sabbaths and New Moons. Solomon himself sacrificed burnt offerings to the Lord on the altar he had built in front of the portico. This was not the altar within the holy place that was reserved for the priests.

Following David's instructions, Solomon appointed the divisions of the priests for their duties and the Levites to undertake their musical duties. Gatekeepers also were appointed by divisions for duty at the various gates (cf. 1 Chr 26:1–3,9–11). Attention also was given to the treasuries (cf. 1 Chr 26:20–32).

8:16 This is the second occasion on which the Chronicler reports the completion of the temple (cf. 7:11). The verse is unique to Chronicles and forms a balancing counterpart to 5:1 in accordance with the Chronicler's chiastic arrangements.[43] This verse represents an important literary mark in the story of the Chronicler, concluding the long section that began at 2:1. A similar phrase to "so the temple of the LORD was finished" occurs in 29:35, as the Chronicler concluded his account of the restoration of the temple service under Hezekiah.

4. Solomon's Wisdom and Wealth and His Death (8:17–9:31)

(1) Maritime Mission to Ophir (8:17–18)

[17]**Then Solomon went to Ezion Geber and Elath on the coast of Edom.** [18]**And Hiram sent him ships commanded by his own officers, men who knew the sea. These, with Solomon's men, sailed to Ophir and brought back four hundred and fifty talents of gold, which they delivered to King Solomon.**

8:17–18   Solomon and Hiram engaged in a joint maritime venture. Hiram provided ships and personnel although Solomon was the initiator of the venture. Even though Solomon had mastery over the land routes to the north, he apparently was able also to tap into the trade with Africa. The ships referred to in v. 18 sailed to Ophir and brought back four hundred and fifty talents of gold for Solomon's use. The location of Ophir is a subject of debate. It has been identified variously with India (Josephus, *Ant.* 8.164), Punt (Somaliland on the coast of Africa), and West or South Arabia. According to 9:21 and 1 Kgs 10:22, the voyages took three years. The list of commodities given in 1 Kgs 10:23 may provide a clue, but these items could have been transported to Ophir, which may have been a transfer point in a trade with more distant regions. The identification of Ophir remains an open question.

(2) Visit of the Queen of Sheba (9:1–12)

[1]**When the queen of Sheba heard of Solomon's fame, she came to Jerusalem to test him with hard questions. Arriving with a very great caravan—with camels carrying spices, large quantities of gold, and precious stones—she came to Solomon and talked with him about all she had on her mind.** [2]**Solomon answered all her questions; nothing was too hard for him to explain to her.** [3]**When the queen of Sheba saw the wisdom of Solomon, as well as the palace he had built,** [4]**the food on his table, the seating of his officials, the attending servants in their robes, the cupbearers in their robes and the burnt offerings he made at the temple of the LORD, she was overwhelmed.**

[5]**She said to the king, "The report I heard in my own country about your**

---

[43] See Dillard, *2 Chronicles,* 5–6.

achievements and your wisdom is true. ⁶But I did not believe what they said until I came and saw with my own eyes. Indeed, not even half the greatness of your wisdom was told me; you have far exceeded the report I heard. ⁷How happy your men must be! How happy your officials, who continually stand before you and hear your wisdom! ⁸Praise be to the LORD your God, who has delighted in you and placed you on his throne as king to rule for the LORD your God. Because of the love of your God for Israel and his desire to uphold them forever, he has made you king over them, to maintain justice and righteousness."

⁹Then she gave the king 120 talents of gold, large quantities of spices, and precious stones. There had never been such spices as those the queen of Sheba gave to King Solomon.

¹⁰(The men of Hiram and the men of Solomon brought gold from Ophir; they also brought algumwood and precious stones. ¹¹The king used the algumwood to make steps for the temple of the LORD and for the royal palace, and to make harps and lyres for the musicians. Nothing like them had ever been seen in Judah.)

¹²King Solomon gave the queen of Sheba all she desired and asked for; he gave her more than she had brought to him. Then she left and returned with her retinue to her own country.

Chapter 9 follows the parallel in 1 Kgs 10:1–29; 11:41–43. This chapter balances 2 Chronicles 1. The Chronicler probably wished to make the general point that as Solomon readily gave his resources to build the temple, so now he was rewarded abundantly with God's gifts to him as well as the esteem of the nations. Also just as David prospered because he established correct religious priorities, causing the nation Israel to prosper, so under Solomon with his building of the temple the whole nation prospered. By contrast Saul brought disaster on Israel because of his own carelessness in religious matters.

The visit of the queen of Sheba to Solomon follows 1 Kgs 10:1–13 fairly closely. The story lends support to the Chronicler's picture of Solomon's wisdom, wealth, and international prestige. Commercial interests probably played a more significant motivation than the queen's desire to tap a new source of wisdom.

9:1 Sheba probably is to be identified with the South Arabian kingdom of Saba. The consonant *s* in Arabic becomes *šh* in Hebrew. Ancient Saba is roughly equivalent to modern Yemen.

Solomon, being a great king, should have excelled in wisdom. The Chronicler highlights this in the course of these verses. Evidently the queen of Sheba was a woman of great wealth like Solomon. She came with caravans of camels laden with spices, gold, and precious stones. Female rulers in pre-Islamic times played important roles. Several classical writers testify to their wealth and power. The kingdom of Saba was renowned for frankincense and myrrh. Negotiations with Solomon concerning trade in aromatic resins were to be expected. Frankincense and myrrh were in high demand for use in pharmacopoeia and cosmetics, embalming and religious offerings (Isa 60:6; Jer 6:20). Frankincense and myrrh ranked alongside gold for trade and as gifts for a king.

9:2–4 Solomon's wisdom is highlighted by the Chronicler. His evident wealth, his fine eating, his retinue of officials, servants, cupbearers in their robes and the sacrificial offerings (see NIV text note on "burnt offerings") Solomon made at the temple overwhelmed the queen of Sheba (lit. "there was no breath in her," i.e., she was breathless).

9:5 It probably is quite deliberate that the Chronicler reported this encounter with the queen of Sheba immediately following the reference to Solomon's seaport at Ezion Geber, whose traffic with Ophir threatened the lucrative overland trade of the South Arabians. The reports that came to the queen of Sheba about Solomon's wealth and achievements were true. Excavations in southern Arabia in recent years have revealed that this was a land with an advanced civilization and prosperous economy.[44]

9:6–8 These words form a strong hyperbole and enhance the status of Solomon still further. Even the queen of Sheba recognized that Solomon had been appointed to his position by God. Solomon, as God's vice-regent, was to maintain justice and righteousness.

9:9 The gifts the queen of Sheba gave to Solomon—gold, spices, and precious stones—would be the kinds of gifts one would bring from southern Arabia.

9:10–11 The parallel account in 1 Kgs 10:11 notes that Hiram's fleet brought gold, precious stones, and algum wood. Here it states simply that the servants of Hiram and the servants of Solomon brought gifts. For algum wood see 2:8–9.

9:12 Solomon's gifts were generous. He gave the queen of Sheba all she asked plus other gifts in value greater than she had brought to him.

(3) Solomon's Splendor (9:13–28)

[13]The weight of the gold that Solomon received yearly was 666 talents, [14]not including the revenues brought in by merchants and traders. Also all the kings of Arabia and the governors of the land brought gold and silver to Solomon.

[15]King Solomon made two hundred large shields of hammered gold; six hundred bekas of hammered gold went into each shield. [16]He also made three

---

[44] See summary in Myers, *II Chronicles*, 56–57.

hundred small shields of hammered gold, with three hundred bekas of gold in each shield. The king put them in the Palace of the Forest of Lebanon. [17]Then the king made a great throne inlaid with ivory and overlaid with pure gold. [18]The throne had six steps, and a footstool of gold was attached to it. On both sides of the seat were armrests, with a lion standing beside each of them. [19]Twelve lions stood on the six steps, one at either end of each step. Nothing like it had ever been made for any other kingdom. [20]All King Solomon's goblets were gold, and all the household articles in the Palace of the Forest of Lebanon were pure gold. Nothing was made of silver, because silver was considered of little value in Solomon's day. [21]The king had a fleet of trading ships manned by Hiram's men. Once every three years it returned, carrying gold, silver and ivory, and apes and baboons.

[22]King Solomon was greater in riches and wisdom than all the other kings of the earth. [23]All the kings of the earth sought audience with Solomon to hear the wisdom God had put in his heart. [24]Year after year, everyone who came brought a gift—articles of silver and gold, and robes, weapons and spices, and horses and mules.

[25]Solomon had four thousand stalls for horses and chariots, and twelve thousand horses, which he kept in the chariot cities and also with him in Jerusalem. [26]He ruled over all the kings from the River to the land of the Philistines, as far as the border of Egypt. [27]The king made silver as common in Jerusalem as stones, and cedar as plentiful as sycamore-fig trees in the foothills. [28]Solomon's horses were imported from Egypt and from all other countries.

This section gathers together a variety of items. It owes much to 1 Kgs 10:14–28 and seems to be designed to enhance the prestige and wealth of Solomon still further.

9:13–14 Revenues (666 talents yearly) brought in by merchants and traders, gold and silver from the kings of Arabia and the governors of the land, flowed into Solomon's kingdom.

9:15–16 From the gold Solomon made two hundred large shields, each weighing six hundred bekas. A beka was the equivalent of a half-shekel (Gen 24:22; Exod 38:26) and weighed about six grams. There also were three hundred small shields each weighing three hundred bekas (or three minas; cf. 1 Kgs 10:17). These shields had a sad end. They were carried off by Pharaoh Shishak when he attacked Jerusalem shortly after Solomon's death (12:9–11). The Chronicler does not provide a description of the "Palace of the Forest of Lebanon" like that given in 1 Kgs 7:1–12.

9:17–19 The ivory throne reflected the glory and splendor of Solomon. The Assyrian ruler Ashurbanipal had a throne like this.[45] It was overlaid

---

[45] J. A. Montgomery and H. S. Gehman, *The Books of Kings,* ICC (London: T & T Clark, 1951), 221–22; Myers, *II Chronicles,* 58.

with pure gold, was approached by six steps, and had a footstool of gold attached. There were armrests on either side with a lion standing beside each. The Kings account (1 Kgs 10:19) notes that "at the back of the throne was a calf's head," but this is omitted by the Chronicler, perhaps because of unsavory religious overtones.

9:20   The goblets and household articles in the Palace of the Forest of Lebanon were made of pure gold. In what is surely hyperbole, the text tells us that gold was so abundant that silver was considered too cheap to be of use.

9:21–24   Further details of Solomon's trading fleet are given. The Hebrew text states that the ships belonging to the king traveled to Tarshish while the Hebrew text of 1 Kgs 10:22 speaks of "ships of Tarshish." The 2 Chr 9:21 reference need not refer to a specific country but rather to a type of ship, a ship that could go to the "ends of the earth." The cargoes carried suggest voyages south to Ophir from Ezion Geber rather than across the Mediterranean to Tarshish (Tartessus) in Spain. Translation of the last item of cargo is uncertain. For "baboon" the NRSV has "peacocks." For the last two items Myers has simply "two species of monkeys."[46]

9:25–28   On the number of Solomon's horses and chariots see the comments at 1:14.

The end of the Chronicler's account of Solomon, like the beginning of chap. 1, spotlights Solomon's great wisdom and wealth as a result of God's favor.

(4) Solomon's Death (9:29–31)

[29]As for the other events of Solomon's reign, from beginning to end, are they not written in the records of Nathan the prophet, in the prophecy of Ahijah the Shilonite and in the visions of Iddo the seer concerning Jeroboam son of Nebat? [30]Solomon reigned in Jerusalem over all Israel forty years. [31]Then he rested with his fathers and was buried in the city of David his father. And Rehoboam his son succeeded him as king.

Some sections that deal with Solomon's life and which appear elsewhere are omitted, for example, 1 Kings 11, which speaks of Solomon's many foreign wives. This would have served to downgrade Solomon when the Chronicler wished to present his positive characteristics. To a degree the picture painted is an idealized one. In any case it indicated the sort of person one should expect to find on David's throne. The unsavory features were set

---

[46] Myers, *II Chronicles*, 53-54.

aside as being atypical of a Davidic king. The Chronicler therefore passes straight from the account of Solomon in all his wisdom and greatness to the concluding summary of Solomon's reign.

This brief passage is based on 1 Kgs 11:41–43 and follows the pattern of the death notices of kings recorded in the Book of Kings.

9:29   At first glance it appears the Chronicler used material from independent collections of prophetic materials, the records of Nathan, the prophecy of Ahijah the Shilonite, and the visions of Iddo the prophet (cf. 1 Chr 29:29; 2 Chr 13:22; 26:22; 33:19). The records of Nathan the prophet point to 1 Kings 1 and hence to the opening of Solomon's reign; the prophecy of Ahijah the Shilonite is based on 1 Kgs 11:29–40. Iddo the seer (12:15; 13:22) is not mentioned in Kings, but some have speculated that he was the unnamed prophet of 1 Kgs 13:1–10. Such sources are not known independently, although they may have existed once. Some commentators propose that they were incorporated into anthologies or other annalistic sources. However, the Chronicler's citations may have come from the Books of Samuel and Kings and not from an independent source. Certainty is not possible. But if the Chronicler did draw on these earlier books, we have here an indication that he regarded these texts as prophetic in nature.

9:30   Solomon reigned over "all Israel" for forty years. That was the ideal for the nation. After Solomon's death the ideal was shattered. For the Chronicler the past ideal was a vision for the future.

9:31   Solomon died and rested with his father. He was succeeded by his son Rehoboam, who was to preside over the disruption of a united Israel.

V. THE DIVIDED MONARCHY (10:1–28:27)
  1. The Rebellion of Israel (10:1–19)
  2. The Reign of Rehoboam: Establishing the Kingdom (11:1–23)
      (1) The Prophecy of Shemaiah (11:1–4)
      (2) Cities for Defense (11:5–12)
      (3) Migration of Priests and Levites (11:13–17)
      (4) Rehoboam's Family (11:18–23)
  3. The Reign of Rehoboam: Shisak's Invasion (12:1–12)
  4. The Conclusion of Rehoboam's Reign (12:13–16)
  5. The Reign of Abijah (13:1–14:1a)
  6. The Reign of Asa (14:1b–16:14)
      (1) The Early Years (14:1b–15)
      (2) Asa's Reformation (15:1–19)
      (3) The Later Years (16:1–14)
  7. The Reign of Jehoshaphat (17:1–21:1)
      (1) Character and Organization (17:1–19)
      (2) Alliance with the Northern Kingdom (18:1–34)
      (3) The Reign of Jehoshaphat: God's Rebuke and Jehoshaphat's
          Reformation (19:1–11)
      (4) Jehoshaphat's Piety Rewarded (20:1–21:1)
  8. The Reign of Jehoram (21:2–20)
      (1) Jehoram Establishes His Rule (21:2–4)
      (2) The Character of Jehoram's Reign (21:5–11)
      (3) The Letter from Elijah (21:12–15)
      (4) The End of Jehoram's Life (21:16–20)
  9. The Reign of Ahaziah (22:1–9)
  10. The Interregnum of Athaliah (22:10–12)
  11. The Reign of Joash (23:1–24:27)
      (1) Jehoida's Coup and the Enthronement of Joash
          (23:1–11)
      (2) The Reaction of Athaliah (23:12–15)
      (3) The Reformation (23:16–21)
      (4) The Later Years (24:1–27)
  12. The Reign of Amaziah (25:1–28)
      (1) Amaziah's Accession (25:1–4)
      (2) The Edomite Campaign (25:5–16)

───────── V. THE DIVIDED MONARCHY (10:1–28:27) ─────────

Solomon's death marked the end of a united Israel. After his death a schism rent the nation into two parts. In telling his story, the Chronicler concentrated on the Southern Kingdom of Judah. It was not that for him the concept of "all Israel" had ceased to be important. But the purposes of God were to be worked out now through the Davidic dynasty and the Jerusalem temple. Israel's true religious traditions would be maintained through these two institutions. At times in the years that followed it was possible to glimpse the hope of a renewed unity, as in the days of Hezekiah when representatives of the Northern Kingdom came to Jerusalem to keep the Passover (2 Chr 30).

The history of the Northern Kingdom as an independent, separated nation did not concern the Chronicler, although he was careful to record any references to contacts between north and south. The northerners were not simply written off. They remained part of "all Israel" but represented the part of Israel that had forsaken God. The hope of a return and a true repentance was seen by the Chronicler as a desirable, eventual outcome of the seeming tragedy of the schism. Repentance would lead to restoration. The political entity of the Northern Kingdom was different from the population of the Northern Kingdom. The northern people were still Israel, still a significant element of "all Israel."

In the early days of Rehoboam's reign (ca. 922–915 B.C.) the schism between south and north came about. The north rebelled against Rehoboam and remained separated, never to be reunited. The exile of the north at the fall of their capital, Samaria, in the days of the Assyrian king Sargon II (721–705 B.C.) took place in 722/721 B.C.

Rehoboam's folly and its consequences illustrate the point that the Chronicler was no narrow Davidic nationalist who believed that in order to prosper Israel only needed a true son of David on the throne. Rehoboam, though in every sense the legitimate Davidic king, did considerable damage to the kingdom. Pedigree is not enough. In fact, it is of no value without the wisdom that comes from the fear of the Lord.

On the other hand, the Chronicler's portrait of the schism lays more blame on Jeroboam than Rehoboam. While Rehoboam is not exonerated, the total picture of this monarch is not altogether negative, and the text speaks of him more as young and foolish than as wicked (2 Chr 13:7). The point is that the Chronicler never regarded the northern monarchy as anything but illegitimate and a rebellion against God's chosen dynasty. As far as he was concerned, all Israel had one and only one ruling family.[1]

1. The Rebellion of Israel (10:1–19)

[1]Rehoboam went to Shechem, for all the Israelites had gone there to make him king. [2]When Jeroboam son of Nebat heard this (he was in Egypt, where he had fled from King Solomon), he returned from Egypt. [3]So they sent for Jeroboam, and he and all Israel went to Rehoboam and said to him: [4]"Your father put a heavy yoke on us, but now lighten the harsh labor and the heavy yoke he put on us, and we will serve you."

[5]Rehoboam answered, "Come back to me in three days." So the people went away.

[6]Then King Rehoboam consulted the elders who had served his father Solomon during his lifetime. "How would you advise me to answer these people?" he asked.

[7]They replied, "If you will be kind to these people and please them and give them a favorable answer, they will always be your servants."

[8]But Rehoboam rejected the advice the elders gave him and consulted the young men who had grown up with him and were serving him. [9]He asked them, "What is your advice? How should we answer these people who say to me, 'Lighten the yoke your father put on us'?"

[10]The young men who had grown up with him replied, "Tell the people who have said to you, 'Your father put a heavy yoke on us, but make our yoke lighter'—tell them, 'My little finger is thicker than my father's waist. [11]My father laid on you a heavy yoke; I will make it even heavier. My father scourged you with whips; I will scourge you with scorpions.'"

[12]Three days later Jeroboam and all the people returned to Rehoboam, as the king had said, "Come back to me in three days." [13]The king answered them

---

[1] See G. N. Knoppers, "Rehoboam in Chronicles: Villain or Victim?" *JBL* 109 (1990): 423–40.

harshly. Rejecting the advice of the elders, [14]he followed the advice of the young men and said, "My father made your yoke heavy; I will make it even heavier. My father scourged you with whips; I will scourge you with scorpions." [15]So the king did not listen to the people, for this turn of events was from God, to fulfill the word the LORD had spoken to Jeroboam son of Nebat through Ahijah the Shilonite.

[16]When all Israel saw that the king refused to listen to them, they answered the king:

> "What share do we have in David,
>   what part in Jesse's son?
> To your tents, O Israel!
>   Look after your own house, O David!"

So all the Israelites went home. [17]But as for the Israelites who were living in the towns of Judah, Rehoboam still ruled over them.

[18]King Rehoboam sent out Adoniram, who was in charge of forced labor, but the Israelites stoned him to death. King Rehoboam, however, managed to get into his chariot and escape to Jerusalem. [19]So Israel has been in rebellion against the house of David to this day.

10:1 This account in 2 Chr 10:1–19 follows closely the account in 1 Kgs 12:1–19. It was necessary for a new king to receive approval and acceptance at a national assembly. Rehoboam therefore was required to appear at Shechem, for "all Israel" had assembled there to make him king. Shechem was strategically located at the eastern entrance to the pass that ran between Mount Gerizim and Mount Ebal. It lay in the midst of a fertile plain with a good water supply. It was a military, political, and religious center for ancient Israel from early times (Gen 12:6–7; 33:18–29; Josh 24). No reference is made in this passage to a covenant, but no doubt some kind of covenant ceremony took place (cf. 2 Sam 3:6–21; 5:1–3; 2 Chr 23:3). The use of the phrase "all Israel" here is quite deliberate and refers to the full number of tribes. Later the name "Israel" was used for the Northern Kingdom (10:16; 11:13) and at times for the Southern Kingdom (11:3; 12:1).

10:2 Jeroboam, son of Nebat, who was to lead the northern tribes out of the union of "all Israel," was in Egypt when he heard of the death of Solomon and the assembly meeting at Shechem. He had fled to Egypt to escape from King Solomon. On Solomon's death he felt it was safe for him to return. In any case Jeroboam had secret plans to lead the northern tribes out of the united kingdom. The Chronicler seems to lay the blame for the division of the kingdom on Jeroboam. He also held Jeroboam responsible for the continuation of the breach (2 Chr 13:5–12). The story in 1 Kgs 11:26–40, in which Ahijah the prophet tore his own garment and gave Jeroboam ten pieces of the twelve into which it was torn, is omitted but apparently assumed by the Chronicler.

10:3 When Jeroboam returned home, the people sent for him; and he and all Israel set about bargaining with Rehoboam, Solomon's son, about easing their burdens.

10:4–5 The issues were heavy taxation and forced labor. The delegates from the northern tribes demanded a reduction in both as a condition of their recognition of Rehoboam's sovereignty. Such reductions were not unknown among the rulers of the nations round about. In some periods of Assyrian history a new king would publish a decree canceling various excessive measures under which their subjects suffered. In Israel itself release from debt and servitude was to be practiced on Sabbatical and Jubilee years (Lev 25:8–55).

10:6–7 The advice of the elders who had served Rehoboam's father, Solomon, was conciliatory. "Be kind to these people and please them" has essentially the same sense as the words in 1 Kgs 12:7, "Be a servant . . . and serve them," although it appears less strong. The elders were important in Israel's earlier patriarchal and tribal society (2 Sam 3:17; 5:3; 17:4,15; 1 Kgs 20:7–8; 1 Chr 11:3). It would have been a wise and gracious decision by Rehoboam to follow the elders' advice.

10:8–11 Rejecting the advice of the elders, Rehoboam consulted the young men, whose identity is uncertain to us. They may have been royal princes, half-brothers of Rehoboam, or civil servants. They had grown up with him and were contemporaries. Rehoboam was forty-one years old at the time of his accession (12:13). These counseled harsh words and a threat that he would increase their burdens. Some have suggested that these two groups of advisers may have been two levels of authority in a bicameral authority. The idea is attractive, but not entirely certain.[2]

10:12–15 When the people returned after three days, Rehoboam replied in terms of the advice given by the "young men." It was the end of a united Israel. The Chronicler essentially repeated the theological explanation from 1 Kgs 12:15 that "this turn of events was from God" and linked it to the prophecy given through Ahijah the Shilonite (a knowledge of 1 Kgs 11:21–29 is presupposed). The whole incident raises questions about where the responsibility for the division of the kingdom lay. In one sense the northern tribes, unwilling to continue under the harsh conditions imposed on them, brought about the break in rebellion against divinely ordained Davidic rule and Jerusalem temple worship. In another sense Rehoboam and the young men brought about the breach through their heartless and intransigent attitudes (cf. 13:7). Behind both of these causes lay the purposes of God in

---

[2] A. Malamat, "Kingship and Council in Israel and Sumer: A Parallel," *JNES* 22 (1963): 247–53.

judgment against the idolatry that entered Israel under Solomon's rule (1 Kgs 11:29–33). Further, Jeroboam carried much of the responsibility on the northern side both for the initial breach and for its continuation (cf. 13:5–6; 1 Kgs 12:25–33).

10:16 The rejection formula is a poetic statement, the antithesis of the acceptance formula declared by "all Israel" when they accepted David as king. Israel's response to David in 1 Chr 12:19 was:

> We are yours, O David!
> We are with you, O son of Jesse!

The rejection formula used by the northern tribes in this verse is:

> What share do we have in David,
> what part in Jesse's Son?

Here "Israel" means the northern tribes. The passage concludes, "So all the Israelites went home."

10:17 The rest of Israel, the people of Israel who were living in the towns of Judah, accepted the rule of Rehoboam. This shows that there was more involved in the split than rebellion against oppression. A spirit of independence had been brewing among the nation's tribes for many years (cf. Josh 17:14–18; Judg 8:1; 12:1; 17–19).

10:18–19 Adoniram (the Heb. has "Hadoram") was dispatched, probably to attempt a reconciliation. Perhaps as one in authority he might have been expected to attempt this, but the people stoned him to death. Apparently the king was there as well and might have been assassinated had he not escaped.

2. The Reign of Rehoboam: Establishing the Kingdom (11:1–23)

The political loss of the northern tribes left only Judah and Benjamin loyal to Solomon's son. His response was to seek to restore the rebels by military action. This was averted by a word from God through Shemaiah, a prophet. However, Rehoboam set about a program of defense by fortifying cities in Judah and Benjamin. Rehoboam had several wives by whom he had sons and like his father, Solomon, placed these in strategic centers to maintain his position and to guard against disloyalty.

(1) The Prophecy of Shemaiah (11:1–4)

¹When Rehoboam arrived in Jerusalem, he mustered the house of Judah and Benjamin—a hundred and eighty thousand fighting men—to make war against Israel and to regain the kingdom for Rehoboam.

²But this word of the LORD came to Shemaiah the man of God: ³"Say to

Rehoboam son of Solomon king of Judah and to all the Israelites in Judah and Benjamin, ⁴"This is what the LORD says: Do not go up to fight against your brothers. Go home, every one of you, for this is my doing.'" So they obeyed the words of the LORD and turned back from marching against Jeroboam.

11:1 For the first fifty years of the coexistence of the divided kingdoms there was internecine warfare. The first possible encounter was averted. The southerners here described as "the house of Judah and Benjamin" and in v. 3 as "all the Israelites in Judah and Benjamin" prepared for war. One hundred and eighty thousand fighting men prepared to make war against Israel to regain the rebel kingdom for Rehoboam. "Israel" here refers to the Northern Kingdom (cp. "the house of Israel" in 1 Kgs 12:21). The exact strength of Rehoboam's army is uncertain despite the figure given. We have here the well-known question about the meaning of "thousand," some kind of military unit (see comment at 1 Chr 5:18). The parallel account in 1 Kgs 12:20, omitted by the Chronicler, mentions that the northern tribes had made Jeroboam king over all Israel. This probably means only the northern tribes although the description "all Israel" is a favorite expression of the Chronicler for the whole people.

11:2 Shemaiah is one of the many prophets and men of God mentioned, almost in passing, in the preclassical period of the prophets. These men left no collection of their prophecies although extracts of their words are to be found scattered through the pages of Samuel, Kings, and Chronicles.

11:3-4 Shemaiah addressed his words to Judah and all the Israelites of Judah and Benjamin. The phrase "Judah and Benjamin" is here geographical in intention (cf. 10:17). The prophet exhorted Judah not to fight against their "brothers." The northern tribes were part of "all Israel" (1 Chr 1-9) and therefore "brothers" in the mind of the Chronicler and just as capable of repentance (28:6-15) as the south was of apostasy (28:1-5,16-25). The phrase "to your tents, O Israel" (10:16) was a call to rebellion, but "go home, every one of you" was a call to abandon war. The response of the southerners to Shemaiah's word, which was "the words of the LORD," was to obey God's word and turn back.

(2) Cities for Defense (11:5–12)

⁵Rehoboam lived in Jerusalem and built up towns for defense in Judah: ⁶Bethlehem, Etam, Tekoa, ⁷Beth Zur, Soco, Adullam, ⁸Gath, Mareshah, Ziph, ⁹Adoraim, Lachish, Azekah, ¹⁰Zorah, Aijalon and Hebron. These were fortified cities in Judah and Benjamin. ¹¹He strengthened their defenses and put commanders in them, with supplies of food, olive oil and wine. ¹²He put shields and spears in all the cities, and made them very strong. So Judah and Benjamin were his.

This passage is unique to the Chronicler and points to the fact that he had access to sources that were either ignored by or unknown to the writer of Kings. They make an interesting replacement for material on Jeroboam in Kings (1 Kgs 12:25–33; 13:1–34; 14:1–20). The building motif is prominent, as an indication of national prosperity granted to kings who enjoyed God's blessing because of their obedience to him.

11:5-6 Rehoboam lived in Jerusalem but built defense towns throughout Judah. These were strategically placed to protect the Shephelah (foothills on the west) and the Judean hills on the south and east. There were no fortresses to the north, suggesting that Rehoboam hoped to regain the areas lost to the north. Little protection was offered in the Negeb, and the fortresses hardly protected the coastal road. But they defended important mountain passes and roads into the heart of Judah.

The order in which the towns are named has not been satisfactorily explained, although some order is discernible. Bethlehem, Etam, Tekoa, and Beth Zur form a north-south row giving protection on the east in front of the wilderness of Judea, Soco, Adullam, Gath, and Mareshah, protecting the western flank from north to south, with Aijalon and Zorah above these in the west. Hebron is joined with Lachish in this list.[3] Aijalon protected the road up the Beth Heron ridge into the central plateau north of Jerusalem. Further south, Zorah protected the Soreq Valley to guard the east-west road connecting the coastal highway to the hill country. Azekah and Soco protected the entrance to the Elah Valley leading to Bethlehem.[4] Archaeological work has been undertaken at several of these sites. Excavations at Azekah, Mareshah, Lachish, Beth Zur, and others have uncovered fortifications that some scholars date to Rehoboam's time, although there is uncertainty.[5]

11:7 Archaeological evidence is not clear for Beth Zur.

11:8 Gath may not be the same as the Philistine Gath but could be Moresheth-Gath by association with Mareshah, which follows. It has been identified with Tell Judeidah, which has an Israelite period,[6] but the Rehoboam period is in dispute.

11:9 Lachish formed the southwestern corner of Rehoboam's fortification. It lay at a road junction north to other fortresses, south to Egypt, and was connected with the coastal highway to the west.

11:11–12 If some doubts remain because of the uncertainty of evidence,

---

[3] H. G. M. Williamson provides a useful listing of these fortresses according to his own order (*1 and 2 Chronicles*, NCBC [Grand Rapids: Eerdmans, 1982], 242).

[4] See R. B. Dillard, *2 Chronicles*, WBC (Waco: Word, 1987), 96–97, for further interesting details.

[5] J. M. Myers, *II Chronicles*, AB (New York: Doubleday, 1965), 69–70.

[6] M. Broshi, *EAEHL* 3.694–96.

the list seems to reflect the realities of Rehoboam's position. He needed defense in all of these areas, and at the present moment there is no strong reason to redate this list to a later date, say, in the days of Josiah or Hezekiah. Each fortification was stocked with supplies of food, olive oil, and wine and with a supply of weapons, shields, and spears. The test would come if a strong invader sought to enter Judah as Pharaoh Shishak did (chap. 12).

(3) Migration of Priests and Levites (11:13–17)

¹³The priests and Levites from all their districts throughout Israel sided with him. ¹⁴The Levites even abandoned their pasturelands and property, and came to Judah and Jerusalem because Jeroboam and his sons had rejected them as priests of the LORD. ¹⁵And he appointed his own priests for the high places and for the goat and calf idols he had made. ¹⁶Those from every tribe of Israel who set their hearts on seeking the LORD, the God of Israel, followed the Levites to Jerusalem to offer sacrifices to the LORD, the God of their fathers. ¹⁷They strengthened the kingdom of Judah and supported Rehoboam son of Solomon three years, walking in the ways of David and Solomon during this time.

11:13–14 The priests and Levites in view of the threatened apostasy "stood" with Rehoboam. The MT indicates that these were in "all Israel." Evidently the faithful priests and Levites of the northern tribes abandoned their pasturelands and property and came to Judah and Jerusalem. Jeroboam had rejected them as priests of the Lord (1 Kgs 12:25–33). His sons probably held positions of authority like other royal sons (2 Sam 15:1–6; 1 Kgs 1:9). The verb translated "sided with" (from *yāṣab*) means to "take a stand" (cf. Ps 94:16). It is not clear that these northerners took up permanent residence with Rehoboam though this is not excluded (cf. v. 16). But it is clear that there was a good deal of sympathy in the north with Rehoboam.

11:15 There were several indications of the apostasy of Jeroboam. He appointed his own priests for the high places, which were not acceptable to official Yahweh worshipers. At these places there were goat and calf idols in violation of Lev 17:7. These "goats," or "hairy ones," were demons or satyrs, idols of some kind. The calf idols are reminiscent of the golden calf of the exodus period (Exod 32:1–10; Deut 9:11; cf. Hos 8:5–6).

11:16 The Chronicler stresses that members from every tribe and thus from all Israel remained faithful even in the midst of apostasy and rebellion. In a typical expression the Chronicler commends those who seek the Lord. Wherever they lived, these people felt the obligation to worship at Jerusalem, where they could offer sacrifices to the Lord, the God of their fathers.

11:17 They supported Rehoboam at least by their allegiance if not by their physical presence. There is a chronological note here. For three years after his accession Rehoboam remained true to the faith of Israel, walking in the ways of David and Solomon. In his fourth year he abandoned the law of God (cf. 12:1–2). The invasion of Pharaoh Shishak followed. The period when divine blessing accompanied obedience gave way to a period of sin and consequent punishment, thus illustrating the Chronicler's doctrine of divine retribution.

(4) Rehoboam's Family (11:18–23)

[18]Rehoboam married Mahalath, who was the daughter of David's son Jerimoth and of Abihail, the daughter of Jesse's son Eliab. [19]She bore him sons: Jeush, Shemariah and Zaham. [20]Then he married Maacah daughter of Absalom, who bore him Abijah, Attai, Ziza and Shelomith. [21]Rehoboam loved Maacah daughter of Absalom more than any of his other wives and concubines. In all, he had eighteen wives and sixty concubines, twenty-eight sons and sixty daughters.

[22]Rehoboam appointed Abijah son of Maacah to be the chief prince among his brothers, in order to make him king. [23]He acted wisely, dispersing some of his sons throughout the districts of Judah and Benjamin, and to all the fortified cities. He gave them abundant provisions and took many wives for them.

11:18 For the Chronicler, as for some other Old Testament writers, a large family was a sign of divine blessing (cf. 13:21; 1 Chr 14:3–7). Mahalath was a great-granddaughter of Jesse through both parents, a second cousin to Rehoboam. Jerimoth is not known elsewhere as a son of David (e.g., 1 Chr 3:1–9). He may have been the son of a concubine. His mother, Abigail, was the daughter of David's eldest brother Eliab (cf. 1 Chr 2:13) so that her own parents were second cousins within the family of Jesse.

11:19 This is all we know of these three sons.

11:20–21 Maacah was either the granddaughter of Absalom, David's son, or the daughter of another Absalom. Rehoboam married the beloved Maacah, who bore him four children. This illustrates part of the tragedy of polygamy, that favoritism is inevitable. Jacob's wives experienced the same conflicts. Nothing is known about Rehoboam's children by Maacah apart from Abijah, Rehoboam's successor (chap. 13), who is known in Kings as Abijam.

11:22–23 Like his father, Solomon (1 Kgs 4:11,13), Rehoboam placed his sons in strategic centers. He planned ahead by appointing Abijah chief prince among his brothers with a view to his becoming king. Other sons he dispersed throughout the districts of Judah and Benjamin and to all the fortified cities. With wide dispersal of his sons, he could maintain his own position and guard against disloyalty, thus reducing the risk of a coup d'etat.

3. The Reign of Rehoboam: Shishak's Invasion (12:1–12)

[1]After Rehoboam's position as king was established and he had become strong, he and all Israel with him abandoned the law of the LORD. [2]Because they had been unfaithful to the LORD, Shishak king of Egypt attacked Jerusalem in the fifth year of King Rehoboam. [3]With twelve hundred chariots and sixty thousand horsemen and the innumerable troops of Libyans, Sukkites and Cushites that came with him from Egypt, [4]he captured the fortified cities of Judah and came as far as Jerusalem.

[5]Then the prophet Shemaiah came to Rehoboam and to the leaders of Judah who had assembled in Jerusalem for fear of Shishak, and he said to them, "This is what the LORD says, 'You have abandoned me; therefore, I now abandon you to Shishak.'"

[6]The leaders of Israel and the king humbled themselves and said, "The LORD is just."

[7]When the LORD saw that they humbled themselves, this word of the LORD came to Shemaiah: "Since they have humbled themselves, I will not destroy them but will soon give them deliverance. My wrath will not be poured out on Jerusalem through Shishak. [8]They will, however, become subject to him, so that they may learn the difference between serving me and serving the kings of other lands."

[9]When Shishak king of Egypt attacked Jerusalem, he carried off the treasures of the temple of the LORD and the treasures of the royal palace. He took everything, including the gold shields Solomon had made. [10]So King Rehoboam made bronze shields to replace them and assigned these to the commanders of the guard on duty at the entrance to the royal palace. [11]Whenever the king went to the LORD'S temple, the guards went with him, bearing the shields, and afterward they returned them to the guardroom.

[12]Because Rehoboam humbled himself, the LORD'S anger turned from him, and he was not totally destroyed. Indeed, there was some good in Judah.

The invasion of Shishak was, in the eyes of the Chronicler, retribution for Rehoboam's sin (11:14–16). Against such a foe Rehoboam's defenses were only a partial match. The account here in 2 Chronicles 12 is parallel to 1 Kgs 14:21–28 but owes something to a source that preserved some details of Shishak's invasion and the prophecy of Shemaiah (vv. 3–8,12). It shows a concern for Judah's abandonment of the law of the Lord. The passage makes use of terms that are characteristic of the Chronicler's theology of divine retribution, namely, "forsake" or "abandon" (vv. 1,5), "be unfaithful" (v. 2), and "humble oneself" (vv. 6–7,12). The Shishak incident provided a model of the sort of thing that could happen again.

12:1   After the schism and the threat of military attack on the northern tribes, things needed to settle down. The kingdom needed to be established, and Rehoboam needed to become strong. Presumably these benefits were granted to Rehoboam. But lacking in gratitude, he and "all Israel" abandoned the law of the Lord. The phrase "all Israel" refers here to Judah and Benjamin, the Southern Kingdom.

The verb "abandon" (*ʿāzab*) is theologically significant. Externally Rehoboam and his nation suffered defeat at the hands of Shishak, a foreign enemy (cf. 7:19–22; 21:10; 24:24; 28:6; 29:6,8–9; 34:25). But the real punishment was that God had abandoned Rehoboam. Abandoning God is the exact opposite of "seeking" God. The phrase "the law of the Lord" points to a canonical corpus that was fixed by the Chronicler's time.

12:2 This verse comes from 1 Kgs 14:25. The campaign of Shishak, king of Egypt, is well attested,[7] especially in his own account. Shishak (also known as Sheshonq I) reigned from 945–925 B.C. He was able to sweep through and around Israel and Judah at will. Shishak's own record of his campaign is written on the walls of a temple at Karnak. More than 150 towns are named although Jerusalem is not mentioned. Of the cities that Rehoboam fortified, only Aijalon is mentioned, but Shishak attacked cities west and south of Rehoboam's defensive line. The main thrust of the campaign seems to have been against the Northern Kingdom.

12:3 The exact size of the Pharaoh's force is hard for us to define because of uncertainty about the meaning of "thousand." The figure for the chariots compares reasonably with that of other chariot-forces of the period known from extrabiblical sources.[8] The sixty thousand horsemen may be a scribal error for six thousand. If so, the proportion of horsemen to chariots is feasible. Pharaoh Shishak had mercenary forces of Libyans, Sukkites, and Cushites. The Sukkites were perhaps the Tjakten, Libyans from the oasis of the western desert. The Cushites were Nubians (Ethiopians). With these forces Shishak was able to capture the fortified cities of Judah (11:6–10). He reached as far as Jerusalem although this city evidently was not taken and is not on his list.

12:5–8 The prophet Shemaiah (cf. 11:2) brought the Lord's message to Rehoboam, and the leaders of Judah assembled in the fortified city of Jerusalem. The king and the leaders of Israel (here the Southern Kingdom) humbled themselves. Here was another reminder of the situation envisaged in Solomon's prayer and God's response to the act of being humbled before him (cf. 7:14). The king and the leaders learned that the Lord does take account of humility when he lessened the consequences of Shishak's attack (v. 7). The response "the LORD is just" (v. 6) was appropriate in view of

---

[7] B. Mazar, "The Campaign of Pharaoh Shishak to Palestine," *VTSup* IV (1957): 57–66; K. A. Kitchen, *The Third Intermediate Period in Egypt* (Warminster: Aris & Phillips, 1973), 293–300; 432–47.26

[8] See Kitchen, *Third Intermediate Period,* 295.

their abandoning him and his law (cf. Ps 51:4). Jerusalem was spared severe destruction although Rehoboam and his leaders became subject to Shishak. This was to teach them that it was better to be servants of the Lord than to be subject to foreign kings.

12:9–11 It would appear that Rehoboam bought off Shishak with Solomon's gold shields and other treasures since Jerusalem is not mentioned on Shishak's list. His main areas of campaign were elsewhere, in the north and in the Negeb. The replacement of gold shields with shields of bronze signified the loss of splendor that the Lord had bestowed on the kingdom of David and Solomon.

12:12 The Chronicler reiterates his conclusion that by humbling himself before the Lord, Rehoboam escaped the ravages of the invader (12:7). He adds the note that there was some good in Judah. This possibly refers to cultic faithfulness (cf. 19:3).

4. The Conclusion of Rehoboam's Reign (12:13–16)

[13]King Rehoboam established himself firmly in Jerusalem and continued as king. He was forty-one years old when he became king, and he reigned seventeen years in Jerusalem, the city the LORD had chosen out of all the tribes of Israel in which to put his Name. His mother's name was Naamah; she was an Ammonite. [14]He did evil because he had not set his heart on seeking the LORD.

[15]As for the events of Rehoboam's reign, from beginning to end, are they not written in the records of Shemaiah the prophet and of Iddo the seer that deal with genealogies? There was continual warfare between Rehoboam and Jeroboam. [16]Rehoboam rested with his fathers and was buried in the City of David. And Abijah his son succeeded him as king.

12:13 The concluding assessment of Rehoboam's reign is based on 1 Kgs 14:21–22. Normally such an assessment is given at the opening of the account of the reign.

12:14 The evil associated with his reign is explained in the parallel account in 1 Kgs 14:22–24 to be idolatry, but there it is attributed to the whole nation of Judah. The Chronicler focuses only on the sins of Rehoboam. He had not set his heart on seeking the Lord. Despite his early good impression (11:5–23) he finally was judged in unfavorable terms (see 13:5–7).

12:15–16 Where the author of Kings cites "the book of the annals of the kings of Judah" (1 Kgs 14:29), the Chronicler cites more specifically the writings of the prophets, Shemaiah the prophet and Iddo the seer. Sources like Samuel and Kings were called "the former prophets" perhaps because they were based largely on such prophetic sources.[9] The expression that here

---

[9] D. M. Howard, Jr., *Introduction to the Historical Books* (Chicago: Moody, 1994), 238–42.

describes the records of Iddo is translated as "that deal with genealogies." Its use in this context is uncertain. It may point to a source used by the Chronicler that dealt with family material or military material. In any case the expression points to the breadth of sources that were available. Rehoboam's successor was Abijah.[10]

5. The Reign of Abijah (13:1–14:1a)

[1]In the eighteenth year of the reign of Jeroboam, Abijah became king of Judah, [2]and he reigned in Jerusalem three years. His mother's name was Maacah, a daughter of Uriel of Gibeah.

There was war between Abijah and Jeroboam. [3]Abijah went into battle with a force of four hundred thousand able fighting men, and Jeroboam drew up a battle line against him with eight hundred thousand able troops.

[4]Abijah stood on Mount Zemaraim, in the hill country of Ephraim, and said, "Jeroboam and all Israel, listen to me! [5]Don't you know that the LORD, the God of Israel, has given the kingship of Israel to David and his descendants forever by a covenant of salt? [6]Yet Jeroboam son of Nebat, an official of Solomon son of David, rebelled against his master. [7]Some worthless scoundrels gathered around him and opposed Rehoboam son of Solomon when he was young and indecisive and not strong enough to resist them.

[8]"And now you plan to resist the kingdom of the LORD, which is in the hands of David's descendants. You are indeed a vast army and have with you the golden calves that Jeroboam made to be your gods. [9]But didn't you drive out the priests of the LORD, the sons of Aaron, and the Levites, and make priests of your own as the peoples of other lands do? Whoever comes to consecrate himself with a young bull and seven rams may become a priest of what are not gods.

[10]"As for us, the LORD is our God, and we have not forsaken him. The priests who serve the LORD are sons of Aaron, and the Levites assist them. [11]Every morning and evening they present burnt offerings and fragrant incense to the LORD. They set out the bread on the ceremonially clean table and light the lamps on the gold lampstand every evening. We are observing the requirements of the LORD our God. But you have forsaken him. [12]God is with us; he is our leader. His priests with their trumpets will sound the battle cry against you. Men of Israel, do not fight against the LORD, the God of your fathers, for you will not succeed."

[13]Now Jeroboam had sent troops around to the rear, so that while he was in front of Judah the ambush was behind them. [14]Judah turned and saw that they were being attacked at both front and rear. Then they cried out to the LORD. The priests blew their trumpets [15]and the men of Judah raised the battle cry. At

---

[10]This name appears as Abijam in 1 Kgs 14:31. The final element in this name may represent the Canaanite god Yam, here replaced by the more acceptable name Yah.

the sound of their battle cry, God routed Jeroboam and all Israel before Abijah and Judah. [16]The Israelites fled before Judah, and God delivered them into their hands. [17]Abijah and his men inflicted heavy losses on them, so that there were five hundred thousand casualties among Israel's able men. [18]The men of Israel were subdued on that occasion, and the men of Judah were victorious because they relied on the LORD, the God of their fathers.

[19]Abijah pursued Jeroboam and took from him the towns of Bethel, Jeshanah and Ephron, with their surrounding villages. [20]Jeroboam did not regain power during the time of Abijah. And the LORD struck him down and he died.

[21]But Abijah grew in strength. He married fourteen wives and had twenty-two sons and sixteen daughters.

[22]The other events of Abijah's reign, what he did and what he said, are written in the annotations of the prophet Iddo.

[1]And Abijah rested with his fathers and was buried in the City of David.

Abijah (ca. 915–913 B.C.) is presented in Chronicles in a favorable light. As with David and Solomon, the Chronicler chose to disregard Abijah's sins that are described in Kings, where he is dismissed in eight verses and said to have walked in all the sins of his father (1 Kgs 15:1–8). The Chronicler preferred to recount what was perhaps Abijah's one moment of glory when he trusted the Lord and was victorious in a war against Jeroboam I, king of the breakaway northern tribes (but see 14:3–5).

For the Chronicler the high point of Abijah's reign was his sermon to the northern tribes, in which he upheld the ideal of the Davidic king as God's anointed ruler for his people and the Solomonic temple as God's chosen place for worship. To be sure, he did not deny that the Davidic king could behave with weakness and folly, but the truth still remains that this is the only chosen line. To abandon it is to turn away from God's kingdom. Abijah's message speaks to our day as well. Many people have grievances against the church and feel that this legitimizes their rejection of it. To be sure, the church has many faults, just as the house of David had many faults. Yet both are at the heart of God's plan. In the end the kingdom of God will triumph, and those who oppose or reject his institutions will suffer for it.

Some scholars have questioned the historical validity of the Chronicler's account of Abijah's reign, but given the negative assessment in Samuel-Kings, the Chronicler had no reason to give this kind of report on Abijah unless he had historical evidence for doing so. He evidently had traditions and other forms of information at his disposal.[11]

13:1–2a This is the only instance in which the Chronicler provides a

---

[11] See D. G. Deboys, "History and Theology in the Chronicler's Portrayal of Abijah," *Bib* 71 (1990): 48–62.

synchronism with the northern king. The practice is quite common in Kings. Maacah, Abijah's mother, was the wife of Rehoboam (11:20). She appears in 15:16 as "mother" of Asa, where the word must be understood as grandmother. Abijah and Asa were not brothers. Maacah appears both as "daughter of Abishalom" (a variant of Absalom; 1 Kgs 15:2) and "daughter of Uriel of Gibeah." One attempt to explain the discrepancy is that she was the granddaughter of Absalom, her parents being Uriel and Tamar (2 Sam 14:27). She remained in the court as queen mother even after her son's death.[12]

13:2b–3 War between the south and the north is here announced. Abijah matched four hundred thousand fighting men against Jeroboam's eight hundred thousand, double the numbers. Again the numbers seem unusually large, and there may be symbolism and hyperbole or the word translated "thousand" may be otherwise understood.[13] Jeroboam made a full-scale effort against the south. The victory achieved by the south under these circumstances stood to their great credit.

13:4 Before the battle was joined, Abijah delivered a speech to the northern troops. On the surface it appears to have been an attempt to dissuade them from fighting. The speech was delivered from Mount Zemaraim in the hill country of Ephraim, a place of uncertain identity but possibly a town on the northern borders of Benjamin (Josh 18:22). The address was directed to Jeroboam and all Israel. The speech has been described as a "Levitical Sermon" with the elements of doctrine, application, and exhortation accompanied by an appeal to earlier biblical texts. The doctrinal basis is the divinely established legitimacy of the dynasty of David and the purity of the Jerusalem cult. Both of these were rejected by the northerners. In the present situation Jeroboam had led the people to abandon the temple worship and the kingdom of Yahweh (13:6–9). The basis for both these doctrines lies in 2 Samuel 7 (cf. 1 Chr 17; Exod 28:1; 29:1–21b; Lev 8–9). The address is directed to Jeroboam and "all Israel." Here the northern tribes are in focus (cf. v. 12, where the people addressed are simply "men of Israel"). Perhaps the intention was to isolate the people from Jeroboam and thus let the blame for the troubles rest on Jeroboam, attempting in this way to win support back from the people to himself.

13:5 Ultimately it was the Lord who had given the kingship of Israel, that is, the whole nation, to David, so that the division was an act of defiance of the Lord. This may carry more weight than blaming Rehoboam. The king-

---

[12] There has been debate about the exact relationship here. See J. M. Myers, *II Chronicles*, AB (New York: Doubleday, 1965), 79, for a useful discussion.

[13] See J. W. Wenham, "Large Numbers in the Old Testament," *TB* 18 (1967): 19–53; J. B. Payne, "The Validity of the Numbers in Chronicles, Part Two," *BSac* (1979): 217.

dom was given to David and his descendants forever (1 Chr 17; 2 Chr 6:42). The context implies that a "covenant of salt" was eternal. The precise social or religious character of such a covenant is not known. The covenant made with David was as permanent as the covenant of Sinai (cf. Num 18:19; Lev 2:13). There was a covenant among the Arabs that acknowledged the sacredness of a bond between parties who had "eaten salt" together.

13:6 Jeroboam was formerly an official of Solomon, son of David (1 Kgs 11:26). The "master" here is Rehoboam, against whom Jeroboam rebelled.

13:7 The "worthless scoundrels" were the young men, contemporaries of Rehoboam, the true Davidic king. They persuaded Rehoboam to reject the wise and mature advice of the elders. Abijah attached blame not so much to the northerners as to their leader, Rehoboam, Abijah's father. This reflects both humility and tact on Abijah's part.

13:8 There is a play on words here. The verb "resist" (*ḥāzaq*) is used at the end of v. 7 in reference to Rehoboam's inability to resist the worthless scoundrels and again, in v. 8, of the rebels resisting the Lord's kingdom, which was in the hands of David's descendants. That Israel was the Lord's kingdom was one of the Chronicler's favorite themes (1 Chr 17:14; 28:5; 29:11,23; 2 Chr 9:8). But the Northern Kingdom had committed the effrontery of going into battle led by bull idols.

13:9 They had driven out the priests of the Lord and the Levites (cf. 11:14b). Priests of their own were installed like the peoples of other lands. "What are not gods" may be a general statement referring to all gods other than Yahweh, particularly the satyrs (cf. 11:15; Hos 8:6). The priesthood was for sale to whomever would bring the appropriate offering, but such a priest would be recognized only by a "nothing god" and not by Yahweh.

13:10–11 The contrasting picture of what took place in the south is now drawn. They followed the commandments of their God, the God of Israel (cf. 2:4; 4:7). By contrast the northerners had forsaken the Lord.

13:12 God was with Abijah's army as leader. The war that was about to ensue was seen as a holy war. The priests with their battle trumpets would sound the battle cry (cf. Num 10:8–9) against Abijah's opponents. A final appeal was made for the northerners not to fight against the Lord, the God of their fathers; they could not succeed.

13:13–16 Jeroboam attempted an ambush, a common military strategy, especially in a holy war (cf. Josh 8:2; Judg 20:29). The picture of the battle being fought before and behind is a well-known strategy (cf. 2 Sam 10:9) as is the sounding of the trumpets and the battle cry (cf. Josh 6:16). It was God who granted Abijah the victory over Jeroboam. Jeroboam and all Israel (the northerners) fled before Judah, and God delivered them into Judah's hands.

13:17–18 Abijah and his men inflicted heavy losses on Israel (regarding the excessive numbers see comments on 13:2b–3). The outcome of the battle was defeat and humiliation for Jeroboam and victory for Abijah and the men of Judah because they relied on the Lord, the God of their fathers. The verb translated "relied on" (*šāʿan*) appears also at 14:11 and 16:7–8. It is used of leaning upon something (cf. 2 Sam 1:6; 2 Kgs 5:18; 7:2,17; Ezek 29:7; figuratively in Prov 3:5). By contrast, when Judah turned aside to wickedness, they might well have lost a battle (cf. 28:19).

13:19 The cities are all known from the preexilic period. Abijah pursued Jeroboam and took from him Bethel, Jeshanah, Ephron, and their surrounding villages. Nor did Jeroboam regain control of them during the days of Abijah. Bethel later returned to northern hands (cf. Amos 7:10–13). Jeshanah has been identified with Burj el-Isane; Ephron (or Ophrah) is not at present identifiable.

13:20 According to 1 Kgs 15:9, Jeroboam outlived Abijah. In fact, nothing is said here about the priority of Jeroboam's death. This verse simply concludes the account of the battle with a reference to the eventual death of Jeroboam. The sense of "struck down" (*nāgap*) is not made clear. The same verb appears in v. 15 in the sentence "God routed Jeroboam and all Israel."

13:21–22 Signs of God's blessing are that Abijah grew in strength and was blessed with a large family (cf. 11:18–23). A summary of Abijah's life is given in 13:21–14:1a. At v. 22 the narrative runs parallel to 1 Kgs 15:7, although the source quoted there is "The Book of the Chronicles of the Kings of Judah," whereas Chronicles quotes from "the annotations of the prophet Iddo." Once again the Chronicler refers to a prophetic source (see comments at 12:15–16).

14:1a This half of v. 1 records the death and burial in the City of David of Abijah, king of Judah.

6. The Reign of Asa (14:1b–16:14)

The reign of Asa (ca. 913–873 B.C.) poses a number of questions for the reader. As in the case of Abijah, the Chronicler devotes much more space to Asa than the parallel passage in 1 Kgs 15:9–24. Kings covers Asa's reign in sixteen verses, whereas the Chronicler takes forty-seven verses. The enlarged coverage in Chronicles enables the Chronicler to develop his theological ideas, notably his theology of retribution. He is able to demonstrate the blessings attending Asa's fidelity early in his reign and the punishment that followed his failure to trust the Lord later in his reign.

Some questions arise about chronology in the Chronicles account. In 16:1, for example, in the thirty-sixth year of Asa's reign, Baasha, king of Israel, launched a campaign against Judah. But 1 Kgs 16:6,8 refers to the death of Baasha in the twenty-sixth year of Asa. We will take up this question in 16:1. Other chronological questions also will be discussed as they arise.

The material on Asa is arranged into three parts: (1) the early years (14:1b–14), (2) the reformation (15:1–19), and (3) the later years (16:1–14).

(1) The Early Years of Asa's Reign (14:1b–15)

Asa his son succeeded him as king, and in his days the country was at peace for ten years.

²Asa did what was good and right in the eyes of the LORD his God. ³He removed the foreign altars and the high places, smashed the sacred stones and cut down the Asherah poles. ⁴He commanded Judah to seek the LORD, the God of their fathers, and to obey his laws and commands. ⁵He removed the high places and incense altars in every town in Judah, and the kingdom was at peace under him. ⁶He built up the fortified cities of Judah, since the land was at peace. No one was at war with him during those years, for the LORD gave him rest.

⁷"Let us build up these towns," he said to Judah, "and put walls around them, with towers, gates and bars. The land is still ours, because we have sought the LORD our God; we sought him and he has given us rest on every side." So they built and prospered.

⁸Asa had an army of three hundred thousand men from Judah, equipped with large shields and with spears, and two hundred and eighty thousand from Benjamin, armed with small shields and with bows. All these were brave fighting men.

⁹Zerah the Cushite marched out against them with a vast army and three hundred chariots, and came as far as Mareshah. ¹⁰Asa went out to meet him, and they took up battle positions in the Valley of Zephathah near Mareshah.

¹¹Then Asa called to the LORD his God and said, "LORD, there is no one like you to help the powerless against the mighty. Help us, O LORD our God, for we rely on you, and in your name we have come against this vast army. O LORD, you are our God; do not let man prevail against you."

¹²The LORD struck down the Cushites before Asa and Judah. The Cushites fled, ¹³and Asa and his army pursued them as far as Gerar. Such a great number of Cushites fell that they could not recover; they were crushed before the LORD and his forces. The men of Judah carried off a large amount of plunder. ¹⁴They destroyed all the villages around Gerar, for the terror of the LORD had fallen upon them. They plundered all these villages, since there was much booty there. ¹⁵They also attacked the camps of the herdsmen and carried off droves of sheep and goats and camels. Then they returned to Jerusalem.

EARLY YEARS AND REFORMS (14:1b–8). Some eight verses are devoted to Asa's reforms. As a reward for Asa's faithfulness, God granted him victory over Zerah, the Cushite.

14:1b [13:23]   The Chronicler provides an expanded account of Asa's reforms by comparison with that provided in 1 Kgs 15:11–12. The Chronicles account anticipates the reforms of Hezekiah and Josiah later in Judah's history.

The peace referred to was the political consequence of Abijah's victory over Jeroboam (13:13–20). But there was another aspect to this peace. It was a reward for Asa's faithfulness to the God of Israel. The period of peace probably lasted until the time of Zerah's invasion (vv. 9–15). The word "ten" here may simply be a round number (cf. 15:10; Gen 31:7).

14:2–3 [14:1–2]   This is the theological assessment of Asa's reign (cf. 1 Kgs 15:11). Asa destroyed the illegitimate cult objects—altars, high places, the standing stones representing Baal, and the Asherah poles, wooden poles representing the goddess Asherah.

14:4[3]   There are nine references to seeking the Lord in the three chapters devoted to Asa (14:4,7 [twice]; 15:2,4,12,13,15; 16:12). The phrase was a summary description of how one was to respond to God and thus defined one who was a member of the believing community. It involved more than a specific act of seeking God's help and guidance but stood for one's whole duty toward God (cf. v. 7; 15:2,12–13). According to 1 Chr 28:9 it is equivalent to knowing God and serving him "with wholehearted devotion." Part of that attitude was the keeping of God's laws and commands.[14] S. Wagner notes that the concept is "so complex that very important consequences are causally connected with it": success (2 Chr 17:5), peace (2 Chr 14:5-6), and life (1 Chr 10:13-14; 2 Chr 15:13). He also explains that it denotes "the Chronicler's typical ideal of piety."[15]

14:5[4]   The "incense altars" may have been shrines of some kind. Some have seen them as a type of high place.[16] The removal of these cultic centers from every town of Judah brought peace to Asa and his kingdom.

14:6–7[6]   A building program was a sign of God's blessing. In particular Asa strengthened Judah's defenses with walls, towers, gates, and bars. This program of building was made possible because there was no war. By a

---

[14] See the uses of דרשׁ, translated "seek," "inquire," or "consult," in 1 Chr 10:13–14; 13:3; 15:13; 21:30; 22:19; 28:9; 2 Chr 12:14; 14:3; 15:12; 16:12; 17:3–4; 18:4,6–7; 19:3; 20:3; 22:9; 26:5; 30:19; 31:21; 34:3,21,26. The verb בקשׁ is translated "seek" in 1 Chr 16:10–11; 2 Chr 7:14; 11:16; 15:15; 20:4.

[15] S. Wagner, "דרשׁ dārash," *TDOT* 3.301. W. C. Kaiser, Jr. presents his study of Asa's revival as three results of seeking the Lord: a time of peace (14:2–7), God's presence again (15:2–7), and prevailing against enemies (14:9-15; 16:1-10; see *Quest for Renewal: Personal Revival in the Old Testament* [Chicago: Moody, 1986], 77-88.

[16] Williamson, *1 and 2 Chronicles,* 260. The building program was a sign that they had prospered.

slight emendation of the Hebrew text some commentators translate v. 7b, "[Because] we have sought Yahweh our God . . . *he* has sought us."

14:8[7]   An account of Asa's army is here given. The possession of a strong army was a further indication that he was a "good" king (cf. 17:14–19; 26:11–15). The usual uncertainty about the arithmetical size of Asa's army applies here (see n. 2 on 13:2b–3).

WAR WITH ZERAH (14:9–15).   Solomon had prayed that the Lord would hear his people's prayer in the hour of battle (6:34). The Chronicler reports several such incidents that show God's response to the call of his people (13:14–18; 18:31; 20:5–20; 32:20–22; 1 Chr 5:20—all passages unique to the Chronicler or modified from the parallel form in Kings).

The invasion of Zerah the Cushite evidently was included by the Chronicler to illustrate a further aspect of Asa's faithfulness, namely, his complete reliance upon God (v. 11). This attitude resulted in a remarkable victory (cf. Abijah's reliance upon God in 13:18).

14:9[8]   The absence of clear extrabiblical evidence has led to a good deal of speculation both about the identity of Zerah and the nature of the military campaign described here. The identity of the Cushites could provide a clue. They often have been identified with Ethiopians (cf. 16:8). This is rejected by recent commentators. The reference in 14:15 to a Bedouin group with sheep, goats, and camels that Asa drove off has led several recent writers to suggest that Cush may have been an ethnic group living in the vicinity of Judah (cf. Hab 3:7). The source of the Chronicler's information is not known.[17] "The vast army" is literally "an army of a thousand thousands" ("an array of a million men," NRSV). The NIV translation is quite appropriate.[18] The three hundred chariots, though a modest number for a major encounter, probably carries some symbolic meaning as well. The encounter took place near Mareshah (Tell Sandahannah), one of the sites of Rehoboam's defensive fortifications.

14:10[9]   "Zephathah" is not identifiable. The LXX has "north of," which in Hebrew script is similar to Zephathah. The proposal is widely accepted.

14:11[10]   Asa's prayer is appropriate for the occasion and in keeping with Solomon's advice. The Lord is called upon as the one who could help the powerless against the mighty. The literal Hebrew reads, "It is not with you to help between the great and him that has no strength." The meaning is that the strong as well as the weak need the Lord's assistance to gain victory.

---

[17] Williamson, *1 and 2 Chronicles,* 263–65, provides a valuable review.

[18] Payne prefers to translate אֲלָפִים here as "specially trained soldiers" ("Validity: Part Two," 215–16).

In this situation the appeal is to the Lord to help the weak. Asa's appeal was that as he relied on the Lord and in the Lord's name had come against the vast army of the Cushites, so may the Lord not allow people to prevail against him (the Lord). This is the standard theological approach of the Chronicler. The war was a holy war, and the victory must have been assured when the Lord's people relied on him however small Israel's forces may have been.

14:12[11]   A good parallel has already been given in 13:15–16, which stresses the small role of the army of Judah. This perspective occurs in other places in the Old Testament (Exod 14:14; Deut 20:4; 1 Sam 17:47). The outcome was that the Cushites fled the battlefield.

14:13[12]   Asa and his army pursued them as far as Gerar, now identified with Tell Abu Hureira. The holy war theme continues with the words "they were crushed before the LORD and his forces." "His forces" refers to Asa's army, which was also the Lord's army. A large amount of plunder was carried off by the men of Judah, a regular concomitant of a successful holy war.

14:14[13]   The "terror of the LORD" was another feature of the holy war. It seized Israel's enemies and resulted in panic among the enemy (cf. Exod 23:27; Deut 7:20,23; Judg 7:20–22). The men of Judah destroyed all the villages around Gerar and plundered them because of the holy panic.

14:15[14]   This verse seems to provide a valuable clue about who the Cushites were. Asa attacked the camps of the herdsmen and drove off sheep, goats, and camels, all of which points to nomadic herdsmen of some kind. The campaign was over, and Asa and his men returned to Jerusalem.

(2) Asa's Reformation (15:1–19)

[1]The Spirit of God came upon Azariah son of Oded. [2]He went out to meet Asa and said to him, "Listen to me, Asa and all Judah and Benjamin. The LORD is with you when you are with him. If you seek him, he will be found by you, but if you forsake him, he will forsake you. [3]For a long time Israel was without the true God, without a priest to teach and without the law. [4]But in their distress they turned to the LORD, the God of Israel, and sought him, and he was found by them. [5]In those days it was not safe to travel about, for all the inhabitants of the lands were in great turmoil. [6]One nation was being crushed by another and one city by another, because God was troubling them with every kind of distress. [7]But as for you, be strong and do not give up, for your work will be rewarded."

[8]When Asa heard these words and the prophecy of Azariah son of Oded the prophet, he took courage. He removed the detestable idols from the whole land of Judah and Benjamin and from the towns he had captured in the hills of Ephraim. He repaired the altar of the LORD that was in front of the portico of the LORD's temple.

9Then he assembled all Judah and Benjamin and the people from Ephraim, Manasseh and Simeon who had settled among them, for large numbers had come over to him from Israel when they saw that the LORD his God was with him. **10**They assembled at Jerusalem in the third month of the fifteenth year of Asa's reign. **11**At that time they sacrificed to the LORD seven hundred head of cattle and seven thousand sheep and goats from the plunder they had brought back. **12**They entered into a covenant to seek the LORD, the God of their fathers, with all their heart and soul. **13**All who would not seek the LORD, the God of Israel, were to be put to death, whether small or great, man or woman. **14**They took an oath to the LORD with loud acclamation, with shouting and with trumpets and horns. **15**All Judah rejoiced about the oath because they had sworn it wholeheartedly. They sought God eagerly, and he was found by them. So the LORD gave them rest on every side.

16King Asa also deposed his grandmother Maacah from her position as queen mother, because she had made a repulsive Asherah pole. Asa cut the pole down, broke it up and burned it in the Kidron Valley. **17**Although he did not remove the high places from Israel, Asa's heart was fully committed [to the LORD] all his life. **18**He brought into the temple of God the silver and gold and the articles that he and his father had dedicated.

19There was no more war until the thirty-fifth year of Asa's reign.

The middle period of Asa's reign is covered in chap. 15, which falls readily into three sections: (1) Azariah's sermon (15:1–7); (2) the reformation (15:8–15), and (3) the removal of Maacah, the king's mother (15:16–19). The returning victorious army was met by an otherwise unknown prophet, Azariah. His words encouraged Asa to continue with reforms he had already commenced (14:1–4).

AZARIAH'S SERMON (15:1–7). **15:1** The phrase "the Spirit of God came upon . . ." was common in the Old Testament for an activity of the Spirit particularly in reference to prophetic inspiration. The Chronicler used it several times (20:14; 24:20; cf. 1 Chr 12:18; 28:12).

15:2 The prophet did not leave the deliverance of his message to a chance meeting but took the initiative himself and went out to meet Asa. He spoke not merely to the king but to all Judah and Benjamin, the loyal southern tribes. He presented a fundamental theological view: If anyone seeks the Lord, he will be found (1 Chr 28:9; cf. Deut 4:29; Jer 29:13–14). Some commentators translate the verse as, "He will let himself be found by you," which is an appropriate understanding of the Hebrew verb here (*yimmāsē*, a reflexive of *mṣ*).[19]

15:3 The verse seems to have in focus the troubled period of the judges,

---

[19] Myers, *II Chronicles,* 86.

when they ignored their God and his law. It is not that the Torah did not exist at this time, any more than that God did not exist (cf. Jer 10:10), but that it was not taught.

15:4 When placed within the background of the cyclical pattern of rebellion, affliction, repentance, and deliverance, these verses are readily linked to the stories of deliverance throughout Judges (Judg 2:11–21).

15:5–7 These verses depict days of turmoil in many lands when one city was being crushed by another. It was God who was the source of these troubles, but as in the days of the judges deliverance also could be found in the days of Asa. The command to be strong in the Lord is found many times in Scripture (e.g., Deut 31:6–7,23; Josh 1:6–7,9; 1 Chr 22:13; 28:10,20; 2 Chr 32:7; Hag 2:4; Zech 8:9,13; Eph 6:10).

THE REFORMATION (15:8–15). It was not that Asa needed courage to face another war but to undertake more fully a reform he had begun earlier. His reform program began at the start of his reign, but he was young and not able to resist the influence of his mother, Maacah, who encouraged various illegitimate religious practices (cf. v. 16).

15:8 Some textual problems are found at the start of this verse. Some commentators omit "Oded the prophet" (the reading of the MT) as an explanatory gloss on v. 1. The Vulgate reads "the prophecy of Azariah the son of Oded." Despite these uncertainties it is clear that it was the prophecy of Azariah (v. 1) that gave Asa the courage he needed in the face of his powerful mother to remove the abominable idols from the whole land of Judah and Benjamin and from the towns he had captured in the hills of Ephraim. Evidently the conquests of Abijah (13:19) were not held for long. It seems reasonable to suppose that they were lost during Asa's minority. According to 1 Kgs 15:16,32, "there was war between Asa and Baasha king of Israel throughout their reigns," though no doubt it was intermittent. In one phase of that war Asa captured towns in the hill country of Ephraim. While there is no exact record of this, the Chronicler evidently was here drawing on another source.

Another aspect of Asa's reforms was the repair of the altar for burnt offerings, which had to be undertaken from time to time. There is no implication here of a prior destruction (cf. 8:12).

15:9 The "all Israel" theme finds a place here. Asa called for a special religious ceremony and gathered all Judah and Benjamin as well as people from Ephraim, Manasseh, and Simeon who had settled among the southern tribes. The Davidic kings showed an inclusive concern for the whole of Israel. This appears repeatedly from 1 Chr 13:1–5 onward. A special point is made of the inclusion of people from the north (cf. 11:13–17). These northerners came in large numbers from Israel to Jerusalem when they saw that

Asa's God was with him. The presence of Simeon raises a question. Traditionally he was located to the south of Judah (1 Chr 4:24–43), although the Simeonites appear at times in the north (cf. 34:6). Perhaps some incursion of people like the Edomites into Judah displaced the Simeonites northwards. Certainty is not possible.

15:10   In the third month in Asa's fifteenth year the peoples assembled for a covenant ceremony of some kind. The date was close to, if not concurrent with, the Feast of Weeks, that is, Pentecost (Exod 23:16; 34:22; Lev 23:15–21; Num 28:26–31; Deut 16:9–10), one of the pilgrim festivals that would have brought crowds loyal to the Jerusalem temple from surrounding regions. The Chronicler possibly intended to make a connection with the Feast of Weeks because of the verbal similarity in Hebrew between "Weeks" (*šābuʿōt*) and the verb "swear" (*šābaʿ*), which is prominent in vv. 14–15.

15:11   A large number of animals was offered, plunder taken from the victory over Zerah: seven hundred head of cattle and seven thousand sheep and goats. The numbers are not unduly excessive. The victory over Zerah seems to have been brought together with this cultic ceremony. It is difficult to give an exact date of these events.[20] The fifteenth year seems to have been the date of Zerah's invasion, but the Chronicler leaves the date deliberately vague.

15:12   The people entered into a covenant to seek the Lord, the God of their fathers, with all their heart and soul. The sense seems to be that the people entered into a binding agreement among themselves to continue wholeheartedly the life of faithfulness demonstrated by the king (on the phrase "seek the Lord" see comment at 14:4).

15:13   The penalty of death seems harsh to us but is reminiscent of Deut 13:6–10 and 17:2–7. We have no evidence of whether or how frequently this penalty was carried out. The expression may have been a way of stressing the extreme abhorrence Israel had to wanton rejection of the Lord's complete sovereignty.

15:14   The taking of an oath to the Lord was the vital element in all covenant ceremonies. The ceremony was no doubt conducted with proper decorum and ritual. The loud acclamation with shouting, trumpets, and horns was normal in such important religious celebrations (cf. 1 Chr 15:28).

15:15   Great joy was evident everywhere at their wholehearted swearing of the oath (cf. 1 Chr 15:25; 16:10; 29:9; 2 Chr 23:13,18,21; 30:21). The Chronicler observes that this fervent response of the king and the people of the Lord was matched by the Lord's response to them.

---

[20] Williamson, *1 and 2 Chronicles*, 257–58.

THE REMOVAL OF MAACAH (15:16–19). **15:16–18** The Chronicler drew his material for this section of his work from 1 Kgs 15:13–15. The importance attainable by a queen mother is seen in other women besides Maacah (see note on 11:20). Other prominent queen mothers were Bathsheba, Jezebel, and Athaliah. The Asherah symbol was a wooden pole here described as "repulsive." This was broken up and burned in the Kidron Valley, which runs north-south on the eastern side of Jerusalem between the city and the Mount of Olives. In this area items cleared out in other reforms also were burned (2 Kgs 23:4–6; 2 Chr 29:16; 30:14).

Asa's failure to remove the high places from Israel (v. 17) appears to be a contradiction of 14:2, which states that he did remove the foreign altars and high places. Rather than seeing here a contradiction, it probably is better to see in the two statements in 14:2 and 15:17 evidence of the persistence of the indigenous cults over several years. Since 15:17 refers to the latter part of Asa's life and 14:2 refers to early reforms, the two statements simply indicate a state of affairs up to thirty years apart. Further, the words "from Israel" could well refer to Asa's failure to carry out his reforms in northern areas over which he exercised authority for a time (cf. v. 8). The gifts he gave were no doubt the spoils of war from his campaign against Zerah. His father, Abijah, would have dedicated booty taken from the war against Jeroboam (13:2–20).

15:19 There was no war again in Asa's kingdom until his thirty-fifth year. There was an era of peace, a reward for Asa's faithfulness. The invasion of Baasha in Asa's thirty-sixth year must have had other causes.

(3) The Later Years (16:1–14)

¹In the thirty-sixth year of Asa's reign Baasha king of Israel went up against Judah and fortified Ramah to prevent anyone from leaving or entering the territory of Asa king of Judah.

²Asa then took the silver and gold out of the treasuries of the LORD'S temple and of his own palace and sent it to Ben-Hadad king of Aram, who was ruling in Damascus. ³"Let there be a treaty between me and you," he said, "as there was between my father and your father. See, I am sending you silver and gold. Now break your treaty with Baasha king of Israel so he will withdraw from me."

⁴Ben-Hadad agreed with King Asa and sent the commanders of his forces against the towns of Israel. They conquered Ijon, Dan, Abel Maim and all the store cities of Naphtali. ⁵When Baasha heard this, he stopped building Ramah and abandoned his work. ⁶Then King Asa brought all the men of Judah, and they carried away from Ramah the stones and timber Baasha had been using. With them he built up Geba and Mizpah.

⁷At that time Hanani the seer came to Asa king of Judah and said to him: "Because you relied on the king of Aram and not on the LORD your God, the

army of the king of Aram has escaped from your hand. [8]Were not the Cushites and Libyans a mighty army with great numbers of chariots and horsemen? Yet when you relied on the LORD, he delivered them into your hand. [9]For the eyes of the LORD range throughout the earth to strengthen those whose hearts are fully committed to him. You have done a foolish thing, and from now on you will be at war."

[10]Asa was angry with the seer because of this; he was so enraged that he put him in prison. At the same time Asa brutally oppressed some of the people.

[11]The events of Asa's reign, from beginning to end, are written in the book of the kings of Judah and Israel. [12]In the thirty-ninth year of his reign Asa was afflicted with a disease in his feet. Though his disease was severe, even in his illness he did not seek help from the LORD, but only from the physicians. [13]Then in the forty-first year of his reign Asa died and rested with his fathers. [14]They buried him in the tomb that he had cut out for himself in the City of David. They laid him on a bier covered with spices and various blended perfumes, and they made a huge fire in his honor.

In its present literary form this third section of Asa's life is presented in three parts: (1) war with Baasha (16:1–6), (2) Hanani's sermon (16:7–10), and (3) the conclusion of Asa's reign (16:11–14). The Chronicler continues his close dependence on 1 Kgs 15:17–22. It was marked by Asa's league with Ben-Hadad, king of Aram-Damascus, which for the Chronicler demonstrated a falling away from the complete reliance upon his God that he had shown earlier in his reign (cf. 14:11). Because of this the years of peace came to an end.

The chronological problems are difficult in this chapter, which introduces the invasion of Asa's territory by Baasha of Israel in the thirty-sixth year of Asa's reign. According to 1 Kgs 15:33 and 16:8, Baasha was dead long before Asa's thirty-sixth year. No widely accepted solution has yet emerged, although many have adopted the view of E. R. Thiele that the "thirty-fifth year" refers to the division of the kingdom and that "of Asa" was a later addition to the text. It also is possible that *malkŭt* may refer to Asa's kingdom (Judah) rather than his "reign," thus measuring the years since the division, or that the numbers are transcriptional errors for "fifteen" in 15:19 and "sixteen" in 16:1.[21]

WAR WITH BAASHA (16:1–6). **16:1** H. G. M. Williamson proposes a chronology which, though speculative to a degree, provides a helpful outline. He proposes that the invasion by Zerah came in the middle of a period

---

[21] E. R. Thiele, *The Mysterious Numbers of the Hebrew Kings* (Grand Rapids: Zondervan, 1983), 84. Good summaries of the arguments are available in Williamson, *1 and 2 Chronicles,* 255–58; Dillard, *2 Chronicles,* 123–25; S. J. De Vries "The Chronology of the O.T.," *IDB* I.580–99; and *IDBSup,* 161–66.

of peace. After Asa's victory the celebration of 15:9–15 was the climax of Asa's reform as well as a victory festival. It is based on a working hypothesis that the chronological references to the thirty-fifth and thirty-sixth years relate not to Asa's reign but to the division of the monarchy. These two dates would then correspond to the fifteenth and sixteenth years of Asa.[22]

16:2 Asa withdrew silver and gold from the treasuries of the Lord's temple and his own palace and sent it to Ben-Hadad, king of Aram-Damascus, to encourage him to break the treaty he had with Baasha. The Arameans were implacable foes of the Northern Kingdom, and the drawing of Damascus into a hostile attitude to Judah would provide conflict for Baasha on a second front and ease pressure on Judah. By this political maneuver Asa's enlistment of Ben-Hadad's aid outmaneuvered Baasha. But however shrewd this scheme was politically, it displayed a lack of trust in the Lord and merited divine retribution.

16:3 The terms of Asa's treaty with Ben-Hadad are set out in this verse. Asa referred back to a former treaty between Ben-Hadad's father and Asa's father Abijah, and he asked Ben-Hadad to break the current treaty he had with Baasha and make a treaty with him. This would cause Baasha to withdraw from his hostile action against Asa. For that purpose Asa sent him gifts of silver and gold.

16:4–5 The plan and the gift Asa proposed were acceptable to Ben-Hadad. He sent the commanders of his forces against the towns of Israel, capturing Ijon, Dan, Abel-Maim (also known as Abel Beth Maacah). The route taken by Ben-Hadad's forces followed one branch of the main international highway, a significant strategic concern for Baasha, which caused him to relieve his pressure on Asa. He stopped building Ramah and abandoned his work.

16:6 At once Asa destroyed the defensive works Baasha had been building at Ramah and reused the stones and timber to build Geba and Mizpah to the north of Ramah. Mizpah is generally identified with Tell en-Nasbeh some eight miles (thirteen km) north of Jerusalem. The precise identification of Geba is uncertain.

HANANI'S SERMON (16:7–10).   From the military point of view Asa's treaty with Ben-Hadad was successful, but his action was a rejection of confident trust in the Lord in a time of crisis. God's spokesman appeared at this time to declare God's mind about the incident. Hanani, the seer, was one of the many spokesmen for God in the days of the kings of Israel and Judah whose words are preserved like those of other "minor" prophets we meet in Chronicles as a brief entry in a wider narrative.

---

[22] Williamson, *1 and 2 Chronicles,* 255–58.

16:7 Nothing is known about Hanani apart from this entry in Chronicles, although his son, Jehu, is given a brief mention elsewhere (19:2; 20:34). This insertion of Asa into the story served to underline the consequences of falling away from the Lord. The verb "rely on" (*šaʿan*) that occurs in 14:11 is used again as an expression for trust, except this time Asa's trust was not in the Lord. Asa's sin was to rely on the king of Damascus-Aram rather than on the Lord. The incident is reminiscent of Isaiah's condemnation of Ahaz when faced with a threat from the north (Isa 7). Had Asa remained faithful, he would have conquered Baasha as well as Aram. As it was, Syria (Aram) escaped from Asa's hand and remained a threat to both Judah and Israel in costly wars later on.

16:8 The two periods of Asa's life are here contrasted. Early in his reign when he relied on the Lord, a great army (Cushites and Libyans) with many chariots and horsemen were delivered into his hand (14:9–15). Now in the latter period of his reign, despite appearances, he was a defeated man. He had done a foolish thing, and henceforth war would plague him (cf. 1 Sam 13:13).

16:9 God knows what is happening in the hearts of all people. He supports those who are wholeheartedly committed to him, but he will not support those who carelessly reject his sovereignty and lean on another. The notion that the Lord's eyes roam through all the earth are echoed in Zech 4:10. Williamson, regarding the Zechariah passage as the earlier, argues that this may be a pointer to the date of the Chronicler. He claims that sufficient time must have elapsed for Zechariah's prophecy to take its place among other Scriptures and therefore to be an appropriate quotation in a "Levitical sermon."[23] Other references to the "eyes of the LORD," however, are found in Pss 33:18; 34:15; Prov 15:3 (cf. also 1 Pet 3:12). Also arguments for dependence are always tenuous.

16:10 Asa became angry with Hanani, however, for rejecting his sovereignty and cast him into prison. Others who may have been supporters of the prophet were brutally oppressed.

THE CONCLUSION OF ASA'S REIGN (16:11–14). **16:11** In this concluding section on Asa's reign the Chronicler refers to a source, "the book of the kings of Judah and Israel" (cf. the parallel text in 1 Kgs 15:23, which calls it "the book of the annals of the kings of Judah"). This is the first mention of this source, but in the following chapters this title or similar titles occur several times. He also refers to "the book of the kings of Israel" (20:34; cp. 1 Kgs 22:45). He does not refer to the book of the kings of Judah (or its equivalent) at all. Evidently he wished to insist that Judah was part of the inclusive Israel.

---

[23] Williamson, *1 and 2 Chronicles*, 274–75.

16:12 In the thirty-ninth year Asa was afflicted with a disease in his feet. There has been some discussion about the nature of the disease, and various diagnoses have been proposed, none of which is entirely satisfactory.[24] The best we can do is refer to a "foot disease." But even this sickness, which might have been seen as a warning from God and an expression of his displeasure at recent events, did not cause Asa to seek help from the Lord. He had fallen a long way from the promise of his early years and had earned the disapproval of the Chronicler.

16:13–14 Asa's death and burial are given greater prominence in Chronicles than in Kings (cp. 1 Kgs 15:24). He was buried in a tomb he had cut out for himself in the City of David. At the last, and despite his failings, he was honored at his death. The huge fire was not a cremation but a memorial and honorific rite customarily, but not always, granted to kings (cf. 21:19; see also Jer 34:5). The spices and various blended perfumes had no particular significance. The festivities connected with his entombment reflect the esteem in which he was held by the people.

7. The Reign of Jehoshaphat (17:1–21:1)

Jehoshaphat (873–849 B.C.), king of Judah, takes his place alongside Hezekiah and Josiah as one of the Chronicler's favorite kings. The treatment of his reign in Chronicles is comparatively extensive when set alongside the account in Kings. The Chronicler devotes four chapters to Jehoshaphat (chaps. 17–21) in contrast to the rather scanty account in Kings, where the kings of Israel are more prominent (1 Kgs 22:1–38; 2 Kgs 3:4–27). Apparently the Chronicler had more material to work with than that provided in Kings. This material was favorable to Jehoshaphat, and the Chronicler gives him high marks (22:9), although he does describe problems in Jehoshaphat's reign as well (19:1–3; 20:37).

The Chronicler does not follow a clear chronology, with several references that are general: "some years later" (18:2); no time reference at 19:4, where one might be expected; "after this" (20:1); and "later" (20:35). There is apparently a specific date at 17:7, "in the third year of his reign," but this has its own problems. A noteworthy feature of this narrative is the Chronicler's use of parataxis, in which elements of the story are set alongside one another without transition or explanation. In particular, the Chronicler describes Jehoshaphat's faith and devotion but then recounts how Jehoshaphat allied himself with the northern kings. From the overall presentation it is clear that the Chronicler regarded this as a disastrous policy, but

---

[24] Myers, *II Chronicles*, 99–100.

he simply let the facts do his talking for him. The lesson that comes through is that one must not only be devoted to the Lord; one also must avoid all entanglements with apostate groups.[25]

The story of Jehoshaphat is presented in four phases: (1) character and organization (17:1–19, (2) alliance with the Northern Kingdom (18:1–34), (3) God's rebuke and Jehoshaphat's reformation (19:1–11), and (4) Jehoshaphat's piety rewarded (20:1–37; 21:1).

(1) Character and Organization (17:1–19)

¹Jehoshaphat his son succeeded him as king and strengthened himself against Israel. ²He stationed troops in all the fortified cities of Judah and put garrisons in Judah and in the towns of Ephraim that his father Asa had captured.

³The LORD was with Jehoshaphat because in his early years he walked in the ways his father David had followed. He did not consult the Baals ⁴but sought the God of his father and followed his commands rather than the practices of Israel. ⁵The LORD established the kingdom under his control; and all Judah brought gifts to Jehoshaphat, so that he had great wealth and honor. ⁶His heart was devoted to the ways of the LORD; furthermore, he removed the high places and the Asherah poles from Judah.

⁷In the third year of his reign he sent his officials Ben-Hail, Obadiah, Zechariah, Nethanel and Micaiah to teach in the towns of Judah. ⁸With them were certain Levites—Shemaiah, Nethaniah, Zebadiah, Asahel, Shemiramoth, Jehonathan, Adonijah, Tobijah and Tob-Adonijah—and the priests Elishama and Jehoram. ⁹They taught throughout Judah, taking with them the Book of the Law of the LORD; they went around to all the towns of Judah and taught the people.

¹⁰The fear of the LORD fell on all the kingdoms of the lands surrounding Judah, so that they did not make war with Jehoshaphat. ¹¹Some Philistines brought Jehoshaphat gifts and silver as tribute, and the Arabs brought him flocks: seven thousand seven hundred rams and seven thousand seven hundred goats.

¹²Jehoshaphat became more and more powerful; he built forts and store cities in Judah ¹³and had large supplies in the towns of Judah. He also kept experienced fighting men in Jerusalem. ¹⁴Their enrollment by families was as follows:

From Judah, commanders of units of 1,000:
Adnah the commander, with 300,000 fighting men;

---

[25] For a careful analysis of the Jehoshaphat narrative in Chronicles, see G. N. Knoppers, "Reform and Regression: The Chronicler's Presentation of Jehoshaphat," *Bib* 72 (1991): 500–524.

¹⁵next, Jehohanan the commander, with 280,000;
¹⁶next, Amasiah son of Zicri, who volunteered himself for the service of the LORD, with 200,000.
¹⁷From Benjamin:
   Eliada, a valiant soldier, with 200,000 men armed with bows and shields;
   ¹⁸next, Jehozabad, with 180,000 men armed for battle.

¹⁹These were the men who served the king, besides those he stationed in the fortified cities throughout Judah.

The Chronicler begins his account of Jehoshaphat in an entirely favorable light and attempts to show a parallel between Asa and Jehoshaphat. Hence Jehoshaphat appears as a builder, as a defender of Judah, and as one who undertook a program of teaching the nation (vv. 7–9). There are also some reminiscences of the character and achievements of his great forebear, Solomon.

Chapter 17 may be divided into four sections: (a) character and rule of Jehoshaphat (17:1–6), (b) teaching mission (17:7–9), (c) tribute (17:10–13a), and (d) details of Jehoshaphat's army (17:13b–19).

JEHOSHAPHAT'S CHARACTER AND RULE (17:1–6). **17:1** Jehoshaphat, the son of Asa, followed his father in the strict line of succession.[26] The expression "strengthened himself against Israel" indicates that he established himself as ruler over the Southern Kingdom. The verb "strengthened" is used a number of times by the Chronicler (cf. 1:1). "Israel" here seems to refer to the Northern Kingdom. However, it is not impossible that the Chronicler was using "Israel" here to refer to the Southern Kingdom, which, in his view, was Israel too. The Hebrew preposition here translated "against" also can mean "over," and one possible meaning is that Jehoshaphat established himself firmly over Judah. In fact, Judah is called Israel in 21:2. In the next verse the north is called Ephraim.

17:2 The points at which Jehoshaphat made himself strong were more than fortification along the northern border. It was a general protective measure that extended into Ephraim, into areas his father had occupied (cf. 15:8). For the meaning of "troops" see comment at vv. 13–19. Jehoshaphat's ability to maintain an army was a sign that God had prospered him.

17:3–4 The Lord was with Jehoshaphat (cf. 1:1) because he walked in the ways of his father. Some manuscripts omit "David," in which case the reference is to Asa. This may gain support from the phrase "in his early years." David, of course, is presented always in a favorable light while Asa was not

---

[26] According to Thiele, Jehoshaphat actually began his reign as a co-regent alongside his father, Asa, when his father contracted his foot disease (*Mysterious Numbers*, 96–98).

always viewed favorably. The statements that Jehoshaphat did not consult the Baals or follow the practices of Israel are mutually explanatory. But by contrast he sought the God of his father (Asa) and followed his commands—a favorite expression of the Chronicler in assessing the faithfulness of Israel's kings. There were parallels to Baal worship ready at hand, for these were the days of Ahab and Jezebel in the Northern Kingdom. R. B. Dillard points out several ways that Jehoshaphat's reign paralleled that of Asa. (1) Both kings' reigns follow similar patterns of reform, victory in battle, and transgression. (2) Both kings are said to have suppressed (14:2–5; 17:6) and to have failed to suppress (15:17; 20:33) the high places. (3) Both enjoyed prosperity, great building programs, and victory as a result of their obedience. (4) Both were involved in foreign alliances. (5) The two kings are linked together as the standard of piety to which Jehoram failed to attain.[27]

17:5 Wealth, honor, and fame are regular elements in the Chronicler's picture of the benefits God bestowed on a faithful king. They were enjoyed by David and Solomon (9:13–27), at this time by Jehoshaphat (17:5; 18:1), and later on by Uzziah (26:8,15) and Hezekiah (32:27).

17:6 The expression in the NIV "his heart was devoted" is literally in Hebrew "his heart was lifted up." Here it is used in a positive sense. Elsewhere in Chronicles (26:16; 32:25) and often in the Old Testament it has a negative meaning, "be haughty." One evidence of this was that he removed the high places and the Asherah poles from Judah. The word "furthermore" may be changed to "again" with the action of Asa, his father, in mind because Asa, in the days of his reform, carried out similar reforms (cf. 14:3). But a similar reform evidently was needed later in Asa's reign. It was a recurring problem in Israel. The people tended to revert to pagan ways and constantly were in need of reform.

JEHOSHAPHAT'S TEACHING PROGRAM (17:7–9). **17:7–8** The particular reference to "the third year of his reign" has been taken by commentators to point to a co-regency with his father Asa, following Asa's debilitating disease (16:12–13; see comments on 17:1). If so, this year marks the beginning of his own effective rule. In that case zeal for reform marked Jehoshaphat's reign from the beginning. He carried on the affairs of state during the years 873–870 B.C. His own reign lasted for twenty-five years (873–849 B.C.).

Jehoshaphat's teaching mission was headed up by five officials (i.e., laymen) and ten religious personnel (eight Levites and two priests). He was acting here as the ideal king (Deut 17:18–20). Even beyond Israel the ancient ·Near East viewed the ideal king as one concerned for law and justice. The

---

[27] R. B. Dillard, "The Chronicler's Jehoshaphat," TJNS 7 (1986): 17–22.

teaching duty of the cultic personnel is well known in the Old Testament (Deut 33:10; Lev 10:11; Jer 18:18; Hos 4:6; Mal 2:7). J. G. McConville takes the inclusion of officials to mean that "this king was prepared to organize his whole kingdom for the purpose of propagating the law."[28] The names of v. 7 do not prevent our attributing them to the ninth century B.C. On the basis of seals and inscriptions we have to revise our view that such lists are late. They could well be quite early.

17:9 It is not certain whether the book of the law of the Lord was the book of the covenant or an edition of it (Exod 20:22–23:33; 34). It may have been a royal law code like other royal edicts. No firm conclusions can be arrived at although there is reason to think that it represents authoritative writings that regulated Israel's life.[29] What is clear from the text is that this group of men—officials, Levites, and priests—went around to all the cities of Judah and taught the people. In this way Israel's faith was kept alive and nurtured.

TRIBUTE (17:10–13a). Here is another indication of God's blessing on a faithful king. The surrounding nations observed Jehoshaphat's strength and recognized the presence of the Lord with him.

17:10 In the period of the conquest as well, God protected his people by filling their enemies with fear (Josh 2:9,24; 5:1). This too was evidence of God's blessing on him.

17:11 The Philistines to the southwest brought gifts and silver as tribute (cf. 1 Chr 14). The Arabs too in the Negeb area to the south and southwest of Judah in territories contiguous with the Philistines brought flocks of animals, 7,700 rams and 7,700 goats, a fairly modest number. These Arabs were neighbors of the Cushites (14:9–15). Asa, Jehoshaphat's father, had conducted campaigns in the area of the Arabs in his day. The Hebrew text indicates that it was "some of the Philistines" who brought gifts. The source of this information is not given. The Chronicler probably used an earlier extra-biblical tradition.

17:12–13a The considerable wealth that flowed into Judah enabled Jehoshaphat to strengthen his defenses in the manner of Rehoboam (11:5–12) and Asa (14:6). He built forts and store-cities and established large supplies in the towns of Judah.

DETAILS OF JEHOSHAPHAT'S ARMY (17:13b–19). This section is a detailed listing of Jehoshaphat's forces mentioned in v. 2. This listing of Judah's army is one of four in the Chronicler's narrative (14:8; 17:14–19; 25:5; 26:11–15). Jehoshaphat's army comprised two elements, the standing

---

[28] McConville, *I & II Chronicles,* DSB (Philadelphia: Westminster, 1984), 179.

[29] R. B. Dillard explains that this passage "speaks of the concept of canonical writings at a time far earlier than critical reconstructions have ordinarily allowed" (*2 Chronicles,* 134).

army and the conscript army.

17:13b The experienced fighting men were stationed in Jerusalem. They are to be linked with "the men who served the king" (v. 19) and the list of the commanders of units of a thousand (vv. 14–18).

17:14–18 Details of the conscript army are hidden behind the "enrolment by families" (the muster by fathers' houses), the divisions based on tribal affiliation with Judah and Benjamin. The large numbers need to be understood in terms of the meaning of "thousand."[30] The description of Amasiah, son of Zicri, as one "who volunteered himself for the service of the LORD" (v. 16) may have come from a source comparable to the list of David's heroes (1 Chr 11:11–13). A few details of the military equipment of Jehoshaphat's troops are provided in v. 17. Evidently the central control of Jehoshaphat's army was located at Jerusalem. The organization was centered about the tribal associations and was directed by a chief of staff (Adnah) and two assistants (Jehohanan and Amasiah) in the case of Judah, with Eliada as chief and Jehozabad as assistant for Benjamin.

(2) Alliance with the Northern Kingdom (18:1–34)

[1]Now Jehoshaphat had great wealth and honor, and he allied himself with Ahab by marriage. [2]Some years later he went down to visit Ahab in Samaria. Ahab slaughtered many sheep and cattle for him and the people with him and urged him to attack Ramoth Gilead. [3]Ahab king of Israel asked Jehoshaphat king of Judah, "Will you go with me against Ramoth Gilead?"

Jehoshaphat replied, "I am as you are, and my people as your people; we will join you in the war." [4]But Jehoshaphat also said to the king of Israel, "First seek the counsel of the LORD."

[5]So the king of Israel brought together the prophets—four hundred men— and asked them, "Shall we go to war against Ramoth Gilead, or shall I refrain?"

"Go," they answered, "for God will give it into the king's hand."

[6]But Jehoshaphat asked, "Is there not a prophet of the LORD here whom we can inquire of?"

[7]The king of Israel answered Jehoshaphat, "There is still one man through whom we can inquire of the LORD, but I hate him because he never prophesies anything good about me, but always bad. He is Micaiah son of Imlah."

"The king should not say that," Jehoshaphat replied.

[8]So the king of Israel called one of his officials and said, "Bring Micaiah son of Imlah at once."

[9]Dressed in their royal robes, the king of Israel and Jehoshaphat king of

---

[30] See comment at 1 Chr 4:18; 7:1–5; 2 Chr 13:2b and discussion in Dillard, *2 Chronicles,* 135.

Judah were sitting on their thrones at the threshing floor by the entrance to the gate of Samaria, with all the prophets prophesying before them. [10]Now Zedekiah son of Kenaanah had made iron horns, and he declared, "This is what the LORD says: 'With these you will gore the Arameans until they are destroyed.'"

[11]All the other prophets were prophesying the same thing. "Attack Ramoth Gilead and be victorious," they said, "for the LORD will give it into the king's hand."

[12]The messenger who had gone to summon Micaiah said to him, "Look, as one man the other prophets are predicting success for the king. Let your word agree with theirs, and speak favorably."

[13]But Micaiah said, "As surely as the LORD lives, I can tell him only what my God says."

[14]When he arrived, the king asked him, "Micaiah, shall we go to war against Ramoth Gilead, or shall I refrain?"

"Attack and be victorious," he answered, "for they will be given into your hand."

[15]The king said to him, "How many times must I make you swear to tell me nothing but the truth in the name of the LORD?"

[16]Then Micaiah answered, "I saw all Israel scattered on the hills like sheep without a shepherd, and the LORD said, 'These people have no master. Let each one go home in peace.'"

[17]The king of Israel said to Jehoshaphat, "Didn't I tell you that he never prophesies anything good about me, but only bad?"

[18]Micaiah continued, "Therefore hear the word of the LORD: I saw the LORD sitting on his throne with all the host of heaven standing on his right and on his left. [19]And the LORD said, 'Who will entice Ahab king of Israel into attacking Ramoth Gilead and going to his death there?'

"One suggested this, and another that. [20]Finally, a spirit came forward, stood before the LORD and said, 'I will entice him.'

"'By what means?' the LORD asked.

[21]"'I will go and be a lying spirit in the mouths of all his prophets,' he said.

"'You will succeed in enticing him,' said the LORD. 'Go and do it.'

[22]"So now the LORD has put a lying spirit in the mouths of these prophets of yours. The LORD has decreed disaster for you."

[23]Then Zedekiah son of Kenaanah went up and slapped Micaiah in the face. "Which way did the spirit from the LORD go when he went from me to speak to you?" he asked.

[24]Micaiah replied, "You will find out on the day you go to hide in an inner room."

[25]The king of Israel then ordered, "Take Micaiah and send him back to Amon the ruler of the city and to Joash the king's son, [26]and say, 'This is what the king says: Put this fellow in prison and give him nothing but bread and water until I return safely.'"

[27]Micaiah declared, "If you ever return safely, the LORD has not spoken

through me." Then he added, "Mark my words, all you people!"

²⁸So the king of Israel and Jehoshaphat king of Judah went up to Ramoth Gilead. ²⁹The king of Israel said to Jehoshaphat, "I will enter the battle in disguise, but you wear your royal robes." So the king of Israel disguised himself and went into battle.

³⁰Now the king of Aram had ordered his chariot commanders, "Do not fight with anyone, small or great, except the king of Israel." ³¹When the chariot commanders saw Jehoshaphat, they thought, "This is the king of Israel." So they turned to attack him, but Jehoshaphat cried out, and the LORD helped him. God drew them away from him, ³²for when the chariot commanders saw that he was not the king of Israel, they stopped pursuing him.

³³But someone drew his bow at random and hit the king of Israel between the sections of his armor. The king told the chariot driver, "Wheel around and get me out of the fighting. I've been wounded." ³⁴All day long the battle raged, and the king of Israel propped himself up in his chariot facing the Arameans until evening. Then at sunset he died.

The story here is comparatively long. It was taken over without much change from 1 Kings 22, to which the Chronicler added an introduction and conclusion. The mention of Jehoshaphat's wealth and honor takes up themes again from chap. 17. The chapter also devotes some space to Ahab, king of the rebellious north, an unusual concern for the Chronicler, who largely ignored the north. Even here Jehoshaphat takes the central place.

This chapter describes Jehoshaphat's failed policy toward the Northern Kingdom and in so doing underscores a significant theological theme for the Chronicler. Jehoshaphat apparently could not bring himself to recognize the depth of the Northern Kingdom's apostasy. Perhaps he harbored ideas that since they were all Israelites then they ought to get along well and be in an alliance together. He may even have supposed that this could bring about the reunification of the nation. Therefore he not only went to war alongside the northern forces but he also entered into a commercial alliance with them (20:35–37) and even married his son Jehoram to Athaliah, daughter of Ahab.³¹ Disaster came from all three efforts, and yet Jehoshaphat never seemed to realize how dangerous it was to say, "I am as you are, and my people as your people" (18:3). The point for the Chronicler was that there could be only one king and one temple for the people of God. The point for us is that flirtation with those in apostasy is flirtation with catastrophe. The requirement to show Christian affability and fellowship must be balanced with discernment and fidelity to God's truth.

MICAIAH PROPHESIES AGAINST AHAB (18:1–27). **18:1** The Chronicler wished to stress that Jehoshaphat had great wealth and honor, for

---

³¹ See Wilcock, *Message of Chronicles,* 190–93, for further discussion.

he repeated 17:5b. Yet he at once mentioned Jehoshaphat's marriage alliance with Ahab. Mixed marriages were always frowned on and were a continuing cause for concern (Ezra 10:2–5; Neh 13:23–27). The problems of mixed marriages with "those who hate the LORD" (19:2) continued on beyond the days of Ezra and Nehemiah. The Chronicler was here giving a message to his own readers. J. M. Myers translates this verse with a concessive clause: "Now although Jehoshaphat had great wealth and honor . . ."[32] Jehoshaphat had no need to enter such an alliance for financial reasons for political or defense reasons because the Lord would defend him. In the world of Jehoshaphat such marriages brought a big dowry as well as political and military gain. For the Chronicler the action was indefensible. Humanly speaking a marriage alliance with Ahab may have brought peace between the two kingdoms, but it was not necessary and was offensive to the Lord. The marriage between Jehoshaphat's son Jehoram and Athaliah, one of Ahab's daughters (21:6), it was to have tragic consequences (22:10–12; 23:1–21).

18:2–3 A general chronological reference appears at this point, "some years later." According to 1 Kgs 22:2 this was three years later. Large numbers of animals, sheep, and cattle were slaughtered by Ahab on the occasion of that visit to provide a big banquet as a gesture of honor. But Ahab wished to entice Jehoshaphat to join him in an attack on Ramoth Gilead, which was currently in the control of the Aramean king of Damascus. The verb "urge" (*hiphil* of *sût*) in the NIV conveys a sense of "entice" or "induce." The same verb is used at times to mean "to entice into sin or apostasy" (Deut 13:6; 1 Chr 21:1). The Chronicler thus indicates strong condemnation of Jehoshaphat's action.

Ramoth Gilead was located in Transjordan in the eastern territory of Gad, one of the Levitical cities of refuge (Deut 4:43; Josh 21:38). It was a strategic city on the King's Highway. Because of its strategic importance to both Israel and Aram (Damascus), it was fought over repeatedly. At some point it was annexed by Damascus, perhaps during the attacks on Ben-Hadad I (1 Kgs 15:20). It would have been among the cities promised to Ahab after the battle at Aphek (1 Kgs 20:26–34). At v. 3 the Chronicler picks up his source in 1 Kgs 22:4 and follows it closely to the end of that chapter. He omits most of 1 Kgs 22:3, in which Ahab claims that Ramoth Gilead was his. In this way he minimizes Ahab's significance.

18:4–6 Jehoshaphat would first seek the Lord's counsel from one of his prophets. The role of the prophets in the military strategy of ancient Israel is well attested. Prophets often are found providing war oracles for the Divine Warrior (2 Chr 11:1–4; 1 Kgs 20:13,28; 2 Kgs 3:11–19; 6:12–

---

[32] Myers, *II Chronicles,* 101.

22; 7:1–7; 13:14–20; 2 Chr 20:14–19). Ahab's response was to call four hundred of his prophets, not one of whom was an acceptable prophet of Yahweh. One of the marks of a true prophet was that he often stood alone against the opinion of others who made prophetic claims (36:16; 2 Kgs 17:13–15; Neh 9:26; Jer 25:4; 26:4–5; 28; 29:24–32; cf. Matt 23:33–37). For Jehoshaphat the fact that all those prophets agreed was sufficient evidence they were in collusion.

18:7–8   Ahab admitted that there was one man whom he hated because he was always criticizing him. Jehoshaphat's rebuke of Ahab demonstrates his genuine fear of the Lord. Ahab ordered the recalcitrant prophet to be brought to him.

18:9–11   While they went to bring Micaiah, Ahab and Jehoshaphat sat on their thrones at the threshing floor by the entrance to the gate of Samaria prophesying with all Ahab's prophets. Zedekiah, son of Kenaanah, portrayed the Lord as a bull goring the nations, in this case the Arameans, until they were destroyed (cf. Deut 33:17). True prophets also at times acted out their prophecies (Jer 28:10).

18:12–13   The messenger who had gone to bring Micaiah urged him to agree with the other prophets who were predicting success for King Ahab. Micaiah's reply befits his status as a genuine prophet.

18:14   The Chronicler introduces a minor but probably significant change from 1 Kgs 22:15. Three different times the record in Kings indicates that the prophets urged King Ahab to attack Ramoth Gilead, "for the LORD will give it into the king's hand" (1 Kgs 22:6,12,15). The Chronicler copied only the first two (2 Chr 18:5,11). The third from Micaiah is recorded in the passive, "They will be given into your hand." This was an ironic reply, but the Lord's name was thus divorced from this false utterance from the mouth of a true prophet. A slight alteration was made in the text in light of the Chronicler's theological concern to protect the integrity of the Lord.

18:15–16   Ahab recognized the sarcasm in Micaiah's tone and demanded that he speak plainly. Micaiah, using the familiar imagery of sheep without a shepherd (Num 27:16–17; Isa 13:14; Zech 10:2; 13:7), gave a grim forecast of Israel scattered and leaderless.

18:17   Ahab saw this as a personal affront rather than a word from God.

18:18–22   Here we are granted a glimpse into the heavenly council, which played an important role in Israel's understanding of warfare. It was normally involved in the mustering of the heavenly army to fight on Israel's behalf. Sometimes it aroused even the forces of the cosmos to join the Divine Warrior in a united campaign against the enemies of God (2 Kgs 6:15–19; 7:6; Isa 13:1–13; Joel 3:9–12). In the present instance the heavenly council devises the death of Ahab and the defeat of Israel's (the north's) armies.[33] The lying prophets were not just deceitful men but men inspired by demons. Yet everything was under the control of the Lord.

18:23–24 Zedekiah, enraged at what Micaiah's remarks implied, struck him on the face with the sarcastic remark that reminds one of the mocking of Jesus (Matt 26:67–68). The point is that Zedekiah, and not Micaiah, possessed the Spirit. Micaiah replied with a pun. Zedekiah was a "seer" who could not see. But on the day the Lord brought vengeance on Israel, he would finally "find out" (lit., "see") what God's Spirit was doing, and he would perish.

18:25–26 The exact meaning of "the king's son" is not certain. It may have been used as a title. A seal and a seal impression discovered in Palestine both carry a proper name followed by "king's son." The person may have been a police officer.[34] Micaiah was to be confined and on limited rations until Ahab returned from battle. Prisoners often received reduced rations (Isa 30:20; Jer 38:9; Matt 25:43).

18:27 The words "mark my words, all you people" are missing in some Greek texts but occur in 1 Kgs 22:28. But the words are significant. They add weight to the claim that Micaiah was indeed a prophet of the Lord and that the words of the other prophets were without substance. In fact, of course, Ahab was killed in the battle (v. 34).

AHAB'S DEATH AT RAMOTH GILEAD (18:28-34). **18:28** Various reasons may be offered to explain Ahab's desire to disguise himself.[35] Such a ruse would help someone escape detection or identification in war or in some other circumstance (Gen 38:14; 1 Sam 28:8; 1 Kgs 14:2). It might also be used in an attempt to evade a prophetic utterance (35:22). Ahab may have anticipated the command of the king of Aram to ignore everyone in the battle except the king of Israel. The one at risk, however, was Jehoshaphat in his royal robes as the subsequent narrative shows. But even that ruse did not guarantee safety to Ahab. It is impossible to flee from the Lord (Ps 139:7).

18:31–32 God's help in answer to an anguished prayer in the hour of battle was a favorite theme of the Chronicler. The parallel text in 1 Kgs 22:32 does not have the elaboration, "The LORD helped him. God drew them away from him." Even in a battle that Jehoshaphat should not have been fighting, the Lord was his helper.

18:33–34 The random arrow shot by an anonymous archer was guided by the Lord to its target, and Ahab was mortally wounded. The parallel

---

[33] Dillard, *2 Chronicles,* 142.

[34] R. de Vaux, *Ancient Israel* (New York: McGraw Hill, 1962), 119–20; J. Gray, *I and II Kings,* OTL (London: SCM, 1964), 453–54.

[35] Williamson gives a good summary of the debate (*1 and 2 Chronicles,* 276-77).

account in 1 Kgs 22:35–38 gives more detail regarding Ahab's death and shows it as a fulfillment of Elijah's prophecy in 1 Kgs 21:19. But the Chronicler omitted the Elijah material and thus also these verses. His own conclusion to this incident comes in 19:1–3. The moral is apparent. The reader is given a bare outline of Ahab's misfortune and is spared from the gory detail of his death supplied by Kings.

(3) *The Reign of Jehoshaphat: God's Rebuke and Jehoshaphat's Reformation (19:1-11)*

¹When Jehoshaphat king of Judah returned safely to his palace in Jerusalem, ²Jehu the seer, the son of Hanani, went out to meet him and said to the king, "Should you help the wicked and love those who hate the LORD? Because of this, the wrath of the LORD is upon you. ³There is, however, some good in you, for you have rid the land of the Asherah poles and have set your heart on seeking God."

⁴Jehoshaphat lived in Jerusalem, and he went out again among the people from Beersheba to the hill country of Ephraim and turned them back to the LORD, the God of their fathers. ⁵He appointed judges in the land, in each of the fortified cities of Judah. ⁶He told them, "Consider carefully what you do, because you are not judging for man but for the LORD, who is with you whenever you give a verdict. ⁷Now let the fear of the LORD be upon you. Judge carefully, for with the LORD our God there is no injustice or partiality or bribery."

⁸In Jerusalem also, Jehoshaphat appointed some of the Levites, priests and heads of Israelite families to administer the law of the LORD and to settle disputes. And they lived in Jerusalem. ⁹He gave them these orders: "You must serve faithfully and wholeheartedly in the fear of the LORD. ¹⁰In every case that comes before you from your fellow countrymen who live in the cities— whether bloodshed or other concerns of the law, commands, decrees or ordinances—you are to warn them not to sin against the LORD; otherwise his wrath will come on you and your brothers. Do this, and you will not sin.

¹¹"Amariah the chief priest will be over you in any matter concerning the LORD, and Zebadiah son of Ishmael, the leader of the tribe of Judah, will be over you in any matter concerning the king, and the Levites will serve as officials before you. Act with courage, and may the LORD be with those who do well."

Second Chronicles 19:1–3 is the conclusion to the narrative about Micaiah, in which a prophet of the Lord gives the Chronicler's own theological comment on the incident recorded in chap. 19. The continuation of the account of Jehoshaphat and his judicial reforms commences at 19:4 and continues to 19:11.

CONCLUSION TO THE ACCOUNT OF JEHOSHAPHAT'S ABORTIVE ALLIANCE WITH AHAB (19:1-3). **19:1** Micaiah's words, "Let each one go home in peace" (18:16), match the comment, "Jehoshaphat returned to his palace in safety." The words "home" and "palace" are the same in Hebrew (*bêt*), and so also are the words for "peace" and "safety" (*běšālôm*). The contrast with Ahab's fate is clear.

19:2   Jehu ben Hanani was one who rebuked Asa for his involvement in a foreign alliance (16:7–10). By this time Jehu must have been an old man, for he was active during the reign of Baasha (1 Kgs 16:1), a contemporary of Asa against whom Hanani had prophesied.

The use of the verb "love" (*ʾāhab*) here is of some interest. In some places in the Old Testament it carries a political rather than an emotional sense.[36] No king of Israel who was loyal to the Lord should "love," that is, enter into a political and helping alliance, with one who "hated" (*śānēʾ*) the Lord. This breach of a covenant relationship could only bring the wrath of Yahweh upon the disloyal offender. It was always to be hoped that such evil alliances might be put aside. In Jehoshaphat's case there was a change of heart so that the Chronicler could give him general approval at the end.

19:3   Jehoshaphat displayed some good things too (cf. 17:3,6). The generally favorable assessment of Jehoshaphat and the reasons for it are set out in chap. 17, where the Chronicler affirms that he sought the God of his father and followed his commands, a favorite assessment of a king who displayed faithful religious practice.

JEHOSHAPHAT APPOINTS JUDGES (19:4–11).   This brief pericope of eight verses has raised a number of questions for commentators. The major questions are concerned with the source of the material, the relation of these verses to Deut 16:18–17:13, and the historicity of the account. We will take these up in the course of the exposition of these verses.

19:4   The statement seems to mean that although Jehoshaphat did not make excursions to the Northern Kingdom after the disaster of Ramoth Gilead (chap. 18), he did go among the people of Judah, not indirectly through emissaries (cf. 17:7–9) but personally. His purpose was to turn the people back to the Lord, the God of their fathers. The expression "from Beersheba to the hill country of Ephraim" describes the land from south to north rather than the more usual north to south (cf. 30:5). On one occasion the Chronicler even reverses what he found in Samuel (cp. 2 Sam 24:2; 1 Chr 21:2).

19:5   According to this statement Jehoshaphat appointed judges in the land and in each of the fortified cities of Judah (cf. Deut 16:18). In contrast with some earlier commentators, W. F. Albright holds that the narrative of 2 Chronicles 19 is a substantially correct account of Jehoshaphat's judicial reforms.[37] However, the Chronicler did not give all the details of that reform.

---

[36] See J. A. Thompson, "Israel's 'Haters,'" *VT* 29 (1979): 200–205.

[37] W. F. Albright, "The Judicial Reform of Jehoshaphat," *Alexander Marx Jubilee Volume,* (1950): 61–82.

19:6 Verses 6–11 contain a good deal of parenetic (preaching) material in the style of Deuteronomy (vv. 6–7,9–10,11b), to be compared with the brief framework of vv. 5,8,11a. There are some parallels in thought between this verse and Deut 1:17. Both passages make it clear that judicial authority depended upon the rule of the Lord and was to reflect his own attributes of righteousness, justice, and fairness. Judges acted on behalf of kings and human authorities only in a derivative sense. They were, in fact, the Lord's agents. The Lord was with them whenever they gave a verdict. He was loved and was known by justice (Pss 9:16; 11:7).[38]

19:7 The frequent injunctions against bribery in the Old Testament indicate that the practice was widespread. In general only the rich benefitted from, or could afford, a bribe. The poor often were at a disadvantage because they could not offer bribes (Exod 23:6–8; Deut 1:17; 16:18–20; 1 Sam 8:3; Ps 15:5; Prov 17:23; Isa 1:21–23; 5:22–23; Mic 3:11; 7:3).[39]

19:8 A court was set up in Jerusalem that was representative of both religious and lay leadership in Israel (cf. Ezra 10:25).

The statement that the leaders lived in Jerusalem represents a slight emendation to the text. The MT reads, "They returned to Jerusalem" (with the verb *šûb*). But both the LXX and the Vulgate attest to an alternative text, which the NIV has followed (using the verb *yāšab*, "lived"). The leaders who lived in Jerusalem on a permanent basis apparently constituted a court of appeal. Capital cases and disputed cases under appeal were transferred there from the municipal courts (see vv. 5,10). There were different judges for the different types of cases (v. 11). Many commentators, following the LXX, the Vulgate, and also the NEB, adopt a slight emendation at the end of v. 8 to read "and [to decide] the disputed cases of the inhabitants of Jerusalem." This Jerusalem also had a municipal court.[40]

19:9–10 These verses constitute a second parenetic section (cf. Deut 17:8–13). Judges were exhorted to make their judgments in the fear of the Lord. Moreover, they were to warn their countrymen not to sin and incur God's wrath (v. 2). It was precisely to help avert this possibility that Jehoshaphat undertook his judicial reform.

19:11 Two jurisdictions are here spelled out, over each of which was a presiding officer or president. The "matter concerning the LORD" were cultic in character. The other jurisdiction was in "any matter concerning the king," that is, civil matters. The common term in Chronicles used here for the high priest is literally "head priest" (*kōhēn hārō'š*). It also is found in

---

[38] Dillard, *2 Chronicles,* 149.
[39] Ibid.
[40] Williamson, *1 & 2 Chronicles,* 290–91.

24:6,11; 26:20; 31:10. The designation "high priest" (*hakkōhēn haggādôl*) common in the Pentateuch occurs only once in Chronicles (2 Chr 34:9). Here this person is called "the head priest." The Levites were the court functionaries who carried out the decisions of the court. In all cases judgment was given on the principle of avoiding guilt before the Lord so as to maintain public welfare. The shape of the divine wrath varied. It could be foreign invasion, internal collapse and revolt, or something else.

(4) Jehoshaphat's Piety Rewarded (20:1–21:1)

¹After this, the Moabites and Ammonites with some of the Meunites came to make war on Jehoshaphat.

²Some men came and told Jehoshaphat, "A vast army is coming against you from Edom, from the other side of the Sea. It is already in Hazazon Tamar" (that is, En Gedi). ³Alarmed, Jehoshaphat resolved to inquire of the LORD, and he proclaimed a fast for all Judah. ⁴The people of Judah came together to seek help from the LORD; indeed, they came from every town in Judah to seek him.

⁵Then Jehoshaphat stood up in the assembly of Judah and Jerusalem at the temple of the LORD in the front of the new courtyard ⁶and said:

"O LORD, God of our fathers, are you not the God who is in heaven? You rule over all the kingdoms of the nations. Power and might are in your hand, and no one can withstand you. ⁷O our God, did you not drive out the inhabitants of this land before your people Israel and give it forever to the descendants of Abraham your friend? ⁸They have lived in it and have built in it a sanctuary for your Name, saying, ⁹'If calamity comes upon us, whether the sword of judgment, or plague or famine, we will stand in your presence before this temple that bears your Name and will cry out to you in our distress, and you will hear us and save us.'

¹⁰"But now here are men from Ammon, Moab and Mount Seir, whose territory you would not allow Israel to invade when they came from Egypt; so they turned away from them and did not destroy them. ¹¹See how they are repaying us by coming to drive us out of the possession you gave us as an inheritance. ¹²O our God, will you not judge them? For we have no power to face this vast army that is attacking us. We do not know what to do, but our eyes are upon you."

¹³All the men of Judah, with their wives and children and little ones, stood there before the LORD.

¹⁴Then the Spirit of the LORD came upon Jahaziel son of Zechariah, the son of Benaiah, the son of Jeiel, the son of Mattaniah, a Levite and descendant of Asaph, as he stood in the assembly.

¹⁵He said: "Listen, King Jehoshaphat and all who live in Judah and Jerusalem! This is what the LORD says to you: 'Do not be afraid or discouraged because of this vast army. For the battle is not yours, but God's. ¹⁶Tomorrow

march down against them. They will be climbing up by the Pass of Ziz, and you will find them at the end of the gorge in the Desert of Jeruel. [17]You will not have to fight this battle. Take up your positions; stand firm and see the deliverance the LORD will give you, O Judah and Jerusalem. Do not be afraid; do not be discouraged. Go out to face them tomorrow, and the LORD will be with you.'"

[18]Jehoshaphat bowed with his face to the ground, and all the people of Judah and Jerusalem fell down in worship before the LORD. [19]Then some Levites from the Kohathites and Korahites stood up and praised the LORD, the God of Israel, with very loud voice.

[20]Early in the morning they left for the Desert of Tekoa. As they set out, Jehoshaphat stood and said, "Listen to me, Judah and people of Jerusalem! Have faith in the LORD your God and you will be upheld; have faith in his prophets and you will be successful." [21]After consulting the people, Jehoshaphat appointed men to sing to the LORD and to praise him for the splendor of his holiness as they went out at the head of the army, saying:

"Give thanks to the LORD,

for his love endures forever."

[22]As they began to sing and praise, the LORD set ambushes against the men of Ammon and Moab and Mount Seir who were invading Judah, and they were defeated. [23]The men of Ammon and Moab rose up against the men from Mount Seir to destroy and annihilate them. After they finished slaughtering the men from Seir, they helped to destroy one another.

[24]When the men of Judah came to the place that overlooks the desert and looked toward the vast army, they saw only dead bodies lying on the ground; no one had escaped. [25]So Jehoshaphat and his men went to carry off their plunder, and they found among them a great amount of equipment and clothing and also articles of value—more than they could take away. There was so much plunder that it took three days to collect it. [26]On the fourth day they assembled in the Valley of Beracah, where they praised the LORD. This is why it is called the Valley of Beracah to this day.

[27]Then, led by Jehoshaphat, all the men of Judah and Jerusalem returned joyfully to Jerusalem, for the LORD had given them cause to rejoice over their enemies. [28]They entered Jerusalem and went to the temple of the LORD with harps and lutes and trumpets.

[29]The fear of God came upon all the kingdoms of the countries when they heard how the LORD had fought against the enemies of Israel. [30]And the kingdom of Jehoshaphat was at peace, for his God had given him rest on every side.

[31]So Jehoshaphat reigned over Judah. He was thirty-five years old when he became king of Judah, and he reigned in Jerusalem twenty-five years. His mother's name was Azubah daughter of Shilhi. [32]He walked in the ways of his father Asa and did not stray from them; he did what was right in the eyes of the LORD. [33]The high places, however, were not removed, and the people still had not set their hearts on the God of their fathers.

[34]The other events of Jehoshaphat's reign, from beginning to end, are writ-

ten in the annals of Jehu son of Hanani, which are recorded in the book of the kings of Israel.

35Later, Jehoshaphat king of Judah made an alliance with Ahaziah king of Israel, who was guilty of wickedness. **36**He agreed with him to construct a fleet of trading ships. After these were built at Ezion Geber, **37**Eliezer son of Dodavahu of Mareshah prophesied against Jehoshaphat, saying, "Because you have made an alliance with Ahaziah, the LORD will destroy what you have made." The ships were wrecked and were not able to set sail to trade.

1Then Jehoshaphat rested with his fathers and was buried with them in the City of David. And Jehoram his son succeeded him as king.

Most of the material of this lengthy chapter is unique to Chronicles. The account of Jehoshaphat's battle with a Transjordan coalition is not found in Kings, although the disaster that befell Jehoshaphat's trading fleet (20:35–37) is dealt with in 1 Kgs 22:48–49, albeit differently. The Chronicler lays great stress on Jehoshaphat's self-humbling, repentance, and dependence on God in the face of a grave threat to Judah (cf. 7:14). This is in keeping with other incidents in Judah's history as interpreted by the Chronicler.

There is no inherent reason for rejecting the possibility of an invasion of Judah by a Transjordan coalition, although the incident has been questioned by some. Much enmity existed between Judah and its eastern neighbors over the centuries. Indeed the compiler of 1 Kings invites his readers to consult his sources for other military exploits of Jehoshaphat (1 Kgs 22:46). The Chronicler evidently tapped into such sources (cf. 20:34). Apart from historical and geographical considerations, this chapter is an example of seeking the Lord and a demonstration of the Lord's willingness and desire to respond. "The LORD will be with you" (v. 17) is a key affirmation.

The chapter falls readily into four sections: (1) Jehoshaphat's great victory (20:1–30), (2) final observations on Jehoshaphat's reign (20:31–34), (3) Jehoshaphat's disastrous maritime venture (20:35–37), and (4) Jehoshaphat's death (21:1).

JEHOSHAPHAT'S GREAT VICTORY (20:1–30). **20:1–2** This incident must be read against the background of 17:3,10, which distinguish between the early and later years of Jehoshaphat. Before his disobedience recounted in chap. 18 and condemned in 19:1–3, his kingdom was protected from attacking enemies by the fear of the Lord "on all the kingdoms of the lands surrounding Judah." Then after the response of faith recounted in this chapter, this situation was renewed (20:29–30).

Jehoshaphat was warned of an invading army from the direction of Transjordan, a coalition of Moabites, Ammonites, and Meunites. There is some speculation about the third group. The MT reads "Ammonites," which is repetitive and probably the result of dittography. That there was a third group is clear from vv. 2,10,22–23, which indicate the third group was from Mount Seir, that is, Edom. The LXX reads "the Meunites," who are mentioned together with the Ammonites during the time of Hezekiah (26:7; cf. 1 Chr 4:41). The location of such a group has been linked with the Arab town Maʿan, twelve miles southeast of Petra. Their link with Mount Seir need not be a problem. Seir was located somewhere in the southern Negeb. Maʿan is situated in the Negeb in several places (Josh 15:55; 1 Sam 23:24; 25:2; 1 Chr 2:45). Most commentators accept the hint in the LXX and translate "Meunites."[41] The coalition was very diverse, and the difference in origins may account for the strife referred to in v. 23. An advance up the western side of the Dead Sea as far as Hazazon Tamar (En Gedi) is feasible. The location of Hazazon Tamar is uncertain, but it may be el-Hasasa between En Gedi and Bethlehem. En Gedi lay in the center of the western side of the Dead Sea. The ascent to the top of the mountains was by way of the pass of Ziz (v. 16).

20:3–4 Jehoshaphat's first response was fear, an appropriate response in the circumstances. Jahaziel later counseled, "Do not fear" (v. 17), counsel that occurs 365 times in the Bible, enough for each day's quota of fearful situations.[42] Jehoshaphat's second response was (literally) to "give his face to seek Yahweh." In fact, the two verbs "feared and gave" begin the verse in Hebrew almost as one verb. Jehoshaphat knew how to deal with fear. Seeking the Lord is stressed here with two synonyms, the first (*dāraš*) translated "inquire" and the other (*biqqēš*) translated "seek" (see comments at 14:4). In this emergency situation Judah expressed their serious need for divine help by fasting.

20:5–9 Jehoshaphat led the prayer on that day. The gathering at the temple recalls Solomon's prayer for divine help in situations just like this (6:14–42). Jehoshaphat apparently saw in the present predicament a judgment from God. The "new courtyard" probably is the "great court" of 4:9. Jehoshaphat's prayer has the form of a national lament (cf. Pss 44; 83). It is addressed to "LORD, God of our fathers," an address used also by David in 1 Chr 12:17; 2 Chr 11:16; 13:18; 14:4). God's omnipotence is affirmed as the prayer unfolds. The Lord refers to Abraham as "my friend" in Isa 41:8 in a context of assurance of deliverance from enemies, which also includes the encouragement, "Do not fear, for I am with you" (Isa 41:10). After recounting God's favors in the past (vv. 6–7), the prayer moves on to affirm confi-

---

[41] Dillard, *2 Chronicles*, 155–56. He also notes that reading "Edom" rather than the MT אֲרָם ("Aram") is not properly a text-critical decision in itself but is a conjectural one formed by geopolitical factors.

[42] L. C. Allen, *1, 2 Chronicles*, CC (Dallas: Word, 1987), 306.

dence in God, especially in light of his having allowed Israel to live in the land and to build a sanctuary for his name. The substance of Solomon's prayer at the dedication of the temple (chap. 6) is recalled (20:9). In times of peril the people will stand in God's presence and cry to him, and he will hear and save.

20:10–12 Developing his plea, Jehoshaphat used the common introduction "But now." There was the predicament. Invaders from the other side of the Dead Sea were at the door, people Israel formerly had spared when they were traveling to the promised land (Num 20:14–21; Deut 2:1–19; Judg 11:14–17). The behavior of these nations toward Israel was reprehensible. Jehoshaphat turned to God to judge them, recognizing that without him he was powerless.

20:13–17 Having laid their concerns before the Lord, the people waited humbly on him. The expression to "stand before the LORD" is found frequently in Scripture (cf. Gen 19:27; Lev 9:5; Deut 4:10; 2 Chr 18:20). The divine response to Jehoshaphat's prayer came by way of Jahaziel, a Levite with an unusually long genealogy reaching back to Asaph in the days of David. He addressed King Jehoshaphat and the people of Judah and Jerusalem with an oracle of salvation containing three main components: the addressees, a "fear not" element at the beginning and again at the end (cf. v. 3), and the substantiation ("the battle is not yours, but God's"; cf. 1 Sam 17:47; 1 Chr 5:22). Here was the perspective of the "holy war" and the speech of the priest before battle (Deut 20:2–4). The literary forms of the salvation oracle and the holy war are woven together in one speech.[43] Even if there was a disparity in the forces, with the Lord fighting for Israel they were assured of success. The substance of the oracle is restated in v. 17 with a quotation from Exod 14:13. The God who had parted the Red Sea had not changed in hundreds of years, and he is still the same today (cf. Isa 52:10; Zech 9:9). The assurance of God's presence was more than a theological statement; it was to be a source of strength.

20:18–21 The lament changes to praise and worship led by the Levites, some Kohathites, and some Korahites, probably Levitical singers, although elsewhere they were gatekeepers (cf. 1 Chr 9:19; 26:1). Rising early in the morning (cf. 2 Kgs 3:22), they left for the wilderness of Tekoa. Jehoshaphat's word as they set out to meet the enemy climbing up the Pass of Ziz echoed that of Jahaziel. The exhortation to "have faith" uses another form of the same verb (ʾmn) meaning "you will be upheld" in v. 20. The "prophets" (v. 20) could be the earlier prophets, whose writings already had become canonical, but probably it refers to the more immediate prophecy of

---

[43] Dillard, *2 Chronicles,* 157.

Jahaziel. In most battles a battle cry is heard. Here it is replaced by singing and praise. After consulting the people, Jehoshaphat appointed men to sing to the Lord and to praise him for the splendor of his holiness as they went out at the head of the army. The song they sang had been heard also in the days of David and Solomon (1 Chr 16:34,41; 2 Chr 5:13).

20:22–26 The ambush was a common feature of the holy war (Josh 8:2,7,12,14,19,21; Jer 51:12; cf. 2 Chr 13:13). But here it was the Lord who "set ambushes" against the foe. These ambushes have been variously identified. We can only speculate, but supernatural agencies probably are implied, comparable with the "panic" that sometimes affected Israel's enemies in a holy war (Exod 23:27; Josh 10:10). Confusion in battle sometimes brought armies to self-destruction (Judg 7:22; 1 Sam 14:20; 2 Kgs 3:23). Jehoshaphat's men were not called upon to participate in the battle (cf. 13:14–18; 14:12–14). The huge quantities of spoil listed serve to emphasize the magnitude of the victory. The Valley of Beracah is represented today by Khirbet Berekut and Wadi Berekut, both situated near Tekoa.

20:27–28 Jehoshaphat and the men of Judah returned to the temple joyfully to celebrate their victory with harps, lutes, and trumpets. In the temple they had sought God's deliverance (v. 5), and now they celebrated there.

20:29–30 The rhetorical question of v. 6 is thus answered in the affirmative. The Lord does rule over the kingdoms of the nations. Evidence of his favor is the victory and peace Jehoshaphat again enjoyed.

FINAL OBSERVATIONS ON JEHOSHAPHAT'S REIGN (20:31– 34). **20:31** A reign of twenty-five years is recorded, whereas in 2 Kgs 3:1; 8:16 it is twenty-two years. The discrepancy is due to a co-regency to ensure a smooth succession. These concluding notices about Jehoshaphat follow 1 Kgs 22:41–50.[44]

20:32–33 Jehoshaphat received general approval from the Chronicler, although it is noted that he did not remove the high places as he might have done by exercising royal power. Also a reformer at the top cannot guarantee that the common people would truly repent, and no general revival occurred here.

20:34 The Chronicler's source for at least some of his material was a prophetic work, "The annals of Jehu son of Hanani," which seems to have been part of a larger work, "The book of the kings of Israel." The term "Israel" here means Judah in particular, but since Judah also was Israel in its wider sense, the designation is correct.

JEHOSHAPHAT'S DISASTROUS MARITIME VENTURE (20:35– 37). **20:35–37** The alternative story in 1 Kgs 22:47–48 records how

---

[44] Thiele, *Mysterious Numbers,* 96–98.

Jehoshaphat built a fleet that was wrecked before it sailed at Ezion Geber. Ahaziah, king of Israel, offered help in a joint venture, which Jehoshaphat at first refused (1 Kgs 22:48–49). Yet once again Jehoshaphat was drawn into an alliance with the king of Israel. He sought a human ally and not God. There is no mention of the Lord's help. Jehoshaphat agreed on an alliance to make ships to go to Tarshish (a fleet of trading ships). Jehoshaphat's devout life did not sanctify this venture; rather, Ahaziah's corrupt life defiled it. The prophet Eliezer, son of Dodavahu of Mareshah, is otherwise unknown.

JEHOSHAPHAT'S DEATH (21:1).   **21:1**   The notice of Jehoshaphat's burial in the City of David follows the typical pattern used in Chronicles and is not especially significant.

8. The Reign of Jehoram (21:2–20)

The Chronicler's account of Jehoram's reign (ca. 849–842 B.C.) represents a considerable expansion over the brief treatment in 2 Kgs 8:16–24. Even so, it is a mere twenty verses in length. There is good reason to believe that the Chronicler drew on earlier authentic sources but handled the material in his own way. In particular he wished to make the point again that faithlessness leads to personal tragedy and to domination by foreign enemies. The story of Saul provides another good example (1 Chr 10).

An unusual feature of this record is the letter from Elijah. The narrative falls into four brief sections: (1) the establishment of Jehoram's rule (21:2–4), (2) the character of Jehoram's reign (21:5–11), (3) the letter from Elijah (21:12–15), and (4) the end of Jehoram's reign (21:16–20).

(1) Jehoram Establishes His Rule (21:2–4)

2Jehoram's brothers, the sons of Jehoshaphat, were Azariah, Jehiel, Zechariah, Azariahu, Michael and Shephatiah. All these were sons of Jehoshaphat king of Israel. 3Their father had given them many gifts of silver and gold and articles of value, as well as fortified cities in Judah, but he had given the kingdom to Jehoram because he was his firstborn son.

4When Jehoram established himself firmly over his father's kingdom, he put all his brothers to the sword along with some of the princes of Israel.

21:2   Verses 2–4 are found only in Chronicles. The normal introductory remarks about a king's reign do not come until v. 5. As Williamson observes, they introduce a theme in chaps. 21–22 of violence, endangering the Davidic line (cf. v. 17; 22:8–11).[45]

---

[45] Williamson, *1 & 2 Chronicles,* 304.

The first piece of information about Jehoram is a list of his numerous brothers. This was a sign of God's favor toward his father, Jehoshaphat (11:18–22; 13:21; cf. 1 Chr 25:5). Jehoram saw the brothers only as a threat and murdered them (v. 4). It seems unusual for two brothers to have the same name, yet Azariahu is just a longer form of Azariah. Some commentators have proposed that the second Azariah should be emended to Uzziah. But there is no inherent reason why these two sons, born perhaps to different wives of Jehoshaphat, should not have the same name. Also the Chronicler's description of Jehoshaphat as king of "Israel" need not be corrected to "king of Judah" (see comment on 20:34). The Chronicler often used "Israel" with reference to the Southern Kingdom.

21:3 It was politically expedient for the king to disperse his sons throughout his kingdom both to extend the royal power and presence in outlying districts and to encourage a smooth transition of reigns to Jehoram, the firstborn son. Yet there may have been problems over the succession very early in Jehoram's reign. That Jehoram is said to have received the kingdom as a gift from Jehoshaphat rather than from God may be an early hint of the lack of divine favor (cf. 1 Sam 28:17; 1 Kgs 14:8; 2 Chr 17:5).

21:4 Sensing that all was not well, Jehoram "established himself" (see comments on 2 Chr 1:1) over his father's kingdom and then killed his brothers as well as some of the leaders of Israel (another reference to Judah). Solomon similarly eliminated potential rivals at the time of his accession (1 Kgs 2). As Dillard says: "There is both irony and retributive justice in that Jehoram sets in motion events that would ultimately lead to the near obliteration of his own line (22:10; 2 Kgs 11:1)."[46]

(2) The Character of Jehoram's Reign (21:5–11)

⁵Jehoram was thirty-two years old when he became king, and he reigned in Jerusalem eight years. ⁶He walked in the ways of the kings of Israel, as the house of Ahab had done, for he married a daughter of Ahab. He did evil in the eyes of the LORD. ⁷Nevertheless, because of the covenant the LORD had made with David, the LORD was not willing to destroy the house of David. He had promised to maintain a lamp for him and his descendants forever.

⁸In the time of Jehoram, Edom rebelled against Judah and set up its own king. ⁹So Jehoram went there with his officers and all his chariots. The Edomites surrounded him and his chariot commanders, but he rose up and broke through by night. ¹⁰To this day Edom has been in rebellion against Judah.

Libnah revolted at the same time, because Jehoram had forsaken the LORD,

---

[46] Dillard, *2 Chronicles*, 165.

the God of his fathers. ¹¹He had also built high places on the hills of Judah and had caused the people of Jerusalem to prostitute themselves and had led Judah astray.

21:5–6 Jehoram had a comparatively short reign of eight years. The story in Chronicles follows 2 Kgs 8:17–19 quite closely. The assessment of Jehoram's reign is negative. The daughter he married was Athaliah, described as the "daughter" of both Ahab (21:6) and Omri (22:2; 2 Kgs 8:26). Like *ben* ("son") *bat* ("daughter") also can mean "descendant." So Athaliah probably was the daughter of Ahab and the granddaughter of Omri. The Syriac Peshitta calls her the "sister of Ahab," which is possible. The point is that she was a member of his corrupt household. Jehoshaphat also was foolish enough to marry into Ahab's house (18:1; cf. 22:3–5; 28:2).

21:7 God was patient with Jehoram for the sake of the Davidic dynasty. The Chronicler has made two textual changes from 2 Kgs 8:19 so that "Judah" becomes "the house of David" and "for the sake of his servant David" becomes "because of the covenant the LORD had made with him," which reiterates God's promise to David to give him a dynasty that would continue over the centuries. The ambiguity in the NIV pronoun "him" does not exist in Hebrew, which has the independent clause with its reference to David first in the opening sentence of v. 7. David's "lamp" is a reference to 1 Kgs 11:36. A burning lamp in the home would indicate its occupancy by a resident. To have a lamp suggests that life would continue and the home would be occupied. The promise was that the Davidic line would not be extinguished until the time of the Messiah, who would occupy the throne forever.

21:8–11 As a result of Jehoram's disobedience, Judah lost some of its political influence. Two areas are presented as illustrations of the principle of immediate retribution,⁴⁷ Edom to the southeast and Libnah on the west.

Edom had been subservient to Judah. David had subdued Edom (2 Sam 8:13–14; 1 Kgs 11:15–17), but rebellion was brewing before Solomon's death (1 Kgs 11:14–22). Under Asa and Jehoshaphat, Judah regained control. In the time of Jehoshaphat, Edom had been ruled by a royal deputy (1 Kgs 22:47; but see 2 Kgs 3:9). Then under Jehoram, Edom rebelled again and set up its own king. Jehoram responded by invading Edom with his officers and chariots but was not able to bring the Edomites under his control. On the contrary, Edomite forces surrounded Jehoram's forces, although he broke out of the trap and escaped, a sign of God's grace and faithfulness to David. There is no evidence that Edom was subdued by Jehoram again.

---

⁴⁷ See Dillard, *2 Chronicles,* 76–81.

Edom remained in rebellion "to this day."

Libnah, possibly to be identified with Tell es-Safi to the west of Judah at the western end of the Valley of Elah, rebelled next, and Jehoram had revolts on two fronts. By Hezekiah's time the city was regained (2 Kgs 19:8).

The refurbishing of the high places (2 Chr 21:11) reversed the policy of Asa and Jehoshaphat.The building of high places was, for the Chronicler, a clear sign of the king's unfaithfulness. The phrase "prostitute themselves" denotes an act of disloyalty and unfaithfulness after the manner of harlots or prostitutes.

(3) The Letter from Elijah (21:12–15)

¹²Jehoram received a letter from Elijah the prophet, which said:

"This is what the LORD, the God of your father David, says: 'You have not walked in the ways of your father Jehoshaphat or of Asa king of Judah. ¹³But you have walked in the ways of the kings of Israel, and you have led Judah and the people of Jerusalem to prostitute themselves, just as the house of Ahab did. You have also murdered your own brothers, members of your father's house, men who were better than you. ¹⁴So now the LORD is about to strike your people, your sons, your wives and everything that is yours, with a heavy blow. ¹⁵You yourself will be very ill with a lingering disease of the bowels, until the disease causes your bowels to come out.'"

The days of Jehoram were days of severe apostasy in Israel. The evil influence of Ahab, Athaliah, and the prophets of Baal was still rampant; and Elijah, the prophet of the Lord, was contesting the claims of Baal. According to 2 Kgs 1:17, Joram of Israel came to the throne of Israel in the second year of Jehoram, king of Judah. Joram had succeeded Ahaziah, whose death Elijah prophesied (2 Kgs 1:16). Hence Elijah was alive during the early years of Jehoram's reign, at least during the years of a possible co-regency. Some have questioned the genuineness of a letter from Elijah, since it is not attested elsewhere,[48] but we should be careful about rejecting the testimony of our primary evidence, the Bible. According to 2 Kgs 1:17, Elijah gave a prophecy about the death of Ahaziah and the accession of Jehoram. This suggests that Elijah was alive for part, at least, of Jehoram's reign.

21:12 Reference to "the God of your father David" rather than the more common "God of Israel" indicates that Jehoram's lineage carried responsibilities of faithfulness on his part as well as the Lord's.

21:13 Elijah compared Jehoram's sins to those of Ahab, with whom he

---

[48] Williamson, *1 and 2 Chronicles*, 306–7; Dillard, *2 Chronicles*, 167; Myers, *II Chronicles*, 121–22.

was quite familiar. The point is that he expected better behavior from the house of David than that of the wayward Northern Kingdom but instead saw God's chosen house imitating the sins of the rebellious tribes. Although the NIV translation "prostitute themselves" appropriately indicates that the people were responsible for their actions, the Hebrew would more literally be translated "made [them] prostitutes," a more graphic description of God's attitude toward these two kings. Jehoram's second and more specific sin of murder is then declared, for which his own family would suffer.

21:14–15 The two consequences of Jehoram's two sins are introduced by the climactic "so now," Hebrew *hinnê,* sometimes translated "behold." The consequences are given in reverse order of the sins. As a result of Jehoram's having murdered his own brothers, the Lord would strike down his sons, his family, and his possessions. The phrase "everything that is yours" is literally "and all your possessions," employing a word (*rĕkûš*) translated "equipment" in 20:25. There it refers to the plunder of the Moabites, Ammonites, and Meunites God gave to Jehoshaphat in response to his faith. Here it refers to the "goods" (*rĕkûš*) that the Philistines and Arabs would plunder from Jehoram (v. 17) in response to his wickedness. Jehoram himself would die with a disease of the bowels that would last (literally) "days upon days" until his bowels came out. As with most illnesses mentioned in the Old Testament, we are left to conjecture about the clinically imprecise vocabulary. Ulcers, colitis, chronic diarrhea, and dysentery have been proposed.

(4) The End of Jehoram's Life (21:16–20)

¹⁶The LORD aroused against Jehoram the hostility of the Philistines and of the Arabs who lived near the Cushites. ¹⁷They attacked Judah, invaded it and carried off all the goods found in the king's palace, together with his sons and wives. Not a son was left to him except Ahaziah, the youngest.

¹⁸After all this, the LORD afflicted Jehoram with an incurable disease of the bowels. ¹⁹In the course of time, at the end of the second year, his bowels came out because of the disease, and he died in great pain. His people made no fire in his honor, as they had for his fathers.

²⁰Jehoram was thirty-two years old when he became king, and he reigned in Jerusalem eight years. He passed away, to no one's regret, and was buried in the City of David, but not in the tombs of the kings.

Two brief paragraphs conclude the story of Jehoram's reign. The first (vv. 16–17) deals with judgment against the people, and the second (vv. 18–20) provides more detail about Jehoram's tragic final days.

21:16–17 Further attacks against Jehoram's kingdom came from the Philistines and the Arabs to the southeast and southwest of his land, that is, in the same general areas as Edom and Libnah. Jehoram's inability to prevent the initial rebellions in these areas encouraged other rebellions. These renewed attacks reached as far as the king's palace, from which the attackers carried off booty and took captive his sons and wives. The sons and wives eventually were killed except for Ahaziah, the youngest, whom God faithfully preserved alive. These attacks probably were against outlying fortified cities to which Jehoram had dispersed his sons and their mothers. Jehoram's youngest son, with his mother, as chap. 22 makes clear, remained with the king in Jerusalem. The "king's palace" need not refer to the palace in Jerusalem where the king still resided after the raid and where Ahaziah was to be made king.[49]

21:18–19a According to the prophecy of v. 15, Jehoram was judged personally and died in agony. There is a textual problem in v. 19a. Jehoram is said to have died after two days, which appears to contradict the picture of a protracted disease. The most common solution is to translate "two years" (NIV, NEB, KJV, NRSV), following similar usage of "days" as "years" elsewhere in the Old Testament (cf. Judg 17:10; 2 Sam 14:26). There is, however, no secure position.[50]

21:19b–20 These verses are to be compared with 2 Kgs 8:23–24. Even during his short reign Jehoram became unpopular. At his death the unusual honor granted to popular kings, the making of a fire in his honor, was not accorded to him (cf. 16:14). He was buried in the City of David, but not in the tombs of the kings. A final comment indicates that he passed away "to no one's regret," a tragic end for a descendant of David. Indicative of the Chronicler's contempt for Jehoram is that he made no mention of other sources that could be consulted for additional information (cp. 2 Kgs 8:23).

9. The Reign of Ahaziah (22:1–9)

1The people of Jerusalem made Ahaziah, Jehoram's youngest son, king in his place, since the raiders, who came with the Arabs into the camp, had killed all the older sons. So Ahaziah son of Jehoram king of Judah began to reign.

2Ahaziah was twenty-two years old when he became king, and he reigned in Jerusalem one year. His mother's name was Athaliah, a granddaughter of Omri.

3He too walked in the ways of the house of Ahab, for his mother encouraged him in doing wrong. **4**He did evil in the eyes of the LORD, as the house of Ahab had done, for after his father's death they became his advisers, to his undoing. **5**He also followed their counsel when he went with Joram son of Ahab king of

---

[49] Ibid., 308.

[50] Williamson preserves the word "days" and suggests the sense is that his bowels came out two days before he died (ibid., 309).

Israel to war against Hazael king of Aram at Ramoth Gilead. The Arameans wounded Joram; [6]so he returned to Jezreel to recover from the wounds they had inflicted on him at Ramoth in his battle with Hazael king of Aram.

Then Ahaziah son of Jehoram king of Judah went down to Jezreel to see Joram son of Ahab because he had been wounded.

[7]Through Ahaziah's visit to Joram, God brought about Ahaziah's downfall. When Ahaziah arrived, he went out with Joram to meet Jehu son of Nimshi, whom the LORD had anointed to destroy the house of Ahab. [8]While Jehu was executing judgment on the house of Ahab, he found the princes of Judah and the sons of Ahaziah's relatives, who had been attending Ahaziah, and he killed them. [9]He then went in search of Ahaziah, and his men captured him while he was hiding in Samaria. He was brought to Jehu and put to death. They buried him, for they said, "He was a son of Jehoshaphat, who sought the LORD with all his heart." So there was no one in the house of Ahaziah powerful enough to retain the kingdom.

The Chronicler's account of the reign of Ahaziah (ca. 842 B.C.) is shorter than the account in 2 Kgs 8:24b–10:14, for since it is concerned mainly with the Southern Kingdom, the considerable detail given in Kings about the Jehu coup is omitted. In any case Ahaziah reigned only one year before he met his death at the hands of Jehu, the usurper king of Israel. During his short reign, Ahaziah's mother, Athaliah, had a powerful influence on him. He was the sole survivor of Jehoram and of the Davidic dynasty. Following his death Queen Athaliah, his mother, destroyed the whole royal family of the house of Judah except Joash (vv. 10–11).

22:1 It was "the people of Jerusalem" who made Ahaziah, Jehoram's youngest son, king in place of Jehoram. Who these were is not clear. This precise description is not used elsewhere (contrast 26:1; 33:25; 36:1). They may be the same as "the people of the land" who took part in royal succession during times of crisis (23:20–21; 26:1; 33:25; 36:1). They often are associated with the landed aristocracy or ruling class. It is even possible that the "inhabitants of Jerusalem" were a group in Jerusalem who acted without consultation with anyone in the outer districts.[51]

The raiders who came with the Arabs into the camp represented an invasion that may not have been great and probably included the Philistines (21:16–17). This raid was for the Chronicler further evidence of God's retributive justice. Jehoram, who killed all his brothers, lived to witness the death of his own sons (21:4,13,16–17).

22:2 The MT gives Ahaziah's age as forty-two, but the NIV has correctly followed 2 Kgs 8:26, the LXX, and the Syriac. The figure forty-two

---

[51] Dillard, *2 Chronicles,* 173.

would make Ahaziah older than his father (cf. 21:5,20). Athaliah, the mother of Ahaziah, is here called "granddaughter" of Omri, a possible translation of Hebrew *bat,* which usually means "daughter" (cf. 21:6).

22:3 By his comment that "he too walked in the ways of the house of Ahab," the Chronicler sees Ahaziah and Jehoram as an "evil pair."[52] With these two kings "the influence of northern kingship, which like the proverbial camel poked its nose into the Judean royal tent in Jehoshaphat's reign, now makes its presence so blatantly felt that the Davidic dynasty is almost obliterated."[53] The influence of Athaliah, the queen mother, is clear. She encouraged Ahaziah in wrongdoing and was his counselor as some other queen mothers had been (1 Kgs 1:11–31; 2:13–21; 15:13; 21:5–7; 2 Kgs 10:13; 24:12,15; Jer 13:18). The queen mother often held a position of considerable political power. Athaliah followed her mother, Jezebel, in this respect.

22:4–6 The house of Ahab of which Athaliah was the leading representative became advisers to Ahaziah. He followed their counsel and went with Joram of Israel to fight against Aram-Damascus. Perhaps he thought it was in Judah's interest to resist the power of Aram, and perhaps he could even justify his action by an appeal to the solidarity of the twelve tribes of Israel. In any case he should not have aligned himself with this apostate dynasty. Jezreel, to which Joram retreated and where Ahaziah visited him, lay at the foot of Mount Gilboa in the Plain of Jezreel.

22:7–9 The Chronicler did not give details of the story of Jehu's usurpation of the throne of Israel. He probably expected that his readers knew the details from 2 Kgs 9:1–28 and 10:12–14 (also Hos 1:4) and included only sufficient material to trace the fortunes of Ahaziah and his family, although a sentence is added at the beginning and end of the paragraph to tie the material into its context.

This account in Chronicles and the one in Kings contain differences. In 2 Kgs 10:12–14 the "princes of Judah" were murdered after Ahaziah, whereas the Chronicler recounts the killing of the princes first. The word "then" at the beginning of v. 9 is not in the Hebrew text (cf. NASB), so the Chronicler may have intentionally given the events out of order, perhaps to conclude his story with judgment on Ahaziah.[54] In 2 Kgs 9:27 Ahaziah is wounded near Ibleam as he fled to Megiddo, where he died. In Chronicles he is captured hiding in Samaria. He is then brought to Jehu at an unspecified location and put to death. In 2 Kgs 9:28 Ahaziah is taken to Jerusalem by his

---

[52] Allen, *1, 2 Chronicles,* 317.
[53] Ibid., 313.
[54] Dillard, *2 Chronicles,* 173.

servants and buried "with his fathers in the City of David," whereas in 2 Chr 22:9 the simple statement is made that "they buried him." The place of burial is not given. Apparently the Chronicler was content to note the main facts and leave the chronological and geographical details for the reader to sort out in Kings. He may have been more concerned to draw out the theological implications of the events. The fact that Ahaziah met his death in association with a visit to the northern king was reprehensible. For this misdeed he suffered the judgment of God.

It was in God's purpose to destroy the house of Ahab, and Jehu had been "anointed" (*māšaḥ*) to carry out God's intention. If Ahaziah placed himself at risk by foolishly visiting the king of Israel, it was almost inevitable that events would turn out as they did. The Chronicler was thus able to provide one more expression of his theology of immediate retribution.

The comment in v. 9 gives us the reflections of the Chronicler. Whatever his defects, Ahaziah was a descendant of Jehoshaphat. As a descendant of one who sought the Lord with all his heart, his corpse could hardly be left exposed. Respect for the godliness of Jehoshaphat extended even to his unworthy descendants.

With the death of Ahaziah the promise of God that David would never lack a descendant to rule over Israel (1 Chr 17:11–14; 2 Chr 21:7) seemed to be failing. The lamp God had given David (21:7) was now only a flickering wick. But God would not allow that, faint as it was, to be extinguished. He had Joash, only a child, waiting to be crowned (22:10–24:27).

10. The Interregnum of Athaliah (22:10–12)

¹⁰When Athaliah the mother of Ahaziah saw that her son was dead, she proceeded to destroy the whole royal family of the house of Judah. ¹¹But Jehosheba, the daughter of King Jehoram, took Joash son of Ahaziah and stole him away from among the royal princes who were about to be murdered and put him and his nurse in a bedroom. Because Jehosheba, the daughter of King Jehoram and wife of the priest Jehoiada, was Ahaziah's sister, she hid the child from Athaliah so she could not kill him. ¹²He remained hidden with them at the temple of God for six years while Athaliah ruled the land.

Neither the Chronicler nor the writer of Kings provides the usual regnal formulae giving the monarch's age, length of reign, and so forth in Athaliah's case (842–837 B.C.). She was not regarded as a legitimate ruler, so the usual introductory and concluding notices about her reign are omitted. She was, in fact, an illegitimate usurper of royal power. Only three verses are given to her six-year reign (22:10–12). The material is drawn from 2 Kgs 11:1–3. With chap. 23 we embark on the account of Joash's reign.

22:10 Athaliah's first act when she usurped power following the death of Ahaziah was to destroy the whole royal family, probably concentrating on potential male successors to Ahaziah. This was not an unknown response by usurpers either in Israel or elsewhere in the ancient Near East. The Hebrew verb for "destroy" (*tĕdabbēr*) is unusual and seems to be cognate with an Akkadian verb *dabaru*, "overwhelm." Some manuscripts and 2 Kgs 11:1 employ a well-known synonym (*tĕʾabbēr*) that some commentators favor.[55]

The narrative in Kings omits a reference to the house of Judah. The Chronicler evidently wished to stress the point. It was to the Davidic family that God had committed royal authority. Even if Athaliah destroyed the earthly manifestation of God's kingdom, it was not in her power to destroy the true kingdom of God that had been committed to the Davidic family (1 Chr 17:14).

22:11 Jehosheba (Heb. text has Jehoshabeath), the daughter of King Jehoram and wife of Jehoiada the priest, survived the slaughter of the royal family. This supports the view that it was the male members of the royal family that Athaliah destroyed. The heroine Jehosheba was able to spirit the infant Joash away from the royal princes who were about to be murdered. Dillard observes: "The fact that royal infants may regularly have been put into the care of wet nurses or foster mothers becomes the key to Jehosheba's frustrating Athaliah's plans; the suckling child was overlooked and could have escaped detection as he grew by mingling with other priests' children or perhaps as a temple devotee like the young Samuel"[56] (1 Sam 1:21–28; 3:1).

22:12 The infant Joash remained hidden with Jehoida the priest and Jehosheba for six years while Athaliah ruled the land. He remained safe in God's care until the time was right for him to be brought forth and publicly anointed as king. No details are given about Athaliah's reign. Such matters were irrelevant to the Chronicler's purpose.

11. The Reign of Joash (23:1–24:27)

Chronicles devotes two chapters to the reign of Joash (837–800 B.C.). The reign is divided into three main periods. Following the brief account of Athaliah's interregnum when the Davidic house was reduced to its lowest ebb ever, the story develops in three stages: (1) Jehoiada's coup and the presentation and enthronement of Joash (23:1–21), (2) temple repairs (24:1–16), and (3) the apostasy of Joash from the Lord (24:17–27).

The reign of Joash begins with the priestly and popular revolt against

---

[55] See BH3 at 2 Chr 22:10.
[56] Dillard, *2 Chronicles,* 179–80.

Athaliah and her atrocities. The Chronicler drew upon 2 Kings 11 for his story, but there are significant additions and omissions in harmony with his theological purposes. In particular he avoids the impression left by 2 Kgs 11:4–8 that only military officials were involved and that they were allowed into the temple. As R. D. Patterson and H. J. Austel have explained: "Both accounts are merely summary statements of the essential details, the account in Kings emphasizing the part played by the military in defense of the king and palace, and that in Chronicles, the role of the Levites in making the temple secure."[57]

The first part of the story of the reign of Joash is presented in three parts: the presentation of Joash (vv. 1–11), the reaction of Athaliah (vv. 12–15), and the reformation (vv. 16–21).

(1) Jehoida's Coup and the Enthronement of Joash (23:1–11)

[1]In the seventh year Jehoiada showed his strength. He made a covenant with the commanders of units of a hundred: Azariah son of Jeroham, Ishmael son of Jehohanan, Azariah son of Obed, Maaseiah son of Adaiah, and Elishaphat son of Zicri. [2]They went throughout Judah and gathered the Levites and the heads of Israelite families from all the towns. When they came to Jerusalem, [3]the whole assembly made a covenant with the king at the temple of God.

Jehoiada said to them, "The king's son shall reign, as the LORD promised concerning the descendants of David. [4]Now this is what you are to do: A third of you priests and Levites who are going on duty on the Sabbath are to keep watch at the doors, [5]a third of you at the royal palace and a third at the Foundation Gate, and all the other men are to be in the courtyards of the temple of the LORD. [6]No one is to enter the temple of the LORD except the priests and Levites on duty; they may enter because they are consecrated, but all the other men are to guard what the LORD has assigned to them. [7]The Levites are to station themselves around the king, each man with his weapons in his hand. Anyone who enters the temple must be put to death. Stay close to the king wherever he goes."

[8]The Levites and all the men of Judah did just as Jehoiada the priest ordered. Each one took his men—those who were going on duty on the Sabbath and those who were going off duty—for Jehoiada the priest had not released any of the divisions. [9]Then he gave the commanders of units of a hundred the spears and the large and small shields that had belonged to King David and that were in the temple of God. [10]He stationed all the men, each with his weapon in his hand, around the king—near the altar and the temple, from the south side to the north side of the temple.

---

[57] R. D. Patterson and H. J. Austel, "1, 2 Kings," EBC (Grand Rapids: Zondervan, 1988), 4:217.

¹¹**Jehoiada and his sons brought out the king's son and put the crown on him; they presented him with a copy of the covenant and proclaimed him king. They anointed him and shouted, "Long live the king!"**

23:1 In the seventh year of the interregnum of Athaliah, Jehoiada "showed his strength" ("took courage," NRSV)[58] and plotted the usurper's overthrow. The text reads literally, "He took the commanders of the hundreds . . . into a covenant [*babbĕrit*] with himself." For "into a covenant" the LXX follows the parallel text in 2 Kgs 11:4, which reads, "And he brought them to him [at] the temple [*bêt*]." In 23:3 both "covenant' and "temple" occur. Evidently it was in the temple that Jehoiada made this agreement (covenant) with the commanders. The text in 2 Kgs 11:4 has Jehoiada making an agreement with the commanders of "the Carites and the guards." Although the ones mentioned by the Chronicler could be a totally separate group (Williamson notes that with one exception the names also are found in priestly or Levitical lists[59]), it also is possible that the Chronicler gives the names of those referred to in Kings,[60] who were perhaps part of the royal bodyguard.[61]

23:2–3 This selected group was able to circulate in the towns of Judah without arousing any suspicion and to gather priests and Levites to Jerusalem, as well as the heads of the Israelite families. The presentation of Joash was thus an act of all the people, not just a piece of palace intrigue. The assembly of such a group need not have aroused Athaliah's suspicions because large gatherings at the temple were common for religious purposes. Plots were generally associated with smaller groups.

The Chronicler regarded Joash as the legitimate Davidic king. The priests, the Levites, and the people, representing "all Israel," were united in their resolve to restore a true king of David's line to the throne. The reference in v. 3 to the Davidic covenant does not appear in the story in 2 Kgs 11:5. It reveals the Chronicler's attitude to messianic and Davidic hopes during the postexilic period.[62]

23:4–5 The arrangement for carrying out the crowning of Joash and the removal of Athaliah centered on the change in the shifts of temple personnel

---

[58] The *hitpael* of פזח also is used in 16:9 of the Lord's strengthening "those whose hearts are fully committed to him." It also describes Amaziah's act of courage in 25:11. The form וַיִּתְחַזֵּק is used several times (e.g., 2 Chr 1:1) with the meaning "established himself."

[59] Williamson, *1 & 2 Chronicles*, 315.

[60] Dillard, *2 Chronicles*, 180. He also argues that there must have been non-Levitical military officers present and that it surely would have been unnecessary for Jehoiada to make a covenant with Levites connected with the temple.

[61] Patterson and Austel, "1, 2 Kings," 4:217.

[62] See H. G. M. Williamson, "Eschatology in Chronicles," *TB* 28 (1977): 148–49.

There would be the maximum number of armed personnel for the coup as well as a large number of persons moving about in the temple so as not to arouse any suspicion in the mind of Athaliah, who would see these changes taking place daily. However, neither the details here nor in 2 Kgs 11:5–8[63] are clear, no doubt due to our ignorance about their procedures.

23:6 There would be little point in overthrowing Athaliah if in so doing the people of God themselves ignored the law of Moses. Any who were not priests or Levites were forbidden to enter the temple of the Lord. They were not consecrated and had to remain in the courtyard guarding what the Lord had assigned to them.

23:7 The Levites were to stand around the king with their weapons in their hands and stay close to the king wherever he went. Patterson and Austel follow Edersheim in proposing that 2 Kgs 2:7–9 speaks of an additional military guard that surrounded the king inside the Levites, whose main concern was temple security.[64]

23:8 Whether the parallel group in 2 Kgs 11:9 (called "the commanders of units of a hundred") was an additional group or the same by another name, these men did just as Jehoiada, the high priest, had ordered. Those going off duty did not leave the temple area.

27:9 The weapons handed out to the "commanders of units of a hundred" consisted of spears and the large and small shields that belonged to King David, which probably were ceremonial in character (cf. 1 Chr 18:7).

23:10 Jehoiada placed all the armed men around the king near the altar and the temple, from the south side to the north side of the temple.

The Chronicler used the word ʿām twelve times in chap. 23, four more than the parallel text in Kings. He added it in vv. 5,6,10,20. It is translated as "men" in the NIV and "people" in the NRSV (vv. 5–6,10,12,16–17). Probably the best translation is "people." It need not indicate "armed force." More often than not it means simply "citizens." The Chronicler indicated by its frequent usage that it was not merely the priests and Levites who were involved in the coup but the whole nation.

---

[63] See Dillard, *2 Chronicles,* 182, for a useful discussion.
[64] Patterson and Austel, "1, 2 Kings," 4:218.

23:11 The hour had come, and all was in readiness for the great denouncement. Jehoiada and his sons brought out Ahaziah's legitimate successor. They presented him with a copy of the covenant (ʿēdût, "testimony"), proclaimed him king, anointed him, and shouted, "Long live the king!" The copy of the covenant may have been the arrangement agreed to in 23:3, although the word there is bĕrît. The word ʿēdût is used in Scripture of the tablets containing the Ten Commandments (Exod 25:16,21). Thus the ark where they were placed could be called "the ark of the testimony"; and the tabernacle, the "tabernacle of the testimony" (cf. Exod 16:34; 25:22; 26:34; 31:18; 32:15; 34:29; 2 Chr 24:6). It is also used of the law of God (Pss 19:8; 78:5; 119:14; 132:12; Isa 8:16,20). What Joash was given, then, may relate to the copy of the Torah to be given to the king according to Deut 17:18.

(2) The Reaction of Athaliah (23:12–15)

¹²When Athaliah heard the noise of the people running and cheering the king, she went to them at the temple of the LORD. ¹³She looked, and there was the king, standing by his pillar at the entrance. The officers and the trumpeters were beside the king, and all the people of the land were rejoicing and blowing trumpets, and singers with musical instruments were leading the praises. Then Athaliah tore her robes and shouted, "Treason! Treason!"

¹⁴Jehoiada the priest sent out the commanders of units of a hundred, who were in charge of the troops, and said to them: "Bring her out between the ranks and put to the sword anyone who follows her." For the priest had said, "Do not put her to death at the temple of the LORD." ¹⁵So they seized her as she reached the entrance of the Horse Gate on the palace grounds, and there they put her to death.

23:12–13 This scene is reminiscent of the anointing of Solomon, which sounded the final note on Adonijah's vain attempt to gain the throne (1 Kgs 1:39–40,45–46). Athaliah went to the temple to investigate. This was to her undoing (2 Chr 23:15). There she saw the legitimate boy-king standing by "his pillar," the customary place for a king to stand when making a public proclamation. The place was "at the entrance," that is, the entrance from the court of the city to the inner court. The captains and trumpeters were near the king, and the people of the land were rejoicing and blowing trumpets while the singers with all their instruments of song were leading the celebration. Athaliah could not help being taken aback and cried aloud, "Treason!" Such a cry from the mouth of Athaliah was full of irony. Athaliah's very presence there was an act of treason in itself because she had usurped the legitimate authority of the boy-king Joash.

23:14–15 Here is more irony. Jehoiada was anxious to protect the sanctity of the temple from any murder. However, his own son experienced that very sacrilege[65] (24:21). In the case of Athaliah the commanders of units of hundreds in charge of the army brought her out from the temple precincts and slew her at the entrance of the horse gate of the palace (different from the horse gate in the city wall; cf. Jer 31:40; Neh 3:28). In this case the omission of a summary statement for Athaliah indicates not only disfavor (see comment at 21:20) but also illegitimacy as ruler.

(3) The Reformation (23:16–21)

[16]Jehoiada then made a covenant that he and the people and the king would be the LORD'S people. [17]All the people went to the temple of Baal and tore it down. They smashed the altars and idols and killed Mattan the priest of Baal in front of the altars.

[18]Then Jehoiada placed the oversight of the temple of the LORD in the hands of the priests, who were Levites, to whom David had made assignments in the temple, to present the burnt offerings of the LORD as written in the Law of Moses, with rejoicing and singing, as David had ordered. [19]He also stationed doorkeepers at the gates of the LORD'S temple so that no one who was in any way unclean might enter.

[20]He took with him the commanders of hundreds, the nobles, the rulers of the people and all the people of the land and brought the king down from the temple of the LORD. They went into the palace through the Upper Gate and seated the king on the royal throne, [21]and all the people of the land rejoiced. And the city was quiet, because Athaliah had been slain with the sword.

23:16 Jehoiada, the high priest and initiator of the coup, proceeded at once to the national rededication to God by making a covenant. According to 2 Kgs 11:17, the covenant was made "between the LORD and the king and the people" and "between the king and the people." The Chronicler speaks of a covenant (literally) "between himself, all the people, and the king," which refers to the same thing, the priest perhaps serving as the Lord's representative.

23:17 An important aspect of the reform was the destruction of the Baal temple permitted by Athaliah. She was the granddaughter of the king of Tyre

---

[65] Dillard, *2 Chronicles,* 183.

and the daughter of Ahab, and surrendering Baal worship evidently had not been part of her marriage contract with Ahaziah (cf. 1 Kgs 11:1–8). One important feature of the suppression of Baalism in this case was the slaying of Mattan, the priest of Baal, in front of his altars (cf. Deut 13:5–10).

23:18–19 Except for the simple notice that Jehoiada appointed watchmen at the temple (2 Kgs 11:18), vv. 18–19 are not found in the parallel account. These verses note the importance of the priests and Levites, of following the instructions of Moses and David, and of protecting the sanctity of the temple. The oversight of the temple was in the hands of priests and the Levites,[66] each of whom had traditional tasks that David had organized (cf. 1 Chr 15–16; 23–27). The Chronicler regularly traces the general arrangements for the house of the Lord and for the singing back to David. The burnt offerings go back to what was written in the law of Moses (cf. 1 Chr 6:48–49; 16:39–40). The gatekeepers (see 1 Chr 26) were stationed at the gates of the Lord's temple to insure that no ritually unclean person entered (v. 19; cf. vv. 6,14).

23:20–21 Jehoiada finally organized a procession that brought the king down from the temple to the king's palace. All the people of the land rejoiced, a characteristic response found in Chronicles whenever the Lord's will was being followed. The personnel listed here are described a little differently from 2 Kgs 11:19, which mentions only the royal bodyguard. Also the "Upper Gate" replaces "the gate of the guards," perhaps a case of updating a name to one in use at the time of writing. The verb translated "be quiet" (*šāqaṭ*) is used several times by the Chronicler to denote the divine blessing God grants to those following his will (13:23; 14:1,4–5; 20:30; cf. 1 Chr 4:40; 22:9).

Athaliah's interregnum was now over. In a sense there never was an interruption of Davidic kingship because Joash was living throughout that sad period even if formally another, a usurper, was on the throne.

(4) The Later Years (24:1–27)

1Joash was seven years old when he became king, and he reigned in Jerusalem forty years. His mother's name was Zibiah; she was from Beersheba. **2**Joash did what was right in the eyes of the LORD all the years of Jehoiada the priest. **3**Jehoiada chose two wives for him, and he had sons and daughters.

4Some time later Joash decided to restore the temple of the LORD. **5**He called together the priests and Levites and said to them, "Go to the towns of Judah and collect the money due annually from all Israel, to repair the temple of your God. Do it now." But the Levites did not act at once.

---

[66] The MT reads "Levitical priests." We have inserted the conjunction "and" with some Heb. MSS, the LXX, Syr, and Vg. The problem arises also at 5:5; 30:27; Ezra 10:5.

⁶Therefore the king summoned Jehoiada the chief priest and said to him, "Why haven't you required the Levites to bring in from Judah and Jerusalem the tax imposed by Moses the servant of the LORD and by the assembly of Israel for the Tent of the Testimony?"

⁷Now the sons of that wicked woman Athaliah had broken into the temple of God and had used even its sacred objects for the Baals.

⁸At the king's command, a chest was made and placed outside, at the gate of the temple of the LORD. ⁹A proclamation was then issued in Judah and Jerusalem that they should bring to the LORD the tax that Moses the servant of God had required of Israel in the desert. ¹⁰All the officials and all the people brought their contributions gladly, dropping them into the chest until it was full. ¹¹Whenever the chest was brought in by the Levites to the king's officials and they saw that there was a large amount of money, the royal secretary and the officer of the chief priest would come and empty the chest and carry it back to its place. They did this regularly and collected a great amount of money. ¹²The king and Jehoiada gave it to the men who carried out the work required for the temple of the LORD. They hired masons and carpenters to restore the LORD'S temple, and also workers in iron and bronze to repair the temple.

¹³The men in charge of the work were diligent, and the repairs progressed under them. They rebuilt the temple of God according to its original design and reinforced it. ¹⁴When they had finished, they brought the rest of the money to the king and Jehoiada, and with it were made articles for the LORD'S temple: articles for the service and for the burnt offerings, and also dishes and other objects of gold and silver. As long as Jehoiada lived, burnt offerings were presented continually in the temple of the LORD.

¹⁵Now Jehoiada was old and full of years, and he died at the age of a hundred and thirty. ¹⁶He was buried with the kings in the City of David, because of the good he had done in Israel for God and his temple.

¹⁷After the death of Jehoiada, the officials of Judah came and paid homage to the king, and he listened to them. ¹⁸They abandoned the temple of the LORD, the God of their fathers, and worshiped Asherah poles and idols. Because of their guilt, God's anger came upon Judah and Jerusalem. ¹⁹Although the LORD sent prophets to the people to bring them back to him, and though they testified against them, they would not listen.

²⁰Then the Spirit of God came upon Zechariah son of Jehoiada the priest. He stood before the people and said, "This is what God says: 'Why do you disobey the LORD'S commands? You will not prosper. Because you have forsaken the LORD, he has forsaken you.'"

²¹But they plotted against him, and by order of the king they stoned him to death in the courtyard of the LORD'S temple. ²²King Joash did not remember the kindness Zechariah's father Jehoiada had shown him but killed his son, who said as he lay dying, "May the LORD see this and call you to account."

²³At the turn of the year, the army of Aram marched against Joash; it invaded Judah and Jerusalem and killed all the leaders of the people. They

sent all the plunder to their king in Damascus. ²⁴Although the Aramean army had come with only a few men, the LORD delivered into their hands a much larger army. Because Judah had forsaken the LORD, the God of their fathers, judgment was executed on Joash. ²⁵When the Arameans withdrew, they left Joash severely wounded. His officials conspired against him for murdering the son of Jehoiada the priest, and they killed him in his bed. So he died and was buried in the City of David, but not in the tombs of the kings.

²⁶Those who conspired against him were Zabad, son of Shimeath an Ammonite woman, and Jehozabad, son of Shimrith a Moabite woman. ²⁷The account of his sons, the many prophecies about him, and the record of the restoration of the temple of God are written in the annotations on the book of the kings. And Amaziah his son succeeded him as king.

The first period of Joash's reign was under the guidance of the high priest Jehoiada. The sinister influence of Athaliah had gone, and the wholesome influence of Jehoiada could mold the young king. The role of Jehoiada, the Chronicler's ideal high priest (cf. 24:15–16), was in no way a substitute for the king. He was certainly a king maker and faithful adviser to the young king but made no pretensions to be a usurper of royal power, as Athaliah had done. The Chronicler, however, had a vision of a balance between royal and religious leadership.

The early years of the young Joash were years in which he enjoyed God's blessing. It was to be different after Jehoiada's death. Those early years were occupied with the restoration of the temple (vv. 4–14).

THE RESTORATION OF THE TEMPLE AND JEHOIADA'S DEATH (24:1–16). A brief paragraph (vv. 1–3) introduces the account of the restoration of the temple, and a brief concluding paragraph records the death of Jehoiada.

24:1 This verse is parallel with 2 Kgs 12:1 but lacks, as usual, the characteristic synchronism with the Northern Kingdom.

24:2 The presence of Jehoiada alongside Joash certainly was a powerful restraining influence on the young king. It is not possible to say why Joash abandoned God after Jehoiada's death (24:17–22), and we should be careful about psychoanalysis from afar. We cannot tell whether Joash secretly hated Jehoiada or simply lacked the character to carry on without him. The parallel passage in 2 Kgs 12:2–3 also qualifies a positive evaluation of Joash by pointing out his failure to remove the high places. The Chronicler also refers to these negative aspects of the reign (vv. 18–19), but he prefers to group the good aspects together first of all and the bad aspects later.

Although 2 Kgs 12:2 (Heb. v. 3) can reasonably be interpreted as the equivalent of 2 Chr 24:2, the RSV, followed by Williamson,[67] translates the

---

[67] Williamson, *1 and 2 Chronicles*, 319.

Hebrew particle *ʾăšer* as "because" rather than its more usual "which." This, together with the fact that the NIV's "all the years" in 2 Kgs 12:2 (but not in 2 Chr 24:2) is literally "all his days," yields the RSV translation, "And Jehoash did what was right in the eyes of the LORD all his days, because Jehoiada the priest instructed him." This results in an apparent contradiction between the Chronicler's evaluation of Joash and that in Kings. This is not a necessary reading of the text and is successfully avoided by the NIV translation "all the years Jehoiada the priest instructed him."

24:3 Apparently the reason Jehoiada was involved in securing two wives for Joash and the reason the Chronicler mentioned it was the danger to the Davidic dynasty after the murders of the time of Jehoram (21:17), Ahaziah (22:9), and Athaliah (22:10).

24:4 In the course of time buildings require a certain amount of repair and restoration. Furthermore, the "sons of Athaliah" had broken in and may have done some damage (v. 7). The time reference in the words "some time later" is quite unspecified, but the decision probably came early in Joash's reign, well before his twenty-third year (2 Kgs 12:6).

24:5–6 Rather than taking the money for the restoration from the royal treasury, however, which Athaliah may have depleted, Joash determined that the priests and Levites should be involved in collecting it from the public. He found precedence for this in the tax Moses had levied for the care of the tabernacle (v. 6; 2 Kgs 12:4; Exod 30:11–16). The Kings passage specifies two additional sources of temple revenue for the project: "money received from personal vows" (cf. Lev 27:1–8; Num 18:15–16) and "money brought voluntarily to the temple." Joash's instructions to the priests and their helpers the Levites presumably would have been conveyed by Jehoiada. Whether he objected to the plan we do not know, but we do know that he did not see to its rapid accomplishment as Joash instructed.

It is often argued that vv. 5b–6 do not fit the context and were a later addition by a "pro-priestly reviser" intended "to draw the whole account closer to that in 2 Kg. 12" and "to soften the criticism of the priesthood expressed in the earlier version."[68] This may be a case, however, of reading too much into minor differences between Kings and Chronicles and also differences between vv. 5b–6 and their context. For example, while v. 5b appears to blame the Levites for the delay instead of "the priests and Levites" in v. 5a and "the priests" in 2 Kgs 12:4–7, v. 6 still appears to hold the chief priest Jehoiada responsible because he did not "require" the Levites to do their duty. Following a review and response to the main arguments, Dillard concludes, "Vv 5b–6 are not smooth and do present some difficulties, but the

---

[68] Ibid., 320–21.

difficulties may not be so great as to require positing a later author for the section."[69]

Joash grounded his rebuke on the Mosaic regulations for the maintenance of the "Tent of the Testimony." This latter expression occurs only here in Chronicles and four times in Numbers (9:15; 17:7,8; 18:2). The term translated "testimony," however, also occurs in 2 Chr 23:11, where the NIV translates it "covenant." The Chronicler uses several terms for the tabernacle, most of "the tabernacle of the LORD" (1 Chr 16:39; 21:29; 2 Chr 1:5) and "the Tent of Meeting" (1 Chr 6:32; 9:21; 23:32; 2 Chr 1:3,6,13; 5:5).

24:7 The reason given for shortage of funds for the temple repair was that the sons of Athaliah had broken into the temple and used even the sacred objects for Baal worship. Such a break-in is not mentioned elsewhere, but the Chronicler had other records (cf. 24:27). The meaning of "her sons" (*bāneyhā*) in this context raises some questions. Athaliah murdered the family of the house of Judah (22:10). Some commentators suggest that the term "son" is flexible in meaning and could refer to "adherents" (NEB). Yet others, by a very slight emendation, read "her builders" (*bōneyhā*), suggesting that the temple materials as well as its "dedicated things" had been used in building temples for the Baals.

24:8 Apparently when Joash discovered that his plan for temple fundraising had not been implemented, he abandoned it in favor of one more dependent on individual initiative. At the king's command a chest was constructed and placed outside, at the gate of the temple (cf. 2 Kgs 12:9, "beside the altar"). The use of such boxes or baskets was common in the ancient Near East.[70] This change may indicate merely that the Chronicler was accommodating the story to the practice of his own day when the laity were not allowed inside the court.[71] According to Patterson and Austel, however, the verse in Kings means that "the chest was set against the altar wall at the entrance that lay to the right side of the altar, or the southern entrance to the middle court."[72] Donations were brought not in coins at this date but in various forms of refined or unrefined metals.

24:9 The reference probably is to the half-shekel tax of Exod 30:11–16; 38:25–26. Here, as in other places, the Chronicler draws a parallel between the tabernacle and the first temple, furthering his tabernacle-temple typology.

24:10 In a striking parallel with the occasion when Israel brought gifts for the building of the first temple, the officials and all the people brought

---

[69] Dillard, *2 Chronicles,* 190.

[70] Ibid., 191.

[71] Ibid., 191.

[72] Patterson and Austel, "1, 2 Kings," EBC 4:222.

their contributions gladly (cf. 1 Chr 29:9). The spirit of joyous giving marked other occasions when some important cultic service was undertaken. The chest in which the gifts were deposited was soon filled.

24:11–12 The Levites were responsible for bringing the full chest to the king's officials. Here too the Chronicler brings the Levites to the fore. They were vitally involved in the restoration of the temple as they were in various other temple ministries. The king's officials are here defined as the royal secretary and the officer of the chief priest (cf. 2 Kgs 12:10). These two officials would be representative of the royal and the priestly authority and would demonstrate the broad basis of support for this reformation. The abundant giving of the people was a sign of God's favor on the undertaking. Joash and Jehoiada gave the "great amount of money" (v. 11) to the various craftsmen to restore the general fabric of the Lord's temple.

24:13 The "original design" came from God (1 Chr 28:11–19), and the reformers did not want to try to improve on it. The diligence of the workers further reveals the celebratory atmosphere of this revival.

24:14 The obedience of God's people brought a greater supply of funds than the leaders had anticipated. The gifts were so lavish that money was left after the building had been repaired. With these surplus moneys articles used in the temple rituals were made (cf. Exod 25; 31:1–10). The account in 2 Kgs 12:13–16, which seems at first to contradict this verse, probably means only that these articles were not made from the money contributed until the work of construction was complete. The workers' integrity was such that they could be relied on to use only what was needed for the job. As the Chronicler informs us, they finished their work considerably under budget. The reference to the regular burnt offerings is intended as an indication that there was full cultic faithfulness throughout Jehoiada's lifetime.

24:15–16 Details of the death and burial of Jehoiada were taken from a source not known to us. Certainly none is given. When Jehoiada died, he was "old and full of years." This expression implies great honor (cf. Gen 24:1; 25:8; 35:29; Job 42:17). It is one of several symbolic expressions here. The age 130 may be symbolic of God's blessing. Several of the Old Testament figures lived to a great age: Aaron to 123 (Num 33:39), Moses to 120 (Deut 34:7), and Joshua to 110 (Josh 24:29). Jehoiada both by virtue of his regency over the young king Joash and for his faithfulness to the Lord was given a royal burial among kings in the City of David. This contrasts with Joash himself, who was buried in the City of David, but not in the tomb of the kings (24:25).

APOSTASY AND DIVINE JUDGMENT (24:17–27). **24:17–18** There is a striking contrast between v. 2 and v. 17. Things changed dramatically for Joash both in his religious outlook and in his fortunes. The leaders of Judah came to the king to pay homage and to offer advice. In the context it seems that the advice they gave was not helpful and once again led to unhappy results for one of Judah's kings (10:8–11; 18:4–11; 22:3–4).

These leaders of Judah may have exercised considerable influence under Athaliah but apparently had been held in check by Jehoiada. With his controlling hand removed, they were again free to entice the king with flattery. The verb "abandon" ('āzab) is a characteristic one of the Chronicler (2 Chr 12:1; 15:2; 21:10; 24:20; 28:6; 29:6). In this case a prophet is sent to urge repentance leading to forgiveness. The cases of Rehoboam (12:1–12) and Jehoshaphat (chaps. 17–20), among others, are cases in point. The rejection of a prophetic warning led to judgment (cf. Asa, 16:7–15). It is evident that despite Jehoiada's restraining influence, the Asherah poles and idols continued to be served. A common story in Israel and elsewhere is that despite religious reforms directed from the top by a leader or leaders, popular forms of religion linger on and break out again when restraints are lifted.

24:19 The prophetic voice was heard often among God's people whether in Judah or in the north. It was still being heard before the fall of Jerusalem (36:15–16). Time and again the people did not listen. Many prophets evidently had confronted Joash (cf. v. 27), but the Chronicler deals only with one.

24:20 Zechariah, the son of Jehoiada, the priest, is not mentioned elsewhere in the Old Testament. As in other such cases the prophet delivers a sermon (for the expression "came upon" see comment at 1 Chr 12:18). Here it is very short. No doubt it is a summation of the original sermon. The theology of retribution here is very simple: those who abandon the Lord are themselves abandoned by him (cf. v. 18). The reverse also is true, that those who seek him prosper. The verb translated "prosper" (ṣālaḥ) is extremely common in Chronicles (cf. 1 Chr 22:11,13; 29:23; 2 Chr 14:7; 20:20; 26:5; 31:21; 32:30).

24:21 Zechariah, the son of the priest who had saved the throne for Joash, ironically was stoned to death by order[73] of the king in the very courtyard of the temple where "Jehoiada and his sons" (23:11) had anointed Joash and protected him from Athaliah. Another irony finds expression here. At the king's order the officials "plotted" against Zechariah. Another form of the same verb (qāšar) occurs in v. 25, where the officials "conspired" against him. Conspiracy followed by stoning had been used to dispose of Naboth in the days of Ahab (1 Kgs 21:8–14).

Matthew 23:35 and Luke 11:51 may refer to this incident. If that is the

---

[73] The word for "order" is מִצְוַה, the same as in v. 20, where it is used of the Lord's commandments. The king had substituted his own will and word for that of the Lord.

case, then Jesus was referring to all the martyrs from the beginning of the canon (Abel, in Genesis) to its end (Zechariah, son of Jehoiada, in Chronicles). This probably indicates that Chronicles stood last in the Hebrew canon in Jesus' time, as it does today. A difficulty is that Matthew's version mentions "Zechariah the son of Berachiah," that is, not the Zechariah of this text but the author of the Book of Zechariah. But as far as we know, the son of Berachiah was not martyred in the temple courtyard, and it seems apparent that Zechariah, son of Jehoiada, is intended.[74]

24:22 This was a dastardly act. Joash had "forgotten" the kindness shown to him by Jehoiada. In short, he had no sense of loyalty or gratitude. The verb used for "killed" (*hārag*) is used also of the execution of the idolatrous priest Mattan in 23:17 and of the death of Joash in v. 25. Wilcock points out that Zechariah's words, "May the LORD see this and call you to account," are not a spiteful call for vengeance but a commitment of the matter into the hands of God (cf. Acts 7:60).[75] The verb translated "call to account" here (*dāraš*) is the verb most frequently used in Chronicles for "seeking" the Lord (see comment at 14:4). Since Joash would not "seek" the Lord in faith, the Lord would "seek" him in judgment. The words of the dying prophet were soon to find fulfillment (2 Chr 24:27).

24:23 "At the turn of the year" means "in the spring," at the beginning of the dry season after the harvest had been gathered in, "the time when kings go off to war" (2 Sam 11:1; 1 Kgs 20:26; 1 Chr 20:1). The Lord had been using Hazael, king of Aram in Damascus, against King Jehoahaz of Israel, the wicked son of Jehu (2 Kgs 13:1–9). On one of these military campaigns Hazael invaded the coastal plain and threatened Jerusalem. Joash managed to avoid disaster by plundering the temple (2 Kgs 12:17–18), but Hazael killed "the leaders," apparently the very ones who had led Joash into apostasy ("leaders" is *śarê,* translated "officials" in v. 17; "officials" in v. 25 is from *ʿebed*).

24:24 When Israel was faithful to the Lord, they could win great victories with only a few men (Deut 7:17–21; 28:7; Judg 7; 1 Sam 14:6,15; 2 Chr 13:3–18; 14:8–15; 1 Kgs 20:26–28). But when they were unfaithful, they were powerless regardless of the odds (Deut 28:20,25; Josh 7:1–5) because the Lord was their strength, and success came only through him (cf. Exod 15:2,6,16; Num 23:22; 24:8; 1 Chr 16:11; 29:11; 2 Chr 20:6,12; 25:8; Pss 28:7–8; 46:1; 68:34–35; Isa 45:24; Jer 9:23–24; 17:5–8). This incident is reported in 2 Kgs 12:17–18, but there it lacks the theological

---

[74] For alternative interpretations of the Matthew account, see C. Blomberg, *Matthew,* NAC (Nashville: Broadman, 1992), 349.

[75] Wilcock, *Message of Chronicles,* 215.

evaluation offered here in Chronicles.

24:25 In the attack of the Aramean king (Hazael, 2 Kgs 12:17–18), Joash was severely wounded. This left him incapacitated and unable to stay ahead of palace intrigue, and his own officials conspired against him. The outrage of his murdering the son of Jehoiada, the priest, was too much for them. He was slain, not gloriously on the field of battle but ignominiously in his own bed.

24:26 Names of the conspirators differ slightly from the ones in 2 Kgs 12:21. Only in Chronicles are they identified as an Ammonite and a Moabite.

24:27 The account of Joash's reign ends with a reference to the writer's sources. This is very general, without details. The many prophecies (*maśśāʾ*, "burden, oracle") about Joash may refer back to v. 19. His source, "the annotations [*midraš*, elsewhere only in 13:13] on the book of kings," is lost.

12. The Reign of Amaziah (25:1–28)

The Chronicler's account of Amaziah's reign (ca. 800–783 B.C.) is based closely on the record in 2 Kgs 14:1–20, although 25:5–16 contains a more detailed account of Amaziah's defeat of the Edomites than that in 2 Kgs 14:7. Second Chronicles 25:5–16 evidently came from a source available to the Chronicler.

Like that of Joash, Amaziah's reign falls into two parts. The first of these is, on the whole, favorably regarded by the Chronicler (cp. vv. 3–13 and vv. 14–28). The second part of the reign displays some unacceptable features, such as the worship of Edomite idols and the rejection of a prophetic warning. The king became proud and suffered military defeat and personal tragedy. The story is presented from a literary point of view in three sections: (1) Amaziah's accession (25:1–4), (2) the Edomite campaign (25:5–16), and (3) war with Jehoash of Israel (25:17–28).

(1) Amaziah's Accession (25:1–4)

¹Amaziah was twenty-five years old when he became king, and he reigned in Jerusalem twenty-nine years. His mother's name was Jehoaddin; she was from Jerusalem. ²He did what was right in the eyes of the LORD, but not wholeheartedly. ³After the kingdom was firmly in his control, he executed the officials who had murdered his father the king. ⁴Yet he did not put their sons to death, but acted in accordance with what is written in the Law, in the Book of Moses, where the LORD commanded: "Fathers shall not be put to death for their children, nor children put to death for their fathers; each is to die for his own sins."

25:1 Again the Chronicler omits any synchronism with the Northern Kingdom though he had cause to mention Jehoash (Joash) of Israel (vv.

17,18,25). He confines himself to a simple statement about Amaziah's age at accession, the length of his reign, and his mother's name.

25:2   Whether the phrase "but not wholeheartedly"[76] applies to Amaziah's whole reign is unclear. His prideful response to his victory over Edom (v. 19) was followed by apostasy, which is anything but wholehearted obedience; and v. 27 suggests that his capture by King Joash of Israel may not have led to his repentance. Second Kings 14:3 has a parallel phrase qualifying Amaziah's obedience: "But not as his father David had done." It adds then the explanation that "in everything he followed the example of his father Joash," a discipleship that included the rejection of a divine prophet (v. 16).

25:3   Amaziah, following biblical law and ancient Near Eastern custom, executed the officials who had murdered his father. He may have been motivated to avenge the death of his father or by considerations of the elimination of potential rivals after he had consolidated his own power.

25:4   Nevertheless, in keeping with the law of Moses here (Deut 24:16), Amaziah did not follow ancient Near Eastern custom in killing the children of these men either in retribution or political expediency.

(2) The Edomite Campaign (25:5–16)

⁵Amaziah called the people of Judah together and assigned them according to their families to commanders of thousands and commanders of hundreds for all Judah and Benjamin. He then mustered those twenty years old or more and found that there were three hundred thousand men ready for military service, able to handle the spear and shield. ⁶He also hired a hundred thousand fighting men from Israel for a hundred talents of silver.

⁷But a man of God came to him and said, "O king, these troops from Israel must not march with you, for the LORD is not with Israel—not with any of the people of Ephraim. ⁸Even if you go and fight courageously in battle, God will overthrow you before the enemy, for God has the power to help or to overthrow."

⁹Amaziah asked the man of God, "But what about the hundred talents I paid for these Israelite troops?"

The man of God replied, "The LORD can give you much more than that."

¹⁰So Amaziah dismissed the troops who had come to him from Ephraim and sent them home. They were furious with Judah and left for home in a great rage.

¹¹Amaziah then marshaled his strength and led his army to the Valley of Salt, where he killed ten thousand men of Seir. ¹²The army of Judah also captured ten thousand men alive, took them to the top of a cliff and threw them

---

[76] The phrase לְבָב שָׁלֵם ("a whole heart") also is found in 1 Chr 12:39 [Eng. v. 38], where it is translated "fully determined." It is parallel there to לֵב אֶחָד ("one mind"). See also 1 Chr 29:19; 2 Chr 19:9.

down so that all were dashed to pieces.

13Meanwhile the troops that Amaziah had sent back and had not allowed to take part in the war raided Judean towns from Samaria to Beth Horon. They killed three thousand people and carried off great quantities of plunder.

14When Amaziah returned from slaughtering the Edomites, he brought back the gods of the people of Seir. He set them up as his own gods, bowed down to them and burned sacrifices to them. 15The anger of the LORD burned against Amaziah, and he sent a prophet to him, who said, "Why do you consult this people's gods, which could not save their own people from your hand?"

16While he was still speaking, the king said to him, "Have we appointed you an adviser to the king? Stop! Why be struck down?"

So the prophet stopped but said, "I know that God has determined to destroy you, because you have done this and have not listened to my counsel."

Only one verse is given to this episode in 2 Kgs 14:7. The Chronicler has expanded this notice considerably from one of his other sources no doubt partly because of the religious interests involved. In fact, we are not informed of the Edomite campaign until v. 11. Amaziah's military strength is first listed (vv. 5–6). This force contained mercenaries from Israel that were dismissed at the word of a man of God, but this dismissal had evil consequences (v. 13). The Chronicler explains that the victory over Edom involved Amaziah in apostasy, which would bear much trouble for Amaziah in the future.

25:5–6 Amaziah's military enrollment is similar to that of David (1 Chr 21; 27:23–24), Solomon (2:17–18), Asa (14:8), and Jehoshaphat (17:14–19). The army was raised from Judah and Benjamin by mustering those twenty years old and upwards. Again the size of Judah's army is uncertain and depends on the interpretation of the word *ʾallûpîm*, translated "thousand" (see discussion at 1 Chr 5:18; 7:1–5).

25:7–8 A man of God, an unnamed prophet (cf. 1 Sam 2:27; 1 Kgs 13:1; 17:24),[77] explained why troops from Israel should not go to fight Edom. First, the Lord was not with Israel, that is, with the Northern Kingdom, as the term "Ephraim" indicates. Similar statements of divine abandonment are found in Num 14:42–43; Deut 1:42 accompanied by an assurance of military failure. Such statements form a striking contrast to numerous assurances of divine presence and resulting success (cf. Gen 21:22; 26:24; 31:3; 48:21; Exod 3:12; 33:14; Deut 20:4; 31:6). That God was not with Israel, however, apparently meant more than his unavailability. If God was not *with* Israel, he was *against* them and against anyone associated with

---

[77] The term "man of God" is used in Chronicles, for Moses (1 Chr 23:14; 2 Chr 30:16), David (2 Chr 8:14), Shemaiah (2 Chr 11:2), and the prophet here. The term is found fifty-five times, however, in Kings. It is used only fourteen times elsewhere in the OT.

them. Such association would mean sure failure for Judah regardless of how courageously they fought. By implication a second reason for not employing troops from Israel is that they were not necessary, for power is in God and not in numbers (see comment on 24:24).

25:9   Naturally Amaziah was concerned about his contract with the mercenaries. There was no question of Amaziah's failing to honor any obligation to the mercenaries. He already had paid a hundred talents, and presumably the mercenaries were ready to fulfill their part of the agreement. The man of God assured Amaziah that he would not sustain any loss, for the Lord could give much more than the hundred talents he had paid out. The mercenaries, however, had to go.

25:10   The mercenaries from Ephraim were dismissed and sent home. They departed in a great rage, perhaps because the dismissal was a slight on their reliability, but also they would be deprived of any share in the spoils of battle.

25:11–12   This account of these events is parallel to 2 Kgs 14:7, which reports Amaziah's victory over Edom in the Valley of Salt. The defeat of the Edomites was particularly brutal: ten thousand killed and ten thousand captured and cast from the top of a cliff called Sela. According to 2 Kgs 14:7, Amaziah named the rock "Joktheel," which may mean "God destroyed." The identity of the place is uncertain despite many attempts to identify it. The identification with Petra is old but not generally accepted. Biblical and postbiblical evidence favors an identification with es-Sela, two and a half miles northwest of Bozra (Buseirah).[78]

25:13   The dismissed troops from the north carried out some destructive retaliation by raiding Judean towns from Samaria to Beth Horon. This verse has raised some questions of geography. Samaria is well inside the Northern Kingdom and hardly could be thought of as embracing Judean towns. Perhaps "Samaria" is a substitute for a Judean town, Migron, a town in Judah near Gibeah (1 Sam 14:2; Isa 10:28). Another possibility is that these mercenaries from the north had not left Samaria when Amaziah's army left for the battle to the south, but once they had left, the mercenaries had a plundering and killing spree as they moved from their home base in Samaria down south as far as Beth Horon, raiding Amaziah's undefended northern frontier.

25:14–15   The carrying off of a vanquished people's deities is well attested in the literature of the ancient Near East,[79] but it is not spoken of elsewhere in reference to a king of Judah (cf. v. 20; cf. 1 Chr 14:12). The

---

[78] A. F. Rainey, "Sela (Edom)," *IDBSup*, 800.

[79] See D. I. Block, *The Gods of the Nations* (Jackson, Miss.: The Evangelical Theological Society, 1988), 88–92, 129–48.

removal of such images often symbolized that the defeated people had been abandoned by their gods, who had thrown their support to the victors. This apparently was the theory behind Amaziah's actions and the reason for the Lord's anger. It would mean not only that Amaziah's victory was due in part to the help of Edom's gods[80] but that those gods were able now to help him further. Then the Lord sent a prophet to rebuke Amaziah not only for his violation of Israel's covenant to worship only the Lord (Deut 5:6–10; 6:4–5) but also for his stupidity. His victory over Edom was not a result of their gods' transfer of support but of their impotence before the God of Israel. The word for "consult" (*dāraš*) is the one found so often in Chronicles for Israel's prescription to "seek" the Lord (cf. 2 Chr 14:4).

25:16 Amaziah was in no mood to listen to the prophet and doubtless would have followed through with his threat and had him killed as his father had done if he persisted (24:20–21). The king's rejection of the prophetic warning was tantamount to a rejection of God's counsel and fraught with danger. There is a play on a Hebrew root here and in v. 17. From the same root (*yᶜṣ*) are derived the words "adviser," "has determined," "counsel," and "consulted his advisers." Also the verb "destroy" (*šaḥat*) is used elsewhere by the Chronicler to describe punishment for worshiping foreign gods (12:7).

(3) War with Jehoash of Israel (25:17–28)

[17]After Amaziah king of Judah consulted his advisers, he sent this challenge to Jehoash son of Jehoahaz, the son of Jehu, king of Israel: "Come, meet me face to face."

[18]But Jehoash king of Israel replied to Amaziah king of Judah: "A thistle in Lebanon sent a message to a cedar in Lebanon, 'Give your daughter to my son in marriage.' Then a wild beast in Lebanon came along and trampled the thistle underfoot. [19]You say to yourself that you have defeated Edom, and now you are arrogant and proud. But stay at home! Why ask for trouble and cause your own downfall and that of Judah also?"

[20]Amaziah, however, would not listen, for God so worked that he might hand them over to [Jehoash], because they sought the gods of Edom. [21]So Jehoash king of Israel attacked. He and Amaziah king of Judah faced each other at Beth Shemesh in Judah. [22]Judah was routed by Israel, and every man fled to his home. [23]Jehoash king of Israel captured Amaziah king of Judah, the son of Joash, the son of Ahaziah, at Beth Shemesh. Then Jehoash brought him to Jerusalem and broke down the wall of Jerusalem from the Ephraim Gate to the Corner Gate—a section about six hundred feet long. [24]He took all the gold and silver and all the articles found in the temple of God that had been in the care of Obed-Edom, together with the palace treasures and the hostages, and

---

[80] Ibid., 33–35.

returned to Samaria.
²⁵**Amaziah son of Joash king of Judah lived for fifteen years after the death of Jehoash son of Jehoahaz king of Israel.** ²⁶**As for the other events of Amaziah's reign, from beginning to end, are they not written in the book of the kings of Judah and Israel?** ²⁷**From the time that Amaziah turned away from following the LORD, they conspired against him in Jerusalem and he fled to Lachish, but they sent men after him to Lachish and killed him there.** ²⁸**He was brought back by horse and was buried with his fathers in the City of Judah.**

Encouraged by his success in his encounter with Edom, Amaziah tried his strength against Jehoash, king of Israel. The account in Chronicles is drawn from 2 Kgs 14:8–14,17–20. This time Amaziah was not successful but was captured and suffered the loss of temple treasures. He later was released but was greatly humiliated.

25:17 The challenge Amaziah issued to Jehoash,[81] "Come, meet me face to face," sometimes means simply "meet one another." It can, however, carry the sense of meeting in battle as it does here and in v. 21.

25:18–19 Jehoash's fable about the arrogant thistle is similar to Jotham's allegory about the thornbush in Judg 9:7–15. The Chronicler viewed pride as a grievous sin and can be heard speaking through Jehoash. To have supposed that a victory over Edom was a warrant for attacking Jehoash and a guarantee of another victory was arrogant and foolish. Amaziah would be wiser to remain at home. His action would bring about his own downfall and that of his nation Judah as well (cf. 26:16).

25:20 Behind the human affairs of this world is the overruling hand of God. Indeed, God guided even Amaziah's own pride in such a way that it brought about his downfall. In judgment for his apostasy God made Amaziah blind to the truth and deaf to wisdom (cf. 1 Kgs 12:15).

25:21 Realizing that war was inevitable, Jehoash went on the offensive. Beth Shemesh was inside Judah instead of along their contiguous borders. Jehoash may have had broader goals of territorial expansion.

25:22–24 The Ephraim Gate (the modern Damascus Gate) was in the northern wall of the city facing Ephraim, and the Corner Gate probably was in the western wall (26:9; Jer 31:38; Zech 14:10). The six hundred feet of wall was not completely repaired until Uzziah's day (26:9). Obed-Edom originally was a Levitical singer (1 Chr 15:18), and later he and his family became gatekeepers with particular responsibility for the store houses (1 Chr 26:15). Some recent commentators believe they had a quasi-military role of guarding the gates.

---

[81] The name of the king of Israel in the Hebrew text is "Joash" here and in vv. 18,21,23,25. "Joash" is a variant of "Jehoash."

The word for "hostages" (*ta⁽ărûbôt*) is found elsewhere only
lel passage in 2 Kgs 14:14. The hostages' purpose probably wa.
that Judah would cause no more trouble for Israel. E. R. Thiele h.
that it was at this time that the people made Uzziah ruler during his   ₃
absence (26:1).[82]

25:25–28   No reference is made to the length of time Amaziah was held
in captivity, although the notice that he outlived Jehoash by fifteen years
often is taken as a clue that he was released when Jehoash died.[83] The conspiracy against Amaziah evidently was of some years' duration going back
to the time when he had given a measure of allegiance to the gods of Edom
(vv. 14,20). Presumably the conspirators had no opportunity to carry out
their purpose while Amaziah was hostage to Jehoash, but the conspiracy
lasted beyond the time of the death of Jehoash of Israel. Amaziah heard of
the conspiracy and sought refuge in Lachish (cf. 11:9), but apparently its citizens were no help. A widely attested emendation for the MT "Judah" in v.
28 is "David." However, the description "the city of Judah" occurs in some
extrabiblical sources such as the Chronicles of the Neo-Babylonian Kings
(626–556 B.C.).[84]

Overall the record of Amaziah's reign is negative, with the exception of
the victory over Edom. "Instead of royal building programs, the walls of
Jerusalem are destroyed; instead of wealth from the people and surrounding
nations, the king is plundered; instead of a large family, there were hostages;
instead of peace, war; instead of victory, defeat; instead of loyalty from the
populace and long life, there is a conspiracy and regicide."[85] An overwhelming message comes through: God asks for the exclusive loyalty of king and
people to their covenant Lord.

13. The Reign of Uzziah (26:1–23)

Uzziah had a long reign of fifty-two years (ca. 783–742 B.C.). The record
in Kings is brief (2 Kgs 14:21–22; 15:1–7). He was elevated to the throne of
Judah when he was only sixteen (vv. 1,3) in the place of his father Amaziah.
Two significant events in his life, one positive and one negative, mark the
narrative. He subdued Elath (2 Kgs 14:22), and "the LORD afflicted the king
with leprosy until the day he died" (2 Kgs 15:5). The length of Uzziah's reign

---

[82] E. R. Thiele, *The Mysterious Numbers of the Hebrew Kings* (Grand Rapids: Zondervan,
1983), 113–23.

[83] Ibid., 115.

[84] D. J. Wiseman, *Chronicles of the Chaldaean Kings, 626–556 B.C.* (London: British
Museum, 1956), 73.

[85] Dillard, *2 Chronicles*, 203.

and the restoration of Elath would have suggested that he enjoyed God's blessing. But on the other hand, his contraction of leprosy (v. 19) would suggest that he was being punished for some sin that is not recorded. The Chronicler portrays an early period of success in war, of building and organizing a well-trained army (26:1–15). But pride led to his downfall. He entered the temple to burn incense, for which he was rebuked by Azariah, the chief priest, and other courageous priests. For this act Uzziah contracted leprosy, which eventually took his life (26:16–23). As L. C. Allen has explained, the "royal trilogy" of Joash, Amaziah, and Uzziah, all of whom served the Lord faithfully only during the first part of their reigns, dramatically presents a message to believers to "hold firmly til the end the confidence we had at first" (Heb 3:14).[86]

The bulk of the Chronicler's account is unique (26:5–20). But additional records evidently were available. That is not surprising since Uzziah's reign covered fifty-two years.[87] There are four sections: (1) introduction (26:1–5), (2) campaigns (26:6–8), (3) internal developments (26:9–15), and (4) pride and downfall of Uzziah (26:16–23).

(1) Introduction (26:1–5)

[1]Then all the people of Judah took Uzziah, who was sixteen years old, and made him king in place of his father Amaziah. [2]He was the one who rebuilt Elath and restored it to Judah after Amaziah rested with his fathers.

[3]Uzziah was sixteen years old when he became king, and he reigned in Jerusalem fifty-two years. His mother's name was Jecoliah; she was from Jerusalem. [4]He did what was right in the eyes of the LORD, just as his father Amaziah had done. [5]He sought God during the days of Zechariah, who instructed him in the fear of God. As long as he sought the LORD, God gave him success.

26:1–2 As in vv. 1,3, the Chronicler's source in Kings has two references to Uzziah becoming king at age sixteen, but there the references (2 Kgs 14:21; 15:2) are separated by a section on Jeroboam II of Israel. The first reference, then, serves to conclude the account of Amaziah and the second to introduce the brief account of Uzziah. The repetition in Chronicles would not seem so awkward if the chapter division paralleled that of Kings. The unusual notice that Uzziah was made king by the people is considered by many to suggest that Amaziah was still alive at the time, exiled in Samaria. This is supported by the mention in v. 2 that it was after Amaziah died that Uzziah

[86] Allen, *1, 2 Chronicles*, 345.
[87] Williamson, *1 and 2 Chronicles*, 333.

restored Elath. His name, "Uzziah," is an abbreviated form of "Azariah," which appears in 2 Kings. In Chronicles the name is consistently "Uzziah" (except in 1 Chr 3:12). The two names were used interchangeably since the two verbal roots ʿzr and ʿzz that underlie the names had similar meanings. The name "Azariah" meant "the Lord helps," and "Uzziah" meant "the Lord is strong." Perhaps the Chronicler preferred Uzziah to avoid confusion with the high priest Azariah in vv. 17–20. He also is known as Uzziah in 2 Chronicles 26; Isa 6:1; Hos 1:1; Amos 1:1; Zech 14:5; 2 Kings 15.

The rule of Uzziah was for the most part contemporaneous with Jeroboam II, both of whom ruled for approximately forty years. Amaziah, his father, had campaigned in the area of Edom but had not subdued Elath (see 25:11–12). Elath was the port at the head of the Red Sea that gave access to the maritime commerce to the East. Once subdued by Solomon (8:17–18), it had revolted under Jehoram (21:8–10). Uzziah was able to bring it once again under the control of Judah, although it was lost again under Ahaz (28:17). No mention is made of the extent of rebuilding that was needed.

26:3–4 That the Chronicler would describe Uzziah as a king "who did what was right in the eyes of the LORD just as his father Amaziah had done" is somewhat surprising. The words are quoted from 2 Kgs 15:3 without the qualifying remark of 2 Kgs 15:4 regarding the high places. Again the Chronicler reserves most or all negative judgments until later (cf. 24:1–2; 25:1–2).

26:5 Uzziah had a wise adviser, Zechariah, who instructed him in the fear of God. Nothing more is known of this Zechariah. We are reminded of the faithful witness of Jehoiada to the young Joash (24:2). The key ideas of seeking the Lord and the Lord granting him success are highlighted again in this verse (see comments at 14:4; 24:20). Obedience to God was, in his view, associated with divine blessing; but disobedience, with judgment.

(2) Uzziah's Military Campaigns (26:6–8)

⁶He went to war against the Philistines and broke down the walls of Gath, Jabneh and Ashdod. He then rebuilt towns near Ashdod and elsewhere among the Philistines. ⁷God helped him against the Philistines and against the Arabs who lived in Gur Baal and against the Meunites. ⁸The Ammonites brought tribute to Uzziah, and his fame spread as far as the border of Egypt, because he had become very powerful.

Significant conquests of Uzziah directed against Philistines and Arabs on his southwestern borders are now taken up. His conquests in these areas were strengthened by the construction of fortresses in the conquered territory. The whole paragraph was intended to demonstrate how Uzziah prospered in foreign affairs. Military activity to the north was not possible because

Jeroboam II was too strong for Uzziah.

26:6 Philistine areas remained a threat to Judah over the centuries. The towns mentioned here all relate to the south and southwestern borders of Judah and make good geopolitical sense in the context. Gath was an ancient enemy of Judah. To strengthen his control of these Philistine cities, Uzziah rebuilt towns near Ashdod and elsewhere among the Philistines. There is archaeological evidence for building in the area. Tell Mor near Ashdod is thought by some scholars to have been the work of Uzziah. Jabneh is mentioned only here in the Old Testament, although it probably is to be equated with Jabneel (Josh 15:11). It became the Jewish center Jamnia after the fall of Jerusalem in A.D. 70. Control of Jabneh had an important strategic consequence, for it gave control of the area through which Jehoash of Israel had attacked Uzziah's father, Amaziah (25:21).

26:7 Further evidence of the blessing of God on Uzziah is success against Arab groups that dwelt in Gur and against the Meunites (see 1 Chr 4:41; 2 Chr 20:1). Gur has been identified with Gari of the Amarna letters, situated to the east of Beersheba. The Meunites may have been a group in the region of Kadesh Barnea, an important trading center.[88]

26:8 The LXX text suggests that we should read "Meunites" here. This would add to the comment "his fame spread as far as the border of Egypt" (cf. 1 Chr 14:17). By that time Uzziah had become very powerful. Contrast this statement with v. 16, where the remark is made that after Uzziah became powerful, his pride led to his downfall. These two statements mark off vv. 9–15, which deal with the internal developments in Uzziah's day.

In his account of the first part of Uzziah's reign, the Chronicler seems to have been comparing Uzziah favorably with his paradigmatic kings, David and Solomon. As Solomon too had subdued Elath, so David subdued the Philistines and achieved great fame (1 Chr 14:8–17).

(3) Internal Developments (26:9–15)

⁹Uzziah built towers in Jerusalem at the Corner Gate, at the Valley Gate and at the angle of the wall, and he fortified them. ¹⁰He also built towers in the desert and dug many cisterns, because he had much livestock in the foothills and in the plain. He had people working his fields and vineyards in the hills and in the fertile lands, for he loved the soil.

¹¹Uzziah had a well-trained army, ready to go out by divisions according to their numbers as mustered by Jeiel the secretary and Maaseiah the officer under the direction of Hananiah, one of the royal officials. ¹²The total number of family leaders over the fighting men was 2,600. ¹³Under their command was

---

[88] Williamson, *1 and 2 Chronicles*, 335.

an army of 307,500 men trained for war, a powerful force to support the king against his enemies. [14]Uzziah provided shields, spears, helmets, coats of armor, bows and slingstones for the entire army. [15]In Jerusalem he made machines designed by skillful men for use on the towers and on the corner defenses to shoot arrows and hurl large stones. His fame spread far and wide, for he was greatly helped until he became powerful.

This second paragraph deals further with Uzziah's prosperous period when he enjoyed God's blessing. It concentrates on internal affairs, which no doubt were being attended to at the same time as external affairs. We lack that kind of chronological specification.

26:9 Building projects were signs of prosperity and thus of divine favor. The raid by Jehoash of Israel doubtless destroyed more than the wall (24:23–24), and there also had been an earthquake during Amaziah's reign (Amos 1:1; Zech 14:5). Uzziah may have built new buildings as well. The Corner Gate (25:23) was still spoken of in the days of Zechariah the prophet (Zech 14:10). The Valley Gate may have been in the south (Neh 3:13) and is spoken of in Neh 2:13. The "angle" mentioned in Neh 3:19–20,24–25 can no longer be precisely identified.

26:10 There is widespread archaeological support for building activity in Uzziah's day.[89] A seal with Uzziah's name was found in a cistern at Tell Beit Mirsim. The towers referred to here may have been defensive but possibly were watchtowers for the royal shepherds and farmers (1 Chr 27:25–31). Many cisterns have been discovered that were in use in Uzziah's time, judging from the debris found in them. A cistern was dug into the limestone and sealed with lime plaster to provide a continuing supply of water (Jer 2:13; 38:6) caught during rainstorms. There evidently was a sizeable group of workers tending Uzziah's fields and pastures. The "fertile lands" (*karmel*) may be a place, Carmel (not to be confused with Mount Carmel in the north) south of Hebron (cf. 1 Sam 25). This verse gives an excellent summary of the agricultural zones and the agricultural activities in Judah, whose royal property (1 Sam 8:12–14; 22:7; 1 Kgs 21; 2 Kgs 8:3–6; 1 Chr 27:25–31) supported the king and provided rewards for faithful service.[90]

26:11 Another mark of Uzziah's prosperity was a well-trained and well-equipped army (cf. 17:14–19; 25:5; 26:11–15 for other accounts of Judah's army). Uzziah's army participated in the victories referred to in vv. 6–8, but he may have ventured further afield. A text from early in the reign of Tiglath-

---

[89]See Williamson, *1 and 2 Chronicles*, 336–37; Myers, *II Chronicles*, 152–53, for bibliography.

[90]See J. Graham, "Vinedressers and Plowmen," *BA* 47 (1984): 55–58; A. Rainey, "Wine from the Royal Vineyards," *BASOR* 245 (1982): 57–62.

Pileser III of Assyria (745–727 B.C.) mentions his campaign against a coalition to his west that included a certain Azriyau of Yaudi (ca. 742 B.C.) who has been identified with Uzziah.[91] The military officials are named individually, confirming the Chronicler's access to ancient documents.

26:12–13 The usual question arises here about how such numbers should be interpreted. Payne renders it "300 alluphs" or "special warriors" and "7,5000 men trained for war"[92] (see comments on 5:18; 7:1–5). Taking the NIV as it stands, the ratio of officers to men was one officer to 118 men.

26:14 Uzziah the king provided the weapons. No longer did the soldiers provide their own arms as in the days of the conscript armies (Judg 20:8–17; 1 Chr 12:2,8,24,33; 1 Sam 13:19–22), which reflects on Uzziah's prosperity under divine blessing.

26:15 The machines installed on the towers have provoked much discussion. Devices such as catapults seemingly did not appear in the ancient Near East before about 400 B.C. The matter is not finally settled, but probably the best explanation available at present is that these devices were defensive constructions on the towers and corners to protect the troops as they shot arrows or hurled stones, as portrayed in Assyrian reliefs of Lachish from the period just after Uzziah.[93]

The conclusion of v. 15 repeats the conclusion of v. 8 with certain changes. Synonyms are used for "spread," the extent of Uzziah's fame is greater but more general in v. 15, the divine source of his power is suggested by a passive in v. 15, and what was still growing power in v. 8 (lit., "he became powerful to above [i.e., increasingly]") seems to have reached its height in v. 15. The verb "helped" is from the same root (ʿzr) as his alternate name, Azariah (see comments at 26:2), and the verb "became powerful" (ḥāzaq) in vv. 8,15 is a synonym of the verb in the name "Uzziah." As v. 16 explains, at the height of his power Uzziah was struck down by his own pride. If he had only remembered the message of his names, that he was powerful because of the Lord's help, he would not have fallen.

(4) Pride and Downfall of Uzziah (26:16–23)

16But after Uzziah became powerful, his pride led to his downfall. He was unfaithful to the LORD his God, and entered the temple of the LORD to burn incense on the altar of incense. 17Azariah the priest with eighty other courageous priests of the LORD followed him in. 18They confronted him and said, "It

---

[91] See Dillard, *2 Chronicles*, 209.

[92] Payne, "1, 2 Chronicles," 4:522.

[93] Y. Yadin, *The Art of Warfare in Biblical Lands* (London: Weidenfeld & Nicolson, 1963), 325–28.

is not right for you, Uzziah, to burn incense to the LORD. That is for the priests, the descendants of Aaron, who have been consecrated to burn incense. Leave the sanctuary, for you have been unfaithful; and you will not be honored by the LORD God."

[19]Uzziah, who had a censer in his hand ready to burn incense, became angry. While he was raging at the priests in their presence before the incense altar in the LORD'S temple, leprosy broke out on his forehead. [20]When Azariah the chief priest and all the other priests looked at him, they saw that he had leprosy on his forehead, so they hurried him out. Indeed, he himself was eager to leave, because the LORD had afflicted him.

[21]King Uzziah had leprosy until the day he died. He lived in a separate house —leprous, and excluded from the temple of the LORD. Jotham his son had charge of the palace and governed the people of the land.

[22]The other events of Uzziah's reign, from beginning to end, are recorded by the prophet Isaiah son of Amoz. [23]Uzziah rested with his fathers and was buried near them in a field for burial that belonged to the kings, for people said, "He had leprosy." And Jotham his son succeeded him as king.

After Uzziah became powerful, there was a change. The account of Uzziah's pride and downfall is found only in Chronicles. The Kings' record is brief: "The LORD afflicted the king with leprosy until the day he died, and he lived in a separate house."

Verses 16–21 use vocabulary characteristic of the Chronicler. Judgment fell on Uzziah only after the rejection of a warning from God (vv. 18–19). This brief passage is marked by a clear demarcation between royal and priestly functions.[94]

26:16 The word translated "became powerful" provides the link to the previous section. It also gives an insight regarding the character of Uzziah and of all strong leaders. He had always been a strong leader, and this had enabled him to do great works. He had not been one of the weak kings of Judah who was easily swayed by others (like Jehoshaphat) or too open and accommodating with the leaders in the north. But as is often the case with strong leaders, this virtue gave way to a headstrong, I-can-do-no-wrong attitude. It was precisely his strength that blinded him to the effrontery of his action.[95] Uzziah's pride was expressed in usurping the role of the priest. The verb translated "was unfaithful" (*ma'al*) is used frequently in Chronicles (1 Chr 2:7; 5:25; 28:19–25; 29:6; 36:14) for various serious violations of covenant loyalty and responsibilities. Only the priests were to burn incense (Exod 30:1–10; Num 16:40; 18:1–7).

26:17–18 Just as when Saul (1 Sam 13:9) and Jeroboam (1 Kgs 12:33)

---

[94]Williamson, *1 and 2 Chronicles,* 338.
[95]See Wilcock, *Message of Chronicles,* 229–32.

usurped the priestly role, Uzziah was confronted by a priest. Azariah the priest is not mentioned elsewhere. The opposite of honor (*kābôd,* often rendered "glory") is disgrace, which often is the result of trying to honor oneself (cf. 1 Chr 29:12,28; 2 Chr 1:11–12; 2 Chr 17:5).

26:19 Like King Asa (16:7–10), Uzziah was angered by the rebuke. But before he could act against Azariah and the others, his forehead erupted with a mark of God's anger (cf. Num 12:10). The translation "leprosy" is not to be accepted as equivalent to the modern disease of the same name but is a skin disease that, however it is described in modern terms, was a visible manifestation of divine judgment in the form of a skin eruption.[96]

26:20 Infectious diseases made an individual ceremonially unclean and required isolation "outside the camp" (Lev 13:46; Num 5:1–14; 12:15; 2 Kgs 7:3). Uzziah would be unable to discharge the duties of kingship, particularly those connected with the temple. His son, Jotham, had to take over in a co-regency arrangement. He had charge of the palace and governed the people.

26:21–22 Among his sources the Chronicler lists Isaiah, the prophet-son of Amoz. Similar lists appear in 1 Chr 29:29; 2 Chr 9:29; 12:15; and elsewhere. He also appeals to writings by Isaiah in his account of Hezekiah (32:32). This is not the canonical Book of Isaiah, which gives no information about Uzziah except that he died (cf. 1:1; 6:1; 7:1). Either the Chronicler was referring to some writings of Isaiah not known to us or the Isaiah traditions had perhaps already been incorporated into Kings or another history[97] (20:34; 24:27; 32:32).

26:23 Uzziah was a great king in human terms. The kingdom of Judah prospered during his reign. Isaiah seems to have lamented his death. It was in the year King Uzziah died that Isaiah was called to prophesy. Yet it was because Isaiah knew what lay ahead for Judah (Isa 6:11–12).[98]

Uzziah's son, Jotham, reigned in Jerusalem sixteen years, which included a ten-year co-regency with Uzziah. In addition there was an overlap of three to four years with that of his own son and successor, Ahaz (735–732/731 B.C.), a fact that would allow for the synchronism with Jotham's twentieth year (2 Kgs 15:30).

14. The Reign of Jotham (27:1–9)

¹Jotham was twenty-five years old when he became king, and he reigned in Jerusalem sixteen years. His mother's name was Jerusha daughter of

---

[96] E. V. Hulse, "The Nature of Biblical Leprosy," *PEQ* 107 (1975): 87–105.

[97] Dillard, *2 Chronicles,* 211.

[98] Ibid., 211–12.

Zadok. [2]He did what was right in the eyes of the LORD, just as his father Uzziah had done, but unlike him he did not enter the temple of the LORD. The people, however, continued their corrupt practices. [3]Jotham rebuilt the Upper Gate of the temple of the LORD and did extensive work on the wall at the hill of Ophel. [4]He built towns in the Judean hills and forts and towers in the wooded areas.

[5]Jotham made war on the king of the Ammonites and conquered them. That year the Ammonites paid him a hundred talents of silver, ten thousand cors of wheat and ten thousand cors of barley. The Ammonites brought him the same amount also in the second and third years.

[6]Jotham grew powerful because he walked steadfastly before the LORD his God.

[7]The other events in Jotham's reign, including all his wars and the other things he did, are written in the book of the kings of Israel and Judah. [8]He was twenty-five years old when he became king, and he reigned in Jerusalem sixteen years. [9]Jotham rested with his fathers and was buried in the City of David. And Ahaz his son succeeded him as king.

The story of Jotham (ca. 750–731 B.C.) is brief, only nine verses. He was a good king. He followed the ways of his father, Uzziah, in piety and did not follow him in sacrilege. The Chronicler paints a wholly positive account of him. The Chronicler's story is largely dependent on the parallel account in 2 Kgs 15:32–38, although he omits the remark that trouble began then with Israel and Syria, preferring to save it for the story of Ahaz.

27:1 The usual introductory notices are provided: his age at accession (twenty-five years), his length of reign (sixteen years in Jerusalem), and his mother's name (Jerusha, daughter of Zadok, a prominent family).

27:2 Jotham's behavior was exemplary, like the early behavior of Uzziah. By contrast, the people were still entangled in paganism. The Chronicler does not condemn Jotham for the people's misdeeds. Here the Chronicler once again contradicts a superficial reading of his book, one that would assert that all the successes or failures of Judah could be attributed to whether the king had been "good" or "bad." Instead, the people can contradict the attitudes of their rulers, whether the ruler be the wicked Athaliah or the good Jotham. The rulers of Israel were tremendously important in determining the attitudes and destiny of the nation, but the citizens could not be absolved of responsibility for their actions and attitudes.

27:3–4 As in the account of Uzziah, divine blessing on Jotham's reign is demonstrated with building projects (vv. 3–4) and military success (v. 5; note the reverse order in 26:6–10). The first part of v. 3 is taken from 2 Kgs 15:35b, which refers to the repair of the Upper Gate of the temple located at the north entrance to the temple enclosure. He also did extensive work on the wall at the hill of Ophel. The Ophel normally is associated with the hilly spur running south from the temple mount.

27:5 While Uzziah's main success in battle was against the Philistines (26:6–7) and the Ammonites paid him tribute (26:8), Jotham fought only the Ammonites (war against the Ammonites is recorded only here). Apparently they had stopped paying the tribute. This tribute seems to us to be very large. A hundred talents of silver is about 3.4 metric tons, and 10,000 cors of barley probably is about 62,000 bushels. The tribute apparently ceased again after three years, perhaps due to the rising power of Aram-Damascus in the area.[99]

27:6 This concluding theological evaluation by the Chronicler again expresses the thematic principle that *success follows obedience to the Lord.* Like his father, Jotham became powerful with the Lord's help; but unlike Uzziah, Jotham apparently did not forget the true source of his strength.

27:7–9 The Chronicler omits any reference to difficulties with Rezin and Pekah (2 Kgs 15:37), perhaps because he did not understand it as judgment on Jotham but on Judah generally and especially on Jotham's successor, Ahaz. The account of Jotham is clearly a truncated one. Details of his death are not given, but he was buried with his fathers in the City of David, a burial that befitted his life and character (cp. 26:23).

15. The Reign of Ahaz (28:1–27)

King Ahaz (735–715 B.C.) probably is most familiar to Bible students as the faithless king to whom the prophet Isaiah delivered the prophecy of Immanuel in Isa 7:14. But the biblical historians, especially the Chronicler, furnish much more information about him. He was king at a critical time in Judah's history, which saw a corrupt Israel fall to a revived Assyrian Empire, thus ending the divided monarchy. Any hopes on the part of the faithful that Judah might learn from this event and return to the Lord were dashed by the reign of Ahaz, who patterned himself after everyone but his righteous predecessors.

The chapter is presented in five sections: (1) character of Ahaz (28:1–4), (2) Syro-Ephraimite war (28:5–8), (3) prophecy of Oded (28:9–15), (4) appeal to the king of Assyria (28:16–21), and (5) apostasy and death of Ahaz (28:22–27). While following the basic outline of 2 Kgs 16:1–2, he diverges from it and supplements it considerably, probably from other sources.

---

[99] Dillard, *2 Chronicles*, 215.

(1) The Character of Ahaz (28:1–4)

¹Ahaz was twenty years old when he became king, and he reigned in Jerusalem sixteen years. Unlike David his father, he did not do what was right in the eyes of the LORD. ²He walked in the ways of the kings of Israel and also made cast idols for worshiping the Baals. ³He burned sacrifices in the Valley of Ben Hinnom and sacrificed his sons in the fire, following the detestable ways of the nations the LORD had driven out before the Israelites. ⁴He offered sacrifices and burned incense at the high places, on the hilltops and under every spreading tree.

28:1 The material in vv. 1–4 is dependent on 2 Kgs 16:2–4 except for an addition in vv. 2b–3a and the typical absence of the correlation with Israel. Ahaz is the only king for which the evaluation is "he did not do what was right," although it often is said of others that they "did evil in the eyes of the LORD" (Judg 2:11 and often in Judges; 1 Kgs 11:6; 14:22; 15:26; and elsewhere). This verse also is unique in that only here and in the parallel verse in 2 Kgs 16:2 is criticism expressed for *not* following David's example, although many times in Kings (but only once in Chronicles, in 2 Chr 29:2) there is commendation for following his example.

28:2–3 That he walked in the ways of the kings of Israel was a severe condemnation. To illustrate what he meant the Chronicler instanced several examples of Ahaz's apostasy. He offered sacrifices (or burned incense) in the Valley of Ben Hinnom, the deep valley, immediately to the south of the temple hill, where fires burned the city refuse. He also sacrificed his sons in the fire. The ritual of child sacrifice is elsewhere associated with the Ben Hinnom Valley (33:6; Jer 7:31–32; cf. Lev 20:1–5; 2 Kgs 3:26–27; 23:10; Mic 6:7; Ezek 16:20–21). Even worse than imitating the apostasy of the Northern Kingdom, Ahaz is condemned for behaving as the cursed Canaanites, whose culture was so vile that God had ordered its elimination (Lev 18:28; 20:23; Deut 7:22–26; 12:2–4; 18:9–14). Little wonder that Yahweh visited Ahaz with judgment in the form of an Aramean attack.

(2) The Syro-Ephraimite War (28:5–8)

⁵Therefore the LORD his God handed him over to the king of Aram. The Arameans defeated him and took many of his people as prisoners and brought them to Damascus.

He was also given into the hands of the king of Israel, who inflicted heavy casualties on him. ⁶In one day Pekah son of Remaliah killed a hundred and twenty thousand soldiers in Judah—because Judah had forsaken the LORD, the God of their fathers. ⁷Zicri, an Ephraimite warrior, killed Maaseiah the king's son, Azrikam the officer in charge of the palace, and Elkanah, second to the king. [8]The Israelites took captive from their kinsmen two hundred thousand wives, sons and daughters. They also took a great deal of plunder, which they carried back to Samaria.

28:5–6 Various aspects of the Syro-Ephraimite war are referred to in other places in the Old Testament—2 Kgs 15:37; 16:5; Isa 7; Hos 5:8–6:6. The political causes of the war are unclear,[100] but its divine purpose was retribution on Ahaz and Judah. The Chronicler's account differs from that in Kings in describing attacks from Syria and from Israel separately rather than as a coalition. He does not deny, however, that Syria and Israel were in fact joined. Dillard suggests that the Chronicler told his story because he was not happy about foreign alliances, which demonstrated a failure to trust in Yahweh[101] (16:2–9; 19:1–2; 22:3–6; 25:6–10). In this section the Northern Kingdom is presented in a moderately favorable light (vv. 9–15), and the Chronicler may have given further evidence of such a view by separating the Syro-Ephraimite campaign into two parts, thus avoiding the impression of any coalition between an Israelite state and a pagan state. The Chronicler's account also differs from Kings in that it stresses the losses Judah suffered. The phrase "given into the hands of" does not appear to mean that Ahaz himself was given physically into the hands of these enemies but rather that his forces were defeated in battle. These defeats happened "because Judah had forsaken the LORD, the God of their fathers." By way of contrast Abijah, king of Judah, once condemned the north in similar terms (13:10–12; cf. 1 Chr 28:9; 2 Chr 7:19–22; 12:1–2; 21:10; 24:24).

28:7 The specific details of the names in this verse suggest another source to which the Chronicler had access. The title "second to the king" occurs elsewhere only in Esth 10:3. The "king's son" may be a title also, but it could be taken literally.

28:8 The use of the term "kinsmen" may be a deliberate attempt to remind the postexilic readers that Israel was one nation despite the division that then existed (cf. 2 Chr 11:4).

(3) The Prophecy of Oded (28:9–15)

[9]But a prophet of the LORD named Oded was there, and he went out to meet the army when it returned to Samaria. He said to them, "Because the LORD, the God of your fathers, was angry with Judah, he gave them into your hand. But you have slaughtered them in a rage that reaches to heaven. [10]And

---

[100] See B. Oded, "The Historical Background of the Syro-Ephraimite War Reconsidered," *CBQ* 34 (1972): 153–65.

[101] Dillard, *2 Chronicles*, 221

now you intend to make the men and women of Judah and Jerusalem your slaves. But aren't you also guilty of sins against the LORD your God? [11]Now listen to me! Send back your fellow countrymen you have taken as prisoners, for the LORD'S fierce anger rests on you."

[12]Then some of the leaders in Ephraim—Azariah son of Jehohanan, Berekiah son of Meshillemoth, Jehizkiah son of Shallum, and Amasa son of Hadlai—confronted those who were arriving from the war. [13]"You must not bring those prisoners here," they said, "or we will be guilty before the LORD. Do you intend to add to our sin and guilt? For our guilt is already great, and his fierce anger rests on Israel."

[14]So the soldiers gave up the prisoners and plunder in the presence of the officials and all the assembly. [15]The men designated by name took the prisoners, and from the plunder they clothed all who were naked. They provided them with clothes and sandals, food and drink, and healing balm. All those who were weak they put on donkeys. So they took them back to their fellow countrymen at Jericho, the City of Palms, and returned to Samaria.

28:9 This otherwise unknown prophet went out to meet the returning victorious army of Israel. There was an Oded the prophet referred to in 15:8, but the two are not the same. This is the ninth of ten episodes in Chronicles in which a prophet or man of God brings a divine message (cf. 1 Chr 17:1; 2 Chr 11:2; 12:5; 15:8; 18:6; 21:12; 25:7–9,15–16; 36:12), but only here is the message delivered to someone other than a king. Even in rebellion the Northern Kingdom is viewed as part of the people of God who can perform God's will on occasion. However, in carrying out God's will, they exceeded what was reasonable and "slaughtered them in a rage that reaches to heaven." God's agent, whether an invader or Israel, is not authorized to go beyond certain limits (cf. Isa 10:5–19; Hos 1:4).

28:10–11 Any intention to make the people of Judah slaves was a breach of the law that forbade the enslaving of fellow Israelites (Lev 25:39–55). Short-term slavery of one Israelite to another was allowable, but ruling over one's brothers "ruthlessly" (Lev 25:43) was forbidden. Israel itself was only a hairsbreadth from judgment. Repentance toward God and magnanimity toward their brethren was called for. They had taken prisoners. These should be sent back. Repentance required some display of appropriate action.

28:12–13 The "leaders in Ephraim," with no mention of the king, confronted the returning army. This taking of authority by the leaders of Ephraim seems to indicate that the throne was already in precarious circumstances. This repentance was a hint that the spiritual unity of Israel and Judah was not totally lost (cf. 30:1–11;31:1). The list of names provided suggests another source containing these details, which are not given in Kings.

28:14–15 In a remarkable reversal of their intention the soldiers of Israel gave up the prisoners captured from Judah and the plunder. Such magnanimous behavior is unusual in the ancient world, since plunder was the payment for service soldiers expected. In recording this incident, it is clear that the Chronicler did not regard the *people* of the Northern Kingdom as an affront to God but only treated their counterfeit monarchy (a rival to the house of David) and their counterfeit shrines at Dan and Bethel (rivals to the temple of Solomon) as illicit. The people themselves were brothers and sisters to the people of Judah, and sometimes they acted like it. The Chronicler, who has stressed from the beginning the unity of "all Israel," was surely delighted to recount this episode (e.g., 2 Chr 30:11). This story may well have been the basis for Jesus' parable of the good Samaritan.[102]

(4) Appeal to the King of Assyria (28:16–21)

[16]**At that time King Ahaz sent to the king of Assyria for help.** [17]**The Edomites had again come and attacked Judah and carried away prisoners,** [18]**while the Philistines had raided towns in the foothills and in the Negev of Judah. They captured and occupied Beth Shemesh, Aijalon and Gederoth, as well as Soco, Timnah and Gimzo, with their surrounding villages.** [19]**The LORD had humbled Judah because of Ahaz king of Israel, for he had promoted wickedness in Judah and had been most unfaithful to the LORD.** [20]**Tiglath-Pileser king of Assyria came to him, but he gave him trouble instead of help.** [21]**Ahaz took some of the things from the temple of the LORD and from the royal palace and from the princes and presented them to the king of Assyria, but that did not help him.**

Having suffered heavy losses at the hands of Syria and Israel and now troubled by invasions from the Philistines and the Edomites, Ahaz appealed to Tiglath-Pileser III of Assyria (745–727 B.C.) for help, a dangerous move.

28:16 Ahaz was in dire straits. His predecessors who had been faithful to the Lord had seen God subdue such enemies many times. But Ahaz did not trust in the Lord (cf. Isa 7:10–16). With Philistines and Edomites in the south and the Syro-Ephraimite invasion in the north (vv. 5–8), he faced a two-front war.[103] The verb "help" is important to the Chronicler. God was ever available to "help" faithful kings (1 Chr 5:20; 2 Chr 14:11; 18:31; 25:8; 26:7,15; 32:8). Such "help" (*ʿāzar*) was not available from other sources (vv. 21,23). Ahaz had turned to human—indeed foreign—help instead of to the God of Israel.

28:17 The Edomites chose the time for an attack on Judah while they

---

[102] Wilcock, *Message of Chronicles,* 240–41; S. Spenser, "2 Chronicles 28:5–15 and the Parable of the Good Samaritan," *WTJ* 46 (1984): 317–49.

[103] According to Williamson, texts from Nimrud have confirmed the historical substance of this paragraph (*1 and 2 Chronicles,* 347–48).

were weak and distracted by other enemies. At this time Edom was probing into the Negeb area.[104]

28:18 The Philistines wanted to recover their losses under Uzziah (26:6). The cities mentioned lay along the borders of the hill country west of Jerusalem. The areas occupied by the Edomites and Philistines possibly were intended to open up overland trading routes that were full of Judahite influence.

28:19 The purpose of these attacks was to discipline Judah (cf. 7:14; 12:6–7,12) because of Ahaz. Once again the Chronicler pressed the point of Ahaz's wickedness and complete unfaithfulness. But Ahaz is here called "king of Israel," using the comprehensive term "Israel," which covers the whole or part of God's people. Even when the monarch was one such as Ahaz, the Chronicler recognized only the Davidic king, who thus had a great responsibility to the Lord and to the people.

28:20 This verse is a summary statement of the net result of Assyrian intervention. The account in Kings explains that the Assyrian king did take Damascus, eliminating that source of trouble. In fact, Assyrian presence brought temporary peace to the entire region as evidenced by an Assyrian text describing their new vassals—Judah, Ammon, Moab, Ashkelon, Edom, and Gaza—bringing tribute to Assyria at Damascus.[105]

28:21 The first cost to Judah (the Heb. text of v. 21 begins with *kî,* "for") was the plundering of temple, palace, and citizenry necessary to pay the tribute. But this was only the beginning of the consequences Judah would suffer for relying on the wrong remedy. The resources of Judah were depleted to no avail.

(5) The Apostasy and Death of Ahaz (28:22–27)

[22]In his time of trouble King Ahaz became even more unfaithful to the LORD. [23]He offered sacrifices to the gods of Damascus, who had defeated him; for he thought, "Since the gods of the kings of Aram have helped them, I will sacrifice to them so they will help me." But they were his downfall and the downfall of all Israel.

[24]Ahaz gathered together the furnishings from the temple of God and took them away. He shut the doors of the LORD'S temple and set up altars at every street corner in Jerusalem. [25]In every town in Judah he built high places to burn sacrifices to other gods and provoked the LORD, the God of his fathers, to anger.

---

[104] J. R. Bartlett, "The Rise and Fall of Edom," *PEQ,* 104 (1972) 26–37; note p. 33 (26:7–8). See also J. A. Thompson, "Israel's 'Haters,'" *VT* 29 (1979): 200–205.

[105] D. J. Wiseman, *1 & 2 Kings,* TOTC (Leicester: InterVarsity, 1993); *ANET,* 282.

²⁶**The other events of his reign and all his ways, from beginning to end, are written in the book of the kings of Judah and Israel.** ²⁷**Ahaz rested with his fathers and was buried in the city of Jerusalem, but he was not placed in the tombs of the kings of Israel. And Hezekiah his son succeeded him as king.**

The response of Ahaz to his new Assyrian lord and the aftermath of his unfaithfulness present a melancholy spectacle. The author of Kings explains that while Ahaz was in Damascus he was so impressed with the Aramean religion of Damascus and especially their altar that he ordered a duplicate constructed in the place of the altar of the Lord (2 Kgs 16:10–16).

28:22–23 Verse 22 is striking. One might expect it to read, "In his time of trouble King Ahaz" *humbled himself before the Lord.* But Ahaz's spirit apparently was cold and dead. A list of his apostasies is given. He offered sacrifices to the gods of Damascus whom he regarded as his conquerors, obviously blind to the truth that it was the Lord who was responsible for his defeat. It was a case of extreme apostasy, for it involved repudiation of the religious regulations the Lord gave Israel through Moses and David, although Ahaz probably worshiped the Lord along with the gods of Aram. Certainly Ahaz seems to have turned in all directions for help—the Assyrians, the gods of the kings of Aram—everywhere except to the Lord, the God of Israel, the only source of the "help" he needed. These others served only to ruin Ahaz and all Israel.

28:24–25 Rejection of the true God leads not to "secular" thinking so much as to pagan thinking. The Chronicler interpreted the plundering of the temple to raise tribute for Assyria (2 Kgs 16:17–18) as religious desecration. His shutting the temple doors, however, may not have meant the cessation of sacrifices at the temple (cf. 2 Kgs 16:14–16) but that the people could no longer bring sacrifices there (contrast Uzziah in 26:21), and the priests ceased their ministry in the holy place (29:3–7,18–19). Under Ahaz, Judah had sunk to the depths, in much the same way as Israel had under Jeroboam at the time of the division (1 Kgs 12:25–33).

28:26–27 The closing remarks about the reign of Ahaz are drawn from 2 Kgs 16:19–20 although with some changes. Ahaz was buried in Jerusalem but like Jehoram (21:20), Joash (24:25), Uzziah (26:23), and Manasseh (33:20) was not placed in the tombs of the kings of Israel. This was no doubt because of his apostasy. According to 2 Kgs 16:20 Ahaz was buried with his fathers in the City of David. The reason for this difference is not clear to us, but apparently the statement "buried with his fathers" meant only that his tomb was in Jerusalem. Under Ahaz, Judah appeared to have reached its nadir. But for the Chronicler there was always hope of tragedy and despair being turned to rejoicing through repentance. Such a return would occur preeminently under Hezekiah, the king most like David (cf. 29:2,25–30).

VI. THE SINGLE KINGDOM: HEZEKIAH TO THE BABYLONIAN EXILE (29:1–36:23)

1. The Reign of Hezekiah (29:1–32:33)
   (1) The Rehabilitation of the Temple (29:1–36)
   (2) The Celebration of the Passover by "All Israel" (30:1–31:1)
   (3) Reform Activities (31:2–21)
   (4) Hezekiah's Victory, Illness, and Faithfulness (32:2–33)
2. The Reign of Manasseh (33:1–20)
   (1) Relapse under Manasseh (33:1–10)
   (2) Manasseh's Captivity, Repentance, and Restoration (33:11–13)
   (3) Manasseh's Reforms (33:14–17)
   (4) Summary and Conclusion (33:18–20)
3. The Reign of Amon (33:21–25)
4. The Reign of Josiah (34:1–36:1)
   (1) Introduction (34:1–2)
   (2) The Removal of Pagan Cults from Jerusalem (34:3–7)
   (3) Temple Repairs and the Discovery of the Law Book (34:8–28)
   (4) Covenant Renewal (34:29–33)
   (5) Josiah's Passover (35:1–19)
   (6) The Account of Josiah's Death (35:20–36:1)
5. The Reign of Jehoahaz (36:2–4)
6. The Reign of Jehoiakim (36:5–8)
7. The Reign of Jehoiachin (36:9–10)
8. The Reign of Zedekiah (36:11–21)
9. Appendix (36:22–23)

VI. THE SINGLE KINGDOM: HEZEKIAH TO THE BABYLONIAN EXILE (29:1–32:23)

With the accession of Hezekiah to the throne, there appeared to be hope that a united Israel was about to emerge. The Chronicler's interest throughout the period of the divided monarchy has been primarily centered on Judah, the Southern Kingdom. No account is given of the fall of Samaria in the days of Hoshea, king of Israel (732–724 B.C.), to the Assyrian ruler Shalmaneser V (726–722 B.C.). Samaria fell in the late summer or autumn of the year 722/721. At the time, Ahaz was ruling in Judah (735–715 B.C.); but he had signed away his liberty, and Judah was a vassal state of the Assyrian Empire. Some encouraging signs would occur, however, once Hezekiah became king of Judah.

The Chronicler had a deep interest in Hezekiah. He devoted more space to his account of Hezekiah's reign than he did to any king of Judah other than David and Solomon (chaps. 29–32). But his interest is different from that of 2 Kings 18–20. The Book of Kings devotes only a single verse to Hezekiah's religious reform, concentrating rather on political and military affairs. Here the account of the reform occupies three chapters (29–31) that deal with the rehabilitation of the temple (chap. 29), the celebration of the Passover by "all Israel" (chap. 30), and the renewal of regular worship (chap. 31). The remaining chapter on Hezekiah's reign refers to the deliverance of Hezekiah from Sennacherib, king of Assyria, and Hezekiah's sickness, pride, success, and death. Hezekiah is presented as the king most like David and Solomon (29:2,11–14; 30:18–20,26).[1] The Chronicler had great hopes of a united Israel once again under a Davidic king and united around the temple of the Lord, other unauthorized places of worship being abandoned.

1. The Reign of Hezekiah (29:1–32:33)

(1) The Rehabilitation of the Temple (29:1–36)

The Chronicler depicts in 29:3 the work of cleansing and restoring the temple at the very beginning of Hezekiah's reign (ca. 715–687 B.C.). This is described in four steps: (1) the instruction and ritual purification of the priests and Levites (29:3–15), (2) the purification of the temple and its precincts (29:16–19), (3) the rededication of the temple (29:20–30), and (4) the participation of the people (29:31–36).[2]

Some commentators have argued that chap. 29 includes some secondary expansion of the Chronicler's original account.[3] Several features of Hezekiah's charge in vv. 5–11 have been seen as the Chronicler's deliberate intention to mold the material into the form of a "Levitical sermon" with its characteristic introduction (v. 5), its use of canonical texts (v. 8), and its pare-

---

[1] There is disagreement among scholars over whether Hezekiah is likened in Chronicles to David or to Solomon. Dillard and others favor "an indissoluble unity of the two," so that both are true (*2 Chronicles,* 229).

[2] This outline is from Dillard, *2 Chronicles,* 232.

[3] See discussions in H. G. M. Williamson, *1 and 2 Chronicles,* NCBC (Grand Rapids: Eerdmans,1982), 351–52; R. B. Dillard, *2 Chronicles,* WBC (Waco: Word, 1987), 232–33.

netic preaching style (v. 11). Normally such sermons are found in the utterances of prophets or other inspired speakers. However, although the exact wording probably is the Chronicler's, it is by no means unlikely that Hezekiah delivered just such an exhortation to the priests and Levites and that the term "Levites" in v. 5 applied to both.[4]

[1]Hezekiah was twenty-five years old when he became king, and he reigned in Jerusalem twenty-nine years. His mother's name was Abijah daughter of Zechariah. [2]He did what was right in the eyes of the LORD, just as his father David had done.

[3]In the first month of the first year of his reign, he opened the doors of the temple of the LORD and repaired them. [4]He brought in the priests and the Levites, assembled them in the square on the east side [5]and said: "Listen to me, Levites! Consecrate yourselves now and consecrate the temple of the LORD, the God of your fathers. Remove all defilement from the sanctuary. [6]Our fathers were unfaithful; they did evil in the eyes of the LORD our God and forsook him. They turned their faces away from the LORD'S dwelling place and turned their backs on him. [7]They also shut the doors of the portico and put out the lamps. They did not burn incense or present any burnt offerings at the sanctuary to the God of Israel. [8]Therefore, the anger of the LORD has fallen on Judah and Jerusalem; he has made them an object of dread and horror and scorn, as you can see with your own eyes. [9]This is why our fathers have fallen by the sword and why our sons and daughters and our wives are in captivity. [10]Now I intend to make a covenant with the LORD, the God of Israel, so that his fierce anger will turn away from us. [11]My sons, do not be negligent now, for the LORD has chosen you to stand before him and serve him, to minister before him and to burn incense."

[12]Then these Levites set to work:

from the Kohathites, Mahath son of Amasai and Joel son of Azariah;
from the Merarites,
Kish son of Abdi and Azariah son of Jehallel;
from the Gershonites,
Joah son of Zimmah and Eden son of Joah;
[13]from the descendants of Elizaphan,
Shimri and Jeiel;
from the descendants of Asaph,
Zechariah and Mattaniah;
[14]from the descendants of Heman,
Jehiel and Shimei;
from the descendants of Jeduthun,
Shemaiah and Uzziel.

---

[4] A negative assessment of the historical worth of the reformation of Hezekiah is L. K. Handy, "Hezekiah's Unlikely Reform," *ZAW* 100 (1988): 111–15.

[15]When they had assembled their brothers and consecrated themselves, they went in to purify the temple of the LORD, as the king had ordered, following the word of the LORD.

THE INSTRUCTION AND RITUAL PURIFICATION OF THE PRIESTS AND LEVITES (29:1–15).   **29:1**   The Chronicler's account of Hezekiah's reign is almost completely independent of the parallel history in 2 Kings 18–20, but the introductory material appears to come from 2 Kgs 18:1–3.

29:2   At once Hezekiah is given a high commendation. Although several kings are compared favorably to David in the Book of Kings, Hezekiah and Josiah are the only ones given this honor in Chronicles.

29:3   Probably, in light of chap. 30, the Chronicler intended "the first month of the first year" to be understood as the first month of Hezekiah's first regnal year rather than the first month after the death of his father. From the very commencement of his reign, the new king set about putting things right in the temple and in the observance of religious obligations. In his concern for temple and worship from the time of his accession, Hezekiah is parallel to Solomon (2 Chr 1–2). Ahaz had shut the doors of the temple (28:24). More important to the Chronicler was that Hezekiah had them opened so that regular worship could proceed.

29:4   From its misuse and disuse under Ahaz, the temple was still unclean, but the task of consecration had to be done by the priests and Levites, who were themselves in need of cleansing. The assembly of the priests and Levites in the square on the east side of the temple was perhaps the same as the "square near the Water Gate" in Neh 8:1,3, a location outside the temple precincts. Such squares often were located just inside the city gates.

29:5   Hezekiah's charge to the Levites is carefully presented by the Chronicler with details of procedures they followed. The instructions are introduced in Hebrew by the well-known term "now." Two different tasks of consecration (*qadaš,* "be holy") are involved. In both cases the thought of making holy is prominent. The Levites needed to be holy themselves before they could undertake the task of making the temple holy. As J. G. McConville has stated: "It was one thing to *be* a priest or Levite, but quite another to be fit, at any given time, to *act* as such."[5] All defilement was to be removed from the sanctuary. The term for "defilement" is quite general, although the effects of Ahaz's desecration would have been very much in mind (cf. 28:23–24). It was to be a new beginning, a fresh chapter in the Chronicler's story.

29:6   Hezekiah did not excuse himself or his generation when he

---

[5] J. G. McConville, *I & II Chronicles,* DSB (Philadelphia: Westminster, 1984), 231.

described the sins of their fathers. Rather, he asserted that the nation must acknowledge its corporate guilt and take steps to rectify what had been done. Admitting that one's nation and cultural heritage have turned away from God is not easy, but true repentance must place the glory of God above national and family pride.

29:7 The details spelled out here were typical of Ahaz's conduct. The ritual obligations of a worshiping community were neglected. Ahaz reversed the pattern of worship that Solomon initiated and his son Abijah carried on (13:11). Hezekiah's task was the restoration of these earlier patterns practiced by Solomon.

29:8–9 The current situation was desperate. The condition of Judah and Jerusalem was comparable to the situation in the north (cf. 28:9,11,13). The anger of the Lord made Judah and Jerusalem "an object of dread and horror and scorn," language used elsewhere of the exiles in Babylon (Jer 29:18; cf. Jer 19:8; 25:9,18; 34:17; Ezek 23:46). The Chronicler's audience would not have missed the comparison and the applicability of Hezekiah's call to purity and unity of worship (30:6–9).

29:10 Here Hezekiah begins a new element in his exhortation with the repeated introductory particle "now" ('attâ). Hezekiah, as the leader of the nation, would stand in their behalf to seek to turn back the wrath of God against Israel. In this he was like Moses, interceding for the people (Num 14:11–19). Hezekiah expressed his intention of taking a solemn oath to put right what was wrong. It was not a renewal of the covenant between God and Israel but a commitment by the king and the nation to seek God again with all their heart (15:12). Remarkably, Hezekiah's first response to the Assyrian threat was to return to the proper worship of God. Wilcock's comment is perceptive and applicable:

> When there is a financial crisis, the first thing we think about is money. When there is a communications crisis, our prime concern is to learn how to talk the language of the modern generation. When there is a church attendance crisis, we make it our chief aim to get numbers up. If Hezekiah had responded to a military threat in a military way, the Assyrians would have understood that. Army would have been matched against army, with dire consequences for Judah. But instead he and his people first look up to God.[6]

To be sure, Hezekiah also made practical military preparations for the coming siege (32:1–5). We might say that he prayed hard and then he worked hard. But he put his prayers in the first place.

29:11 The "clergy," which had long neglected its duty, needed encour-

---

[6] Wilcock, *Chronicles*, 247.

agement. The time had come for renewal. The fact that the ministry of the temple had fallen on bad times did not mean that it had to stay that way. Again the verse is introduced in Hebrew by the important term "now" (ʿattâ), since this is his concluding exhortation. The command he gave them at the beginning (v. 5) must be followed with all diligence and haste because the Lord had entrusted to them the responsibility of temple worship.

29:12–14 Fourteen Levites are listed in two groups. The first eight consist of two from each of the Levitical families, the Kohathites, the Merarites, the Gershonites, and the descendants of Elizaphan. The second group is made up of two each from the three families of the Levitical singers, Asaph, Heman, and Jeduthun.

29:15 These Levites then set to work. They assembled their brothers and consecrated themselves and went as the king had ordered and according to the Lord's instructions (cf. 1 Chr 28:12,19) to purify the temple of the Lord.

16The priests went into the sanctuary of the LORD to purify it. They brought out to the courtyard of the LORD'S temple everything unclean that they found in the temple of the LORD. The Levites took it and carried it out to the Kidron Valley. 17They began the consecration on the first day of the first month, and by the eighth day of the month they reached the portico of the LORD. For eight more days they consecrated the temple of the LORD itself, finishing on the sixteenth day of the first month.

18Then they went in to King Hezekiah and reported: "We have purified the entire temple of the LORD, the altar of burnt offering with all its utensils, and the table for setting out the consecrated bread, with all its articles. 19We have prepared and consecrated all the articles that King Ahaz removed in his unfaithfulness while he was king. They are now in front of the LORD'S altar."

THE PURIFICATION OF THE TEMPLE AND ITS PRECINCTS (29:16–19). **29:16** Having purified themselves, they were ready to purify the temple. The priests alone were responsible for going into the inner part (sanctuary) of the temple, that is, the most holy place, where the ark was kept (3:8–13; cf. Lev 10:18). The text does not specify here what "everything unclean" refers to, but evidently the idols associated with Ahaz are meant. The Kidron Valley was a burial place and therefore an appropriate place for things unclean (cf. 15:16; 30:14). On several occasions items of foreign worship were taken there for destruction, for example, at the time of Asa (15:16) and Josiah (30:14; 2 Kgs 23:4,6,12).

29:17 The purification of the temple required sixteen days. The first half was spent in the courts up to the portico. The second half was devoted to the temple of the Lord itself, finishing on the sixteenth day of the first month. Since Passover was to begin on the fourteenth day (Num 9:1–11), it had to be delayed. Had more priests been available for the purification operations, it might have been on time (29:34; 30:3).

29:18–19   The text stresses the proper recovery and cleansing of the temple implements as part of a restoration to the original Solomonic conditions (4:19–22; 1 Chr 28:14–17).

[20]**Early the next morning King Hezekiah gathered the city officials together and went up to the temple of the LORD.** [21]**They brought seven bulls, seven rams, seven male lambs and seven male goats as a sin offering for the kingdom, for the sanctuary and for Judah. The king commanded the priests, the descendants of Aaron, to offer these on the altar of the LORD.** [22]**So they slaughtered the bulls, and the priests took the blood and sprinkled it on the altar; next they slaughtered the rams and sprinkled their blood on the altar; then they slaughtered the lambs and sprinkled their blood on the altar.** [23]**The goats for the sin offering were brought before the king and the assembly, and they laid their hands on them.** [24]**The priests then slaughtered the goats and presented their blood on the altar for a sin offering to atone for all Israel, because the king had ordered the burnt offering and the sin offering for all Israel.**

[25]**He stationed the Levites in the temple of the LORD with cymbals, harps and lyres in the way prescribed by David and Gad the king's seer and Nathan the prophet; this was commanded by the LORD through his prophets.** [26]**So the Levites stood ready with David's instruments, and the priests with their trumpets.**

[27]**Hezekiah gave the order to sacrifice the burnt offering on the altar. As the offering began, singing to the LORD began also, accompanied by trumpets and the instruments of David king of Israel.** [28]**The whole assembly bowed in worship, while the singers sang and the trumpeters played. All this continued until the sacrifice of the burnt offering was completed.**

[29]**When the offerings were finished, the king and everyone present with him knelt down and worshiped.** [30]**King Hezekiah and his officials ordered the Levites to praise the LORD with the words of David and of Asaph the seer. So they sang praises with gladness and bowed their heads and worshiped.**

THE REDEDICATION OF THE TEMPLE (29:20–30).   Most commentators understand vv. 20–24 and vv. 25–30 to be describing simultaneous events. The first stage of the rededication was the offerings of the leaders. This is described here with the focus on the priests and the animals that were offered (vv. 20–24), then on the Levites and the music and worship that accompanied the sacrifices (vv. 25–30). The second stage of the rededications was the offerings brought by the people (vv. 31–36).[7]

29:20–21   The rededication of the temple involved secular and religious representatives—the king, the city officials, the priests, and the Levites. The

---

[7] See Williamson, *1 & 2 Chronicles,* 357–58.

bulls, rams, and lambs probably were the burnt offering. The "kingdom" here probably refers to the "royal house"; the sanctuary included the cultic personnel; and Judah, the nation as a whole. These offerings are similar to those in Ezekiel for the cleansing of the altar and the sanctuary (Ezek 43:18–27), the return of a priest to his duties after defilement and purification (44:27), and the preparation of the prince and people for the celebration of the Passover (45:21–23). There is some emphasis on employing the correct personnel in the designation "priests, the descendants of Aaron" (cf. Lev 1:7–9).

29:22 In the priestly laws in Leviticus (Lev 1:5) the one who brought the offerings killed the animal, but the priest sprinkled the blood. If this was the procedure here, the king and the officials of v. 20 are the subject of the impersonal "they" of vv. 21–22, but the text is not explicit.

29:23 The goats for the sin offering were brought before the king and the assembly, who laid their hands on them. This was done also for the burnt offering (Lev 1:4) as an indication of the identification of the offerer (the king and the assembly) with the victim (the he-goats).

29:24 In this case it is clear that the priests both slaughtered the animals (cf. v. 22) and presented their blood on the altar for a sin offering. This procedure was followed on the annual day of atonement when the high priest, representing all Israel, killed the goat of the sin offering (Lev 16:15). The king had ordered on this occasion that the burnt offering and the sin offering were to be offered for "all Israel." This fact is stressed by repetition and also by the word order of the final clause (lit., "because for all Israel the king had ordered . . ."). Hezekiah (and the Chronicler) viewed the occasion as referring to the total entity "Israel," that is, Judah plus the people of the old Northern Kingdom, constituting the one people of God.

29:25–26 Again in vv. 25–30 Hezekiah is shown following David's example (cf. 29:2). This verse takes up the role of the Levites who led the musical aspects of the rededication ceremonies. They provided music and singing as the offering began (v. 27). Hezekiah stationed the Levites in the temple of the Lord with their cymbals, harps, and lyres as Solomon had done at the original dedication of the temple (7:6). In his day David and Gad, the king's seer, and Nathan, the prophet, had prescribed music for their worship (1 Chr 29:29). The Levites stood ready with David's instruments and the priests, as usual, had their trumpets (5:12). In effect, Hezekiah restored the pure worship associated with David and Solomon.

29:27–28 The occasion was solemn and grand. Hezekiah had fulfilled his covenant, and worship of the true God in the manner he had prescribed resumed.

29:29 Yahweh, not the king, was Lord here. Hezekiah bowed in worship with everyone else.

29:30 This verse is simply a summarizing conclusion. The associated joyous response, singing praises with gladness as they bowed their heads and worshiped, was a regular response on such occasions.

[31]Then Hezekiah said, "You have now dedicated yourselves to the LORD. Come and bring sacrifices and thank offerings to the temple of the LORD." So the assembly brought sacrifices and thank offerings, and all whose hearts were willing brought burnt offerings.

[32]The number of burnt offerings the assembly brought was seventy bulls, a hundred rams and two hundred male lambs—all of them for burnt offerings to the LORD. [33]The animals consecrated as sacrifices amounted to six hundred bulls and three thousand sheep and goats. [34]The priests, however, were too few to skin all the burnt offerings; so their kinsmen the Levites helped them until the task was finished and until other priests had been consecrated, for the Levites had been more conscientious in consecrating themselves than the priests had been. [35]There were burnt offerings in abundance, together with the fat of the fellowship offerings and the drink offerings that accompanied the burnt offerings.

So the service of the temple of the LORD was reestablished. [36]Hezekiah and all the people rejoiced at what God had brought about for his people, because it was done so quickly.

THE PARTICIPATION OF THE PEOPLE (29:31–36).   Following the formal acts of sin offering and the rededication of the sanctuary, the king invited the people to bring their own sacrifices and thank-offerings to the temple. The regular temple services were now renewed (v. 35b).

29:31 Now that the "whole assembly" had dedicated themselves to the Lord verbally, it was time for them to express their faith by bringing sacrifices. The Hebrew idiom for "dedicated yourselves" is "you have filled your hand." It is ordinarily used for priestly investiture (13:9), but here it applies to the whole assembly and not just to the priests. The same idiom is used in this wider sense in 1 Chr 29:5. The word for "sacrifices" here ($z\check{e}b\bar{a}\d{h}\hat{i}m$) probably refers to fellowship offerings in general (v. 35) of which thank offerings form a subgroup (Lev 7:11–18).[8] The responsiveness of the people recalls events at the time of Moses, David, and Solomon (Exod 36:6–7; 1 Chr 29:1,5–9; 2 Chr 7:7). Here was a pattern to be followed by the Chronicler's postexilic audience.

29:32 Burnt offerings were intended to express total self-giving worship of God. Unlike the fellowship offerings, in which the offerer shared, the burnt offerings were given to God in their entirety and completely burned on the altar.

---

[8] Williamson, *1 and 2 Chronicles,* 359.

29:33 "The animals consecrated as sacrifices" may have been the fellowship offerings referred to in vv. 31,35. If so, the worshipers consumed much of these offerings.

29:34 According to Leviticus 1, the offerer had to skin (flay) the beast, not the priest. Apparently the large numbers of offerings precluded having the courtyard filled with laypeople doing this work. Here is another word of commendation for the Levites from the Chronicler. Apparently the priests in particular had grown spiritually lax during the days of Ahaz, and many were slow to respond to the revival under Hezekiah.

29:35 As a final comment the writer notes the abundance of burnt offerings and that they were accompanied by fellowship and drink offerings. It was, indeed, a large task. But it was all-important for the reestablishing of the temple of the Lord.

29:36 As on various other important cultic occasions, the king and all the people rejoiced. The credit for what had taken place was given to God, who still cared it about his people. Another important feature of the rededication of the temple was that it was all done so quickly, in less than three weeks (vv. 17,20), dating from the first day of Hezekiah's first regnal year. Judah had plummeted morally and spiritually under Ahaz and had become like the Northern Kingdom. But God had retrieved his people.

(2) The Celebration of the Passover by "All Israel" (30:1–31:1)

With the restoration of the temple now achieved, Hezekiah undertook strenuous efforts to reunite "all Israel," both south and north, in national worship, which the Chronicler centered on the observance of the Passover. It is the dominant theme of the early part of the chapter (vv. 1–13) and is prominent in the latter section of chap. 30 (note especially 30:25; 31:1) but is present also in the central section of the chapter, which deals with the celebration itself. Hezekiah is portrayed here as a second Solomon (v. 26), and the celebration of the Passover is a watershed between the disruption of Israel after Solomon's death and a return to the spiritual conditions that existed in Solomon's day.

Historically, Hezekiah's particular interest in the north is reasonable. The time was opportune for a probe into the north. The Northern Kingdom had fallen to Assyria, and Assyria itself was preoccupied for a time with events in other parts of their own extensive empire.[9] It is of some interest that Hezekiah named his son Manasseh (32:33). This name, linked with that of

[9] D. J. Wiseman, ed., *Peoples of Old Testament Times* (London: Oxford University Press, 1973), 182.

Ephraim, represented the northern tribes (30:1; 31:1).

The likelihood and nature of Hezekiah's Passover has been the subject of much debate among scholars.[10] A widely held view, which is not espoused in this commentary, is that a Passover celebration at the central sanctuary did not occur until the time of Josiah (2 Kgs 23:21–23. It seems reasonable to argue, however, that the Chronicler had access to an account of such an event and that Hezekiah did celebrate the Passover in Jerusalem. As Dillard has argued, the deviations of Hezekiah's Passover from orthodox practice (the delay in its observance, participation by some who were ceremonially unclean, and the extension of the feast to a second week) would be highly unlikely if he had fabricated the account.[11] It was part of his strenuous effort to reunite the separated people of the north and the south in worship, a first step toward political and national unity. The preoccupation of modern commentators with the question of the historicity of the Passover often has led to their missing the significance of the event for the Chronicler.

The narrative falls readily into three parts: (1) the preparations for the Passover (30:1–12), (2) the celebration of the Feast of Unleavened Bread and the Passover (30:13–22), and (3) the second period of celebration (30:23–27).

¹Hezekiah sent word to all Israel and Judah and also wrote letters to Ephraim and Manasseh, inviting them to come to the temple of the LORD in Jerusalem and celebrate the Passover to the LORD, the God of Israel. ²The king and his officials and the whole assembly in Jerusalem decided to celebrate the Passover in the second month. ³They had not been able to celebrate it at the regular time because not enough priests had consecrated themselves and the people had not assembled in Jerusalem. ⁴The plan seemed right both to the king and to the whole assembly. ⁵They decided to send a proclamation throughout Israel, from Beersheba to Dan, calling the people to come to Jerusalem and celebrate the Passover to the LORD, the God of Israel. It had not been celebrated in large numbers according to what was written.

⁶At the king's command, couriers went throughout Israel and Judah with letters from the king and from his officials, which read:

"People of Israel, return to the LORD, the God of Abraham, Isaac and Israel, that he may return to you who are left, who have escaped from the hand of the kings of Assyria. ⁷Do not be like your fathers and brothers, who were unfaithful to the LORD, the God of their fathers, so that he made them an object of horror, as you see. ⁸Do not be stiff-necked, as your fathers were; submit to the LORD. Come to the sanctuary, which he has consecrated forever. Serve the LORD your God, so that his fierce anger will turn away from you. ⁹If

---

[10] Useful outlines of the issues appear in Dillard, *2 Chronicles,* 240–43; Williamson, *1 and 2 Chronicles,* 360–65; Myers, *II Chronicles,* 176–78.

[11] Dillard, *2 Chronicles,* 240.

you return to the LORD, then your brothers and your children will be shown compassion by their captors and will come back to this land, for the LORD your God is gracious and compassionate. He will not turn his face from you if you return to him."

¹⁰The couriers went from town to town in Ephraim and Manasseh, as far as Zebulun, but the people scorned and ridiculed them. ¹¹Nevertheless, some men of Asher, Manasseh and Zebulun humbled themselves and went to Jerusalem. ¹²Also in Judah the hand of God was on the people to give them unity of mind to carry out what the king and his officials had ordered, following the word of the LORD.

THE PREPARATIONS FOR THE PASSOVER (30:1–12).   **30:1**   This verse is a summary statement introducing the entire narrative. An oral proclamation was issued accompanied by letters to the northern tribes (cf. Esth 1:22). The expression "all Israel" here refers to the northern territory. That such an invitation could be sent indicates that Assyria had not maintained tight control in these areas. Otherwise such an invitation could have been seen as a rebellious act. Little wonder that Hezekiah saw the time as opportune for the reunification of God's people.

30:2   A Passover celebration in the second month was irregular (Exod 12:2; Lev 23:5; Num 9:1–5), but not without precedence. Two reasons are given for this in v. 3.

30:3–4   Their delay was partly because not enough priests had consecrated themselves (cf. 29:34). The second reason for being a month late was that the people had not assembled in Jerusalem. But the law allowed for a Passover in the second month for those who had become unclean through contact with a corpse or who had been on a journey (Num 9:9–12). These exceptions for individuals were here extrapolated into principles that could apply to the whole nation. Also the Northern Kingdom probably had fallen behind by one month since Jeroboam I (1 Kgs 12:32–33) had disturbed the religious calendar.¹²

30:5   The proclamation was sent throughout all Israel from Beersheba to Dan, the ideal extent of all Israel (1 Chr 21:2). The Passover was kept "to the LORD [Yahweh], the God of Israel," a significant phrase. Yahweh was the God of the whole people Israel, south and north. The phrase "in large numbers according to what was written" is difficult to interpret (cf. NJKV, "for a long time in the prescribed manner"). It may mean "en masse as prescribed," that is, as a pilgrimage festival (cf. Deut 16:5–8). Or it could mean that this was the first observance of Passover as a united people since Solomon's day.

---

¹² See S. Talmon, "Divergencies in Calendar Reckoning in Ephraim and Judah," *VT* 8 (1958): 48–74.

30:6 The use of the verb "return" (*šub*) is the first of many words repeated in this passage from 2 Chr 7:14 ("return" in vv. 6,9, "humbled" in v. 11, "prayed" in v. 18, "seeking" in v. 19, and "heard" and "healed" in v. 20). Dillard notes, "The author seems to go out of his way to introduce the language of that text."[13] Williamson proposes that the verb sub is used with the same theological significance as it has in 7:14 elsewhere only in 15:4; 30:6,9; and 36:13.

The letter is quoted (vv. 6–9) and is somewhat like the so-called "Levitical sermon" in 29:5–11. It could apply to Judah as well as to Israel since Judah also had known desolation (v. 7), had experienced God's fierce anger (v. 8), had been captive to foreigners (v. 9; cf. 28:5; 29:6,8–10), and had escaped from the hand of the kings of Assyria (v. 6). The designation "you who are left, who have escaped" would have conveyed simultaneously a sense of fear often experienced by those who have just had a narrow escape and also a sense of gratitude that God had delivered them. They should have identified easily with those escapees from Egypt who first celebrated the Passover, as should the Chronicler's own audience of postexilic Judah.

30:7 Hezekiah exhorted the people on the basis of the clear results of their predecessors' apostasy (cf. 29:6–9). His message was very similar to the opening words of Zechariah in Zech 1:2–6.

30:8–9 Israel had a long history of being "stiff-necked" (cf. Exod 32:9; 34:9; Deut 9:6; 31:27; 2 Kgs 17:14; 2 Chr 36:13), that is, unresponsive to God. But there were always a few who would "submit" (lit., "give the hand") to the Lord and grasp his extended hand of mercy and forgiveness. If they would only "return" (*šub*) to him he would "turn" (*šub*) back to them and those dispersed by the Assyrians could "come back" (*šub*) home. Sometimes people refuse to repent out of a sense of hopelessness, but Hezekiah reminds that it is never too late to return to God. Repentance is a major theme of the prophets.[14] If, however, the people refused to repent, the same troubles that afflicted their parents would also come upon them.

30:10–12 In general, the people in the north did not receive the envoys, although there were exceptions. Returning to Jerusalem after so many years of independence required more humility than the majority of northerners could muster (cf. 2 Kgs 5:11–12). How often pride has expressed itself in scorn and ridicule (cf. Deut 28:37; Pss 69; 123; Luke 23:11). The positive response of those in Israel as well as Judah was due to the "hand of God," as are all true revivals. The result was a spiritual unity that had not existed for many years (cf. 1 Chr 12:38).

---

[13] Dillard, *2 Chronicles,* 226.

[14] W. L. Holladay, *The Root šûbh in the Old Testament* (Leiden: Brill, 1958).

¹³A very large crowd of people assembled in Jerusalem to celebrate the Feast of Unleavened Bread in the second month. ¹⁴They removed the altars in Jerusalem and cleared away the incense altars and threw them into the Kidron Valley.

¹⁵They slaughtered the Passover lamb on the fourteenth day of the second month. The priests and the Levites were ashamed and consecrated themselves and brought burnt offerings to the temple of the LORD. ¹⁶Then they took up their regular positions as prescribed in the Law of Moses the man of God. The priests sprinkled the blood handed to them by the Levites. ¹⁷Since many in the crowd had not consecrated themselves, the Levites had to kill the Passover lambs for all those who were not ceremonially clean and could not consecrate [their lambs] to the LORD. ¹⁸Although most of the many people who came from Ephraim, Manasseh, Issachar and Zebulun had not purified themselves, yet they ate the Passover, contrary to what was written. But Hezekiah prayed for them, saying, "May the LORD, who is good, pardon everyone ¹⁹who sets his heart on seeking God—the LORD, the God of his fathers—even if he is not clean according to the rules of the sanctuary." ²⁰And the LORD heard Hezekiah and healed the people.

²¹The Israelites who were present in Jerusalem celebrated the Feast of Unleavened Bread for seven days with great rejoicing, while the Levites and priests sang to the LORD every day, accompanied by the LORD'S instruments of praise.

²²Hezekiah spoke encouragingly to all the Levites, who showed good understanding of the service of the LORD. For the seven days they ate their assigned portion and offered fellowship offerings and praised the LORD, the God of their fathers.

THE CELEBRATION OF THE FEAST OF UNLEAVENED BREAD AND THE PASSOVER (30:13–22).   **30:13**   At this point in the narrative reference to the Feast of Unleavened Bread is made (vv. 13,21) although the Passover is referred to in vv. 15,17–18 (cf. vv. 1–2,5). The close association of the two festivals allowed either designation. The change here may reflect a different source.[15]

30:14   As Hezekiah's reform proceeded, it was clear that he would need to remove the altars in Jerusalem set up by Ahaz (28:24) as well as the altars on the high places for burning incense (28:4,25; 14:5). These the Levites threw into the Kidron Valley (cf. 15:16; 29:16; 2 Kgs 23:4,6,12).

30:15   After thus removing the pagan altars, the people, that is, the laypeople of v. 13, killed the Passover lamb on the fourteenth day of the second month, which, as we have seen, was a deviation from normal practice. Evidently the priests and Levites had neglected to make necessary preparations

---

[15] Dillard, *2 Chronicles*, 245.

for Passover by offering the appropriate sacrifices of cleansing. They were put to shame by the people's zeal. "Popular enthusiasm, indeed, has often outstripped—even found itself in conflict with—the ecclesiastical authorities."[16]

30:16–17 The Chronicler delighted to recount that the law of Moses was being followed. However, normally laymen would have sacrificed their own Passover lambs for their own households and handed the blood to the priests (Deut 16:5–6). Since many were unclean, however, the Levites had to do it for them.

30:18–20 Most of the people from Ephraim, Manasseh, and Issachar were not ritually purified, due either to ignorance or lack of time. Although God's law was binding, there also was some flexibility in extraordinary circumstances. Hezekiah offered a special prayer on their behalf, asking that God would pardon all those whose hearts were ready to seek God even if they were ritually unclean according to the ceremonial purification laws of the sanctuary. Prayer was effective in overriding purely ritual considerations according to the Chronicler. For all his concern with the cult and its personnel, the Chronicler was not content with a religion of mere external correctness but delighted in the one who "sets his heart on seeking God." In hearing Hezekiah and healing the people, God was answering Solomon's prayer as he promised in 7:14.

30:21 This verse summarizes the proceedings of the festival but concentrates on the Feast of Unleavened Bread. The seven days of celebratory singing implies that when a people returns to God their worship is a thing of joy and beauty.

30:22 The Levites continued the festival for seven days and showed great skill in serving the Lord, for which Hezekiah commended them.

[23]The whole assembly then agreed to celebrate the festival seven more days; so for another seven days they celebrated joyfully. [24]Hezekiah king of Judah provided a thousand bulls and seven thousand sheep and goats for the assembly, and the officials provided them with a thousand bulls and ten thousand sheep and goats. A great number of priests consecrated themselves. [25]The entire assembly of Judah rejoiced, along with the priests and Levites and all who had assembled from Israel, including the aliens who had come from Israel and those who lived in Judah. [26]There was great joy in Jerusalem, for since the days of Solomon son of David king of Israel there had been nothing like this in Jerusalem. [27]The priests and the Levites stood to bless the people, and God heard them, for their prayer reached heaven, his holy dwelling place.

[1]When all this had ended, the Israelites who were there went out to the

---

[16]McConville, *I & II Chronicles*, 236–37.

towns of Judah, smashed the sacred stones and cut down the Asherah poles.
They destroyed the high places and the altars throughout Judah and Benjamin
and in Ephraim and Manasseh. After they had destroyed all of them, the Israelites returned to their own towns and to their own property.

THE SECOND PERIOD OF CELEBRATION (30:23–31:1). The celebrations continued for an additional seven days. This narrative provides a further comparison with Solomon (7:8–10), as v. 26 implies. The phrase "the
whole assembly" occurs in Chronicles only in connection with David (1 Chr
13:2,4; 29:1,10,20), Solomon (2 Chr 1:3; 6:3,12-13), Joash's coronation
(2 Chr 23:3), and Hezekiah (2 Chr 29:28; 30:2,4,23,25).

30:23 The whole assembly is further defined in v. 25. The decision to
extend the festival was in effect unanimous and spontaneous. In the days of
Solomon at the original dedication of the temple there was an extended festival (7:8–9). Here is a further illustration of the joy that was displayed in
Israel on major occasions (1 Chr 29:22; 2 Chr 7:8–10).

30:24 Festivals in which a large number of people participated required
large quantities of food (cp. 7:5). More priests consecrated themselves and
thus made amends for early dilatoriness.

30:25–26 It is of some interest to note that non-Israelite resident aliens
who had adopted Israel's faith shared in the Passover (Exod 12:48–49).

30:27 The phrase in NIV "the priests and Levites" lacks the "and" in the
MT and could be translated "the Levitical priests." This phrase appears in
Deut 17:9, and the same expression occurs in 2 Chr 23:18. Some commentators have drawn attention to what appears to be the language of Deuteronomy in Chronicles. The priestly blessing of the people goes back to Num
6:22–27. The request for a divine response comes often in Solomon's prayer
of dedication in 2 Chronicles 6 (cf. vv. 19–40), and God assured him that he
heard (7:12). God also is described as one who hears in 1 Chr 28:8; 2 Chr
30:20; 34:27.

31:1 Before the people returned home, they destroyed the pagan cult
items in the towns of Judah and Benjamin and also in Ephraim and
Manasseh. The parallel account in 2 Kgs 18:4 refers to the destruction of the
bronze serpent, Nehushtan, that Moses had made (Num 21:9) when fiery ser-
pents bit the Israelites in the wilderness. This incident is omitted, but additional details are given. Hezekiah was fostering some form of cult
centralization, designed no doubt to undo the work of Jeroboam I and to
reunite the people around Jerusalem as the religious centre of the nation.
This movement was taken further under King Josiah (chaps. 34–35).

(3) Reform Activities (31:2–21)

After the cleansing of the land (31:1) arrangements had to be made for the collection and storage of tithes and offerings for the support of the priests and Levites. Chapter 31 is concerned with such matters.

²Hezekiah assigned the priests and Levites to divisions—each of them according to their duties as priests or Levites—to offer burnt offerings and fellowship offerings, to minister, to give thanks and to sing praises at the gates of the LORD'S dwelling. ³The king contributed from his own possessions for the morning and evening burnt offerings and for the burnt offerings on the Sabbaths, New Moons and appointed feasts as written in the Law of the LORD.

VARIOUS ASSIGNMENTS (31:2–3). **31:2** The priests and Levites were appointed to their divisions. It was a return to the order destroyed by Ahaz but set up originally by Solomon according to the commandment of Moses and following the ordinance of David (8:13–14). The Lord's "dwelling" here is literally "camp," a figurative expression for the temple based, perhaps, on the picture of the tabernacle in the wilderness (Num 2). Compare 1 Chr 9:18–19. The Greek reads "courts of the temple."

31:3 Just as David and Solomon provided for the temple from their own wealth (1 Chr 29:1–5; 2 Chr 9:10–11), so did Hezekiah. The likeness of Hezekiah to David and Solomon is further illustrated by Hezekiah's oversight of the cultic personnel (2 Chr 8:14; cf. 1 Chr 23–26) and his care in following the "Law of the LORD" (1 Chr 16:40; 22:12; 30:16; 31:4,21; cf. 2 Chr 12:1; 17:9; 19:8; 23:18; 34:14–15; 35:26).

⁴He ordered the people living in Jerusalem to give the portion due the priests and Levites so they could devote themselves to the Law of the LORD. ⁵As soon as the order went out, the Israelites generously gave the firstfruits of their grain, new wine, oil and honey and all that the fields produced. They brought a great amount, a tithe of everything. ⁶The men of Israel and Judah who lived in the towns of Judah also brought a tithe of their herds and flocks and a tithe of the holy things dedicated to the LORD their God, and they piled them in heaps. ⁷They began doing this in the third month and finished in the seventh month. ⁸When Hezekiah and his officials came and saw the heaps, they praised the LORD and blessed his people Israel.

⁹Hezekiah asked the priests and Levites about the heaps; ¹⁰and Azariah the chief priest, from the family of Zadok, answered, "Since the people began to bring their contributions to the temple of the LORD, we have had enough to eat and plenty to spare, because the LORD has blessed his people, and this great amount is left over."

¹¹Hezekiah gave orders to prepare storerooms in the temple of the LORD, and this was done. ¹²Then they faithfully brought in the contributions, tithes and dedicated gifts. Conaniah, a Levite, was in charge of these things, and his

brother Shimei was next in rank. [13]Jehiel, Azaziah, Nahath, Asahel, Jerimoth, Jozabad, Eliel, Ismakiah, Mahath and Benaiah were supervisors under Conaniah and Shimei his brother, by appointment of King Hezekiah and Azariah the official in charge of the temple of God.

[14]Kore son of Imnah the Levite, keeper of the East Gate, was in charge of the freewill offerings given to God, distributing the contributions made to the LORD and also the consecrated gifts. [15]Eden, Miniamin, Jeshua, Shemaiah, Amariah and Shecaniah assisted him faithfully in the towns of the priests, distributing to their fellow priests according to their divisions, old and young alike.

[16]In addition, they distributed to the males three years old or more whose names were in the genealogical records—all who would enter the temple of the LORD to perform the daily duties of their various tasks, according to their responsibilities and their divisions. [17]And they distributed to the priests enrolled by their families in the genealogical records and likewise to the Levites twenty years old or more, according to their responsibilities and their divisions. [18]They included all the little ones, the wives, and the sons and daughters of the whole community listed in these genealogical records. For they were faithful in consecrating themselves.

[19]As for the priests, the descendants of Aaron, who lived on the farm lands around their towns or in any other towns, men were designated by name to distribute portions to every male among them and to all who were recorded in the genealogies of the Levites.

PROVISION FOR SUPPORT OF RELIGIOUS PERSONNEL (31:4–19). **31:4** Hezekiah restored the system of offerings that supported the priests and Levites (Lev 6:14–7:36; Num 18:8–32; Deut 14:27–29; 18:1–8; 26:1–15), and which Ahaz apparently had stopped. These offerings also were subject to neglect in the postexilic era (Neh 13:10–13; Mal 3:8–12). The command was issued in the first instance to the people living in Jerusalem. The portion due to the priests and Levites consisted of tithes, firstfruits, and parts of some of the sacrifices. The freedom to study "the Law of the LORD" was not a matter of academic leisure for the priests; rather, it was crucial for the well-being of the whole nation that the clergy thoroughly understand what God requires (cf. Mal 2:6–7). Similarly, any church today that does not afford its pastor the opportunity for study and growth will suffer for it.

31:5 Evidently "Israelites" here includes many northerners. It was forbidden in the law to eat the tithe of grain, wine, and oil (Deut 12:17). These commodities were to be brought in kind to the sanctuary. The best of the oil, the wine, and the grain, the firstfruits of what Israel gave to the Lord, was for the priests (Num 18:12–13); and the tithe was for the Levites (Num 18:21; cf Deut 18:4). Honey was excluded from burnt offerings (Lev 2:11–12) but was brought as part of the firstfruits. The generosity with which these gifts were given also is stressed in 1 Chr 29:14 (cf. Deut 15:10; Ps 37:21,26; Prov 11:25; 22:9).

31:6 The tithe here refers to the tithe of cattle and sheep as distinct from produce. To bring actual livestock to the sanctuary was not practical for everyone. If the way was too long (Deut 14:24–26), provision was made to turn the tithe into money and take this to the place the Lord appointed. It is clear here that many of "the men of Israel" were those who came from the north and had settled in the towns of Judah.

31:7 The amassing of the firstfruits and tithes continued from the time of the Feast of Pentecost and the grain harvest through the time of the Feast of Tabernacles and of the fruit and vine harvests (Exod 23:16).

31:8 When a leader has determined to try to provoke his people to return to God, nothing can stir his heart as much as a willing, positive response. Like Jesus at the well in Samaria, Hezekiah here had food and drink of a spiritual kind (John 4:32).

31:9–10 The source of the people's generosity is acknowledged to be the Lord's blessing (cf. 1 Chr 29:14). The chief priest (i.e., the high priest), Azariah, is not the same as the priest of 26:17, but the practice of naming a child after his grandfather was well known. This Azariah is not mentioned in the list of high priests in the genealogical lists of 1 Chr 6:3–15.

31:11 The narrative here commences to detail the arrangements made for the collection and storage of the tithes and other contributions. Nothing in the text indicates whether new storerooms had to be built or whether existing facilities were adapted and reused.

31:12–13 These names are for the most part well known elsewhere, chiefly in Levitical lists. King Hezekiah had a hands-on involvement, being involved in the appointment of these officials.

31:14–15 Kore the Levite, keeper of the east gate, an important official (cf. 1 Chr 9:18), had six helpers named. Their task was to arrange for the distribution of the freewill offerings made to the Lord and also the consecrated gifts to their fellow priests in the towns according to their divisions, with no distinction of age.

31:16 The distribution included all males "three years old and more." The lower cutoff point was from the time they were weaned. Some emend this figure to "thirty," the age at which they began their priestly duties.

31:17 The priests were organized by families in the genealogical records. The Levites shared in the distribution and were divided on the basis of their duties and their divisions, twenty years old and upwards (on the variation in age for Levites see comments at 1 Chr 23:3–6).

31:18 The children were not neglected in the distribution, nor were the wives, their sons, and their daughters. This was for the whole community, those who lived in Jerusalem and those who resided in the cities of the priests.

31:19   The priests in the rural areas were not forgotten. Hezekiah's reformation was nothing if not thorough.

20This is what Hezekiah did throughout Judah, doing what was good and right and faithful before the LORD his God. 21In everything that he undertook in the service of God's temple and in obedience to the law and the commands, he sought his God and worked wholeheartedly. And so he prospered.

CHARACTERIZATION OF HEZEKIAH (31:20–21).   **31:20–21** L. C. Allen suggests that these verses resume and expand on 29:1–2 and so mark off chaps. 29–31 as demonstrating Hezekiah's righteousness. The last clause of v. 21, he says, introduces chap. 32 and also is resumed at 32:30—"He succeeded in everything he undertook."[17] Thus Hezekiah serves as prime example of the Chronicler's "retribution theology." We are reminded again of the parallel between Hezekiah and Solomon (7:11). Consequently he prospered in all that he did.

(4) Hezekiah's Victory, Illness, and Faithfulness (32:2–21)

Other aspects of Hezekiah's reign were reserved for this final chapter because the Chronicler was anxious to give the first place in his account to Hezekiah's reform program. A traumatic experience in Hezekiah's reign was the threat of King Sennacherib of Assyria. In the King's account this incident is placed in the forefront of the account where little notice is taken of the reforms of the king (2 Kgs 18:4).

1After all that Hezekiah had so faithfully done, Sennacherib king of Assyria came and invaded Judah. He laid siege to the fortified cities, thinking to conquer them for himself. 2When Hezekiah saw that Sennacherib had come and that he intended to make war on Jerusalem, 3he consulted with his officials and military staff about blocking off the water from the springs outside the city, and they helped him. 4A large force of men assembled, and they blocked all the springs and the stream that flowed through the land. "Why should the kings of Assyria come and find plenty of water?" they said. 5Then he worked hard repairing all the broken sections of the wall and building towers on it. He built another wall outside that one and reinforced the supporting terraces of the City of David. He also made large numbers of weapons and shields.

6He appointed military officers over the people and assembled them before him in the square at the city gate and encouraged them with these words: 7"Be strong and courageous. Do not be afraid or discouraged because of the king of Assyria and the vast army with him, for there is a greater power with us than

---

[17] L. C. Allen, *1, 2 Chronicles,* CC (Dallas: Word, 1987), 366.

with him. [8]With him is only the arm of flesh, but with us is the LORD our God
to help us and to fight our battles." And the people gained confidence from
what Hezekiah the king of Judah said.

PREPARATIONS FOR SENNACHERIB'S INVASION (32:1–8). **32:1** In
view of the Chronicler's retribution theology, this verse is striking after such
a glowing account of faithfulness. But the invasion of Sennacherib is reminiscent of the invasion of Zerah in Asa's day (14:9–15), where trust in God
led to victory. God does not promise that his faithful ones will not have trials
but that he will not forsake them. The details supplied by the Chronicler are
somewhat abbreviated by comparison with the accounts in 2 Kgs 18–19 and
Isa 36–37. There is no mention here of the siege of Jerusalem, of Hezekiah
paying tribute, or of Sennacherib's capture of many towns in Judah. Only
after Hezekiah had carried out so many faithful acts did the events of this
chapter unfold. Faithful deeds are followed by divine help and deliverance.

According to Sennacherib's annals, he conquered forty-six Judahite cities.[18] At the same time, it certainly is true that Sennacherib "thought" he
would take Jerusalem, but he failed to do so. The Kings record gives a date,
"the fourteenth year of King Hezekiah (2 Kgs 18:13), but the Chronicler was
more concerned about theology. He was concerned to show how deliverance
from Assyria followed Hezekiah's reforms, regardless of specific chronological details (31:20).

32:2–4 It is no denial of one's trust in God if one makes certain precau-
tionary preparations. "Pray to God and keep your powder dry" is a wise
response in the face of danger at any time. Blocking off the water from the
springs outside the city was a wise defensive measure because a plentiful
water supply made the task of invaders easier.

The exact identity of the springs referred to is not given, but v. 30 may
shed some light on the question. At one stage Hezekiah dug the famous
"Hezekiah's tunnel," which took water from the Gihon spring into the city
(2 Kgs 20:20). This may be the channel referred to in v. 30. But there was an
earlier system that took water from the Gihon spring round to the south of the
city, remains of which can still be seen. It was partly an open channel and
partly tunneled with outlets to take the water down into the Kidron Valley for
irrigation. Perhaps "the waters of Shiloah that flow gently" (Isa 8:6) may represent this system. Another source of water was En-Rogel to the south of the
city. Uncertainty prevails about the precise nature of Jerusalem's water supply at this time, and considerable scholarly discussion has grown up over the
years.[19]

---

[18]*ANET,* 288.
[19]See Williamson, *1 and 2 Chronicles,* 380–81; Dillard, *2 Chronicles,* 256–57.

32:5 The countermeasures taken by Hezekiah were threefold. He had to care for the water problem, both from a defensive and offensive point of view. Then he had to repair weak spots in the wall, erect towers, construct an outside wall, and build up the Millo, that is, "the supporting terraces" as David and Solomon once had done (1 Chr 11:8; 1 Kgs 11:27). There is good archaeological evidence of considerable wall-building activity in Jerusalem. Part of a massive wall called the "Broad Wall" has recently been discovered in the modern Jewish quarter of the Old City of Jerusalem that has been dated to the days of Hezekiah.[20] K. M. Kenyon has explained the nature of the Millo as terraces expanding the city and supporting structures on the eastern slope of Jerusalem above the Kidron Valley.[21] Finally, Hezekiah reorganized the army, placed the nation on a wartime footing, and supplied his forces with weapons of war.

32:6–8 Hezekiah appointed officers over the people (a citizens' conscript army), and assembled his troops before him in the square at the city gate. In a typical speech like that delivered before a battle (20:15–17; cf. 13:4–12), Hezekiah addressed the defenders of Jerusalem. The speech was comprised of phrases and concepts found elsewhere in Old Testament contexts (Josh 10:25; Deut 31:6; 2 Kgs 6:16; Isa 7:14; 8:8–10; 31:3; Jer 17:5). In this speech there is no reference to Egyptian help (see 2 Kgs 18:20–25). Despite all the military preparations, Hezekiah urged the people to be courageous in the Lord who was their real "secret weapon" against the apparently overwhelming force of Assyria.

[9]**Later, when Sennacherib king of Assyria and all his forces were laying siege to Lachish, he sent his officers to Jerusalem with this message for Hezekiah king of Judah and for all the people of Judah who were there:**

[10]**"This is what Sennacherib king of Assyria says: On what are you basing your confidence, that you remain in Jerusalem under siege? [11]When Hezekiah says, 'The LORD our God will save us from the hand of the king of Assyria,' he is misleading you, to let you die of hunger and thirst. [12]Did not Hezekiah himself remove this god's high places and altars, saying to Judah and Jerusalem, 'You must worship before one altar and burn sacrifices on it'?**

[13]**"Do you not know what I and my fathers have done to all the peoples of the other lands? Were the gods of those nations ever able to deliver their land from my hand? [14]Who of all the gods of these nations that my fathers destroyed has been able to save his people from me? How then can your god**

---

[20] N. Avigad, "Jerusalem—'The City Full of People,'" ed. H. Shanks and B. Mazor, Eng. ed. (Washington, D.C./Jerusalem: Biblical Archaeological Society/Israel Exploration Society, 1984), 133–34. This was a massive wall of unhewn stones averaging seven meters thick that enclosed the pool of Siloam.

[21] K. M. Kenyon, *Archaeology in the Holy Land*, 5th. ed. (Nashville: Nelson, 1985), 237.

deliver you from my hand? [15]Now do not let Hezekiah deceive you and mislead you like this. **Do not believe him, for no god of any nation or kingdom has been able to deliver his people from my hand or the hand of my fathers. How much less will your god deliver you from my hand!"**

[16]Sennacherib's officers spoke further against the LORD God and against his servant Hezekiah. [17]The king also wrote letters insulting the LORD, the God of Israel, and saying this against him: "Just as the gods of the peoples of the other lands did not rescue their people from my hand, so the god of Hezekiah will not rescue his people from my hand." [18]Then they called out in Hebrew to the people of Jerusalem who were on the wall, to terrify them and make them afraid in order to capture the city. [19]They spoke about the God of Jerusalem as they did about the gods of the other peoples of the world—the work of men's hands.

SENNACHERIB'S TAUNTS (32:9–19). **32:9** Sennacherib's strategy was to secure the coastal road against any invasion from Egypt (2 Kgs 19:8). A significant strong point was Lachish to the southwest of Jerusalem.[22] While Sennacherib was laying siege to Lachish he engaged in a piece of psychological warfare by sending messengers to Jerusalem to intimidate Hezekiah and Jerusalem.[23]

32:11–15 Sennacherib's message was typical of those who place their faith in human power rather than the invisible power of God. Like many such people, he considered faith in the living God to be the same as all "religion," and he mocked the reforms of Hezekiah as meaningless in the face the power of the sword he carried. There is great irony in these verses. Whereas Sennacherib is engaging in psychological warfare, he is doing so by quoting truths thinking they are lies. The phrase "the LORD our God will save us from the King of Assyria" is truth, but Sennacherib quoted it as if it were an impossibility. Similarly, in v. 12 Hezekiah's reforms were not against the wishes of this "god" but were conducted in fear of the Lord. Sennacherib alluded to history in vv. 13–14 and the fact that no god had stopped them yet. The problem for Sennacherib was that he had never confronted the One true God, Yahweh, the God of Israel. When he did, he returned defeated and disgraced (v. 21).

32:16–17 Sennacherib's propaganda machine was as efficient and persistent as any in the modern world. All of this was intended to intimidate Hezekiah and the people of Jerusalem and to equate their God with the pow-

---

[22] Sennacherib commemorated the siege of Lachish with a mural over fifty feet long carved in stone in one of his palaces. On the question of two campaigns against Jerusalem by Sennacherib, see J. Bright, *A History of Israel*, 3d ed. (Philadelphia: Westminster, 1981), 298–309.

[23] Dillard, *2 Chronicles*, 257.

erless gods of the peoples of other lands.

32:18–19 According to 2 Kgs 18:28 it was Rabshakeh, one of Sennacherib's officials, who sought to intimidate the people with his propaganda. The Chronicler comments that the propagandists did not understand the difference between the true God and man-made religion ("the work of men's hands").

[20]**King Hezekiah and the prophet Isaiah son of Amoz cried out in prayer to heaven about this.** [21]**And the LORD sent an angel, who annihilated all the fighting men and the leaders and officers in the camp of the Assyrian king. So he withdrew to his own land in disgrace. And when he went into the temple of his god, some of his sons cut him down with the sword.**

[22]**So the LORD saved Hezekiah and the people of Jerusalem from the hand of Sennacherib king of Assyria and from the hand of all others. He took care of them on every side.** [23]**Many brought offerings to Jerusalem for the LORD and valuable gifts for Hezekiah king of Judah. From then on he was highly regarded by all the nations.**

HEZEKIAH'S DELIVERANCE (32:20–23). **32:20** Hezekiah and the prophet Isaiah responded to human threats with prayer to God. The Kings account is given in 2 Kgs 19:2–4,14–15. The action of Hezekiah and Isaiah follows the advice of 2 Chr 7:14 for God's people in trouble to pray and seek his face.

32:21 A divine intervention ensued, a vindication of the faith of Hezekiah and Isaiah. The Lord sent an angel who annihilated all the fighting men and the leaders and officers of the camp of the Assyrian king. Sennacherib withdrew in disgrace and returned to Assyria, where he met his death at the hands of plotting sons. That God delivered his people from Sennacherib is a fulfillment of the promise made at the Solomonic dedication of the temple (2 Chr 6:28–31; 7:13–15).

32:22–23 Further evidence of blessing for a faithful king was that many brought an offering for the Lord and valuable gifts for Hezekiah. A final indication of the blessing of God on him was that he was held in high regard by all the nations. This episode was another example of national deliverance and prosperity as a reward for faithfulness (cf. Asa, 14:1,5–7; 15:15; Jehoshaphat, 20:30; and particularly Solomon, 1 Chr 22:9).

[24]**In those days Hezekiah became ill and was at the point of death. He prayed to the LORD, who answered him and gave him a miraculous sign.** [25]**But Hezekiah's heart was proud and he did not respond to the kindness shown him; therefore the LORD's wrath was on him and on Judah and Jerusalem.** [26]**Then Hezekiah repented of the pride of his heart, as did the people of Jerusalem; therefore the LORD'S wrath did not come upon them during the days of Hezekiah.**

²⁷Hezekiah had very great riches and honor, and he made treasuries for his silver and gold and for his precious stones, spices, shields and all kinds of valuables. ²⁸He also made buildings to store the harvest of grain, new wine and oil; and he made stalls for various kinds of cattle, and pens for the flocks. ²⁹He built villages and acquired great numbers of flocks and herds, for God had given him very great riches.

³⁰It was Hezekiah who blocked the upper outlet of the Gihon spring and channeled the water down to the west side of the City of David. He succeeded in everything he undertook. ³¹But when envoys were sent by the rulers of Babylon to ask him about the miraculous sign that had occurred in the land, God left him to test him and to know everything that was in his heart.

³²The other events of Hezekiah's reign and his acts of devotion are written in the vision of the prophet Isaiah son of Amoz in the book of the kings of Judah and Israel. ³³Hezekiah rested with his fathers and was buried on the hill where the tombs of David's descendants are. All Judah and the people of Jerusalem honored him when he died. And Manasseh his son succeeded him as king.

HEZEKIAH'S ILLNESS, REPENTANCE, WEALTH, HONOR, AND DEATH (32:24–33). **32:24–26** The words "in those days" suggest that the paragraphs that follow in v. 24 and following should be read in close connection with the preceding narrative. Hezekiah's illness followed soon after Sennacherib's visit to Jerusalem.

The reference to Hezekiah's illness is brief in Chronicles and assumes familiarity with the account in 2 Kgs 20:1–11, which gives details of the miraculous sign (*môpēt*). The Chronicler made use of the sign to link together the two separate accounts in Kings of Hezekiah's illness and the visit of the Babylonian envoys. The healing God gave to Hezekiah became an occasion for pride. When Hezekiah, with the citizens of Jerusalem, humbled himself in respect to his pride, the wrath of God did not fall on the people in the days of Hezekiah. Repentance was often a sincere act of David (2 Sam 12:13; Ps 51:1-12).

32:27–29 God's forgiveness resulted in blessings for Hezekiah and the people as it had for David, Solomon, Jehoshaphat, and Uzziah. In order to draw parallels with Solomon, the Chronicler detailed Hezekiah's "very great riches." These were some of the treasures he showed to Babylonian envoys (2 Kgs 20:13). Some evidence of the wealth of Hezekiah comes from archaeological evidence from the days of Hezekiah, Manasseh, and possibly Josiah.[24] Further evidence of God's blessing on Hezekiah is given in his building program—storehouses especially for the storage of agricultural

---

[24] Myers, *II Chronicles,* 293; J. Gray, "Recent Archaeological Discoveries and Their Bearing on the Old Testament," in *Tradition and Interpretation,* ed. G. W. Anderson (London and New York: Oxford University Press, 1979), 77.

products, stalls for his cattle, and pens for his flocks (v. 28).

32:30 The reference probably is to "Hezekiah's tunnel"; cf. 2 Kgs 20:20. This amazing engineering achievement was evidence of God's blessing (see the comments at 31:21). The famous Siloam inscription cut into the wall of the tunnel probably was cut as the work was being completed.[25]

32:31 The Chronicler's assertion that God "left Hezekiah" in order to "test" him has significant theological implications. God wants genuine character and faithfulness in his people, and he will expose them to trials in order to train and shape them. The path of sanctification is not an easy one (cf. Gen 22:1).

32:32 Verses 32–33 form a typical conclusion to a king's reign. The reference to the "vision" of Isaiah is a reminder that there was a considerable amount of material about Hezekiah and other kings in the Book of Isaiah.

32:33 Hezekiah was buried with his fathers on the hill where David's descendants were buried. The precise meaning of the word translated "hill" (*ma'ălēh*) in the NIV is not certain. It may have been a topographical feature in the area of the royal tombs such as "the upper part" or the "upper tier" of a two-level tomb, or even an expression of quality, "better" or "finer."[26]

2. The Reign of Manasseh (33:1–20)

Under Manasseh (697/696–643/642) Judah suffered a severe relapse. Whereas the evaluation of his reign in 2 Kgs 21:1–18 is completely negative, however, the account of the Chronicler is somewhat kinder. It opens with an account of Manasseh's apostasy (vv. 1–10) that led to an Assyrian invasion and his captivity; but it also reveals that in captivity he repented, was restored to his throne, and undertook a partial reform of the cult.

A historical question has been raised in regard to Manasseh's captivity in Babylon, taken there by Assyrian forces, since there is no extrabiblical documentation for these events. This fact is not, of course, a sufficient reason for rejecting their historicity. Assyrian records are by no means sufficiently comprehensive to allow any argument from silence to decide the issue. There is valuable circumstantial evidence which has persuaded a good number of scholars that historical events underlie the Chronicler's narrative. The Assyrian records mention Manasseh. He is listed among twenty-two kings of Hatti, the seashore, and the islands, who were summoned to Nineveh by Esarhad-

---

[25] J. C. L. Gibson, *Textbook of Syrian Semitic Inscriptions: Volume 1: Hebrew and Moabite Inscriptions* (Oxford: Oxford University Press, 1971), 21–23. In line 5 of this inscription the same word for "outlet" is used as appears here.

[26] Dillard, *2 Chronicles*, 260.

don (650–669 B.C.)[27] to bring building materials for a new palace. Asshur–banipal (668–627 B.C.) mentions him among vassal kings who participated in a campaign against Egypt.[28]

In these references Manasseh appears as submissive to the Assyrian king. The question is asked regarding what historical circumstances would have brought about his humiliation and punishment by Assyria. Various proposals have been made. Manasseh quite possibly may have been on the side of Shamash-shum-ukin, who revolted against his brother Asshur-banipal. The inscriptions of both Esarhaddon and Asshur-banipal abound in references to Egypt and the Palestinian states in the time of Manasseh, who reigned for fifty five years.

One other important Assyrian source is the vassal-treaties of Esarhaddon dated in the year 672 B.C. The crown prince of Assyria, Asshur-banipal, was inducted at a special ceremony where representatives of all the lands under Assyrian control were present. These representatives were sworn not to arouse the anger of the gods and goddesses against him and to serve Ashur as their god. They were bound by fearful oaths to support the crown prince after the death of his father. These treaties are not entirely intact, and the name of Manasseh does not appear. But the interest and activity of both Esarhaddon and Asshur-banipal in the west may well have forced compliance with their demands on Judah. Naturally vassals took opportunity to deviate from the treaty obligations laid upon them and even to rebel. In fact, numerous rebellions are attested in the reigns of Esarhaddon and Asshur-banipal.[29]

By all accounts, the Chronicler's narrative is historically reliable, but it of course includes a theological wording. Where other nations' historians saw political and military movements, the Chronicler saw the hand of God behind every event.[30]

The chapter before us divides into four sections: (1) relapse under Manasseh (vv. 1–10); (2) Manasseh's captivity, repentance, and restoration (vv. 11–13); (3) Manasseh's reforms (vv. 14–17); and (4) summary and conclusion (vv. 18–20).

(1) Relapse under Manasseh (33:1–10)

[1]Manasseh was twelve years old when he became king, and he reigned in Jerusalem fifty-five years. [2]He did evil in the eyes of the LORD, following the

---

[27] *ANET,* 291.

[28] Ibid., 294.

[29] Useful summaries of the period occur in Myers, *II Chronicles,* 198–99; Dillard, *2 Chronicles,* 264–65.

[30] See W. M. Schniedewind, "The Source Citations of Manasseh: King Manasseh in History and Homily," *VT* 41 (1991): 450–61, and Dillard, *2 Chronicles,* 265.

detestable practices of the nations the LORD had driven out before the Israelites. ³He rebuilt the high places his father Hezekiah had demolished; he also erected altars to the Baals and made Asherah poles. He bowed down to all the starry hosts and worshiped them. ⁴He built altars in the temple of the LORD, of which the LORD had said, "My Name will remain in Jerusalem forever." ⁵In both courts of the temple of the LORD, he built altars to all the starry hosts. ⁶He sacrificed his sons in the fire in the Valley of Ben Hinnom, practiced sorcery, divination and witchcraft, and consulted mediums and spiritists. He did much evil in the eyes of the LORD, provoking him to anger.

⁷He took the carved image he had made and put it in God's temple, of which God had said to David and to his son Solomon, "In this temple and in Jerusalem, which I have chosen out of all the tribes of Israel, I will put my Name forever. ⁸I will not again make the feet of the Israelites leave the land I assigned to your forefathers, if only they will be careful to do everything I commanded them concerning all the laws, decrees and ordinances given through Moses." ⁹But Manasseh led Judah and the people of Jerusalem astray, so that they did more evil than the nations the LORD had destroyed before the Israelites.

¹⁰The LORD spoke to Manasseh and his people, but they paid no attention.

33:1 Manasseh ruled longer than any other king of Judah. Although the Chronicler usually cites the name of the King's mother, he does not do so here or in the remainder of 2 Chronicles.[31]

33:2 In comparing Manasseh's works to those of the pre-Israelite Canaanites, the Chronicler (here citing 2 Kgs 21:2) implies that the Israelites deserve the same fate as the Canaanites who preceded them. The repetition in v. 9 is even more condemning.

33:3–6 The practices of v. 2 are now specified. If Manasseh had searched the Scriptures for practices that would most anger the Lord and then intentionally committed them, he could not have achieved that result any more effectively than he did. The high places Hezekiah had destroyed were rebuilt, the altars for Baal and the poles for Asherah were reerected. He also reestablished Astral worship, the practice of sacrificing sons in the fire (or of making sons pass through the fire), sorcery, divination, and witchcraft, and the consulting of mediums and spiritists (dealing in necromancy and familiar spirits). The rite of child sacrifice evidently was a divinatory practice.[32]

---

[31] Dillard, *2 Chronicles,* 267.

[32] See J. A. Thompson, *Deuteronomy,* TOTC (Downers Grove: InterVarsity, 1974), 210–12. On the cult of the dead see E. M. Bloch-Smith, "The Cult of the Dead in Judah: Interpreting the Material Remains," *JBL* 111 (1992): 213–24.

The use of plural nouns for Baals and Asherahs may indicate that numerous separate examples of these cult objects were erected (v. 6). This whole passage is strongly reminiscent of Deut 18:9–13. All in all, the sins of Manasseh detail the depths to which counterfeit religion will take a person. Here was the Davidic king, the heir and keeper of the promises of the covenant with David, worshiping poles and stones and the stars. Worse yet, he was murdering his own sons, one of whom otherwise might have been heir to the throne and the covenant. Paganism, whether in its ancient or modern manifestations, is not only an offense to God but is a degradation to humankind.

33:7–10 These verses serve as an indictment against Manasseh. What God had covenanted with David and Solomon was being ignored by Manasseh. God had put his "Name," his very character, his very essence, in the temple. Manasseh was in effect replacing God with the "carved image." Whereas God had promised not to send the people into exile if they remained faithful, v. 8 implies that they would indeed find their "feet . . . leave the land" (cf. Jer 18:5-10). Manasseh did indeed lead Judah into rebellion against God (v. 9) and when God spoke to him and the people they ignored the offer of grace. This action sealed their fate.

(2) Manasseh's Captivity, Repentance, and Restoration (33:11–13)

[11]So the LORD brought against them the army commanders of the king of Assyria, who took Manasseh prisoner, put a hook in his nose, bound him with bronze shackles and took him to Babylon. [12]In his distress he sought the favor of the LORD his God and humbled himself greatly before the God of his fathers. [13]And when he prayed to him, the LORD was moved by his entreaty and listened to his plea; so he brought him back to Jerusalem and to his kingdom. Then Manasseh knew that the LORD is God.

33:11 Which king of Assyria is intended here is uncertain, but it was likely Asshur-banipal, who brought Babylon under his control in 648 B.C.[33] The plausibility of this incident is confirmed by an Assyrian bas-relief[34] where both hooks and shackles are depicted on prisoners. Treatment like this was meted out to Jehoiachin (Ezek 19:4,9). The hook in his nose would serve to humiliate him completely before his captors (2 Kgs 19:28). The fetters recall Jehoiakim bound in bronze shackles and taken to Babylon (2 Chr 36:6). In fact, this incident has been described as a "foreshadowing in microcosm" of Judah's exile.[35]

---

[33] E. H. Merrill, *Kingdom of Priests* (Grand Rapids: Baker, 1987), 435.

[34] *ANET in Pictures,* 447.

[35] Merrill, *Kingdom of Priests.*

33:12–13 In his distress Manasseh sought the favor of Yahweh his God–a different response from that of Ahaz (28:22). The expression "sought the favor of" is the equivalent of "seek my face" (7:14).

Manasseh provides a convincing example of the efficacy of repentance, indeed, the best example in the Chronicler's whole work, of which there are several (12:1–12; 19–20, 32:25–26). Initially Manasseh refused God's warning and went into exile before he repented.

A foreshadowing of the themes of exile and restoration already was illustrated in the two preceding reigns, those of Ahaz (chap. 28) and Hezekiah (chaps. 29–32); but here the pattern of exile and restoration is presented in the life of a single ruler. The Chronicler's message for his readers was that just as restoration followed repentance in the life of Manasseh, so also the repentance of the people brought about restoration after the Babylonian captivity.

(3) Manasseh's Reforms (33:14–17)

[14]Afterward he rebuilt the outer wall of the City of David, west of the Gihon spring in the valley, as far as the entrance of the Fish Gate and encircling the hill of Ophel; he also made it much higher. He stationed military commanders in all the fortified cities in Judah.

[15]He got rid of the foreign gods and removed the image from the temple of the LORD, as well as all the altars he had built on the temple hill and in Jerusalem; and he threw them out of the city. [16]Then he restored the altar of the LORD and sacrificed fellowship offerings and thank offerings on it, and told Judah to serve the LORD, the God of Israel. [17]The people, however, continued to sacrifice at the high places, but only to the LORD their God.

The promise of 7:14 concludes with the promise that God would "heal their land." Verses 14–17 provide ample evidence of the truth of that promise. From the point of view of the Assyrians these rebuilding activities in Judah would have afforded a protection on their southern borders provided by their vassal Manasseh.

33:14 According to the Chronicler this building program occurred after Manasseh's return from Babylon, as the word "afterwards" indicates. It was partly a repair program. The wall that Hezekiah seems to have started was made higher and encircled the city on the west side. Verse 14 is useful topographically although the exact position of some of the places mentioned is not clearly indicated. Manasseh also strengthened his military security by stationing military commanders in the fortified towns of Judah.

33:15–16 Manasseh attempted to undo some of the damage his earlier apostasy had caused. He removed the foreign gods, the image he had erected in the temple of the Lord, and the altars he had built on the temple hill and in

Jerusalem. He restored the altar of the Lord. But whatever the extent of Manasseh's religious reforms, some of these items seem to have returned. It is easier to lead a people into sin than to lead them back out of it.

33:17 The qualification that such sacrifices were made "only to the LORD their God" has a ring of compromise or at least of misunderstanding. In any clear and comprehensive reform, all these foreign cult practices would have been removed completely never to return. Even a cursory glimpse of 34:3–5 and 2 Kgs 23:4–7 will show how Manasseh's reforms lacked real depth.

(4) Summary and Conclusion (33:18–20)

[18]The other events of Manasseh's reign, including his prayer to his God and the words the seers spoke to him in the name of the LORD, the God of Israel, are written in the annals of the kings of Israel. [19]His prayer and how God was moved by his entreaty, as well as all his sins and unfaithfulness, and the sites where he built high places and set up Asherah poles and idols before he humbled himself—all are written in the records of the seers. [20]Manasseh rested with his fathers and was buried in his palace. And Amon his son succeeded him as king.

This summary represents an expansion of 2 Kgs 21:7–8. The Chronicler is able here to restate some of his leading themes: prayer, faithfulness, and humbling oneself before God. The "seers" who spoke to Manasseh would be included in v. 10. The "annals of the kings of Israel" was concerned with the kings of Judah. Judah was, of course, Israel also in the Chronicler's view.

Beyond the obvious lesson that God always is ready to hear a repentant sinner, Manasseh's story was of great significance for the Chronicler. Manasseh, according to Kings, bore the greatest responsibility for the fall of the nation (2 Kgs 21:10–16; 23:26–27; 24:3–4). By emphasizing his repentance, however, the Chronicler drove home at least two lessons. First, he reminded his readers that, notwithstanding his great guilt, Manasseh did not bear *sole* responsibility for the calamity that followed. Already in Ezekiel's day people had begun to blame all their troubles on the sins of the fathers, and the Chronicler no less than Ezekiel rejected this kind of evasion of responsibility (see Ezek 18:1–4). Second, he reminded his postexilic readers that even though judgment had come and the worst had happened, there was still hope. After all, Manasseh, the chief of sinners himself, repented in exile and was restored. The nation could do the same and experience the same restoration.[36]

---

[36] For further discussion see Wilcock, *Chronicles*, 255–64.

33:18–19   No doubt this intriguing reference to "his prayer" is what prompted some anonymous Jew of the late second temple period to compose the Prayer of Manasseh, which is now found in the Apocrypha. This brief work (fifteen verses) is a prayer for forgiveness, although it does not mention anything specifically associated with Manasseh. It apparently was not part of the original Septuagint, and it was not in all copies of the Vulgate Apocrypha, but it apparently finally was included in the Deuterocanonical works on the strength of its inclusion in the Codex Alexandrinus.[37]

33:20   Manasseh was buried "in his palace," but not among the tombs of David's descendants as were worthy kings. Second Kings 21:18 says that Manasseh was buried "in his palace garden, the garden of Uzza."[38] Although J. McKay has identified an Arabian astral deity by this name,[39] the significance of a garden by this name is really unknown.

3. The Reign of Amon (33:21–25)

[21]Amon was twenty-two years old when he became king, and he reigned in Jerusalem two years. [22]He did evil in the eyes of the LORD, as his father Manasseh had done. Amon worshiped and offered sacrifices to all the idols Manasseh had made. [23]But unlike his father Manasseh, he did not humble himself before the LORD; Amon increased his guilt.

[24]Amon's officials conspired against him and assassinated him in his palace. [25]Then the people of the land killed all who had plotted against King Amon, and they made Josiah his son king in his place.

33:21   Amon's reign (642–640 B.C.) was brief, only two years. The Chronicler's account is based on 2 Kgs 21:19–26.

33:22–23   Just as Manasseh could not go back and undo the damage he had done to his nation, even so he could not go back and change the son he had raised to be a pagan. Amon followed in his father's footsteps, but not the steps that Manasseh would have liked him to follow.

33:24   The reasons that Amon's officials conspired against him and assassinated him in his palace are not given, but they may have had a political motivation in the international politics of the day. Amon was perhaps pro–Assyrian in his policies at a time when Assyria's power was declining and many Israelites were looking toward Egypt for leadership.[40] If so, anti-

---

[37] R. K. Harrison, "Manasseh, Prayer of," *ISBE* 3.235–36.

[38] Williamson, *1 and 2 Chronicles,* 395.

[39] J. McKay, *Religion in Judah under the Assyrians* (Naperville: Alec R. Allenson, 1973), 24–25.

[40] A. Malamat, "The Historical Background of the Assassination of Amon, King of Judah," *IEJ* 3 (1953): 26–29, and Dillard, *2 Chronicles,* 269-70.

Assyrian opponents of Amon's foreign policy lay behind the plot.

33:25   Another group killed all the plotters, perhaps in order to avoid a direct confrontation with Assyria. Just who "the people of the land" were has been the subject of some debate. Most commentators agree that these were the free landholders of Judah who always acted decisively in times of crisis to maintain the Davidic dynasty in the land.

The phrase "and they made Josiah his son king in his place" is a note of transition. Josiah, it might be expected, would follow in his father's footsteps. Nothing could have been further from the truth.

4. The Reign of Josiah (34:1–36:1)

The Chronicler's account of Josiah (640–609 B.C.) covers two chapters (chaps. 34–35) and parallels the earlier account in 2 Kgs 22:1–23:30. Both books provide a positive evaluation of Josiah, but Chronicles commences its story earlier. In his twelfth year (at age twenty) the reforms began, whereas Kings begins with the finding of the book of the law in Josiah's eighteenth year (age twenty-six). The Passover celebration is described in greater detail by the Chronicler, who also gives a more detailed account of Josiah's death in the battle of Megiddo.

After a brief introduction (34:1–2) the Chronicler's narrative is presented in five sections spread over chaps. 34–35: (a) introduction (34:1–2); (b) the removal of pagan cults from Jerusalem, Judah, and Israel (34:3–7); (c) temple repairs and the discovery of the law book (34:8–28); (d) covenant renewal (34:29–33); (e) Josiah's Passover (35:1–19); and (f) Josiah's death (35:20–27).

The chronological differences between Chronicles and Kings have provoked some discussion. The initiative for reform may not have been entirely due to Josiah, for in his boyhood he would have been under the influence and constraint of a regent or regents who might well have been from among the "people of the land," who no doubt saw the dangers of the religious policies followed by Manasseh and Amon and were anxious to return to a Yahweh-centered religious practice. One persuasive proposal is that the prophets Zephaniah and Jeremiah had an influence on Josiah before the finding of the book of the law in 621 B.C.[41]

The decline of Assyrian power in the latter half of the seventh century certainly favored the reestablishment of a strong Judahite state. Josiah's "seeking the God of his father David" in his eighth year (v. 3) would have followed the death of Asshur-banipal in 633 B.C. or 627 B.C. Josiah's extend-

---

[41] D. W. B. Robinson, *Josiah's Reform and the Book of the Law* (London: Tyndale, 1951).

ing of his reform into former Assyrian provinces in the north in his twelfth year (v. 3) took place on the death of Asshur-etil-ilani, and the further reforms in his eighteenth year (v. 8) followed the failure of Assyrian control in Babylonia in 623 B.C. Even with some modification in the absolute dates, the lessening of Assyrian influence may have been a contributing factor. There would be widespread acceptance among scholars of an early move toward reform predating the finding of the law book in 621 B.C.

(1) Introduction (34:1–2)

¹Josiah was eight years old when he became king, and he reigned in Jerusalem thirty-one years. ²He did what was right in the eyes of the LORD and walked in the ways of his father David, not turning aside to the right or to the left.

34:1–2   Several elements of Josiah's reign have parallels with the reign of Joash (chaps. 23–24). Both came to the throne as boys. Both collected funds for temple restoration. Both are reported as having stood in the king's place in the temple precincts (34:31; 24:13), both led the nation in a covenant renewal in the temple (23:16–17; 34:29–32). But whereas Josiah remained true to the Lord, not turning to the right or to the left, Joash was faithful only as long as Jehoiada, the priest, lived (24:2,15–18). Hezekiah is the only other king in Chronicles besides Josiah to be compared favorably to David (cf. 29:2; Sirach 49:4).

(2) The Removal of Pagan Cults from Jerusalem (34:3–7)

³In the eighth year of his reign, while he was still young, he began to seek the God of his father David. In his twelfth year he began to purge Judah and Jerusalem of high places, Asherah poles, carved idols and cast images. ⁴Under his direction the altars of the Baals were torn down; he cut to pieces the incense altars that were above them, and smashed the Asherah poles, the idols and the images. These he broke to pieces and scattered over the graves of those who had sacrificed to them. ⁵He burned the bones of the priests on their altars, and so he purged Judah and Jerusalem. ⁶In the towns of Manasseh, Ephraim and Simeon, as far as Naphtali, and in the ruins around them, ⁷he tore down the altars and the Asherah poles and crushed the idols to powder and cut to pieces all the incense altars throughout Israel. Then he went back to Jerusalem.

34:3   In the eighth year he would have been sixteen. He was still a young man and had not undertaken public duties. He probably was under the control and direction of a regent. However, in matters of personal religion he displayed personal piety. When he was twenty-one, he began his active reforms in Judah and Jerusalem, which he purged of high places, Asherah poles, the carved idols, and the images.

34:4-5 Josiah was determined to complete the work of uprooting the apostasy of Manasseh's reign. Ultimately, he was unable to free the people of their attachments to paganism. It is in this sense that Kings rightly attributes the decline and fall of Judah to Manasseh's reign. Notwithstanding Manasseh's later repentance, neither he nor anyone else was able to pull back the forces Manasseh had released early in his career.

Verses 4–5 take up the picture in the Kings account (cp. v. 4b with 2 Kgs 23:6 and v. 5a with 2 Kgs 23:14,16,20). Though not explicitly stated, the Chronicler implied that Josiah executed the priests of Baal (cf. 2 Kgs 23:20) following the precedent set by Jehu (2 Kgs 10) and Jehoiada (23:17). The punishment is fitted to the crime: the priests who burned sacrifices to Baal had their own bones burned on the same altar. According to 2 Kgs 23:16 the bones of priests who had died were removed from their graves and burned.

34:6-7 These reforming activities were carried north to Manasseh, Ephraim, and Simeon as far as Naphtali. The appearance of Simeon here is unexpected. That tribe was normally located to the south of Judah (1 Chr 4:24–33). Meanwhile, Nineveh was besieged by Cyaxares and the Medes in 625 B.C. The Babylonians had broken free, and tribes from the north were raiding former Assyrian lands. It was a golden opportunity for Josiah to extend his control into Israel, even as far as Upper Galilee (Naphtali).

(3) Temple Repairs and the Discovery of the Law Book (34:8–28)

These verses are based on 2 Kgs 22:3–7. There was repair work to be done at the temple. Josiah sent one of his officials to make arrangements for the commencement of the repairs. The law book was discovered in the midst of the reform. This chapter sets the scene for the announcement its discovery.

[8]In the eighteenth year of Josiah's reign, to purify the land and the temple, he sent Shaphan son of Azaliah and Maaseiah the ruler of the city, with Joah son of Joahaz, the recorder, to repair the temple of the LORD his God. [9]They went to Hilkiah the high priest and gave him the money that had been brought into the temple of God, which the Levites who were the doorkeepers had collected from the people of Manasseh, Ephraim and the entire remnant of Israel and from all the people of Judah and Benjamin and the inhabitants of Jerusalem. [10]Then they entrusted it to the men appointed to supervise the work on the LORD'S temple. These men paid the workers who repaired and restored the temple. [11]They also gave money to the carpenters and builders to purchase dressed stone, and timber for joists and beams for the buildings that the kings of Judah had allowed to fall into ruin.

[12]The men did the work faithfully. Over them to direct them were Jahath and Obadiah, Levites descended from Merari, and Zechariah and Meshullam,

descended from Kohath. The Levites—all who were skilled in playing musical instruments— [13]had charge of the laborers and supervised all the workers from job to job. Some of the Levites were secretaries, scribes and doorkeepers.

TEMPLE REPAIRS (34:8–13). **34:8** In the eighteenth year of Josiah's reign temple repairs were undertaken. He was then twenty-six years old and fully in control of the nation. The repair of the temple was part of the total reform program begun earlier. Only Shaphan is mentioned in 2 Kgs 22:3, but the Chronicler adds Maaseiah, the ruler (governor) of the city, and Joah, the recorder. These offices are well attested in preexilic times. A seal inscribed in Hebrew attests the title "governor of the city."

34:9 The Chronicler aimed at a comprehensive definition of Israel both north and south. The northern tribes are described as the "remnant of Israel" (cf. v. 21; see also Isa 10:20-22; 11:11,16; 37:4,31-32). Some of the northerners had been taken into captivity after the fall of Samaria (2 Kgs 17:6), but there were many who remained. The Chronicler is speaking here of a unified "Israel," which already had been realized in principle in the activities of Hezekiah.

34:10–11 The temple obviously needed more than a simple "cleansing." It apparently had fallen into a state of disrepair, as indicated by the need for carpenters and stonemasons. Manasseh and Amon had seriously neglected the temple.

34:12–13 The reference here is to the faithful discharge of the actual work of repair. The parallel text in 2 Kgs 22:7 focuses on the careful handling of the money. But both diligent labor and careful accounting were involved in the total program. In keeping with his desire to honor the Levites, he stressed that they had the oversight of the work. The stage is now set for the discovery of the law book.

[14]While they were bringing out the money that had been taken into the temple of the LORD, Hilkiah the priest found the Book of the Law of the LORD that had been given through Moses. [15]Hilkiah said to Shaphan the secretary, "I have found the Book of the Law in the temple of the LORD." He gave it to Shaphan.

[16]Then Shaphan took the book to the king and reported to him: "Your officials are doing everything that has been committed to them. [17]They have paid out the money that was in the temple of the LORD and have entrusted it to the supervisors and workers." [18]Then Shaphan the secretary informed the king, "Hilkiah the priest has given me a book." And Shaphan read from it in the presence of the king.

[19]When the king heard the words of the Law, he tore his robes. [20]He gave these orders to Hilkiah, Ahikam son of Shaphan, Abdon son of Micah, Shaphan the secretary and Asaiah the king's attendant: [21]"Go and inquire of the LORD for me and for the remnant in Israel and Judah about what is written in this

book that has been found. Great is the LORD'S anger that is poured out on us because our fathers have not kept the word of the LORD; they have not acted in accordance with all that is written in this book."

[22]Hilkiah and those the king had sent with him went to speak to the prophetess Huldah, who was the wife of Shallum son of Tokhath, the son of Hasrah, keeper of the wardrobe. She lived in Jerusalem, in the Second District.

[23]She said to them, "This is what the LORD, the God of Israel, says: Tell the man who sent you to me, [24]'This is what the LORD says: I am going to bring disaster on this place and its people—all the curses written in the book that has been read in the presence of the king of Judah. [25]Because they have forsaken me and burned incense to other gods and provoked me to anger by all that their hands have made, my anger will be poured out on this place and will not be quenched.' [26]Tell the king of Judah, who sent you to inquire of the LORD, 'This is what the LORD, the God of Israel, says concerning the words you heard: [27]Because your heart was responsive and you humbled yourself before God when you heard what he spoke against this place and its people, and because you humbled yourself before me and tore your robes and wept in my presence, I have heard you, declares the LORD. [28]Now I will gather you to your fathers, and you will be buried in peace. Your eyes will not see all the disaster I am going to bring on this place and on those who live here.'"

So they took her answer back to the king.

DISCOVERY OF THE BOOK OF THE LAW (34:14–28). **34:14–15** The Chronicler follows 2 Kgs 22:8–20 quite closely in these verses. The question is the identity of the book of the law of the Lord. The general consensus is that it was Deuteronomy (or some earlier stage version of it). Dillard lists seven elements that favor that the book was Deuteronomy: (1) that book's emphasis on centralization of worship at the place chosen by God, that is, the temple in Jerusalem (Deut 12); (2) the destruction of the high places and all rival cultic installations (Deut 12); (3) the strong emphasis on curses (Deut 27:9–26; 28:15–68) including the threat of exile; (4) the character of the Passover observance (Deut 16); (5) a prophet consulted to know the will of God (Deut 18:9–22); (6) the Deuteronomic flavor of the Book of Kings; and (7) the covenant nature of Deuteronomy in view of the designation "the Book of the Covenant" in 34:30.[42] It may be, however, that the Chronicler understood the expression to refer to the whole of the Pentateuch and not merely a part of it (see note on 2 Chr 34:30). How the book came to be lost can only be a matter of speculation, although it is conceivable that during the threat of invasion in Hezekiah's time or during the apostasy under Amon and Manasseh it was hidden in the temple.

---

[42] Dillard, *2 Chronicles*, 280. For a discussion of the date of Deuteronomy see Thompson, *Deuteronomy*, 47–68.

34:16–18   Shaphan took the book to the king and reported on how the repairs were proceeding. The text makes no great issue of informing the king that Hilkiah the priest had given him a book. Yet it was a most important discovery with profound results as Shaphan probably knew since 2 Kgs 22:8 says that he had already read it.

34:19–21   The tearing of one's garments was a sign of great distress and took place in a variety of troubled circumstances. Josiah then demanded that his priests inquire (*dāraš*) of the Lord and give him further information on what God required. The phrase "the remnant in Israel and Judah" was significant for the Chronicler, who saw that the sins revealed in the book referred to the whole of God's people.

34:22   Hilkiah, as was proper in such circumstances, consulted the prophetess Huldah, the wife of Shallum who was "keeper of the wardrobe." Evidently his official role was as the temple functionary responsible for the production and maintenance of the priestly and Levitical vestments. The exact location of the second district is uncertain. Hezekiah had extended the walls of Jerusalem and enclosed an area on the west side of the Tyropoean Valley, perhaps the second quarter of Zeph 1:10 and Neh 11:9. Nevertheless, the entourage of Josiah would "inquire" of the Lord through Huldah.

34:23–28   Huldah's response was concerned with "all the curses written in the book" in such passages as Leviticus 26 and Deuteronomy 27–29. It was an ominous message. The sins of Israel for which judgment would fall are detailed in v. 25. But there was hope for Josiah himself, whose heart was responsive and who humbled himself before God, tore his robes, and wept in God's presence. The verb "humble" (*kāna⁽*) expresses an important theological concept (2 Chr 7:14; 12:6-7,12; 28:19; 30:11; 33:12,19; 34:27). It appears twice in v. 27. Josiah's attitude was an example for all wrongdoers to follow. The promised reward was that God would spare Josiah from witnessing the disaster he would bring on Jerusalem and its people, and Josiah would be buried in peace. Huldah's prophecy is reminiscent of Jer 18:1–11 where the prophetic promise, whether hope or judgment, is contingent upon human response by either repentance to God or the forsaking of God. Although Josiah's reign was one marked by religious reform based on the law of Moses, he disobeyed God when he fought Neco of Egypt (2 Chr 35:20-24). Huldah's prophecy was fulfilled, since Judah did not suffer judgment from God, i.e., exile, until after the death of Josiah.

(4) Covenant Renewal (34:29–33)

²⁹**Then the king called together all the elders of Judah and Jerusalem.** ³⁰**He went up to the temple of the LORD with the men of Judah, the people of Jerus-**

alem, the priests and the Levites—all the people from the least to the greatest. He read in their hearing all the words of the Book of the Covenant, which had been found in the temple of the LORD. ³¹The king stood by his pillar and renewed the covenant in the presence of the LORD—to follow the LORD and keep his commands, regulations and decrees with all his heart and all his soul, and to obey the words of the covenant written in this book.

³²Then he had everyone in Jerusalem and Benjamin pledge themselves to it; the people of Jerusalem did this in accordance with the covenant of God, the God of their fathers.

³³Josiah removed all the detestable idols from all the territory belonging to the Israelites, and he had all who were present in Israel serve the LORD their God. As long as he lived, they did not fail to follow the LORD, the God of their fathers.

34:29-30 Josiah gathered the elders, the priests and Levites, and "all the people from the least to the greatest" to hear "all the words of the Book of the Covenant." Three things are evident here. First, the reading was for everyone, not the religious leaders only. The Word of God is meant for everyone and is not to be locked up in churches, hidden behind pulpits, or confined to professors' offices. It demands to be heard by all. Second, the phrase "Book of the Covenant" deserves special attention. This phrase occurs only four times in the Old Testament (Exod 24:7; 2 Kgs 23:2,21; 2 Chr 34:30). Its exact meaning is uncertain, but according to Ben Sira (ca. 190–180 B.C.) the phrase referred to the entire five books of the Pentateuch that was given to Moses (Sirach 24:23).[43] This may be the meaning here in Chronicles and in Kings. Third, what the people heard was the very inspired and authoritative word of God, given to be normative for life and faith. One must remember that this "Book" did not in itself create this change, but rather true transformation comes only by the power of the Holy Spirit (2 Cor 3:1-3) as must have been the case for Josiah, whose own personal transformation, as well as the reform itself, began before the "Book" was found (2 Chr 34:1-7).

34:31-32 The immediate result of the reading of the "Book of the Covenant" was the commitment made first by Josiah, and then by all the people, to keep the Word of God. This covenant renewal is reminiscent of former renewals in Israel's past (Exod 34; Josh 24). W. Kaiser interprets this story as an early type of "revival," but "reform" could be used and often is. Kaiser examines 2 Chr 34:1-33 in three steps centered on the theme of human humbleness: (1) humbling oneself before God [vv. 1–13]; (2) humbling ourselves

---

[43] G. Sheppard, *Wisdom as a Hermeneutical Construct* (Berlin and New York: DeGruyter, 1980), 62.

before God's word [vv. 14–28]; and humbling ourselves before God's people [vv.29–33].[44] As noted at vv. 23-28, "to humble oneself" is a key theological concept in Chronicles, and it also is essential in being a believer living in the will of God.

34:33   This verse summarizes and concludes the events of chap. 34. The covenant renewal called for pure and unadulterated monotheism for the rest of his reign. The expression "all the territories belonging to the Israelites" draws attention to the Chronicler's belief that Israel was now one and that all in Israel would serve the Lord their God as long as Josiah lived (640–609 B.C.).

(5) Josiah's Passover (35:1–19)

[1]**Josiah celebrated the Passover to the LORD in Jerusalem, and the Passover lamb was slaughtered on the fourteenth day of the first month.** [2]**He appointed the priests to their duties and encouraged them in the service of the LORD'S temple.** [3]**He said to the Levites, who instructed all Israel and who had been consecrated to the LORD: "Put the sacred ark in the temple that Solomon son of David king of Israel built. It is not to be carried about on your shoulders. Now serve the LORD your God and his people Israel.** [4]**Prepare yourselves by families in your divisions, according to the directions written by David king of Israel and by his son Solomon.**

[5]**"Stand in the holy place with a group of Levites for each subdivision of the families of your fellow countrymen, the lay people.** [6]**Slaughter the Passover lambs, consecrate yourselves and prepare [the lambs] for your fellow countrymen, doing what the LORD commanded through Moses."**

[7]**Josiah provided for all the lay people who were there a total of thirty thousand sheep and goats for the Passover offerings, and also three thousand cattle—all from the king's own possessions.**

[8]**His officials also contributed voluntarily to the people and the priests and Levites. Hilkiah, Zechariah and Jehiel, the administrators of God's temple, gave the priests twenty-six hundred Passover offerings and three hundred cattle.** [9]**Also Conaniah along with Shemaiah and Nethanel, his brothers, and Hashabiah, Jeiel and Jozabad, the leaders of the Levites, provided five thousand Passover offerings and five hundred head of cattle for the Levites.**

[10]**The service was arranged and the priests stood in their places with the Levites in their divisions as the king had ordered.** [11]**The Passover lambs were slaughtered, and the priests sprinkled the blood handed to them, while the Levites skinned the animals.** [12]**They set aside the burnt offerings to give them to the subdivisions of the families of the people to offer to the LORD, as is written in the Book of Moses. They did the same with the cattle.** [13]**They roasted the Pass-**

---

[44] W. Kaiser, *Quest for Renewal* (Chicago: Moody, 1986), 111–23.

over animals over the fire as prescribed, and boiled the holy offerings in pots, caldrons and pans and served them quickly to all the people. [14]After this, they made preparations for themselves and for the priests, because the priests, the descendants of Aaron, were sacrificing the burnt offerings and the fat portions until nightfall. So the Levites made preparations for themselves and for the Aaronic priests.

[15]The musicians, the descendants of Asaph, were in the places prescribed by David, Asaph, Heman and Jeduthun the king's seer. The gatekeepers at each gate did not need to leave their posts, because their fellow Levites made the preparations for them.

[16]So at that time the entire service of the LORD was carried out for the celebration of the Passover and the offering of burnt offerings on the altar of the LORD, as King Josiah had ordered. [17]The Israelites who were present celebrated the Passover at that time and observed the Feast of Unleavened Bread for seven days. [18]The Passover had not been observed like this in Israel since the days of the prophet Samuel; and none of the kings of Israel had ever celebrated such a Passover as did Josiah, with the priests, the Levites and all Judah and Israel who were there with the people of Jerusalem. [19]This Passover was celebrated in the eighteenth year of Josiah's reign.

The account of Josiah's Passover is given in much more detail than in the brief notice in 2 Kgs 23:21–23. The section in its opening verse and its closing verses (vv. 18–19) is clearly dependent on the Kings version. Verses 2–17 show a considerable expansion but read as a unity. The important role of the Levites is stressed in keeping with the Chronicler's interests. Following the Kings narrative, the legal prescriptions are those taken from Deuteronomy.

35:1 The Chronicler provides the exact date of the observance of the Passover. These facts are absent from the parallel text in 2 Kgs 23:21–23. They contrast with the delayed observance of the Passover in the days of Hezekiah (30:2–3; cf. Exod 12:6; Lev 23:5; Num 9:3). There is no reference here to these details being found in the book of the covenant (2 Kgs 23:21), but their having followed Moses' instructions is made clear in vv. 6,12.

35:2 We may have here a reflection of the failures of the priests in the days of Hezekiah in contrast to the conscientious behavior of the Levites (29:12–19,34; 30:3).

35:3 The Levites are pictured here as having a teaching function (17:7–8; Neh 8:7–9). Other texts speak of the teaching duties of the priests (Hos 4:6; Jer 5:31; 18:18). The instruction to the Levites to "put the sacred ark in the temple" requires some explanation. There is no statement elsewhere that the ark had ever been removed, although it is possible that Manasseh's "carved image" (33:7) had displaced the ark. This would not explain, however, the instruction not to carry it on their shoulders. In many of the pagan rituals of the ancient Near East the image of a deity was carried in procession on special occasions.[45] Perhaps Manasseh had begun such a practice with the ark of the Lord contrary to the law. If so, it is possible to translate the verb *nātan* ("put") as "leave." That these instructions are given to the "Levites" suggests that here again (cf. 29:5) the term is being used in a general sense to include the priests, who were the only ones allowed to enter the sanctuary.

35:4 The roles of David and Solomon in assigning the courses and divisions of the priests and Levites have been described in 1 Chr 24:4,19–20,30–31; 28:19–21; and 2 Chr 8:14.

35:5 Each family grouping of the laypeople was to be served by a part of a Levitical family.

35:6 Though the Passover animal was ordinarily slaughtered by the lay offerer (Exod 12:3–6,21; Deut 16:5–6), the Chronicler indicates that the practice of slaughter by the Levites as begun under Hezekiah continued. In Hezekiah's time this was done because of the ritual impurity of some participants, but the practice evidently was normalized by the time of Josiah. It was not the custom, however, in later times. The Pentateuch does not legislate for the slaughter of the Passover lamb by the Levites. The words "what the LORD commanded through Moses" evidently refer to the principle of sacrificing a Passover lamb rather than to the one who should perform the task.

35:7–9 Also in the case of Hezekiah's Passover, the king and his officials contributed liberally for the sacrifices. Here offerings are said to have come from four sources: Josiah (v. 7), his "officials" (v. 8), the temple "administrators" (v. 8), and the "leaders of the Levites." The Chronicler often reported the voluntary and joyful giving of king and people (24:8–14; 29:31–36; 31:3–21) as an example no doubt to be followed by others. It is possible that the cattle (bulls) referred to in vv. 7–9 were part of the burnt offerings made for the concurrent Feast of Unleavened Bread. The total number of small animals offered was 37,600 and of bulls, 3,800. This was nearly double the number of offerings made at the Passover under Hezekiah (30:24) but much less than the offerings made at the dedication of the temple in Solomon's day (2 Chr 7:5). The logistics for the resident population in these operations must have been considerable.[46]

35:10 The actual celebration of the Passover ceremony is described in vv. 10–15. The priests stood in their places with the Levites in their divisions as the king had ordered.

---

[45] E. R. Clendenen, "Religious Background of the Old Testament," in *Foundations for Biblical Interpretation,* ed. D. S. Dockery et al. (Nashville: Broadman & Holman, 1994), 282, 292.

[46] Dillard, *2 Chronicles,* 290.

35:11–12 The Levites both killed the Passover lambs (v. 6) and skinned them while the priests manipulated the blood (cf. 29:22; 30:16). For a time the streaming of celebrants to receive the animals for the ceremony, the process of slaying and skinning the animals, and the removal of the portions used as burnt offerings turned the temple into a vast hive of activity. All these actions were largely dictated by the centralized nature of the celebration. The prescriptions of Exodus 12 would have been inappropriate in the temple setting. Details of the complicated ritual are not available to us in any prescribed legislation pertaining to the Passover. The offerings probably included fellowship offerings, the fat portions of which were burned on the altar (Lev 3:6–16). The burnt offerings and the fat offerings (v. 14) may refer to the more regular sacrifices.

35:13 The verb translated "roast" (*bāšal*) also can mean "boil" (cp. Exod 12:8–9 and Deut 16:7). It actually was a general term for preparing food, its precise significance depending on the context (cf. 2 Sam 13:8). The translation makes allowance for the Hebrew phrase "according to custom." Hence "they roasted the Passover animals over the fire as prescribed" gives the true meaning. On the other hand, the "holy offerings were boiled in pots, cauldrons and pans." In the context these were the bulls of v. 12, which certainly was the ancient practice (1 Sam 2:13–14; 1 Kgs 19:21). The willing service of the Levites is emphasized by the phrase "they served them quickly to all the people." The element of haste in the original Passover story (Exod 12:11) may be found here in the quick service of the Levites.

35:14 There is a note of selflessness here. After all the people had been attended to, the Levites could provide for themselves and for the priests. The enormity of the task for the priests is demonstrated by the fact that they were sacrificing the burnt offerings and the fat portions till nightfall.

35:15 The musicians, the descendants of Asaph, took their places prescribed by David. The Chronicler connects the Levites with prophetic authority.[47] The preparation of the Passover for the priests, singers, and gatekeepers surpassed the king's command in vv. 3–6.

35:16–18 This concluding summary draws in part on 2 Kgs 23:21–23. The Israelites who were present included people from both north and south. The record in 2 Kgs 23:22 refers to the Passover celebrated "in the days of the Judges [the equivalent in Chronicles of the days of Samuel the prophet] and in the days of the kings of Israel or of the kings of Judah." The celebration of Passover here was magnificent in that it marked a true restoration of the ancient tradition, but the need for restoration shows how negligent Israel had been about keeping its laws and traditions.

---

[47] Dillard, *2 Chronicles*, 291.

35:19   The chronological note "in the eighteenth year of Josiah's reign" forms an inclusio with 34:8. Josiah was then twenty-six years old; it was an eventful year.

(6) The Account of Josiah's Death (35:20–36:1)

[20]After all this, when Josiah had set the temple in order, Neco king of Egypt went up to fight at Carchemish on the Euphrates, and Josiah marched out to meet him in battle. [21]But Neco sent messengers to him, saying, "What quarrel is there between you and me, O king of Judah? It is not you I am attacking at this time, but the house with which I am at war. God has told me to hurry; so stop opposing God, who is with me, or he will destroy you."

[22]Josiah, however, would not turn away from him, but disguised himself to engage him in battle. He would not listen to what Neco had said at God's command but went to fight him on the plain of Megiddo.

[23]Archers shot King Josiah, and he told his officers, "Take me away; I am badly wounded." [24]So they took him out of his chariot, put him in the other chariot he had and brought him to Jerusalem, where he died. He was buried in the tombs of his fathers, and all Judah and Jerusalem mourned for him.

[25]Jeremiah composed laments for Josiah, and to this day all the men and women singers commemorate Josiah in the laments. These became a tradition in Israel and are written in the Laments.

[26]The other events of Josiah's reign and his acts of devotion, according to what is written in the Law of the LORD— [27]all the events, from beginning to end, are written in the book of the kings of Israel and Judah.

[1]And the people of the land took Jehoahaz son of Josiah and made him king in Jerusalem in place of his father.

The account now moves from the year of the reform (622 B.C.) to the year of his death (609 B.C.). We can only speculate about his movements between the reformation and the time of his death. No doubt he was involved in organizing and strengthening his administration. Some valuable archaeological data are provided by a wide variety of stamp seals and scroll seals discovered in excavations.[48] The most significant material available to us is concerned with the encounter with Pharaoh Neco at the battle at Megiddo, where Josiah was mortally wounded. His premature death came as a profound shock to his contemporaries, who found it difficult to accept and to explain.

C. Begg shows that the death of Josiah follows a characteristic pattern in Chronicles. First, his death is another example of "immediate retribution for sin." Second, Josiah's reign follows the pattern of a king who begins well but ends up doing something wrong, as did Asa, Jehoshaphat, Joash, and Uzziah.

---

[48] A useful summary is provided in Myers, *II Chronicles*, 215.

Third, the king hears a "warning speech" before his tragic military error, just as we see also in 2 Chr 11:1–4 and 18:16–22. Fourth, the Chronicler juxtaposes a laudable effort at religious reform with a perceived threat by an external enemy; the same thing occurred in the reigns of Asa, Jehoshaphat, and Hezekiah.[49]

35:20 One of the great theological issues for the Chronicler was how to explain the premature death of Josiah, a pious and faithful king, at the hands of Pharaoh Neco. This was difficult to accept or explain. The Chronicles account given in vv. 20–24 is more detailed than that in 2 Kings 23. The latter follows the final summary of Josiah's reign in 2 Kgs 23:28 as an appendix, which states the fact of his death but offers no explanation. Verse 20 introduces the campaign of Pharaoh Neco, who was on his way to fight at Carchemish on the Euphrates.

35:21 Neco's movement into these areas has become clear since the publication of the Babylonian Chronicles.[50] He was going the aid of Assyria. The Babylonians had overrun the southern part of Assyria and pushed the Assyrians back from Haran. Fearing the advance of the Babylonians, Pharaoh Neco and the Egyptian army were on their way to assist the Assyrians. Josiah, who apparently was an ally of the Babylonians (or at least an opponent of the Assyrians), attempted to impede the march of Neco. He may have succeeded, for the Assyrian-Egyptian forces were thwarted in their endeavor to retake Haran. But Josiah's involvement in the incident led to his being wounded in battle and to his eventual death. The theological explanation offered by the Chronicler is in terms of Josiah's refusal to accept the divine warning offered in an unusual way by the words of the pagan king Neco, who told Josiah that he had no quarrel with him personally but with the Babylonian king.[51] Perhaps more important to the Chronicler than the word of a foreign king was the lack of any statement that Josiah had "sought the LORD" before engaging an enemy in battle.

35:22–23 Ironically, Josiah followed the path of Ahab here, who also disguised himself and charged into battle, only to be slain by a random arrow (18:1–34).

35:24 The wounded Josiah was taken from his own chariot, placed in another chariot, perhaps one carrying supplies, and taken to Jerusalem, where he died. He was buried honorably in the tombs of his fathers, and all

---

[49] C. T. Begg, "The Death of Josiah in Chronicles: Another View," *VT* 37 (1987): 1–8. See especially pp. 1–3.

[50] D. J. Wiseman, *Chronicles of the Chaldean Kings,* 19, 63. A succinct account is given in Myers, *II Chronicles,* 216.

[51] According to 1 Esdr 1:28, Jeremiah also warned Josiah against going into battle, but this could be only a later historian's speculation on the basis of v. 25.

Judah and Jerusalem mourned. This much can be said for the manner of his death: his body did not lie on the battlefield to run the risk of desecration but was buried in peace in Jerusalem (cf. the fate of Saul in 1 Chr 10:8-12).

35:25 Interestingly, Jeremiah is not mentioned in the Kings parallel text. Some laments of Jeremiah are recorded in the Book of Lamentations, but the one for Josiah is lost. Jeremiah's prophetic ministry paralleled the reign of Josiah. In fact, Jeremiah was a prophet before Josiah's reforms and lived to see both the reforms of Josiah and his death. They apparently had a good relationship and Jeremiah truly mourned the passing of a great king. Jeremiah lived on through the fall of Jerusalem over twenty years later and witnessed the exile to Babylon.

"The Laments" is another lost collection. These are not to be confused with the Book of Lamentations, although in purpose they may have been similar. It must be remembered however, that not only did Jeremiah lament over Josiah's death, but so did "all the men and women singers," signifying that this was a dark day in Israel's history.[52]

35:26–36:1 This concluding notice corresponds to 2 Kgs 23:28. The translation of the NIV, "his acts of devotion," draws attention to Josiah's "faithfulness" or "loyalty" to the Lord. He acted according to what was written in the Law of the Lord, probably alluding to the book of the law discovered in the temple (34:14). The "people of the land," that significant group of citizens who played such a prominent role in the appointment of the kings (23:13,21; 33:25; 36:1), took Josiah's son Jehoahaz and made him king in Jerusalem.

After the untimely death of Josiah, the "people of the land" acted quickly in the interests of national stability to fill the vacancy by putting Jehoahaz on the throne. The last chapter of the Chronicler covers briefly the last four kings of Judah and the exile. The last two verses in 2 Chronicles represent an appendix.

The treatment of these four kings is quite brief. The usual formulaic references to maternal lineage and the death notices are lacking. Each of these kings finished his life in exile except perhaps for Jehoiakim. Each was involved in the loss of a considerable amount of tribute largely through a despoiling of the temple. Any references to the activities of their reign are confined to information about the temple. The fate of the temple and the fate of the Davidic dynasty are, in a sense, parallel. H. G. M. Williamson has pointed to a parallel between the close of Saul's life with Israel's total defeat and "exile" (1 Chr 10) and the fate of the nation finally as it was overthrown by Nebuchadnezzar. The faithfulness of David in his day lifted Israel from its

---

[52] That the lament was made an ordinance in Israel, cp. Judg 11:39-40.

sad state and restored it; the Chronicler did not spell out the way of restoration for Israel after its latest "exile."[53]

The last chapter in Chronicles is presented in four vignettes to which a significant appendix is added: Jehoahaz (36:2–4), Jehoiakim (36:5–8), Jehoiachin (36:9–10), Zedekiah (36:11–21), and an appendix (36:22–23).

5. The Reign of Jehoahaz (36:2–4)

²Jehoahaz was twenty-three years old when he became king, and he reigned in Jerusalem three months. ³The king of Egypt dethroned him in Jerusalem and imposed on Judah a levy of a hundred talents of silver and a talent of gold. ⁴The king of Egypt made Eliakim, a brother of Jehoahaz, king over Judah and Jerusalem and changed Eliakim's name to Jehoiakim. But Neco took Eliakim's brother Jehoahaz and carried him off to Egypt.

36:2 The account of Jehoahaz (609 B.C.) follows 2 Kgs 23:30–34 but in keeping with the Chronicler's policy omits any reference to his mother and also to the negative remarks in 2 Kgs 23:32 (an unexpected omission). The reign of Jehoahaz was very brief, only three months.

36:3 The reason Pharaoh Neco dethroned Jehoahaz was no doubt that he espoused an anti-Egyptian or pro-Babylonian policy. Neco deposed him while he himself was still in northern Aram (2 Kgs 23:33). He was placed in bonds at Riblah and taken to Egypt, where he later died in exile (Jer 22:11–12; cf. Ezek 19:1–4). The levy of a hundred talents of silver and a talent of gold was less than that imposed on Hezekiah by Sennacherib (2 Kgs 18:14). The origin of this tribute is not given, but it probably was paid, at least in part, out of the temple treasury. The plundering of the temple took place under each of these last kings at an increasing volume (vv. 3,7,10,18–19).

36:4 The king of Egypt chose Eliakim (Jehoiakim) to rule over Judah, now a vassal state of Egypt. Normally the people of the land would make the choice. Neco's hegemony over Judah ended the years of independence enjoyed under Josiah. The Chronicler did not pass any moral judgment on Jehoahaz but confined his attention to the themes of exile and tribute that characterize his treatment of the last four kings of Judah.[54]

6. The Reign of Jehoiakim (36:5–8)

⁵Jehoiakim was twenty-five years old when he became king, and he reigned in Jerusalem eleven years. He did evil in the eyes of the LORD his God. ⁶Nebuchadnezzar king of Babylon attacked him and bound him with bronze

---

[53] Williamson, *1 and 2 Chronicles,* 96, 412.
[54] Dillard, *2 Chronicles,* 299.

shackles to take him to Babylon. [7]Nebuchadnezzar also took to Babylon articles from the temple of the LORD and put them in his temple there.

[8]The other events of Jehoiakim's reign, the detestable things he did and all that was found against him, are written in the book of the kings of Israel and Judah. And Jehoiachin his son succeeded him as king.

The basis for this paragraph is 2 Kgs 23:36–24:7, although this is abbreviated. Further details of Jehoiakim (609–598 B.C.) may be found in the Book of Jeremiah. The twin themes of the exile of the king and the despoiling of the temple are continued.

36:5 The Chronicler omitted much of the detail contained in the Kings account (2 Kgs 23:36–24:7). Jehoiakim's death is not reported, which is in keeping with the Chronicler's method. He does not report the death of any of the last four kings of Judah. Nor is the length of Jehoiakim's life reported, although it must have been at least thirty-six years. Kings reports his death but in no detail (2 Kgs 24:6). According to Jer 22:18–19 he was to be buried as the burial of an ass, dragged and cast forth beyond the gates of Jerusalem.

36:6 Nebuchadnezzar visited Jerusalem more than once. Here he is reported as having attacked Jehoiakim and having bound him with bronze shackles "to take him to Babylon." There is no extrabiblical evidence of an exile for Jehoiakim, and some biblical passages suggest that he in fact died in Jerusalem (Jer 22:18–19).[55]

36:7 Taking temple objects was common in times such as this, as it represented the complete military and religious conquest of a city (cf. Dan 1:1–2; Ezra 1:7). Although such "aids" to worship are important, their absence does not mean that God too is absent.

36:8 The prophet Jeremiah paints a similarly unfavorable picture (Jer 22:18–19; 25:1–26:24; 36:1–32). Jehoiakim's death left his eighteen-year-old son to bear the brunt of Babylon's reaction.

7. The Reign of Jehoiachin (36:9–10)

[9]Jehoiachin was eighteen years old when he became king, and he reigned in Jerusalem three months and ten days. He did evil in the eyes of the LORD. [10]In the spring, King Nebuchadnezzar sent for him and brought him to Babylon, together with articles of value from the temple of the LORD, and he made Jehoiachin's uncle, Zedekiah, king over Judah and Jerusalem.

Jehoiakim was taken into exile with the payment of tribute from the temple vessels (cf. 2 Kgs 24:8–17; 25:27–30). That Jehoiachin (598 B.C.) was exiled to Babylon is attested by two Babylonian records. The Babylonian

---

[55] On the fate of Jehoiakim, see F. B. Huey's discussion on Jer 22:18-19 (*Jeremiah, Lamentations,* NAC [Nashville: Broadman, 1993] 207). Also, cf. Jer 22:20-23; 25:1-26:24; 36:1-33.

Chronicle provides an accurate contemporary record of the capture of Jerusalem and its king (March 16, 597 B.C.).[56] Further, some receipts found in Babylon refer to the issue of rations to "Iakin king of Judah" and his five sons.[57]

36:9 There is a difference between the biblical texts about the age at which Jehoiachin acceded to the throne. According to 2 Kgs 24:8 and the LXX, he was eighteen years of age, while the MT reads eight years, which may be the result of a translation error. The Babylonian receipts show that in 592 B.C. Jehoiachin had five sons, that is five years after his exile in 597 B.C. Hence the age of his accession must have been eighteen.

36:10 "At the turn of the year," that is, in the spring, Nebuchadnezzar had the young king brought to Babylon, indicating that a military campaign was involved (cf. 1 Chr 20:1). Details are given in 2 Kgs 24:10–17 but are omitted by the Chronicler, whose main concern was the king's exile and the taking of booty from the temple, described as "articles of value."

Nebuchadnezzar made Jehoiachin's uncle the next king. The Chronicler records the royal genealogy through Jehoiachin's line into the postexilic period (1 Chr 3:1b–24). Seven sons are recorded, to be compared with five in the Babylonian receipts. There is some evidence that the people of Judah continued to regard Jehoiachin as their legitimate king. He was given royal treatment in Babylon, which encouraged the people of Judah to hope for his return (Jer 28:4). Seals have been found bearing the words "Eliakim steward of Yaukin," which may refer to King Jehoiachin. If so, it suggests that his property was administered fro him while in exile.[58] The people seem to have regarded Zedekiah merely as a regent.

8. The Reign of Zedekiah (36:11–21)

[11]Zedekiah was twenty-one years old when he became king, and he reigned in Jerusalem eleven years. [12]He did evil in the eyes of the LORD his God and did not humble himself before Jeremiah the prophet, who spoke the word of the LORD. [13]He also rebelled against King Nebuchadnezzar, who had made him take an oath in God's name. He became stiff-necked and hardened his heart and would not turn to the LORD, the God of Israel. [14]Furthermore, all the leaders of the priests and the people became more and more unfaithful, following all the detestable practices of the nations and defiling the temple of the LORD, which he had consecrated in Jerusalem.

[15]The LORD, the God of their fathers, sent word to them through his messengers again and again, because he had pity on his people and on his dwelling

---

[56] Wiseman, *Chronicles*, 73.

[57] *ANET*, 308.

[58] Myers, *II Chronicles*, 220.

place. ¹⁶But they mocked God's messengers, despised his words and scoffed at his prophets until the wrath of the LORD was aroused against his people and there was no remedy. ¹⁷He brought up against them the king of the Babylonians, who killed their young men with the sword in the sanctuary, and spared neither young man nor young woman, old man or aged. God handed all of them over to Nebuchadnezzar. ¹⁸He carried to Babylon all the articles from the temple of God, both large and small, and the treasures of the LORD'S temple and the treasures of the king and his officials. ¹⁹They set fire to God's temple and broke down the wall of Jerusalem; they burned all the palaces and destroyed everything of value there.

²⁰He carried into exile to Babylon the remnant, who escaped from the sword, and they became servants to him and his sons until the kingdom of Persia came to power. ²¹The land enjoyed its sabbath rests; all the time of its desolation it rested, until the seventy years were completed in fulfillment of the word of the LORD spoken by Jeremiah.

Only the barest outline of the story of Zedekiah (598–587 B.C.) is given by the Chronicler. More background to his reign is available in 2 Kgs 24:18–25:7; Jer 39:1–7; 52:1–11. Narratives and sermons in Jeremiah fill out the picture (Jer 27:1–28:17; 34:1–22; 37:1–38:28). The present passage is largely concerned with the exile and the desecration of the temple, which reaches its climax in vv. 18–19. There is some interest in the "land" (v. 21) and in the general population, who had regularly rejected the warnings of the prophets and had thus brought the exile on themselves.

36:11 It was Zedekiah who accompanied Judah into exile. The Book of Jeremiah provides a valuable insight into the character of Zedekiah. The prophet repeatedly urged Zedekiah to submit to Babylonia rather than look to Egypt for help during the latter part of his eleven-year reign.

36:12 Zedekiah is given a bad assessment. The Chronicler turns again to terms he used often to express his theology. The first of these is that Zedekiah did not "humble" himself before the prophet Jeremiah, God's messenger (cf. 7:14). But it was not only Zedekiah who failed to humble himself. The whole nation behaved in the same way (vv. 15–16; cf. Jer 37:2).

36:13 Zedekiah's rebellion was no doubt encouraged by some of his political advisers in this respect. The oath of allegiance that he swore to Nebuchadnezzar in the name of his God was normal in political treaties, but his breaking of the oath only serves to reinforce the portrait of him as an apostate (cf. Ezek 17:11–21).

36:14 Not only did Zedekiah display disloyal and unfaithful attitudes and responses, but all the leaders of the priests and the people behaved in the same way. In Zedekiah the people had the kind of king they deserved.

36:15–16 The root cause of the exile is summarized in these verses. In the parable of the "wicked tenants," Jesus spoke of the owner of the vineyard sending slave after slave in vain to collect his due share. Perhaps Jesus had this or similar verses in mind.

36:17 It was God who brought up against the people the king of the Chaldeans. In the vivid language of the peoples of the East, the Chaldeans killed without mercy many Judahites in the very sanctuary itself. God handed all of them over to Nebuchadnezzar. Some escaped from the sword and were carried as exiles to Babylon (v. 20) to become servants to the Babylonians. The Chronicler drew a broad picture and showed no interest in the part of the population that remained in the land.

36:18–19 It was significant to the Chronicler that the temple was plundered and destroyed. Nebuchadnezzar carried to Babylon all the articles from the temple of God as well as the treasures of the king and his officials. The two themes of the exile of the king and the spoiling of the temple, which the Chronicler has followed for Judah's last four kings, now both reach their climax.

36:20–21 The Chronicler finished his story with many Judahites in exile in Babylon. However, there is some hope of restoration. The exiles would be servants of the ruler in Babylon "until the kingdom of Persia came to power." While they awaited that day, the land enjoyed its Sabbath rests and continued to enjoy its rest all the time of its desolation. The phrase is reminiscent of Lev 26:34–35, which forms an element in a long list of punishments that would attend Israel's disobedience. One consequence of an exile would be to give the land the rest it should have enjoyed but was denied. The end point of the land's desolation would be reached when the seventy years spoken of by Jeremiah were fulfilled. Jeremiah's "seventy years" have been variously understood, and a considerable literature has grown up around the issue.[59]

The biblical text itself has been understood in various ways. At least three possibilities have been proposed: (1) the exile ran from the first deportation (605/604 B.C.) until the decree of Cyrus in 539 B.C. This period is not exactly seventy years but close enough. The Chronicler marked the end of the period with the decree of Cyrus. (2) The exile ran from the destruction of the temple in 586 B.C. to the dedication of the second temple in 516 B.C. (3) It is possible that the seventy years is not intended to be literal but symbolic for some less defined period of judgment. Jeremiah's original intention may have been a general period of judgment based on an individual's life-span or on three generations, as in some Old Testament as well as extrabiblical usages. In fact, the exile itself in most respects lasted only some fifty years. However, reckoning from the Babylonian victory at Carchemish (605 B.C.), the time of

---

[59] An excellent summary of some of the more significant contributions of recent years is given in Williamson, *1 and 2 Chronicles,* 417–18.

servitude was quite close to seventy years.

9. Appendix (36:22–23)

[22]In the first year of Cyrus king of Persia, in order to fulfill the word of the LORD spoken by Jeremiah, the LORD moved the heart of Cyrus king of Persia to make a proclamation throughout his realm and to put it in writing:

[23]"This is what Cyrus king of Persia says:

"'The LORD, the God of heaven, has given me all the kingdoms of the earth and he has appointed me to build a temple for him at Jerusalem in Judah. Anyone of his people among you—may the LORD his God be with him, and let him go up.'"

The work of the Chronicler probably finishes at v. 21. These two verses correspond to Ezra 1:1–3, where the hope for the future is introduced by quoting one form of the decree of Cyrus. The negative note with which the Chronicler ended his work is thus completed by making explicit the hope hinted at in v. 21.

36:22   The first year of Cyrus king of Persia was 539 B.C. During that year he issued decrees to put his realm on a new footing. One of his decrees referred to the exiled Jews. This reference to Persia is the first in any of the historical and prophetical books, apart from Ezekiel (Ezek 27:10; 38:5), where the references are to Persia before the conquests of Cyrus and its emergence as a world power. The decree of Cyrus was seen by the writer to be a fulfillment of God's word spoken by Jeremiah (Jer 25:11–14; 29:10). Cyrus was acting in harmony with God's word to one of the prophets, moved by God to make a proclamation throughout his realm and to put it in writing.

36:23   The decree of Cyrus is found in a longer form in Ezra 1:2–4; 6:2–5. As regularly happened in decrees in the ancient Near East, the one who issued a decree claimed that the God of the people in whose favor the decree was issued had instructed the decree maker to act in a particular way. This was a useful public relations exercise. The particular interest for Israel was that the Lord had appointed Cyrus to build a temple for him in Jerusalem. In fact, the tabernacle and the first and second temples were all built in part with funds provided by Gentile nations. Cyrus's authorization for the rebuilding of the temple included not only the building but also the return of the implements taken from the first temple by Nebuchadnezzar and the funding of the project from the Persian treasury (Ezra 6:4–5).

The book thus ends with the possibility of a new exodus. As God had once forced the hand of a reluctant pharaoh, now he moved the heart of a Persian king. The Book of Chronicles thus ends with the promise that the people of God would again go free to build a sanctuary where they could worship him in the land he had promised to their ancestors.

Selected Subject Index

Person Index

Scripture Index